JOURNAL FOR THE STUDY OF THE NEW TESTAMENT
SUPPLEMENT SERIES
166

Executive Editor
Stanley E. Porter

Editorial Board
David Catchpole, R. Alan Culpepper, Margaret Davies,
James D.G. Dunn, Craig A. Evans, Stephen Fowl, Robert Fowler,
Robert Jewett, Elizabeth Struthers Malbon, Robert W. Wall

Bloomsbury T&T Clark
An imprint of Bloomsbury Publishing Plc

B L O O M S B U R Y
LONDON · NEW DELHI · NEW YORK · SYDNEY

John's Use of the Old Testament in Revelation

G.K. Beale

Journal for the Study of the New Testament
Supplement Series 166

Bloomsbury T&T Clark
An imprint of Bloomsbury Publishing Plc

Imprint previously known as T&T Clark

50 Bedford Square	1385 Broadway
London	New York
WC1B 3DP	NY 10018
UK	USA

www.bloomsbury.com

**BLOOMSBURY, T&T CLARK and the Diana logo are trademarks of
Bloomsbury Publishing Plc**

First published in 1998 by Sheffield Academic Press Ltd
Paperback edition first published by Bloomsbury T&T Clark 2015

British Library Cataloguing-in-Publication Data
A catalogue record for this book is available from the British Library.

ISBN: HB: 978-1-8507-5894-5
PB: 978-0-5676-5752-7
ePDF: 978-1-4411-6724-8
ePub: 978-0-5673-4169-3

Library of Congress Cataloging-in-Publication Data
A catalog record for this book is available from the Library of Congress.

Series: The Library of New Testament Studies

Typeset by Bookcraft Ltd, Midsomer Norton, Bath

CONTENTS

ACKNOWLEDGMENTS

This book has been inspired by my research over the last twenty years on the Book of Revelation, and especially by a commentary on Revelation which has dominated the second decade of my research. My work on John's Revelation began formally when I commenced doctoral work at Cambridge University in the Fall of 1977. John Sweet was my supervisor during most of my time at Cambridge, and he has continued throughout the years to provide helpful advice and comment on my ongoing work. I am grateful to him for his help, which has also made its impact on the present monograph.

Even before beginning doctoral work, I had the privilege of studying under S. Lewis Johnson during Seminary days. It was he who originally suggested to me that the use of the Old Testament in Revelation might be an excellent area to study for doctoral research. Little did I know that I would spend twenty years studying this important yet difficult subject. His method of studying the use of the Old Testament in the New has been formative for my own approach, and I have passed it down to my own students at Gordon–Conwell Theological Seminary. Thank you, Dr Johnson.

I am also grateful to many of my past students at Gordon–Conwell who have sat through my lectures and read some of my work, and who have made helpful comments which have caused me to reflect further with profit on John's Apocalypse. I am particularly grateful to Elizabeth Shively, Juan Hernández Jr., Joel White, Jeffrey Herron, Erik Panikian, Janling Fu, David Smith, Dan Gurtner, Hunter Weïmar, Scott Foster and John Lin who helped with proofreading; John Lin was especially helpful with the production of the final manuscript. In addition, Meredith Kline, Jr, and Freeman Barton of the library staff offered invaluable assistance in obtaining interlibrary loans and other material from the library.

To God be the glory.

MATERIAL IN THIS VOLUME PREVIOUSLY PUBLISHED

Chapter 2 (The Various Ways John Uses the Old Testament) is a major revision of
'[The Use of the Old Testament in] Revelation', in D.A. Carson and H.G.M.
Williamson (eds.), *It is Written: Scripture Citing Scripture: Essays in Honor of
Barnabas Lindars* (Cambridge: Cambridge University Press, 1988), pp. 318-36.

Chapter 3, section A (The Eschatology of Revelation in Relation to the Rest of
the New Testament: The 'Already and Not Yet') is a minor revision of 'Eschatology (of Acts, Hebrews, Catholic Epistles, and Revelation)', in R.P. Martin and
P.H. Davids (eds.), *Dictionary of the New Testament*, Vol. 3 (Downers Grove, IL:
InterVarsity Press, 1997), pp. 330-45.

Chapter 3, section B (The Interpretation of Revelation 1.19: Its Old Testament
Background and its Disputed Significance as an Interpretative Key to the Whole
Book) is a revision of 'The Interpretative Problem of Rev. 1:19', *NovT* 34 (1992),
pp. 360-87. (Permission sought.)

Chapter 3, section E (The Old Testament Background of Revelation 3.14: The
Already and Not Yet New Creation of Revelation) was previously published as
'The Old Testament Background of Rev 3.14, *NTS* 42 (1996), pp. 133-52.

Chapter 4, section B (The Hearing Formula in the Letters of Revelation and its
Implications for the Purpose of Symbolism in the Visionary Portion of the Book) is
a minor revision of G.K. Beale, 'The Hearing Formula and the Visions of John in
Revelation', in M. Bockmuehl and M.B. Thompson (eds.), *A Vision for the Church:
Studies in Early Christian Ecclesiology in Honour of J.P.M. Sweet* (Edinburgh:
T. & T. Clark 1997), pp. 167-80.

Chapter 5 (The Influence of the Old Testament on the Grammar of Revelation:
Solecisms in Revelation as Signals for the Presence of OT Allusions) is a revision of
'Solecisms in the Apocalypse as Signals for the Presence of OT Allusions (A
Selective Analysis of Rev. 1–22)', in C.A. Evans and J.A. Sanders (eds.), *Early
Interpretation of the Scriptures of Israel* (JSNTSup, 148; Studies in Scripture in
Early Judaism and Christianity, 5; Sheffield: Sheffield Academic Press, 1997), pp.
421-43.

I am thankful to these journals and publishers for permission to republish
material.

ABBREVIATIONS

AB	Anchor Bible
ABD	David Noel Freedman (ed.), *The Anchor Bible Dictionary* (New York: Doubleday, 1992)
AUSS	*Andrews University Seminary Studies*
BAGD	Walter Bauer, William F. Arndt, F. William Gingrich and Frederick W. Danker, *A Greek–English Lexicon of the New Testament and Other Early Christian Literature* (Chicago: University of Chicago Press, 2nd edn, 1958)
BDF	Friedrich Blass, A. Debrunner and Robert W. Funk, *A Greek Grammar of the New Testament and Other Early Christian Literature* (Cambridge: Cambridge University Press, 1961)
BETL	Bibliotheca ephemeridum theologicarum lovaniensium
BFCT	Beiträge zur Förderung christlicher Theologie
Bib	*Biblica*
BibRes	*Biblical Research*
BJRL	*Bulletin of the John Rylands University Library of Manchester*
BSac	*Bibliotheca Sacra*
BW	James A. Brookes and Carlton L. Winbery, *Syntax of New Testament Greek* (Washington: University Press of America, 1979)
BZAW	Beihefte zur *ZAW*
BZNW	Beihefte zur *ZNW*
CBQ	*Catholic Biblical Quarterly*
ConBNT	Coniectanea biblica, New Testament
CR:BS	*Currents in Research: Biblical Studies*
CTM	*Concordia Theological Monthly*
DM	H.E. Dana and J.R. Mantey, *A Manual Grammar of the Greek New Testament* (Toronto: Macmillan, 1927)
EvQ	*Evangelical Quarterly*
ExpTim	*Expository Times*
FzB	Forschung zur Bibel
GKC	*Gesenius' Hebrew Grammar* (ed. E. Kautzsch, revised and trans. A.E. Cowley; Oxford: Clarendon Press, 1910)
GTJ	*Grace Theological Journal*
HDR	Harvard Dissertations in Religion

HNT	Handbuch zum Neuen Testament
HSM	Harvard Semitic Monographs
HTR	*Harvard Theological Review*
IBS	*Irish Biblical Studies*
ICC	International Critical Commentary
Int	*Interpretation*
JAAR	*Journal of the American Academy of Religion*
JBL	*Journal of Biblical Literature*
JETS	*Journal of the Evangelical Theological Society*
JSNT	*Journal for the Study of the New Testament*
JSNTSup	*Journal for the Study of the New Testament*, Supplement Series
JSOTSup	*Journal for the Study of the Old Testament*, Supplement Series
JTS	*Journal of Theological Studies*
LSJ	H.G. Liddell, Robert Scott and H. Stuart Jones, *Greek–English Lexicon* (Oxford: Clarendon Press, 9th edn, 1968)
MHT	J.H. Moulton, W.F. Howard and M. Turner, *A Grammar of New Testament Greek*, I–IV (Edinburgh: T. & T. Clark, 1906–1976)
MNTC	Moffatt NT Commentary
NCB	New Century Bible
Neot	*Neotestamentica*
NICNT	New International Commentary on the New Testament
NIDNTT	Colin Brown (ed.), *The New International Dictionary of New Testament Theology* (3 vols.; Exeter: Paternoster Press, 1975)
NIGTC	The New International Greek Testament Commentary
NovT	*Novum Testamentum*
NovTSup	*Novum Testamentum*, Supplements
NRT	*La nouvelle revue théologique*
NTS	*New Testament Studies*
OTP	James Charlesworth (ed.), *Old Testament Pseudepigrapha*
RB	*Revue biblique*
RevExp	*Review and Expositor*
RevQ	*Revue de Qumran*
RivB	*Rivista biblica*
RTR	*Reformed Theological Review*
SANT	Studien zum Alten und Neuen Testament
SBLSP	SBL Seminar Papers
SBT	Studies in Biblical Theology
SEÅ	*Svensk exegetisk årsbok*
SJT	*Scottish Journal of Theology*
SNT	Studien zum Neuen Testament
SNTSMS	Society for New Testament Studies Monograph Series

Str–B	[Hermann L. Strack and] Paul Billerbeck, *Kommentar zum Neuen Testament aus Talmud und Midrasch* (7 vols.; Munich: Beck, 1922–61)
TDNT	Gerhard Kittel and Gerhard Friedrich (eds.), *Theological Dictionary of the New Testament* (trans. Geoffrey W. Bromiley; 10 vols.; Grand Rapids: Eerdmans, 1964–)
TDOT	G.J. Botterweck and H. Ringgren (eds.), *Theological Dictionary of the Old Testament*
TLG	*Thesaurus Linguae Graecae*
TynBul	*Tyndale Bulletin*
TZ	*Theologische Zeitschrift*
WBC	Word Biblical Commentary
WMANT	Wissenschaftliche Monographien zum Alten und Neuen Testament
WTJ	*Westminster Theological Journal*
WUNT	Wissenschaftliche Untersuchungen zum Neuen Testament
ZNW	*Zeitschrift für die neutestamentliche Wissenschaft*

The stylistic conventions of the NA[27] edition of the Greek New Testament (*Novum Testamentum Graece*) in *not* accenting secondary textual variants has been followed in this monograph.

When the author did not supply his own translation the New American Standard Bible was used.

Citations for the Shepherd of Hermas are taken from *The Apostolic Fathers: Greek Texts and English Translations of their Writings* (ed. J.B. Lightfoot, J.R. Harmer and Michael W. Holmes; Grand Rapids, MI: Baker Book House, 2nd edn, 1992).

Chapter 1

INTRODUCTION: RECENT DISCUSSION AND DEBATE ABOUT
THE USE OF THE OLD TESTAMENT IN REVELATION

Introduction

In comparison with the rest of the New Testament, the use of the Old
Testament in the Apocalypse of John had not been given a proportion-
ate amount of attention up through the late nineteen-seventies: merely
two books had been published, one in 1912, another in 1972.[1] In addition, six significant articles had been dedicated to the topic.[2] Otherwise,
important discussion of the subject could be found only in portions
of books and commentaries, the more valuable of which were Swete,
Charles, Vos, Caird, van der Waal, Ford, Beasley-Murray,[3] and, to

1.   A. Schlatter, *Das Alte Testament in der johanneischen Apokalypse* (BFCT
16.6; Gütersloh: Bertelsmann, 1912); F. Jenkins, *The Old Testament in the Book of
Revelation* (Marion, IN: Cogdill Foundation Publications, 1972). Jenkins's work is
on a more popular level.
2.   A. Vanhoye, 'L'utilisation du livre d'Ezéchiel dans l'Apocalypse', *Bib* 43
(1962), pp. 436-76; A. Lancellotti, 'L'Antico Testamento nell'Apocallise', *RivB* 14
(1966), pp. 369-84; L.P. Trudinger, 'Some Observations Concerning the Text of the
Old Testament in the Book of Revelation', *JTS* 17 (1966), pp. 82-88; A. Gangemi,
'L'utilizzazoine del Deutero-Isaia nell'Apocalisse di Giovanni', *Euntes Docete* 27
(1974), pp. 109-44, 311-39; B. Marconcini, 'L'utilizzazione del T.M. nelle citazioni
isaiane dell'Apocalisse', *RivB* 24 (1976), pp. 113-36; M.D. Goulder, 'The Apocalypse as an Annual Cycle of Prophecies', *NTS* 27 (1981), pp. 342-67; cf. also
J. Cambier, 'Les images de l'Ancien Testament dans l'Apocalypse de Saint Jean',
NRT 77 (1955), pp. 113-22, and E. Lohse, 'Die alttestamentliche Sprache des Sehers
Johannes: Textkritische Bemerkungen zur Apokalypse', *ZNW* 52 (1961), pp. 122-
26, which are of more limited value.
3.   H.B. Swete, *The Apocalypse of St. John* (London: Macmillan, 1906), *passim*, but especially pp. cxl-clvi; R.H. Charles, *A Critical and Exegetical Commentary on the Revelation of St. John* (2 vols.; Edinburgh: T. & T. Clark, 1920),

somewhat lesser degree, Delling, Comblin, Farrer and Holtz.[4] Since the middle of the 1980s, however, six significant books and an important unpublished dissertation have been written on the topic: G.K. Beale, *The Use of Daniel in Jewish Apocalyptic Literature and in the Revelation of St. John* (1984; based on a 1980 Cambridge dissertation); J.M. Vogelgesang, 'The Interpretation of Ezekiel in the Book of Revelation' (unpublished PhD dissertation; Cambridge, MA: Harvard University, 1985); J. Paulien, *Decoding Revelation's Trumpets: Literary Allusions and Interpretation of Revelation 8:7-12* (1987); J.-P. Ruiz, *Ezekiel in the Apocalypse: The Transformation of Prophetic Language in Revelation 16, 17-19, 10* (1989); J. Fekkes, *Isaiah and Prophetic Traditions in the Book of Revelation: Visionary Antecedents and their Development* (1994); R.J. Bauckham, *The Climax of Prophecy: Studies in the Book of Revelation* (1993); and S. Moyise, *The Old Testament in the Book of Revelation* (1995)[5] In addition, since the same period of the mid-1980s, a number of articles on the same subject have appeared.

---

passim, but especially pp. lxv-lxxxii; L.H. Vos, *The Synoptic Traditions in the Apocalypse* (Kampen: Kok, 1965), pp. 16-53; G.B. Caird, *A Commentary on the Revelation of St. John the Divine* (London: A. & C. Black; New York: Harper & Row, 1966), *passim*; C. van der Waal, *Openbaring van Jezus Christs: Inleiding en Vertaling* (Gröningen: De Vuurbaak, 1971), pp. 174-241; D. Ford, *The Abomination of Desolation in Biblical Eschatology* (Washington, DC: University Press of America, 1979), pp. 243-306; G.R. Beasley-Murray, *The Book of Revelation* (London: Marshall, Morgan & Scott, 1974), *passim*.

4.   G. Delling, 'Zum Gottesdienstlichen Stil der Johannes-Apokalypse', *NovT* 3 (1959), pp. 107-37; J. Comblin, *Le Christ dans l'Apocalypse* (Bibliotheque de Théologie, Théologie Biblique, 6.3; Paris: Desclée de Brouwer, 1965); A. Farrer, *The Revelation of St. John the Divine* (Oxford: Clarendon Press, 1964); T. Holtz, *Die Christologie der Apokalypse des Johannes* (Texte und Untersuchungen, 85; Berlin: Akademie-Verlag, 1971).

5.   Evaluation of these six works to varying degrees can also be found throughout G.K. Beale, *The Book of Revelation* (NIGTC; Grand Rapids: Eerdmans; Carlisle: Paternoster, 1998) and in the following discussion herein (where also full bibliographical references will appear). See also the discussion of recent literature in F.J. Murphy, 'The Book of Revelation', *CRBS* 2 (1994), pp. 181-225 (200-201). Among recent articles see: G.K. Beale, '[The Use of the Old Testament in] Revelation', in D.A. Carson and H.G.M. Williamson (eds.), *It Is Written: Scripture Citing Scripture* (Essays in honour of Barnabas Lindars; Cambridge: Cambridge University Press, 1988), pp. 318-36; A.S. Bøe, 'Bruken av det Gamle Testamente i Johannes' Åpenbaring', *Tidsskrift for Teologi og Kirke* 63 (1992), pp. 253-69; and T.E.

The purpose of this chapter is to survey and evaluate briefly the most significant studies written since the mid-1980s.

A. *Recent Exegetical Studies on the Use of the Old Testament in Revelation*

1. *G.K. Beale*

My own study was the first to appear in the decade of the eighties.[6] I attempted to demonstrate that a number of works in Jewish apocalyptic literature and some passages in John's Revelation reflected similar exegetical patterns of the use of Daniel. In particular, I concluded that whole segments in these works were based on sections from the book of Daniel, especially Daniel 7 and Daniel 10–12. This was consistent with the work of Lars Hartman who also found that the synoptic eschatological discourse was based broadly on Daniel 7–12.[7] I argued that there was no mechanical dependence nor copying but a creative use of Daniel in the light of the purposes and circumstances of each apocalyptic writer. For example, the various writers always wove in other Old Testament texts from outside of Daniel to enrich and supplement their understanding of the Daniel prophecies. Furthermore, in the case of John, the understanding of Christ's death and resurrection and the resulting formation of the church in the midst of persecution certainly influenced his understanding of Daniel and how he viewed it as beginning fulfillment. On the other hand, despite varying degrees of creative exegesis, the apocalyptic authors and John were seen to show respect for the Old Testament contexts to which they were making reference.

It is not my intent nor my place to evaluate my own work, since this has already been done by others. Amidst mixed reviews, the most trenchant summary and critique of my own work has been done by J.-P. Ruiz and, to lesser degree, Steve Moyise. Their critiques, along with others, will be summarized at a more appropriate place later in this book (Chapter 2, sect. D.1.a), where also my responses can be found.

McComiskey, 'Alteration of OT Imagery in the Book of Revelation: Its Hermeneutical and Theological Significance', *JETS* 36 (1993), pp. 307-16.

6. *The Use of Daniel in Jewish Apocalyptic Literature and in the Revelation of St. John* (Lanham, MD: University Press of America, 1984).

7. L. Hartman, *Prophecy Interpreted* (ConBNT, 1; Lund: C.W.K. Gleerup, 1966).

2. J.M. Vogelgesang

Before discussing published works since the late 1980s, there is an unpublished dissertation by J.M. Vogelgesang which deserves brief mention.[8] The primary contribution of this study is to lend further supporting evidence to prior studies which have argued for the dominant influence of Ezekiel on either the entire Apocalypse or upon segments of the book. Vogelgesang believes John used Ezekiel as the model for Revelation's overall structure and that Ezekiel is the key to interpreting Revelation. Though there is not space to summarize or evaluate the interpretative conclusions thoroughly, J.-P. Ruiz has provided that service,[9] whose criticisms of Vogelgesang are cogent. Therefore, only a summary of Ruiz's evaluation is given here, along with some of my own critiques.

First, Vogelgesang draws a number of contrasts between Ezekiel 40–48 and Rev. 21.1–22.5 in order to show that John intends a radical and absolute universal salvation in contrast to the ethnic particularism of Ezekiel, whose vision is centered on the temple in Israel. Many of the contrasts, however, are overdrawn and are not persuasively demonstrated: that John places his city on a plain and not on a mountain; that John depicts an urban instead of rural scene; that John's city is 'Babylon redeemed' instead of true Israel redeemed, so that all humanity is redeemed, even the enemies of God and Christ (which does not sufficiently acknowledge the antithetical parallelism between the woman of chs. 17–18 and the woman of chs. 21–22 and the fact that God will defeat and judge his enemies); and that John's portrayal of the New Jerusalem without a temple and holy mountain corresponds with the secularized pictures of earlier mythical city-models (such as the Greek and Babylonian), though this appears incompatible with John's lack of accommodation with secular society elsewhere in Revelation.

Nevertheless, some of Vogelgesang's insights could be quite suggestive if fitted within another perspective. For example, there certainly is a universalization, but more likely not one in which all without exception are redeemed but in which the sphere of salvation is no longer lim-

---

8.   Vogelgesang, 'Interpretation of Ezekiel'.

9.   J.-P. Ruiz, *Ezekiel in the Apocalypse: The Transformation of Prophetic Language in Revelation 16,17–19,10* (European University Studies, 23.376; Frankfurt am Main: Peter Lang, 1989), pp. 129-80, which is especially to be consulted for a more thorough summary of the positive arguments of Vogelgesang's unpublished dissertation than can be given here.

ited to national Israel's geographical boundaries, the boundaries being widened to include all from the nations who identify with Jesus as the true Israel and as the true temple, everything the old temple pointed to. The primary reason that John throughout Rev. 21.9–22.5 excludes most of the detailed descriptions of the Ezekiel 40–48 temple and its ordinances is because he understands it being fulfilled in God and Christ's presence and not fulfilled in the form of a physical structure.[10] This expectation of a non-literal temple is, for the most part, a break with Judaism, which consistently affirmed the hope of a final, material temple structure on a scale greater than any before.[11]

Vogelgesang observes that the size of John's city is approximately the size of the then-known Hellenistic world,[12] which could easily be viewed as another way of saying that the temple-city in Revelation represents, not merely Israelite saints, but the redeemed from throughout the nations who identify with Jesus. Since Jesus is the temple, a Gentile does not have to move to geographical Israel to find true worship but only has to move spiritually to Jesus the true Israel. Likewise, the notion that John has depicted a city modelled on other known secularized city plans from the Babylonian and Hellenistic world could suggest that such earlier depictions contained within them faint though 'fallen' and distorted outlines of the ideal city of God. John's city is, not merely the perfected New Jerusalem, but the ideal cosmopolitan-Gentile city, in order to indicate that not only Israel's hopes but also God's original design for humanity in general are finally fulfilled.

Ruiz's next criticism of Vogelgesang concerns his main thesis that Revelation is an 'anti-apocalypse', which is based on his contention that John has re-utilized the apocalyptic tradition by making his own work 'anti-esoteric, universally accessible, and understandable' to all in the believing community.[13] Part of the problem with this proposal is the very definition of 'apocalyptic' itself which is not clearly defined by Vogelgesang, nor is Revelation's precise place within the apocalyptic literary movement discussed. Vogelgesang tries to demonstrate his

---

10. The observations concerning John's exclusion of cultic details from the Ezek. 40–48 vision by Vogelgesang, 'Interpretation of Ezekiel', p. 116, fit better with this perspective than his own.

11 See O. Michel, 'ναός', *TDNT*, IV, pp. 880-90 (889); Holtz, *Die Christologie der Apokalypse des Johannes*, pp. 195-96.

12. Vogelgesang, 'Interpretation of Ezekiel', p. 95.

13. Vogelgesang, 'Interpretation of Ezekiel', p. 282.

thesis partly from the observation that Revelation extends promises made to Israel to the nations (e.g. Rev. 5.9; 7.9), which he refers to as a hermeneutic of 'democratization'. John's so-called democratizing tendency can be seen, for example, in his viewing the entire community as priests instead of only a select group within the community (e.g. cf. 22.3-4; cf. also 7.15). While 'democratization' may be suitable, it is better to view these kinds of applications as universalizations or extensions to the world of what in the Old Testament was limited in reference to Israel. Old Testament texts pertaining to ethnic Israel's redemption and restoration are applied in Revelation to the world's redemption on the basis of defining the true people of God according to their faith in Christ and according to their corporate representation by Christ, the one who sums up true Israel in himself. This is why the church comes to be viewed as the true Israel. And, since Christ is also the last Adam, all humanity finds its hopes summed up in him. Therefore, these hermeneutical extensions are best understood, not so much as reactions against earlier Jewish apocalyptic tendencies of esoterism, but more in the light of the redemptive-historical movement toward, not only the restoration of Israel, but of the entire creation itself.[14]

Ruiz's final criticism of Vogelgesang concerns his further 'anti-apocalyptic' contention that John contradicts the apocalyptic tendency to exalt the visionary as one having unique access to the heavenly throne by portraying no essential difference between the liturgical experience of all believers and that of the seer's own visionary experience on 'the Lord's day' (cf. Rev. 1.10). Hence, he finds another democratizing strategy whereby everything about the seer's visionary experience is supposedly available to all worshippers in the church community. The primary evidence adduced in favor of this is Rev. 1.10. Vogelgesang concludes from this verse that the description of John's visionary encounter taking place 'on the Lord's day' is to indicate that this was a worshipful experience on no higher plane than the worship experience of other believers on 'the Lord's day'.

Revelation 1.10, however, does not clearly support such a conclusion, which is pointed to by the observation that the conclusion runs counter to the majority of commentary opinion on this verse. Above all, when it is recalled that Rev. 1.10 ('I came to be in the Spirit') is an allusion to Ezekiel (e.g. Ezek. 3.12), it is obvious that the interpretation

---

14. For the full rationale for John's 'universalizing' tendency, see below at Chapter 2, sect. D.4 ('*Universalization of the Old Testament*').

proposed contradicts the way the wording is used in Ezekiel. In Ezekiel the phrase refers to the commissioning of the prophet and his consequent divine authority, so that he is singled out among the rest of Israel. Likewise, the point of Rev. 1.10 is to underscore John's unique prophetic authority in order that the hearers would recognize the inspired nature of the message, and seek to understand and obey it (cf. 1.3; 2.7 [and the following 'hearing' formulas]; 13.18; 17.9; etc.). While the writer shares in a solidarity and equality with the hearers (they are all believers in Christ: cf. 1.9!), they are recipients of his uniquely and divinely inspired message. Interestingly, Jesus is not called a prophet in order to highlight that his status is higher than that of a prophet nor are the readers called prophets because they are those who are the recipients of John's unique prophetic ministry. This is a far cry from any form of thoroughgoing democratization.

The reason that John's visionary experience is set on 'the Lord's day' is to underscore the christological (and theological) focus of the following vision (1.12ff.), which is picked up again in Revelation 4–5.

Ruiz's evaluation of Vogelgesang is justified and yet balanced, since he acknowledges Vogelgesang's contribution of demonstrating even further than others previously the extensive influence of Ezekiel in the Apocalypse. What is questionable is not whether or not Ezekiel is used often and directly but Vogelgesang's interpretative conclusions about the significance of this usage.

3. *J. Paulien*

J. Paulien's *Decoding Revelation's Trumpets*[15] sets out to propose an exegetical method for interpreting Revelation by offering criteria to identify more objectively Old Testament allusions according to the categories of 'certain', 'probable', 'uncertain' and 'non-allusion'. He also includes the category of 'echo', which he associates closely with the category of 'probable' allusions, an association he never clearly explains. Nevertheless, these categories and the criteria connected with them, which are a distillation of methodologies gathered from prior studies, are helpful in analyzing allusions.

In essence, the degree of allusive probability is determined by the criteria of verbal, thematic, and structural parallels. The presupposition

15. *Decoding Revelation's Trumpets: Literary Allusions and Interpretation of Revelation 8:7-12* (Andrews University Seminary Doctoral Dissertation Series, 21; Berrien Springs, MI: Andrews University Press, 1987).

for considering the validity of an allusion is the demonstration that the author could have had familiarity with the body of literature from which the purported allusion is a part.

Paulien tests his method by applying it to Rev. 8.7-12. He first examines past identifications of allusions in Rev. 8.7-12 by prior commentators, and he then proposes new allusions himself. His concluding chapter aims to interpret Rev. 8.7-12 in the light of the re-examination of proposed allusions conducted in ch. 2 and by applying the method formulated in the earlier part of the book. Paulien's study of the first four trumpets is helpful, though he places too many allusions in the 'probable' category and does not pay sufficient attention to tracing Jewish exegetical tradition of Old Testament texts alluded to by John.

Perhaps, Paulien's primary contribution is in his study of 'echoes'. He defines an 'echo' as a symbol or wording which has been separated from its original context, and whose core meaning is determined by observing a recurring similar pattern of use elsewhere in the Old Testament. Paulien's analysis of 'echoes' is an advancement in the study of allusions, though his definition is too brief and further clarification is still needed. One problem is that, though he views 'echoes' as unconscious and unintentional, he nevertheless seems to consider them to have a similar degree of allusive validity as his category of intentional 'probable allusions'.

For example, in Rev. 8.7 he classifies as echoes the images of hail, fire, blood, earth, grass and trees. He claims that these echoes are collective allusions to the extensive occurrence of these words and images in the Old Testament, which shed light on the meaning of Rev. 8.7. In particular, he notes that 'trees' and 'grass' are used occasionally in the Old Testament as symbols of sinful people whom God judges. Against this background, Paulien concludes that the same symbolism is reflected in Rev. 8.7 and that this symbolism supplements the idea of the clear Old Testament allusions already recognized (in this case, Exod. 9.22-25 [LXX]).

It is not clear, however, whether or not this method of recognizing and applying 'echoes' has sufficient controls. More objective criteria need to be offered for recognizing the probable existence of an echo. It is wiser to err on the side of minimalism rather than maximalism in judging the validity of allusions. The only reasonable certainty about the symbols in Rev. 8.7 (and elsewhere) derives from three sources: (1) their usage in the Old Testament text clearly alluded to; (2) their usage in Jewish exegetical tradition to which reference has been made; and (3) from the immediate New Testament context. The method is too uncontrolled if several echoes from different portions of the Old Testament are posited which have no ostensible link with Old Testament allusions already clearly identified in a verse.

Most commentators, including Paulien, agree that Rev. 8.7 definitely alludes to Exod. 9.22-25: the hail, fire, and burning of the earth, trees, and grass of Rev. 8.7 is based on the Egyptian plague of hail and fire which struck the land, plants, and trees in part of Egypt. The echoes which Paulien proposes do not have any clear thematic links with Exodus 9. In addition, doubt about their validity is enhanced when it is recognized that these echoes are metaphors symbolizing a different meaning than the images in Exodus itself: as noted above, the trees and grass are used occasionally in the Old Testament as symbols of sinful people whom God judges, and Paulien sees this background as combined with the Exodus background. This is problematic, however, since the trees and grass of Exodus are not metaphorical for wicked people but refer to literal trees and grass in Egypt.

Consequently, a less speculative method is to interpret the symbols of a passage mainly against the background of their meaning in the Old Testament text to which there has been explicit reference rather than to supplement that meaning with echoes whose existence is difficult to establish and whose collective meaning is incompatible with the clearly recognized Old Testament allusions.

Despite some of the methodological problems inherent in Paulien's study, his work has advanced our understanding of exegetical method in analyzing Old Testament allusions.[16]

4. *Richard Bauckham*

In 1993 Richard Bauckham published a major work on John's use of the Old Testament and related Jewish traditions (*The Climax of Prophecy*),[17] as well as a smaller volume written along similar lines.[18] The

---

16. For a fuller summary and evaluation of Paulien see G.K. Beale, review of *Decoding Revelation's Trumpets*, in *JBL* 111 (1992), pp. 358-61. In a written communication, Paulien contends that I have misunderstood his discussion of 'echoes' in the *JBL* review.

17. R.J. Bauckham, *The Climax of Prophecy: Studies in the Book of Revelation* (Edinburgh: T. & T. Clark, 1993).

18. R.J. Bauckham, *The Theology of the Book of Revelation* (Cambridge: University Press, 1993).

focus of this summary will be on his *Climax of Prophecy*, since the smaller work is an abbreviation of many of the interpretations and arguments developed in detail in the larger work. Bauckham's work is a landmark study for three reasons: (1) because he studies the use of the Old Testament in a trenchant manner; (2) because he demonstrates the notion that the entire book was 'composed with such meticulous attention to the detail of language and structure that scarcely a word can have been chosen without deliberate reflection on its relationship to the work as an integrated, interconnected whole';[19] and (3) because he argues persuasively that John does not mechanically and mindlessly depend on the ideas of other contemporary apocalyptic works but utilizes them in an extremely creative manner to supplement his explicit use of the Old Testament and to enhance the unified literary nature of his work. The observation of such meticulous interpretative treatment of the Old Testament bears out Barnabas Lindars' notion that John's literary work was not the result of urgent, *ad hoc* apologetic concerns, as he claims is the case with other New Testament works, for example like Galatians or 2 Corinthians, but arose out of meditation worked out quietly in the study at a slightly later stage of Christian apocalyptic.[20] In this light it is understandable that readers might not notice all of the allusions on a first reading or even on many subsequent readings.[21]

In fact, Bauckham is not certain that John was familiar with any particular non-canonical Jewish or Christian works but did share with them independently knowledge of oral traditions which they reflect. Through study of the development of these traditions in these other apocalyptic works much light, nevertheless, can be cast on John's use of these common traditions, most of which have their roots in the Old Testament.[22]

Bauckham observes that John uses the Old Testament in a careful and not haphazard way throughout, so that an understanding of these Old Testament texts is crucial to the interpretation of the Apocalypse at every point along the way and is necessary for understanding his literary strategy. Consequently, the Old Testament 'forms a body of literature which John expects his readers to know and explicitly to

19. Bauckham, *Climax of Prophecy*, p. x.

20. B. Lindars, 'The Place of the Old Testament in the Formation of New Testament Theology', *NTS* 23 (1977), pp. 59-66 (63).

21. Bauckham, *Theology of the Book of Revelation*, p. 18.

22. Bauckham, *Climax of Prophecy*, pp. xi-xii.

recall in detail while reading his own work'.[23] Furthermore, a study of Jewish exegetical tradition of various Old Testament texts can also shed light on John's own understanding of the same texts.

Therefore, Bauckham emphasizes that John is an exegete who has set out to interpret the Old Testament in order to understand how its prophecies have found inaugurated fulfillment and will find consummated realization at the end of time:

> It is a book designed to be read in constant intertextual relationship with the Old Testament. John was writing what he understood to be a work of prophetic scripture, the climax of prophetic revelation, which gathered up the prophetic meaning of the Old Testament scriptures and disclosed the way in which it was being and was to be fulfilled in the last days. His work therefore, presupposes and conveys an extensive interpretation of large parts of Old Testament prophecy. Allusions are meant to recall the Old Testament context, which thereby becomes part of the meaning the Apocalypse conveys, and to build up, sometimes by a network of allusion to the same Old Testament passage in various parts of the Apocalypse, an interpretation of whole passages of Old Testament prophecy.[24]

In doing this, John is following others before him in the Old Testament prophetic tradition who reinterpreted earlier Old Testament prophecies and updated them for their own time.[25]

Bauckham's assessment lines up with that of the prior works of Beale and Fekkes (on the latter see below), who also contend that John contextually utilizes the Old Testament and focuses upon it as an object of interpretation. Nevertheless, the context of Bauckham's analysis shows also that John's own Christian presuppositions and his contemporary and historical context shed light on his own view of the Old Testament, a point also argued by the present monograph, as well as my earlier works.[26]

Most of Bauckham's interpretations of how John uses the Old Testament are convincing, many of which are novel, and there are very few conclusions which are debatable. Some of his findings support prior

23. Bauckham, *Climax of Prophecy*, p. xi.

24. Bauckham, *Climax of Prophecy*, p. xi. This is a conclusion which the present work also attempts to corroborate (e.g. see Chapter 2).

25. Bauckham, *Theology of the Book of Revelation*, pp. 4-5.

26. E.g. see Chapter 2 below, which is a revision of my earlier article 'Revelation' (e.g. see pp. 325-33).

conclusions reached by earlier commentators. There are so many studies which are given substantial treatment that they cannot be summarized adequately here without detracting from the excellent manner in
which they are discussed by Bauckham. Nevertheless, one of his analy-
ses deserves brief comment, since it is so novel and so well argued, and
is representative of the fresh approaches he takes elsewhere in the
book.[27]

Bauckham argues persuasively that the numbering of Rev. 7.4-8 suggests that those numbered are an army who are to conduct ironic holy
war.[28] The evidence for the view is primarily fourfold.

(1)   The purpose of numbering for a census in the Old Testament
       was always for counting up the military force of the nation:
       e.g. Num. 1.3, 18, 20, etc.; 26.2, 4; 1 Chron. 27.23; 2 Sam.
       24.1-9. For example, the purpose in the wilderness was to
       organize a military force to conquer the promised land; like-
       wise, when David took his census in 2 Samuel 24, it was for
       the purpose of reckoning the military strength of Israel. The
       repeated phrases ἐκ φυλῆς ('from the tribe of') in Rev. 7.4-8
       may echo the almost identical repeated phrase ἐκ τῆς φυλῆς
       ('from the tribe of') from Num. 1.21, 23, etc.

(2)   This is suggested further by the fact that those counted in the
       Old Testament were males of military age, and the 144,000 in
       Rev. 14.1-4 are 'male virgins'. According to Bauckham, the
       number of 144,000 is symbolic of perfection, though he qual-
       ifies this from the possible perspective of a first-century reader.

(3)   The military census of Numbers 1 has influenced the account
       in 1QM of the Qumran community's understanding of the fu-
       ture, imminent messianic war, when they would re-conquer
       the land of promise. For instance, 1QM organizes the army of
       the Qumran sect into the traditional grouping of twelve tribes
       (2.2-3, 7; 3.13-14; 5.1-2; 6.11).

27. Bauckham's first chapter on the 'Structure and Composition' of Revelation
is also outstanding and creative, but is not summarized here, since it does not focus
on use of the Old Testament.

28. Bauckham, *Climax of Prophecy*, pp. 217-29; so also in less developed form
by J. Valentine, 'Theological Aspects of the Temple Motif in the Old Testament
and Revelation' (Unpublished PhD dissertation; Boston, MA: Boston University
Graduate School, 1985), pp. 219-23.

(4)   There is evidence that the end-time expectation of the return of the ten tribes also included a hope that they would take part in a final war to defeat decisively God's enemies (though this point is less convincing, except for the appeal to Isa. 11.14, which is preceded by reference to 'the root of Jesse', probably alluded to in Rev. 5.5). Together with Isa. 11.14, Bauckham's last point finds more support from Isa. 14.2 and Mic. 5.6-9, the latter of which refers to a 'ruler in Israel' from 'Judah', whose 'exoduses are from *the beginning*' (5.2), who will 'shepherd His flock' (5.4), which is called 'the tribes of Israel' (4.14, LXX), 'the sons of Israel' (5.3), a 'remnant...*as lambs*' and a 'remnant...*as a lion*'(5.6-7, LXX). These Old Testament prophetic descriptions behind Rev. 7.4-8 not only provide more rationale for why Judah is placed first in the tribal list but also hint at an identification of a remnant from 'every tribe of the sons of Israel' in Rev. 7.4-8 both with 5.5 and the group in 7.9-17, who are also alluded to as sheep who will be shepherded (7.17).

In the context of Revelation, this military force of Rev. 7.4-8 conquers its enemy ironically in the same way in which the lamb ironically conquered at the cross: by maintaining their faith through suffering, they overcome the Devil (e.g. see also 5.5-6; 7.14; 12.11). Consequently, they are those 'following the lamb wherever he goes' (14.4). In particular, 7.4-8 portrays an army ready to fight, and 7.14 interprets the manner of their fighting: they conquer in no other way than that of the lamb, through persevering in the midst of suffering (see 7.14).[29]

Bauckham's analysis of the structure of the book, of key repetitive phrases throughout the book, and of the significance of numbers is very creative and suggestive, as well as convincing.[30]

Many other exegetical features of Bauckham's work deserve further summary and evaluation, but the scope of the present discussion does not allow for this, though this has been done elsewhere.[31]

---

29. For identification of the group in 7.4-8 with that in 7.9-17, see further on the introductory discussion to 7.9 in Beale, *Book of Revelation*.

30. Bauckham, *Climax of Prophecy*, pp. 1-37.

31. Summary and evaluation of many features of Bauckham's work appears throughout Beale, *Book of Revelation*.

5. *Jan Fekkes*

Still more recently Jan Fekkes has written a book on the use of Isaiah in the Apocalypse: *Isaiah and Prophetic Traditions in the Book of Revelation: Visionary Antecedents and their Development.*[32] Fekkes's work is important because a study of the use of Isaiah in Revelation has never been done in a full-scale manner. The book is divided into four main sections. First, there is discussion of the role of early Christian prophets in comparison to John as a Jewish-Christian prophet, which rightly concludes that John appeals to the Old Testament in order to underscore his absolute authority as a prophet in line with Old Testament prophets.

In the second segment there is a general survey of John's use of the Old Testament, initially focusing on the criteria for assessing the validity of Old Testament allusions; later in the book he places allusions into the following categories:[33] (1) certain/virtually certain; (2) probable/possible; and (3) unlikely/doubtful. The remainder of this section surveys the Old Testament uses of John and categorizes them thematically into the following classifications: (1) prophetic call narratives (Rev. 1.10-19; 10.1-11; based especially on Ezekiel, as well as Isaiah, and Daniel); (2) christological titles and descriptions (1.13-18; chs. 2–3; 5.5-6; 19.11-16; based especially on Isaiah, Daniel, Psalms, as well as Genesis, Zechariah, Jeremiah and Ezekiel); (3) throne-room theophanies (Rev. 4.1–5.2; based especially on Ezekiel, as well as Isaiah and Daniel); (4) Day of the Lord and holy war (Rev. 6.12-17; 14.14-20; 16.14; 19.11-21; based especially on Isaiah and Joel, as well as Hosea); (5) serial judgments (chs. 8–9; 16; based especially on Exodus, as well as Joel); (6) eschatological enemies (Rev. 12–13; 17.6-16; based especially on Daniel); (7) oracles against the nations (Rev. 14.8-11; 17.1-5, 16b-19.3; based especially on Jeremiah and Isaiah, as well as Ezekiel; (8) oracle of salvation (New Jerusalem; Rev. 7.14-17; 21.1-22.5; based especially on Isaiah and Ezekiel, as well as Zechariah).

The third segment, the major part of the book sets out to investigate in each chapter of the Apocalypse the validity of previously proposed allusions to Isaiah and to propose some new ones. A mass of worthwhile exegetical data is found in this portion of the book. The discus-

---

32. J. Fekkes, *Isaiah and Prophetic Traditions in the Book of Revelation: Visionary Antecedents and their Development* (JSNTSup, 93; Sheffield: JSOT Press, 1994).

33. Fekkes, *Isaiah and Prophetic Traditions*, pp. 279-81.

sion is characterized by judicious exegetical and technical textual analysis which interacts with most of the important primary and secondary sources. While not all will agree with every conclusion reached, the conclusions are almost always well reasoned and supported with good evidence. Among the examples of many good discussions is the analysis of the proposed use of Isa. 48.6 in Rev. 1.19 (which Fekkes rightly doubts) and the discussion of an Isa. 65.16 background behind Jesus' title in Rev. 3.14 (which he accepts and for which he offers further evidence). A number of his discussions result in a better understanding, not only of the use of the Old Testament in Revelation, but also of the meaning of Revelation itself.

The fourth and concluding section pulls together the preceding inductive exegetical analysis of Isaiah allusions in an attempt to discern significant patterns. The important conclusions reached are the following.

(1) Of the approximately 73 previously proposed allusions (not including repeated allusions to the same Old Testament text), Fekkes finds 43 to be 'authentic', 9 'probable, though not certain', and 23 'doubtful'.[34] Apart from allusions to Isa. 26.17 and 66.7-8 in Revelation 12, there are no probable allusions to Isaiah elsewhere in Revelation 8–13.[35]

(2) Fekkes discerns several exegetical uses of the Old Testament, among which the following are most significant, but certainly not novel: combination of two or more texts by analogy; bridging two passages together by means of a third; clarification of one Old Testament text by means of another more developed parallel Old Testament text; and extending the scope of a passage by subtle additions.

(3) The conclusions reached about the various uses of Isaiah corroborate his earlier analysis of Old Testament usage in general in the Apocalypse. Many of the same thematic classifications of Old Testament use discovered in the earlier analysis are found again in the case of Isaiah (prophetic call, christological descriptions, eschatological judgment and eschatological salvation). John does not so much focus on special books of the Old Testament as on special themes, so that themes dictate his

---

34. Fekkes, *Isaiah and Prophetic Traditions*, pp. 279-81.
35. Fekkes, *Isaiah and Prophetic Traditions*, p. 282.

selection of Old Testament texts instead of particular Old Testament books or authors.

(4)   Fekkes' work makes a contribution to the vexed question of whether or not John uses the Old Testament contextually in line with the original meaning of Old Testament passages or whether he merely uses Old Testament wording for his own purposes, twisting and disregarding the original meaning to suit the new situation. The commentary literature has been divided over the latter issue, as have been the more recent specialized works on the use of the Old Testament in the Apocalypse.[36]

In particular, Fekkes concludes that the cumulative weight of his evidence argues against two prominent presuppositions undergirding the view of some that John uses the Old Testament haphazardly: (a) that John does not interpret the Old Testament because he does not employ quotation formulae, uses Scripture anthologically and develops meanings inconsistent with the Old Testament context; and (b) that John does not interpret the Old Testament because he is a prophet, and such an appeal to another authority outside of himself would be inconsistent with his unique claim to authority. The latter notion is proved invalid by the observation that Old Testament prophets also reused earlier prophetic oracles in developing their own authoritative prophecies.[37]

Fekkes's discovery of thematic uses of Isaiah points further to a contextual use of the Old Testament, since this suggests that John was familiar with thematic emphases of Old Testament segments and not merely with single 'prooftexts', verses or mere individual wording which he exploits for his own unique thematic purposes.

While these four conclusions by Fekkes should be judged to be convincing, the following weaknesses of the work are observable.

First, the design of the thesis itself is not very creative: a mere examination and evaluation of previously proposed Isaiah allusions.

Second, Fekkes never attempts to respond trenchantly to one of the main objections to the notion that John interpreted the Old Testament

---

36. E.g. Beale, and, apparently, Paulien, arguing for the former, and Ruiz and Moyise the latter, though Moyise attempts a synthesis of the two approaches (on which see below).

37. Fekkes, *Isaiah and Prophetic Traditions*, p. 288.

contextually (though he shows awareness of the problem): John's pre-dominantly Gentile audience would have been generally unfamiliar with the Old Testament and would not have understood or appreciated his allusions, many of which are subtle and theologically sophisticated. Fekkes merely makes the assertion that there were 'biblically oriented conventicles' among the communities to which John was writing, which would have perceived his artful and penetrating Old Testament allusions.[38] Fekkes needs to take this objection much more seriously (and I believe there is a plausible and persuasive response to this objection).[39]

Third, there are some significant omissions in relevant bibliographical awareness:[40] these omitted sources primarily concern the use of the Old Testament in Revelation and were all published at least five years before Fekkes's work, which appeared in 1994. These would have been very important works for Fekkes to interact with, especially since they concern exegetical methodology in John's use of the Old Testament.

Nevertheless, all things considered, Fekkes's work is a good contribution to the study of the use of the Old Testament in Revelation.

B. *Recent Hermeneutical Studies on the Use of the Old Testament in Revelation*

The two works to be discussed in this section have special focus on the hermeneutical implications of the use of the Old Testament in the Apocalypse.

1. *J.-P. Ruiz*
In 1989 J.-P. Ruiz published an important book on the use of Ezekiel in Revelation.[41] Throughout the work are numerous insights about how the context of Old Testament allusions sheds helpful light on their use by John. The study could have been discussed above in the category of exegetical studies, but Ruiz views his exegetical work to contribute primarily to the specific area of hermeneutics. In particular, he sees his

---

38. Cf. Fekkes, *Isaiah and Prophetic Traditions*, p. 287, where he has one mere footnote validating this view.

39. On which see Chapter 2, sect. C.2.

40. (1) Paulien, *Decoding Revelation's Trumpets*; (2) Beale, 'Revelation'; and (3) Ruiz, *Ezekiel in the Apocalypse*.

41. Ruiz, *Ezekiel in the Apocalypse*.

book contributing, at least, to the following areas:[42] (1) it supports Vanhoye's claims that Revelation uses a Hebrew form of Ezekiel and that John uses Ezekiel in certain ways (large-scale allusions, multiple uses, combined Old Testament references); (2) the findings generally support Beale's view that Daniel is used extensively in Revelation 4–5, 13, and 17, but also that these chapters are *not* a midrash on Daniel, the latter of which is a conclusion which will receive further response at the appropriate point later;[43] (3) the study confirms Vogelgesang's observations of a heavy reliance on Ezekiel but does not confirm his theory that Revelation is an 'anti-apocalypse' which democratized visionary experience by showing its availability to all believers in worship;[44] (4) Ruiz demonstrates that Rev. 16.17–19.10 cannot be divided according to prior sources (as suggested by Boismard and Bergmeier) but is built around the metaphorical unity of prostitute, beast and Babylon, all three of which are inextricably linked realities (which are in antithetical contrast to the inseparable pictorial realities of bride, lamb and New Jerusalem which dominate 21.1–22.5); (5) the work contends that because of the three incorporated elements of cultic terminology (the temple and its associated paraphernalia), liturgical formulae (e.g. the seven blessings throughout the book and the eight 'hearing' formulae) and doxological hymns (e.g. 19.5-7; cf. 12.12; 18.20), the church's liturgical setting is the intended life-situation in which Revelation is to be read and understood.[45] This is a point, however, made also by other commentators who have noticed that Rev. 1.3 underscores such a viewpoint (as also reiterated by Ruiz). Nevertheless, Ruiz focuses more on the readers'/hearers' responsibility of interpreting what is read in Revelation than merely on their reading or hearing the book read, which has not been emphasized as much by earlier commentators.

Ruiz especially sees his contribution to lie in this last area of how the reader/hearer understands Revelation in a liturgical context and how John's own use of the Old Testament could be a hermeneutical clue for how his readers were interpreting his work. In particular, Ruiz contends that the church's liturgical setting is 'the privileged context' for hearing

---

42. For Ruiz's own longer summary, see Ruiz, *Ezekiel in the Apocalypse*, pp. 517-39.

43. On which see Chapter 2, sect: D.1.a.

44. For summary of Ruiz's critique of Vogelgesang, see the preceding section on Vogelgesang.

45. See especially Ruiz, *Ezekiel in the Apocalypse*, pp. 184-89.

and interpreting Revelation; the hearers are called in this context to 'sapiential reflection' on John's writing 'which is at the heart of the hermeneutical actualization of Revelation'.[46] John alludes extensively to Old Testament tradition, with which his readers are also familiar, and he exhorts them 'to reappropriate the tradition which is theirs' in the same way that he has reappropriated Old Testament tradition. John even gives his readers 'the hermeneutical equipment with which to focus that reappropriation'.[47]

What Ruiz claims this means is that, just as John 'creates' and 'produces genuinely new meaning'[48] through his rereading and reuse of Old Testament allusions, so readers of Revelation should see 'meanings behind meanings' in John's own language, so that 'new meanings' are offered 'which are not simply repetitions or combinations of the old ones'.[49] To the degree that 'the "interpreting subject" engages in an active reading of John's book, he or she engages in a dialogue with the text and with the texts [the Old Testament allusions] within the text'.[50] Therefore, in Revelation there is an ongoing 'open-endedness' of meaning or 'continuous fertility of the metaphoric terrain', which will continue as long as there is a 'dialogue between the text and its interpreters'.[51] John's words 'gather more meanings over time', so that they have a polysemy of sense and their full depth can never be plumbed.[52] Consequently, for example, even if one could understand Ezekiel's original intention in the wording of a particular text, new, endless meanings can be derived by different interpretative communities from this text which Ezekiel did not intend.

Ruiz is contending for a hermeneutical approach to Revelation which is aligned with an approach sometimes referred to as 'reader-response criticism'. In essence, the approach generally contends that readers or 'interpretative communities' are the ultimate determiners of a text's meaning and not the original author's intention in that text. Since Ruiz's formal comments in explaining his view are brief, fuller evaluation of this approach will be conducted below with examination of S. Moyise's

---

46. Ruiz, *Ezekiel in the Apocalypse*, p. 224.
47. Ruiz, *Ezekiel in the Apocalypse*, p. 225.
48. Ruiz, *Ezekiel in the Apocalypse*, p. 219.
49. Ruiz, *Ezekiel in the Apocalypse*, p. 228; cf. also pp. 520, 538-39.
50. Ruiz, *Ezekiel in the Apocalypse*, p. 520.
51. Ruiz, *Ezekiel in the Apocalypse*, p. 222.
52. Ruiz, *Ezekiel in the Apocalypse*, p. 223.

work, who attempts a full-blown defense of this perspective in Revelation and quotes Ruiz at various points in support.[53]

It is not clear how Ruiz's correct observation that the church's liturgy is the context for the reception and interpretation of Revelation supports his deduction that John's statements are susceptible to endlessly multiple meanings. He adduces Rev. 19.1-10 as a piece of doxological–liturgical evidence, suggesting that it implies that John's readers are also 'active participants in the interpretation of the book' and not merely hearers and spectators of the drama portrayed before them.[54] It is plausible that John intends that the hearers in this passage are to participate in praise to God (cf. 19.1-7), but it is unlikely that this particular text is encouraging a participation in interpreting the text, much less interpreting a text which has boundless meanings lying inherently within.

Likely also is his suggestion that the readers are included (certainly secondarily) in the exhortation to John about not worshipping an angelic being but only God and to recognize that he was hearing 'God's true words'.[55] Again, however, that this also includes an encouragement to the readers *to interpret* the Revelation text is certainly not clear, but, even if implied, would not support the notion that the text contains a fathomless pit of interpretative possibilities. Surely, the main point of Rev. 19.9b is to affirm the divine authority of the words John has just heard in v. 19a, which is likely an assessment of the whole book, an assessment which the readers are also to accept.

In addition to Ruiz's understanding of the hermeneutical implications of the community's liturgical setting, he offers a second piece of evidence in favor of the contention that the liturgical context has such hermeneutical overtones. He analyzes the imperatives, especially the expressions like the repeated formula 'the one having an ear, let him hear' (cf. the letters and 13.9) and the exhortation for the readers to have 'wisdom' and 'understanding' (13.18; 17.9), as well as the imperatives implied in the macarisms.[56] He calls these hermeneutical imperatives which invite readers to enter into a process of interpretative reflection of John's text, in addition to underscoring the prophetic,

---

53. Further direct evaluation of Ruiz on this issue will occur at various points in conjunction with analysis of Moyise's work.

54. Ruiz, *Ezekiel in the Apocalypse*, p. 523.

55. Ruiz, *Ezekiel in the Apocalypse*, p. 524.

56. Ruiz, *Ezekiel in the Apocalypse*, pp. 190-214, 538.

divinely authoritative, ethical and eschatological nature of the material to be interpreted. All of these implications of the imperatives are likely in mind to one degree or another. If an exhortation to interpret is included, what cannot be deduced is whether or not there are countless interpretations hidden within a text. The undoubted focus of the imperatives and formulaic blessings is *ethical*; readers are exhorted to obey God's message in the text. Certainly, part of this process is for readers to realize what Old Testament prophecy says, to perceive that the fulfillment of those prophecies is beginning to happen in their midst, and then to react to that situation in an obedient manner.

For example, the prophetic background of Rev. 13.18 and 17.9 is Daniel 11–12, which prophesies that there will be a tribulation in which an evil king will persecute saints and deceive others by influencing them to acknowledge his sovereignty and enter into the covenant community to perpetuate that deception. The Daniel prophecy also says that true believers will need to exercise keen 'insight and understanding' in order to discern the deceptive nature of the evil king and of his emissaries who enter into the covenant community and pass themselves off as true saints, but, in reality, are hypocrites (cf. Dan. 11.30-35; 12.10). When John tells the readers to have 'wisdom' and 'understanding', he is primarily exhorting them to be aware that the end-time deception prophesied by Daniel is beginning to take place through the authorities of the Roman empire and in the false teachers within the church community. The readers don't need any sophisticated or penetrating interpretative ability to interpret the hidden meaning of Daniel, but they do need to perceive that what had been understood and expected in previous generations from the prophecy of Daniel 11–12 was beginning to be fulfilled.

Against this background, they needed 'wisdom' to identify who the perpetrators of deception were by comparing carefully the description of the deceivers in Daniel with the similar behavior of those both inside and outside the church. Believers are to have 'wisdom' which enables them to know God's wise, prophetic plan and be prepared to discern divine imposters and their propagandists which have been prophesied by Daniel.[57] If the readers could exercise such 'wisdom', they would be able to prevent themselves and others from coming under the influence of the eschatological deceivers. They must be spiritually on the alert to

---

57. See Ruiz, *Ezekiel in the Apocalypse*, p. 207, who makes this point himself, based on the usage of σοφία elsewhere in Revelation.

discern such deceptive manifestations, which are unexpected by those not cultivating divine wisdom. Therefore, in contrast to Ruiz, the imperatives of 13.18 and 17.9 function primarily to underscore an ethical obligation by the faithful not to be deceived rather than emphasizing any significant interpretative role on their part. Both the exhortations call mainly for moral, not so much intellectual, ability to discern, first, that Old Testament prophecy is beginning fulfillment, and, second, to discern how to apply the truth of Old Testament prophecy while living in the midst of its fulfillment.[58] This corresponds to the common Old Testament definition (e.g. in Proverbs) of 'wisdom': applying to life situations the truth which is already known in the mind.[59]

In a virtually identical vein, including allusion to the expectation of Daniel 11–12, 1 Jn 2.18 says, with respect to false teachers within another covenant community, 'My little children, it is the last hour; and just as you heard that antichrist is coming, even now many antichrists have arisen; from this we know that it is the last hour'. Likewise, these readers are told how to distinguish true from false teachers.

Ruiz also understands John's eight hearing formulas to have virtually the identical function as the expressions in 13.18 and 17.9. As with 13.18 and 17.9, so also the hearing formulas may include an encouragement to interpret along with conveying notions of the prophetic, divine authority and eschatology, but primarily in mind is the obligation to respond in an ethical or moral manner: the hearers are exhorted to faithful loyalty to Christ despite temptations to compromise with idolatry and threats of persecution.[60] In fact, pointing in just the opposite direction of Ruiz's view, the Old Testament and Gospel background of the hearing formula indicates that it was used in conjunction with parabolic communication when straightforward, abstract and rational discourse had proved not to move Israel to righteous, ethical action and loyalty to Yahweh; the same appears to be the case in

58. See further Beale, *Book of Revelation, in loc.*

59. For the specific Old Testament background of 'wisdom' and its relevance for 13.18 and 17.9 see G.K. Beale, 'The Danielic Background for Revelation 13:18 and 17:9', *TynBul* 31 (1980), pp. 163-70.

60. Because of space limitations, full analysis of Ruiz's discussion of the hearing formula cannot be entered into here, but the results are the same. In this respect cf. further Ruiz's analysis of the hearing formula with that of the author's own study below which underscores the ethical nature of the formulas (Chapter 4, sect. B: 'The Hearing Formula in the Letters of Revelation and its Implications for the Purpose of Symbolism in the Visionary Portion of the Book').

Revelation. Therefore, John is aiming the exhortations more at the volition (the heart) than the cognition (the mind). What focus there is on perceiving truth is to be understood more in terms of genuine believers being shaken out of their spiritual anesthesia and realizing the sinful predicament and dangerous idolatrous situation which they are in, and repenting and taking action not to compromise.[61]

Ruiz views these as exhortations to have 'attentive reflection'[62] or 'sapiential reflection'.[63] Ruiz himself rightly acknowledges that the hearing formulas invite readers 'to come thereby to an understanding of their situation and of what the risen Christ expects from them',[64] but he wants to highlight just as much what he sees as the cognitive interpretative elements in the formula. As he rightly says, such elements are there to some degree, since if readers do not use their minds they will not understand what Christ is saying[65] (as is true in any human discourse), but the interpretative element is secondary and certainly would not refer explicitly to 'exegesis' or a creative 'rereading of scripture' in the way those terms are used today nor to the refined notion of whether or not the material to be interpreted was susceptible to endlessly multiple meanings.

In fact, relevant parallels within the text of Revelation itself underline the moral over the cognitive element in all of what Ruiz calls the 'hermeneutical imperatives', but are better termed 'moral imperatives' or merely 'paraenesis'. With respect to the hearing formula in association with the exhortations of 13.18 and 17.9, compare the following:

13.9:	If anyone has ears, let him hear;
13.10b:	Here is the perseverance and faith of the saints;
13.18:	Here is the wisdom: the one having understanding;
17.9:	Here is the mind which has wisdom.

Where Rev. 13.18 and 17.9 have 'wisdom and understanding', 13.10b substitutes 'perseverance and faith', apparently interpreting 'wisdom and understanding' in the moral–volitional sense of obedience and trust in God. Furthermore, Rev. 13.10b is most probably a continued explanation of what it means to 'hear with the ears' in 13.9.

---

61. See Chapter 4, sect. B.
62. Ruiz, *Ezekiel in the Apocalypse*, p. 199.
63. Ruiz, *Ezekiel in the Apocalypse*, p. 224.
64. Ruiz, *Ezekiel in the Apocalypse*, p. 196.
65. Ruiz, *Ezekiel in the Apocalypse*, p. 198.

In addition, the blessings, containing implied imperatives, exhibit almost the same paraenetic emphasis:

> 1.3:   Blessed is the one reading and the ones hearing the words of the prophecy and keeping the things having been written in it, for the time is near;
>
> 22.7:   And, behold, I am coming quickly. Blessed is the one keeping the words of the prophecy of this book.

Both verses emphasize the notion of imminence in the last and first clauses respectively. Also, in both cases, blessing is pronounced on those who 'keep' or respond in obedience to the commandments in the book. While 'hearing' occurs uniquely in 1.3, it likely does not refer explicitly to any kind of exegetical or interpretative procedure on the part of the readers, but, as in the following hearing formulas, to the need for ethical action and loyalty to Yahweh, so that the target of the implied imperatives of the macarisms is the volition (the heart) more than the cognition (the mind). Again, paraenesis is the focus.

Thirdly, Ruiz proposes that Revelation's use of 'mystery' undergirds his contention that the readers are encouraged to enter into a formal interpretation of the text.[66] Before readers begin to interpret the symbols of the book by means of their interpretative 'wisdom', they must first confront the symbol as an unresolved enigma, which is part of the 'mystery' of Revelation.

The main point, however, in the use of 'mystery' in 1.20 and 17.5, 7 is on John, not the readers, being given an interpretation of a prior symbolic vision by a heavenly mediator. Both 10.7 and 17.5 refer to the mystery as something prophetic which will be or is in process of being fulfilled according to God's word (cf. 17.17). This is not merely the revealing of end-time events hitherto hidden in the decretive counsels of God but the revealing of the unexpected manner in which such events will unravel, which applies to the use in 1.20 as well.

In the light of 10.7, the entire book could be considered part of the 'mystery', and this is the verse Ruiz focuses upon and says refers to each uninterpreted symbol of the book which the reader-interpreter needs to unravel. This is possible, but it would be a secondary meaning of 'mystery', since three of the four uses of μυστήριον in Revelation directly refer to the heavenly mediator resolving the symbolic enigma for John (John does not resolve it himself), and the other use in 10.7 is

---

66. Ruiz, *Ezekiel in the Apocalypse*, pp. 212-14, 220, 538.

still directed to John but certainly has a broader reference. I think Ruiz has made a good point here, but it is implicit and not explicit. His contention, however, that μυστήριον has both the objective sense of the revelation of God's unfolding plan and the subjective idea of the process of interpretative reflection whereby parts of that plan are 'received, discerned, and appropriated'[67] is not supported by the texts where μυστήριον occurs, where it always has to do with revelation, which includes its use in Daniel, Qumran and elsewhere in the New Testament.[68] Furthermore, his conclusion does not address the issue of symbols containing ever-new, changing meanings, which is one of the conclusions Ruiz also wants to draw from his discussion of 'mystery' in Revelation.[69]

Lastly, Ruiz adduces one more primary line of evidence in favor of the notion that John formally encourages his readers to interpret his statements which are endlessly open-ended in meaning. The idiosyncratic Greek of the Apocalypse (especially the so-called solecisms) function to make the reader pause because 'the familiar conventions of ordinary discourse are suspended'.[70] Ruiz believes that such awkward language is not merely due to inelegant style or grammatical incompetence but is the result of 'conscious and intentional difficulties placed before the reader as an obstacle to confound an ordinary reading of the text'.[71] Once readers have discerned the clue that John is not composing an ordinary written communication, they interact with the symbolic discourse of Revelation, and so are put on a hermeneutical course 'of coming to understand the new meaning which the text offers'.[72] Accordingly, readers become interpreters in that they 'decode' the significance of the symbolic pictures which confront them, symbols which, Ruiz contends, ultimately have an unlimited array of meanings.

In response, the question of the solecisms of the Apocalypse has been a perennial problem difficult to explain. A full discussion of the solecisms and my own solution to the thorny issue must await a later chap-

---

67. Ruiz, *Ezekiel in the Apocalypse*, p. 214.
68. For my own fuller analysis of the use of μυστήριον, see Chapter 3, sect. D below.
69. Ruiz, *Ezekiel in the Apocalypse*, pp. 220-22; e.g. he says, 'each interpreter, each audience is called upon to "decode" the μυστήριον anew' (p. 222).
70. Ruiz, *Ezekiel in the Apocalypse*, p. 220; cf. also pp. 216, 224.
71. Ruiz, *Ezekiel in the Apocalypse*, p. 220.
72. Ruiz, *Ezekiel in the Apocalypse*, p. 220.

ter,[73] but a brief response to Ruiz's view of the solecisms is better given here. Some have attributed the difficult grammatical constructions to, among other things: (1) a reflection of categories of unusual though acceptable Greek syntax (attested also in contemporary Hellenistic Greek); (2) to *constructio ad sensum*; (3) to John's ineptness or inelegant style; (4) to the intense effect of the apocalyptic vision; (5) to Semitic influence (either the style of the LXX, Hebrew Old Testament or Aramaic); and (6) to his attempt to make the reader focus more on certain phrases. Ruiz's proposal fits within the last category. Very similar to Ruiz is the view of the nineteenth-century commentator Moses Stuart who argued that the syntactical peculiarities were intended to make readers take closer notice of the clause at hand (especially when they were appositional or explanatory clauses). My own view, to be offered in ch. 5 of the present book, is best understood within category §5 and §6 above: the awkward constructions are often part of Old Testament allusions and are due to John's carrying over the exact grammatical form of an Old Testament wording in order to create 'syntactical dissonance', which causes the reader/hearer to pause and increases their chances of recognizing the unusual wording to be an Old Testament allusion.

Both my view and Ruiz's are a refinement of Stuart's, who said that the irregularities influence the readers to focus more on a particular phrase for rhetorical purposes, which he does not further define. Putting aside discussion of my new proposal until later, what can be said for Ruiz's view? He claims that John consciously and intentionally placed difficulties 'before the reader as an obstacle to confound an ordinary reading of the text'. What he means by 'an ordinary reading' apparently is a discourse which is abstract and does not contain metaphors (though to say that metaphorical communication is not a natural part of 'an ordinary reading' is questionable). Once readers have discerned the clue that John is not composing an ordinary written communication, they interact with the symbolic discourse of Revelation. This is reasonable as far as it goes. It is Ruiz's deduction based on this observation which is questionable: he says that, as readers interact with the symbolism, they come to be involved in a process 'of coming to understand the new meaning which the text offers'.[74] Even this *could* be viable in

---

73. See Chapter 5 below ('The Influence of the Old Testament on the Grammar of Revelation').

74. Ruiz, *Ezekiel in the Apocalypse*, p. 220.

the sense that the solecisms make readers pause, and the purpose of the pause is to stimulate readers to reflect on John's meaning and to interpret that meaning. Ruiz, however, understands this, not to refer merely to John's new interpretation of the Old Testament, but to ever new meanings engendered as a result of the ongoing generations of readers' interaction with the text and the text with the readers, *irrespective* of the original Old Testament meaning or John's own interpretation of the Old Testament.

The conclusion that the text-reader dialogue generates ever-new meanings is not sustainable by the text. More evidence must be forthcoming to substantiate such a hermeneutical claim. Where does the text itself say that it contains endless meanings apart from that of the Old Testament and John's? It is almost irresistible to think that a presupposition of reader-response criticism[75] lies at the root of such an attempt to interpret the function of the solecisms in this manner. Furthermore, Ruiz never cites nor explains one actual example in Revelation where a solecism occurs and functions in the manner which he claims. It would have been acceptable if Ruiz had limited his conclusions to saying that there were unlimited 'significances'[76] or 'implications' of an interpretation of a text.[77] It is possible, though unlikely, that Ruiz confuses the hermeneutical concepts of 'meaning' and 'significance' (as defined, e.g., by E.D. Hirsch, on which see below in discussion of Moyise).

Perhaps, the best evidence Ruiz offers for his perspective is the observation, noted above, that John creates new meaning through his rereading and reuse of Old Testament allusions and that his readers are to follow his method in their rereading of the Old Testament and of Revelation itself. This is an interesting suggestion, and it is certainly true that John creates 'new' meanings, but these must be understood as 'new' in the redemptive-historical sense of organically developed meanings of the Old Testament not seen so clearly hitherto, but now seen

75. For fuller evaluation of which see discussion in the following sub-section below of Moyise, who has applied the theory in the most extensive way to Revelation.

76. For the definition of 'significance' and its distinction from 'meaning' or 'interpretation', see discussion below of Moyise.

77. Ruiz does distinguish 'interpretation' and 'significance' (which he calls 'application') but includes the former with the latter in being limitless (Ruiz, *Ezekiel in the Apocalypse*, pp. 211, 220-221).

retrospectively in the light of latter-day fulfillment.[78] Ruiz's conclusion that John's creative handling of the Old Testament suggests that texts have unlimited meanings goes beyond what the text says. In addition, Ruiz is insensitive to discussing the historical particularity of John's writing: if John was a prophet, why should his readers also follow his interpretative procedure?[79] I think there is a partial answer to this,[80] but not the one Ruiz gives (both with respect to his view of the role of solecisms and with respect to the hermeneutical significance of the liturgical setting). Ruiz adds that the readers' active engagement in the interpreting process 'is itself revelatory, is itself a participation in the book's project of revelation'.[81] If such were the case, of course, a solid rationale would be provided for readers to follow John's purported creative method of rereading scripture. Again, the textual support for such a conclusion is lacking; instead, the conclusion is a theological statement without exegetical support, which corresponds better to ecclesiological traditions in which revelation is viewed as an ongoing process throughout the history of the church. Ruiz's position at this point appears close to running counter to his own earlier criticism of Vogelgesang, where he acknowledged that, though John shared in a solidarity and equality with the hearers, they were recipients of his uniquely and divinely inspired message.[82]

78. For elaboration of what is meant here, see the following discussion of Moyise.

79. A general critique posed to any such approach by R. Longenecker, 'Can We Reproduce the Exegesis of the New Testament?', *TynBul* 21 (1970), pp. 3-38.

80. On which see discussion of Moyise below, where I contend that John's 'new' or 'creative' interpretations are not 'new' in the sense of being in a contradictory trajectory to their Old Testament source texts but are organically related in a redemptive-historical sense to original Old Testament meanings, especially when seen in the light of the early Christian communities' hermeneutical presuppositions. Furthermore, that later Christian readers should emulate the exegetical method of the New Testament writers is a viable notion, as long as it is understood that such readers do not share in the same revelatory stance as the biblical writers and that such exegetical methods do not involve an uncontrolled spinning out of texts, whatever meanings are agreed upon by any particular interpretative community. Meaning must be ultimately determined by original authorial intent (for elaboration see also G.K. Beale, 'Did Jesus and his Followers Preach the Right Doctrine from the Wrong Texts? An Examination of the Presuppositions of Jesus' and the Apostles' Exegetical Method', *Themelios* 14 [1989], pp. 89-96).

81. Ruiz, *Ezekiel in the Apocalypse*, p. 216; cf. also p. 530.

82. Ruiz, *Ezekiel in the Apocalypse*, pp. 171-76, where he says that both John

2. *Steve Moyise*

S. Moyise has written the most recent monograph on Revelation. This is different in nature than all prior works, since his intent is not to provide a thorough exegetical analysis of any aspect of John's use of the Old Testament, but to focus on the kind of hermeneutical approach one should take toward understanding the allusions. The primary purpose of the book is to explore whether or not the notion of 'intertextuality' together with recent developments in 'reader-response criticism' can contribute to a deeper understanding of John's references to the Old Testament. In reality, though his work is of a different nature, Moyise's is a development of a hermeneutical approach to Revelation anticipated by earlier commentators, especially J.-P. Ruiz.

Moyise notes that in a technical manner all Old Testament allusions are taken out of context in the sense that they are removed from their original literary context in the Old Testament and placed into a new literary context in the New Testament. Therefore, the Old Testament wording must bear some new meaning by virtue of its new literary context.[83] Furthermore, the juxtaposition of Old Testament texts with Christian tradition produces a tension to which John offers no resolution, since he appears not to indicate which should be interpreted in the light of the other.[84]

According to Moyise, two important positions on this issue are represented by Beale and A.Y. Collins.[85] The former holds that various chapters of the Apocalypse are a midrash on Daniel 7 and that the author is interpreting Daniel for the readers and locating their situation within the prophetic context of Daniel in order to meet their needs, that is, Daniel's prophecies have begun fulfillment and are continuing fulfillment in their midst. Here, the Old Testament is determinative of the

and the readers were participating in a revelatory process, the only difference being that John received revelation through visions and the readers received revelation through reflecting on the words John uses to describe the visions. Such a distinction seems so small that his earlier criticism of Vogelgesang would appear to be rendered ineffective.

83. S. Moyise, *The Old Testament in the Book of Revelation* (JSNTSup, 115; Sheffield: Sheffield Academic Press, 1995), pp. 19-20, 112-13.

84. Moyise, *Old Testament in the Book of Revelation*, pp. 108-46; likewise, Ruiz, *Ezekiel in the Apocalypse*, p. 528, says that metaphors are 'renewed by their recontextualization in John's text and by the permanent tension which each embodies'.

85. Moyise, *Old Testament in the Book of Revelation*, p. 22.

meaning of the New Testament passage, without seeing any significant contribution of meaning from the New Testament context in which the Old Testament reference is placed.[86] Others, like Collins, argue that John employs various significant Old Testament texts merely to express his own unique viewpoint, so that John's intent is not to interpret Old Testament texts nor does their meaning exercise any determinative influence on his understanding but they are only a means to suit his own creative interpretative ends.[87] Similarly, Schüssler Fiorenza understands the New Testament context to be so determinative that the original meaning of an Old Testament passage has essentially faded, so that John has no interest in interpreting the Old Testament but merely 'uses its words, images, phrases, and patterns as a language arsenal in order to make his own theological statement or express his own prophetic vision'.[88]

In response to these two opposite perspectives, Moyise contends that the real question is not, 'has the author respected the Old Testament context', or 'has he not respected the Old Testament context', but 'how does the Old Testament context interact with the New Testament context?'[89] Is the New Testament use a consistent, organic development to one degree or another of the Old Testament passage, or is there such a degree of cognitive dissonance between the two that no harmonious development can be discerned?[90] His answer is that it is likely that John

---

86. Moyise, *Old Testament in the Book of Revelation*, p. 111, though this is a misrepresentation of my view, on which see further below, and on Chapter 2 (e.g. 'Conclusion').

87. See likewise Ruiz, *Ezekiel in the Apocalypse*, p. 121, though he is inconsistent, acknowledging elsewhere that the original meaning of wording in its Old Testament context is the driving force for meaning in the Revelation context (e.g. he affirms that the background of Daniel is very formative in understanding the exhortations of Rev. 13.18 and 17.9 and for understanding the figure of the 'beast' [pp. 210-11, in dependence on my own article, 'Danielic Background'; likewise, he says that there is an originality with John's use of μυστήριον in Rev. 17.5 but that 'That originality is fully in line with the OT background of μυστήριον', p. 337 [again, in dependence on Beale, *Use of Daniel*, pp. 12-19, 168-69]; many more such examples could be given; indeed, ironically, it is one of the strengths of Ruiz's work to see the Old Testament context as informing the New Testament context).

88. Quoting here E. Schüssler Fiorenza, *The Book of Revelation: Justice and Judgment*, p. 135.

89. Moyise, *Old Testament in the Book of Revelation*, p. 19.

90. Moyise contends that this is a different question than whether or not the New Testament respects the Old Testament context (e.g. Moyise, *Old Testament in*

is offering new understandings of Old Testament texts which may have been surprising to an Old Testament readership.

It is important, however, to formulate as precisely as possible what it means to say that John expresses *new understandings* of the Old Testament. Moyise believes that the recently formulated notion of 'intertextuality' can shed light on the issue.[91] Allusion to an earlier text by a later text results in some kind of correspondence between the two. 'Intertextuality' refers to a reader's attempt to follow the meaning of the later text, while being mindful of the prior text and how the later text redefines and distorts the original by putting it within another cultural and linguistic context. An intertextual reading must be careful to analyze the ways in which the two respective contexts interact.[92] 'The task of intertextuality is to explore how the source text continues to speak through the new work and how the new work forces new meanings from the source text.'[93]

At this point, the question must be asked, is the reader to struggle with an 'intersection of textual surfaces' or is the reader led to a fixed interpretative resolution?[94] Moyise, as already observed, says that two predominant answers have been given to this question: the Old Testament is determinative for the meaning of the New Testament text or the New Testament is determinative for the meaning of the Old Testament text.

Moyise contends that there is a middle position between the two different answers. He sometimes refers to this as the new affecting the old and the old affecting the new:[95] the Old Testament reflects on the New Testament context, even as the New Testament context absorbs and changes the Old Testament allusion.[96] There is a tension between these two interpretative angles which is not easily resolved. Moyise gives the example of Rev. 5.5-6, where Christ is compared to a 'lion' and a 'lamb'; even though both are allusions to the Old Testament, they appear to express two very different views of Christ within the space of

the Book of Revelation, p. 142), but I cannot detect a material difference between the two.

91. Moyise, *Old Testament in the Book of Revelation*, pp. 18-19.
92. Moyise, *Old Testament in the Book of Revelation*, pp. 18-19.
93. Moyise, *Old Testament in the Book of Revelation*, p. 111.
94. Moyise, *Old Testament in the Book of Revelation*, p. 23.
95. Moyise, *Old Testament in the Book of Revelation*, p. 19.
96. Moyise, *Old Testament in the Book of Revelation*, p. 116.

only two verses. Some see only the Old Testament–Jewish notion of a conquering messianic figure who defeats enemies in some literal or militaristic fashion, since that background utilizes both lion and lamb images in that manner.[97] On the other hand, some see the New Testament context of the crucified Christ portrayed as a slain lamb to swallow up any original Old Testament notion of a literal conquering messiah, which Gen. 49.9-12, for example, conveys by reference to Judah and to a ruler from Judah being compared to a lion. In this respect, Caird says that it is as if John wants us to read 'Lamb' wherever the Old Testament says 'Lion': 'wherever the Old Testament speaks of the victory of the Messiah or the overthrow of the enemies of God, we are to remember that the gospel recognizes no other way of achieving these ends than the way of the Cross'.[98]

Moyise asks the question, 'Does John intend a resolution of the tension?' His answer is an ambiguous 'yes' and 'no'. On the one hand, he discusses evidence that John resolves the tension. He appeals to Bauckham, who says that John uses militaristic language and applies it to a non-militaristic context: Christians follow Christ by fighting spiritual holy war at the cost even of their physical lives in order to save their souls and in order to defeat the spiritual powers of evil.[99] Nevertheless, in reality, this is nothing more than a version of Caird's solution, which Moyise has already considered extreme and one-sided.

Moyise also discusses evidence that John does not attempt to resolve the tension by adducing other passages in the book which he believes exhibit an unresolvable tension. For example, he sees passages elsewhere in the Apocalypse (e.g. Rev. 19.11-21) which allude to the militaristic notion in the Old Testament of a Messiah with no hint at an attempt to tone down or reinterpret the expectation of a military kind of victory.[100] He also contends that John offered no help to readers as to how the sealed 144,000 about which he hears in 7.1-8 fits with the innumerable multitude which he sees in 7.9-17. Moyise leaves unclear whether or not there is ultimate tension in the 'lion–lamb' and other like texts.[101]

---

97. Cf. Ford's view in *Abomination*, pp. 129-30.
98. Caird, *Revelation of St. John the Divine*, p. 75.
99. Moyise, *Old Testament in the Book of Revelation*, pp. 134-35.
100. Moyise, *Old Testament in the Book of Revelation*, p. 133.
101. Moyise, *Old Testament in the Book of Revelation*, cf. pp. 123-34.

What could be called 'new' interpretations result from the bearing of the new context on the old.[102] Moyise has not gone far enough in explaining how John (or other New Testament writers) has generated his new views of the Old Testament. It is true to say that the Old Testament wording must bear some new meaning by virtue of its placement in the new literary context. This is, however, somewhat general and vague.

More particularly, it should be recognized that these new interpretations are the result of John's new, presuppositional lenses through which he is now looking at the Old Testament, among the most significant of which are: (1) Christ corporately represents true Israel of the Old and New Testament; (2) history is unified by a wise and sovereign plan, so that the earlier parts of canonical history are designed to correspond typologically and point to latter parts of inscripturated history; (3) the age of end-time fulfillment has been inaugurated with Christ's first coming; and (4) in the light of points 2 and 3, the later parts of biblical history interpret earlier parts (a trend already begun by later Old Testament tradition with respect to earlier Old Testament books), so that Christ as the centre of history is the key to interpreting the earlier portions of the Old Testament.

Granted the legitimacy of these presuppositions, John's interpretation of the Old Testament shows respect for Old Testament contexts, and his interpretation shows formative influence from the Old Testament itself; if, however, these presuppositions are spurious, then his interpretation must be seen as foreign to the original intention of the Old Testament writers. Some modern commentators, like Schüssler Fiorenza, view John's own context as injecting new meaning into the Old Testament references which is inconsistent and incompatible with the Old Testament. It is more likely, however, that John would have seen these presuppositions as organically growing out of the Old Testament itself, since the presuppositions are ultimately traceable also to Christ's own interpretative approach which he probably passed on to his disciples. John sees that what the Old Testament prophesied is beginning fulfillment in events of his own time, and his study of the Old Testament helps him better understand these events, even as the details of the events themselves help him better understand the Old Testament.

---

102. Though Moyise says that John does not create 'something completely new' (Moyise, *Old Testament in the Book of Revelation*, p. 138).

There is not space to discuss this at greater length; however, I have addressed these questions in more detail elsewhere.[103] If Moyise had been sufficiently cognizant of these presuppositions, he might not have been so persuaded to see unresolvable tensions of interpretation within the Apocalypse. For instance, his prime representative example of the irreconcilable 'lion–lamb' notion is solved reasonably well by the 'already and not yet' presupposition of John's eschatology. Christ's past defeat of the enemy as a 'lion' has begun in an ironic manner through death and suffering as a 'lamb', but the future, consummate form of the enemy's defeat will be more straightforward: Christ will judge decisively and openly both his earthly and cosmic enemies, including Satan himself. The judgment commences at the cross in veiled form and is consummated before all eyes in more open (and perhaps more literal) form at the very end of history, when Christ returns finally to deliver his people completely and to judge definitively his foes and consign them to eternal punishment.

It is my suspicion that Moyise, though he says formally that John offers no resolution to whether Old Testament interprets New Testament or *vice versa*, may have in mind the reciprocal interpretative interplay of Old Testament influence and the New Testament presuppositions which read the Old Testament in new but not contradictory or inorganic ways, especially since: (1) he acknowledges formally that 'the new affects the old and the old affects the new'[104] and that 'Any description of John's use of Scripture must do justice to both the continuities and the discontinuities';[105] (2) he acknowledges that significant incidents of John's use of the Old Testament 'might come under the category of typology',[106] so that many of his interpretative conclusions may fall under Thomas Greene's literary category of those kinds of texts which are 'not a pale imitation of the old but its true successor';[107] (3) he uncritically acknowledges R.J. Bauckham's view of the organic relationship of John's use of the Old Testament to Old Testament

---

103. Beale, 'Did Jesus and his Followers Preach the Right Doctrine from the Wrong Texts?'.

104. Moyise, *Old Testament in the Book of Revelation*, pp. 19, 58, 82-83, 102, 110-11, 115, 128.

105. Moyise, *Old Testament in the Book of Revelation*, p. 22.

106. Moyise, *Old Testament in the Book of Revelation*, p. 83.

107. Moyise, *Old Testament in the Book of Revelation*, p. 119.

prophetic tradition, which is similar to my own perspective;[108] (4) he acknowledges that I hold to a similar interplay of Old Testament and New Testament texts, though not to the degree which he claims he does;[109] and (5) some of the examples of new interpretation of the Old Testament cited by Moyise, as a result of his purported new hermeneutical perspective, are commonly accepted re-interpretations of the Old Testament which arise from John's obvious Christian presuppositions.[110] Consequently, Moyise seems to be using the newer jargon of contemporary hermeneutics (reader-response theory, etc.) to describe phenomena described formerly with different, traditional terminology.

John's interpretative resolution between the juxtaposition of Old Testament texts and Christian tradition is to be found either in the broader Old Testament context or broader New Testament context, or both. Though there may be times when these contexts yield ambiguous information, it does not mean that John was ambiguous in his own mind. The juxtaposition of texts or ideas which are seemingly incompatible interpretatively is likely best viewed as part of John's overall Semitic style: it is an expression of Semitic paratactic thinking which allowed the setting in close proximity of two different, and sometimes seemingly contradictory, ideas of a word, without the discomfort experienced by some twentieth-century readers; the broader context usually resolved the tension when parataxis was used in the Old Testament.[111] This appears to account better for the evidence than the formulation of a new hermeneutical theory.

Moyise leaves unclear whether or not there is ultimate tension between Old Testament references and their uses in the New Testament context, using as his representative example John's use of the Old Testament military imagery of the Messiah as a military kind of conqueror.[112] The upshot of his overall thesis, however, leans toward con-

---

108. Moyise, *Old Testament in the Book of Revelation*, pp. 98-99.

109. Moyise, *Old Testament in the Book of Revelation*, pp. 62, 111. I elaborate on the interplay in my 'Did Jesus and his Followers Preach the Right Doctrine from the Wrong Texts?', and in my forthcoming *Book of Revelation*; see also G.K. Beale (ed.), *Right Doctrine from Wrong Texts? Essays on the Use of the Old Testament in the New* (Grand Rapids: Baker Book House, 1994).

110. E.g. see Moyise, *Old Testament in the Book of Revelation*, pp. 128-29, 134-35.

111. See G.B. Caird, *The Language and Imagery of the Bible* (Philadelphia: Westminster Press, 1980), pp. 117-21.

112. E.g. cf. Moyise, *Old Testament in the Book of Revelation*, pp. 123-34.

cluding that the hermeneutical tension often remains. This becomes clearer when he sets out to answer the question, 'Irrespective of what John may have intended [as a resolution of the tension between a meaning of an Old Testament passage and its apparently changed meaning in a different New Testament context], does the text offer such a resolution to readers today?' This question is answered with a resounding 'no', since Moyise concludes that such an answer is demanded by the observation that major commentators differ profoundly about whether or not Revelation is essentially Christian or Jewish (as represented, for example, respectively by the different positions of Caird and Ford on the militaristic notion of the Old Testament allusions to the Messiah's victory).[113] This conclusion is bolstered further by the presupposition that 'we have no access to the author's mind'.[114] Furthermore, even if we were able to discover an author's original intentions, it would not help us toward understanding 'how the actual text does work with particular readers'.[115]

Moyise tries to qualify this conclusion by acknowledging that John's purposes, *in some way*, are still of interest to the reader.[116] Yet, as noted above, he is not able to explain exactly how knowing John's intention can help the reader toward better resolving the tension of whether the Old Testament determines meaning in the New Testament or *vice versa*. The reason for this is because Moyise concludes that John himself does not resolve that tension.[117]

Therefore, the reader is left to determine the resolution. Indeed, John 'forces' those reading his work to engage 'in an active reading' of his book and to enter into 'a dialogue with the text and with the texts within the text'.[118] Not coincidentally, Moyise cites Ruiz at this point, whom Moyise also cites at other points, and rightly so, since Ruiz expresses a similar vagueness about this issue, though he does not address John's hermeneutical theory as directly or thoroughly as Moyise.[119]

---

113. Moyise, *Old Testament in the Book of Revelation*, pp. 131-32.

114. Moyise, *Old Testament in the Book of Revelation*, p. 132.

115. Moyise, *Old Testament in the Book of Revelation*, p. 132.

116. Moyise, *Old Testament in the Book of Revelation*, p. 132.

117. Moyise, *Old Testament in the Book of Revelation*, pp. 133-35.

118. Moyise, *Old Testament in the Book of Revelation*, p. 135.

119. Though Ruiz is brief in his comments, my impression is that Moyise's more in-depth elaboration is a generally fair representation of the way Ruiz would elaborate.

Moyise elaborates further on what he means by this:

> The contribution of this study has been to show how the literary concept of 'intertextuality' can be used to illuminate this 'dialogue with the text and texts within the text'. It is not so much applying a method as asking certain types of questions and pondering particularly evocative phrases (like 'connotations bleed over'). Its premise is a very simple one, namely, that if an allusion points the reader to something outside of the text, it inevitably sets up a relationship between the two contexts which is in some sense unpredictable (*and out of the hands of the author*). *The task of the interpreter is to give an account of how these two contexts potentially affect one another, as Hays puts it, the distortions and new figuration that they generate* [my italics].[120]

> By utilizing past texts, the author has produced a fresh composition which invites the reader to participate and *create meaning* [my italics].[121]

Up to this point, Moyise has seemed to maintain a balance throughout his work on granting legitimacy to discerning the original author's intention and to the reader creating meaning. Indeed, Moyise himself has exhibited a tension between these two poles, which is not easily solvable, so that ironically his own authorial intention is hard to discern. At the conclusion of his work, however, he clearly lines up with the notion that the emphasis is to be placed on the reader creating meaning. His reason for doing so is because of a contemporary trend in research within which he positions his own work; accordingly he says,

> emphasis on the author's 'intention' has been largely abandoned in New Testament study and replaced by a focus either on the text itself or on the role of the reader.[122]

His ultimate reason for aligning his own work with this perspective of research is based on two hermeneutical presuppositions: (1) 'we have no access to the author's "intention"', and 'meaning is not a "given" but has to be "created" by the reader'.[123]

One's views about these hermeneutical presuppositions will determine how one responds to Moyise's thesis. This is not the place to enter into a full analysis and evaluation of reader-response criticism and its

---

120. Moyise, *Old Testament in the Book of Revelation*, p. 135.
121. Moyise, *Old Testament in the Book of Revelation*, p. 142.
122. Moyise, *Old Testament in the Book of Revelation*, p. 142.
123. Moyise, *Old Testament in the Book of Revelation*, p. 142. The first presupposition was anticipated earlier by Moyise (p. 132).

relationship to 'intertextuality', especially since Moyise does not give a defense of the theory but merely assumes its validity, taking refuge in what he judges to be the consensus of present New Testament scholarship. Nevertheless, some evaluative comments are appropriate which show the general approach of what a more in-depth response would look like.

First, Moyise certainly makes an overstatement when he says that 'emphasis on the author's "intention" has been largely abandoned in New Testament study and replaced by a focus on either the text itself or on the role of the reader'.[124] This may be true within his own interpretative community, but certainly is not the case generally speaking. At the least, such a conclusion demands a study in its own right, surveying many New Testament scholars' works over the last decade. For example on the one hand, most articles which appear in the quarterly journal *New Testament Studies* are exegetical in the traditional sense in that they seek to explicate the original author's intention. On the other hand, various seminars and program groups on New Testament subjects at the annual Society of Biblical Literature meetings do operate with the presuppositions of 'reader-response criticism', but the question needs to be asked in these cases how representative such groups are of the field of New Testament scholarship.

Second, modern writers who operate with the assumptions of reader-response criticism, especially the notion that readers, not original authors, create meaning, usually also assume that the readers of their own works are not left to create new meanings but can discover rather easily the original intention.[125] This is a significant inconsistency. One possible response might be that there is a difference between interpreting ancient and modern texts in that the former have been read and re-read and re-interpreted differently by various communities throughout centuries, whereas this is not true of the latter. Therefore, one could try to

124. Moyise, *Old Testament in the Book of Revelation*, p. 142.
125. Cf. E.D. Hirsch, *The Aims of Interpretation* (Chicago:University of Chicago Press, 1976), p. 6, who makes the same criticism: 'Whenever I am told by a Heideggerian that I have misunderstood Heidegger, my still unrebutted response is that I will readily (if uneasily) concede that point, since the concession in itself implies a more important point, namely, that Heidegger's text can be interpreted correctly, and has been so interpreted by my accuser. Since the accusation assumes the determinateness and stability of Heidegger's meaning, *and* the possibility of its being correctly interpreted, I admit the practical error for the sake of the theoretical

posit that there is a qualitative difference between some ancient texts and modern writings, the former being more legitimately susceptible to multiple meanings and the latter not so susceptible.[126] This response, however, would still fall short of being convincing, since even more modern writings, such as poetry, have been subjected to varying interpretations, yet most agree that authors of poetry have an original intention to convey to the reader. Despite age, one could perhaps maintain that certain literary genres are capable of legitimate multiple interpretations. But not even consideration of literary genres is helpful as a response, since authors can use all kinds of genres to convey their unitary intention. Of course, an author could set out to write something with the intention of being unclear, so that many competing interpretations of the writing could legitimately and easily result, but such an intent would be rare, and does not represent most of the literary genres of today or of the past.

The notion that readers create meaning is likely due in part to a hermeneutical flaw of confusing original 'meaning' with 'significance'. These two realities are sometimes collapsed into one another and not differentiated. E.D. Hirsch helpfully distinguishes between 'meaning' and 'significance', which also bears on the present discussion. The explanation of original, intentional, *verbal meaning* is distinct from the 'significance' of that meaning.[127] Here we enter into the realm of epistemology, with which implicitly we have been involved all along. By way of illustration, we can compare an author's original, unchanging meaning to an apple in its original context of an apple tree. When

truth. I was once told by a theorist who denied the possibility of correct interpretation that I had not interpreted his writings correctly'. Hirsch contends that Heidegger's disciples, such as Jacques Derrida, had not been able to give a cogent response to this logical criticism at the time he wrote *Aims of Interpretation* (1976; p. 13). The same kind of criticism against reader-response criticism and deconstructionism is made by D.A. Carson, *The Gagging of God* (Grand Rapids: Zondervan, 1996), pp. 102-105.

126. This possibility was mentioned to me by one of my colleagues in biblical studies at Gordon–Conwell Theological Seminary. Moyise, *Old Testament in the Book of Revelation*, p. 118, himself implies this: 'There is no denying that a Christian will read into words like "firstborn" and "faithful witness" connotations that were not present in the psalm [Ps. 89]. This is to be expected for words "gather more meanings over time".'

127. See directly below for a further explanation of verbal meaning as a 'willed type'.

someone removes the apple and puts it into another setting (say, in a basket of various fruits in a dining room for decorative purposes), the apple does not lose its original identity as an apple, the fruit of a particular kind of tree, but the apple must now be understood not in and of itself but *in relation to the new context* in which it has been placed. This new contextual relationship is called 'significance'. The new context does not annihilate the original identity of the apple, but now the apple must be understood in its relation to its new setting. It is the same with meaning and its significance: '"Meaning refers to the whole verbal meaning of a text, and "significance" to textual meaning in relation to a larger context' beyond itself, that is, a context of 'another mind, another era, a wider subject matter, an alien system of values', etc.[128] What Hirsch calls 'significance' some theologians would call 'application' (how does the message of a particular ancient biblical text apply to the lives of people living in the twentieth century?).

Third, it appears that Moyise sometimes understands the proposal of diverse interpretations of a text (or of an Old Testament allusion),[129] all of which have plausible evidence supporting them, to be evidence of inability to discern an author's original intention. Even if this were true in some cases, which it is, it would not be evidence for a general theory that the original authorial intention behind most or all Old Testament allusions is not discoverable. This would be a logical fallacy in which the evidence of a part is used to represent the remaining uninvestigated whole. Moyise would have to investigate a much greater range of allusions in Revelation before he could conclude this with such a proposal

128. Hirsch, *Aims of Interpretation*, pp. 2-3. The scope of the present work is unable adequately to discuss the hermeneutical debates between the classical and modern positions represented respectively, e.g., by Hirsch and Gadamer; these debates themselves have their roots in two alternative epistemological positions represented by Husserl and Heidegger; for discussion from Hirsch's perspective see Hirsch, *Aims of Interpretation*, pp. 4-6; E.D. Hirsch, *Validity in Interpretation* (New Haven: Yale University Press, 1967), pp. 209-74; for an assessment from a similar perspective see Royce G. Gruenler, *Meaning and Understanding* (Grand Rapids: Zondervan, 1991), pp. 74-86, N.T. Wright, *The New Testament and the People of God* (Minneapolis: Fortress Press, 1992), pp. 18-144 *(passim)*, and Carson, *Gagging of God*, pp. 57-137, 163-74. Both Wright and Carson strike a good balance between the subjective and objective epistemological aspects involved in this debate.

129. Such as in the case of the differing interpretations by Caird and Ford of the messianic images of the lion and lamb in Rev. 5.5-6 discussed earlier.

for the whole. In fact, there is not much original exegesis of Old Testament allusions in the work itself; most of the analysis of actual texts is a survey of what commentators say about texts or a summary of very basic and well-known interpretations of certain texts, whether in Qumran, or especially in Revelation. Furthermore, contrary to Moyise, mutually incompatible interpretations of the same passage do not mean that one interpretation is as good as another.[130] Apparently irreconcilable interpretations may indicate that the original author's intention is either unrecoverable in a particular text or very difficult to assess. Or, such contrary interpretations may indicate different but ultimately reconcilable or supplementary aspects of an author's one meaning. Such interpretations should be judged according to degrees of probability and possibility. There is a tradition of commonsense criteria which have already been established to evaluate degrees of probability and possibility of interpretative alternatives in a text.[131]

In this regard, Hirsch's notion of a 'willed type' as a further explanation of intentional, verbal meaning may be helpful. A willed type has two characteristics: (1) an entity with a boundary in which some things

130. In this respect, Moyise says that readers are addressed by a number of voices within a text, and 'how these are "heard" and what the reader makes of them will differ from person to person', depending on one's prior choice of a hermeneutical key to the overall context of the particular focus text (Moyise, *Old Testament in the Book of Revelation*, p. 143). Moyise cites Fiorenza in support: 'Competing interpretations of Revelation are not simply either right or wrong, but they constitute different ways of reading and constructing socio-historical and theo-ethical meaning' (E. Schüssler Fiorenza, *Revelation: Vision of a Just World* [Proclamation; Minneapolis: Fortress Press, 1991], p. 3). While Moyise and Fiorenza grant the capability of modern interpreters to recognize the intention of one another's writings and the different presuppositional or hermeneutical perspectives expressed in these writings, they are inconsistent in not being willing to grant the same ability in recognizing the intention and, apparently even, the presuppositions of ancient writers. Though we all have presuppositions which influence the way we read texts, these presuppositions do not blind us from perceiving authorial intentions incompatible with our hermeneutical lenses and from discerning the different presuppositions of others, both modern and ancient writers. Wright, *New Testament and the People of God*, pp. 18-144 (*passim*), refers to such an approach as 'critical realism'.

131. E.g. see Hirsch, *Validity in Interpretation*; note Hirsch's concepts of 'intrinsic genre' and 'coherence'. Hirsch says that these criteria are part of 'the classical, mixed tradition of evaluation' (*Aims of Interpretation*, p. 12).

belong within the boundary and others are excluded, and it can be represented by only a single instance among the other things which belong within the legitimate boundary; and (2) the type as an entity can be represented by more than a single instance, as long as the other representing instances fall within the boundary.[132]

For example, suppose I say, 'Nothing pleases me so much as the Third Symphony of Beethoven and other similar kinds of classical music.' In response, a friend might ask, 'Does it please you more than a walk during a beautiful spring day?' My friend has misunderstood me by taking me too literally. I was speaking in hyperbole, so that a walk during a beautiful spring day was not one of the things that fell under what I meant by 'things that please me', for, indeed, such a walk might please me just as much as Beethoven's Third. I used 'nothing' as a hyperbole to stand for 'no other comparable work of musical art'. How did I know that 'a walk during a beautiful spring day' was not to be included within the specific class of 'things that please me'? Some overriding principle in my meaning must have determined that 'a walk during a beautiful spring day' was excluded from what I meant and that Elvis Presley's 'You Ain't Nothing but a Hound Dog' was included, along with a number of other non-classical music compositions. This is the case because I intended to refer to a particular *type* of 'thing that pleases me' and 'willed all possible members belonging to that type'[133] and excluded others not falling within the boundary of comparable classical compositions. Certainly, my *conscious* intention did not include all musical works which please me, but only a select few, nor was there before my mind's eye all musical pieces which do not please, but only a few. If my friend were to ask me if I would include Bach's Mass in B Minor as works which especially please me, I would say 'yes', even though my conscious intention was to include explicitly only Beethoven's Third and, implicitly, Handel's *Messiah*, Bach's 'Brandenburg Concertos', and Vivaldi's *Four Seasons*. My friend could suggest more musical pieces which I would also include and exclude in my willed type, but which were neither part of my explicit statement nor even part of my implicit conscious intention.[134] Such implicit meanings within

---

132. Hirsch, *Validity in Interpretation*, pp. 49-50.
133. Hirsch, *Validity in Interpretation*, p. 49.
134. This illustration about classical music has been adapted, with a few changes, from Hirsch, *Validity in Interpretation*, pp. 48-49.

my 'willed type' can be called 'implications' of the explicit verbal meaning.[135]

Therefore, in the words of Hirsch,

> Thus, it is possible to will an et cetera without in the least being aware of all the individual members that belong to it. The acceptability of any given candidate applying for membership in the et cetera depends entirely on the type of whole meaning I willed.[136]

This notion of a 'willed type' is instructive for understanding and analyzing John's use of the Old Testament. First, when John alludes to a particular text, it could be asked which feature of the Old Testament context does he have in mind, since it is apparent that New Testament writers have varying degrees of contextual awareness when they make reference to an Old Testament passage.[137] In each case, John probably has some specific feature in mind explicitly which more often than not is apparent to most readers, and perhaps implicitly he had other features consciously in mind, but which are not apparent in his written expression. If we had opportunity to ask him directly after he had written what other implicit features he had in mind, he would probably acknowledge some. Even if we asked him whether or not some other contextual features could be included in his unconscious intention (or within the scope of his 'willed type'), he would probably acknowledge some more.[138] To go beyond what is apparently his clear, explicit

---

135. Hirsch, *Validity in Interpretation*, pp. 61-67.

136. Hirsch, *Validity in Interpretation*, p. 49. Hirsch's view of a determinant meaning is based on Husserl's epistemological presupposition that the mind can perceive an idea of something experienced and that it can 'demarcate' that mental act so that it remains the same idea over a period of time (Hirsch, *Aims of Interpretation*, pp. 4-5). An explicitly theistic hermeneutical perspective would add to this the presupposition that the omniscient God's immutable, sovereign transcendence is the enduring foundation for 'an absolute transcendent determinant meaning to all texts' (D. McCartney and C. Clayton, *Let the Reader Understand* [Bridgpoint; Wheaton, IL: Victor Books, 1994], p. 284); the determinant meaning of all texts is known completely by the all-knowing God who is 'not mutable or time bound, and so the meaning which He understands of a text is unchanging' (McCartney and Clayton, *Let the Reader Understand*, p. 284).

137. On the feature of degrees of contextual awareness, see Chapter 2, sect. C.2.

138. Perhaps, this is what Moyise has in mind when he says, 'That is not to say that discussion of the effect of intertextual echo must be limited to John's conscious intention. There is no reason to assume that John thought out all the possibilities of

instance of the 'willed type' is a matter of guesswork on the part of the interpreter, involving varying degrees of possibility and probability (indeed, sometimes it is difficult to know whether or not John even is conscious of some of the very Old Testament references themselves, which are apparent to commentators but could be the mere result of a mind so saturated with Old Testament language and ideas that they are unconsciously expressed).[139] Such multiple meanings should not be confused with the kind of contradictory, multiple meanings for which reader-response critics argue.

One of the many examples of this in the Apocalypse is the clear allusion to Isa. 22.22 in Rev. 3.7. The Old Testament allusion sets up a primary correspondence (and contrast) between Eliakim and Christ: like Eliakim, Christ was to have absolute power over the Davidic throne as king. Whereas Eliakim's rule was primarily political and local (over Israel), Christ's was primarily spiritual, as well as universal. He held authority over those entering the kingdom and over those in the realm of death. In addition, however, there are other contextual features both within the immediate context of Isaiah 22 and within the broader context of the entire book of Isaiah which could be implicit as a part of John's 'willed type' (e.g. as Eliakim's power was equal to the Israelite king's, so was Christ's to God's; as Eliakim's office likely included priestly connotations, so did Christ's; as Eliakim was appointed to his political office, so Christ was appointed to a greater office; and so on). Most of these additional contextual features also find varying degrees of contextual support both within the immediate and broad context of Revelation.[140] How possible or probable they are in relation to John's 'willed type' is a matter of possibility and probability judgments. But what we cannot say is that we can make of John's allusion anything we want. There are hermeneutical boundaries which exclude many things which we know for certain John did not intend.

Such a discussion of hermeneutics in the Apocalypse cannot be concluded without reflecting, at least briefly, on the interpretation of symbols. It is surprising that Moyise did not address this issue to some degree, since it is usually in this area which some commentators attempt

bringing Psalm 89 into a relationship with the living Christ [in Rev. 1.5]' (Moyise, *Old Testament in the Book of Revelation*, p. 118).

139. On which see further Chapter 2, sect. C.1.

140. See Chapter 2, sect. D.6.a, for a number of other contextual features in the context of Isaiah which John possibly could also have had in mind.

to substantiate some form of a reader-response hermeneutic. In sum, the appeal is made to the notion that symbols are ambiguous, indeterminate, and hence open-ended, with evocative, multiple meanings. On the basis of this presupposition, the conclusion is sometimes drawn that symbols cannot be fully expressed by only one or even several limited meanings. Furthermore, it is claimed that John's symbols cannot be expressed by finite, space-time bounded logical, propositional language because they refer to a divine transcendent reality.[141]

Again, because of space constraints, only a brief following response can be given which is methodological in orientation and not philosophical or theological.[142] First, it should be acknowledged that the language of biblical literature, including metaphors, 'cannot be reduced to, but certainly includes, the notion of propositional truth'.[143]

The symbols in Revelation are either similes or metaphors (or implied metaphors). All metaphors have a literal subject and a figurative subject, which functions as a pictorial filter through which the literal subject can better be understood. The figurative subjects may have a range of possible points of comparison with which they are commonly associated. The point of comparison usually carries both cognitive and emotional elements. Suppose the phrase 'George is a wolf' is said in a context in which George is understood to be a dangerous criminal. We understand better through the picture of wolf that the literal subject George is someone who hurts people and this image evokes a feeling of fear.

In the above example, the broader context may suggest that George is not only dangerous like a wolf but also that other points of comparison associated with wolves are in mind, that is, that he is cunning, quick,

141. Representative among those holding a reader-response view of John's symbols are: Ruiz, *Ezekiel in the Apocalypse*; M.E. Boring, *Revelation* (The Interpretation Series; Louisville: John Knox Press, 1989), pp. 51-59; E. Schüssler Fiorenza, 'Revelation', in E.J. Epp and G.W. MacRae (eds.), *The New Testament and its Modern Interpreters* (Atlanta: Scholars Press, 1989), pp. 417-18; E. Schüssler Fiorenza, *The Book of Revelation: Justice and Judgment* (Philadelphia: Fortress Press, 1985), pp. 186-92. For further summary and analysis of this hermeneutical perspective, see the introductory section on 'The Interpretation of Symbolism' (and the subsection on 'The "New Hermeneutical" Perspective on John's Symbols') in Beale, *Book of Revelation*.

142. For philosophical and theological evaluation see Beale, *Book of Revelation*.

143. Carson, *Gagging of God*, pp. 163-74, who notes that there is an ethical–moral aspect which is distinct from the propositional.

elusive, scavenging, preying upon others and hungry. Potentially all of these or only some of these points of commonplace comparisons may be in mind. Sometimes John explains his implied metaphors by giving explicit identifications of an image following the visionary depiction of it. When there is no explicit identification, the immediate and broad context of the book is the most important factor in determining which meanings are intended.

The known commonplace associations of a picture also will help to provide the possible alternative points of comparison, when the context of the book does not yield a clear identification. This means that a thorough survey must be made of the commonplace associations in the biblical and ancient world through the primary source documents, especially the Hebrew Old Testament, LXX, Jewish literature and pagan literature, as well as evidence from numismatic, inscriptional and prosopographic sources. When the context of the book does not yield a probable meaning, the Old Testament and Judaism are the primary backgrounds against which to understand the images and ideas of the Apocalypse. In this respect, the task is to trace the exegetical tradition in the later portion of the Old Testament and in Judaism of Old Testament symbolic passages alluded to by John in order to see the commonplace associations of the Old Testament. The Greco-Roman world is also an important quarry providing needed background against which to understand the book.

In addition to context and the known commonplace associations, the most obvious way of discerning the intended point(s) of comparison is the literal subject itself. The literal subject of 'George' the human compared with 'wolf' immediately excludes some wolfly associations such as fur-like, having pointed ears and being large toothed, though even these could be compared to George, if the context so warranted. There are varying degrees of correspondence between the picture and the literal subject. In high degrees of correspondence something essential to the likeness of the picture is applied to the literal subject. In low degrees of correspondence the likeness is restricted to some narrow aspect of the figurative subject.[144]

In studying the language of the Apocalypse careful consideration needs to be given to identifying the point(s) of comparison, which are sometimes multiple for any given symbol. An author may intend one

144. On which see further Caird, *Language and Imagery of the Bible*, pp. 153-59.

metaphor to have more than one point of comparison. Therefore, to identify more than one point of comparison in a single metaphor is not to be guilty of allegorical interpretation nor to acknowledge that a limitless number of meanings is possible but to discover the original intention of an author's rich metaphorical use.

However, it is true that most of Revelation's symbols have multiple associations or meanings and that the interpreter can never be sure that all the multiple meanings of a symbol have been discovered. On the other hand, this does not mean there are inexhaustible meanings (e.g. dependent on the individual interpreter's own subjective stance and situation). The interpreter can arrive at a probable assessment of what are some of the 'core' associations or meanings of the symbols explicitly and implicitly intended by the ancient author within the orbit of his 'willed type'.[145] Such 'core' notions are accessible and comprehensible by paying heed primarily to the immediate context of the book, as well as by recognizing prior use of the symbol in the Old Testament, early Judaism, the New Testament, and the contemporary Greco-Roman environment,[146] all of which yield multiple associations or connotations. Revelation's metaphorical texture is 'like an onion or rose with layers of meaning', or even like a prism refracting meaning in multiple ways,[147] but not in limitless ways.[148]

145. This is arrived at much in the same way as we discussed above that one can make probability and possibility judgments of how many features of an Old Testament context may be in mind in John's use of particular Old Testament allusions.

146. For further discussion about the viability of being able to validate interpretations on the basis of probability judgments see the good analysis of Hirsch, *Validity in Interpretation*.

147. Schüssler Fiorenza, *Revelation*, p. 19.

148. I have found my approach to evaluating the application of 'reader-response criticism' to Revelation throughout this chapter to be compatible with and supplemented by the following works which evaluate its larger application to the New Testament in general: Wright, *New Testament and the People of God*, pp. 18-144 (*passim*); Carson, *Gagging of God*, pp. 57-137, 163-74. Cf. likewise, W.W. Klein, C.L. Blomberg and R.L. Hubbard, *Introduction to Biblical Interpretation* (Dallas, TX: Word Books, 1993), pp. 438-40.

Chapter 2

THE VARIOUS WAYS JOHN USES THE OLD TESTAMENT

Introduction

Before analyzing the uses which John makes of Old Testament scripture, it is necessary first to consider some issues of prolegomena.

A first preliminary consideration is to assess the amount of Old Testament actually utilized in Revelation. There is general acknowledgment that the Apocalypse contains more Old Testament references than any other New Testament book, although past attempts to tally objectively the total amount have varied.[1] The variation in statistics is due to the different criteria employed to determine the validity of an Old Testament reference and the fact that some authors include 'echoes' and parallels of a very general nature.[2] The range of Old Testament usage includes the Pentateuch, Judges, 1–2 Samuel, 1–2 Kings, Psalms, Proverbs, Song of Solomon, Job, the major prophets and the minor prophets. Roughly more than half the references are from the Psalms, Isaiah,

---

1. UBS[3], pp. 901-11 = 394; NA[26], pp. 739-74 = 635; British and Foreign Bible Society Greek text, pp. 734-87 = 493; E. Hühn, *Die altestamentlichen Citate und Reminiscenzen im Neuen Testament* (Tübingen: J.C.B. Mohr [Paul Siebeck], 1900), pp. 269ff. = 455; W.D. Dittmar, *Vetus Testamentum in Novo* (Göttingen: Vandenhoeck & Ruprecht, 1903), pp. 263-79 = 195; Swete, *Apocalypse*, p. xcl = 278; Charles, *Revelation*, pp. lxv-lxxxii = 226; van der Waal, *Openbaring*, pp. 174-241 = 1000 (approx.); for a listing of statistics from other commentators see Fekkes, *Isaiah in Revelation*, p. 62. See J. Paulien, 'Elusive Allusions: The Problematic Use of the Old Testament in Revelation', *BibRes* 33 (1988), pp. 37-38ff., for an example of the varying lists of allusions in a particular segment of Revelation (Rev. 8.7–9.21 and 11.15-18). One reason for the varying statistics is that some of these lists include parallels together with allusions and citations.

2. Cf. the survey and evaluation of Vos, *Synoptic Traditions in the Apocalypse*, pp. 17-19, and Vanhoye, 'L'utilisation du livre d'Ezéchiel dans l'Apocalypse', pp. 438-40.

Ezekiel and Daniel, and in proportion to its length Daniel yields the most.[3]

The evaluation of Daniel as most influential is supported by recent study.[4] Among the allusions to Daniel, the greatest number comes from Daniel 7. Proportionally, Ezekiel ranks second as the most used Old Testament book,[5] although in terms of actual numbers of allusions Isaiah is first, followed by Ezekiel, Daniel and Psalms (although statistics cited by commentators differ; e.g. Swete cites Isaiah = 46,[6] Daniel = 31, Ezekiel = 29, Psalms = 27). There is more agreement that Ezekiel exerts greater influence in Revelation than Daniel (on which see below in this section). The Old Testament in general plays such a major role that a proper understanding of its use is necessary for an adequate view of the Apocalypse as a whole.

A. *The Text Form of Old Testament References in the Apocalypse*

The text form of the Old Testament references in Revelation needs in-depth discussion since there are no formal quotations and most are allusive, a phenomenon often making textual identification more difficult. The complex relationship of the Hebrew text to early Greek versions, the history of which is largely unknown to us, makes it difficult to know whether John depends on the Hebrew or the Greek.[7] Unfortunately, however, the scope of the present discussion precludes thorough analysis of this important subject.[8] The majority of commentators have not followed Swete's assessment[9] that John depended mainly on the LXX but have apparently followed Charles' conclusion that John was

3. So Swete, *Apocalypse*, p. cliii, where numerical statistics are also given for many of the Old Testament books used.

4. Cf. Beale, *Use of Daniel*.

5. Cf. Vanhoye, 'L'utilisation du livre d'Ezéchiel dans l'Apocalypse', pp. 473-75.

6. And the more trenchant analysis of Fekkes, *Isaiah in Revelation*, pp. 280-81, finds 50 'certain and probable' allusions to Isaiah.

7. So J.M. Vogelgesang, 'Interpretation of Ezekiel', pp. 19-22.

8. But see further Trudinger, 'OT in Revelation'; Beale, *Use of Daniel*, pp. 43-259, 306-13; *idem*, '"Kings of Kings and Lord of Lords" in Rev. 17:14', *NTS* 31 (1985), pp. 618-20; *idem*, 'A Reconsideration of the Text of Daniel in the Apocalypse', *Bib* 67 (1986), pp. 539-43.

9. Swete, *Apocalypse*, pp. clv-clvi.

influenced most by the Hebrew rather than the Greek Old Testament,[10] a conclusion based mainly on the observation that John's allusions depart from the wording of the LXX;[11] however, the wording also departs from the Hebrew at significant points.[12] The likelihood is that John draws from both Semitic and Greek biblical sources and often modifies both.[13] Charles himself acknowledged that, though John's pattern was to translate from the Hebrew text and not to quote from the Greek version, nevertheless, 'he was often influenced in his renderings by the LXX and another Greek version' (proto-Theodotion).[14]

B. *Criteria for Discerning the Presence of Old Testament Allusions*

The criteria for identifying the presence of allusions is crucial to consider before studying Old Testament usage. Reasonable criteria of discerning allusive validity is the following: (1) *clear allusion*—when the wording is almost identical to the Old Testament source, it shares some common core meaning, and could not likely have come from anywhere else; (2) *probable allusion*—though the wording is not as close as in category one, it still contains an idea or wording that is uniquely traceable to that Old Testament text; or, the New Testament passage may exhibit a *structure* of ideas uniquely traceable to an Old Testament passage; and (3) *possible allusion*—the language is only generally similar to the purported source, so that it may echo either the wording or the concept of an Old Testament passage. Also, a reasonable explanation of

---

10. Charles, *Revelation*, I, pp. lxvi-lxvii, as well as pp. lxviii-lxxxii; C.G. Ozanne, 'The Language of the Apocalypse', *TynBul* 16 (1965), pp. 3-9.; Trudinger, 'OT in Revelation'; S. Thompson, *The Apocalypse and Semitic Syntax* (SNTSMS, 52; Cambridge: Cambridge University Press, 1985), pp. 1-2, 102-108.

11. Charles, *Apocalypse*, I, p. lxvi.

12. See further Moyise, *Old Testament in the Book of Revelation*, p. 17.

13. So Moyise, *Old Testament in the Book of Revelation*, p. 17, though this is a conclusion reached already by the mid-nineteenth century commentator Moses Stuart (*Commentary on the Apocalypse*, II [Andover: Allen, Morrell & Wardwell; New York: M.H. Newman, 1845], pp. 231-32), and in 1902 by T.C. Laughlin (*The Solecisms of the Apocalypse* [Princeton, NJ: Princeton University Press, 1902], p. 21); cf. likewise J.H. Moulton, W.F. Howard and Nigel Turner, *A Grammar of New Testament Greek. II. Accidence and Word-Formation* (Edinburgh: T. & T. Clark, 1929), p. 480; for LXX influence cf. also Beale, '"Kings of Kings and Lord of Lords"'; Beale, 'Text of Daniel in the Apocalypse'.

14. Charles, *Revelation*, I, p. lxvii.

authorial motive should be given if a proposed Old Testament allusion is to be accepted as clear or probable. For example, in John's case, he appears to allude to the Old Testament to explain how he sees Old Testament prophecy as having been and being fulfilled in the light of Christ's coming, Pentecost and the creation of the church (on which see further on the excursus at the end of this section).[15] These criteria for allusive validity are also applicable to recognizing the presence of allusions to other sources outside the Old Testament (from Judaism[16] and the Greco-Roman background). One must be circumspect in the search for dependence on other prior literary sources, being conscious of resisting the temptation to find parallels where there are none.[17]

C. *Further Preliminary Considerations for Studying Old Testament Usage in the Apocalypse*

1. *Problematic Use of Combined Allusions and the Issue of Literary Consciousness*
We have already acknowledged the non-formal character of the Old Testament references in Revelation. Not only does this make Old Testament textual identification more difficult but it also renders it problematic to determine whether or not the author is consciously or unconsciously referring to an Old Testament text. This problem is compounded since many, indeed most, of the Old Testament reminiscences are found in combination with one another. Sometimes four, five or more different Old Testament references are merged into one picture. Good examples are the descriptions of Christ (1.12-20), God on the throne and the surrounding heavenly host (4.1-11), and the diabolic

---

15. See further Beale, *Use of Daniel*, p. 308; see also Paulien, 'Elusive Allusions', for additional discussion of criteria and validity of allusions.

16. E.g. see H.M. Parker, 'The Scripture of the Author of the Revelation of John', *Iliff Review* 37 (1980), pp. 35-51, who contends that John was saturated with non-canonical apocalyptic Jewish tradition, though direct dependence on this material is small in comparison with direct Old Testament references (for further evaluation see F.D. Mazzaferri, *The Genre of the Book of Revelation from a Source-Critical Perspective* [BZNW, 54; Berlin: W. de Gruyter, 1989], pp. 47-49); in fact, Parker's references to this material fall into the category of broad conceptual parallels and not verbal literary dependence.

17. In this respect, note the warnings of S. Sandmel, 'Parallelomania', *JBL* 81 (1962), pp. 1-13, and T.L. Donaldson, 'Parallels: Use, Misuse and Limitations', *EvQ* 55 (1983), pp. 193-210.

beast (13.1-8).[18] How are such combined allusions to be studied? This phenomenon would be particularly hard to analyze if, as some contend, it is less intentional and more the result of a memory so saturated with Old Testament language and ideas that they are unconsciously organized in the author's visions 'like the changing patterns of a kaleidoscope'.[19] In this case, the Old Testament contextual meanings of the allusions need not be examined to comprehend better John's use, since he himself did not consciously reflect on such Old Testament contexts. Indeed, many have concluded that the lack of formal citation in the Apocalypse points in the same direction.

Caird,[20] however, sees conscious effort in such allusive combinations for the purpose of expressing evocative and emotive power. Therefore, for him it is unnecessary to attempt to comprehend the meaning of each reference in its Old Testament and New Testament context, since the whole picture must be kept together without separating and analyzing various strands in order to evoke the desired emotional effect. Of course, in these mosaics there is always the possibility of a mixture of conscious intention with unconscious activity.

In contrast to Caird's view, often a greater understanding is gained and emotive effect felt when the various allusive parts of these visionary amalgamations *are* studied separately in their Old Testament contexts. Vos cites Rev. 4.2-9 as a fitting illustration of unconscious mixing of Old Testament allusions. However, when the Old Testament context of each allusion is studied one finds that, without exception, they are all from descriptions of theophany scenes, which function as introductory sections to an announcement of judgment either upon Israel or the nations: compare Vos's parallels of (1) Rev. 4.2 with Isa. 6.1 and/or 1 Kgs. 22.19; (2) Rev. 4.3f. with Ezek. 1.28; (3) Rev. 4.5a with Ezek. 1.13 and/or Exod. 19.16; (4) Rev. 4.5b with Ezek. 1.13 and Zech. 4.2, 6 (omitted from Vos); (5) Rev. 4.6a with Ezek. 1.22; (6) Rev. 4.6b with Ezek. 1.5 and 1.18; (7) Rev. 4.7 with Ezek. 1.10; (8) Rev. 4.8a with Isa. 6.2; (9) Rev. 4.8b with Isa. 6.3; and (10) Rev. 4.9 with Isa. 6.1.

18. For a thorough list of other examples, see Vos, *Synoptic Traditions in the Apocalypse*, pp. 39-40.

19. So Swete, *Apocalypse*, p. cliv, and Vos, *Synoptic Traditions in the Apocalypse*, pp. 38-39.

20. Caird, *Revelation*, pp. 25-26.

This common denominator of a theophany-judgment theme is enhanced when one notes also the dominant influence of Dan. 7.9-13 throughout Revelation 4–5 (see below). This clearly common motif in all the Old Testament allusions points toward a more intentional thematic formation of texts to describe a similar theophany in Revelation. This seems even more likely when one considers that in the immediate contexts of three of the Old Testament allusions there appears the image of a 'book' associated with judgment, as in Rev. 5.1 (cf. Dan. 7.10; Ezek. 2.9-10; Zech. 5.1-3). All of the common scenes and themes of these Old Testament contexts intensify the cognitive and emotive aspects of the picture in Rev. 4.2-9.

The same thing can be illustrated through Rev. 1.12-20, 13.1-8, and 17, and other examples cited by Vos to support his proposal of unconscious clustering.[21]

Therefore, caution must be used in making claims of unconscious activity on the author's part, although this is a possibility. For example, it is possible, though speculative, to propose that the above-mentioned exegetical links in Revelation 4–5 were already intact in some previous tradition to which John makes unconscious allusion (e.g. a synagogue or Christian liturgical tradition). Such unconscious activity is more likely to have occurred with the less-clear or non-clustered allusions, although exegetical analysis must determine this in each case. Furthermore, as Vanhoye has concluded, it is not typical for John to use Old Testament allusions in isolation but to fuse them together on the basis of their affinity with one another,[22] as illustrated above in Revelation 4–5.

Although space does not permit, it would be helpful to discuss in this section whether or not the Apocalypse is a literary stereotype or if it can be traced to a visionary experience, or is a combination of both.[23] If there were an experiential basis, which is highly probable, descriptions of such visions were probably coloured both unconsciously and consciously by the traditions which had exerted a formative influence on the author's thinking. Furthermore, actual visions would have been experienced in the author's own thought forms, so that it might be difficult to distinguish description of a visionary experience from that of a

21. See Beale, *Use of Daniel*, pp. 154-270.
22. Vanhoye, 'L'utilisation du livre d'Ezéchiel dans l'Apocalypse', p. 467.
23. Cf. further Hartman, *Prophecy Interpreted*, p. 106; Beale, *Use of Daniel*, pp. 7-9.

retelling of the experience through unconscious or conscious appeal to various traditions (Old Testament, Jewish, and so on). The likelihood is that John had genuine visions and that he subsequently recorded those visions in literary form.[24] No doubt, John would have associated some of his visions and auditions with similar Old Testament passages and employed the language of those passages to record what he saw and heard.

The references to the Old Testament, and its various versions, is not the result of a mere recording of the actual visions themselves which would have been influenced by the author's learned tradition, but also a result of subsequent reflection on the Old Testament during the writing down of the vision. John can allude, not only generally to the LXX, but also to variants therein, and to forerunners of the versions of Theodotion, Symmachus and Aquila, as well as to the Hebrew and Targumic texts. It is improbable that all of these different versional references were already included in prior traditions with which John became familiar at various points. This evidence reflects a knowledge on the author's part of different 'Bibles', just as today a devout student of the Bible might have a knowledge of different English versions. John's use of grammatical solecisms as signals to readers of Old Testament allusions is a telltale example of this:[25] he sometimes maintains the unique grammatical form of Old Testament wording from its context in Hebrew or Greek and transplants it into his own literary context without conforming its grammatical form to the new syntactical context, thus causing 'syntactical dissonance'. The anomaly makes readers pause and reflect, and gives them a chance to recognize the wording as an Old Testament allusion.

Additional evidence in favor of conscious dependence and composition based on the Old Testament is the observation that allusions in Revelation are linked on the basis of specific themes and of specific phrases or key-words shared between the different Old Testament contexts alluded to and combined together by John (e.g. Rev. 1, as well as 1QM 1, *1 En.* 46–47, *4 Ezra* 13.1-12). It is possible but improbable that

---

24. See the excellent analysis of M. Rissi, *Time and History: A Study on the Revelation* (Richmond, VA: John Knox Press, 1966), pp. 18-21, who reviews and evaluates several objections to the genuineness of John's visionary experience and concludes in favor of genuineness.

25. Assuming the plausibility of the analysis of Revelation's solecisms given in Chapter 5 below.

such links typically reflect no conscious intention, but only part of the complex inherited in an apocalyptic tradition. Surely this occurs sometimes, but to deny that John never composes like this is to deny his own theological and exegetical creativity. The burden of proof is on one to show that John could not or did not ever enter into such compositional activity. A more balanced view would be that sometimes he inherited these exegetical links in a prior though unknown tradition and that sometimes he himself created the links. But even in those places where one wants to claim that he inherited a tradition with the links already made, it must obviously be recognized that some creative though unknown composer consciously created the links at an earlier point. Most of the time, however, why speculate about an unknown composer of an unknown tradition when a good candidate like John is known who just as well could have created the interpretative links? The discussion earlier in this section and below lends confirming evidence to this conclusion, as does the work of Bauckham and Fekkes in their own different ways.

John's apparent self-identification with the line of Old Testament visionaries implies that he would be conscious of developing the ideas of the earlier prophets and, therefore, that the clearer Old Testament references in his work are the result of an intentional activity (cf. 1.1-3, 10; 4.1-2; 17.3; 21.10).[26] Furthermore, the chain of associated texts in Revelation 1, 4–5, 13 and 17 discussed above, and evident elsewhere, confirms an intentional activity on the author's part. This conclusion is enhanced by the remaining evidence considered below.

2. A Consideration of Contextual and Non-contextual Use of the Old Testament
Of course, if one concluded that John alluded to the Old Testament only unconsciously, there would be little possibility of studying his method of allusion, since such study assumes conscious activity. In the light of our conclusion in favour of intentionality, however, we must first ask whether or not John uses the Old Testament in harmony with its broader contextual meaning.

There is unanimous consensus that John uses the Old Testament with a high degree of liberty and creativity. As a result, many conclude that he handles numerous Old Testament passages without consideration of

---

26. Vos, *Synoptic Traditions in the Apocalypse*, p. 52.

their original contextual meaning, even assigning meaning quite contradictory to it. The reasons given for this conclusion are at least fourfold.

(1)   John does not use quotation formulas in introducing Old Testament references but only cites Scripture in an informal anthological style, which points to using Old Testament words only as a cloak for his own new thoughts unrelated to the original Old Testament contexts.[27] In response, informal citation or allusion does not logically entail non-contextual use of the Old Testament nor a lack of attempt to interpret the Old Testament, especially since the majority of New Testament references to the Old Testament elsewhere are also informal and allusive.[28] It would be unduly presumptuous to think that all of these Old Testament references elsewhere are *not* being interpreted by New Testament writers with context in mind.

(2)   Another reason adduced for John's supposed lack of concern for Old Testament context is that his apocalyptic style is dependent on his prophetic spirit which creates in order to proclaim for his own purposes, and does not consciously quote from other authorities in order to teach or argue;[29] consequently, there is no attempt to interpret the Old Testament contextually. This, however, does not take into consideration that the 'prophetic spirit' does not necessarily create *ex nihilo*, as apparent from the exilic and post-exilic prophets who reused, reformulated and actualized prior prophetic material.[30] Furthermore, John does not view himself as a prophet independent of his Old Testament tradition or heritage but applies to himself the language of Old Testament prophetic commissions. He does this in order to show that his prophetic authority is equal to that of Old Testament prophets and to

27. Schüssler Fiorenza, 'Apokalypsis and Propheteia', pp. 107-10.
28. So also Fekkes, *Isaiah and Prophetic Traditions*, pp. 286-87.
29. Schüssler Fiorenza, 'Apokalypsis and Propheteia', p. 109, following K. Stendahl.
30. Following Fekkes, *Isaiah and Prophetic Traditions*, p. 288; for a similar critique see Bauckham, *Climax of Prophecy*, pp. 262-63, 297-98, who observes that Fiorenza does not attempt to study John's use of the Old Testament in view of the way the Old Testament was understood and interpreted in the Jewish exegetical tradition of the day.

demonstrate that his message stands in continuity with their message (see 'Excursus' at the end of Chapter 3, sect. B, and see 1.10; 4.1-2; 17.3; 21.10).

(3) A third reason put forward for John's disregard for Old Testament context is that his readers were either illiterate or from a pagan Greek background, or both, and would not have been able to understand the interpretative use of Old Testament literature. This objection does not take into consideration the following factors: (a) the churches in Asia Minor were composed of a core of Jewish believers formerly from the Synagogue, as well as Gentile godfearers who also had association with the Synagogue (cf. evidence in Acts); (b) there is still some relationship with the Synagogue in Smyrna and Philadelphia, though it is antagonistic, which points further to some link with a knowledge of Old Testament tradition (cf. 2.9; 3.9); in fact, in Rev. 3.9 there may be expressed the expectation that more antagonistic Jews from the Synagogue will become Christians imminently, which assumes that the evangelistic message of the Philadelphian church was based to a significant degree upon the Old Testament and its fulfillment in Christ as Messiah;[31] (c) specific reference to a false 'prophet' with an Old Testament name ('Jezebel') in Thyatira suggests a teaching in that church which distorted both Old Testament and New Testament tradition (2.20); (d) the linguistic evidence of the text itself: if John knew these congregations and had a pastoral relationship with them, it is implausible that he would employ on such a vast scale so many Old Testament allusions, especially if he knew that they would not have a clue to what he was referring and would not be benefitted by his massive references to the Old Testament; for example, such clear Old Testament allusions in the letters as 'manna', 'Jezebel', 'Balaam', 'temple' and 'new Jerusalem' are tips of an Old Testament iceberg pointing to some basic knowledge of the Old Testament on the readers' part; (e) if it is true that John communicated his revelation first to a circle of fellow-prophets, who were then to communicate it to the churches (see on 22.16a), then this circle must also be considered as part of the audience, who would have probably

---

31. For which see further on Rev. 3.9 in Beale, *Book of Revelation*.

studied it with an Old Testament 'scripturally learned attention';[32] (f) John's self-understanding as a prophet (see on 1.1,
10; 4.1-2; 17.3; 19.10; 21.10; 22.9), which appears to have
been generally accepted among, at least, the seven churches,
implies that he probably had taught with prophetic authority
among them, especially since he attributes such teaching functions to other so-called prophets among the churches (an infer-
ence based on Rev. 2.20).[33] If so, there was probably greater
awareness of the Old Testament among some groups in the
churches, so that well-selected crucial words and phrases from
Old Testament texts could spark associations and recall to
many in the audience themes and important biblical contexts;[34]
(g) we know from Acts and elsewhere in the New Testament
that Jewish and Gentile believers were trained in their new
faith on the basis of the Old Testament, the Bible of the early
church (e.g. Acts 17.10-12; 18.24-28; 2 Tim. 2.2, 15; 3.16-
17); (h) it is plausible that on subsequent readings of Revelation in the churches that the audience would be able to
discern more of the allusions than on merely hearing the first
reading (this is based on the known fact in the second century
and the probability in the first century that letters were read
repeatedly in the early church: for example, as implied by Col.
4.16; 1 Thess. 5.27; Rev. 1.3); and (i) it seems generally
acknowledged that both the majority of pagan Greeks and
Jews in the Greco-Roman world gained a reading knowledge
(respectively, at least, of Greek or Hebrew, and, in addition,
Latin) in childhood, which even extended in varying degrees
to slaves.[35]

(4)   A final reason for sometimes postulating John's lack of attention to Old Testament context is issued in the form of a warning to those who see him working contextually: only because

32. Bauckham, *Climax of Prophecy*, p. 30, as well as pp. 83-91.

33. Following, in part, Fekkes, *Isaiah and Prophetic Traditions*, p. 287. That
John had a teaching ministry in the churches is consistent with the role of prophets
in churches as described by the Didache (11.10-11; cited by Fekkes).

34. Fekkes, *Isaiah and Prophetic Traditions*, p. 287, and see the further bibliography cited there by Fekkes in further support of this point.

35. See J.T. Townsend, 'Education: Greco-Roman Period', II, pp. 12-17, where
also relevant bibliography can be found.

an author *is influenced literarily* by an Old Testament text does not logically entail the conclusion that he depends *interpretatively* on the meaning of that text nor that he is attempting to interpret or offer a commentary on that text; more evidence than a mere citing of an Old Testament text must be forthcoming.[36] While this is a plausible warning, it may also be said that the mere reference to an Old Testament text legitimately invites the question about whether or not a writer depends on the meaning of that Old Testament text or whether he is attempting to interpret it. The greater number of references an author makes to the Old Testament, the more it points to a familiarity with the meaning of the Old Testament. In particular, the increased number of references a writer appeals to from the same Old Testament text, whether specific verses or a segment, strongly suggests that the writer was absorbed with that Old Testament passage and had probably meditated upon it; this enhances the probability that he was familiar with its meaning and, to varying degrees, dependent on that meaning, or, at least, was attempting to interpret that Old Testament text (e.g. cf. the use of Daniel and Ezekiel in Rev. 4–5). This appears to be true with John's use of the Old Testament, especially in the light of the above three main points. Recent study also supports this conclusion (on which see throughout this section; e.g. Beale, Bauckham and Fekkes). For example, Draper has contended that Revelation interprets the Old Testament in a manner similar to that of Qumran, though the interpretation in the former is carried out implicitly and in the latter explicitly.[37]

The cumulative effect of all of these factors points to the probability of varying degrees of knowledge of the Old Testament by a number of people in the churches; the evidence suggests the ability or potential to learn the Old Testament by those in John's audience who may not have had prior knowledge of it. Even if the preceding evidence were unwisely disregarded, it does not make our study of what John meant by

36. So Ruiz, *Ezekiel in the Apocalypse*, p. 123, who offers this critique of Beale, *Use of Daniel*.

37. J.A. Draper, 'The Twelve Apostles as Foundation Stones of the Heavenly Jerusalem and the Foundation of the Qumran Community', *Neot* 22 (1988), pp. 41-63.

the allusions irrelevant, since 'the process of great literary creation does not necessarily calculate what readers will notice'.[38]

Vos has also argued in a thoroughgoing exegetical manner that John handles Old Testament passages without respect for the Old Testament contextual meaning. Our remaining comments in this section will be focused on an evaluation of his discussion as generally representative of those who hold this viewpoint.

Vos restricts most of his survey to what he considers to be the clearest Old Testament references in the Apocalypse.[39] He concludes that at least 7 of the 22 passages discussed there show a 'disregard for [the Old Testament] context'. Four of these concern references to heavenly beings. The first is the application of a description of Yahweh (Ezek. 43.2) to that of the Son of Man figure (Rev. 1.15). But this is more of a change of application than non-contextual use, since the Son of Man is clearly portrayed as a divine figure in Revelation 1. In Rev. 18.1 a description of Yahweh (Ezek. 43.2b) is applied to an angel descending from heaven, yet, since angels in the Old Testament and Revelation are mere conveyers of divine decrees, it is plausible that they would take on other theophanic characteristics besides that of the divine word. In addition, sometimes in the Old Testament God appears in the form of a heavenly being, and this may be the case also in Revelation (e.g. Rev. 10.1-6, which is based on the heavenly being of Daniel 10–12 who may be divine). Therefore, in spite of the possible change of application, the broad Old Testament idea of a heavenly being revealing a divine decree to a prophet remains intact. The same general conclusion can be reached with respect to the similar usage of Ezek. 37.3 in Rev. 7.14. In Rev. 4.8a descriptions of the Isaiah 6 seraphim are merged with those of the Ezekiel 1 cherubim, but again the primary Old Testament framework of a heavenly being guarding God's throne is still retained.

Vos also argues for a disregard of context in the use of Ezek. 37.10b in Rev. 11.11. The Ezekiel text uses the idea of resurrection as a metaphor for the future ingathering of Israel from throughout the nations, while John applies it to the resurrection of the two witnesses, who probably are symbolic of the witnessing church as the true Israel (so Caird, Sweet, etc.). This kind of reference may fit into the analogical usage category (see below) because of the common idea of *Israel's resurrection*. The shift of application to the church as the true Israel and

---

38. Bauckham, *Climax of Prophecy*, p. 30.
39. Vos, *Synoptic Traditions in the Apocalypse*, pp. 21-37, 41.

the understanding of Ezekiel's language as apparently connoting a literal resurrection may represent eschatological escalation whereby the resurrection terminology now finds an eschatological and not merely historical level. Although there is a possibility of disregard for context because of the different application and even somewhat changed meaning, a correspondence and sense of continuity can be discerned (note also in both passages that those 'resurrected' have previously been slain among the nations; cf. Ezek. 37.9-14, 21-2/Rev. 11.7-10).

Vos also contends that the use of Isa. 22.22 in Rev. 3.7 is non-contextual, since Eliakim's authority over the Israelite kingdom is applied to Christ's authority over God's kingdom. This, however, can also be viewed as an escalated analogy wherein the human, earthly, political and temporal rule over Israel by Eliakim finds a correspondence on a grander scale with Christ's divine, heavenly, spiritual and eternal rule over the whole world (cf. Rev. 1–5). Additional points of note in Isaiah 22 are: (1) the possible priestly connotations of Eliakim's rule (22.21a); (2) Eliakim was to be like a 'father' for the Israelites in the exercise of his office (22.21b); (3) apparently Eliakim's authority was to be equal to that of King Hezekiah's (22.22); and (4) Eliakim is referred to as the 'servant' of Yahweh (22.20). All of these elements, together with the messianic overtones of the 'house of David' (22.22) enhance the idea that John was quite aware of the context of Isa. 22.22 and intentionally escalated these aspects of Eliakim's reign to the grander scale of Christ's reign. Perhaps the correspondences were just too good to miss.[40]

Therefore, we may viably speak about changes of applications but need not conclude that this means a *disregard* for Old Testament context, since this is not a logically necessary deduction. It seems likely that Vos, and others, confuse disregard for context with change of application. That the above texts reflect disregard for Old Testament context is possible but other explanations are more satisfactory. The passages I have discussed are test cases, the conclusions of which are applicable to other Old Testament references where it is probable that the author has made *intentional allusion* and has demonstrated varying

---

40. Cf. G. von Rad, *Old Testament Theology* (2 vols.; New York: Harper & Row Publishers, 1962–1965), II, p. 373, who argues cogently for a typological relationship between Isa. 22.22 and Rev. 3.7.

degrees of respect for the Old Testament context.[41] The overall thrust of the present monograph is an argument in support of this position.

Admittedly, it is sometimes difficult to know whether there has been conscious or unconscious activity. Non-contextual uses of the Old Testament can be expected to occur in those places where there is unconscious allusion. No doubt the apocalyptist's mind was so saturated with Old Testament language from the tradition he had learned that when he described his vision he sometimes spontaneously used this language without much forethought. For example, the phrase 'I turned *to see the voice which was speaking*' (Rev. 1.12a) is probably drawn from Dan. 7.11 (LXX), but there it refers to the 'boastful words' of the beast. This may have been drawn in unconsciously because of the clear influence of Daniel 7 in Rev. 1.7-14.

To clarify what is meant by 'context' is important. What is usually meant is *literary* context: how a passage functions in the logical flow of a book's argument. But there is also *historical* context. For example, the *historical* context of Hos. 11.1 is the Exodus and not the argument of the book of Hosea. In addition, there is also the *thematic Old Testament context* whereby a New Testament writer focuses first on a general Old Testament theme (e.g. judgment or restoration) and then appeals to a number of specific passages from different Old Testament books which pertain to that theme.[42] A New Testament author might reflect on only one of these three contexts; he could focus on all three or entirely disregard them. In the light of the passages discussed above, John appears to display varying degrees of awareness of literary context, as well as thematic context and, perhaps, historical context, although appeal to literary and thematic contexts is predominant. Thematic context is really an explanation for why particular literary contexts are focused upon. Those texts with a low degree of correspondence with the Old Testament literary context can be referred to as semi-contextual, since they seem to fall between the opposite poles of what we ordinarily call 'contextual' and 'non-contextual' usages.[43] The

---

41. An assessment corroborated by Fekkes, *Isaiah and Prophetic Traditions*, e.g., pp. 70-103 (and *passim*) and generally by Paulien, *Decoding Revelation's Trumpets*. See numerous examples of contextual use of the Old Testament in Beale, *Book of Revelation, passim*.

42. For development of thematic Old Testament context see Fekkes, *Isaiah and Prophetic Traditions*, pp. 70-103.

43. See McComiskey, 'Alteration of OT Imagery', for an attempt to perceive

categories of use to be considered below should further clarify and illustrate these initial conclusions.

D. *Various Uses of the Old Testament in the Apocalypse*[44]

1. *The Use of Segments of Old Testament Scripture as Literary Prototypes*

Sometimes the author takes over Old Testament contexts or sequences as models after which to pattern his creative compositions.[45] Such modeling can be apparent either (1) through observing a thematic structure which is uniquely traceable to only one Old Testament context or (2) by discerning a cluster of clear allusions from the same Old Testament context. Sometimes both are observable, thus enhancing the clarity of the Old Testament prototype. It has been argued in some depth that broad patterns from Daniel (especially chs. 2 and 7) have been followed in Revelation 1, 4–5, 13 and 17, the former two sections in particular exhibiting both allusive clusters and structural outlines from segments of Daniel.[46] Incidentally, this would show further design in these chapters and point away from an unconscious use of the Old Testament. The same use of Daniel as a midrashic model is also observable in Jewish apocalyptic, indicating that this kind of use of the Old Testament was not uncommon (e.g. 1QM 1; *4 Ezra* 11–13; *1 En.* 69.26-71.17; 1 En. 90.9-19; *2 Bar.* 36–40).[47] The influence of Daniel may even extend to the structure of the whole Apocalypse, since the same Dan. 2.28-29 allusion punctuates the book at major divisional transitions (Rev. 1.1; 1.19; 4.1; 22.6). Furthermore, the five apocalyptic visions in Daniel (2, 7, 8, 9, 10–12) cover the same time of the eschato-

---

degrees of Old Testament contextual awareness based on the determinative intention of John in the light of his own contextual usage in Revelation, though he deemphasizes the role of the Old Testament too much.

44. In addition to the following uses, see further sub-categories of usage in Fekkes, *Isaiah and Prophetic Traditions*, pp. 70-103.

45. Cf. Schüssler Fiorenza, 'Apokalypsis and Propheteia', p. 108.

46. See Beale, *Use of Daniel*, pp. 154-305, 313-20, for thorough discussions of these uses of the Old Testament. See Ruiz, *Ezekiel in the Apocalypse*, pp. 123-28, who is unconvinced by this evidence, especially the notion that Dan. 7 is the model for Rev. 4–5 instead of Ezekiel; see response to Ruiz below at section D.1.a.

47. Beale, *Use of Daniel*, pp. 67-153.

logical future, which may be the prototypical structure followed by Revelation in some of its purported synchronously parallel sections.[48]

In a somewhat similar vein, Goulder has argued that broad portions of Ezekiel have been the dominant influence on at least 11 major sections of the Apocalypse (Rev. 4; 5; 6.1-8; 6.12–7.1; 7.2-8; 8.1-5; 14.6-12; 17.1-6; 18.9-24; 20.7-10; 21.22).[49] Goulder observes that these uses of Ezekiel are a dominant influence on the structure of Revelation since they are placed to a marked extent in the same order as they are found in Ezekiel itself.[50] However, Goulder proposes that a liturgical rather than a literary explanation can be given to account better for the parallel order of Ezekiel and Revelation. He attempts to demonstrate this by speculating that there is a general alignment of the Apocalypse with the Jewish calendar, especially with respect to the year of festivals and holy days, and that this liturgical-calendrical pattern is even more formative on the structure of Revelation than Ezekiel.[51] Though S. Moyise does not follow Goulder's liturgical theory, he finds that Ezekiel has provided more of the model for Revelation than Daniel.[52] Virtually identical to Goulder, though also not positing a liturgical background, is J.M. Vogelgesang who has gone so far as to conclude that John used Ezekiel as the model for the book's overall structure and 'is the key to understanding the message of the book altogether'.[53]

Others have also recognized Ezekiel's broad influence, especially in Revelation 20–22, where the order of events appears to have been taken from Ezekiel 37–48.[54]

---

48. Beale, *Use of Daniel*, pp. 271-85; G.K. Beale, 'The Influence of Daniel upon the Structure and Theology of John's Apocalypse', *JETS* 27 (1984), pp. 413-23.

49. Cf. Goulder, 'Apocalypse as an Annual Cycle of Prophecies', pp. 343-49.

50. Goulder, 'Apocalypse as an Annual Cycle of Prophecies', pp. 353-54.

51. Goulder, 'Apocalypse as an Annual Cycle of Prophecies', pp. 349-64.

52. Moyise, *Old Testament in the Book of Revelation*, pp. 74-83, wherein also is critique of Goulder's liturgical theory; similarly cf. Mazzaferri, *Genre of Revelation*, p. 365.

53. Vogelgesang, 'Interpretation of Ezekiel', p. 394, as well as pp. 16, 66-71. See Ruiz, *Ezekiel in the Apocalypse*, p. 127, for others who also see that Ezekiel provides the broad outline of Revelation.

54. E.C. Selwyn, 'Dialogues on the Christian Prophets', *Expositor*, Sixth Series 5 (1902), pp. 321-43 (332-34); A. Wikenhauser, 'Das Problem des tausendjährigen Reiches in der Johannes-Apokalyse', *Römische Quartalschrift* 40 (1932), pp. 13-25; K.G. Kuhn, 'Gog-Magog', *TDNT*, I, pp. 789-91; J. Lust, 'The Order of the Final Events in Revelation and in Ezekiel', in J. Lambrecht (ed.), *L'Apocalypse johannique et l'Apocalyptique dans le Nouveau Testament* (BETL, 53; Gembloux:

There are many other commentators who, along with Goulder, see Ezekiel as the paradigm either for Revelation 4[55] or the broader segment of Rev. 4.1–5.1 (e.g. Caird, Sweet). Mounce also sees the prediction of Tyre's judgment in Ezekiel 26-27 as forming the model for the prophecy of Babylon's judgment in 18.9-19,[56] though the model extends through to 18.23. The past downfall of Tyre (and those who mourn over it) is a prefigurement of the fall of the last great economic system. *Thematically*, the section also can be divided into the lament of the kings of the earth (vv. 9-10), the lament of the merchants of the earth (vv. 11-17a) and the lament of the mariners (vv. 17b-19). The same three groups in Ezek. 27.29-30, 35-36 express sadness over Tyre's demise.

Besides Goulder's observations on the formative use of Ezekiel, even another can be added. The broad structure of the New Jerusalem from Rev. 21.9 through 22.5 is based on the vision of Ezekiel 40–48. Ezekiel 40–48 prophesies the pattern of the final temple (chs. 40–44), as well as the arrangement of the eschatological city and divisions of the land around the temple compound (chs. 45–48). Rev. 21.9–22.5 further interprets the yet future fulfillment of Ezekiel by collapsing temple, city and land into one end-time picture portraying the one reality of God's communion with his people. This identification is apparently based on Ezekiel's own identification of temple, city and land as representing the same truth, though Ezekiel never collapses the three explicitly in the reductionistic manner that Rev. 21.9–22.5 does. Ezekiel explains the consummate inheritance of land and the final sanctuary to be indications of God's 'everlasting covenant of peace' in which his 'dwelling place also will be with' Israel (Ezek. 37.25-28; so also 43.7 with respect to the significance of the temple). And the concluding statement of the Ezekiel 40–48 vision likewise interprets the ultimate meaning of the renovated city to be God's presence with his people: cf. 48.35, 'the name of the city from that day [will be], "the Lord is there"'. The fact

Duculot; Leuven: Leuven University Press, 1980), pp. 179-83. Cf. Ruiz, *Ezekiel in the Apocalypse*, pp. 48-49, who mentions M. Boismard's study (M. Boismard, '"L'Apocalypse" ou "Les Apocalypses" de St. Jean', *RB* 56 [1949], pp. 530-32), which attempted to show that Rev. 4–8 and Rev. 17–22 were dominated by Ezekiel Cf. also Vanhoye, 'L'utilisation du livre d'Ezéchiel dans l'Apocalypse'.

55. Vogelgesang, 'Interpretation of Ezekiel', pp. 43-51.

56. R.H. Mounce, *The Book of Revelation* (NICNT; Grand Rapids: Eerdmans, 1977), p. 328.

that John 'saw no temple' in the new Jerusalem 'because the Lord
...and the Lamb are its temple' (21.22) is partial but clear evidence of
John's method of interpretative distillation.

In addition to Goulder's above liturgical view, others of paradigmatic
significance for the book have also been proposed, which are based
either on early Jewish or Christian liturgical tradition.[57]

There is a consensus that the plagues of the 'trumpets' in Rev. 8.6-12
and those of the bowls in 16.1-9 follow the paradigm of the Exodus
plagues and trials (Exod. 7–14), although creatively reworked and
applied (e.g. Beasley-Murray, Caird, Sweet). Already this Exodus
model had been used by Amos (chs. 8–9) and creatively applied in
Wisdom of Solomon 11–19, the latter usage perhaps also exerting influence on John's application.[58] J.S. Casey has argued for a significant
influence of an Exodus typology in the trumpets and bowls, as well as
in other segments of Revelation.[59] J.A. Draper proposes that the eschatological scheme in Zechariah 14 'provides the basis for a midrashic
development in Revelation 7',[60] while J.P.M. Sweet more tentatively
suggests the same thing for Revelation 20–22.[61]

All of the above proposed Old Testament models have woven within
them allusions from other parts of the same Old Testament book and

57. Cf. D.R. Carnegie, 'The Hymns in Revelation: Their Origin and Function'
(Unpublished PhD dissertation for the British Council for National Academic
Awards [supervision under the London Bible College], 1978); S. Läuchli, 'Eine
Gottesdienststruktur in der Johannesoffenbarung', *TZ* 16 (1960), pp. 359-78 (see
Carnegie's evaluation in D.R. Carnegie, 'Worthy is the Lamb: The Hymns in Reve-
lation', in H.H. Rowden (ed.), *Christ the Lord, Studies Presented to D. Guthrie*
[Downers Grove, IL: InterVarsity Press, 1982], pp. 243-56); P. Prigent, *Apocalypse
et Liturgie* (Cahiers Théologiques, 52; Paris: Delachaux & Niestlé, 1964) (see
Beale's evaluation in *idem, Use of Daniel*, p. 184).

58. J.P.M. Sweet, *Revelation* (SCM Pelican Commentaries; London: SCM
Press, 1979), pp. 161-62.

59. J.S. Casey, 'Exodus Typology in the Book of Revelation' (PhD dissertation,
Southern Baptist Theological Seminary, Louisville, Kentucky, 1981). For a conve-
nient summary of Casey's dissertation see Mazzaferri, *Genre of the Book of Revelation*, pp. 367-73.

60. J.A. Draper, 'The Heavenly Feast of Tabernacles: Revelation 7.1-17', *JSNT*
19 (1983), pp. 133-47.

61. J.P.M. Sweet, 'Maintaining the Testimony of Jesus: The Suffering of Christians in the Revelation of John', in W. Horbury and B. McNeil (eds.), *Suffering and
Martyrdom in the New Testament* (Cambridge: Cambridge University Press, 1981),
pp. 101-17 (112).

from elsewhere in the Old Testament corpus, and many of these are based upon common themes, pictures, catch-phrases, etc. Often these other references serve as interpretative expansions of an Old Testament prototype. On the reasonable assumption that these models were intentionally composed, two primary uses of them can be discerned. First, the Old Testament patterns appear to be used as forms through which future (sometimes imminent) eschatological fulfillment is understood and predicted (cf. Rev. 13; 17).[62] Second, the prototypes are utilized as a lens through which past and present eschatological fulfillment is understood (cf. Rev. 1; 4–5). It is not always clear whether or not these Old Testament prototypes are the means or the object of interpretation, and likely there is an oscillation between the two; that is, the Old Testament interprets the New Testament, and the New Testament interprets the Old Testament.

a. *Excursus: Rejoinder to Critical Evaluations of the Use of Segments of Daniel as Midrashic Prototypes for Various Chapters in Revelation.* There have been several criticisms of my notion that John uses segments from Daniel as models for chapters in Revelation. Ruiz has made the most thoroughgoing critical analysis. He criticizes my use of the terms 'midrash', 'apocalyptic' and 'eschatology', since they are generally such 'fuzzy' and debated terms.[63] Since these were debated terms even in the late 1970s, I intentionally decided to give my own definitions. I was not attempting to give a state-of-the-art review of these terms or enter into the mainstream of debate or to use the consensus definitions, but only to let the reader know what I meant by use of these terms.[64] Nevertheless, definitions of these words does not bear one way or another upon the viability of the thesis.

Ruiz follows A.Y. Collins in her critique that my hypothesis depends on a doubtful presupposition, and this is the heart of the problem of the work.[65] Collins says I do not adequately discuss the question of

---

62. Also see the same employment of the Daniel models in 1QM 1; *1 En.* 46–47; 69.26–71.17; 90; *4 Ezra* 11–13; *2 Bar.* 36.1–42.2.

63. Ruiz, *Ezekiel in the Apocalypse*, pp. 119-22.

64. Ruiz contends, however, that the definitions given are unclear. For example, I use the word 'midrash...loosely to refer to the dominant influence of an OT passage on a NT writer and to that writer's interpretative development of the same OT text'. While one may disagree in a variety of ways about whether or not this is an inclusive enough definition, I do not think it is unclear.

65. Ruiz, *Ezekiel in the Apocalypse*, p. 120.

'whether the book of Daniel was for the author of Revelation an object of interpretation or a means' of interpretation, but that I merely presuppose that it is an object of interpretation.[66] Ruiz affirms that a case is never made for the viability of the presupposition that John is giving a Christian interpretation of Daniel.[67] He believes that a more reasonable view, in the light of the importance of references to Daniel in Revelation, 'would recognize that the Daniel material in Revelation is used by John as a means to his own creative ends'.[68] He does not say why this is more 'reasonable' than the other view. In fact, on the surface it would appear that if an author is saturated with a particular Old Testament book, all things being equal, it would seem natural and logical to say that the saturation was the result of meditating on that Old Testament book.

What is actually at issue here is two conflicting sets of presuppositions. The presupposition of Collins and Ruiz is that Daniel was a mere instrument used by John for his own creative, literary purposes. Which is the correct presupposition? Of course, the very nature of a presupposition is that it cannot be proven, only assumed. What makes a presupposition viable is how much of the data can be reasonably explained by the presupposition. That presupposition which coheres best with and makes the most sense out of the inductive data is to be considered the more probable presupposition. Readers will have to read the broad context of my work and that of Ruiz and Collins in order to decide which makes the best case for the coherency of the respective presuppositions (though below I contend that I hold both presuppositions to varying degrees and that they are not mutually incompatible).

Collins elaborates on her critique by saying that my view contains a specific assumption 'which has shaped the research': that Revelation 4–5 portrayed the fulfillment in the church of the Daniel 7 prophecy of a kingdom in which all nations would be subservient to the Son of Man.[69] She is correct that I do hold this presupposition, since it is likely that

---

66. A.Y. Collins, review of *Use of Daniel in Jewish Apocalyptic Literature and the Revelation of St. John* (Lanham: University Press of America, 1984), by G.K. Beale, in *JBL* 105 (1986), pp. 734-35.

67. Ruiz, *Ezekiel in the Apocalypse*, pp. 120-21.

68. Ruiz, *Ezekiel in the Apocalypse*, p. 121.

69. Moyise, *Old Testament in the Book of Revelation*, p. 82, also criticizes me for having the one-sided view that John used the Old Testament 'as a lens through which past and present eschatological fulfillment is understood'.

John's own presupposition was that the age of end-time fulfillment has been inaugurated with Christ's first coming. Indeed, this is one of four hermeneutical presuppositions, to be discussed in the conclusion of this chapter, arguably held by Jesus and the New Testament writers, which underlay their use of the Old Testament. Indeed, eschatological fulfillment of Old Testament prophecy is generally recognized as the broad understanding of the early Christians. This presupposition, however, is one which has emerged as the result of much inductive exegetical work on my part, as well as on the part of many others.

In the light of this, Collins's critique is hard to comprehend. One may not agree with the theological cogency of John's presupposition, but is it really plausible to believe that he did not hold this presupposition in view of its prevalence elsewhere in the New Testament and Qumran, and in light of such passages, for example, as Rev. 1.3 ('the time is near'), 10.7 ('then the mystery of God is finished, as He preached to His servants the prophets') and 22.10 ('Do not seal up the words of the prophecy of this book, for the time is near'), all of which are either closely surrounded by or are part of Old Testament allusions?[70]

Inextricably linked, and sometimes equated, with the debate about whether Daniel was an object or a means of interpretation is the issue over whether or not John used and developed the Old Testament with contextual integrity or whether he employed it without any regard for its original context. This can be a presuppositional issue, but actual exegetical analysis can be adduced (and has been on both sides) either to support or disprove one of these perspectives. My *Use of Daniel* (and all of my subsequent works on the topic) attempts to make the case that John does handle the Old Testament in a compatible way with the original author's intention. This does not mean, however, that Daniel is only an object of interpretation, but it should also be seen as a means to John's creative purposes. Many assume that if Daniel is a mere means to achieve John's purposes, then he is not concerned with Daniel's con-

---

70. E.g. to 'not seal up the words of the prophecy' in Rev. 22.10 means that now, at last, the end-time prophecies of the Old Testament, especially those in Daniel (Theodotion of Dan. 12.4, to which allusion is made in 22.10a; cf. also 12.9; 8.26; cf. LXX), have begun fulfillment and, in the light of the fulfillment, these prophecies can now be understood better. Therefore, the language of unsealing writing indicates, not only beginning fulfillment, but also the revelation of greater insight into the prophecies which was kept from Old Testament saints (so likewise Eph. 3.4-5). Cf. G.B. Caird's similar understanding of the fulfillment of Daniel in Rev. 10.7 (Caird, *Revelation*, pp. 128-29).

textual meaning. This is a mistaken assumption. It is certainly possible that an author can be very creative in reusing earlier literature and yet still adapt it with new meanings in a manner consistent with the broad contextual meaning of the prior literature. One could contend that John always uses his Old Testament allusions without any regard for the original context, but to say that in each case in response to so many Old Testament allusions begs the question and would appear to reflect a presupposition which will not allow John to have a contextual approach.

Consequently, a careful reading of my *Use of Daniel* supports the notion that Daniel was both an object and a means of interpretation, along the lines explained above; indeed, in the conclusion of my book I said: 'It is not always clear in these uses whether Daniel is the means or the object of interpretation, although we have *generally* opted for the latter. Nevertheless, *it is possible that there was an oscillation between the two uses by the apocalyptic authors*' (italics added).[71] I was certainly not absolute in my preference of one perspective over the other, as the preceding qualified statements show, though my view was weighted more on the side of Daniel as an object of interpretation. Today I would qualify my assessment more than I did in 1984, and I have already done so in 1988[72] and 1989,[73] but such qualification is not a radical adjustment of my original 1984 position, and it is important to note that I did originally recognize the viability of both perspectives.

Therefore, a close examination of my book reveals significant comments on the side of a creative handling of Daniel in which Daniel is better understood through John's New Testament situation.[74] The

---

71. Beale, *Use of Daniel*, p. 319. Moyise, *Old Testament in the Book of Revelation*, p. 62, recognized that in my 1988 Lindars' *Festschrift* article I did 'hint at a more dialectical relationship' by saying the Old Testament was both a 'servant and guide' for John (though I think this is more than a hint; see my elaboration in the article Beale, 'Revelation', p. 333).

72. Beale, 'Revelation', e.g., p. 333.

73. Beale, 'Did Jesus and his Followers Preach the Right Doctrine from the Wrong Texts?'

74. Along these lines, with respect to Daniel and its associated traditions, I say in the concluding sections of the book: 'John develops the tradition in a creative way, adding new elements from Daniel and expanding on some which are drawn from the tradition' (Beale, *Use of Daniel*, p. 288); 'John's acquaintance with the Danielic framework of the synoptic eschatological tradition generally influenced him so to frame his own visions and also sparked off a train of thought in which he

meaning of Daniel influenced John's understanding of New Testament realities and the meaning of New Testament realities influenced his understanding of Daniel. This is to say the New Testament interprets the Old and the Old interprets the New. For this reason it is difficult to understand why Ruiz says that to claim Daniel's influence was dominant in various chapters of the Apocalypse makes John too much of a mechanical copyist, 'denies John due mastery over his own work', and 'fails to credit John with sufficient autonomy with respect to the sources from which he drew material'.[75] Why cannot John freely choose to use Daniel as an overshadowing influence in one segment of his work, just as he clearly also freely adapts and combines various Old Testament allusions together without any controlling influence from any one of those Old Testament contexts? And, furthermore, if it can be shown that other apocalyptic writers used Daniel in a similar dominating manner, does this not increase the plausibility, at least, that John could have done the same thing?[76]

Ruiz also makes the observation that I do not consistently draw enough of a distinction between Old Testament 'influence' and 'dependence', but often speak as if they were synonymous: 'Demonstrating the *influence* of a biblical text on a particular passage in Revelation is far easier than to [sic] proving the dependence of a particular passage on a specific biblical text.'[77] An Old Testament text may be an unconscious influence upon a New Testament author, perhaps as the result of learned traditions of which the Old Testament was a part, so that the author is not consciously dependent on a particular text, and, accordingly, cannot be said to be interpreting the Old Testament text.

directly alluded to Daniel...he adapted it [the Daniel-synoptic tradition] quite freely to his own purposes bringing in all sorts of extra OT allusions, both from Daniel and elsewhere' (Beale, *Use of Daniel*, p. 293); 'John developed the Daniel tradition with which he was familiar in the direction of the heavenly enthronement scene, *since he wanted to explain more about the heavenly status of Jesus*' (Beale, *Use of Daniel*, p. 290, italics added); in addition, John sometimes turns statements from Daniel on their heads for creative ironic purposes (Beale, *Use of Daniel*, pp. 320-23).

75. Ruiz, *Ezekiel in the Apocalypse*, p. 121.

76. Ruiz does not evaluate the claim in my *Use of Daniel* that there were several precedents of Jewish adaptations of Daniel as an interpretative model for some compositions, but he does say that even if this were so, it would not prove it for John (Ruiz, *Ezekiel in the Apocalypse*, p. 111); however, it does set a precedent which Ruiz apparently implicitly recognizes; he just denies it for John.

77. Ruiz, *Ezekiel in the Apocalypse*, p. 123.

Ruiz himself, however, seems inconsistent in his application of the distinction between unconscious influence and conscious dependence;[78] in ch. 1 we saw that Ruiz affirms that John creates new meaning through his rereading and reuse of Old Testament allusions, and that his readers are to follow his method in their rereading of the Old Testament and of Revelation itself. Ruiz is saying here that, though John created new meanings from Old Testament texts, nevertheless, *he was dependent on the Old Testament in the sense that he was a conscious interpreter of the Old Testament* and that he was providing a model for other Christians to be conscious interpreters of his own work (regardless of whether or not he or they interpreted the base text along the lines of the original authorial intention). In fact, this is one, if not the most, significant contribution Ruiz believes that his work makes.

Unless I have misunderstood Ruiz, it is inconsistent for him to launch a major criticism against my view that John was a conscious interpreter of Daniel, and yet elsewhere maintain that *he was* a conscious interpreter of the Old Testament. Possibly, in this respect, Ruiz is apparently against only the notion that large segments of Revelation do not reflect models of chapters from Daniel, and that in these specific cases John is not interpreting these purported Old Testament chapters.[79] His critique, however, is more principial than this, since he says that it was not

78. E.g. see Ruiz, *Ezekiel in the Apocalypse*, pp. 210-11, where he positively quotes my discussion in which Dan. 11–12 is proposed as the best background against which to understand Rev. 13.18 and 17.9 (likewise, also in positive reference to my work, cf. pp. 319, 322). The parallels drawn suggest more than unconscious influence, especially in Rev. 13 which is soaked throughout with Daniel. Similarly, he affirms that '13,9 holds a particular interest for this study in that it invites the reader to be particularly attentive to a reference to the prophetic literature' (pp. 201-202). Likewise, conscious interpretation of Old Testament texts is reflected in his statement that, 'John faced the challenge of establishing his authority and that of his message by demonstrating the *authentic continuity* of his work with the written tradition of biblical prophecy' (p. 533; my italics). Finally, he says that μυστήριον is used with 'originality' in Revelation, an originality which 'is nonetheless fully in line with the OT background of μυστήριον' (p. 337, also in reference to my work).

79. Yet Ruiz can say positively what appears to be the opposite: 'As a legitimate heir of the prophetic tradition, he fashioned his reports according to the models of prophetic forms and prophetic metaphors...' (Ruiz, *Ezekiel in the Apocalypse*, pp. 534-35). Why could not John have done this specifically with the prophetic form or context of Daniel 7?

'John's intention to provide a Christian rereading[80] of Daniel' nor to focus on Daniel 'principally [as] an object of interpretation',[81] but that 'the Daniel material in Revelation is used by John as a means to his own creative ends'.[82] It appears that Ruiz has drawn a false distinction between John's possible Christian rereading of Daniel and John's using Daniel to his own creative ends, which are not incompatible. John could be interpreting Daniel's text and in the process be doing so for his own creative ends. The question of whether he interprets in a creative manner compatible with Daniel's original intention[83] is linked to, but is actually a separate question from, the issue of whether or not John consciously reread Daniel or whether Daniel was an object of his interpretation.

Nevertheless, I do allow for the unconscious influence of traditions at various points, though I do not think that this explains the majority of the allusions to Daniel either in early Judaism or in Revelation. Furthermore, there is likely a 'middle road' in the debate over whether or not John was an interpreter of the Old Testament or merely used it purely as a means to his own interpretative ends. On the one hand, it is unlikely that we can regard John as an 'interpreter' or 'commentator' in the modern sense, because his book certainly does not reflect the kind of formal grammatical, lexical and exegetical analysis found in modern monographs and commentaries. On the other hand, it appears improbable that John was not concerned to some important degree about understanding the Old Testament on its own terms and how it related to the redemptive events that had taken place in Christ's coming and that of the Spirit at Pentecost. In attempting to strike the balance between the alternative of an unconscious influence from the Old Testament (John

80. Ruiz actually uses this word positively in explaining John's use of the Old Testament throughout his work (Ruiz, *Ezekiel in the Apocalypse*, p. 182 [John 'reread Ezekiel'], p. 520 ['John grants access to his rereading of the Jewish Scriptures']; so also p. 519 and p. 538).

81. On the other hand, Ruiz refers positively to 'an understanding of Revelation's interpretation of the text(s) of Ezekiel' (Ruiz, *Ezekiel in the Apocalypse*, p. 225), and says further that John's citation of Jer. 15.2 in Rev. 13.10, which is offered as a 'hermeneutical key to unlocking the significance of the first beast [depicted according to the contours of Dan. 7], is an instance of the principle of "Scripture interpreting Scripture"' (p. 203).

82. Ruiz, *Ezekiel in the Apocalypse*, pp. 120-21.

83. This question is addressed at various points in Chapters 1 and 2 of the present work.

as an uninterested interpreter) and that of conscious dependence (John as perceptive interpreter), though leaning more toward the latter in Revelation, I concluded the following in my earlier work on the *Use of Daniel*:

> At times we may have made the apocalyptic authors seem like conscious exegetes or commentators of the O.T. rather than creative composers whose minds are 'soaked' with the O.T. and who re-apply it under the influence of their tradition, as is often the case.[84]
>
> The writers admittedly cannot be understood as 'exegetes' or 'commentators' in the *modern sense*, but neither are their creative compositions devoid of all thought and design with respect to OT usage. Perhaps one of the most creative and least exegetical uses of Daniel can be seen with the Qumran רז and פשׁר, 1 Enoch 69:2–71:17 and Testament of Joseph 19:6-12. Nevertheless, although *the creative element is dominant in these texts* [italics added], all thought for Daniel is not lost. The elements of creativeness and a *kind* of exegetical thought are more apparent in 1QM 1, 1 Enoch 46–47, 52, 90, IV Ezra 11–12, 13, II Baruch 38:1–42:2 and the Revelation texts. These texts to varying degrees reflect a thoughtful, overall organization according to a Danielic *Vorbild*, which has been carried out in a highly creative manner. The most creative of these are 1QM and the Enoch texts, which may reflect less exegetical intention than the others. The extent of exegetical consciousness and intention in these texts [varies].[85]

As noted above (sect. C.1), John can refer, not only generally to the Septuagint, but to its variants, and to forerunners of Septuagintal versions (Theodotion, Symmachus and Aquila), as well as to the Hebrew and Targumic texts, and he can sometimes do this intentionally in an awkward grammatical manner in order to draw attention to various key Old Testament texts.[86] It is improbable that all of these different versional references were already included in prior traditions with which John became familiar at various points. This evidence reflects some

---

84. Beale, *Use of Daniel*, p. 312, which Ruiz (Ruiz, *Ezekiel in the Apocalypse*, p. 123) quotes but says that to say this was too little too late. This comment, however, was at the conclusion of the work and, as the directly following part of the quotation reveals, refers not merely to Revelation but, even more, to early Jewish apocalyptic works. Furthermore, at the conclusion, the reader is directed back to particular studies in Jewish apocalyptic and Revelation which exhibit varying degrees of creativeness, influence and actual dependence.

85. Beale, *Use of Daniel*, pp. 312-13.

86. On which see discussion of the solecisms in Chapter 5.

significant degree of knowledge on the author's part of different 'Bibles'. Additional and striking evidence in favor of conscious dependence and composition based on the Old Testament is the observation made earlier at sect. C.1 and C.2 that allusions in Revelation are connected on the basis of specific themes and of specific phrases or keywords shared between the different Old Testament contexts alluded to and combined together by John.[87] Bauckham's and Fekkes's works support the perspective of John as a prophetic interpreter of the Old Testament, in line, they contend, with later Old Testament interpreters of earlier Old Testament material! On the surface, the mere presence of so many allusions from one chapter of Daniel in one segment of a writing would suggest to logic and to commonsense that the writer's mind was 'soaked' with that chapter of Daniel and that the writer was interested to some significant degree in understanding Daniel and, at the same time, he wanted to show how his own new context sheds interpretative light on Daniel itself.

And, as discussed earlier (sects. C.1 and C.2), if John has inherited interpretative traditions in which combinations of Old Testament allusions and exegetical links have already been composed, then this assumes that an earlier exegete or composer was responsible for this. We have merely moved the exegetical process one step earlier. Some who are skeptical of John as an interpreter are also skeptical of others in the biblical tradition being interpreters. At some point, however, in the light of the specific evidence of (1) exegetical links, (2) reflection of specific yet varied versions of the Old Testament, and (3) the solecisms, one must posit an interpreter. Rather than speculating about an unknown interpreter of an unknown tradition, why not suppose that John was the interpreter–composer, since he is a good potential candidate? Or, one could plausibly contend that John adapts a tradition with some exegetical material, and he is motivated to interpret further the Old Testament on the basis of the tradition.[88]

87. This is such a significant feature pointing strongly to conscious dependence that the fuller discussion in sect. C.1 and C.2 should be consulted.

88. I actually argue this for parts of Revelation in 'The Use of Daniel in the Synoptic Eschatological Discourse and in the Book of Revelation', in D. Wenham (ed.), *Gospel Perspectives. V. The Jesus Tradition outside the Gospels* (Sheffield: JSOT Press, 1985), pp. 129-53, where also Jesus is seen as an earlier interpreter developing a Daniel tradition. Ruiz, *Ezekiel in the Apocalypse*, p. 128, is unconvinced by this proposal, though I still think it remains plausible and attractive.

Ruiz, in particular, while apparently acknowledging the dominant influence of Daniel in Revelation 1 and 13, is unpersuaded by the evidence adduced in the *Use of Daniel* that Daniel 7, instead of Ezekiel 1–2, is the predominant influence in Revelation 4–5, though he is willing to acknowledge that there is clear evidence of influence from Daniel. His main objection is that while Revelation 4–5 can be seen to follow the thematic outline of Dan. 7.9ff., it can just as easily be seen to follow the outline of Isaiah 6. Ruiz's comparisons to Isaiah 6 are too facile and still do not have as much in common with Revelation 4–5 as do the parallels of Daniel 7. Note the following outline:

Daniel 7 and Revelation 4–5

1. Introductory vision phraseology (**Dan. 7.9** [**cf. 7.2, 6-7**]; Rev. 4.1)
2. The setting of a throne(s) in heaven (**Dan. 7.9a**; Rev. 4.2a [cf. 4.4a])
3. God sitting on a throne (**Dan. 7.9b**; Rev. 4.2b)
4. The description of God's appearance on the throne (**Dan. 7.9c**; Rev. 4.3a)
5. Fire before the throne (**Dan. 7.9d-10a**; Rev. 4.5)
6. Heavenly servants surrounding the throne (**Dan. 7.10b**; Rev. 4.4b, 6b-10; 5.8, 11, 14)
7. Book(s) before the throne (**Dan. 7.10c**; Rev. 5.1-5)
8. The 'opening' of the book(s) (**Dan. 7.10c**; Rev. 5.2-5, 9)
9. A divine (messianic) figure approaches God's throne in order to receive authority to reign forever over a kingdom (**Dan. 7.13-14a**; Rev. 5.5b-7, 9a, 12-13)
10. This 'kingdom' includes 'all peoples, nations and tongues' (**Dan. 7.14a** [MT]; Rev. 5.9b)
11. The seer's emotional distress on account of the vision (**Dan. 7.15**; Rev. 5.4)
12. The seer's reception of heavenly counsel concerning the vision from one among the heavenly throne servants (**Dan. 7.16**; Rev. 5.5a)
13. The saints are also given divine authority to reign over a kingdom (**Dan. 7.18, 22, 27a**; Rev. 5.10)
14. A concluding mention of God's eternal reign (**Dan. 7.27b**; Rev. 5.13-14).

Ruiz composes an outline which compares Revelation to Isaiah 6 in order to show that it is similar to the parallels drawn with Daniel 7. He concludes that one should not think that Daniel 7 is any more influential than Isaiah 6 (he could have provided a similar outline with comparison of Ezekiel 1–2). To be precise, and not pedantic, there are a number of significant parallels lacking in Isaiah 6 (and Ezekiel 1–2), which Daniel has in common with Revelation 4–5. The first six items of the Daniel outline he reproduces in Isaiah 6. Even with these items, however, the parallels are not as close, since Isaiah lacks the notion of *the setting up of a throne, and that there were plural thrones*. The fifth item of 'fire before the throne' is only implied at best in Isaiah 6, where 'smoke' and a 'burning coal' is mentioned, whereas both Daniel 7 and Revelation 4–5 explicitly mention a 'burning fire' coming out *from the throne itself*.

The next seven items of the outline have little resemblance to the comparable points from Daniel 7 and Revelation 4–5. The only close points of contact are the seer's reaction and his reception of counsel from a heavenly being (eleventh and twelfth elements). In both cases, however, the Daniel parallels are closer: the seer reacts with emotional distress to a vision *because he cannot understand it*,[89] and *the heavenly being interprets part of the vision* in order to relieve the seer's perplexity. On the other hand, in Isaiah 6 the prophet responds emotionally to a vision because he does understand it (being in the presence of a holy God, he realizes his sin, and the angel solves the problem which the seer understands by conducting a symbolic ritual of forgiveness). Ruiz also admits that there is no mention in Isaiah 6 of books nor the opening of books (seventh and eighth elements).

His elements 9 and 10 (Isaiah 6 and Revelation 4–5 involve conferral of prophetic commission) are not clear, especially since he cites no specific verse references. It is obvious that he has in mind Isaiah's commission in Isa. 6.8-10, but it is not clear what parallel he has in mind in Revelation 4-5. The corresponding items 9 and 10 in the Daniel outline pertain respectively to the approach before God's throne of a divine messianic-like figure to receive authority over an eternal kingdom *and* to this kingdom including 'all people, nations and tongues'. The prophetic commission of Isaiah certainly does not concern the latter item of a kingdom composed of many peoples, nor does it have to

89. For the interpretative aspect of 'opening the book' and 'looking into it' see Beale, *Book of Revelation*, on Rev. 5.2.

do with a divine messianic-like figure being given authority to reign over an eternal kingdom. Perhaps, what Ruiz has in mind is the prophetic recommissioning of John in 4.1-2, but he does not make this evident nor imply it. And, even if he did, it would compose only one item of correspondence, not two.

Finally, the last two elements of his outline he refers to as 'God's demonstration of power has a punitive character'. He apparently sees the idea of power as a distinct item from the notion of punitiveness. These last two elements are too general; they could be found in many Old Testament and New Testament passages. Again, he does not cite the specific parallel verses in Isaiah 6 and Revelation 4–5 which he believes have correspondences in these two areas. The probable reason for not citing specific verses is that the ideas are too general. Only a very general parallel of divine power could be drawn, but where is the explicit reference to judgment in Revelation as there is in Isaiah 6 (e.g. Isa. 6.9-13?).[90] His last two general points are in contrast to the specific Daniel parallels of the saints being given authority to reign over a kingdom *and* a final mention of God's eternal reign.

The outline of Ezekiel 1–2 could be compared more convincingly than Isaiah to Revelation 4–5 and proposed as the dominant background, since it has at least as many parallels as Isaiah and more specific allusions to it are found in Revelation 4–5. As is the case in Isaiah 6, however, the same crucial elements found in Daniel 7 and Revelation 4–5 are also absent in Ezekiel, except for the image of a book. Another significant element missing in Isaiah and Ezekiel is the image of a sea, which both Daniel 7 and Revelation 4–5 include. That Daniel is more dominant than both Isaiah or Ezekiel is also evident from observing that there are more allusions to Daniel in Revelation 4–5 (approximately 23)[91] than either to Isaiah 6 (of which there only at most 5 verbal allusions) or to Ezekiel 1–2 (of which there are approximately

---

90. On which see G.K. Beale, 'Isaiah VI 9-13: A Retributive Taunt against Idolatry', *VT* 41 (1991), pp. 257-78. I believe there is an idea of judgment in Rev. 4–5, but it is implicit and such an implicit notion needs to be demonstrated, and Ruiz does not do this (for such a demonstration, see Beale, *Use of Daniel*, pp. 178-228).

91. Half of the allusions are from Dan. 7 and the rest from other chapters in Daniel.

15), a significant point never mentioned by Ruiz. In addition, the Daniel parallels are in the same basic order as those in Revelation.[92]

Ruiz's point in drawing out the Isaiah 6 parallels was to show that, if the thematic outline of other Old Testament chapters could be shown to be just as similar to Revelation 4–5 as Daniel 7, then Daniel 7 should not be seen as the dominant influence, which enhances his view that, perhaps, neither is John consciously dependent on Daniel. In reality, however, he draws only about 8 significant Isaianic parallels in his outline (and Ezekiel 1–2 has about the same number) in comparison to Daniel's 14. Therefore, Ruiz's evaluation does not take into sufficient consideration the following features: (1) the inductive evidence of numerous specific verbal allusions to Daniel throughout Revelation 4–5; (2) the significantly broader outline of Daniel 7 in comparison with that of Ezekiel 1–2 or Isaiah 6; and (3) the qualifications made about Daniel 7 as a model.[93] In this light, Ruiz would need to adduce more evidence in favor of his critique before it could be convincing.[94]

Moyise also offers a similar, though less trenchant, critique as Ruiz of the proposal that Daniel 7 is dominant in Revelation 4–5.[95] He examines only the comparisons of Daniel to Rev. 4.1-10, focusing more on 4.2-5. He affirms that when the relevant parallels are set out, they do

92. See Beale, *Book of Daniel*, pp. 178-228, for fuller discussion of the use of Daniel in Rev. 4–5 and its relation to the influence of Ezekiel in Rev. 4–5, which a number of commentators see as dominant.

93. Ruiz, *Ezekiel in Revelation*, pp. 224-27, which I have not elaborated on in much detail above.

94. Ruiz, *Ezekiel in Revelation*, pp. 126-27, also is skeptical of my proposal that Dan. 7 is the main influence in Rev. 17, since I ignore the allusions in 17.1-4 (though I do dedicate a paragraph to this) and I do not recognize that Rev. 17 is a unified segment together with ch. 18, all of which are part of the larger segment of 16.17–19.10, which depends on 'a consistent rereading of Ezekiel 16 & 23, and 26,1–28,19, in combination with other texts' (p. 537). These are good observations. However, all I claim is the *probability* that *in Rev. 17.5-16a* Daniel is dominant because the only clear Old Testament allusions in this section are from Daniel and because a broader Danielic *Vorbild* is discernible in the chapter, the latter observation pointing to the *possibility* of a Danielic dominance for the entire chapter. I am open to Daniel being subsumed within a broader Old Testament framework like Ezekiel in Rev. 16.17–19.10. The scope and limits of my work, nevertheless, did not permit wider investigation of the broader context (see Beale, *Use of Daniel*, pp. 249-67). Ruiz does not refute the specific notion of Daniel's dominance in 17.5-16a.

95. Moyise, *Old Testament in the Book of Revelation*, pp. 60-61.

not have much in common other than the observation that they are both visions of God's throne. Moyise also notes that the actual narrative descriptions of Daniel 7 and Revelation 4–5 are different in many ways, to such an extent that to say that one is the model for the other is 'really sleight of hand'.[96] It is true that if the parallels of the outline of Daniel 7 and Ezekiel 1–2 (and, perhaps Isaiah 6) are compared, not only for Rev. 4.2-5, but for all of Revelation 4, that none should be seen as dominant over the other. The contention in the *Use of Daniel*, however, was that Revelation 4–5 should be seen as one whole vision, as most commentators acknowledge. When ch. 5 together with ch. 4 is considered as a unity, the broad outline of Daniel 7 is more apparent and dominant than any others; in addition, more allusions to Daniel 7 appear in ch. 5 by far in comparison to any other Old Testament passage, including Ezekiel or Isaiah. As seen above, the following unique and significant elements are not found in Ezekiel (or Isaiah) which do appear in Daniel 7 and Revelation 4–5: (1) the opening of books; (2) the approach of a divine messianic-like figure before God's throne in order to receive authority to reign over an eternal kingdom; (3) this kingdom consists of all peoples of the earth; (4) the reign of the saints over a kingdom; (5) mention of God's eternal reign; and (6) the image of a sea.

Moyise needed to evaluate this evidence together with the above-mentioned observation that Daniel provides over 30 per cent more verbal allusions than Ezekiel (and almost 80 per cent more than Isaiah 6), which shows that not only a bare comparative outline but also a significant number of allusions point to a Daniel dependence. Furthermore, one does not expect exact photographic reproduction of a prior text for that text to be used as a model. The examination of the way early Judaism used Daniel as a model for various segments of material comports with what John has done in Revelation 4–5.[97] Perhaps Moyise disagrees with the analysis of the use of Daniel in these early Jewish apocalyptic texts, but he does not even acknowledge this evidence and its possible bearing on John's use. As with Ruiz's critique, Moyise needs more detailed interaction with the material on both sides of the argument before his evaluation could be persuasive.

Both Ruiz and Moyise are also critical of the proposal that the Daniel 2 ἃ δεῖ γενέσθαι literary markers at the beginning of the main sections of the book (1.1, 19; 4.1; 22.6) demonstrate that Daniel 2 'provides the

---

96. Moyise, *Old Testament in the Book of Revelation*, p. 61.
97. E.g. see Beale, *Use of Daniel*, pp. 67-153.

framework of thought for the whole of the Apocalypse'.[98] Their argument has merit, though there is plausibility in viewing this evidence as suggesting not that Daniel was *the* framework but *a* framework of thought. There is no doubt that Ezekiel also provided a conceptual framework. Indeed, Moyise and others are correct in saying that there is more evidence for Ezekiel than any other book being the primary Old Testament lens for the entire Apocalypse.[99]

Critical evaluation of both Ruiz and Moyise has been difficult both here and in ch. 1, since the hermeneutical issues are complicated, and there are subtleties which may be hard to express, all of which makes it difficult to know whether or not I have completely understood their own positions and their critique of my views. In the light of this, my criticisms of them should be viewed as considerably softened.

2. *Thematic Use of the Old Testament*

In addition to alluding to specific Old Testament texts and segments, the author of Revelation develops important Old Testament *themes*. Many of these themes are delineated throughout the major commentaries. J. Fekkes has shown that, among others, John develops extensively such Old Testament themes as end-time judgment and end-time salvation, each of which have thematic sub-categories.[100] Some special studies of note are D. Ford's tracing of Daniel's 'abomination of desolation' theme,[101] T. Longman's study of the Old Testament divine warrior concept,[102] R.J. Bauckham's articles on the Old Testament earthquake idea[103] and on John's reinterpretation of the Old Testament 'holy war' theme,[104] recent articles on the employment of the ancient Near East/Old Testament covenant form in Revelation 2–3 and throughout

---

98. See Ruiz, *Ezekiel in Revelation*, pp. 127-28, and Moyise, *Old Testament in the Book of Revelation*, pp. 61-62. For my full argument, see the *Use of Daniel*, pp. 275-85.

99. For this evidence see Chapter 3, sect. D.1.

100. See Fekkes, *Isaiah and Prophetic Traditions*, pp. 70-103, and *passim*, for in-depth discussion of these kinds of uses of the Old Testament.

101. Ford, *Abomination*, pp. 243-314.

102. T. Longman, 'The Divine Warrior: The New Testament Use of an Old Testament Motif', *WTJ* 44 (1982), pp. 290-307.

103. R.J. Bauckham, 'The Eschatological Earthquake in the Apocalypse of John', *NovT* 19 (1977), pp. 224-33.

104. R.J. Bauckham, *Climax of Prophecy*, pp. 210-37.

the book,[105] and the Old Testament concept of the 'day of the Lord'.[106] Of particular note is C.H. Giblin's further development of the 'holy war' theme in which he makes a case that this Old Testament notion 'in all its essential [eightfold] institutional features structures the entire course of events' in Revelation 4–22,[107] and is formative for the overall thought of chs. 1–3 as well.[108]

D.R. Carnegie has offered a most interesting study on the function of hymns in the Old Testament and their re-use in Revelation. He shows that the various songs in Isaiah 40–55 come at the end of subsections and round them off, not only by offering a concluding thanksgiving, but also by giving an interpretative summary of the theme of the whole previous section (cf. Isa. 48.20ff.; 52.9; etc.). The series of hymns in Revelation are seen to have the same function under the inspiration of the Isaianic songs (cf. Rev. 4.11; 5.13; 7.9-12; 11.15-18; 19.1-8; so Carnegie).[109]

3. *Analogical Use of the Old Testament*

This use can be considered the most general description of Old Testament usage in the Apocalypse, since the very act of referring to an Old Testament text is to place it in a comparative relationship to something in the New Testament. However, specific well-known persons, places, and events are the focus here. The pictures undergo creative changes (expansions, condensations, supplemental imagery, etc.) and, of course, are applied to different historical situations (for a superb example of such alteration see Vos's discussion of the Exodus plague imagery in Rev. 8.6-12 and 16.2-13]).[110] Nevertheless, a key idea in the Old Testament context is usually carried over as the main characteristic or principle to be applied in the New Testament situation.[111] Therefore, even

---

105. W.H. Shea, The 'Covenantal Form of the Letters to the Seven Churches', *AUSS* 21 (1983), pp. 71-84; K.A. Strand, 'A Further Note on the Covenantal Form in the Book of Revelation', *AUSS* 21 (1983), pp. 251-64.

106. D.A. Gray, 'The Day of the Lord and its Culmination in the Book of Revelation (Related to the Theology of Hope)' (PhD dissertation; Manchester: University of Manchester, 1974).

107. C.H. Giblin, *The Book of Revelation* (Good News Studies, 34; Collegeville, MN: Liturgical Press, 1991), p. 29, as well as pp. 25-34, 224-31.

108. Giblin, *Revelation*, pp. 25-36, 224-31.

109. Carnegie, 'Worthy is the Lamb', pp. 250-52.

110. Vos, *Synoptic Traditions in the Apocalypse*, pp. 45-47.

111. Vos, *Synoptic Traditions in the Apocalypse*, pp. 47-48.

though John handles these Old Testament figures with creative freedom, almost always these pictures broadly retain an essential Old Testament association and convey principles of continuity between the Old Testament and New Testament.[112]

a. *Illustration of a Typical Analogical Use of the Old Testament.* The use of Deuteronomy in Rev. 22.18-19 is an example of a contextual analogical use, which will receive extended treatment here as an illustrative model of how other analogical applications of the Old Testament could also be discussed.

Verses 18-19 summarize the book of Revelation as a new law code to a new Israel, which is modeled on the old law code to ethnic Israel. Though many commentators note only Deuteronomy 4, John alludes to a series of warning passages throughout Deuteronomy:

Deuteronomy	Revelation 22.18-19
hear the statutes... you shall not add to the word... nor take away from it (4.1-2; likewise 12.32); and it will be when he hears the words... every curse which is written in this book will rest on him, and the Lord will blot out his name from under heaven (29.19-20).	I testify to everyone who hears the words... if anyone adds to them, God will add to him the plagues which have been written in this book, and if anyone takes away from the words of the book ... God will take away his part from the tree of life and from the holy city...

Further similarities enhancing the link between Deuteronomy and Rev. 22.18-19 are:

(1) in the light of the directly preceding and following contexts of each of the three Deuteronomy passages, it is clear that all three are specific warnings against idolatry, as is the case in Revelation 22 (see on 21.8, 27; 22.15);

(2) a positive response to both of the Old Testament and New Testament warnings results in the reward of life in the new land (Deut. 4.1; 12.28-29; cf. Rev. 21.1–22.5 with 22.14, 17-19);

(3) both also use the terminology of 'plagues' to describe the punishment for unfaithfulness (see τὰς πληγὰς in Deut. 29.21 and Rev. 22.18).

112. So Cambier, 'Les images de l'Ancien Testament dans l'Apocalypse de Saint Jean'; pp. 116-20; cf. Gangemi, 'L'utilizzazoine del Deutero-Isaia nell'Apocalisse di Giovanni', pp. 322-39.

What is the meaning of 'adding to' and 'taking away from' the revelatory words of John's Apocalypse? The answer must be sought in Deuteronomy. In both Deut. 4.1-2 and 12.32 the language serves as a twofold warning against deceptive teaching which affirmed that idolatry was not inconsistent with faith in the God of Israel (see Deut. 4.3, which alludes to the Baal-Peor episode of Num. 25.1-9, 14-18, and Deut. 13). Those who deceive in this way are false prophets (so Deut. 13.1-5); note that Deut. 12.32 of the English text is placed by the Hebrew Bible, the LXX (cf. Rahlf's edition) and the Targums (Onqelos and Neofiti) as the first verse of ch. 13, which introduces the subject of false prophets (cf. the false prophet Balaam who was behind the deception of Baal-Peor: see on Rev. 2.14). Such false teaching amounts to 'adding to' God's Law. Furthermore, it is tantamount to 'taking away from' God's Law, since it violates the positive laws against idolatry, consequently nullifying their validity. The disobedience of following this false teaching is probably included in the dual warning of Deut. 4.2 and 12.32, as Deut. 29.19-20 confirms.

Therefore, 'adding and taking away' refers not to mere general disobedience to the divine word, but to false teaching about the inscripturated word and following such deceptive teaching. Belief in the abiding truth of God's word is the presupposition for positive obedience to it: compare Deut. 4.2, 'you shall not add...nor take away *in order that* you may keep the commandments of the Lord'. The ancient near-eastern treaty documents, after which Deuteronomy 4 is modeled, were also protected against intentional alterations by means of inscriptional sanctions and curses.[113]

The twofold warning of 22.18-19 is directed against those who foster or follow such seductive teaching. This Deuteronomic background is remarkably comparable to Rev. 22.18-19, since the descriptions in the three vice lists of Rev. 21.8, 21.27 and 22.15 all conclude by emphasizing the deceptiveness of the ungodly in connection with idolatry. Consequently, 'to add' to the words of John's prophecy is to promote the false teaching that idolatry is not inconsistent with faith in Christ. 'To take away from the words of the book of this prophecy' is also to advance such deceptive teaching, since it would violate and vitiate the validity of Revelation's exhortations against idolatry. Alternatively, it

---

113. M.G. Kline, *The Structure of Biblical Authority* (Grand Rapids: Eerdmans, 1972), pp. 27-38.

may be best to see 'adding' and 'taking away' as a hendiadys referring
to a warning not to be associated with false teaching.

Strikingly analogous also to Rev. 22.18-19 is *1 En.* 104.11, where 'to
change or take away from my words' means the readers should not
'lie', should not 'take account of…idols', not 'alter and pervert the
words of righteousness' and not 'practice great deceits'. Though Moffatt sees allusion in Rev. 22.18 to the *1 Enoch* text,[114] it is better to see
it together with Revelation as part of the larger exegetical tradition
based on Deuteronomy.

Also in remarkably similar fashion, Josephus (*Apion* 1.42-43) alludes to the same wording of Deut. 4.2 and sees it as a warning against
doctrinally malicious scribes, as well as any Israelite who would think
about not regarding the entire Old Testament 'as the decrees of God',
not abiding by them and uttering 'a single word against them'.

This analysis fits well also with the situation of the churches portrayed in chs. 2–3, which depict idolatry as a significant threat to the
churches. Analogously, some of the false teachers and their followers
encouraging idolatry in the church of Pergamum are identified as those
'who hold the teaching of Balaam, who kept teaching Balak to put a
stumbling-block before the sons of Israel, to eat things sacrificed to
idols, and to commit immorality' (see 2.14). The same deceptive teaching was also prevalent in the church of Thyatira (see on 2.20-23). Such
false prophets who distort the truth are either adding false theology or
taking away from the revealed truth.

Against the background of the letters, the rewards of 22.12-19 are
best understood, since they correspond to the promises to the 'overcomers' in chs. 2–3: (1) 'rendering to each as his work deserves' (2.23;
22.12); (2) eating of the tree of life (2.7; 22.14, 19); and (3)
identification with 'the city of God' (3.12; 22.14, 19). Those who overcome the threat of idolatry will inherit these promises. Indeed, in this
context, the 'washing of the robes' in Rev. 22.14 must refer to keeping
oneself undefiled by the pollution of idol worship, resulting in the same
twofold reward which will be withheld from the transgressors in 22.19
(see also 3.4-5 and 7.14 for the 'washing' imagery).

Consequently, the warnings of 22.18-19 are directed, not primarily to
pagans outside the church, but to all in the church community, as the
warnings of Deuteronomy were addressed to all Israelites. Those who

---

114. J. Moffatt, *The Revelation of St. John the Divine* (The Expositor's Greek
Testament, V; Grand Rapids: Eerdmans, 1970), p. 32.

do not heed the warnings are people who profess to be Christian but their allegiance to other gods betrays their confession. As a result, the inheritance they lay claim to by their apparent testimony will, in fact, not be given to them because they deny by their actions the faith they profess. Not only will they not receive their purported inheritance at the end of the age, but also they will suffer 'the plagues which are written in this book' (v. 19). These 'plagues' include not merely the suffering of the last judgment in the 'lake of fire', as v. 19 implies, but penal inflictions incurred by the ungodly throughout the time prior to that judgment. In line with this are uses of the πληγή ('plague') word group elsewhere in the book which are applied to the era preceding Christ's last coming (e.g. see on 8.12; 9:18, 20; 11.6; 13.3, 12, 14; cf. also 16.21).[115]

Therefore, the whole range of plagues recorded in the book will come on the apostate, which is supported by the Deut. 29.20 allusion: 'every curse which is written in this book will rest on him' (likewise Deut. 28.58-61; 29.21; Jer. 25.13).[116] Possible allusion to Deut. 28.58-61 also suggests an all-encompassing reference to the plagues in Revelation.[117]

115. This analysis of 'adding and taking away' is supported by Prov. 30:6: 'Do not add to His words lest he reprove you, and you be proved a *liar*'. Even in *Did.* 4.13 and *Barn.* 19.11 the formulaic 'neither adding to them nor taking away from them' has a focus respectively upon shunning 'hypocrisy' by not 'forsaking the commandments' and upon urging saints to 'hate utterly the evil one'.

116. One Armenian version makes the all-encompassing reference explicit by paraphrasing with 'all the plagues which have been written in this book' (see H.C. Hoskier, *Concerning the Text of the Apocalypse* [2 vols.; London: Bernard Quaritch, 1929], II, p. 642; likewise JB: 'every plague mentioned in the book').

117. Some commentators view vv. 18-19 as merely a familiar way that literary works in Judaism and early Christianity were concluded in order that later scribes would be sure to copy the documents carefully (as in the Letter of Aristeas 310-11, as well as Eusebius, *Hist. Eccles.* 5.20.2 [citing Irenaeus]; cf. *1 En.* 104.10-13, Josephus, *Apion* 1.42; *2 En.* 48.6-9 and *b. Meg.* 14a; Caird, *Revelation*, pp. 278-79). Perhaps, this could be the case, but if so, the above Deuteronomy background shows that this literary convention has been intensified by a theological intention (on which see the discussion directly above). However, John is not warning future scribes about exact copying but is warning all Christians 'who hear the words of the prophecy of this book' (so also 1.3; 22.9; as noted by numerous commentators)! The need for such a warning for Christians, including Christian scribes, is apparent from those who 'distorted' Paul's letters and 'the rest of the Scriptures to their own destruction' (2 Pet. 3.16; cf. Rist, *Revelation*, p. 550). The urgency of the warning

b. *A Brief Survey of Other Analogical Uses of the Old Testament.* The following is a sampling of other analogies with a brief description of the primary point of correspondence or continuity:

(1) *judgment*—theophanies introducing judgment (Isa. 6, Ezek.1, Dan. 7/Rev. 4–5), books of judgment (Ezek. 2, Dan. 7, Dan.12/Rev. 5.1-5 and Ezek. 2/Rev. 10), lion from Judah exercising judgment (Gen. 49.9/Rev. 5.5), 'Lord of lords and King of kings' exercising judgment (Dan. 4.37 [LXX]/Rev. 17.14; 19.16), horsemen as divine agents of judgment (Zech. 1 and 6/Rev. 6.1-8), Exodus plagues inflicting judgment (Exod. 7.14–12.51/Rev. 8.6-12; 16.1-14), locusts as agents of judgment (Joel 1–2/Rev. 9.7-10), prophets giving testimony through judgment (Exod. 7.17; 1 Kgs 17.1/Rev. 11.6), 'Babylon' judged by God in 'one hour' (Dan. 4.17a [LXX]/Rev. 18.10, 17, 19).

(2) *tribulation and persecution of God's people*—ten days of tribulation (Dan. 1.12/Rev. 2.10), three-and-a-half years of tribulation (Dan. 7.25; 12.7/Rev. 11.2; 12.14; 13.5), Sodom, Egypt and Jerusalem as infamous places where persecution occurs (Rev. 11.8), persecuting rulers symbolized as beasts (Dan. 7/Rev. 11–13, 17) and 'Babylon the Great' (Dan. 4.30, etc./Rev. 14.8; 16.19; 17.5; 18.2).

(3) *seductive, idolatrous teaching*—Balaam (Num. 25; 31.16/Rev. 2.14) and Jezebel (1 Kgs 16.31; 2 Kgs 9.22/Rev. 2.20-23).

(4) *divine protection*—the tree of life (Gen. 2.9/Rev. 2.7; 22.2, 14, 19), the 'sealed' Israelites (Ezek. 9/Rev. 7.2-8) and the wings of the eagle (Exod. 19.4; Deut. 32.11/Rev. 12.14).

5) *victorious battle of God's people over the enemy*—Armageddon (Zech. 12.11/Rev. 16.16 [19.19]; cf. Gog and Magog in Ezek. 38–39:16/Rev. 20.8).

(6) *apostasy*—the harlot (Ezek. 16.15; etc./Rev. 17).

(7) *the divine Spirit as the power for God's people*—Zech. 4.1-6/Rev. 1.12-20; 11.4.

is also apparent from the early Gnostics, who advanced their false teaching by reproducing New Testament books by adding to or eliminating material from them (see Beasley-Murray, *Book of Revelation*, pp. 346-47). Indeed, as some commentators point out, if vv. 18-19 were a warning only to prevent scribal miscopying, it was lost on the scribes, since vv. 18-19 are filled with textual variants.

Some analogies are repeated in the book and creatively developed in different ways, though usually within the conceptual boundaries of the Old Testament context to some degree.

One other analogical use is also instructive. The image of the deceiving 'serpent of old' in Rev. 12.9 (cf. 20.2) evokes an episode of primitive religious history which maintains the same meaning for the final, eschatological phase of theological history.[118] The author's theological basis for maintaining such continuities lies in his conviction that Old Testament and New Testament history is but the working out of God's unified design of salvation and deals throughout with the unchanging principles of faith in God, God's faithfulness in fulfilling his salvific promises, the anti-theocratic forces attempting to thwart such promises and the victory of God's kingdom over that of Satan.[119]

4. Universalization of the Old Testament

Vanhoye is apparently the only author to discuss this as a formal category of Old Testament usage. The apocalyptist has a tendency to apply to the world what in the Old Testament was limited in reference to Israel or other entities.[120] There are several examples of this phenomenon. The title which Yahweh gave Israel in Exod. 19.6 ('kingdom of priests') is applied in Rev. 1.6 and 5.10 to the church, composed of kingly priests 'from every tribe and people and nation' (Rev. 5.9). Indeed, this very phrase of universality in Rev. 5.9 is most likely taken from Dan. 7.14, where it referred to the nations of the world subjugated to Israel's rule, which is now extended to the rule by all these very nations.[121]

a. Two Illustrations of Typical Universalisations of the Old Testament

(i). *Revelation 1.7.* Rev. 1.7 reads, 'Behold, he is coming with the clouds, and every eye will see him, even those who pierced him, and all the tribes of the earth will mourn over him.' Prophetic fulfillment is generally indicated by John's combination of two clear Old Testament

---

118. So Cambier, 'Les images de l'Ancien Testament dans l'Apocalypse', pp. 118-19.

119. Gambier, 'Les images de l'Ancien Testament dans l'Apocalypse', pp. 119-20.

120. Cf. A. Vanhoye, 'L'utilisation du livre d'Ezéchiel dans l'Apocalypse', pp. 446-67.

121. Cf. Rev. 5.10; Beale, *Use of Daniel*, pp. 214-19.

references. The first is from Dan. 7.13, which in its Old Testament context refers to the enthronement of the son of man over all the nations (cf. Dan. 7.14) after God's judgment of evil empires (Dan. 7.9-12). The application of this text to Jesus shows that he is its fulfillment and emphasizes his eschatological kingship, a theme already introduced in v. 5 (Judaism also had a messianic understanding of the Daniel son of man: e.g. *4 Ezra* 13 and throughout *1 Enoch* 37–71). The following citation is from Zech. 12.10, which in Zechariah pertains to the end-time period when God will defeat the enemy nations around Israel and when Israel will be redeemed after repenting of her sinful rejection of God and his messenger (i.e. 'the one they have pierced').

The identical combination of Daniel 7 and Zechariah 12 in Mt. 24.30 may have influenced John to do the same here (the same combination occurs also in Justin Martyr, *Dial. Trypho* 14.8; Mt. 24.30 may also refer to repentance in the light of 24.31). Whether or not this was the case, the author discerned that both passages concerned the common theme of God's end-time defeat of Israel's enemies, and, therefore, these were attractive texts to supplement those Old Testament allusions already used to refer to the inaugurated end-time kingdom.[122] That the one 'mourned' for is compared to a 'firstborn son' (πρωτότοκος) in Zech. 12.10 is also not coincidence, since the same word is used to describe the king in the LXX of Psalm 88 (89), 28 (27, Eng.) and Jesus in Rev. 1.5.

The Zechariah text has been altered in two significant ways. The phrases πᾶς ὀφθαλμὸς ('every eye') and τῆς γῆς ('of the earth') have been added to universalize its original meaning. The rejection of God's messenger and the consequent repentant mourning is not limited to Israelites but affirmed of all nations. Those who mourn are not those who literally crucified Jesus but who are guilty of rejecting him. This is probably not a reference to every person without exception but to all among the nations who believe, as indicated clearly by 5.9 and 7.9 (cf. the plural of φυλή ['tribe'] as a *universal* reference to unbelievers in 11.9; 13.7; 14.6). γῆ ('earth, land') cannot be a limited reference to the land of Israel but is a universal denotation, since this is the only meaning which the phrase πᾶσαι αἱ φυλαὶ τῆς γῆς ('all the tribes of the earth') has in the Old Testament (against the 70 AD preterist view which understands it as the land of Israel; cf. LXX of Gen. 12.3; 28.14;

---

122. See Beale, *Use of Daniel*, pp. 155-56, for other possible connections between these two texts which may have motivated John to combine them.

Ps. 71[72, Eng.].17; Zech. 14.17). The phrase 'all the tribes of Israel' occurs repeatedly in the Old Testament (approx. 25 times), which highlights also the different wording of Rev. 1.7b. This implies an extension of the Old Testament concept of 'Israel', since what applied to that nation in Zechariah 12 is now transferred to the peoples of the earth, who assume the role of repentant Israel.[123] The addition of τῆς γῆς ('of the earth') to πᾶσαι αἱ...φυλὰ ('all the...tribes') of Zech 12.14 was likely motivated by πασῶν τῶν φυλῶν τῆς γῆς ('all the tribes of the earth') from Zech. 14.17 and perhaps πάντες...φυλαὶ ('all...tribes') of Dan. 7.14 (Theodotion), where universal designations are intended (this is the case even if γῆ ['earth'] of Zech. 12.12 stands partially behind the wording of 1.7b). This continues the same trend of application seen with the use of Exod. 19.6 in Rev. 1.6.

Some believe that the Zechariah quotation is utilized contrary to its original intention to connote the grief of the nations over their impending judgment. But John typically adheres to and consistently develops the contextual ideas of his Old Testament references and proposed exceptions to this rule must bear the burden of proof (according to the thesis throughout this section and book).[124] Indeed, the nations in 1.7b do not mourn over themselves but Jesus, which fits better into an understanding of repentance than judgment.[125] And the extended application of the mourning from the nation Israel to the believing nations is not an inconsistent development, since the latter now are understood to be the true Israel.[126]

There is an additional problem in the relation of the Zechariah text to Revelation. In the Hebrew text of Zech. 12.10 there is ambiguity in that God is the one who is pierced, yet he identifies himself apparently with an associate ('they will look on *Me* whom they have pierced, and they will mourn for *Him*'). John cites the Old Testament passage to identify

---

123. Independent confirmation of this analysis of the use of Zech. 12.10 can be found in Bauckham, *Climax of Prophecy*, pp. 319-22, who helpfully notes that the use in the messianic Ps. 71[72].17 is an intentional development of Gen. 12.3 and 28.14, where the Abrahamic promise of blessing to the nations is affirmed; Bauckham concludes the same development occurs in Rev. 1.7.

124. The same thesis is argued in the larger work by Beale, *Book of Revelation*.

125. So Caird, *Revelation*, p. 18.

126. Note also the emphasis on the salvation of the nations in 21.24–22.3; see Sweet, *Revelation*, p. 63.

Jesus with the pierced God of Zechariah,[127] thus clarifying the ambiguity by seeing that it was not the Father who was pierced but the divine Son, who nevertheless shares divine status together with the Father.[128]

Therefore, repentant Gentiles are viewed as fulfilling the Zechariah prophecy at the second coming of Christ. However, the Daniel 7 reference may include the whole course of the church age during which Christ guides the events of history in judgment and blessing, since the son of man allusion in 1.13 has present application (although cf. 14.14), as do the Old Testament references in 1.5-6 and 1.14-20 (cf. below); the same citation from Dan. 7.13 in Mk 13.26 and 14.62 refers, not to the final coming of Christ, but to the son of man's coming in judgment of Jerusalem in 70 AD;[129] and the identical combination of Dan. 7.13 with Zech. 12.10 found in Mt. 24.30 is susceptible of the same meaning, although the final parousia could be in mind. Of course, there are also clear synoptic references to the son of man's coming to conclude history (e.g. Mt. 19.28; 25.31). These references in the Synoptics could have prepared John's readers for another application of the son of man prophecy to a time preceding, as well as including, his final coming at the climax of history.

Furthermore, Christ's 'coming' in the letters appears to refer to his conditional visitation in judgment of the churches, though a second coming allusion could be included (cf. 2.5, 16; 3.11; see likewise 16.15). Observable also is the use of the identical phrase ἔρχομαι ταχύ ('I come quickly') in 2.16 and 3.11 (cf. 2.5) to indicate Jesus' conditional comings, as well as in 22.7, 12 and 20 to refer apparently to the certainty of his final coming. This points to a close conceptual link between the comings in the letters and in the conclusion to the book. Therefore, Christ's 'coming' in 1.7 and elsewhere in the Apocalypse is understood better as a process occurring throughout history so that his so-called 'second coming' is actually a final coming concluding the

127. So see A. Hultberg, 'The Significance of Zech. 12:10 for the Theology of the Apocalypse' (A paper presented at the 47th Annual Meeting of the Evangelical Theological Society, Philadelphia, PA, 16 November 1995), whose discussion is more nuanced.

128. This is a notion found elsewhere in the book: cf. 3.7 (on which see discussion below); cf. 4.11 with 5.12-14; 6.16b-17; 17.14; 19.16; 21.2-23; 22.3.

129. Cf. R.T. France, *Jesus and the Old Testament* (London: Tyndale Press, 1971), pp. 140-42, 227-39.

whole process of comings.[130] In Dan. 7.13 the son of man's 'coming' primarily indicates his reception of authority to exercise end-time kingship over the world. This is understood in 1.7 and in the other 'comings' of Revelation to begin fulfillment at the resurrection and continue fulfillment until the son of man's last coming at the end of history.[131]

Consequently his 'comings' in blessing and judgment throughout the course of the interadvent period are but manifestations of him exercising this latter-day authority. The Zechariah quotation perhaps connotes the climax of the historical process expressed in the Daniel 7 allusion. However, in Jn 19.37 the Zech. 12.10 quotation refers to the Gentile soldier near the cross who 'pierced' Jesus and then apparently repented, which is viewed as a formal, direct beginning prophetic fulfillment of the Zechariah prophecy[132] (note the πληρόω formula in Jn; cf. Jn 19.34-37 and Mk 15.39). A strikingly similar application of Zech. 12.10 is found in Rev. 1.7.[133] Consequently, the Zechariah 12 quotation could also include application to a period preceding the final parousia when Gentiles believe in the Messiah. If so, the 'seeing' would have to be taken more figuratively and perceived as being future only from John's standpoint. Some commentators have rightly suggested that 1.7 serves as the keynote of the book, but this keynote must be understood in the

---

130. So also C. Brütsch, *Clarte de l'Apocalypse* (Geneva: Labor et Fides, 1955), p. 31, who also cites Godet and von Speyr in support.

131. Compatible with the above analysis of 1.7 is S.E. Porter, *Verbal Aspect in the Greek of the New Testament, with Reference to Tense and Mood* (Studies in Biblical Greek, I; New York: Peter Lang, 1989), p. 231, who does not see ἔρχεται ('he comes') clearly as a futuristic present and paraphrases 1.7 accordingly as 'behold he is in progress coming with the clouds and every eye will see him' (cf. also p. 437). In contrast, Thompson, *Semitic Syntax*, pp. 34-35, sees ἔρχεται ('he comes') as a futuristic present under Semitic influence.

132. So J.R. Michaels, 'The Centurian's Confession and the Spear Thrust', *CBQ* 29 (1967), pp. 102-109; Sweet, 'Maintaining the Testimony of Jesus', p. 112.

133. For a survey of the various interpretations of Zech. 12.10, especially concerning the piercing, see J.G. Baldwin, *Haggai, Zechariah, Malachi* (London: Tyndale Press 1972), pp. 190-94; in *b. Suk.* 52a Zech. 12.10, 12 is applied to Israel's mourning over the death of the Messiah ben Joseph. See A.Y. Collins, 'The "Son of Man" Tradition and the Book of Revelation', in J.H. Charlesworth (ed.), *The Messiah* (Minneapolis: Fortress Press, 1992), pp. 536-47, for further analysis of the wording of the Old Testament references to Daniel 7 and Zechariah 12, especially in comparison to variant Old Testament Greek versions, the Hebrew and parallels in the Gospels.

light of the above discussion about John's already-and-not-yet view of the combined Old Testament quotation.

(ii). *Revelation 1.12: The Seven Golden Lampstands.* John's use of the lampstand image and the picture of the 'seven stars' in Revelation 1 also fits into his trend of universalizing what the Old Testament restricted for the nation Israel. The first thing John sees is that of 'seven golden lampstands' (v. 12b), which has its general background in Exodus 25, 37, and Numbers 8, but the image is more specifically drawn from Zech. 4.2, 10, which is borne out by three observations: (1) the mention of 'seven spirits' in Rev. 1.4 (cf. Zech. 4.6); (2) the lampstand vision of v. 12b is interpreted in v. 20, which follows the same vision-interpretation pattern of Zech. 4.2, 10; and (3) clear allusion to Zech. 4.2, 10 is found in Rev. 4.5 and 5.6 in close association with allusions to Daniel.

The 'seven lampstands' represent the church (cf. 1.20). In Zech. 4.2-6 the lampstand with its seven lamps is a figurative synecdoche by which part of the temple furniture stands for the whole temple, which by extension also represents faithful Israel (cf. Zech. 4.6-9) who is required to live '"not by [earthly] might nor by power, but by My Spirit" says the Lord' (Zech. 4.6). Judaism also understood the lampstand of Zechariah to symbolize Israel, especially the righteous gathered from all generations at the end time.[134]

The lampstand in the Tabernacle and temple was in the presence of God, and the light which emanated from it apparently represented the presence of God (see Num. 8.1-4; in Exod. 25.30-31 the lampstand is mentioned directly after the 'bread of Presence'; likewise 40.4; 1 Kgs 7.48-49). Likewise, the lamps on the lampstand in Zech. 4.2-5 are interpreted in 4.6 as representing God's presence or Spirit, which was to empower Israel (as the lampstand) to finish re-building the temple, despite resistance (cf. Zech. 4.6-9). So new Israel, the church, is to draw its power from the Spirit, the divine presence, before God's throne in its drive to stand against the resistance of the world. This is highlighted by 1.4 and 4.5, where the seven lamps are identified as the

---

134. *R. Lev.* 30.2, *Num. R.* 13.8, *Cant. R.* 4.7 §1, *Pes. K., Piska* 27.2, *Pes. R. Piska* 7. 7 and *Piska* 8.4 interpret the lampstand of Zech. 4.2 to represent Israel; *Midr. Pss.* 16.12; *R. Lev.* 32.8, *R. Qoh.* 4.1§1, *Sifre Deut., Piska* 10, and *Pes. R., Piska* 51.4 compare the lampstand of Zech. 4.2-3 to Israelites from all epochs gathered at the end of time.

Spirit, as in Zechariah 4 (see Rev. 1.4). This emphatic notion of the lampstand connoting God's presence with the church is confirmed from 11.4, where the 'lampstands...stand before the Lord of the earth'.[135]

Consequently, the 'lampstand' (the church) is given power by 'the seven lamps' (see Rev. 4.5) on it, a power primarily to witness as a light uncompromisingly to the world so that the gates of hell (cf. 2.9-11, 13) would not prevail against the building of God's temple, the true Israel, which is identified with the heavenly temple. This reiterates the mission of true Israel as expressed by the use of Exod. 19.6 in Rev. 1.6. This also suggests that the end-time temple has been inaugurated in the church[136] (*Num. R.* 15.10 expresses the hope that when God restores the end-time temple, he will also restore the candlestick').

135. *Num. R.* (on Num. 8.2-3) affirms that the reward for Israel continually lighting the seven lamps on the lampstand would be that God would preserve their 'souls from all evil things' (15.4) and that their blessings would 'never be abolished' (15.6). It was in the light of these seven lamps that God's presence dwelt (15.9). *Targ. Jerusalem Lev.* 24.2-4 directly links the dwelling of God's glory in Israel to the continued burning of the seven lamps on the lampstand. The Qumran Teacher of Righteousness affirms that, despite his opponents, he 'will shine with a seven-fold light...for Thou *art* an everlasting light unto me and hast established my feet' (1QH 7.24-25). Likewise, the continued burning of the lamps (= the Spirit) on the seven lampstands (= churches) will mean that Christ's (= the divine Ancient of Days [v. 14]) presence will be continually with the churches and protecting them spiritually.

136. For the church as a temple identified with the heavenly temple see Beale, *Book of Revelations*, on Rev. 1.16. For the church as the new spiritual temple see further on 11.1-2 in Beale, *Book of Revelation*; likewise cf. 1 Cor. 3.16-17; 6:19; 2 Cor. 6.16; Eph. 2.21-22; 1 Pet. 2.5; Ignatius *Eph.* 9; Ignatius, *Eph.* 15. Already in Jn 2.19-22, and elsewhere in the Gospels, Christ has identified his resurrection body as the true temple, and this is developed in Rev. 21.22. The notion of saints composing a spiritual temple also has analogy in Judaism. The temple of Ezekiel's prophecy is spiritualized in Rev. 11.1-2 (which cannot be argued here) and in Judaism. Qumran declared the Jerusalem temple apostate. They believed themselves to represent the true, spiritual temple: cf. 1QS 5.5-6; 8.4-10; 9.3-6; 11.7ff.; CD 3.19-4.6; 4Q Flor. 1.2-9 (so B. Gärtner, *The Temple and the Community in Qumran and the New Testament* [SNTSMS, 1; Cambridge: Cambridge University Press, 1965], pp. 16-44, 45-53). The presence of God in the Qumran temple would insure the invincibility of it against the deceptive designs of Belial (4Q Flor. 1.7-9; CD 3.19; Gärtner, *Temple*, pp. 34-35). This spiritual invincibility is seen as a fulfillment of the prophecy of the temple in Ezek. 44 (cf. CD 3.19-4.6; cf. 4Q Flor. 1.15-17)! Metaphors of measurement are even used to express the inviolable

Rev. 11.1-13 confirms that the lampstands represent the church as the true temple and the totality of the people of God witnessing between the period of Christ's resurrection and His final coming. *Targ. Jon. Zech.* 4.7 foresees that the successful building of the temple in the midst of the world's opposition will be achieved ultimately by 'the Anointed One' who 'shall rule over all kingdoms'. In the light of Rev. 1.5-6, Christ's death and resurrection have laid the foundation for the new temple, which He will build through the Spirit (the lamps on the lampstand).[137] Zech. 6.12-13 calls a messianic-like figure 'Branch', and repeats twice that 'He will build the temple...and rule...[and] be a priest on His throne' (the Targum substitutes 'Anointed' for 'Branch'). Likewise, *Targ. Isa.* 53.5 affirms that the Servant 'will build the sanctuary'.

The shift from one lampstand in Zechariah to seven in Revelation stresses not only that this letter is intended for the church universal of the escalated end times, but also the idea that true Israel is no longer limited to a nation but encompasses all peoples.[138]

Like the seven lampstands, the number of 'seven *stars*' may also have arisen in part from the 'seven *lamps*' of Zechariah 4.[139] In later

security of this temple (cf. 'cord of righteousness' and 'plumbline of truth' in IQH 11.26; cf. 11.19-27; cf. McKelvey, *New Temple*, p. 52).

Also, to engage continually in the study of the Law was equivalent to building the temple prophesied in Ezek. 40–47 (*Lev. R.* 7.3). Repentance could be 'accounted unto a person as if he had...built the Temple and the altar and offered thereon sacrifices' (*Lev. R.* 7.2).

137. *Midr. Tanḥ. Gen., Parasha* 6, *Toledoth* §20 and Qumran also saw in Zech. 4.1-14 a messianic prophecy (cf. 1QS 9.10-11 and A. Dupont-Sommer, *The Essene Writings from Qumran* [trans. G. Vermes; Oxford: Basil Blackwell, 1961] p. 317); in development of Zech. 4.9, *Gen. R.* 17 says the Messiah would be descended from Zerubbabel and would rebuild the temple; *ARN* 30b identifies one of the figures of Zech. 4.14 as the Messiah.

138. The escalation of lampstands already had a precedent in Solomon's temple which had ten lampstands (1 Kgs 7.49) in comparison to the Tabernacle's one.

139. In this regard, it may not be too speculative to view the number of 'seven *stars*' as having arisen in part from the 'seven *lamps*' of Zechariah 4 in light of the fact that the two symbols have been directly related in Rev. 1.20 (λαμπρότης ['brightness'] of Dan. 12.3 [Theodotion] and λαμπάδιον ['candlestick'] of Zech. 4.2-3 may have served as further attracting factors, in addition to the 'stone' associations between Zechariah 4 and the Daniel 'son of man' [the latter of which is a parallel figure to the 'stone' of Daniel 2]). Perhaps, since the one lampstand from Zechariah 4 was increased to seven in order to indicate universality, the stars of

Judaism the Zech. 4.2 lampstand is said to symbolize the righteous in Israel and is equated with the wise who will shine like the stars in Dan. 12.3: compare *Lev. R.* 30.2; *Sifre Deut., Piska* 10; *Pes.K., Piska* 27.2; *Pes.R., Piska* 51.4. McNamara sees the Palestinian Targum to Exod. 40.4 as the background for 1.20a, where the 'seven lamps' of the tabernacle are viewed as 'corresponding to the seven stars which resemble the just that shine unto eternity in their righteousness', the latter phrase being a clear allusion to Dan. 12.3![140] These references show that the Zechariah lampstand and stars of Dan. 12.3 were equated in Judaism, so that their combination in 1.20 is natural and may suggest that the 'stars', even if angelic, represent the church's heavenly existence and the 'lampstands' its earthly existence.[141]

Therefore, it is unnecessary to view the 'stars' as simply imbibed from a mythological-astrological background. Nevertheless, the picture could be a polemic against the imperial myth of an emperor's son who dies and becomes a divine ruler over the stars of heaven,[142] since it is likely that the title 'ruler of the kings of the earth' in 1.5 also has such a polemical connotation.[143] If so, Christ's universal sovereignty would also be accented.

Daniel 12 may have undergone the same hermeneutical development. A similar phenomenon appears discernible in *1 En.* 90.20-25, where 'seven white ones' (= angels) and seventy 'stars' (= angels) are based on the context of Daniel (Dan. 7.10; 9.2, 24; 12.1-3; see Beale, *Use of Daniel*, pp. 67-88; cf. also *1 En.* 21.3 where seven stars are equivalent to seven angels). This evidence suggests that these stars are heavenly angelic beings (see *1 En.* 86.1-3 and 88.1, where stars also symbolize angels).

140. M. McNamara, *The New Testament and the Palestinian Targum to the Pentateuch* (AnBib, 27; Rome: Pontifical Biblical Institute, 1966), pp. 197-99.

141. Contrast McNamara, *New Testament and the Palestinian Targum*, pp. 197-99, who sees that the Targum reference suggests that the stars and the angels of Rev. 1.20 should be identified as righteous human representatives of the church communities.

142. Caird, *Revelaton*, p. 15; E. Lohmeyer, *Die Offenbarung des Johannes* (HNT, 16; Tübingen: J.C.B. Mohr [Paul Siebeck], 1970), p. 18.

143. So R. Shütz, *Die Offenbarung des Johannes und Kaiser Domitian* (FRLANT, 32; Göttingen: Vandenhoeck & Ruprecht, 1933), pp. 35-36; Brütsch, *Clarte de l'Apocalypse*, p. 28; J. Roloff, *Revelation* (Minneapolis: Fortress Press, 1993), p. 36, cites a Mithras liturgy in which the god Mithras was depicted as holding the seven stars of the 'bear' constellation in his hand.

Early Judaism's symbolic identification of the seven lamps in the temple with the seven planets probably does not allude to pagan mythological ideas but to the Old Testament–Jewish belief that Israel's earthly temple and its furniture were the microcosmic copy of the archetypical heavenly temple-house of God.[144] If this background is in mind, then the imagery of the seven lampstands adjacent to Christ and the seven stars evokes the idea that, in contrast to Israel's temple and lampstand which was geographically limited, the churches have a position in the cosmic, heavenly or spiritual temple, in the midst of which Christ is ruling and present.

The stars symbolize angelic beings who are corporate representatives in heaven of the churches on earth, which is the most probable way of understanding the reference to 'angels' in Rev. 1.20:[145] 'The mystery of the seven stars which you saw in my right hand and the seven golden lampstands is: the seven stars are angels of the seven churches, and the seven lampstands are the seven churches.'

b. *A Brief Survey of Other Examples of Universalizing the Old Testament.* Another classic example of this tendency is the extension of the Exodus plague imagery from the land of Egypt to the whole 'earth' in Rev. 8.6-12 and 16.1-14: for example, in 8.9 a third of the sea, including fish and ships, is affected instead of merely a river and fish; in 16.10 rather than the sun being darkened, it is the kingdom of the satanic beast which becomes darkened. The 'ten days of tribulation' experienced by Daniel and his friends (Dan. 1.12, 14) and the three-and-a-half years of Israel's tribulation (Dan. 7.25; 12.7) are both extended to an entire church (and likely the Church at large)—the

144. For early Judaism's symbolic identification of the seven lamps in the temple with the seven planets see Josephus, *Ant.* 3.145; *War* 5.217; Philo, *Rer. Div. Her.* 45. 221-25; *Vit. Mos.* 2.102-105; Philo, *Quaest. in Exod.* 2.73-81; *Targ. Pal. Exod.* 4.4; *Num. R.* 12.13 equates the seven lamps with the 'lights of the firmament of the heaven'; cf. M. Eliade, *The Myth of the Eternal Return* (London: Routledge & Kegan Paul, 1955), pp. 6-17; O. Keel, *The Symbolism of the Biblical World* (New York: Crossroad, 1985), pp. 171-76; L. Goppelt, 'τύπος', *TDNT*, VIII, pp. 256-57).

145. See Beale, *Book of Revelation* (on Rev. 1.20) for substantiation of this identification of the 'stars', especially with respect to: (1) the use of ἄγγελος elsewhere in Revelation; (2) stars as metaphorical for both saints and angels in the Old Testament and Judaism; and (3) angels as corporate representatives of saints in the Old Testament, New Testament and Judaism.

eschatological, true Israel—throughout the world. And part of this tribulation is instigated by the latter-day 'Babylon the Great' (Dan. 4.30) who persecutes not merely ethnic Israelite believers, but also saints throughout the earth (Rev. 17.5-8; 18.24), and harmfully affects 'nations', 'kings of the earth' and the world's economy (18.1-23). Therefore, when 'Babylon the Great' falls, rather than the effect being provincial, 'the cities of the nations' also fall (16.19). Likewise, the former persecutors of God's people in the Old Testament (Sodom, Egypt and Jerusalem) are now defined as 'peoples and tribes and tongues and nations' (Rev. 11.8-10).

The Apocalypse concludes with references from the predicted end-time temple reserved for Israel, although now its cultic benefits are extended to the Gentiles: compare Ezek. 37.27, 44.9 and 48.35 in Rev. 21.3; compare Rev. 22.2 where the 'leaves of healing' foretold in Ezek. 47.12 to be an aid to the Israelites are transformed into 'leaves...for the healing of the *nations*'.

Sometimes the rationale for universalism is found already in the Old Testament contexts from which the allusions are drawn (cf. Ezek. 14.12-21 in Rev. 6.8), although the inspiration can also arise from combining a narrowly designed Old Testament Israelite reference with another very similar Old Testament text which, however, is universal. For example, the Israelite-orientated book of judgment from Ezek. 2.9-10 is given cosmic dimensions in Rev. 5.1 and 10.8-11 because it has been attracted to other Old Testament judgment-book allusions which have a wider cosmic application (compare Dan. 7.10, 12.4, 9 in Rev. 5.1-5 and Dan. 12.4-9 in Rev. 10.1-6). Nevertheless, the primary reason for the extended applications is the New Testament's and John's presupposition concerning the cosmic dimensions of Christ's lordship and death: cf. Rev. 1.5; 5.9-10; for other examples of universalization see 1.12-13, 20 (lampstands), 2.17 (manna), 7.9, 15 (Ezek. 37.26), 17.1ff. (harlot), 18.9 (Ezek. 26.16ff.; 27.29-35), 19.7 (bride), 3.12 and 21.2 (Jerusalem).

It is tempting to conclude that John does not handle the Old Testament according to its original contextual meaning when he universalizes. Vanhoye's evaluation, however, is plausible. He says that while the universalization is motivated by the Christian spirit to explain redemptive fulfillment, it is not contrary to the Old Testament sense. Although the author certainly makes different applications and executes developments beyond those of his Old Testament predecessors, he stays within the same interpretative framework and is conscious of being profoundly faithful to the overall parameters of their message).[146] This is a viable analysis since all of these universalizations can be considered sub-categories of the above-discussed analogical use of the Old Testament, where it was proposed that, although John creatively reworks the Old Testament and changes the application of it, his pictures retain significant points of correspondence with the Old Testament context and express salvation-historical principles of continuity. All of the cited examples of universalization appear to be harmonious developments of these principles. This is the case, for example, with the Old Testament texts pertaining to ethnic Israel's redemption and applied in Revelation to the world's redemption, on the basis of defining the true people of God according to their faith in Christ and according to their corporate representation by Christ, the one who sums up true Israel in himself. This is why the church comes to be viewed as the true Israel.

5. *Informal, Direct Prophetic Fulfillment Uses of the Old Testament*
Although there are no formal Old Testament quotations (i.e., with introductory formulae) used as prooftexts to indicate direct prophetic fulfillment, it is still probable that some Old Testament texts were *informally* referred to in order to designate present or future fulfillment of Old Testament verbal prophecy. The determination of whether a text refers to future or present fulfillment often depends on one's overall view of the book (e.g. preterist, historicist, idealist, futurist).

a. *Illustration of a Typical Direct Prophetic Use of the Old Testament.* The concluding mention in Rev. 2.17 of the 'new name having been written' on a stone is an example of a brief allusion conveying substantial prophetic overtones from the Old Testament. Rev. 3.12 reveals that the name in 2.17 is a pregnant reference to 'the name of My God, and the name of the city of My God, the new Jerusalem, which comes down out of heaven from My God, and My [Christ's] new name', which is written on the believer.[147] Separate meanings are not to be assigned to each of these names but they all refer to the intimate, eschatological presence of God and Christ with his people, as expressed most clearly by 22.3-4: 'the throne of God and of the Lamb shall be in it, and His bondservants shall serve Him; and *they shall see His face, and His name*

---

146. Vanhoye, 'L'utilisation du livre d'Ezéchiel dans l'Apocalypse', p. 467.
147. E.g. Lohmeyer, *Offenbarung des Johannes*, p. 27.

shall be on their foreheads' (so cf. likewise the significance of 14.1-4). The Pseudo-Titus Epistle[148] paraphrases Rev. 2:17 accordingly: 'They will receive the white stone... upon which is written the ineffable name of God, which no man knows save he who has received it.'

The 'new name' is a mark of genuine membership in the community of the redeemed without which entry into the eternal 'city of God' is possible. It stands in contrast to the satanic 'name' which unbelievers receive, which identifies them with the character of the devil and with the ungodly 'city of man': compare ὄνομα καινὸν γεγραμμένον...ὁ λαμβάνων ('a new name having been written...the one receiving') in 2.17 and λαμβάνει τὸ χάραγμα τοῦ ὀνόματος αὐτοῦ ('he receives the mark of his name') in 14.11; compare 13.16-18.

This conclusion is also pointed to by observing that the 'new name' of 2.17 is an allusion to the prophecy of Isa. 62.2 and 65.15 about Israel's new standing in the future.[149] The saints of Israel are referred to figuratively (by metonymy) as Jerusalem which 'will be called by a new name' (not different, personal new names!). There, the 'new name' designates Israel's future kingly status (62.3), restoration to Yahweh's covenantal presence (62.4a; cf. the same significance for 'name' in 56.4-8; 65.15-19) and especially emphasizes its new 'married' relationship with the Lord (cf. 62.4b-5, which also refers to Israel as a 'bride' and God as the 'bridegroom'). The promised blessings of this prophecy will be fulfilled among those in the church, the latter-day Israel, who do not compromise. Isaiah's prophecy of Israel's restoration to God's latter-day presence lies as the substratum also for all the other references in the book to the believers' 'name' (3.12; 14.1; 22.4) and God's or Christ's 'name' (3.12 and 22.4, as well as 19.12-13, 16).

Therefore, καινός ('new') in this context predominately carries the nuance of newness of prophetic fulfillment. This usage is found in other New Testament contexts describing end-time or redemptive-historical transitions, where prophetic fulfillment is indicated as essential to or inextricably linked with new covenantal realities in contrast to the old covenantal era of unrealized prophecy (e.g. cf. 2 Cor. 3.6; Heb. 8.8, 13; 9.15; Rev. 21.1).

---

148. E. Hennecke, *New Testament Apocrypha* (2 vols.; ed. and revised W. Schneemelcher; trans. R.McL. Wilson; Philadelphia: Westminster Press, 1963), II, p. 166.

149. Cf. καλέω ('to call') + ὄνομα καινόν ('new name') in both texts; cf. perhaps 56.5; see also E.W. Hengstenberg, *The Revelation of St. John* (2 vols.; New York: R. Carter and Brothers, 1853), I, p. 190.

Jesus is the first one to fulfill the 'new name' prophecy of Isaiah. This must mean that he represents latter-day Israel. Rev. 3.12 makes this most explicit, where, also in allusion to the same Isaiah prophecy, Christ says that believers will have written upon them 'the name of the city of my God, the new Jerusalem... and *my new name*' (likewise 14.1; 22.4). Here 'new Jerusalem' and 'my new name' are likely in synonymous parallelism. Among all the passages in the New Testament, this one comes closest to equating Christ with true Jerusalem or Israel. Jesus' followers come to be identified with his new name when they believe, as apparent from their identification with Christ's name in the present (see 'My name' in 2.13 and 3.8, which anticipates the new name prophecy at the end of each of the respective letters). Identification with fulfillment of the Isaiah prophecy escalates at one's death and at Christ's final coming (in this respect, see 3.12 and 19.12-16). The identification of Christ with the Isaianic new name in 2.17 is also suggested by 19.12, where the same epistemological language about the name is used: Christ has a 'name written upon Himself *which no one knows except* Himself', yet is immediately revealed to be 'the word of God' and 'Lord of Lords and King of Kings'. It cannot be accidental that in 19.12-15 Christ is portrayed at the end of time as fulfilling prophecies from Isaiah 11, 49 and 63.

Such a multi-perspectival fulfillment view of the Isaiah prophecy is reflected by *b. B.Bat.* 75b, which affirms partly on the basis of a parallel 'name' prophecy in Isa. 43.7 that 'three are named after the name of God, and these are the righteous, and the Messiah, and Jerusalem'. *T.d.Eliyy.*, p. 121 understands that God's 'servants' (of Isa. 65.15) who will receive a 'name' will also be 'worthy—Jew and heathen alike—in the days of the Messiah'. *Pes.K.*, *Piska* 22[5a] says that God 'will renew in the time-to-come... the name of the Messiah, and the name of Jerusalem', and offers Isa. 62.2 as a prooftext for the latter.

This part of Isaiah's prophecy may have come to mind because of the earlier references to the 'sword' of Isa. 49.2 (cf. 11.4) in Rev. 2.12, 16, which are also from contexts concerning Israel's future restoration, and together they serve to emphasize the thought that this church is to behave faithfully in order to inherit the restoration promises and to avoid judgment.

The prophetic segment of Isaiah 62 and 65 was also chosen because of its suitability to the problem at Pergamum, especially with respect to compromising participation at idolatrous feasts. The context of Isa.

65.15 primarily contrasts God's faithful servants in Israel with Israelites who compromise by dedicating meals and cup offerings to idols and false gods.[150] In the eschaton the faithful will be comforted from their former troubles (vv. 16-19) by 'eating' and 'drinking' whereas the compromisers will be punished by being 'hungry' and 'thirsty' (v. 13) and slain by the 'sword' (v. 12), which is equated with the 'second death' by *Targ. Isa.* 65.6, 15! That the same dual idea rounds off the two concluding verses of the letter to Pergamum shows an awareness that Old Testament prophecy is going to be fulfilled in this community and lays before the readers a prophetic warning of judgment for disobedience and of blessing for faithfulness.[151]

There may also be a priestly connotation attached to the 'new name', especially when looked at from the Old Testament background. First, the 'new name' in Isaiah was associated with Gentiles who would not only be related to God covenantally, but would perform priest-like tasks apparently together with redeemed Israelites, who are to be called 'priests of the Lord' (cf. Isa. 56.5-7 with 61.6 and 66.18-21; *T. d. Eliyy.*, p. 121 on Isa. 65.15). A priestly association would be consistent with the reference elsewhere in the book to Christians as priests of the new covenant (see Rev. 1.6; 5.10; 20.6). That being 'granted a new name' has a priestly association is apparent from *T. Levi* 8.12-14, where it is promised that the posterity of Levi would 'be *granted a new name*, because from Judah a king will arise and shall found a new priesthood in accord with the gentile model and for all nations'.[152] Perhaps a priestly association also helps explain the hidden aspect of the manna, since manna was put in the ark, where no one could see it except the high-priest who entered once a year into the holy of holies.[153]

150. So Isa. 65.3-4, 7, 11; *Targ. Isa.* 65.4 is applied to those who pay homage to a memorial erected in honor of the emperor Tiberias (so B.D. Chilton, *The Isaiah Targum* [The Aramaic Bible, II; Wilmington, DE: Michael Glazier, 1987]), p. 123.

151. Cf. W. Hendriksen, *More than Conquerors: An Interpretation of the Book of Revelation* (Grand Rapids: Baker Book House, 1962), pp. 84-87, 265, for supplemental discussion of the 'new name'.

152. *OTP*, I, p. 791.

153. J. Gill, *An Exposition of the New Testament*. III. *The Revelation of St. John the Divine* (Philadelphia: William W. Woodward, 1811), pp. 691-886, 711. See Beale, *Book of Revelation* (at Rev. 2.17), for further discussion of the priestly as well as the magical background.

b. *A Brief Survey of Other Examples of Direct Prophetic Uses of the Old Testament.* Of special note is the introduction to the book, where allusion is made to Dan. 2.28-29, 45: compare Rev. 1.1, δεῖξαι...ἃ δεῖ γενέσθαι ('to show...what must take place'), followed directly by ἐν τάχει ('quickly'), with Dan. 2.28 [LXX], ἐδήλωσε...ἃ δεῖ γενέσθαι ἐπ' ἐσχάτων τῶν ἡμερῶν ('he showed...what must take place in the latter days'). John's 'quickly' has been substituted for Daniel's 'in the latter days', so that what Daniel expected to occur in the distant future, the defeat of cosmic evil and ushering in of the kingdom, John expects to begin in his own generation, and perhaps has already been inaugurated. Such imminence and even *incipient inauguration*, is corroborated by the phrase ὁ γὰρ καιρὸς ἐγγύς ('for the time is near') in 1.3, which elsewhere includes *both* the 'already' and 'not-yet' element (so Mk 1.15; Mt. 26.45; Lam. 4.18; cf. Mt. 3.2 with 4.17.[154]

Dan. 12.4, 9 is used likewise in 22.10: whereas Daniel is commanded to 'conceal these words and seal up the book until the end of time' (12.4), John is given the consummatory command to 'not seal up the words of the prophecy of this book, for the time is near'. This use in 22.10 intensifies that of 1.1-3 since it is directly linked to a verbatim repetition of 1.1 in 22.6.

The reference to the Son of Man (1.13-14) probably indicates John's belief that Jesus had begun to fulfill the Dan. 7.13 prophecy of the son of man's exaltation, although the similar reference in 1.7 may include reference to a further phase of the same prophecy which still awaits realization. The same kind of 'already and not yet' idea is found in 2.26-27 where Jesus says he has started to fulfill the Ps. 2.7 prediction but that his followers will also take part in the fulfillment at a future time (probably at death). The use of Dan. 7.13 and Zech. 12.10 also fits into this category (on which see discussion above at sect. D. 4a).

If the argument that Revelation 1 and 4–5 are each modeled on Daniel 7 can be sustained,[155] then John's intention may be to indicate that Jesus' death, resurrection and gathered church is the inaugurated fulfillment of Daniel.

There is also evidence of expectations of exclusive future fulfillment, of which only the clearest examples are listed here: Ps. 2.1/Rev. 11.18;

---

154. Cf. Beale, 'Influence of Daniel upon the Structure and Theology of John's Apocalypse', pp. 415-20, and see below the analysis of Rev. 1.19 (Chapter 3, sect. B).

155. Beale, *Use of Daniel*, pp. 154-228.

Ps. 2.9/Rev. 12.5 and 19.15; Isa. 11.4 and 49.2/Rev. 19.15; Isa. 25.8/ Rev. 21.4; Isa. 63.2-6/Rev. 19.15; Isa. 65.17 and 66.22/Rev. 21.1; Ezek. 47.1, 12/Rev. 22.1-2.

6. *Informal, Indirectly Prophetic (Typological) Fulfillment Uses of the Old Testament*
All of the illustrations so far have concerned fulfillments of Old Testament texts which are clearly direct verbal prophecies in their Old Testament context. It is also viable to consider that there are texts which John understands as prophetic but which do not appear as such in the Old Testament. These uses also are not part of formal Old Testament quotations (with introductory formulae), but are in the form of allusions. It is worth considering whether parts of certain Old Testament historical narratives are viewed as *indirect typological prophecies*. Many of the Old Testament passages listed in our above discussion of analogical uses are potential candidates in this category. That is, are all of these texts merely analogies? We have already found that the essence of the analogies has to do with a basic *correspondence* of meaning between Old Testament prophecy or *historical* narrative and something in the New Testament. Some of these Old Testament historical elements have also undergone an escalation, even a universalization, under John's hand. Perhaps there was a prophetic rationale in escalating these historical texts. At any rate, such uses are worth further inquiry in this regard, especially against the background of John's and the New Testament's awareness that the 'latter days' had been inaugurated, that the church was the latter-day Israel and that the whole Old Testament pointed toward this climax of salvation history.[156] The precedent of overt typological-prophetic uses in Matthew, Hebrews and elsewhere in the New Testament should leave open the same possibility in Revelation.

a. *A Representative Illustration of an Indirect Prophetic (Typological) Fulfillment Use of the Old Testament*. Though discussed briefly earlier, Isa. 22.22 is an Old Testament reference which deserves serious consideration as a typological use in Rev. 3.7b, and serves as an example of how other similar Old Testament passages in Revelation could be

---

156. For inaugurated eschatological language cf. Mk 1.15; Acts 2.17; 1 Cor. 10.11; 2 Cor. 6.2; Gal. 4.4; 1 Tim. 4.1; 2 Tim. 3.1; Heb. 1.2; 9.26; Jas 5.3; 1 Pet. 1.20; 1 Jn 2.18; Jude 18; Rev. 1.1; 1.19; 4.1; 22.6, 10; cf. Beale, 'Influence of Daniel Upon the Structure and Theology of John's Apocalypse', pp. 415-20.

treated: 'the one having the key of David, the one who opens and no one will shut, and who shuts and no one opens'.

This second part of Christ's self-description of v. 7 is not identical to any phrases from ch. 1 but is based on 1.18b, where Jesus claims to 'have the keys'.[157] That this imagery is based on 1.18b is apparent from two observations. First, virtually the exact expressions occur in both texts: ὁ ἔχων τὴν κλεῖν ('the one having the key') and 'I have the keys' (ἔχω τὰς κλεῖς) in 1.18b. Second, all Christ's other introductory self-descriptions develop phrases from ch. 1; even the immediately preceding ὁ ἀληθινός ('the true') in 3.7b develops ὁ πιστός ('the faithful'), in 1.5, as apparent from 3.14 (on which see sect. E of ch. 3).

Whereas these keys are called the 'keys of death and of Hades' in 1.18b, in 3.7b a quotation from Isa. 22.22 is substituted for 'of death and of Hades':[158] 'the one having the key *of David, who opens and no one shuts, and who shuts and no one opens*' (the difference in singular 'key' and plural 'keys' is probably not significant). The substitution is meant to amplify the idea of the original phrase in 1.18b by underscoring the sovereignty which Christ holds over the sphere 'of death and Hades'.

The point of the quotation is that Jesus holds the power over salvation and judgment. In 1.18 the stress is on his sovereignty over death and judgment, while in 3.7b the emphasis is on his authority over those entering the kingdom. John compares the historical situation of Eliakim in relation to Israel with that of Christ in relation to the church in order to help the readers better understand the position which Christ now holds as head of the true Israel and how this affects them. The quotation could be a polemic against the local synagogue which claimed that only those worshipping within their doors could be considered God's true people, and which even may have excommunicated Christian Jews.[159] In this respect, the Targumic paraphrase of Isa. 22.22 rendered the

---

157. Against F. Hahn, *The Titles of Jesus in Christology* (London: Lutterworth, 1969), p. 245, who does not see a development of 1.18.

158. Part of the textual tradition of 3.7 testifies to a clear link between this verse and 1.18, since some MSS replace Δαυίδ ('David') with ᾅδου ('Hades'; e.g. 104*, 218, 336, 459, 620, 2050, 2067*) or with τοῦ θανάτου καὶ τοῦ ᾅδου ('death and Hades'; e.g. 111, 1893). *Odes* 17.9-13 and 42.11-20 understand the 'open door' image of Rev. 3.7 as Christ's liberation of souls from the region of the dead.

159. Cf. Mounce, *Revelation*, p. 116. Interestingly, *Sifre Deut.*, Piska 321 applies the 'opening and shutting' of Isa. 22.22 to the teaching authority of Jewish scholars or scribes: cf. Mt. 23.13; cf. Str-B, I, 741, note c.

quotation even more appropriate to the situation of the church: 'I will place the key of the *sanctuary* and the authority of the house of David in his hand'. Ethnic Israel, which claims to be the divine agent wielding the power of salvation and judgment, no longer maintains this position, although it claims to. Christ's followers can be assured that the doors to the true synagogue are open to them, whereas the doors remain closed to those who reject him. Because Christ has become the ruler over Satan's realm of 'death and Hades', he has power over those still in Satan's realm, such as the unbelieving Jews whom Jesus calls 'the synagogue of Satan'. Christ will express this power by strengthening the witness of the Philadelphian church so that the unbelieving Jews will be released from Satan's sway, and recognise God's true work in Christ (cf. 3.7-9).[160]

The Isa. 22.22 quotation is not merely analogically applied but is likely better understood as an indirect typological prophecy; John apparently understands Isa. 22.22, not originally as a verbal prophecy, but retrospectively as a historical narration about Eliakim which contained a pattern foreshadowing what the Messiah would do on a grander scale. Such a conclusion is pointed to by six observations.

First, the reference to Eliakim as 'My servant' in Isa. 22.20 would have been easily associated with Isaiah's servant prophecies of chs. 40–53, since the phrase occurs there 13 times (the same phrase occurs only twice elsewhere, in Isaiah in reference to the prophet himself [20.3] and to David [37.35]).

Second, the description of placing 'the key of the house of David [= administrative responsibility for the kingdom of Judah] on his [Eliakim's] shoulder', the allusion to him as a 'father' to those in 'Jerusalem and to the house of Judah', and the reference to him as 'becoming a throne of glory' would all have subtly facilitated a prophetic understanding of Isa. 22.22, since this language is so strikingly parallel to that of the prophecy of the future Israelite ruler of Isa. 9.6-7: 'the government will be on *his shoulders*...and his name will be called... Eternal *father*', who sits 'on the *throne of David*'.

Third, that Isa. 22.22 is viewed in an indirectly prophetic, typological manner is further evident by observing the intentional allusions to

---

160. There is not space to argue that actual 'conversion' of the Jews is in mind, which is debated; for further discussion in this respect, see Beale, *Book of Revelation, in loc.*

prophetic 'servant' passages (Isa. 43.4; 45.14; 49.23) in the immediately following context of Rev. 3.9. This time, however, these allusions are applied to the church, although the rationale for the application lies in an understanding of the church's corporate identification with Jesus as God's servant and true Israel, that is, 'the holy one, the true one', according to 3.7.[161]

Fourth, the main typological correspondence between Eliakim and Christ is that Christ, like Eliakim, was to have absolute power over the Davidic throne as king. Whereas Eliakim's rule was primarily political, Christ's was to be primarily spiritual, as well as ultimately universal in all aspects; whereas Eliakim was to rule over Jerusalem, Judah and the house of David, Christ's sovereignty was to extend over all peoples. The context of Isa. 22.22 reveals other correspondences between Eliakim and Christ; although it is difficult to know whether or not all of these were consciously in mind, together the parallels show why this Old Testament passage would have been so attractive to apply to Christ. (1) As Eliakim was specially appointed to his royal office by Yahweh, so Christ was appointed to a greater royal office by God. (2) As Eliakim's power was equal to the king's, so would Christ's be to that of God's. (3) As Eliakim's office may have included some sort of priestly connotations (cf. the associations of Eliakim's 'tunic' and 'sash'), such connotations are also discernible with Christ's royal office in Revelation (note, e.g., the probable priestly description of Christ's attire in Rev. 1.13 and his priestly activity of offering sacrifice for the people in Rev. 1.5b).

An early Jewish understanding of the priestly nature of Eliakim's office is testified to by the Targumic paraphrase of Isa. 22.22, 'I will place the key of the *sanctuary* and the authority of the house of David in his hand'. *Exod. R.* 37.1 understands Eliakim in Isa. 22.23 as a 'high priest'. And it is likely not coincidence that in Rev. 3.12 Christ also is seen as having power over who enters God's temple, thus pointing further to priestly associations: 'He who overcomes, I will make him a

---

161. E.g. Isa. 49.3-6 and the use of 49.6 in Lk. 2.32, Acts 13.47 and 26.23; Christ and the church often fulfill what is prophesied of Israel in the Old Testament. Cf. France, *Jesus and the Old Testament*, pp. 50-60, 75; H.K. LaRondelle, *The Israel of God in Prophecy* (Berrien Springs, MI: Andrews University Press, 1983); G.K. Beale, 'The Old Testament Background of Reconciliation in 2 Corinthians 5–7 and its Bearing on the Literary Problem of 2 Corinthians 6:14-18', *NTS* 35 (1989), pp. 550-81.

pillar in the temple of My God'.[162] The permanent establishment of the overcomer as a pillar in the temple in Rev. 3.12 may also continue the imagery of Isa. 22.22-25, where Eliakim's relatives achieve glory by 'hanging on him as a *peg* firmly attached to a wall'.[163] In contrast to Eliakim's dependents who eventually lost their glory and position in the palace when he was finally removed (cf. Isa. 22.23-25), the followers of Jesus will never be removed from their position in the temple-palace because Jesus, the 'true' messiah, will never lose his regal position in the presence of his Father (hence 'pillar' is metaphorical for permanence).

Fifth, whenever David is mentioned in connection with Christ in the New Testament there are usually discernible prophetic, messianic overtones with it: cf. Mt. 1.1; 22.42-45; Mk 11.10; 12.35-37; Lk. 1.32; 20.41-44; Jn 7.42; Acts 2.30-36; 13.34; 15.16; Rom. 1.1-4; 2 Tim. 2.8. The only other occurrences of 'house of David' in the New Testament have the same prophetic nuance (Lk. 1.27, 69; so also 'tabernacle of David' in Acts 15.16), as do the only remaining references to David in Revelation, both of which are allusions to Isaianic messianic prophecies (Rev. 5.5; 22.16 [cf. Isa. 11.1, 10]).

Sixth, the first part of Christ's self-description in this verse also points to a typological use of Isa. 22.22: 'These things says the holy one, the true one'. This, like the second part of the verse, is not as much of a verbatim development of ch. 1 as the previous self-descriptions have been. Further analysis, however, shows that the verse does have a link with ch. 1. If ὁ ἅγιος, ὁ ἀληθινός ('the holy, the true') is original (so C 𝔐 latt sy co Epiph), then it probably is a paraphrastic development of 'faithful witness' in 1.5a, especially since ἀληθινός in the self-description of 3.14 clearly develops the same clause from 1.5a. In 1.5a Jesus is seen as a fulfillment of the 'faithful witness' and 'first-born' who was prophesied in Ps. 88 (89, MT) 28, 38 to come as the seed of

---

162. The Targum even refers to Eliakim twice as 'a *faithful* officer *ministering* in an enduring place' (following Chilton, *Isaiah Targum*, p. 44).

163. Some Greek Old Testament witnesses even refer to Eliakim as being set up as a 'pillar' in Isa. 22.23 (Vaticanus, Origen and Q read στηλῶ, 'I will set up as a pillar' or 'I will inscribe on a pillar'; following H. Kraft, *Die Offenbarung des Johannes* (HNT, 16a; Tübingen: J.C.B. Mohr [Paul Siebeck], 1974), p. 82; cf. Fekkes, *Isaiah and Prophetic Traditions*, pp. 130-33, though skeptical about LXX influence).

David to reign on his throne forever.[164] That thought of fulfillment is picked up again here. Jesus as the holy and true witness will empower those faithful to him to be a similar witness. The word ἀληθινός can have the sense both of *genuine* (from a Greek perspective) and *trustworthy* (according to the Hebrew conception), so that the idea of a *true* and *faithful* witness may be included in it.[165] In addition, he together with his people stand as the 'true Jewish witnesses' in contrast to those 'who say that they are Jews, and are not, but lie' (3.9) by saying that Jesus is a false messiah and his followers pseudo-Israelites.

The phrase 'the holy, the true' is a divine attribute elsewhere in Revelation (so 6.10), so that the use of it here suggests Jesus' deity. In fact, ἅγιος ('holy') is used of Yahweh almost exclusively in Isaiah as part of the title 'the Holy One of Israel' (approx. 20 times). This background is probably present here in anticipation of the Isa. 22.22 quotation and of the Isaiah allusions in 3.9,[166] where Jesus assumes the role of Yahweh and his followers represent the true Israel (see on 3.9; ὁ ἅγιος τοῦ θεοῦ ['the holy one of God'] is also a messianic title in contexts of fulfillment: Mk 1.24; Lk. 4.34; Jn 6.69). The idea of 'true' carries connotations of Jesus being the true Messiah, who has begun to fulfill messianic prophecy (see further on 3.14 at Chapter 3, sect. E), though he is rejected by the Jews as a false messianic pretender.

164. See Chapter 3, sect. E for further analysis of the use of Ps. 89 in Rev. 1.5, and the link of 1.5 to 3.7 and 3.14.

165. The Septuagint sometimes translates forms of the root אמן ('to be faithful') by ἀληθινός; see further discussion of 3.14, see Chapter 3, sect. E below.

166. In view of the heavy influence of Isaiah 40–60 in Rev. 3.7-9, allusion to Isa. 45.1 may also be discerned in 3.8: cf. ἀνοίξω ἔμπροσθεν αὐτοῦ θύρας καὶ πόλεις οὐ συγκλεισθήσονται ('I shall open to him doors and cities shall not be closed') with δέδωκα ἐνώπιόν σου θύραν ἠνεῳγμένην, ἣν οὐδεὶς δύναται κλεῖσαι ('I have given before you an opened door, which no one is able to shut') in 3.8. Just as Israel was weak in comparison to its opponents but would be made strong by God's restoring work through Cyrus, so would God make the witness of the small church in Philadelphia effective among its opponents (so E. Lövestamm, 'Apokalypsen 3:8b', *SEÅ* 30 (1965), pp. 91-101; cf. Isa. 45.2-7). If this passage is also in mind, then it is likewise applied in a reverse, ironic manner to the church. Perhaps, the language of Isa. 45.1 has become merged with that of Isa. 22.22, or the latter has led the author's thought to the former.

Therefore, John cites Isa. 22.22 in the second part of Rev. 3.7 because he sees in it a historical portrayal which prefigured what the Messiah would do on a grander scale.[167]

7. *Inverted Use of the Old Testament*
There are some allusions which on the surface are distinctly contradictory to the Old Testament contextual meaning. Further study again reveals, however, the imprecise nature of such categories.

a. *Example of a Typical Inverted Use of the Old Testament*. The clear example of an inverted use of the Old Testament is Rev. 3.9, which collectively makes reference to the Isaianic prophecies that the Gentiles would come and bow down before Israel and recognize them as God's chosen people. First, that the Jews 'will come and bow down before your feet' is a collective allusion to Isa. 45.14, 49.23, 60.14 (cf. LXX Göttingen apparatus) and Ps. 86.9. However, the hope from Isaiah has been turned upside down, since it is the Jewish persecutors of the Christians whom God will make to submit to the church, and not, in this instance, the unbelieving Gentiles. This reversal of Isaiah's language is most likely attributable to a conscious attempt to express the irony that the submission which unbelieving ethnic Jews hoped to receive from Gentiles they themselves would be forced to render to the church.[168] John concludes that ethnic Jews had become as unbelieving Gentiles because of their rejection of Christ and persecution of Christians; the unbelieving Jews are not true Israel and the believing church now represents God's true people. This prophecy has been fulfilled ironically in the predominantly Gentile church, which has become true Israel by virtue of its faith in Christ. In contrast, ethnic Israel fulfills the role of the Gentiles from Isaiah's perspective because of their unbelief.

In fact, this ironic element is intensified at the end of v. 9 through John's reference to the Gentile-dominated church as apparently being in the position of true Israel. This is accomplished by making a reverse application of Isa. 43.4 (perhaps, together with the LXX of Isa. 41.8, 44.2, 60.10 and 63.9; cf. 48.14; *Jub.* 1.25), which originally spoke of

---

167. Von Rad, *Old Testament Theology*, II, pp. 372-73, has also argued for a typological understanding of this Old Testament text in Rev. 3.7 but on an even different, viable basis.

168. So also Vos, *Synoptic Traditions in the Apocalypse*, p. 25; Mounce, *Revelation*, p. 118.

God's prophesied love and honour for Israel above the nations in the latter days. Vos is, therefore, inconsistent in recognizing an irony in the first part of v. 9 but concluding with respect to the Isa. 43.4 citation that 'the context of the alleged quotation has been totally disregarded'.[169] Isaiah's prophecies that the end-time salvation of Israel would spark off the salvation of the Gentiles has been fulfilled in an ironic manner. This is likely true even if a remnant of Jewish-Christians composed a part of the Philadelphian church, since the majority would have been Gentile. And, while the church assumes the role of Israel in these fulfilled prophecies, Christ performs the role which Isaiah foretold of Yahweh. Christ is the one causing the unbelieving Jewish community to recognize that the Gentile church composes his beloved people. John's use here shows a consistent ironic understanding of some of the major themes in Isaiah 40–66. And while such a view arises out of a contextual awareness of the Old Testament, the New Testament use is so diametrically opposite that it is best to categorize this as an inverted or ironic use.

b. *A Brief Survey of Other Inverted Uses of the Old Testament*. The terminology of cosmic universality from Dan. 7.14 in Rev. 5.9 reveals an intended inversion. Whereas in Daniel the phrase refers to the nations subjugated to Israel's rule, now these very nations rule together with the Messiah.

A sampling of other such uses is noteworthy. Dan. 7.21 refers to an oppressive 'horn' which 'was waging war with the saints and overpowering them'. This is applied in reverse fashion in Rev. 12.7-8 to describe the overthrow of Satan by Michael and his angels. Such reverse application probably does not reflect unconscious activity or an atomistic exegesis, but polemical irony, expressed by portraying the theocratic forces' defeat of the cosmic enemy through the same imagery from Daniel 7 which was used to describe how this enemy began to defeat God's forces. This may be a figurative way of expressing a *lex talionis* irony whereby the point is to show that the same way in which the enemy will try to subdue God and His people will be used by God himself to subdue the enemy. That this language is intentionally drawn in reverse manner from Dan. 7.21 is evident not only from the verbal likeness (cf. Theodotion) but also from the immediately following allusion to Dan. 2.35 (Rev. 12.8b) *and* from the same Dan. 7.21 reversal in

169. Vos, *Synoptic Traditions in the Apocalypse*, p. 26.

Rev. 17.14, where the Danielic 'Lord of lords and King of kings' (= Dan. 4.37 [LXX]) is the subject of the polemical overthrow.

The same kind of retributive ironies can be observed elsewhere in the Apocalypse: (1) Dan. 8.10 in Rev. 12.4, 9, 10; Dan. 7.7ff. in Rev. 5.6-7 (so 1 *En.* 90.9-13, 16; *T. Jos.* 19.6-8; *Gen. R.* 99.2; 4 Ezra 13.1ff.);[170] (2) Dan. 7.14 in Rev. 1.7-8; (3) Exod. 8.10 and 15.11, etc. in Rev. 13.4; (4) Exod. 3.14 (esp. *Exod. R.* 3.14) in Rev. 17.8.[171] The point of these kind of ironic uses is to mock the enemy's proud attempt to overcome God and his people and to underscore the fitting justice of the punishment.

There may be other examples of this reversal phenomenon but the ones discussed should alert one to caution in making facile statements about non-contextual, atomistic or straightforward contextual use, since the apocalyptic style is not always susceptible merely to such categories.

Nevertheless, all of the above cases studied here and throughout section D can be categorized as, at least, *broadly* contextual. Vanhoye has noted that John always employs Old Testament references with a view to making them contribute to the unified argument of his work,[172] and that every page 'witnesses to a penetrating intelligence of the ancient prophecies and of a perfect familiarity with their mode of expression'.[173] Gangemi observes that John does not choose Old Testament allusions at random but in accord with the main themes of the Apocalypse: divine transcendence, redemption, Yahweh's servant, Babylon's judgment, and new creation of the heavenly Jerusalem.[174] And it is clear that John drew these unifying themes of his work from the Old Testament (in this case Isaiah 40–66). Indeed, John is continuing to develop fundamental lines of Old Testament salvation history.[175]

---

170. Cf. G.K. Beale, 'The Problem of the Man from the Sea in IV Ezra 13 and its Relation to the Messianic Concept in John's Apocalypse', *NovT* 25 (1983), pp. 182-88.

171. Cf. 1.4, 8; 4.8; 11.17; 16.5; cf. also Ezra 9.14b in 1QM 1.6b and Dan. 11.40, 44-45 in 1QM 1.4.

172. Vanhoye, 'L'utilisation du livre d'Ezéchiel dans l'Apocalypse', pp. 463-64.

173. Vanhoye, 'L'utilisation du livre d'Ezéchiel dans l'Apocalypse', p. 462.

174. Gangemi, 'L'utilizzazione del Deutero-Isaia nell'Apocalisse di Giovanni', pp. 322-38.

175. Cambier, 'Les images de l'Ancien Testament dans l'Apocalypse ,de Saint Jean', pp. 118-21; Gangemi, 'L'utilizzazione del Deutero-Isaia nell'Apocalisse di Giovanni', pp. 332-39.

8. *Stylistic Use of Old Testament Language*

This use represents the most general category so far discussed. It has long been recognized that the Apocalypse contains a multitude of grammatical solecisms. Charles claimed it contained more grammatical irregularities than any other Greek document of the ancient world.[176] He accounted for this with his famous dictum 'while he writes in Greek, he thinks in Hebrew, and the thought has naturally affected the vehicle of expression',[177] a judgment which has met with subsequent agreement, especially recently.[178]

But was this intentional on the author's part or an unconscious by-product of his Semitic mind? It seems that his grammatical 'howlers' are deliberate attempts to express Semitisms and Septuagintalisms in his Greek, the closest analogy being that of the LXX translations, especially Aquila.[179] The fact that most of the time the author does keep the rules further points to the solecisms being intentional.

Why did John write this way? Sometimes his purpose was deliberately to create a 'biblical' effect in the hearer and thus to demonstrate the solidarity of his work with that of the divinely inspired Old Testament Scriptures.[180] A polemical purpose may also have been included. John may have been expressing the idea that Old Testament truth conveyed through the channel of the church as the new Israel was uncompromisingly penetrating the Gentile world, and would continue to until the final parousia.[181]

I will argue in a later chapter that many of the solecisms are used as signals for the presence of Old Testament allusions (Chapter 5). Apparently unrecognized for the most part previously, a significant number of

---

176. Charles, *Revelation*, I, p. cxliii.

177. Charles, *Revelation*, I, p. cxliii.

178. Cf. Sweet, *Revelation*, pp. 16-17; A.Y. Collins, *Crisis and Catharsis* (Philadelphia: Westminster Press, 1984), p. 47, and above all Thompson, *Semitic Syntax, passim*); though S. E. Porter has issued a dissenting voice, arguing that what some have called Semitisms fall 'within the range of possible registers of Greek usage in the 1st century' (S.E. Porter, 'The Language of the Apocalypse in Recent Study', *NTS* 35 [1989], pp. 582-603). For further discussion of this issue see below on the analysis of solecisms in Chapter 5.

179. Sweet, *Revelation*, p. 16; see especially Thompson, *Semitic Syntax*, p. 108 and *passim*.

180. Sweet, *Revelation*, p. 16.

181. Cf. somewhat similarly Collins, *Crisis and Catharsis*, p. 47; Thompson, *Semitic Syntax*, p. 108.

these irregularities occur in the midst of Old Testament allusions. Accordingly, a number of the expressions appear irregular because John is carrying over the exact grammatical form of the Old Testament wording or intentionally reproducing a Septuagentalism in order to create syntactical dissonance. This 'dissonance' is one of the ways that John gets the readers' attention, causing them to pause and focus on the phrase and to recognize more readily the presence of an Old Testament allusion.

Conclusion

Perhaps one of the reasons for the high degree of Old Testament influence in the Apocalypse is that the author could think of no better way to describe some of his visions, which were difficult to explain, than with the language already used by the Old Testament prophets to describe similar visions. The present study, particularly of categories of usage in the Apocalypse, favours the evaluation of I. Fransen:

> The familiarity with the Old Testament, with the spirit which lives in the Old Testament, is a most essential condition for a fruitful reading of the Apocalypse.[182]

This is a conclusion which runs counter to that of Barnabas Lindar's general evaluation of the primary role of the Old Testament in the majority of the New Testament corpus:

> The place of the Old Testament in the formation of New Testament theology is that of a servant, ready to run to the aid of the gospel whenever it is required, bolstering up arguments, and filling out meaning through evocative allusions, but never acting as the master or leading the way, nor even guiding the process of thought behind the scenes.[183]

However, Lindars appears to exclude the Apocalypse from his analysis.[184] He expresses apparent openness to discovering more respect for Old Testament contextual meaning in the Apocalypse because he judges

---

182. I. Fransen, 'Cahier de Bible: Jésus, le Témoin Fidèle (Apocalypse)', *BVC* 16 (1956–57), pp. 66-79; likewise Sweet, 'Maintaining the Testimony of Jesus', p. 111.

183. Lindars, 'Place of the Old Testament in the Formation of New Testament Theology', *NTS* 23 (1977), pp. 59-66.

184. Cf. Lindars, *New Testament Apologetic* (Philadelphia: Westminster Press, 1961), *passim*; B. Lindars, 'Formation of New Testament Theology', pp. 63-64.

John's writing not to be the result of urgent, *ad hoc* apologetic concerns but to have arisen out of meditation worked out quietly in the study at a slightly later stage of Christian apocalyptic.[185]

Therefore, the conclusion of this brief overview is that the place of the Old Testament in the formation of thought in the Apocalypse is both that of a servant and a guide: for John, the Christ event is the key to understanding the Old Testament, and yet reflection back upon the Old Testament context leads the way to further comprehension of this event and provides the redemptive-historical background against which the apocalyptic visions are better understood; the New Testament interprets the Old and the Old interprets the New.[186] The analysis throughout the present monograph lends further evidence pointing in this direction. Whether or not there is the same reciprocal relationship elsewhere in the New Testament is a question which cannot be addressed here. However, the observation that much of the New Testament was written, not only with an apologetic motive, but also in an apocalyptic atmosphere should cause us to be open to this possibility.

This is a conclusion which is not far in some respects from that of the work of Moyise, who also wants to see a reciprocal interpretative relationship of Old Testament and New Testament.[187] What to some may appear to be John's novel interpretations of the Old Testament are the result of his new presuppositional lenses through which he perceives the Old Testament, among the most significant of which are:[188] (1) Christ corporately represents true Israel of the Old and New Testament; (2) history is unified by a wise and sovereign plan, so that the earlier parts of canonical history are designed to correspond typologically and point to later parts of inscripturated history; (3) the age of

185. Lindars, 'Formation of New Testament Theology', p. 63.

186. Ruiz, *Ezekiel in the Apocalypse*, pp. 120-21, holds, unconvincingly in my view, the one-sided perspective that the Old Testament was not an object of interpretation by John but *only* the means of his own creative interpretation.

187. Moyise, *Old Testament in the Book of Revelation*, e.g., pp. 19, 58, 82-83, 102, 110-11, 115, 128, though it is not clear why he wants to deny that John is offering an interpretation of the Old Testatment books which he intentionally quotes (e.g. see p. 58).

188. The following four presuppositions have been noted already in the discussion of Chapter 1, where also is further discussion of the problem of whether or not John is contextually sensitive to the Old Testament.

end-time fulfillment has been inaugurated with Christ's first coming;[189] and (4) in the light of points 2 and 3, the later parts of biblical history interpret earlier parts, so that Christ as the centre of history is the key to interpreting the earlier portions of the Old Testament.

Granted the viability of these assumptions, John's interpretation of the Old Testament shows a careful understanding of Old Testament contexts, and his interpretation shows significant influence from the Old Testament itself; if, however, these presuppositions are hermeneutically fallacious, then his interpretation must be seen as alien to the intention of the Old Testament. John probably saw his presuppositions as organically growing out of the Old Testament itself and out of Christ's own approach to interpreting the Old Testament. Consequently, it is likely that John is offering new understandings of Old Testament texts and fulfilments of them which may have been surprising to an Old Testament audience, but not to a New Testament audience which retrospectively looks at the Old Testament in the light of the above presuppositions.

189. Moyise comes close to recognizing the programmatic nature of this presupposition for John (Moyise, *Old Testament in the Book of Revelation*, p. 58).

Chapter 3

THE INFLUENCE OF THE OLD TESTAMENT UPON THE ESCHATOLOGY
OF REVELATION

A. *The Eschatology of Revelation in Relationto the Rest of the New
Testament:The 'Already and Not Yet'*

Before looking explicitly at the bearing of the Old Testament on the eschatology of Revelation, it should be helpful at the beginning of this
chapter (section A) to locate Revelation's eschatology in relation to the
eschatology of the rest of the New Testament. Contrary to some views
which understand Revelation to consist primarily of futuristic eschatology, we will find that the 'already and not yet' conception found elsewhere in the New Testament also runs throughout Revelation. After
this initial analysis, the following sections of this chapter (sections B,
C, D and E) will investigate explicit and particular cases where the Old
Testament influences John's perspective of the latter days. The last
chapter of the book will also address this topic with respect to the
'millennium' in Revelation 20.

1. *Introduction*
In order to understand the New Testament rightly one must have some
acquaintance with how the New Testament authors viewed eschatology
or the 'end-times'.[1] This may sound like a surprising proposition to
some non-specialists in biblical studies, since such people often think

---

1.   On the vagueness of the term 'eschatology' and clarification of its definition
see I.H. Marshall, 'Slippery Words', *ExpTim* 89 (1978), pp. 264-69; for the relation
of the term to 'apocalyptic' see D.E. Aune, 'Apocalypticism', in G.F. Hawthorne,
R.P. Martin and D.G. Reid (eds.), *Dictionary of Paul and his Letters* (Downers
Grove, IL: InterVarsity Press, 1993), pp. 25-35, and see L.J. Kreitzer, 'Eschatology', in G.F. Hawthorne, R.P. Martin, and D.G. Reid (eds.), *Dictionary of Paul
and his Letters* (Downers Grove, IL: InterVarsity Press, 1993), pp. 253-69.

of the end-times as a period which will happen only at the very climax of history. After all, can one not have an excellent understanding of the New Testament without knowing about exactly how the world is going to end? Are not questions about the time of the so-called "rapture", tribulation and millennium secondary to the salvation which Christ accomplished at the cross? These questions could be answered with a 'yes' if the end-times were a period coming only at the final phase of history. Indeed, many outside scholarly circles assume this to be true, so that Christ's death and resurrection are events which happened at His first coming and are not closely connected with those events leading up to His second coming.

However, such an understanding of the latter days which views them as arriving only at the very end of history needs radical rethinking. And with respect to Revelation, both popular and scholarly thought too often have approached its 'eschatology' as though it could only refer to what will happen at the very end of history as we know it. The phrase 'latter days' (and similar phrases) occurs numerous times in the New Testament and rarely refers *exclusively* to the very end of history, as we typically think of it. This wording is almost always used to describe the end-times as beginning already in the first century. Consequently, a survey of these phrases in the New Testament, as well as a brief overview of the language in the Old Testament, Judaism and Apostolic Fathers, demands that the sometimes popular and scholarly view be reassessed. We could widen our following study to include other conceptual references to eschatology, but the present survey of explicit eschatological terms will be sufficient to make the point. At the conclusion of the survey, a similar survey will be done in John's Apocalypse for purposes of comparison and contrast.

2. *Background for New Testament Eschatology: Eschatology of the Old Testament*

The first observation that can be made about these phrases in the New Testament is that they are alluding specifically to identical phrases in the Old Testament or echoing the general Old Testament usage of 'latter days'. Therefore, the meaning of the Old Testament expression 'latter days' must be understood before the New Testament use can begin to be explained. In the Old Testament this wording is prophetic and refers to a future time when: (1) there will be a tribulation for Israel consisting of their own judgment leading to captivity (Jer. 23.20; cf.

30.24), as well as subsequent oppression (Ezek. 38.14-17ff.), persecution (Dan. 10.14ff.; 11.27–12.10), false teaching, deception and apostasy (Dan. 10.14ff.; 11.27-35); (2) after the tribulation Israel will seek the Lord (Hos. 3.4-5), they will be delivered (Ezek. 38.14-16ff.; Dan. 10.14ff.; 12.1-13) and their enemies will be judged (Ezek. 38.14-16ff.; Dan. 10.14ff.; 11.40-45; 12.2); (3) this deliverance and judgment will occur because a leader (Messiah) from Israel will finally conquer all of its Gentile enemies (Gen. 49.1, 8-12; Num. 24.14-19; Isa. 2.2-4; Mic. 4.1-3; Dan. 2.28-45; 10.14–12.10); (4) the saints of Israel will be raised from the dead (Dan. 12.2); (5) God will establish a new covenant with Israel (cf. Jer. 31.31-34 with Jer. 30.24); (6) God will establish a kingdom on the earth and rule over it (Isa. 2.2-4; Mic. 4.1-3; Dan. 2.28-45) together with a Davidic king (Hos. 3.4-5); (7) even some of Israel's Gentile enemies will experience deliverance during these eschatological days (Jer. 48.47; 49.39; cf. Isa. 19.19-25).

The Old Testament does not always employ the more technical terminology of 'latter days' when discussing eschatological subjects. For example, Isaiah's prophecy of the new creation is overtly eschatological, but there is no eschatological formulae used to introduce the prophecy (cf. Isa. 65.17 and 66.22). Joel's prophecy of the Holy Spirit is introduced only by 'after this' Joel 2.28, which, however, Peter in Acts 2.17 paraphrases by 'in the latter days' (see directly below at sect. 5).[2]

3. Background for New Testament Eschatology: Eschatology of Judaism
The writings of intertestamental Judaism express a hope in and an expectation of God's bringing history to a final consummation through a final, great tribulation,[3] followed by judgment of the wicked and salvation of the faithful. This is especially true in the apocalyptic literature. Jewish apocalyptic usually views the 'end' as imminent, though there

2.   Among others, for discussion of the subject of Old Testament eschatology, as well as references to other relevant secondary sources, see N. Pryor, 'Eschatological Expectations in the Old Testament Prophets', in J.P. Lewis (ed.), *The Last Things: Essays Presented to W.B. West, Jr.* (Austin, TX: Sweet Publishing, 1972), pp. 32-59, and D.E. Gowan, *Eschatology in the Old Testament* (Philadelphia: Fortress Press, 1986); see also for further bibliographical sources C. Brown, 'The Parousia and Eschatology in the NT', *NIDNTT*, II, pp. 901-35.
3.   On which see D.C. Allison, *The End of the Ages Has Come* (Philadelphia: Fortress Press, 1985), pp. 5-25.

are examples of something approaching an idea of 'inaugurated eschatology'.[4] The notion that the latter days actually have begun to be fulfilled on earth is found in the Qumran community; the consummation is understood to be 'around the corner', but the latter day period is seen already to have commenced in the midst of the Qumran covenanters.[5]

Constraints of space do not allow a further analysis of the language for or the concept of eschatology in the literature of post-biblical Judaism (especially from 200 BC up to 150 AD).[6]

4. *Eschatology of the Gospels and Paul*

The New Testament repeatedly uses precisely the same phrase 'latter days' as found in the Old Testament prophecies. The meaning of the phrase is identical, except for one difference: in the New Testament the end days predicted by the Old Testament are seen as beginning fulfillment with Christ's first coming. All that the Old Testament foresaw would occur in the end-times has begun already in the first century and continues on until the final coming of Christ. This means that the Old Testament expectations of the great tribulation, God's domination of the Gentiles, deliverance of Israel from oppressors, Israel's resurrection, the new covenant, the new creation and the establishment of God's kingdom, have been set in motion by Christ's death, resurrection and formation of the Christian church. Christ's first coming marked the beginning of his messianic reign, which was underscored by the presence of the Holy Spirit in his ministry (e.g. at his baptism [Mt. 3.13-17] and in the casting out of demons [Mt. 12.22-32]). The resurrection marked a heightened level of Jesus' inaugurated reign. On the other hand, persecution of Jesus and his followers indicated the beginning of the final tribulation. What the Old Testament did not foresee so clearly was the reality that the kingdom and the tribulation could co-exist at the same time (e.g. Rev. 1.6-9). Therefore, the latter days do not take place only at some point in the future but occur throughout the whole church age.

---

4.   Cf. A. Lincoln, *Paradise Now and Not Yet* (SNTSMS, 43; Cambridge: Cambridge University Press, 1981), pp. 177-78.

5.   See J. Carmignac, 'La notion d'eschatologie dans la Bible et à Qumran', *RevQ* 7 (1969), pp. 17-31, for discussion of eschatology in Qumran.

6.   See further G. Howard, 'Eschatology in the Period between the Testaments', in J.P. Lewis (ed.), *The Last Things: Essays Presented to W.B. West, Jr.*, (Austin, TX: Sweet Publishing, 1972), pp. 60-73, who also cites other relevant sources.

Paul says that the Old Testament was written to instruct the Corinthian Christians about how to live in the end-times, since upon them 'the ends of the ages have come' (1 Cor. 10.11). He refers to Jesus' birth as occurring 'when the fullness of the time came' in fulfillment of the messianic prophecies (Gal. 4.4). Likewise, 'the fullness of the times' alludes to when believers were delivered from Satan and sin through Christ's death and resurrection (Eph. 1.7-10; 1.20–2.6), which commenced his own rule over the whole earth (Eph. 1.19-23). Christ's death and resurrection launched the beginning of the latter-day new creation prophesied by Isaiah (cf. 2 Cor. 5.17 with Isaiah 43; 65–66). The end-time prophecies of Israel's restoration from exile reach beginning fulfillment in Christ's, the true Israel's, resurrection and in those in the church who identify by faith with him (e.g. see 2 Cor. 6.16-18).[7] The presence of tribulation in the form of false, deceptive teaching at the church of Ephesus is also one of the signs that the long-awaited latter days had finally come (1 Tim. 4.1-3; 2 Tim. 3.1-9). That this idea in 1 and 2 Timothy is not a reference to only a distant, future time is evident from recognizing that the Ephesian church is already experiencing the latter-day tribulation of deceptive teaching and apostasy (see 1 Tim. 1.3-4, 6, 7, 19-20; 4.7; 5.13-15; 6.20-21; 2 Tim. 1.15; 2.16-19; 2.25-26; 3.2-9).

This brief review of eschatology in the Gospels and Paul demonstrates that the last days predicted by the Old Testament began with Christ's first coming, although there is other terminology besides 'latter days' in many other passages which could also be adduced as further evidence (e.g. see Paul's use of 'now' in 2 Cor. 6.2; Eph. 3.5, 10; etc.) that Christ's death and resurrection and his community of faith have ushered in the fulfillment of the Old Testament's prophecies about the end times. In this initial eschatological phase, Christ and the church fulfill the prophecies concerning Israel's tribulation, deliverance from oppressors, and kingdom, since Jesus is seen by the New Testament as the true, spiritual Israel who represents his people as such (see Rom. 2.25-29; 9.6, 24-26; Gal. 3.29; 6.15-16; Eph. 2.16-18; 3.6; 1 Pet. 2.9; Rev. 1.6; 3.9, 12; 5.9-10).[8]

Of course, there are passages in the New Testament which speak of the future consummation of the present latter-day period. There are still many end-time prophecies which have not yet been fulfilled but will be

7. Cf. Beale, 'Old Testament Background of Reconciliation'.
8. See further LaRondelle, *Israel of God in Prophecy*.

when Christ returns a second time: e.g. the bodily resurrection of all people, the destruction of the present cosmos, the creation of a completely new heavens and earth, and the final judgment (e.g. Rev. 21.1ff.).

Until the final conclusion of history, Christ's followers experience only a part of what will be completely experienced in the new heavens and earth. There is what some call an 'already-and-not-yet' dimension of the end-times.[9] In this respect Oscar Cullmann has metaphorically described Jesus' first coming as 'D-day', since this is when Satan was decisively defeated. 'V-day' is the second coming when Jesus' enemies will totally surrender and bow down to Him. 'The hope of the final victory is so much more the vivid because of the unshakably firm conviction that the battle that decides the victory has already taken place.'[10]

The point is that the great end-time predictions of the Old Testament have already begun the process of fulfillment and await their consummation.[11]

The same notion found in the Gospels and Paul, that the end times have begun but are not finally consummated, occurs likewise in the rest of the New Testament.

---

9. On this see C.F.D. Moule, 'Influence of Circumstances on the Use of Eschatological Terms', *JTS* 15 (1964), pp. 1-15, and Lincoln, *Paradise Now and Not Yet*, pp. 181-84, who both see that different aspects of eschatological thought are generated in response to the particular circumstances in churches which faced various New Testament authors.

10. O. Cullmann, *Christ and Time* (Philadelphia: Westminster Press, 1964), p. 87.

11. For the 'already' and 'not yet' notion of eschatology in the Gospels and Paul see: Allison, *End of the Ages*; Allison, 'Eschatology', in J.B. Green, S. McKnight and I.H. Marshall (eds.), *Dictionary of Jesus and the Gospels* (Downers Grove, IL: InterVarsity Press, 1992), pp. 206-209; Kreitzer, 'Eschatology'; G. Vos, 'The Eschatological Aspect of the Pauline Conception of the Spirit', in R.B. Gaffin (ed.), *Redemptive History and Biblical Interpretation: The Shorter Writings of Geerhardus Vos* (Phillipsburg, NJ: Presbyterian and Reformed Publishing, 1980), pp. 91-125; G. Vos, *The Pauline Eschatology* (Grand Rapids: Baker Book House, 1979); G.E. Ladd, *Presence of the Future* (Grand Rapids: Eerdmans, 1974); G.E. Ladd, 'Eschatology and the Unity of New Testament Theology', *ExpTim* 68 (1957), pp. 268-78; Caird, *The Language and Imagery of the Bible*, pp. 241-71; A.A. Hoekema, *The Bible and the Future* (Grand Rapids: Eerdmans, 1979); A. König, *The Eclipse of Christ in Eschatology* (Grand Rapids: Eerdmans; London: Marshall, Morgan & Scott, 1980); C.M. Pate, *The End of the Ages Has Come: The Theology of Paul* (Grand Rapids: Zondervan, 1995).

5. *The Eschatology of Acts*

a. *Past and Present*. The first time the wording 'last days' appears in the New Testament (in canonical order) is Acts 2.17. Here Peter understands that the tongues being spoken at Pentecost are a beginning fulfillment of Joel's end-time prophecy that a day would come when God's Spirit would gift not merely prophets, priests and kings, but all of God's people: 'And it shall be in the last days, God says, that I will pour forth of My Spirit upon all mankind...' (Acts 2.15-17a; cf. Joel 2.28). The resurrection marked the beginning of Jesus' messianic reign, and the Spirit at Pentecost signaled the inauguration of His rule through the church (see Acts 1.6-8; 2.1-43). At significant transitional points in Acts where the gospel is being extended to new regions or ethnic groups, the pouring out of the Spirit is repeatedly mentioned in order to indicate subsequent events to Pentecost which followed in its pattern, perhaps to be considered as 'little Pentecosts' (e.g. Acts 8.17; 10.44-46; 1.9.6). These later outpourings continue to serve to demonstrate Christ's exalted reign, but they also indicate that Gentile as well as Jew are accepted by faith and are included as subjects in the Messiah's new kingdom. This is a point implied from Acts 2, where Jews representing all parts of the known Gentile world were present at Pentecost. The clearest example of a subsequent Spirit-outpouring modeled on Acts 2 is Acts 10.34-47, where the Roman soldier Cornelius and his Gentile associates believed in Christ and 'the gift of the Spirit [was]...poured out on the Gentiles also'.

It is unlikely that Acts represents a 'de-eschatologizing' by substituting a history of the church for a near expectation of the end (e.g. as represented by Sabourin).[12] Indeed, Luke sees that the pouring out of the Spirit is a further stage of eschatological fulfillment, which makes the time of the church an eschatological era.[13]

The reason that the coming of the Spirit is perceived in such a highlighted eschatological manner is because one of its purposes was to demonstrate the exalted, heavenly messianic kingship of Jesus, as a result of the resurrection from the dead. This is natural since the Spirit

---

12. L. Sabourin, 'The Eschatology of Luke', *BTB* 12 (1982), pp. 73-76.

13. For both sides of the debate see B.R. Gaventa, 'The Eschatology of Luke–Acts Revisited', *Encounter* 43 (1982), pp. 27-42; on the problem of the purported delay of Christ's final coming see further on L. Kreitzer, 'Parousia', in P. Davids and R.P. Martin (eds.), *Dictionary of the Later New Testament and its Developments* (Downers Grove, IL: InterVarsity Press, 1997), pp. 330-45.

was linked with the future hope of resurrection life in the Old Testament and in Judaism, a link found elsewhere also in the New Testament (cf. Romans, 1 Tim. 3; etc.).[14] As a consequence of Jesus' resurrection, the eschatological center of gravity had shifted from Jesus' ministry on earth to his reign in heaven. The very notion that Jesus had been *raised from the dead* was itself a highly charged end-time idea, whose roots lay in the Old Testament (Isa. 25.7-8; 26.18-19; Ezek. 37.1-14; Dan. 12.1-2) and post-biblical Judaism (e.g. 2 Macc. 7.9, 14; 1QH 11.12; *1 En.* 51.1; *2 Bar.* 30.1-3; 50.1-4; *T. Jud.* 25.1; *LAE* 41.3). Consequently, other references to Jesus' resurrection throughout the book, though not formally linked with technical eschatological terminology as in Acts 2, are still eschatological in nature, especially since they are often associated in context with Old Testament hopes and promises (see Acts 1.3-11, 22; 3.15, 26; 4.2, 10, 33; 5.30-31; 7.55-56; 9.3-6; 10.40-41; 13.30-37; 17.31-32; 22.6-11; 25.19; 26.6-18, 22-23). Likewise, the resurrection of some Christians was probably identified with Jesus' eschatological resurrection (Acts 9.37-41; 20.9-12; cf. Mt. 27.52-53).

That fulfillment of other latter-day Old Testament prophecies, in addition to that of the resurrection and the Spirit, had been inaugurated was certainly also an indication that the last times had begun (Acts 3.18, 22-26; 4.25-28; 13.27-29, 46-48; 15.14-18; 26.22-23). Possibly, even the mention of entering 'the kingdom of God' after enduring 'tribulation' is an allusion, not merely to a reality at the end of history, but also to that inaugurated messianic, heavenly realm which one enters upon death (Acts 14.22; cf. Stephen's vision, directly preceding his death, of Christ as the presently reigning 'son of man' in Acts 7.55-56).

It is likely that the most encompassing idea for eschatology in Acts, and the New Testament as a whole, is that of new creation, since this notion best ties together all the various thematic strands linked to eschatology. For example, the resurrection is essentially an act of new creation (the creation of new life) which is brought about by the life-giving agency of the Spirit. Even the healings in Acts (cf. 3.1-16; 5.16; 9.33-34;14.8-11; 19.11-12), as well as throughout the Gospels, are best understood within the larger redemptive–historical framework of the beginning new creation wherein the curses of the fallen creation (sickness, death, and so on) begin to be reversed.

---

14. On which see Vos, 'Eschatological Aspect'.

b. *Future*. In Acts 1.6 the disciples ask Jesus if it is 'at this time that you are restoring the kingdom to Israel?' Jesus replies in v. 7 that 'It is not for you to know times or epochs which the Father has fixed by His own authority', and then he promises in v. 8 that the Spirit would come upon them and empower them to witness. Some commentators understand v. 7 together with v. 8 as a response which explains that there will be an indefinite delay of the coming of Israel's restored kingdom in its consummated form, but that during the interim period the Spirit would maintain the witness of Jesus' followers.[15] Accordingly, the time of the restoration of the kingdom is equated with the time of Jesus' final coming to conclude history, which is mentioned in the directly following v. 11. In addition, Acts 3.19-21 is seen to continue the theme of the yet-future coming kingdom; along these lines, in Acts 3.19-21, the 'times of refreshing' and the 'times of restoration of all things' are to occur when Jesus returns to conclude history, apparently in the same way as he left at the ascension (1.11).

Another perspective on Acts 1.6-8, however, is plausible, if not more probable. Jesus responds in vv. 7-8 to three misunderstandings inherent in the apostles' question of v. 6. First, v. 7 is a response to their wrong assumption that it was proper for them to know the precise time (cf. 1 Thess. 5.1-8) about when the kingdom would be restored to Israel: such knowledge is reserved for the Father alone. Secondly, Acts 1.8 appears to be a response to an implicit assumption in the question of v. 6 that future stages of the kingdom would be only physical in their expression. Though some understand the continued response of v. 8 to refer to the notion of a parenthetical period characterized by the Spirit which is not part of the messianic kingdom, it is more likely that the verse asserts that *a* future form of the kingdom is to be 'spiritual' in nature ('you will receive *power* [of the kingdom !] when the Holy Spirit has come').

The promise of Acts 1.8, of course, begins fulfillment at Pentecost, which Peter understands to be an escalation of the 'latter days' first inaugurated by Jesus, when he himself began to receive the Spirit at his baptism. In fact, 'the latter days' was not only the time of the expected outpouring of God's Spirit in the Old Testament and Judaism, but the Old Testament inextricably linked the repeated phrase 'latter days' with the prophesied kingdom, so that Peter's reference to the phrase in 2.17 conveys the notion of fulfillment of the foreseen kingdom (e.g. see the

15. Cf. A. Buzzard, 'Acts 1:6 and the Eclipse of the Biblical Kingdom', *EvQ* 66 (1994), pp. 197-215.

Old Testament references in sect. A.2 and A.3 above). Thirdly, v. 8
appears to be a reply to an apparent ethnocentric presupposition in v. 6
that the nature of the kingdom would be essentially Israelite racially
and nationally. Jesus' reply is that the kingdom would encompass subjects who lived even 'unto the end of the earth' (in partial allusion to
Isa. 49.6; cf. Acts 13.47 which refers back to the conclusion of 1.8 and
where the Old Testament reference is explicit). Hence, Acts 1.8 affirms
what will be an ongoing, progressive and non-consummative fulfillment of the prophecy of the Old Testament kingdom, which had already
begun establishment in Jesus' earthly ministry.[16]

Acts 3.20-21 clearly refers to the yet-future consummation, when
Christ comes a final time and achieves 'the restoration of all things'.
Acts 3.19, however, may include an 'already and not yet' notion, especially because of its placement directly following an assertion that God
had already 'fulfilled' Old Testament prophecy about Christ's suffering:
'Repent therefore and return, that your sins may be wiped away, *in
order that times of refreshing may come from the presence of the Lord*'
(which may be parallel to Acts 2.38: 'Repent, and...be baptized...for
the forgiveness of your sins, and you will receive the gift of the Holy
Spirit'). Likewise, 3.22-26 refers to beginning fulfillments of Old Testament messianic prophecy.[17] Even the reference 'until the times of
restoration of all things' in 3.21 has an 'already and not yet' notion,
since the 'restoration' had likely begun with Jesus' coming, resurrection and giving of the Spirit.[18]

---

16. See D. Hill, 'The Spirit and the Church's Witness: Observations on Acts
1:6-8', *IBS* 6 (1984), pp. 16-26, upon which the preceding discussion of Acts 1.6-8
is partly based, though he denies that Luke has an inaugurated eschatological perspective; cf. F.F. Bruce, 'Eschatology in Acts', in W.H. Gloer (ed.), *Eschatology
and the New Testament: Essays in Honor of G.R. Beasley-Murray* (Peabody, MA:
Hendrickson, 1988), pp. 51-63, for a balanced 'already and not yet' view of Acts
1.6-8, and of the entire book.

17. For further argument in support of this analysis cf. W.S. Kurz, 'Acts 3:19-
26 as a Test of the Role of Eschatology in Lukan Christology', in *SBLSP* 11
(Chico, CA: Scholars Press, 1977), pp. 309-323, and sources cited therein; cf. also
H.F. Bayer, 'Christ-Centered Eschatology in Acts 3:17-26', in J.B. Green and
M. Turner (eds.), *Jesus of Nazareth: Lord and Christ* (Grand Rapids: Eerdmans,
1994), pp. 236-50.

18. So Bayer, 'Christ-Centered Eschatology in Acts 3:17-26'.

In contrast, an incontestably future reference to a future judgment is Acts 17.30-31, where Paul affirms that people should repent in the present because God has determined a specific day at the end of history when 'he will judge the world in righteousness' through Jesus Christ (likewise Acts 24.25).

Paul also affirms 'the hope of the promise' of the final resurrection for the nation Israel in 26.6-7, yet even this has been inaugurated in Christ's, the true Israel's, resurrection (as clear from Acts 13.32-33, 23.6-7 and 26.22-24).[19]

6. *The Eschatology of Hebrews*

a. *Past and Present.* The second verse of the epistle begins with the statement that God 'in these *last days* has spoken to us in his son, whom he appointed heir of all things' (Heb. 1.2). Consequently, as seen elsewhere in the Gospels, Acts and Paul, Christ's first coming commences the beginning of the end times, which had been prophesied by the Old Testament. In this respect, Heb. 1.5-13 cites Old Testament prophecies primarily concerning the messianic son's kingship which have begun fulfillment in Jesus' first advent (cf. also 5.5; 8.1; 10.12-13;

---

19. On the futurist aspects of eschatology in Acts see also A.E. Nielsen, 'The Purpose of the Lucan Writings with Particular Reference to Eschatology', in P. Luomanen (ed.), *Luke–Acts* (Helsinki: The Finnish Exegetical Society, 1991), pp. 76-93; on the 'already and not yet' notion of eschatology in Acts, which has its precedent in Luke's Gospel (e.g. E.E. Ellis, 'Present and Future Eschatology in Luke', *NTS* 12 [1965], pp. 27-41), see further H.J. Cadbury, 'Acts and Eschatology', in W.D. Davies and D. Daube (eds.), *The Background of the New Testament and its Eschatology: Studies in Honour of C.H. Dodd* (Cambridge: Cambridge University Press, 1956), pp. 300-21; K. Giles, 'Present–Future Eschatology in the Book of Acts (I)', *RTR* 40 (1981), pp. 65-71; K. Giles, 'Present–Future Eschatology in the Book of Acts (II)', *RTR* 41 (1982), pp. 11-18; E. Franklin, 'The Ascension and the Eschatology of Luke–Acts', *SJT* 23 (1970), pp. 191-200; F.O. Francis, 'Eschatology and History in Luke–Acts', *JAAR* 37 (1969), pp. 49-63; Gaventa, 'Eschatology of Luke–Acts Revisited' (which also gives also a good overview of the history of the debate); cf., similarly to Gaventa, R.H. Smith, 'The Eschatology of Acts and Contemporary Exegesis', *CTM* 29 (1958), pp. 641-63; R.H. Smith, 'History and Eschatology in Luke–Acts', *CTM* 29 (1958), pp. 881-901; J.T. Carroll, *Response to the End of History: Eschatology and Situation in Luke–Acts* (Atlanta: Scholars Press, 1988), pp. 121-67 (though, cf. the apparently inconsistent p. 137); cf. also A.J. Mattill, *Luke and the Last Things* (Dillsboro, NC: Western North Carolina Press, 1979), who focuses, however, on Luke's near expectation and hope of the end.

12.2). Likewise, the portrayal of the ideal Adam's reign as 'the son of man' from Psalm 8, never completely realized in the Old Testament period, is applied to Christ as the one finally who has started to 'fill the shoes' of this exemplary human figure (Heb. 2.6-9). Christ has done what the first Adam and Israel, the corporate Adam, failed to achieve.[20] It is in this sense of Christ's 'fulfillment' of end-time prophecy that he is also to be understood to be a 'son' who was 'made [eschatologically] complete' (not 'perfected') and who has begun to lead and will finish leading his people to their end-time completed salvation (cf. further 2.10; 5.8-9, 14; 6.1; 7.11, 19, 28; 9.9; 10.1, 14; 11.40; 12.2).[21] In this manner, Christ has decisively defeated the power of the Devil and death (2.14), a reality not expected to occur until the eschatological new creation. The writer to the Hebrews can even refer in 9.26 to Christ's mission 'to put away sin by the sacrifice of himself' as happening at the 'consummation of the ages' (cf. similarly 10.10, 12, 14). This is why the author refers to the beginning fulfillment of Jeremiah's prophecy of a new covenant which is concluded in Jeremiah and Hebrews with an underscoring of the forgiveness of sin ('I will be merciful to their iniquities, and their sin I will remember no more'; cf. Jer. 31.31-34 with Heb. 8.8-12 and 10.16-17). In line with the end-time tone of Heb. 9.26, Jeremiah's prophecy was also one which was inextricably linked to 'latter-day' happenings (cf. Jer. 30.24 ['in the latter days'] with 31.31 ['days are coming'], 31.33 ['after those days']). Another mark that the last age has arrived is the resurrection of Christ (Heb. 13.20).

Jesus' followers have also 'tasted the powers of the *age to come*' (6.5), among which, apparently, is 'the heavenly gift... of the Holy Spirit' (6.4).[22] This is the closest the New Testament comes formally to identifying the Holy Spirit as a mark of the inbreaking eschatological age (though cf. also Rom. 8.23; 2 Cor. 1.20-22; Eph. 1.13-14). Even the Christians' 'hope' of a future consummated salvation is rooted in Christ as already having begun to realize that hope (cf. 6.17-20).[23] In fact,

---

20. For the notion of Israel as a corporate Adam, see N.T. Wright, *The Climax of the Covenant* (Minneapolis: Fortress Press, 1992), pp. 21-26.

21. See, e.g., M. Silva, 'Perfection and Eschatology in Hebrews', *WTJ* 39 (1976), pp. 60-71.

22. Cf. P. Ellingworth, *The Epistle to the Hebrews* (NIGTC; Grand Rapids: Eerdmans; Carlisle: Paternoster Press, 1993), p. 320.

23. Cf. further W.C. Robinson, 'Eschatology of the Epistle to the Hebrews: A Study in the Christian Doctrine of Hope', *Encounter* 22 (1961), pp. 37-51.

Christians have already 'come to Mount Zion and to the city of the living God, the heavenly city' (the new Jerusalem; cf. 12.22), so that the expected latter-day city of God has invaded invisibly into the present age in order that saints may now be able to participate in it. Likewise, Christ's priestly work of sacrificing himself has inaugurated the eschatological temple (cf. 9.8, 23).[24] Those who spurn Christ's 'once for all' sacrifice at the 'consummation of the ages' (9.26) are not able to be 'renewed to repentance', since there is no other sacrifice which will be offered again other than the one they have despised (6.4-6; 10.26-29).[25]

One striking feature of the eschatology of Hebrews, though also a trait of New Testament eschatology elsewhere, is that of its two-dimensional nature: it is characterized both by a vertical and horizontal plane, or both a spatial and temporal element. The preceding discussion has focused on the temporal aspect that the 'end-times' had begun in Christ's past work but also the final 'end' was still to come in the future. In the light of the spatial perspective, the end-time temple, for example, can be viewed both as a reality in present time and as being in a spatial dimension different from that of the material, earthly dimension (Heb. 9.1–10.26) because of the work of Christ.[26]

b. *Future.* There is debate about whether the 'rest' of Hebrews 3–4 has been inaugurated with Christ's first coming[27] or whether it is a reality only at the final consummation.[28] Both views are supported by viable arguments, though the futuristic conception of the rest is, perhaps, more likely. The emphasis throughout chs. 3–4, as well as the entire epistle, is upon persevering until the end when the final reward is to be received

24. See L.D. Hurst, 'Eschatology and "Platonism" in the Epistle to the Hebrews', in *SBLSP 23* (Chico, CA: Scholars Press, 1984), pp. 41-74.

25. Cf. C.E. Carlston, 'Eschatology and Repentance in the Epistle to the Hebrews', *JBL* 78 (1959), pp. 296-302.

26. See further Kreitzer, 'Eschatology', for the notion in Paul.

27. So C.K. Barrett, 'The Eschatology of the Epistle to the Hebrews', in W.D. Davies and D. Daube (eds.), *The Background of the New Testament and its Eschatology: Studies in Honour of C.H. Dodd* (Cambridge: Cambridge University Press, 1956), pp. 363-93; 366-73; A.T. Lincoln, 'Sabbath, Rest, and Eschatology in the New Testament', in D.A. Carson (ed.), *From Sabbath to Lord's Day* (Grand Rapids: Zondervan, 1982), pp. 197-220.

28. So R.B. Gaffin, 'A Sabbath Rest Still Awaits the People of God', in C.G. Dennison and R.C. Gamble (eds.), *Pressing toward the Mark* (Philadelphia: Committee for the Historian of the Orthodox Presbyterian Church, 1986), pp. 33-51.

(3.6, 14). Furthermore, the 'rest' is referred to as 'a promise' which 'remains', that is, has not yet been fulfilled (4.1, 6, 9). While it is true that the 'rest' is spoken of as being present (4.3: 'we... enter that rest') and even past (4.10: 'the one who has entered his rest'), these uses are best understood as being viewed from a future vantage point (e.g. 4.10 can easily be understood in the sense of a Hebrew prophetic perfect, referring to the certainty of a future event by speaking of it as if it had already happened). The dominant theme of these two chapters is that, in contrast to Israel's failure to enter the 'rest' of the promised land after its wilderness sojourn, and subsequently in its history, the Hebrew Christians are exhorted to persevere in their earthly sojourn so that they will enter the 'rest' of the antitypical 'heavenly country' (Heb. 11.16), which the land of Canaan typologically foreshadowed. Only then will the intended Sabbath rest of the new creation be enjoyed.

The coming judgment of unbelievers and apostates at the end of the age is a repeated theme in the epistle (6.2; 9.27), especially as a warning serving as encouragement to persevere (10.27-31, 36-38; 12.25-29; 13.4).[29] Those who pay heed to the warnings of judgment and the exhortations to persevere will receive at the consummation of history full salvation (9.28), their 'reward' (10.35; 11.26), and the complete inheritance of what was promised (6.11-12, 17-18; 9.15; 10.23, 34-35; 11.39). The inheritance of the promised land of the new earth is the author's irreducible summary of what true believers will receive at the eschaton (11.9-16; 13.14). God will raise them from the dead in order that they will be able to participate in the inheritance (11.35; cf. 6.20). This final inheritance will be indestructible (12.27-28) and eternal. There, God's presence can be more fully experienced (cf. 12.14). The readers should not be lax about these exhortations because the final 'day' is 'near' (10.25).[30]

---

29. Cf. S.D. Toussaint, 'The Eschatology of the Warning Passages in the Book of Hebrews', *GTJ* 3 (1982), pp. 67-80.

30. For further discussion of an 'already and not yet' notion of eschatology in Hebrews, see: Barrett, 'Eschatology of the Epistle to the Hebrews'; G.W. MacRae, 'Heavenly Temple and Eschatology in the Letter to the Hebrews', *Semeia* 12 (1978), pp. 179-99; and C. Woods, 'Eschatological Motifs in the Epistle to the Hebrews', in J.P. Lewis (ed.), *The Last Things: Essays Presented to W.B. West, Jr.* (Austin, TX: Sweet Publishing, 1972), pp. 140-51.

7. *The Eschatology of the Catholic Epistles*

a. *Past and Present*. An indication of the incipient form of the new creation occurs in Jas 1.18: 'as a result of exercising his will, he has given
birth to us by means of the word of truth in order that we should be a
kind of firstfruit among his creatures'. A full-blown allusion to the true
temporal nature of the time in which author and readers live appears in
ch. 5. There, James chastises people for living in ungodly ways and not
redeeming the opportunities for doing righteousness in view of the
significant time period in which they are presently living: 'It is in the
last days that you have stored up your treasure' (5.3). Because it is already the last period of history, the final 'coming of the Lord' and the
time of judgment for such unrighteous people is imminent (cf. 5.7-9).[31]

Like James, 1 Peter commences with a mention that the latter-day
new creation of believers has taken place: God has 'caused us to be
born again, unto a living hope, by means of the resurrection of Jesus
Christ from the dead'. Their new birth and consequent '*living* hope' are
integrally linked to Christ's resurrection as a basis. This new-age notion
is developed further in 1.20-21, where Christ's resurrection 'from the
dead' is portrayed as part of 'the end of the times' and where it is
through the resurrected Christ that the readership have become believers with a hope. It is through this same resurrection that Jesus has been
placed at God's right hand to begin ruling (3.18-19, 21-22). The latter-
day Spirit is the agent bringing about the resurrection of Christ (3.18),
as well as the resurrection life of his followers (4.6; whether physically
dead or alive) and their ongoing conduct in the sphere of that life (1.2).
Similar to Hebrews, Peter also speaks of Christ's death for sins with the
age-turning expression 'once for all' (3.18). Not only this, but the final
judgment even has been set in motion with the divinely ordained sufferings directed toward the Christian community, which serves to test their
faith (4.12-19).

2 Peter makes the most far-reaching reference to Christ's kingship by
observing that it commenced at the very beginning of his earthly ministry, when he was baptised (1.16-17). Christ and the apostles prophesied that false teachers would infiltrate the church community in 'the
last days' (2 Pet. 3.3; Jude 18 has 'last time'). Both 2 Peter and Jude
contend that this expected latter-day tribulation of apostate teaching

---

31. On the problem of imminence mentioned here and elsewhere in Hebrews,
the Catholic Epistles and Revelation, see Kreitzer, 'Parousia', as well as Allison,
'Eschatology', and Kreitzer, 'Eschatology'.

already has been expressed through the appearance of false teachers who were then attempting to pervert the truth in the very midst of the Christian community (cf. 2 Pet. 3.2-7, 16-17 with 2.1-22; 3.16-17; cf. Jude 17–18 with 4, 8, 10-13).

The Johannine epistles reveal an acute awareness that the eschaton has already broken into history. The most notorious expression indicating this is the repeated references to the 'Antichrist', especially in 1 Jn 2.18: 'Children, it is the last hour, and just as you have heard that Antichrist is coming, even now many antichrists have come; from this we know that it is the last hour.' There are false teachers, little 'antichrists', from within the community, who have since departed but are still threatening to deceive Christians about the nature of Christ's person and his commandments (cf. 2.22-23, 26; 4.1-6; 2 Jn 7–11). These deceivers, likely holding to a proto-gnostic form of doctrine, are the corporate embodiment of the beginning fulfillment of the Daniel 7–12 prophecy of an eschatological opponent of God's people who would deceive and arouse covenant disloyalty within the ranks of the community of faith; Jesus and Paul also further developed the Daniel prophecy (cf. Mk 13; Mt. 24; Lk. 21; 2 Thess. 2). 1 Jn 3.4 even identifies these false teachers with the covenantal 'lawlessness' which Daniel prophesied would characterize the deceivers who would arise from within the ranks of the faithful (cf. Dan. 12.10 [esp. cf. LXX with Theodotion]): 'Everyone who does the sin also does the lawlessness, and the sin is the lawlessness';[32] in this respect, the notion of 'lawlessness' is to be identified with the end-time sin of the 'lawless one' of 2 Thessalonians 2.

The upshot is that the readers need to be aware that they are living in the midst of the 'great tribulation' which has been expressed among them in the form of false teachers in order that they will not be taken off guard and be deceived. In fact, 'the sin to death' in 5.16 is best understood in the light of this highly charged latter-day context to refer to covenant community apostasy, that is, either deceiving others or allowing oneself to be deceived by the false teachers and, therefore, as never really having belonged truly to the community of faith and, subsequently, experiencing spiritual death (cf. 2.19; although not discussing

32. Cf. I.H. Marshall, *The Epistles of John* (NICNT; Grand Rapids: Eerdmans, 1978), pp. 176-77; I.H. Marshall, *1 and 2 Thessalonians* (NCBC; Grand Rapids: Eerdmans; London: Marshall, Morgan & Scott, 1983), pp. 188-90; S.S. Smalley, *1, 2, 3 John* (WBC, 51; Waco, TX: Word Books, 1984), p. 155; R.E. Brown, *The Epistles of John* (AB, 30; Garden City, NY: Doubleday, 1982), pp. 399-400.

the eschatological context, cf. Scholer who argues that 'the sin to death' is that committed only by pseudo-believers).[33]

From another perspective, Christ's life and death have such a cosmic impact on the world through his followers that it can be said that the old fallen *world of darkness* 'is passing away' (cf. 2.2, 8, 12-14, 17). The basis for the cosmic upheaval is that Christ's redemptive work has dealt a mortal blow to the evil ruler of the old age (3.8). Those who identify with Christ's redemptive work also participate in the victory over the Devil (2.13-14).

Alternatively, though the old world has begun to disintegrate spiritually, Christ's death and resurrection have also set in motion a new creation, so that there is an overlap of the old with the new: 'the darkness is passing away and the true light is already shining' (1 Jn 2.8). The resurrection life of the eternal age to come has begun in Jesus' resurrection and in the spiritual resurrection of his followers who identify with his death and resurrection (see 1 Jn 1.2; 2.17, 25; 3.14; 4.9; 5.11-13, 20, especially in the light of Jn 5.21-29). It is also the Spirit, which was prophesied to be poured out in the eschatological age (cf. Joel 2.28-32 in Acts 2.16-21 in sect. A.5 above), who gives assurance that one truly has entered into the midst of the divine presence characterizing the new age (3.24; 4.13).

b. *Future*. Judgment is also a significant theme in James (cf. 2.13; 3.1). People will be judged because of their selfishness, greed and persecution of the righteous (5.1-9). The day of the final judgment is near (5.7-9). In contrast, those who demonstrate true faith through good works will receive a reward at the Last Day (cf. 1.12; 5.7-9).[34]

1 Peter affirms that a day will come when God will impartially judge everyone by their works, whether or not they lived lives of godly obedience (1.17; cf. 4.17-18). Even now God 'is ready to judge the living and the dead' (4.5), since 'the end of all things has come near' (4.7). In the light of such an imminent judgment, believers are advised to live

---

33. D.M. Scholer, 'Sins within and Sins without: An Interpretation of 1 John 5:16-17', in G.F. Hawthorne (ed.), *Current Issues in Biblical and Patristic Interpretation* (Grand Rapids: Eerdmans, 1975), pp. 230-46.

34. See T.C. Penner, *The Epistle of James and Eschatology* (JSNTSup, 121; Sheffield: Sheffield Academic Press, 1996), who contends that an 'already-and-not-yet' eschatology is the primary framework within which to understand James, especially the ethical injunctions of the epistle.

circumspectly in order that they are not found deserving judgment
when it unexpectedly occurs. Those who are able to persevere in faithfulness will receive definitive 'salvation ready to be revealed in the last
time' (1.5; cf. 1.9) when Christ returns again (1.13) and his followers
can fully rejoice in the greater manifestation of his glory (4.13; cf. 5.1).
At this 'proper time' (5.6), believers 'will receive the unfading crown
of glory' (5.4), and God will 'perfect, confirm, strengthen, and establish' for all time those who have persevered to the end (5.10; cf. 5.6).
Another image of this final reward is that of receiving an 'inheritance'
which 'will not fade away' (1.4; cf. 3.9). The believers' 'hope' is
focused on this goal (3.15). When the final day comes, God's 'dominion' will be decisively manifested as being 'forever and ever' (5.11; cf.
4.11). Both the 'already' and 'not yet' aspects of the latter days in 1
Peter provide a theological framework for better understanding the
Christian's ethical obligation.[35]

The notion of the coming final judgment is picked up again in 2 Peter
(2.3, 9; 3.7)[36] and Jude (6, 14-15). At the time of this judgment, 'the
earth and its works will be burned up' (2 Pet. 3.7-13). This is likely a
literal expectation on the part of the author, though some understand it
figuratively, viewing it as a picture of an ethical purification of the
earth. A figurative view of the fiery judgment is especially affirmed by
some who favor the textual reading in 3.10 of 'the earth and its works
will be *found* [*or discovered*]', but this, if the original reading, probably
does not refer to the earth and what people have done as literally surviving through a judgment, but to the works of the wicked which *will
be laid bare*, so that the ungodly will not be able to escape judgment.[37]
The purpose of reflecting on the cosmic conflagration is pastoral and
ethical: to encourage saints to be holy in order that they should 'be
found' faithful when the expected judgment day occurs (cf. 3.11-12,
14). In contrast to the ungodly, they will find mercy on this dreadful

35. Cf. R. Russell, 'Eschatology and Ethics in 1 Peter', *EvQ* 47 (1975), pp. 78-
84; for an 'already and not yet' notion of eschatology in 1 Peter, see E.C. Selwyn,
'Eschatology in 1 Peter', in W.D. Davies and D. Daube (eds.), *The Background of
the New Testament and its Eschatology: Studies in Honour of C.H. Dodd* (Cambridge: Cambridge University Press, 1956), pp. 394-401.

36. Cf. J.R. Michaels, 'Eschatology in 1 Peter III.17', *NTS* 13 (1967), pp. 394-
401.

37. Cf. R.J. Bauckham, *Jude, 2 Peter* (WBC, 50; Waco, TX: Word Books,
1983), pp. 301, 316-21; cf. D. Wenham, 'Being "Found" on the Last Day: New
Light on 2 Peter 3:10 and 2 Corinthians 5:3', *NTS* 33 (1987), pp. 477-79.

day (Jude 21). The old creation, which is to be destroyed, will be replaced by 'a new heavens and a new earth' (2 Pet. 3.13), language reminiscent of Rev. 21.1, though both are based on the new creation prophecy of Isa. 65.17 and 66.22. At this time, the kingdom which was inaugurated at Jesus' first coming will be established in its completeness (2 Pet. 1.11), and God's people will stand in the immediate presence of his glory (Jude 24). The attribute of glory is an eternal, divine characteristic, which is possessed both by the Father (Jude 25) and the Son (2 Pet. 3.18), and which will be revealed clearly at the end of time.

1 Jn 2.28 and 4.17a together speak of the possibility of Christ's final 'parousia' occurring at any time, and that his readers should persevere ('abide') in their faith, so that when he should come, they should have confidence in obtaining salvation and not be ashamed and find themselves deserving wrath on 'the day of judgment'. Such perseverance until his coming will result in their becoming fully conformed to his likeness when he comes a final time because the faithful will finally be able fully 'to see him just as he is' (3.2). Those who maintain this 'hope' will be motivated in the present to begin to resemble his holy image (3.3; similarly 4.17b).

8. *The Eschatology of the Apostolic Fathers*

a. *Past and Present.* Like the New Testament, the Apostolic Fathers also understand that the blessings of the age to come have begun but have not reached their consummate form. Not uncommon is mention that the age in which the writers were living was also the time of the 'last days', which had commenced with the initial coming of Christ (e.g. *2 Clem.* 14.2; *Barn.* 12.9; 16.5). For example, it can be said that 'these are the last times' (Ignatius, *Eph.* 11.1), that 'Christ appeared at the end of time' (Ignatius, *Magn.* 6.1; likewise Hermas 89.3), and that Christians have a 'foretaste of things to come' (*Barn.* 1.7).

Comparable to the New Testament also, the early Fathers held so intensely to the inaugurated aspect of the end times that they even believed that the promised new creation had been set in motion. *Barn.* 6.13 can say that 'He made a second creation in the last days', which was modelled on the first creation: 'Behold, I make the last things as the first'. Hence, Christians had become 'new, created again from the beginning' (*Barn.* 16.8; likewise 6.11, 14) likely on the basis that their progenitor himself, Jesus Christ, was the representative 'new man' from whom they received their identity (cf. Ignatius, *Eph.* 20). Such thinking motivated some writers to assert that believers were already participating in the blessings of the Garden of Eden (*Diogn.* 12; Frag. Papias, *Trad. of Elders* 2). Such a heightened notion of inaugurated eschatology is apparently the basis for the seer's misguided question in the Shepherd of Hermas concerning whether or not 'the consummation had *already* arrived' (16.9).

Again, following the lead of New Testament writers, the Apostolic Fathers see an inextricable link between the beginning phase of the latter-day new creation and the resurrection of saints. Resurrection is the means by which believers become a part of the new creation, first spiritually at conversion, then physically at the end of the age at the final resurrection. Christ brought 'the newness of eternal life' (Ignatius, *Eph.* 19.3) by himself becoming a 'new man' (Ignatius, *Eph.* 20.1), as a result of his own resurrection. The inaugurated and consummated resurrection of Christians occurs because of their identification with Christ's resurrection (see respectively Ignatius, *Magn.* 9; Ignatius, *Trall.* 9.2; cf. *1 Clem.* 24.1; Polycarp, *Phil.* 2.2; *Barn.* 5.6-7). Those who believe in Jesus 'will live forever' (*Barn.* 11.11). Conversely, God has also commenced with the destruction of the old creation 'for his elect', (Hermas 3.4), which is likely best understood as beginning through Christ's own death (i.e. destruction of his old body) and resurrection; the resurrection put an end to the curse of death for God's people (Ignatius, *Eph.* 19.3; *Barn.* 5.6), so that even when believers die physically, ironically they enter into an escalated phase of their new birth and of their immortality (*Mart. Pol.* 19.2). Christ's resurrection is the decisive blow in defeating the Devil (Frag. Pap. 24), the prince of death, and those who remain faithful to Christ participate with him in completing this defeat (Ignatius, *Eph.* 13.1; Ignatius, *Trall.* 4.2). In this respect, Christ's resurrection is also the basis of his messianic reign (Polycarp, *Phil.* 2.1). Those who trust in Christ also enter into the kingdom during the present age (Hermas 93.2-4).

Not only is there a link between the eschatological new creation and resurrection, but also between the new creation and the notion that the church has become the 'temple' of God (Ignatius, *Eph.* 15.3; Ignatius *Trall.* 7.2; Ignatius, *Phil.* 7.2; *Barn.* 4.11), though this connection is explicitly made only in *Barnabas* (6.8-19; 16.1-10). The likely reason for associating the two concepts is that the Garden of Eden of the first creation was identified by later Old Testament writers as sanctuary-like,[38] and it became natural for New Testament writers and the early Fathers to make the same connection. Indeed, John's Apocalypse and *Barnabas* draw a parallel between the first creation, when Adam and Eve were placed in Eden, and the second creation of Christians as a temple (Rev. 21.1–22.5; *Barn.* 6.8-19). The same segment from *Barnabas* draws a parallel between Israel's promised land and the new creational temple of the church because the Old Testament depicts that land as 'Eden' (Gen. 13.10; Isa. 51.3; Ezek. 36.35; Joel 2.3) and Israel as a corporate Adam, who was chosen ideally to succeed where the first Adam failed.[39]

Presumably, these writers also view the gift of the Holy Spirit to be among the eschatological blessings (*1 Clem.* 2.2; 46.6), though this connection is drawn possibly only in *Barnabas* (cf. 1.3 with 1.7; likewise see Heb. 6.4-5).

In the Old Testament, the apparent chronology of predicted end-time events placed the final tribulation before the resurrection of the dead and the new creation (e.g. Dan. 11.35–12.12). Now, however, the Fathers, once again, follow the New Testament in placing the beginning of the final tribulation at the same time as the inaugurated new creation and its attendant blessings (as, e.g., also in Rev. 1.9!). The author of *Barnabas* understands that he is living in the 'last days', the 'age of lawlessness' (4.9), and 'the deception of the present age' (4.1; cf. 18.2), which is the inception and harbinger of the soon to be fulfilled Antichrist prophecy from Dan. 7.7-8, 24 (4.4-6; likewise cf. 2 Thess. 2.3-7 and 1 Jn 2.18, where 'lawlessness' is also used and is rooted in Dan. 12.10 [Theodotion]); that prophecy was apparently to begin more concrete fulfillment imminently, though not necessarily consummately, through the infiltration of false teachers in the church (cf. 4.1, 9-11; 18.1-2). Similarly, the Shepherd of Hermas contends that 'great tribulations' have already been suffered (7.1) which apparently prepare saints for '*the* coming great tribulation' (6.7; cf. 7.4; for a similar correspondence between a present 'great tribulation' and '*the* great tribulation' to come cf. respectively Rev. 2.22 and 7.14). Likewise, Hermas 'escaped a great tribulation' from a satanic beast which was 'a foreshadowing of *the* great tribulation that is coming' (23.4-5).

---

38. M.G. Kline, *Images of the Spirit* (Grand Rapids: Baker Book House, 1980), pp. 35-56.

39. Wright, *Climax of the Covenant*, pp. 21-26.

b. *Future*. The consummation of all things will be in the 'age to come' (Hermas, 24.5; *2 Clem*. 6.3). The *Epistle of Barnabas* states that at this concluding temporal point there will be a complete new creation: 'at this time all things [will] have been made new' (*Barn*. 15.7); the 'renewed creation' will be exceedingly fertile (Frag. Pap. 14). In connection to the preceding context in *Barnabas*, on the basis that 'a thousand years is like one day' (Ps. 90.4), *2 Enoch* 25–33 appeals to the seven days of creation in Genesis 1 and affirms that history will follow the same sevenfold pattern, the consequent reckoning of the historical age being 7000 years and a following 'eighth day', referring apparently to eternity.[40]

In relation to the same tradition, *Barnabas* 15 reckons history to last 6000 years, at the conclusion of which

> the Lord will bring everything to an end, for with him a day signifies a thousand years...in six thousand years everything will be brought to an end...it is not the present sabbaths that are acceptable to me, but the one [the Sabbath of the last thousand years] that I have made; on that Sabbath, after I have set everything at rest, I will create the beginning of an eighth day, which is the beginning of another world.

The Sabbath of the last thousand years merges into the eternity of the eighth day, 'the day on which Jesus both arose from the dead and ...ascended into heaven'. The last thousand years is figurative for the saints' eternal Sabbath rest and the eighth day of Christ's resurrection becomes figurative, not merely for eternity, but for the age of the saints' resurrection when eternal rejoicing begins; hence, the seventh and eighth day for *Barnabas* overlap and are virtually identical.[41] Irenaeus,

---

40. See A. Wikenhauser, 'Weltwoche und tausendjähriges Reich', *Tübinger Theologische Quartalschrift* 127 (1947), pp. 399-417, for a survey of how Ps. 90 and the days of creation influenced the church Fathers of the third and fourth centuries with respect to the duration of world history and the question of chiliasm.

41. See J. Daniélou, *The Theology of Jewish Christianity: The Development of Christian Doctrine before the Council of Nicea*, I (Chicago: H. Regnery, 1964), pp. 396-401, D.H. Kromminga, *The Millennium in the Church* (Grand Rapids: Eerdmans, 1945), pp. 29-40, and E. Ferguson, 'Was Barnabas a Chiliast? An Example of Hellenistic Number Symbolism in Barnabas and Clement of Alexandria', in D.L. Balch, E. Ferguson and W.A. Meeks (eds.), *Greeks, Romans, and Christians: Essays in Honor of A.J. Malherbe* (Minneapolis: Fortress Press, 1990), pp. 157-67, for a similar view of *Barn*. 15; for discussion of other viewpoints on *Barnabas* see J.W. Mealy, *After the Thousand Years* (JSNTSup, 70; Sheffield: JSOT Press, 1992), p. 48, who himself sees the last thousand years in *Barnabas* as the *beginning*

Against Heresies 5.28.3 and vv. 33-36 may follow the same line of thought as in *Barnabas* 15, though his view seems inconsistent and the consensus is that he was a premillennialist.

Just as an inextricable link has been observed between the inaugurated new creation and the resurrection, so the same connection exists between the final phase of both: 'when the righteous will rise from the dead and reign, when creation, too, [is] renewed' (Frag. Pap. 14). This will be the time of the consummated resurrection (*1 Clem.* 50.4; *2 Clem.* 19.3-4; Polycarp, *Phil.* 2.2; *Mart. Pol.* 14.2), eternal life (Hermas 24.5; cf. *Barn.* 11.11), and immortality (*1 Clem.* 35.1-4; *2 Clem.* 14.5). Interestingly, the tradition purportedly stemming from Papias associates the final resurrection of the righteous with the commencement of the millennial reign of the saints (Frag. Pap. 3.11-16).

Believers will enter the final form of God's kingdom at this time (*2 Clem.* 5.5; 11.7; 12.1-2, 6; Hermas 89.5, 8; 92.2) and will reign with the Lord (Polycarp, *Phil.* 5.2). Before this occurs, however, Christians must pass through a final tribulation of deception and persecution which is greater than any earlier trials (*Did.* 16.3-5; cf. also the notion of '*the coming great tribulation*' in Hermas 6.7; cf. 7.4).[42]

Therefore, the full reward of the true saint lies in the future and must be waited for in the present (*2 Clem.* 20.2-4). This reward will be given by the Son of God, when he comes to draw the present age to its conclusion (*Did.* 16.7-8; Hermas 58.3), though no one knows the time that this is to occur (*Did.* 16.1). Consequently, one must be constantly ready for his coming (*Did.* 16.1; cf. Herm. 114.4).

There will be final judgment for God's enemies and the unfaithful who are not prepared for Christ's coming (*2 Clem.* 18.2; Ignatius, *Eph.* 16.2; *Mart. Pol.* 11.2; *Barn.* 19.10); this judgment is imminent, and, in fact, is already on the way (*2 Clem.* 16.3). Continued awareness of the coming judgment serves as the basis of motivation for a believer's upright conduct (*2 Clem.* 18.2; *Barn.* 19.10). Christ himself will execute this judgment (Polycarp, *Phil.* 2.1; 6.2).

---

of the eternal age but not co-extensive with it, which is plausible; see Kromminga, *Millennium in the Church, passim*, for a thorough survey of the doctrine from the Apostolic Fathers up to the twentieth century.

42. On 'great tribulation' in Hermas, see further R.J. Bauckham, 'The Great Tribulation in the Shepherd of Hermas', *JTS* 25 (1974), pp. 27-40.

Consequently, there will be both salvific reward and judgment at the conclusion of history (*2 Clem.* 10.3-5; *Barn.* 4.12-14; 21.2-3, 6; Hermas 53).[43]

9. *The Eschatology of Revelation*

a. *Past and Present.* The technical vocabulary for the eschatological period ('latter days', etc.) found in most other New Testament books cannot be found in John's Apocalypse. Nevertheless, other kinds of terminology are used and the concepts of inaugurated and consummated eschatology are part of the fabric running throughout the book's texture.

The book opens with mention that Christ's resurrection has begun fulfillment of the prophesied resurrection of the saints (1.5: 'Jesus Christ...the firstborn from among the dead'). This resurrection results in placing Christ in the position of 'ruler of the kings of the earth' (1.5) and as the one who now possesses the keys of 'death and Hades' (1.18). The very same resurrection described in 1.5 is later explained to be none other than 'the beginning of the [new] creation of God' (in Rev. 3.14).[44] By virtue of his resurrection Christ has also continued to fulfill Daniel's prophecy about the end-time, world-wide reign of the Son of Man (cf. Dan. 7.13-14 with Rev. 1.13), as well as the Son of God's rule predicted in Psalm 2 (cf. Rev. 2.26-27; 12.5). Likewise, through the resurrection, Christ has been declared openly to be of equal status with God (e.g. 'I am the first and the last' [Rev. 1.17; 2.8; 22.13], based on the self-attribution of Yahweh in Isa. 41.4, 44.6, and 48.12).

Christ's followers are also identified with him in the present age, not only as subjects in his newly established messianic kingdom, but also as those who rule with him (Rev. 1.6, 9; 5.10, on which see further the debate of whether or not saints are only subjects of Christ's kingdom or whether they also actually rule with him).[45] The predominantly Gentile church has also begun to fulfill the prophecies of Israel's latter-day

---

43. For sources discussing patristic eschatology, see J. McRay, 'Charismata in Second-Century Eschatology', in J.P. Lewis (ed.), *The Last Things: Essays Presented to W.B. West, Jr.* (Austin, TX: Sweet Publishing, 1972), pp. 151-68.

44. On which see G.K. Beale, 'The Old Testament Background of Rev. 3:14', *NTS* 42 (1996), pp. 133-52 and Chapter 3, sect. E below.

45. Accordingly, see G.K. Beale, review of *After the Thousand Years* (JSNTSup, 70; Sheffield: JSOT Press, 1992), by J.W. Mealy, in *EvQ* 66 (1994), pp. 242-45; A.J. Bandstra, '"A Kingship and Priests": Inaugurated Eschatology in the Apocalypse', *Calvin Theological Journal* 27 (1992), pp. 10-25.

restoration (cf. Rev. 3.9 and the Old Testament allusions there to Isa. 45.14; 49.23; 60.14; 43.4; as well as the LXX of Isa. 41.8; 44.2; etc.).

These themes of Christ's resurrection and the beginning of his rule together with the saints as sparking off the beginning of latter-day events are notions we have seen elsewhere in the New Testament and Fathers.

b. *Future*. Revelation expects the final coming of Christ to occur at some point in the near future (e.g. 16.15; 22.7, 12, 17, 20). The visions of the book also express parabolically an expectation of his coming, especially to judge the ungodly (e.g. 6.12-17; 11.15-19; 14.14-20; 17.14; 19.11-21; cf. either Christ or God as the agent of judgment in 6.10-11; 11.11-13; 14.8-11; 16.17-21; 20.9-15; 21.8). Nevertheless, Christ will come also to reward and finally bless his people (11.18; 19.7-9; 21.1–22.5, 12, 14; possibly cf. 7.9-17). At this time, he will establish his kingdom in its final, complete and eternal form (11.15-17; 19.1; 22.5; cf. possibly 7.9-17). Directly preceding the last judgment and the full coming of the kingdom, there will be a tribulation of deception and persecution for God's people (e.g. 11.7-10; 16.12-14; 20.7-9; cf. possibly 3.10; 6.11; 7.14; 13.5-18), as well as a final period of torment for their persecutors (e.g. 16.21; 17.16-17; cf. 3.10). Many of these same future conceptions have been observed also in other New Testament literature.

c. *Some Special Problems of Eschatology in Revelation*. There are a variety of problems in Revelation which pertain to whether or not a number of topics and key passages in the Apocalypse are to be related to inaugurated eschatological realities or only to yet future eschatological fulfillment at the very end of the present age.[46] Some of these problems are dealt with directly below in this section, while others are of such magnitude that they deserve separate treatment on their own (e.g. for the latter cf. the problem of Rev. 1.1, 19 and 4.1 [below at sect. B] and the issue of the millennium, in the last chapter of the book).

(i). *The Problem of the References to Christ's Comings in Revelation 1–3 and 22*. Some of the references to Christ's 'coming' in the letters appear to refer to a conditional coming in judgment: if there is no repentance in response to the present warning, then Christ will come in a

---

46. On the problem in general, see A.J. Bandstra, 'History and Eschatology in the Apocalypse', *Calvin Theological Journal* 5 (1970), pp. 180-83.

pre-parousia judgment upon that particular church (so 2.5, 16; 3.3, 20, though this last reference refers to a conditional blessing). Some, however, argue that it is not Christ's coming which is conditional but only whether or not he will come to judge or reward at the *very end of history*, which is dependent on the response of the readers.[47] While possible, this is an overly subtle perspective since the protasis εἰ δὲ μή in conditional clauses in the New Testament elsewhere outside of Revelation is followed by an apodosis, *the whole* of which is always conditional (so 12 times). Therefore, both the activity of 'removing' *and* 'coming' are probably conditional in Rev. 2.5 (cf. the wording: 'I am coming to you, and I will remove your lampstand from its place, if you should not repent'). If the 'coming' as part of the protasis were not conditional in 2.5, clearer indications from the context would be needed. In contrast, the context of 2.5 points in the other direction, as the majority of commentators acknowledge, as they do also with respect to the similar statements about the comings in 2.16, 3.3 and 3.20 (e.g. Caird and Roloff, *in loc.*). The assertions about Christ's coming in 2.25 and 3.11 could well refer to the final parousia but they are not in the form of conditional statements.

Therefore, it is unlikely that the 'coming' in Rev. 2.5 is unconditional but the 'removing' is conditional. Furthermore, focusing on 2.5 as a test case in the debate, the actual wording 'I will remove your lampstand *from its place*' indicates removal of the church as a light of witness to the world, which points to the removal of it *before* Christ's final coming, since the churches' witness is a relevant activity only before the final advent, not afterward.[48] Indeed, part of the 'witness' is to the promise that Christ will return to judge and to redeem (see the relation of 'witness' to the final coming in 19.7-21 [cf. vv. 9-10]; 22.7-20 [cf.

---

47. Cf. R.J. Bauckham, 'Synoptic Parousia Parables and the Apocalypse', *NTS* 23 (1977), pp. 162-76 (173-74), who argues this for 3.3 and 3.20, and implies it for 2.5, 16; likewise, Holtz, *Christologie der Apokalypse*, p. 207; A. Satake, *Die Gemeindeordnung in der Johannesapokalypse* (WMANT, 21; Neukirchen–Vluyn: Neukirchener Verlag, 1966), p. 153; G.A. Krodel, *Revelation* (Augsburg Commentary on the New Testament; Minneapolis: Augsburg, 1989), p. 109; R.L. Thomas, *Revelation 1–7: An Exegetical Commentary* (Chicago: Moody Press, 1992), pp. 143-47, 154.

48. Thomas, *Revelation 1–7*, pp. 146-47, sees removal of the lampstand as indicating loss of witness, but inconsistently understands this as a judgment only at the final parousia.

vv. 8, 16, 20]).[49] This also suits the visionary context of Christ presently walking in the midst of the lampstands as their priestly custodian who repairs or removes according to their function.[50] This analysis likewise fits 2.21-22, where Jezebel's lack of repentance elicits from Christ a promise to send tribulation on her and her followers, which likely *precedes* the end of history, and appears to be limited to that particular situation. The report of Ignatius that the Ephesian church had repented and regained their love suggests that the early church also understood that the admonition of 2.4-5 was not tied exclusively to a second coming circumstance (see Ignatius, *Eph.*).

Nevertheless, it must be admitted that to attempt to see 2.25 and 3.11 as strictly parallel to the other comings is plausible. And this would be the best argument that in 2.5, 2.16, 3.3, and 3.20 it is not the coming of Christ that is conditional but only the effect of that coming. But should the conditional comings be interpreted by the non-conditional ones or vice-versa? It is probably best to see them as not precisely identical but to view the conditional comings to be local interventions during the church age and the non-conditional ones as referring to the final parousia, although even the latter could allude to pre-parousia comings, which has precedent in the application of the Dan. 7.13 'comings' to Christ's ministry (Mk 10.45; Lk. 7.34; 19.10) and his judgment of Jerusalem (Mt. 10.23; Mk 13.26; 14.62).[51] Perhaps there is an intended ambiguity in these sayings because of the inaugurated nature of Christ's eschatological coming in the New Testament generally, which is evident specifically in Revelation 1 (cf. 1:5, 7, 13-18), as well as in chs. 2-3 (where the descriptions of Christ's inaugurated kingship from ch. 1 introduce each of the letters). The prophesied coming of the messiah has begun fulfillment, is presently being fulfilled, and will be consummated at some point in the future. The ambiguity of the comings in the letters is plausibly to be understood as an expression of this tension between the 'already and not yet', which has been the dominating thought throughout the first three chapters (see the following discussion of 1.7 directly below), and, as we have already seen, is woven throughout the warp and woof of the entire New Testament.

This conclusion is also corroborated by others who have proposed that the dual eucharistic theme of promise and judgment is woven

49. See similarly Bauckham, *Climax of Prophecy*, pp. 166-67.
50. Cf. likewise Mounce, *Revelation*, p. 89.
51. France, *Jesus and the Old Testament*, pp. 227-39.

throughout the letters and that part of the imagery is drawn from a eucharistic background (cf. most prominently 2.17, 20). In the Eucharist believers experience repeated anticipation in the present of the judicial and salvific effects of Christ's final coming.[52] This same background in the letters suggests that Christ is likewise present and 'coming' among the churches, so that his parousia is not merely a definitively future event.[53] The identification of the Spirit with Christ in the conclusion of all the letters would fit well with this line of thought, so that his salvific presence with the churches is through the Spirit, and his threatened judgment will occur also through the Spirit's visitation.

In connection with the repeated affirmations of Christ's 'comings', Rev. 1.7 needs special discussion, since some understand it to be introducing the main idea of the entire book: 'behold, he is coming with the clouds, and every eye will see him, even those who pierced him, and all the tribes of the earth will mourn over him'. This text has already received some analysis above (Chapter 2, sect. D.4a.(i)), where it was found that John's use of Daniel 7 and Zechariah 12 in Rev. 1.7 indicated a beginning fulfillment of those Old Testament prophecies in a somewhat unexpected manner. Consequently, in this light, Christ's 'coming' in that verse is an 'already and not yet' reality.

Furthermore, as discussed above, Christ's 'coming' in the letters appears to refer to his conditional visitation in judgment of the churches, though allusion to Christ's final coming could be included (cf. 2.5, 16; 3.11; see likewise 16.15). Observable also is the use of the same phrase ἔρχομαι ταχύ ('I come quickly') in 2.16 and 3.11 (cf. 2.5) to indicate Jesus' conditional comings, as well as in 22.7, 12, and 20 to refer apparently to the certainty of his final coming. As also mentioned in Chapter 2, this points to a close link between the comings in the letters and in the conclusion to the book. Therefore, not only Christ's 'coming' in 1.7, but his 'comings' elsewhere in the Apocalypse are understood better as a process happening throughout the interadvent age, so that his

52. Cf. Moule, 'Influence of Circumstances'. See also G. Wainwright, *Eucharist and Eschatology* (New York: Oxford University Press, 1981), p. 151. (On the judgment theme of the Lord's Supper, see also pp. 80-83. For a more thorough elaboration on the 'already and not yet eschatological and new creation' nature of the Eucharist, see esp., pp. 37-41, 68-70, 77, 80-83, 106, 147-54.)

53. So Sweet, *Revelation*, pp. 35, 41-42, 82, and Prigent, *Apocalypse et Liturgie*, pp. 14-45, although a number of Prigent's proposed parallels are not convincing (e.g. against Prigent see E.F. Scott, *The Book of Revelation* [London: SCM Press, 1939], pp. 140-41).

so-called 'second coming' is really a final coming, concluding the whole process of comings.[54] In Dan. 7.13 the son of man's 'coming' indicates his reception of authority to exercise end-time rule over the entire world. This idea from Daniel 7 is understood in Rev. 1.7 and in the other 'comings' of Revelation to begin fulfillment at the resurrection and continue fulfillment until the son of man's final coming at the conclusion of history.

(ii). *The Problem of When the Saints Begin to Reign.* There is disagreement among commentators about precisely when the reign of Christians in the messianic kingdom begins in the book of Revelation. J.W. Mealy is a recent example of one who understands the reign of the saints to be limited exclusively to a purported future millennium and on into eternity. However, to be able to do so he de-emphasizes the inaugurated eschatology of the Apocalypse. Among instances of this is his argument that Rev. 1.6 ('He made us to be a kingdom, priests to His God') says nothing about the present reign of the saints but only that they are conferred with 'an identity as priests to the King's God',[55] and that they have 'citizenship' in the kingdom but do not yet possess 'kingship'.[56] Their 'kingship' will come only at the parousia when the millennium is established. It is likely, however, that on a first reading of 1.6 by someone who has no eschatological agenda uppermost in mind the verse would more naturally be understood to affirm that both kingly and priestly authority begin to be conferred on the saints during the present age. Just as the saints already exercise priestly authority, as virtually even all futurist commentators agree, so it is likely that they already exercise authority of the kingdom.

The reign of believers during the interadvent age is also apparent from Rev. 1.9: 'I, John, your fellow-partaker in the tribulation and kingdom and perseverance in Christ Jesus'. Since Christ has begun to reign in fulfillment of Old Testament kingdom prophecies (Rev. 1.5, 13-20), so those who are 'in Him' share in what He possesses. Furthermore, if the 'tribulation' and their active 'perseverance' through tribulation were a present reality, so likely is their active participation in sharing Christ's kingly authority through corporate representation (*'in*

---

54. So also C. Brütsch, *Clarte de l'Apocalypse*, p. 31, citing others also in support.

55. Mealy, *After the Thousand Years*, p. 32.

56. Mealy, *After the Thousand Years*, p. 84.

Christ'). As they persevere through tribulation they reign ironically. To differentiate citizenship in the kingdom from kingship on the basis of 1.6, 9 is possible, but it is an overly scrupulous distinction. In addition, if the elders sitting on thrones with crowns in Rev. 4.4 represent in any way exalted Christians ruling in heaven, then the reign of saints has at least been inaugurated in the heavenly realm (note the elders on heavenly thrones in heaven also in 11.16, and their presence in heaven around God's throne in 7.11 and 19.4).

Similarly, Mealy repeatedly affirms that Rev. 5.10b refers to the rule of Christians on the earth which will begin only at Christ's future coming.[57] He translates the crucial clause in 5.10b as 'they *will* reign on the earth'. But some MSS read a present tense instead of future: 'they *are reigning* on the earth.' In support of the present tense is A 1006. 1611. 1841. 2329. 𝔐^K, while support for the future is found in ℵ 1854. 2050. 2053. 2344. 2351. 𝔐^A lat. co; Hipp Cyp. Both readings have equally good textual support so that internal evidence must be the deciding factor. Commentators are divided on which reading should be preferred.[58] But Mealy does not refer to the textual problem at all. He apparently assumes without any argument the validity of the future tense reading and uses it as a key prooftext to demonstrate that it will be *on the earth* that saints will reign only during a future millennium.

On 1.6 and 5.10 Mealy apparently is following the analysis of R. Schnackenburg,[59] whom he says has a 'judicious discussion' on this subject.[60] However, Schnackenburg does not clearly argue in favor of Mealy's view (e.g. Schnackenburg says that saints 'partake of Christ's eschatological reign' and that their being called a 'kingdom' means that they are presently 'kings' as well as 'priests'). Though he underscores future fulfillment of the saints' reign in his discussion, he appears to include in his view an inaugurated aspect of that reign. Schnackenburg's student, E. Schüssler Fiorenza,[61] does argue along the same lines of Mealy, though he does not cite her at this point, as he does at other

57. Mealy, *After the Thousand Years*, pp. 32, 108, 110, 116, 216, 238.

58. See Beale, *Book of Revelation*, in loc., for further analysis of the textual problem and for an argument on internal grounds that the present tense is more preferable.

59. R. Schnackenburg, *God's Rule and Kingdom* (New York: Herder & Herder, 1963), pp. 330-31.

60. Mealy, *After the Thousand Years*, p. 32.

61. E. Schüssler Fiorenza, *Priester für Gott: Studien zum Herrschafts und Priestermotiv in der Apokalypse* (Münster: Aschendorff, 1972), e.g. pp. 330, 338.

points. His omission in discussing, much less demonstrating, his conclusion about Rev. 1.6 and 5.10 is a significant oversight, since this conclusion is an important part of his argument against the inaugurated reign of the saints and against the notion that the millennial reign of Revelation 20 has been inaugurated in the present age.[62]

He also sees that the promises to the overcomers in the letters of chs. 2 and 3 have fulfillment only in the future, new creation.[63] The promise that overcomers, however, will receive white robes (3.4-5) and crowns (2.10) and will sit on Christ's throne (3.21) appears to be fulfilled in some sense in 4.4 where the elders sit on thrones (so also 11.16), wearing white garments and crowns (cf. also 4.10). If the elders are associated with exalted Christians in any way (whether as identical, personified, representatively, symbolically, etc., as many commentators hold), then the promises to the overcomers begin to come true in the saints' heavenly existence (the promises probably even have application to pre-death existence in the light of such texts as 1.5, 9; 2.9; 3.11, 20; 5.10; cf. 2.17 with 3.1). Indeed, that exalted saints receive white robes at death is clear from 6.11. And the purported *consummate* respite from temporal affliction pictured in 7.15-17 (according to Mealy)[64] also begins instead, according to 6.11 and 14.13, with the saints' pre-parousia 'rest' in heaven (7.15-17 may even be a merged picture of 'already and not yet', though the expectation of rest in 21.4 is clearly future). In 2.17 overcomers are promised an eschatological meal with Christ, and in 3.20 Christ says that believers not yet having experienced death may partake of that meal with him. If saints conclude their 'overcoming' at death (so 12.11), it makes much sense that their reward for overcoming (such as sitting with Christ on his throne in 3.21) would begin to be given in their exalted state at the time of death.

If Revelation portrays an inaugurated and consummate form of Christ's reign, it is logical that the same two-stage reign of the saints could well be posited. But it could be argued that since Christ's inaugurated reign began only after his bodily exaltation in heaven, the inaugurated reign of Christians could begin only after their bodily resurrection at the end of the age. However, Revelation also pictures believers in non-bodily form as exalted in heaven after death but before their bodily resurrection (see references above). This could certainly qualify them to

62. Mealy, *After the Thousand Years*, pp. 31-32.
63. Mealy, *After the Thousand Years*, pp. 82-84, 216-19.
64 . Mealy, *After the Thousand Years*, pp. 216-19.

be eligible candidates for an office of inaugurated kingship. The picture of elders sitting on thrones in heaven confirms that this is in fact the case (see above on 4.4, 10). And when ascriptions like 1.6, 9 and 5.10 are applied to the saints, it is also suitable to understand them in the light of inaugurated kingship.

Therefore, it is an *argumentum ad hominem* when Mealy says that the idea of an inaugurated millennium (commonly known as 'amillennialism') 'has lost nearly all support by Revelation specialists in this century, on the valid grounds that it fails to do justice to the unique [futuristic?] eschatological perspective of Revelation itself'.[65] First, such a sweeping statement, at least, needs to be supported by significant and numerous bibliographical references of scholars on both sides and discussion of these sources. Second, Mealy's definition of 'specialists in this century' is vague, since at crucial points he himself relies on scholars who have written very little on the Apocalypse (e.g. Schnackenburg, Metzger, etc.) or who wrote in the last century (U. Smith). Thirdly, there are significant Revelation 'specialists' who see the saints participating in inaugurated promises to the overcomers and in promised kingship. I chose randomly from commentaries on the Apocalypse and found commentators generally divided over the issue: for example, some held to the present, active reign of saints in 1.6, 9 and 5.10 together with a consummate, future stage of that reign,[66] while others affirmed that only a future reign was in mind in the same passages.[67] We should heed Paul S. Minear's warning about making hard and fast 'temporal and spatial' judgments, especially with respect to some aspect of John's eschatology.[68]

---

65. Mealy, *After the Thousand Years*, p. 19. See ch. 6 below for my own view and analysis of the millennium in Rev. 20.

66. E.g. P.S. Minear, *I Saw a New Earth: An Introduction to the Visions of the Apocalypse* (Washington: Corpus Books, 1969), p. 232; Beasley-Murray, *Revelation*, pp. 57-58, 64; Sweet, *Revelation*, p. 130; Caird, *Revelation*, pp. 17, 20; Alan Johnson, *Revelation* (The Expositor's Bible Commentary, 12; Grand Rapids: Zondervan, 1981), p. 424.

67. E.g. Isbon T. Beckwith, *The Apocalypse of John* (New York: Macmillan, 1919), p. 429; Schüssler Fiorenza, *Priester für Gott*; A.Y. Collins, *The Apocalypse* (New Testament Message, 22; Wilmington, DE: Michael Glazier, 1979), p. 8.

68. P.S. Minear, 'The Cosmology of the Apocalypse', in W. Klassen and G.F. Snyder (eds.), *Current Issues in New Testament Interpretatiom: Festschrift for O.A. Piper* (New York: Harper & Row, 1962), pp. 23-37.

(iii). *The References to the Promises in Relation to the 'Overcomers' in the Letters of Revelation.* This issue has been touched on briefly in the preceding section, but more elaboration is needed. Not only do some commentators view the fulfillment of these promises to occur only in a future millennium or new cosmos, but some also understand the 'overcomers' to refer only to a special sub-class of Christians who are martyrs and who are to suffer in a final tribulation at the very end of the age.

The 'overcoming' repeatedly mentioned at the conclusion of each of the letters, however, probably occurs *before* the believer inherits the consummate form of the promises also cited at the end of each letter. For example, the 'conquering' of sin (so 2.4-5; 2.14-16; 2.20-24) entails being ironically conquered by the world. That is, when believers refuse to compromise with the world, they are really conquering the world in a spiritual manner, even though they are persecuted and defeated by the world on the material level. This is just as true in the other five churches as it is in Smyrna and Philadelphia, even though there is no overt mention of persecution in the other five. But it is clear that these five all have problematic sins which affect their witness in the world, so that, if they overcome their sin, they will encounter suffering from the world, as have Smyrna and Philadelphia. Hence, the church which perseveres in its witnessing faith wins a victory on earth before the consummation of history, even though it suffers earthly defeat.

The use of νικάω ('to conquer, overcome') in 12.11,15.2, and Rom. 8.35-37 confirms that overcoming in the letters is best understood individually, ironically, and as an inaugurated event, not merely a yet future reality on a corporate level. The ironic conception of νικάω ('to conquer') is modelled after that of Christ's end-time 'conquering', as is evident from 3.21. In 5.5-6 and Jn 16.33 Christ's conquering is ironically interpreted as being accomplished through his death on the cross. Likewise, the description of suffering saints who overcome in Rom. 8.36-37 is strikingly similar to that of Rev. 5.5-6: compare 'as sheep of slaughter...*we overwhelmingly conquer*' of Romans with Rev. 5.5-6, '*he overcame*...a lamb standing as having been slain'. Following this line of thought the Syriac Peshitta defines the saints' 'overcoming' and Christ's victory in Rev. 2.26-28 as being 'shattered, even as I [Christ] was disciplined by my Father'.

This usage may be linked to or developing a Jewish exegetical tradition which applied νικάω ('to conquer') to the Maccabean martyrs who were said to have conquered because they maintained their faith in God's law, even though they were defeated from the earthly perspective through suffering and death: in this manner they 'conquered the tyrant' who was persecuting them (*4 Macc.* 1.11; 6.10; 7.3; 9.6, 30; 11.20-21; 16.14; 17.12-18).

This paradoxical and inaugurated latter-day notion of 'overcoming' is enhanced by two observations: (1) the beast of Revelation is spoken of as 'overcoming' the saints by imposing some form of physical suffering upon them (11.7; 13.7) and (2) Christ and the saints are referred to with the identical word as 'overcoming' the beast by maintaining their faithful testimony while enduring such suffering (cf. 5.5-6; 12.11; as well as 15.2; 17.14). The origin of this ironic application of νικάω ('to conquer') to the beast and to Christ and the saints may lie in Dan. 7.21 which refers prophetically to the end-time opponent overcoming the saints. John quotes this contextually in 11.7, 12.7b, and 13.7 but then ironically twists it to refer to Jesus and the saints in 17.14 and to the angels in 12.7-8.[69]

The eschatological promises to the overcomers are not to be viewed as intended only for those who suffer martyrdom for their faith, as Charles, Kiddle, and Caird, among others, contend,[70] but to all true believers.[71] It is not just the way people die which proves them to be overcomers, but the whole of their Christian lives are to be characterized by 'overcoming', which is a process completed upon death. Therefore, overcoming refers to the victory of one's whole life of faith, as is also the case in 1 John (cf. 1 Jn 5.4-5! See also 1 Jn 2.13-14). All the uses of 'overcome' (νικάω) in 1 John refer to not succumbing to false teaching from within the community, which is underscored likewise in the letters to Pergamum and Thyatira in Revelation.

The end-time promises to the overcomer in these letters all pertain to the salvific blessing of communion with God which provides all the essentials of life (security, home, power, food, clothing and a name). Therefore, these promises likely apply to all believers who are included in the household of God.[72]

---

69. In this respect, see Beale, *Book of Revelation*, on 11.7, 12.7-8, 13.7, 17.14.

70. E.g. Charles, *Revelation*, I, p. 54; Caird, *Revelation*, pp. 27-28, 33-34, 58; M. Kiddle and M.K. Ross, *The Revelation of St. John* (MNTC; London: Hodder & Stoughton, 1940), pp. 61-65.

71. See further Beale, *Book of Revelation*, excursus on Rev. 2.28.

72. Minear, *I Saw a New Earth*, p. 60; cf. Rev. 21.3, 7; 22.3-4.

This conclusion is supported by the observation that all the promises to the overcomers in the letters are described in the final vision of the book (21.1–22.5) and generally refer to participation in the eternal kingdom of God. They include protection from judgment (2.10; 3.5), an inheritance in the city of God (3.12), participation in Christ's reign (2.26-28; 3.21) and eternal life (2.7; 3.5).

Christians taste the inaugurated fruits of some of the latter-day promises cited in the seven letters even before they die. The inaugurated aspect of some of the promises can be discerned from an analysis of Rev. 2.7,[73] as well as from the concluding promises in each of the letters (as already elaborated upon earlier at more length): compare the reigns of 2.26-27 and 3.21 with 1.5-6, 9; 2.17b; compare the 'crown' of 2.10 with 3.11 and 4.4; compare the white garments of Rev. 3.4-5, 18 with 4.4 and 6.11. In fact, if the process of 'conquering' for the believer is completed at one's death, then it is probable that the promises to the conquerors begin to some degree also at death. John probably viewed the eternal life mentioned in 2.7 and 2.10-11 as inaugurated in that the believer becomes identified through faith with Jesus' death and resurrection (cf. 1.5, 18), and, therefore, becomes identified with the incipient eschatological realities in which Jesus himself began to participate. If Christ's 'comings' in some of the letters include pre-second coming visitations, then the saints' overcoming and attendant promises would also begin before the final consummation (e.g. see on Rev. 2.5 above at sect. A.9.c.1).

(i). *The Problem of the Delay of the Parousia in Revelation.* Because of the design of the present chapter, discussion of this issue must be found elsewhere in the most relevant literature.[74]

Brief comment, however, is necessary concerning the relationship of apparent statements of imminence in relation to the notion that the final coming of Christ has been delayed. Some of the expressions often classified under the category of 'imminence' may not be references exclusively to the near future, but could be 'already and not yet' allusions,

73. Cf. below; see further on 2.7 in Beale, *Book of Revelation*.

74. In addition to the most prominent commentary literature, cf. also Kreitzer, 'Parousia'; C.L. Holman, *The Origin of Christian Eschatology* (Peabody, MA; Hendrickson, 1996), who contends that the tension between expectation and delay in New Testament eschatology is rooted in the same tension in the Old Testament and Jewish apocalyptic.

which lessens some of the tension inherent in sayings referring only to a near expectation without any element of beginning fulfillment of the expectation (e.g. 'what must occur quickly' [Rev. 1.1; 22.6; on which see sect. B below]; 'the time is near' [Rev. 1.3; on which see sect. B below]; 'he *is coming* with the clouds' [Rev. 1.7; on which see Chapter 2, sect. D.4a.(i) above]; 'I *am coming* quickly' [22.7][75]). The reason that inaugurated eschatology in Revelation, and the New Testament in general, diminishes the tension of an unfulfilled hope of a yet final, consummate end is because now a significant degree of fulfillment has occurred in comparison to the radically unfulfilled hopes of the Old Testament and intertestamental Judaism (though there were lesser degrees of initial fulfillment even in the Old Testament and intertestamental period).[76] In contrast, the notion of beginning fulfillment could paradoxically include the expectation of a consummate, imminent fulfillment, since one might assume that, once initial fulfillment had begun, complete fulfillment could not be far off.[77]

10. *Conclusion*

The 'already and not yet' notion of eschatology is a major theme which runs throughout the New Testament, from the Gospels all the way through to Revelation and the earliest Fathers. Revelation is of a piece with this full-orbed, end-time concept. Many commentators consider Revelation to be a unique New Testament book in the sense that they believe that it is predominately a prophecy about yet-future events (especially the visionary portion of chs. 4–21). The brief discussion of the Apocalypse so far points to it being a book about how the latter days have begun, are continuing their course, and how they will be consummated. The following sections of this chapter will point further in this direction, where additional problems of eschatology in Revelation will be discussed separately because of their important bearing on the overall understanding of eschatology in the book. Some reference

---

75. On which see Beale, *Book of Revelation, in loc.*, as well as on Rev. 6:11; 10.7; 12.12.

76. On which see Holman, *Origin of Christian Eschatology*, pp. 169-70.

77. In this respect, cf. Holman, *Origin of Christian Eschatology*, p. 168, who has made the seminal statement that New Testament inaugurated eschatology (though Holman less accurately refers to this as 'realised eschatology') is the 'best explanation' both for an 'imminent expectation' and 'eschatological delay'. Cf. further Holman, *Origin of Christian Eschatology*, pp. 161-70.

has been made already to the bearing of the Old Testament on problems and issues of eschatology; the following sections of this chapter will focus even more on how John's use of the Old Testament affects his eschatology.

B. *The Interpretation of Revelation 1.19:*
Its Old Testament Background and its Disputed
Significance as an Interpretative Key to the Whole Book

Revelations 1.19 says the following: 'Now write what you see, what is, and what is to take place hereafter' (RSV). The meaning of this verse has been understood as the key verse to the interpretation and the structure of the Apocalypse. Though nearly all agree, however, about the verse's importance in decoding the book, few agree about its exact meaning.

On the whole, scholars have taken several approaches concerning the relation of Rev. 1.19 to the Apocalypse as a whole, some of which have sub-variants. A new view will also be discussed.

It is the purpose of this section to survey some of these approaches, to describe and evaluate each of them, and to suggest ways in which a proper understanding of the verse might involve more than one view. A 'new' view will be described first, and then the other perspectives will be summarized and understood in relation to how the 'new' view could serve as supplemental to each. Finally, from among these views, some preferred views will be selected, all in the hope of making the 'mystery' of Rev. 1.19 much less mysterious.[78] The importance of the following discussion is crucial since it forms part of the foundational argument for why this monograph understands the entire Apocalypse, and not merely chs. 1–3, to pertain to the time of past and present, as well as the future.

1. *The 'New' View: That Revelation 1.19c is a Conscious Eschatological Expression from Daniel 2.28-29, 45 (View i)*
Rev. 1.19 is the most important of a series of verses in the book[79] which also allude to Dan. 2.28-29, 45. This view differs from the previous

---

78. For fuller discussion of all these views, and of sub-variants of them, as well as for explanation of other views, see the more thorough analysis in G.K. Beale, 'The Interpretative Problem of Rev. 1:19', *NovT* 34 (1992), pp. 360-87.

79. The other verses are Rev. 1.1; 4.1; 22.6.

ones based on the assumption that 1.19 has as much or more to do with the *eschatological* nature of the book than with its actual literary or historical *structure*. That is, Rev. 1.19 highlights not so much the chronological order of the visions nor the order of the events that the visions represent, but it focuses upon these events to describe the climactic end of the ages.

That Rev. 1.19 is based upon and shares a common context with Dan. 2.28-29, 45 will be demonstrated by showing the influence of Daniel 2, not only in Rev. 1.19c, but also in three critical parallel passages of Revelation (1.1; 4.1; 22.6); since these key texts in the book allude to Daniel, it is likely that Rev. 1.19c, perhaps the most critical passage of all, does so also.

a. *Revelation 1.1*. The place of Rev. 1.1 in the context of Revelation is generally thought to be well understood, for this verse provides the introduction for, and probably the title to, the book. However, it is the *sources* of the verse, Dan. 2.28-29, 45, which provides the alert reader with a clue to the purpose of Revelation. Indeed, the parallels between Rev. 1.1 and Dan. 2.28-29 make a connection highly likely:

Daniel 2.28 (LXX)[80]	Revelation 1.1
ἐδήλωσε...ἃ δεῖ γενέσθαι ἐπ᾽ ἐσχάτων τῶν ἡμερῶν ('he showed...what things must take place in the latter days')	δεῖξαι...ἃ δεῖ γενέσθαι ἐν τάχει ('to show...what things must take place quickly')

But if the two verses are in fact connected, how does one explain the changes between the two verses?

First, δεῖξαι ('to show') and ἐδήλωσε ('to show') are semantic equivalents.[81] Second, and more importantly, the change in the latter phrase from ἐπ᾽ ἐσχάτων τῶν ἡμερῶν ('in the latter days') to ἐν τάχει ('quickly') is neither random nor purposeless, but provides insight into

80. Virtually identical to the LXX are Theodotion of Dan. 2.28 (cf. 2.29, 45) and the LXX of Dan. 2.45. Ἀποκαλύπτω is used repeatedly in these verses of Dan. 2 (Theodotion) and σημαίνω is also found (2.45 of LXX), thus exhibiting further affinity with Rev. 1.1.

81. Both words describe the role of the prophets in revealing what God has 'shown' them: e.g. see δείκνυμι in Amos 7.1, 4, 7; 8.1; Zech. 1.9; 2, 3; 3.1; Jer. 24.1; Ezek. 11.25; 40.4; 43.10; Dan. 10.1; likewise, δηλόω is used *thirteen* times in Dan. 2 to describe the revelation of the content of Nebuchadnezzar's visionary dream, which the prophet Daniel summarized before the king (cf. similarly in Dan. 7.16). In contrast, δείκνυμι occurs exclusively in Revelation.

the relation John understands to exist between Revelation and Daniel. Some understand ἐν τάχει[82] to designate the speedy manner of its fulfillment (*how* it will be fulfilled), while others view the clause to connote the imminent time of fulfillment (*when* it will be fulfilled). The phrase appears to indicate that fulfillment has begun (that it *is being* fulfilled), or will begin in the near future. Simply put, John understands Daniel's reference to a distant time to refer to his era, and updates the text accordingly.[83]

This change implies that what Daniel expected to occur distantly 'in the latter days'—the defeat of cosmic evil and the ushering in of the divine kingdom—John expects to begin 'quickly', in his own generation, if it has not already begun to happen.[84] Therefore, if this allusion in Rev. 1.1 is understood by John in the light of the eschatological context of Daniel 2, then he may be asserting that the following contents of the whole book are to be conceived of to a significant extent within the thematic framework of Daniel 2 (and its parallel apocalyptic chapters, such as Dan. 7). Indeed, there is much in Revelation 1 to suggest that this is the case: common references to (1) the kingdom (vv. 6, 9; cf. Dan. 7.14) being possessed by (2) a 'son of man' (1.7, 13; cf. Dan. 7.13-14), who is described in a (3) theophanic vision (vv. 13-15; cf. Dan. 7.9-10) strongly suggest that Daniel 2 and Revelation 1 describe the same event, and are linked as promise and fulfillment. Furthermore, that the events of vv. 6, 9, 13-15 are all present realities indicates that the fulfillment of Daniel 2 is not merely imminent, but is taking place in his very presence.

Additional evidence that Rev. 1.1 describes the commencement of the fulfillment promised in Daniel 2 is found in its immediate context, Rev. 1.3, where the phrase ὁ γὰρ καιρὸς ἐγγύς ('for the time is near') is found. The phrase may be taken as an exaggerated expression of imminence: the time is not simply coming soon, but is actually *here*. If someone said that an invading army had drawn near and were just this

---

82. See Mounce, *Revelation*, pp. 64-65, for discussion of various interpretative options concerning this phrase.

83. Cf. M. Wilcock, *I Saw Heaven Opened* (London: Inter-Varsity Press, 1975), pp. 32-33, who seems to have come close to making the same observation in Rev. 1.1.

84. John's understanding of Dan. 2 as having already begun fulfillment is not unique in the New Testament. Lk. 20.18 (= Mt. 21.44) quotes Jesus as equating the 'stone' of Dan. 2.34-35 with his own ministry. The same 'inaugurated end-time' view of Dan. 2.35 is probably also apparent in Rev. 12.8.

minute stepping foot on the beaches along Boston's North Shore, the reference to their 'nearness' would allude both to the fact that the invasion had just commenced and a greater stage of the invasion was even imminent. In support of such a notion being included in the nearness clause of Rev. 1.3, Mk 1.15 reads πεπλήρωται ὁ καιρὸς καὶ ἤγγικεν ἡ βασιλεία τοῦ θεοῦ ('the time is fulfilled, and the kingdom of God has drawn near'), where Jesus uses this phrase to describe not merely the nearness of his ministry and of the kingdom, but *the actual inauguration of them.* In other words, if the kingdom had truly drawn near,[85] and had actually just begun during Christ's earthly ministry, how much more present was the kingdom in John's day, especially since he uses a similar fulfillment formula?[86]

Given these strong textual and thematic parallels between Rev. 1.1, 3 and Daniel, the very least that can be said is that the wording of these Revelation texts refers to the immediate future. It is much more likely, however, that John views the death and resurrection of Christ as inaugurating the long-awaited kingdom of the end-times predicted in Daniel 2.[87]

In summary, understanding Rev. 1.1 in the light of Daniel 2 makes sense for textual reasons (v. 1 is an overt allusion to Dan. 2), contextual reasons (vv. 1, 3b, 6, 9, 13-15 share a common view of Dan. 2 and 7), and thematic reasons (v. 1 describes the beginning of the end that was predicted in Dan. 2).

---

85. The perfect tense ἤγγικεν seems to indicate the completion of a past event (the beginning of the end times), the effects of which were still being felt, both in Mark's day, and John's.

86. It is significant that some see this second phrase in Mk 1.15 as an allusion to the prophecy in Dan. 7.22 (e.g. C.H. Dodd, *According to the Scriptures* [New York: Charles Scribner's Sons, 1953], p. 69, and F.F. Bruce, *New Testament Development of Old Testament Themes* [Grand Rapids: Eerdmans, 1970], pp. 23-30; although cf. *contra* France, *Jesus and the Old Testament* , p. 139).

87. Cf. Rev. 1.5-6, 9, 13-18, which view the promised kingdom as beginning its fulfillment in the present. It is also possible that Rev. 1.3 is an allusion to Lk. 21.8, where ὁ καιρὸς ἤγγικεν also has the significance of 'fulfilment in the present' (for the possibility of the allusion see Vos, *Synoptic Traditions in the Apocalypse*, pp. 178-81). If nothing else, both Mk 1.15 and Lk. 21.8 may be in mind and at least are representative as parallels with Rev. 1.3b. Indeed, the additional verbal parallel in Lam. 4.18 suggests the possibility that this figurative language was idiomatic.

b. *Revelation 1.19*. The conclusion of the Revelation 1 vision comes in vv. 19-20, which could also serve as another introduction. The threefold phrase of v. 19 may represent a further adaptation of the threefold clause in v. 8b (cf. v. 18a) or a commonly used phrase like it.[88] The third part of the formula in v. 19 (ἃ μέλλει γενέσθαι μετὰ ταῦτα)[89] reflects the wording of v. 1 (ἃ δεῖ γενέσθαι ἐν τάχει), which, as shown above, is drawn from Dan. 2.28-29a, 45-47 (ἃ δεῖ γενέσθαι ἐπ᾽ ἐσχάτων τῶν ἡμερῶν).[90] Since the Daniel 2 references treat μετὰ ταῦτα as synonymous with ἐπ᾽ ἐσχάτων τῶν ἡμερῶν (on which see following note and chart), both referring to the general era of the end times, John may also be using μετὰ ταῦτα as an eschatological reference, particularly to the general period of the latter days which had commenced, was presently ongoing, and would continue in the future until the consummation.[91] This would not be an exclusively future reference, but would be consistent with the inaugurated end-time outlook of the Daniel 2 allusion in Rev. 1.1 and of the immediate context

88. See W.C. van Unnik, 'A Formula Describing Prophecy', *NTS* 9 (1963), pp. 86-94, described in detail in view 6 below. The relevant phrase in Rev. 1.8 reads 'the one who is and who was and who is coming', which is identical to 1.4b.

89. Although μέλλει replaces Daniel's δεῖ in most MSS of v. 19, δεῖ is present in some: cf. ℵ* *pc* (δεῖ μέλλειν), 2050 *pc* latt (δεῖ), C (δεῖ μέλλει); cf. Josephus, *Ant.* 10.210.

90. The wording most resembles Dan. 2.45 (Theodotion) ἃ δεῖ γενέσθαι μετὰ ταῦτα.

91. Proof for this all-important assertion is found in that the MT 'after this' (*'aḥᵃrē dᵉnāh*) of Dan. 2.29 is in synonymous parallelism with 'in the latter days' of Dan. 2.28, which strongly implies that the former phrase has eschatological import (cf. C.F. Keil, *Biblical Commentary on the Book of Daniel* [Biblical Commentary on the Old Testament; Grand Rapids: Eerdmans, 1971], pp. 111-12). The Greek translations confirm the synonymous nature of these phrases by using them to translate the MT. Theodotion uses μετὰ ταῦτα for Dan. 2.29, 45, *while in the very same verses the old LXX version reads* ἐπ᾽ ἐσχάτων τῶν ἡμερῶν, making more explicit the latter-day sense implicit in the 'after this' (*'aḥᵃrē dᵉnāh*) of the Aramaic text (note also that Acts 2.17 renders the *'aḥᵃrē-kēn* of Joel 3.1 [= μετὰ ταῦτα in the LXX version] with ἐν ταῖς ἐσχάταις ἡμέραις). Therefore, in Dan. 2 μετὰ ταῦτα is an eschatological expression that is synonymous with, but not as explicit as, ἐπ᾽ ἐσχάτων τῶν ἡμερῶν. Likewise in Revelation, μετὰ ταῦτα may be a packed eschatological expression in Rev. 1.19 and 4.1. That is, with reference to Rev. 1.19 and 4.1, μετὰ ταῦτα likely does not function as a simple literary or general temporal transition marker to the next vision, but is a phrase describing the end times, the eschatological 'after this' of which Daniel spoke.

throughout Revelation 1 and the New Testament generally (on which see further n. 103 below). This notion would be enhanced further by noticing that even the book of Daniel itself understood the general era of the latter days as undergoing incipient inauguration in the time of the Babylonian empire (in this respect, see further on excursus at discussion of Rev. 4.1 at sect. B.l.c.l below). A comparison of the Daniel and Revelation texts may help to highlight the equivalence of the 'latter days' of Dan. 2.28 with the 'after this' of Dan. 2.29, 45 and Rev. 1.19c:

Daniel 2	Daniel 2
Dan. 2.28 (Theodotion): ἃ δεῖ γενέσθαι ἐπ' ἐσχάτων τῶν ἡμερῶν ('what things must take place *in the latter days*')	
Dan. 2.29 (LXX): ὅσα δεῖ γενέσθαι ἐπ' ἐσχάτων τῶν ἡμερῶν ('what must take place *in the latter days*');	*Dan. 2.29 (Theodotion)*: τί δεῖ γενέσθαι μετὰ ταῦτα ('what must take place *after these things*');
Dan. 2.45 (LXX): τὰ ἐσόμενα ἐπ ἐσχάτων τῶν ἡμερῶν ('the things which will be in *the latter days*')	*Dan. 2.45 (Theodotion)*: ἃ δεῖ γενέσθαι μετὰ ταῦτα ('what must take place *after these things*')
	Revelation 1.19c
	ἃ μέλλει γενέσθαι μετὰ ταῦτα ('what is about to [what must] take place *after these things*')

The assertion that Dan. 2.29a, 45 lies behind Rev. 1.19b may be confirmed, not merely from textual similarities between the verses themselves, but also by the similarities of their respective contexts.

In this regard, a term worthy of examination is μυστήριον ('mystery') which is found in Rev. 1.20 and Dan. 2.29, 47, where both references have nearly identical contexts. In Daniel 2, God is twice praised as the consummate revealer of mysteries (μυστήρια), and the references occur at the beginning and end of Daniel's divinely-inspired interpretation of Nebuchadnezzar's dream. Similarly, in Revelation 1, the divine son of man figure begins the interpretation of John's initial vision by revealing (and being the revealer of) the lampstand 'mystery' (μυστήριον). Furthermore, John's vision describes a 'mystery' containing: (1) the inaugurated fulfillment of the office of the Danielic 'son of man' (cf. Dan. 7.13) as messianic king, the beginning fulfillment of which is participated in by (2) the Church (cf. vv. 6, 9) and (3) guardian angels of the churches (cf. 1.20 and the introductions to the letters in chs. 1-3).[92] This contextual understanding of 'mystery' in 1.20 and its direct link with Rev. 1.19c point further to the notion that the Daniel 2 allusion in v. 19c is an inaugurated latter-day reference and not exclusively about the future.

There are two objections to seeing Rev. 1:19 as an allusion to Daniel. The first is that the texts do not agree closely enough; Rev. 1.19 reads μέλλει ('is about' or 'is necessary'), not δεῖ ('is necessary'), the latter of which appears in Daniel (and Rev. 1.1, 4.1, 22.6). In response, it is quite possible that the original text of Revelation may well have included δεῖ. Though possible,[93] it is more probable that δεῖ is a secondary insertion, resulting from a scribal attempt to conform the wording of v. 19c to that of 1.1, 4.1b and 22.6b.[94] A more satisfying explanation regards John's use as a paraphrase, not a literal quotation. Since Josephus twice paraphrases ἃ δεῖ γενέσθαι (or the MT equivalent) of Dan. 2.28, 29, 45 with τὰ μέλλοντα (and later τί γενήσεται),[95] it is certainly plausible for John to have done the same.

The second objection is that, given the fact Rev. 1.19 is one of seven threefold formulae (though the wording varies) in Revelation,[96] since no other formulae allude to Daniel, it is unlikely that Rev. 1.19 does either. In response, it should be noted that there is no necessary reason why a threefold formula could not also contain an allusion to Daniel. Indeed, Josephus' paraphrase of Dan. 2.28-29, 45 is part of a threefold temporal formula, with only the final clause being based on Daniel: 'I [Josephus] am expected to write of what is past and done and not of *what is to*

92. Μυστήριον ('mystery') occurs in the LXX with a latter-day notion only in Daniel. Cf. μυστήρια and τὸ μυστήριον following ἃ δεῖ γενέσθαι in Dan. 2.28-30, but μυστήρια precedes the same phrase in 2.28a. The above evidence shows that Isa. 48.6 (ἃ μέλλει γίνεσθαι) is likely not alluded to in 1.19c, a point with which most commentators agree (Moffatt, *Revelation*, p. 347, seems to be the only commentator who sees Isa. 48.6 as an allusion, though he adduces no argumentation in support). But even if Isaiah were in mind, the idea would be very similar to the Daniel context. Both Daniel and Isaiah prophesy of the coming latter days in which God and Israel will reign over the nations; John's contribution is in saying that this end-time prophecy has begun fulfillment.

93. See above n. 89 and MSS ℵ* C 2050 pc latt; cf. Josephus, *Ant*. 10. 210.

94. At the very least, the variant readings reflect an early interpretative tradition identifying 1.19c with the formulae of 1.1, 4.1b, and 22.6b.

95. *Ant*. 10.210, 267.

96. The other threefold formulae occur in 1.4, 8, 17; 4.8; 11.17; 17.8.

be'.[97] Another example of a threefold formula which alludes to Daniel is *Barn.* 1.7, 'for the Lord made known to us through the prophets' τὰ παρεληλυθότα καὶ τὰ ἐνεστῶτα καὶ τῶν μελλόντων ('things past and present and the things about to be').[98] This reference is highly significant because δοὺς ἀπαρχὰς ἡμῖν γεύσεως ('giving us the firstfruits of the taste [of things about to be]') immediately follows, indicating that the 'things about to be' have, indeed, begun in the midst of the readers' lives;[99] consequently, this bears a roughly contemporary witness within the early Christian community also to an inaugurated understanding of Dan. 2.28-29, 45 like that argued above for Rev. 1.1 and 1.19. That both in Josephus and *Barn.* 1.7, a threefold formula clearly alludes to Daniel 2, makes it quite viable that Rev. 1.19 also may contain such an allusion. It may be a mistake, however, to identify Rev. 1.19 as being composed of a threefold formula (on which see the discussion of view 6 below).

Given the great number of textual and contextual similarities between Rev. 1.19 and Dan. 2.29a, 45, it may be said that Rev. 1.19 clearly draws from Daniel 2.

c. *Revelation 4.1.* In the light of the allusions to Daniel 2 observed in Revelation 1, it seems significant that the introduction of the next major section in the book at Rev. 4.1 also contains an allusion to Daniel 2.[100]

97. Interestingly, the temporal scope of the phrases in Dan. 2.28-29, 45 themselves, while primarily focusing on the future, include secondary reference to the immediate past and the present (so Dan. 2.37-38).

98. The linkage with Daniel is inferred by comparing the last two parts of the formula ἐνεστῶτα καὶ τῶν μελλόντων of *Barn.* 1.7 with τῶν ἐνεστώτων...τοῦ νῦν καιροῦ...εἰς τὸν μέλλοντα in *Barn.* 4.1. The phrases in *Barn.* 4.1 develop the twofold formula of *Barn.* 1.7 and weave it in as part of an introduction to formal quotations from Dan. 7.7-8, 24. The point of the quotations is to identify the 'deception of the present time' in 4.1 as a beginning fulfillment of the fourth and last evil kingdom prophesied by Daniel.

99. This inauguration of 'things about to be' is further emphasized in the immediately following line of *Barn.* 1.7, 'and seeing each of these things severally coming to pass', which refers to fulfillment of each of the three time periods composing the temporal formula at the beginning of 1.7. In *Barn.* 5.3 such fulfillment is the basis for the readers' insight into the prophetic revelations of 'things past... and...present...and...things about to be', which is a repetition of the earlier formula in *Barn.* 1.7.

100. Most commentators see 4.1 as an introduction to a new section in the book, and the majority of these view it as introducing all the visions up to the end of the

Not only does the wording of 4.1 closely reflect Dan. 2.28-29, 45,[101] but also the allusion is apparently used in the same way as in 1.1 and 1.19:

Daniel 2.28 (LXX)	Revelation 4.1
ἐδήλωσε... ἃ δεῖ γενέσθαι ἐπ᾽ ἐσχάτων τῶν ἡμερῶν ('he showed... what things must take place *in the latter days*') *Theodotion of Dan.* 2.29, 45 τί δεῖ γενέσθαι μετὰ ταῦτα ('what must take place *after these things*'); ἐγνώρισεν... ἃ δεῖ γενέσθαι μετὰ ταῦτα ('he made known... what must take place *after these things*'); cf. further the chart of textual comparisons in the discussion on Rev. 1.19 above.	δείξω σοι ἃ δεῖ γενέσθαι μετὰ ταῦτα ('I will show you what must come to pass *after these things*')

As in 1.19, μετὰ ταῦτα is likely synonymous with Daniel's general end-time phrase ἐπ᾽ ἐσχάτων τῶν ἡμερῶν,[102] so that the visions following 4.1 are also not merely about the eschatological future, but are more broadly eschatological visions, some of which have been inaugurated and others which still await consummation.[103]

---

book (e.g. Merril C. Tenney, *Interpreting Revelation* [Grand Rapids: Eerdmans, 1957], pp. 70-71; Beasley-Murray, *Revelation*, pp. 25-26; Sweet, *Revelation*, p. 47).

101. Above all, cf. Dan. 2.29, 45 of Theodotion; see the above textual comparisons for Rev. 1.19, although it could be a composite of all the similar Daniel 2 phrases.

102. See above on n. 91 and the analysis of Rev. 1.19.

103. This receives corroboration, not only from the Dan. 2 allusion in Rev. 1.1 and 1.19, but also from the use of the phrase ἐπ᾽ ἐσχάτων τῶν ἡμερῶν and synonymous expressions elsewhere in the New Testament often in an inaugurated sense: cf. Mk 1.15; Acts 2.17; Gal. 4.4; 1 Cor. 10.11; 2 Cor. 6.2; Eph. 1.10; 1 Tim. 4.1ff.; 2 Tim. 3.1ff.; 1 Pet. 1.20; 2 Pet. 3.3; Heb. 1.2; 9.26; Jas 5.3; 1 Jn 2.18; Jude 18; some exceptions appear to be 1 Pet. 1.5 and Jn 6.39-40, 44, 54, which seem to refer only to the future, but in the light of Jn 11.24-26, 40-44 and 12.1 even the phrases from John 6 have reference to Jesus' own day. Indeed, 1 Pet. 1.5 refers to a period called the 'last time' and it is directly linked to the phrase 'the last of times' in 1.20, which is a period already having been set in motion. Cf. R.L. Thomas, 'The Kingdom of Christ in the Apocalypse', *The Masters Seminary Journal* 3.2 (1992), pp. 117-40 (126-28) who has concurred with my conclusions in earlier publications that Dan. 2 is crucial for the structure and theology of Revelation, but affirms that John did not understand the Dan. 2 prophecy as having begun fulfillment but that it still awaited future realization.

Therefore, if μετὰ ταῦτα in Rev. 4.1b has reference to Daniel's inaugurated eschatology, then all the subsequent visions need not refer to a time period after that of chs. 1–3, but only that they are further visions concerned with an explanation of the 'latter days', both in their 'realized' and 'unrealized' aspects.

Interestingly, the vast majority of futurist commentators have taken Rev. 4.1 as one of the most obvious supports for their position. However, the present overall discussion indicates that the μετὰ ταῦτα clause is a general end-time reference to past, present and future events along the continuum of New Testament redemptive history. Again, the point needs underscoring, that if the present discussion concerning Rev. 4.1 is valid, and given the fact that the end times began before Revelation was written, then this text cannot be made to assert that all of the visions after 4.1 refer either exclusively or predominantly to the future.

It is possible to object to 4.1 as a Daniel allusion, if the text were punctuated with a period following γενέσθαι, with μετὰ ταῦτα εὐθέως ('after these things immediately') beginning the next sentence. Such a reading may have patristic support. Ambrose in his commentary on Luke[104] cites Rev. 4.1b without the final μετὰ ταῦτα, though this may result merely from his own selectivity and not from a text actually omitting the final phrase. Jerome begins a quotation of 4.2 with μετὰ ταῦτα in his commentary on Daniel.[105] Lachmann and Westcott and Hort choose as their preferred readings the omission of μετὰ ταῦτα at the end of v. 1 and the addition of it at the beginning of v. 2.

In response to this objection, the probability that Daniel 2 is in fact alluded to is suggested by observing that the ἃ δεῖ γενέσθαι parallels of 1.1, 1.19 and 22.6 (for the latter see below) are all allusions to Daniel 2, and all occur at major literary joints of the book, as does 4.1. Such an allusion to Daniel 2 would be suitable to introduce chs. 4–5, which themselves are modeled on Daniel 7.[106] Furthermore, the likelihood that a temporal phrase follows ἃ δεῖ γενέσθαι in 4.1 is made likely by observing that the other instances of ἃ δεῖ [or μέλλει] γενέσθαι in Revelation are directly followed by temporal phrases (either ἐν

104. Ambrose, *Exp. Ev. Sec. Luc.* 7.893-99.

105. Jerome, *In Danielem* 2.607-10. Griesbach notes the readings of Ambrose and Jerome in the apparatus of his edition of the Greek New Testament.

106. For such a Daniel model see Beale, *Use of Daniel*, pp. 178-228.

τάχει, as in 1.1 and 22.6, or μετὰ ταῦτα, as in 1.19).[107] Finally, most modern commentators and editions of Greek texts acknowledge either a parallel or allusion to Dan. 2.29, 45 in Rev. 4.1. In conclusion, it is likely that Rev. 4.1 is an allusion to Daniel 2.

(i). *Excursus to Revelation 4.1.* Alan Johnson has argued that the phrase 'what must take place after these things' in Rev. 4.1b refers to what is after the present time of the writer. Therefore, the following visions of chs. 4–22 pertain to a period after the time of the historical churches addressed in the letters.[108] Some commentators even understand the phrase at the end of 4.1 to mean that the events narrated in 4.2–22.5 will not commence until after the entire church age, during a period of tribulation which directly precedes Christ's final coming.[109] Johnson's own view is based on Keil's analysis of the phrase in Dan. 2.28, 29, 45, where the same conclusion is drawn with respect to the Daniel context. However, Keil also affirms that the events 'which must occur after-wards' include the immediate future of the then-reigning king Neb-uchadnezzar, as well, and, therefore, of the writer himself.[110] Conse-quently, Johnson's conclusion that this phrase refers to a period after the time of the historical churches of the letters is not supported by Keil's study. But even in contrast to Keil, strictly speaking, the 'latter days' of Dan. 2.28 (equivalent to 'after this', Dan. 2.29, 45), to which the *entire* dream (consisting of all four kingdoms) and interpretation are said to refer, includes not only the immediate and distant future but also the immediate past and present. This is evident from observing that the head of gold in Dan. 2.37-38 is identified as Nebuchadnezzar in his *present* reign ('You *are* the head of gold'), yet the description of his reign in vv. 37-38 is holistic so that, not only the immediate future, but also the recent past are included in the identification. This could further support our above conclusion that the Dan. 2.28-29, 45 allusion in 1.1, 19 and 4.1 refers to the 'latter days' having been inaugurated in the past and continuing in the present and into the future. Nevertheless, the pri-mary focus of Daniel's 'latter days' is surely on the establishment of

107. Though note the discussion concerning the possible reason behind the vari-ation in 1.19, at sect. B.1.b. above.

108. So Johnson, *Revelation*, pp. 461, 464.

109. So, e.g., see J.F. Walvoord, *The Revelation of Jesus Christ* (London: Mar-shall, Morgan & Scott, 1966), pp. 101-102.

110. Keil, *Commentary on the Book of Daniel*, pp. 111-12.

God's kingdom in the future, which we have argued John views to have been inaugurated.

Therefore, the phrase 'what must take place after these things' in Rev. 4.1b does not indicate that the events pictured in the following chapters of the book occur after the time of the historic seven churches of the letters nor after the whole period of the so-called church age.

d. *Revelation 22.6*. This last reference to Daniel 2 introduces the concluding section of exhortations.[111] The text of 22.6 corresponds precisely to that in 1.1 (δεῖξαι τοῖς δούλοις αὐτοῦ ἃ δεῖ γενέσθαι ἐν τάχει). Surely this is no accident. It is also likely that the phrase again is used similarly, as in 1.1, as a reference to Daniel 2 (see the discussion there [at sect. B.1.a]).

In summary, the above analysis has attempted to establish that Rev. 1.19 is an intentional allusion to Dan. 2.28-29, 45, a conclusion which the majority of commentators accept, though none has attempted to any significant degree to explore the interpretative use of the allusion.[112] However, the preceding discussion has argued on the basis of lexical and structural parallels that 1.1, 1.19c, 4.1, and 22.6 are all conscious allusions to Daniel 2; the parallels between 1.19c and the other three Daniel 2 allusions confirms that 1.19c is also a Daniel 2 allusion. Additionally, the verses all make use of Daniel 2 contextually, and understand the prophecy to have an 'already and not yet' end-time sense, referring to the latter days which had begun but were not yet consummated.[113] The Old Testament context of Daniel 2 is one which fits well thematically with that of Revelation.

The preceding discussion warrants the conclusion that John is *consciously* introducing major sections of his book by the Daniel 2 allusion. A further conclusion can be drawn with respect to the significance of the allusion in 4.1. Although it is no doubt legitimate to divide 4.1–22.5 into various subsections, John also may have conceived of it as a

111. The verse may also serve as a conclusion to the preceding section (as with 1.19 above at sect. B.1.b).

112. Perhaps one reason for this is that some may not think the allusion to be intentional. Of course, if John is not conscious of the allusion, then any attempt to find interpretative implications of it is futile.

113. The only author who comes close to this conclusion is Boring, *Revelation*, p. 84, who paraphrastically renders v. 19 as 'those [visions of chs. 4–22] that picture the eschatological future that is already dawning'. Unfortunately, he does not discuss the reasons which led him to this translation.

broad unity. This unity is evident by observing that 'the visions of destruction (6-20) are bracketed by the overarching vision of God the Creator and Redeemer' in Revelation 4–5 and 21.1–22.5.[114] As mentioned already, using the allusions to Daniel 2 as markers for the broad structure of Revelation gives the following broad outline: (1) 1.1-18 (introduction); (2) 1.19–3.22; (3) 4.1–22.5; (4) 22.6-21 (conclusion).[115]

This structural scheme could receive further corroboration from noting that the phrases in Dan. 2.28-29 introduce the vision proper in the Daniel 2 account (2.31-35), and the same phrase in 2.45b is part of the formal conclusion of the narrated vision. Likewise, the same phrases from Daniel introduce and conclude the vision section of Rev. 4.1–22.6,[116] thus indicating dependence, not just on the words of Daniel 2, but upon its structure as well. The concluding function of the phrase in Rev. 22.6b is highlighted by the initial phrase of that verse affirming that the visions of all the previous chapters are 'faithful and true' (πιστοὶ καὶ ἀληθινοί), a phrase based, not surprisingly, on the conclusion of the Daniel 2 vision.[117]

If it can be concluded that these allusions to Daniel 2 are intentional,[118] forming the outline of Revelation, then there is an exegetical basis for proposing that the content of the dream in Daniel 2 provides a crucial framework within which to interpret the content of the Revelation,[119] a framework of the inaugurated latter-day judgment of cosmic evil and the establishment of God's eternal kingdom. That Daniel 2 is

114. Sweet, *Revelation*, p. 47.

115. So also independently H.W. Günther, *Der Nah—und Enderwartungshorizont in der Apokalypse des heiligen Johannes* (FzB, 41; Würzberg: Echter Verlag, 1980), p. 65.

116. Or even 1.1–22.6, given the parallel wording of 1.1 and 22.6b.

117. Cf. Dan. 2.45b of Theodotion: ἀληθινὸν τὸ ἐνύπνιον, καὶ πιστὴ ἡ σύγκρισις αὐτοῦ ('the dream is true and its interpretation is faithful'). The presence of this phrase in conjunction with ἃ δεῖ γενέσθαι (cf. Dan. 2.45a Theodotion) makes it even more likely that Dan. 2.45 is the source of Rev. 22.6.

118. Some might prefer to see the phrase of 1.19c (and its parallels) as a stereotyped prophetic formula ultimately based on Daniel, though by John's time perhaps used by Christian prophets with no conscious reference to Daniel. However, the above discussion of textual comparisons of 1.1, 1.19, 4.1 and 22.6 pointed to both the probability that Dan. 2 was the source for the expressions, and that its use was, in fact, conscious and overt.

119. Cf. L. Goppelt, *Typos* (Grand Rapids: Eerdmans, 1982), p. 197, who suggests that Dan. 2.28 is 'the guiding principle' of Revelation because of its strategic occurrence in Rev. 1.1; 1.19; 4.1; 22.6.

used contextually is apparent from recognizing that in John's other *conscious* uses of the Old Testament throughout the book varying significant degrees of respect for the Old Testament context are evident.[120] Based on the assumption that John's other Old Testament citations and allusions are used contextually, the conclusion follows that John's use of Daniel 2 in Revelation in general, and in Rev. 1.19 in particular, is also contextual.

It will now be insightful to survey alternative interpretations of Rev. 1.19 in the light of the above analysis of the Daniel 2 allusion in Rev. 1.19c and to consider the bearing of the Daniel 2 allusion upon these other views.

2. *The Chronological Sequence View (View ii)*

19a	19b	19c
ch. 1	chs. 2–3	chs. 4–22

Many commentators see Rev. 1.19 as denoting a straightforward, three-fold, chronological division of Revelation[121] (and the history of the church in relation to the world). It is important to note that in this view, the three clauses of Rev. 1.19 describe consecutive, mutually exclusive periods of the entire history of the church age; they do not overlap:

   (a)   'what you have seen' refers to the previous vision of ch. 1, which concerns the events of the first century;

   (b)   'the things which are' relates to Revelation 2–3, and describes the condition of the churches in Asia Minor (and the world)

---

120. I have attempted to argue this point in depth above (Ch. 2: 'The Various Ways John Uses the Old Testament'). The approach of arguing that the New Testament uses the Old Testament with significant respect for context has been set forth trenchantly by Dodd, *According to the Scriptures*, and most recently, in a more nuanced and updated manner, by R.B. Hays, *Echoes of Scripture in the Letters of Paul* (New Haven: Yale University Press, 1989). For an analysis and evaluation of recent literature on this issue *pro* and *con* see Beale, *Right Doctrine from Wrong Texts?*

121. See also E. Lohse, *Die Offenbarung des Johannes* (Göttingen: Vandenhoek & Ruprecht, 1960), p. 19; R.L. Thomas, 'The Chronological Interpretation of Revelation 2–3', *BSac* 124 (1967), pp. 321-31; G.E. Ladd, *A Commentary on the Revelation of John* (Grand Rapids: Eerdmans, 1972), p. 34. This position has been popularized by H. Lindsey, *There's a New World Coming* (New York: Bantam Books, 1975), e.g., pp. 18-19, 25.

during the 'church age', the time extending from the first century until the commencement of the 'Great Tribulation';

(c) the 'things about to take place after these things' applies exclusively to 4.1–22.5,[122] and narrates the final tribulation,
which will begin directly before the very end of history and
will continue for a brief period until Christ's final coming to
conclude history.

Though the chronological perspective is undoubtedly a popular understanding of Rev. 1.19, making chs. 4–22 come alive with tantalizing
insight into future world events, there are weighty problems with such
an understanding of this verse. The main objection to this view is that it
interprets Revelation without sufficient sensitivity to its literary form,
giving a straightforward, literal reading of the book, rather than using a
figurative approach, more appropriate to its symbolic genre (on which
see ch. 4 below).

Another objection to the chronological understanding of Rev. 1.19 is
that, since both Revelation 2–3 (which supposedly describes only the
'church age') and Revelation 4–22 (the future 'Great Tribulation')
contain repeated references both to the past[123] and future,[124] neither
Revelation 2–3, nor 4–22 can be understood to be strictly chronological. Therefore, since these chapters are described in some sense by Rev.
1.19, if Revelation 2–3 and 4–22 are not strictly chronologically different from one another, then 1.19 may be contemporary with them.

Not only does the larger section of Revelation 4–22 describe events
of past, present and future, but the subsections of that broader segment
recapitulate, describing the same events in different ways (on which see
further on Chapter 3, sect. C below, and secondary source references
therein).

To the potential objection that the past and future references are merely tangential allusions to past or future events[125] occurring throughout

---

122. Though sometimes the last section pertaining to the future is seen to begin
at ch. 6 or even later.

123. With respect to past references, see chs. 2–3, both with respect, e.g., to the
initial vision of Rev. 1 and Christ's redemptive work; cf. 12.1-5 concerning the
latter period of the Old Testament and the life of Christ.

124. E.g. in chs. 2–3, with respect to the promises to the 'conquerors' and the
exhortations about Christ's coming.

125. Much as the New Testament quotes or alludes to the Old Testament (past)
or contains prophecy (future).

the account, and not an essential part of the larger narrative, one might respond that there is no reason that this be the case. An *a priori* assumption that the events of Revelation *must* be in the rigid chronological order of future history wrongly too often prevents one from holding a view of recapitulation. Indeed, it is just as likely that the allusions in the 'chronological' account are in fact organic parts of sections that each deal with past, present and future events occurring throughout Revelation, and throughout history.

Regarding specific textual matters, the chronological perspective wrongly understands μετὰ ταῦτα ('after these things') in 1.19 (and 4.1) to denote consecutive eras in world history. While this phrase can have this meaning, it is not required by the context, which possibly could point to the meaning of μετὰ ταῦτα being the mere order of visions in which John saw them (on which see below, sect. B.4).

If the 'chronological view' were to acknowledge and attempt to incorporate positively, from its own perspective, an intentional allusion to Dan. 2.28-29, 45 into its view, then it would be refined in that the phrase 'after these things' of Rev. 1.19c would refer, not merely to the future in general, but specifically to the future latter days prophesied by Daniel. Given the use of μετὰ ταῦτα in Daniel and especially in the Daniel 2 allusions of Revelation, however, the chronological view's understanding of μετὰ ταῦτα ('after these things') is difficult to sustain. The semantic equivalence of μετὰ ταῦτα with an inaugurated 'latter days' idea, as we have seen in the preceding section, does not fit well with a futuristic chronological outline of the book based on 1.19c. If μετὰ ταῦτα refers to the general eschatological age, which John sees as already being inaugurated, and even Daniel itself is understood to be undergoing incipient inauguration, then v. 19 cannot express such a tidy chronological formula. Accordingly, the third clause in v. 19 would have reference to the eschatological period that includes inauguration in the past, present and future.

Further problems with the threefold chronological view will become evident in the discussions below of other viewpoints, but can be summarized as follows. (1) The initial phrase (v. 19a) 'what things you have seen' probably does not refer only to the initial vision of 1.12-18, and, therefore, to a past part of the book in distinction to present (v. 19b) and future (v. 19c) parts of the book, but to the entire vision of the book. More convincing is the idea that ἃ εἶδες must also include the visions of the whole book. This likelihood is substantiated by the observation that 1.19 does not stand alone, but is part of an overall section in 1.9-20 which is best viewed as a commissioning narrative, so that v. 19a is but a repetition of the initial command in 1.11 to record all of the visions of the book (as argued further below, especially in the excursus at the conclusion of the entire section). (2) In addition, the second phrase 'what things are' likely does not refer to the present time only of chs. 2–3 but of present-time segments scattered throughout the book, and, in fact, may not be a temporal reference at all, but an allusion to the figurative nature of the book which needs to be interpreted (accordingly, some translate the phrase ἅ εἰσὶν as 'what they [the pictorial visions] mean', on which see below, sect. B4).

3. *A Double Reference to the Present and Future (View iii)*

	19a	**19b**	**19c**
View *3a*	chs. 1–22	chs. 1–3	chs. 4–22
View *3b*	chs. 1–22	chs. 1–22	chs. 1–22
		as 'already'	as 'not yet'

In this view, v. 19a is a restatement of the command in 1.11 to record the entire vision that became the Apocalypse. From this beginning, the remainder of the verse can be understood in either of two ways.

View *3a*, like the chronological perspective given above (view *2*), takes Rev. 1.19b-c to represent a consecutive, chronological structure. Thus, v. 19b describes the present reality, 'what is', while v. 19c deals with the future, 'what is to take place after these things'. The application of the Daniel 2 allusion results in the same futuristic refinement as in view *2* above. This view, however, is unlikely, since the remainder of the book itself does not clearly support a twofold structure (any more than it supports a threefold one), and is subject to the same critiques of the chronological view above.[126]

A second and more probable version of this perspective (*3b*) is that vv. 19b-19c describe, not the present and future in a strict, chronological sequence, but together describe the overall nature of the Apocalypse, that is that all of the visions have a present and/or future reference.[127] The Greek allows for such an interpretation, since the καί... καί series of vv. 19b-19c can be rendered 'both...and' or 'even...and' or 'that is...and'. Overall, this view is a strong one, since it is probable

---

126. See view 2, above.
127. So Moffatt, *Revelation*, p. 347; Beckwith, *Apocalypse of John*, p. 442-44;

that 1.19a ('write what you have seen') is a recommission to write repeating 1.11a (on this see the excursus at the conclusion of this section below).

The understanding of v. 19c as an allusion to the eschatological text of Dan. 2.28-29, 45 could be combined with the second option discussed herein (*3b*). This would indicate that there is an emphasis on the significance of the visions for the present ('what is'), but especially because John's present is part of Daniel's latter days. The translation might then read, 'write, therefore, what you have seen [the totality of the vision], both what is and what must occur in the latter days'.

4. *'What You Have Seen' (v. 19a) and 'What Is' (v. 19b) Refer to 1.12-20; 'What Must Happen After These Things' (v. 19c) Refers to Chs. 4-22 (View iv)*

19a	19b	19c
1.11, 12-18, 20	1.20 (inc. chs. 2–3)	chs. 4–22
(past vision)	(past vision continued and interpreted)	(ff. visions to be seen about past, present and future)

In this view, similar to view *3* above, v. 19a is a formal restatement of v. 11, repeating the command to write. The difference between the two verses is that, as a result of the Christophany of vv. 11-18, the visions have begun. In this perspective, the εἰσίν of v. 19b is taken in the sense of 'what they mean', 'what they stand for', or 'what they represent',[128] as occurs often throughout the book: 1.20; 4.5; 5.6, 8;

E.A. McDowell, *The Meaning and Message of the Book of Revelation* (Nashville, TX: Broadman, 1951), pp. 32-33; Caird, *Revelation*, p. 26; Beasley-Murray, *Revelation*, p. 68; Mounce, *Revelation*, p. 82; Rissi, *Time and History*, p. 33.

128. For this meaning of εἰσίν see M. Stuart, *Commentary on the Apocalypse*, II, p. 54; H. Alford, *The Greek Testament. IV. Epistles of St. John and Jude: and the Revelation* (Cambridge: Deighton, Bell, 1886), p. 559 (who also cites a number of older commentators with which he is in agreement and disagreement); Johnson, *Revelation*, p. 429; R.H. Gundry, *The Church and the Tribulation* (Grand Rapids: Zondervan, 1973), p. 66; D.C. Chilton, *The Days of Vengeance* (Fort Worth, TX: Dominion Press, 1987), p. 78. So, most recently, J.R. Michaels, 'Revelation 1:19 and the Narrative Voices of the Apocalypse', *NTS* 37 (1991), pp. 604-20. Cf. Moffatt, *Revelation*, p. 347, who argues against this interpretation of εἰσίν on the basis that it is too limiting to understand εἰσίν as referring only to the interpretation of the 1.12-18 vision and not also of the visions of the whole book. Moffatt is correct to argue against such a limitation, but wrong to reject the interpretation of εἰσίν

7.14; 11.4; 14.4; 16.14; 17.9a, 9b, 12, 15.[129] The alternation from the plural εἰσὶν in the second clause to the singular μελλέι [γενέσθαι] in the last clause may hint that the last two clauses of v. 19 should be distinguished, so that both may not be identified as being temporal references. The implied plural subject 'they' in v. 19b refers to the various parts of the son of man vision needing interpretation, which would immediately be supplied in v. 20. Verse 19c refers to the visions of Revelation 4–22, which John has yet to see, based on the use of μετὰ ταῦτα elsewhere, which throughout the book refers to the temporal order of visions from John's perspective (7.1, 9; 15.5; 18.1; 19.1) and not to the chronological order of events to be fulfilled in history. In other words, v. 19c refers to the visions that John would see after this initial vision, not to the fact that these visions also deal with events which are future.[130]

The strength of this view over the preceding ones lies in the attempt to relate vv. 19a and 19b to their immediate context; its weakness is in restricting the reference of vv. 19a and 19b *exclusively* to the inaugural vision (on which for further explanation see below).[131]

5. *An Expression of the Temporally Gnomic or Supra-historical Character of the Book's Ideas (View v)*

19a	19b	19c
	formula as a whole refers to all of chs. 1–22	
	(prophecy about the totality and meaning of history)	

W.C. van Unnik asserts that the entire formula of v. 19 refers to all of chs. 1–22, and explains that John is commissioned to prophesy about the totality of and the meaning of history, whose truths apply not only within history but also transcend any one historical time period. He argues for this perspective by adducing numerous examples of compara-

---

outright, since εἰσὶν may be taken viably to refer to the interpretation of all the visions of the book (see further below on the application of view *1* to view *4*).

129. These 12 references represent half of the 24 occurrences of εἰσὶν, so that half have this interpretative nuance, 6 of which are preceded by a form of εἶδον, as in 1.19 (εἶδες).

130. So Alford, *Revelation*, p. 559; Johnson, *Revelation*, p. 429; Gundry, *Church and the Tribulation*, pp. 64-66.

131. For further strengths and critiques of this general view see Beale, 'Interpretative Problem of Rev. 1:19', pp. 362-65.

ble threefold prophetic formulae in pagan religious contexts, ranging from the time of Homer to the fourth century AD.[132]

As a typical example, though from within Christian tradition, van Unnik cites from the Gnostic *Apocryphon of Jn* 2.15-20, in which the Revealer says to John: 'Now I have come to reveal to you that which is, that which has been, and that which will be so, that you may know the things which are seen and the things not seen and to reveal to you about the perfect Man.'[133] The purpose of the formula in the *Apocryphon* is not primarily to delineate that the revelation pertains to past, present and future, but to emphasize that the revelation penetrates to the inner meaning of history and ultimate reality, here centering in 'the perfect Man', who is to be identified as Christ. This is a particularly significant reference since it is the earliest interpretation (mid–second century AD) of Rev. 1.19 which we have, and it interprets the three clauses of v. 19, not as a tidy chronological outline for the book, but as having the connotation of a transcendent interpretation of all history and of Christ's role in that history.

As a result of surveying these formulae, van Unnik concludes that the somewhat variously arranged formula 'that which was, is and shall be' does not only express eternal duration, but also a revelation which transcends historical time and uncovers the meaning of existence and of history in its totality. Prophets employed this formula to authenticate the divine inspiration upon them, thus establishing the truth of the mysteries they were revealing.

Van Unnik's view receives corroboration from the observation that v. 19 could function figuratively as a merism (indicating the totality of polarity) supplemented with a middle element, which heightens the figurative significance. This is supported by the appearance of a strikingly similar threefold formula, ὁ ὢν καὶ ὁ ἦν καὶ ὁ ἐρχόμενος ('the one

132. Van Unnik, 'Formula Describing Prophecy', pp. 86-94; see also W.C. van Unnik, *Sparsa Collecta 2* (NovT, 30; Leiden: E.J. Brill, 1980), pp. 183-93; cf. Sweet, *Revelation*, p. 73, who adopts van Unnik's view. Cf. also W.C. van Unnik, *Het Godspredikaat 'Het Begin en het Einde' bij Flavius Josephus en in de Openbaring van Johannes* (Mededelingen der Koninklijke Nederlandse Akademie van Wetenshappen, afd. Letterkunde, Nieuwe Reeks-deel, 39.1; Amsterdam: Noord-Hollandsche Uitgevers-Maatschappij, 1976).

133. This is a significant reference, since the context of 2.1-25 is modelled on Rev. 1.12-19: the threefold formula comes immediately after mention of John seeing an 'old man', who is associated with 'the Son' and 'perfect Man', who lives 'forever' who is 'incorruptible', and who exhorts him, 'be not timid'.

who is and who was and who is coming', in varied order), in Rev. 1.4, 1.8 and 4.8 (and, with minor variations, 11.17), which also serves as an example of a merism with a middle element inserted to intensify the figurative significance of *all-inclusiveness*. In functioning as a heightened merism the phrase emphasizes, not a chronology of God's obvious existence, but His transcendence and sovereignty over all events throughout history. A middle element is added in these formulae to emphasize the present reality of God's sovereign transcendence. He acts in and rules over all history, including, and especially, the present: God was not only present and sovereign at the beginning of world history, and he will not only be sovereign and present at the end of history, but also he is sovereign and present at all points between the beginning and the end. In like manner, v. 19 conveys through a revelation, not a chronology of events, that the hidden meaning of history is centered in Christ: he is the ultimate interpreter of history because he is the transcendent sovereign and omnipresent one who planned and guides history.[134]

Granted that formulae of the type described above abound in pagan prophetic literature, the question may well be asked why John would bother to use a pagan formula in the first place. He may have coined his threefold commissioning statement in the form of the threefold pagan, prophetic formula in order to illicit an ironic, polemical association in the mind of his readers.

In the letters to the churches, John shows an awareness of his readers' acquaintance with the ideas and religions in their regions, and selects Old Testament allusions accordingly, for polemical purposes, as a critique of their pagan societies.[135] John may have been motivated to model his threefold formula after the threefold pagan formulae, in order to show Revelation's pan-historical scope. That is, if a threefold formula validated the messages of the pagan prophets, how much more valid is John's revelation of all human history, because the same Christ

---

134. In partial confirmation of van Unnik, C.R. Smith has proposed a similar, yet revised version of the view (cf. C.R. Smith, 'Revelation 1:19: An Eschatologically Escalated Prophetic Convention', *JETS* 33 [1990], pp. 461-66, and summary by Beale, 'Interpretative Problem of Rev. 1:19', pp. 379-81).

135. In this respect, see further G.K. Beale, review of *The Letters to the Seven Churches of Asia in their Local Setting* (JSNTSup, 11; Sheffield: JSOT Press, 1986), by C.J. Hemer, in *Trinity Journal* 7 (1986), pp. 107-11.

who set in motion the latter days is he who commissioned John to record his revelation.

Though van Unnik's approach is highly interesting, it faces three difficulties, one textual, and two thematic.

Textually, it remains to be seen whether or not van Unnik's threefold pagan formulae actually relate to Rev. 1.19. Van Unnik's formulae (and the formulae of 1.4; 1.8; 4.8, cf. 11.17) have a highly parallel structure, each element of the threefold formula being composed of *temporal* terms in contrast to Rev. 1.19. From the perspective of most commentators, van Unnik fails to do justice to the explicit link between the commissions to write in v. 11 and v. 19a.[136] In particular, v. 19a does not refer formally to a past tense element, but to a recommission to write the whole vision of the book, whereas v. 19b and 19c refer to two temporal parts of the vision (according to view *3* above, and a combination of other views). Consequently, v. 19a does not appear to be part of a threefold temporal formula.

Moreover, van Unnik's interpretation of Rev. 1.19 (in which the vision relates both to eternal events *and* also provides eternal insight) appears to be an example of semantic overload, of placing too much meaning on a given word or phrase.[137] Van Unnik's threefold phrase can refer to either the time span of the visions (i.e., the totality of history) *or* the visions' meaning (to uncover the meaning of existence and of history in its totality), but probably not *both*.[138]

Given that van Unnik believes Rev. 1.19 to be reflective of John's commissioning to write about the totality and meaning of history, it may be difficult to understand of what value an allusion to Daniel's latter days would be for his view, since formulae of this sort already encompass all of world history. However, the Daniel allusion may indicate that, though the *time* of the latter days is included in the formula, the unique *nature* of the latter days prophesied by Daniel remains hidden until John reveals that these latter days have begun (and find their

---

136. So see further on view 6 and the conclusion below.

137. In ordinary conversation, words or phrases typically have but one meaning, with the exception of figurative expressions like symbolic pictures, puns, and double entendres; furthermore, in cases of ambiguous meaning of a word, 'the best meaning is the least meaning' (M. Silva, *Biblical Words and their Meaning* [Grand Rapids: Zondervan, 1983], p. 153, citing M. Joos).

138. The criticisms in this paragraph were conveyed to me by my research student Greg Goss.

ultimate meaning in) Christ's redemptive work.[139] His death and resurrection are the keys to unlocking the meaning of all history.

If we were to assume the correctness of van Unnik's view, John's use of a pagan formula would be highly polemical: he is asserting that his prophetic insight ('what you have seen') covers not only the full breadth of everything pagan prophets purportedly grasped ('what is'—historical past-present-and-future) but also the inbreaking eschatological reality which transcends and supersedes it ('that which must be after this'). In this light, Rev. 1.19 could be rendered, 'You have a divine mandate to write according to the prophetic insight which has been given to you, about the things of this age, and those of the in-breaking age to come'.[140]

6. *A Genre Formula Indicating the Mixture of Literary Genres which Compose the Book (View vi)*

The genre view understands the three phrases of v. 19 differently from all the other views. Whereas the majority of the above views (in 2–5) understand in varying ways the three clauses of v. 19 as temporal designations of past, present and future, this view understands them to be primarily statements about the *genre* of the whole book. Though this view still considers v. 19 to be the key to Revelation, the threefold structure describes the literary nature of the visions, not when they will take place. There are multiple ways to formulate the genre view, but they do not differ significantly nor ultimately with respect to how the whole book is to be approached. For the sake of simplicity only one genre view is presented here:[141]

	19a	19b	19c
Views			
1 + 3 + 4	chs. 1–22	chs. 1–22	chs. 1–22
(genre)	(apocalyptic)	(figurative)	(eschatological formula based on Daniel)

139. This would be a combination of views 1 + 6 + 3b.

140. So Smith, 'Revelation 1:19'.

141. For other forms of the view see Beale, 'Interpretative Problem of Rev. 1:19', pp. 377-79; my former student Greg Goss first suggested one of these other versions of the genre view in application to my view of Dan. 2, which alerted me to the version stated here.

This perspective is a synthesis of views *1 + 3 + 4*, which combines the idea of v. 19c as an allusion to Daniel with the second and third proposals together: 'write, therefore, what you have seen, and what they [the visions] mean, and [or "even"] what must happen in the latter days [past, present and future].' This view does not understand v. 19 to be a threefold *temporal* statement about the whole book. Instead, v. 19 *elaborates the threefold hermeneutical nature or genre* of the entire Apocalypse: because the vision is *apocalyptic* (visionary) in nature (v. 19a), thus the whole book is to be interpreted both *figuratively* (v. 19b; also cf. vv. 12-18 with v. 20) and *eschatologically* (cf. v. 19c, also Dan. 2.28-29, 45). The phrases ἃ εἶδες (v 19a) and ἃ εἰσὶν (v. 19b) are not to be limited only to the vision of 1.12-20 (against view *4*) but include the whole book.

7. *Conclusion*

The most preferable among the views discussed are those that understand 'what must happen after these things' as an allusion to Daniel 2 with an 'already-and-not-yet' sense, and that affirms that each of the three object clauses in v. 19 refers equally to the entire book. Though difficult to rank, the order of preference among these four is as follows:

1. the 'new view' combined with the version of the 'double reference' view that takes the second and third clauses as describing together the overall nature of the whole Apocalypse, both present ('what is') and Daniel's eschatological past, present, and future ('what is to be'), and that takes 'write what you have seen' as a repetition of the commission in 1.11;

2. the 'new view' combined with the same version of the 'double reference' view (though without any temporal notions in mind) *and* the 'genre formula' view, in which case all three clauses refer to the whole Apocalypse, the first regarding it as apocalyptic, the second as figurative language, and the third as Danielic eschatology;

3. the 'new view' combined, again, with the same version of the 'double reference' view, but now also with part of van Unnick's understanding, in which case all three clauses refer to the whole of the Apocalypse as Danielic eschatology, giving the ultimate meaning of history; and

4. the 'new view' combined with part of van Unnik's view, in which case all three parts of the threefold formula refer to the whole Apocalypse from the perspective of prophecy, then from the perspective of this age, and then from the perspective of the 'already-and-not-yet' age to come.

The reason for favoring these four perspectives is that they do the most justice to the way Daniel appears to be used in v. 19c.[142] Of course, if John is not actually dependent upon Daniel, or is not conscious of using Daniel, or alludes to Daniel, but with little or no concern for the Old Testament context, then one of the last five views (2–6) discussed in this section must be preferred, without any incorporation of a Danielic perspective.

8. Excursus on the Relation of Revelation 1.19 to Revelation 1.11
Another reason for choosing these four views is that they are based on v. 19a as a commission to write the entire book (although van Unnik's view is least consistent in this respect). In this regard, v. 19a is a resumption of the commission in v. 11 to write the whole book. But that v. 19a is such a resumption and is precisely synonymous with the commission of v. 11 needs argument in more depth at this point.

The place of v. 19a ('write what you have seen') in the immediate context shows it clearly refers to the inaugural vision of 1.12-20. But the reason that ἃ εἶδες likely includes reference also to the writing of the entire book, and not merely 1.12-20, is the absence of any language suggesting such a limitation. Its inclusive reference is evident further by observing that ὃ βλέπεις γράψον εἰς βιβλίον ('what you see write in a book') in 1.11a is picking up ὅσα εἶδεν...τὰ ἐν αὐτῇ γεγραμμένα ('which things he saw...the things having been written in it') in 1.2b-3, which is an obvious reference to the entire vision of the book. And if 1.11a is an allusion to the whole vision, so likely is 1.19a (γράψον οὖν ἃ εἶδες) because of its verbal parallelism with and close contextual relation to 1.11.[143] The implicit link between 1.2b, 1.11 and 1.19 is

---

142. One approach in considering the above four alternatives may be to see that they are not mutually exclusive of one another. The first or second options explain the primary intention but the way this intention was formulated may have been motivated by the pagan prophetic formula represented by the third and fourth options.

143. So also Moffatt, *Revelation*, p. 347; Beckwith, *Apocalypse of John*,

strengthened by a textual tradition which appends two phrases to the end of v. 2, creating a threefold clause like that of v. 19: cf. οσα ειδεν και ατινα εισι και ατινα χρη γενεσθαι μετα ταυτα in 𝔐ᴬ ('which things he saw *and which are and which must come to pass after these things*'). This, at the least, likely represents the earliest interpretation identifying 1.2, which refers to the entire vision, with 1.19.

The second reason which points to v. 19a being a restatement of the command in v. 11 to write the whole of Revelation (and not just vv. 12-18) is that the plural relative pronoun ἃ at the beginning of each of the three clauses in v 19 strongly suggests also that the verse is not limited to the 1.12-18 scene but to the total panorama of the book. The ἃ of v. 19a picks up the initial ἃ in 1.1, the ὅσα of 1.2, and the ὃ of v. 11 (which must have a collective sense), suggesting that the ἃ of 1.19a (and, therefore, probably also of v. 19b and v. 19c) has the multiple visions of the book in mind, since 1.1-2, 11 clearly refer to such. Furthermore, that the Daniel 2 allusions in 1.1 and 22.6 have an all-inclusive focus[144] makes it likely that the ἃ of 1.19c does as well;[145] and this points further to the first two relative plural pronouns (ἃ) in vv. 19a and 19b as having the same all-inclusive focus.

But the most persuasive indication that all of v. 19 includes the scope of the entire vision of the Apocalypse is the observation that 1.9-11 and 1.12-20 function together as a larger literary unit, which introduces the entire book by serving as the risen Christ's prophetic commission for John to write the visions he would witness, as evidenced by the restatement of the commission in v. 19a, thus forming an *inclusio* with v. 11. The change in v. 19 to the aorist (εἶδες, 'you have seen') from the present (βλέπεις, 'you see') of v. 11 refers not merely to what is past at the

pp. 442-43; Mounce, *Revelation*, p. 82; L. Morris, *The Revelation of St. John* (Grand Rapids: Eerdmans, 1980), pp. 55-56; H. Hailey, *Revelation* (Grand Rapids; Baker Book House, 1979), p. 114.

144. The ἃ in 4.1 can easily be understood as a collective plural, especially if it is understood eschatologically, and not merely as a reference to the visions which follow.

145. A possible objection to this view is that the plural relative οὓς + εἶδες in 1.20 unambiguously refers to elements only of the first vision in vv. 12-16. Therefore, the same could be the case for the plural relatives in v 19. While this is possible, understanding the ἃ as a plural in the light of 1.1-2, 1.11, and 22.6 are equally plausible, and given that these verses share a common context with Daniel 2, it is more likely that the ἃ of v. 19c be understood as having a plural, not a singular, referent.

moment of Christ's speaking (the son of man vision), but primarily to what is or will be past (the vision of the entire book) at the time when John begins to execute the command to write.[146]

The introduction of the commission in v. 10 is coined in the language of Ezekiel's raptures in the Spirit, thus investing John with prophetic authority like that which Ezekiel received when he was commissioned (cf. Ezek. 2.2; 3.12, 14, 24; 11.1; 43.5; see also Rev. 4.2; 17.3; 21.10).[147] Further evidence of John being commissioned in a manner similar to the Old Testament prophets is given in v. 11. The command 'to write in a book' (γράψον εἰς βιβλίον) is reflective of the charge Yahweh gave to his prophetic servants to communicate to Israel the revelation they had received (so cf. the LXX of Exod. 17.14; Isa. 30.8; Jer. 37 [30, Heb.].2; 39 [32, Heb.].44; Tob. 12.20).[148]

That vv. 10-11 and vv. 12-18 are bound together by the theme of the prophetic commission is borne out by v. 17a, where John exhibits the fourfold pattern reflective of Old Testament prophets (especially Daniel) who receive prophetic commissions: (1) seeing a vision; (2) falling down in fear, (3) subsequently being strengthened by a heavenly being; (4) and, finally, receiving further revelation from him (so Dan. 10.5-11; 10.12-20; cf. also Dan. 8.15-18 with 8.19-27).

146. In agreement with Beckwith, *Apocalypse of John*, p. 443. Closely related to this view is the proposal by some that the command to write in v. 19a is proleptic ('write the things you are about to see'), since v. 19a is in parallelism with the present tense command in v. 11a to write the unfolding visions of the whole book (e.g. Moffatt, *Revelation*, p. 341; Mounce, *Revelation*, p. 82). Or, εἶδες could function like a Hebrew prophetic perfect (with the sense 'Write what things you will see') or have a future perfect nuance ('the things you will have seen'; so Morris, *Revelation*, p. 56). It is possible that John wrote the book at intervals, while the whole vision was being unfolded (cf. 10.4). In this case v. 19 would have been written after the whole vision was given, as with 1.1-2, which may be true of all of ch. 1.

147. This identification with prophetic authority is enforced by the additional description of the voice which he heard as 'a great voice as a trumpet', evoking the same voice which Moses heard when Yahweh revealed himself to him on Mount Sinai (Exod. 19.16, 19-20; the voice of 1.11 is that of an angel who functions to introduce the son of man vision [so 4.1-2]).

148. The reader steeped in the Old Testament might discern that all such commissions in the prophets were commands to write testaments of judgment against Israel (so Isa. 30.8; Jer. 37[30].2; 39[32].44; cf. also Exod. 34.27; Isa. 8.1; Hab. 2.2; cf. Jer. 36.1), and that, therefore, at this early point in the book there is already a hint that one of its major themes will be judgment.

In summary, Christ commissions John in vv. 10-11, by displaying his divinity to provide the authority for issuing the commission in vv. 12-18,[149] and, on the basis of (οὖν, v. 19a) this authority, reissues the commission in v 19. Therefore, the οὖν functions in a dual manner, resumptively with respect to v. 11[150] and inferentially with respect to the segment of vv. 11-18. That is, in v. 19 John is now told that he may begin to fulfill the commission given in v. 11, because his paralyzing fear of v. 17a has been removed by Christ's affirmation in vv. 17b-18 that he has authority over death. The presence of the οὖν is also an important feature indicating a connection back to the all-encompassing nature of the v. 11 commission. Of course, v. 20 is limited only to vv. 12-18, since it is a beginning explanation only of that section.[151]

C. *The Problem of the Temporal Scope of the Sevenfold Series of Trumpets and Bowls in the Light of Relevant Old Testament Background*

Are the discernible sections within Revelation 4–16 related to one another chronologically, thematically or both? The main lines of debate revolve around whether Rev. 4–16 represent a sequential forecast of events to happen one after another or whether some segments overlap temporally and thematically. The former position essentially understands that the order of the visions generally represents the order of future end-time events, while the latter views the series of visions as

---

149. I.e. in vv. 12-18 Christ reveals his delegating authority by revealing that by his victory over death he became *the* end-time judge, priest, and king of the churches and of the world.

150. So Moffatt, *Revelation*, p. 346; Charles, *Revelation*, I, p. 33; Swete, *Apocalypse*, p. 21; A.T. Robertson, *The General Epistles and the Revelation of John* (Word Pictures in the New Testament, 6; Nashville: Broadman Press, 1933), p. 294; cf. BAGD, p. 593.

151. The repeated imperatives of γράφω coupled with the same place names as the imperative of 1.11 occur in the seven letters of chs. 2–3. Clearly the imperatives are tied in to 1.19 and introduce developments of the inaugural son of man vision. These imperatives are a beginning fulfillment of the all-encompassing commissions to write given in vv. 11, 19. In contrast to vv. 11, 19, these imperatives are formally restricted to the content of the following words of Christ in each letter and are thereby formally limited also only to the son of man vision. Partial fulfillments of the overall commissions to write of 1.11, 19 appear also in 10.4, 19.9, and 21.5.

I am grateful to my research student Greg Goss for his aid in helping me edit an earlier draft of this segment on 'The Interpretation of Rev. 1.19'.

repeating or 'recapitulating' themselves both with respect to chronology and subject matter. To one degree or another most scholars fall along the spectrum of one of these two positions. Typically the former group views Revelation 4–16 as a panorama of events to happen only in the period immediately preceding and culminating with the final coming of Christ, whereas the latter see a threefold temporal reference to events associated with (1) the redemptive work of Christ's first coming, (2) the course of the inaugurated latter-day interadventual age, and (3) the second coming of Christ and consummation of cosmic history.[152]

The purpose of this section is not to discuss all the most important features of both the chronological sequence view and the recapitulation view,[153] but to focus on those areas of the problem which are potentially affected by Old Testament background.

1. Relevant Old Testament Background in which Recapitulation and Synonymously Parallel Segments Are Characteristic
It is not surprising that recapitulation might appear as a feature in Revelation's structure, since it is a prominent characteristic elsewhere of prophetic and apocalyptic literature. There is general acknowledgment that the Old Testament books to which the Apocalypse is most heavily indebted are the Psalms, Isaiah, Ezekiel and Daniel. Proportionally Daniel is most used, followed by Ezekiel, although in terms of sheer numbers Isaiah ranks first, after which come Ezekiel and Daniel.[154] It is likely no coincidence that the structure of Isaiah, Daniel and Ezekiel is primarily characterized by a format of recapitulation, sometimes in the form of chiasm.[155] Zechariah is also significantly used (approx. 15

152. An exception to this is Beasley-Murray, *Revelation*, who is both a futurist and a recapitulationist, understanding the parallel sections to cover exclusively different aspects of the eschatological future.

153. See Beale, *Book of Revelation*, 'Introduction', for discussion of both sides of the issue.

154. For statistics and related bibliography see Chapter 2, sect. 1.

155. For Isaiah, see N.K. Gottwald, *The Hebrew Bible—A Socio-Literary Introduction* (Philadelphia: Fortress Press, 1985), pp. 505-506; W.J. Dumbrell, 'The Purpose of the Book of Isaiah', *TynBul* 36 (1985), pp. 111-28; for Daniel see A. Lenglet, 'La Structure Litteraire de Daniel 2–7', *Biblica* 53 (1972) pp. 169-90; J.G. Baldwin, *Daniel* (Leicester: Inter-Varsity Press, 1978), pp. 59-63; D. Ford, *Daniel* (Nashville: Southern Publishing Association, 1978), pp. 25-29; J.J. Collins, *The Apocalyptic Vision of the Book of Daniel* (HSM, 16; Missoula, MT: Scholars Press, 1977), pp. 116-17, 133; for Ezekiel cf. the outlines in most commentaries

times) and it likewise exhibits a chiastically parallel structure.[156] Since John has a tendency to appeal to prophetic precedent throughout his work, perhaps the prophetic style of visionary recapitulation was too tempting to miss.

Daniel and Zechariah are especially relevant for consideration in this regard, since they are cast in the style of overt apocalyptic visions closest in form to the genre of the Apocalypse. Daniel's structure of five synonymously parallel visions (Dan. 2, 7, 8, 9, 10–12) may be most influential upon the structure of Revelation, since Daniel is used so much in the book and is employed to designate its broad structural divisions (see on Chapter 3, sect. B. above, and further below). Indeed, an outline of five recapitulated sections for Revelation (4–7; 8.1–11.19; 12.1–14.20; 15–16; 17.1–21.8), with chs. 1–3 and 21.9–22.21 as outer boundary sections respectively of imperfect anticipation and perfect consummation, proposed and argued elsewhere, would seem to be corroborated by this.[157] Daniel's five parallel visions are supplemental

(e.g. J.W. Wevers, *Ezekiel* [NCB; London: Thomas Nelson, 1969]; J.B. Taylor, *Ezekiel* [Leicester: Inter-Varsity Press, 1969]). J.H. Sims, *A Comparative Literary Study of Daniel and Revelation* (Lewiston: Edwin Mellen Press, 1994), pp. 115-19, contends that the structure of Revelation broadly echoes that of Daniel, especially a chiastic structure like that proposed by Schüssler Fiorenza (see below) which reflects that of the Aramaic section of Daniel 2–7.

156. Baldwin, *Haggai, Zechariah, Malachi*, pp. 74-81; Gottwald, *Hebrew Bible*, p. 504; cf. M.G. Kline, 'The Structure of the Book of Zechariah', *JETS* 34 (1991), pp. 179-93.

157. Past attempts to outline Revelation have been characterized by observations which have discerned an organizing principle based on a series of sevens. Prominent among these proposals are the schemes offered, e.g., by Farrer, *Revelation*, Lohmeyer, *Die Offenbarung des Johannes*, and J.W. Bowman, 'The Revelation to John: Its Dramatic Structure and Message', *Int* 9 (1955), pp. 436-53. Cf. also E. Schüssler Fiorenza, *The Book of Revelation: Justice and Judgment* (Philadelphia: Fortress Press, 1985), pp. 175-76, who constructs a sevenfold chiastic structure (others have also proposed a chiastic structure, among which is B.W. Snyder, 'Combat Myth in the Apocalypse: The Liturgy of the Day of the Lord and the Dedication of the Heavenly Temple' [Unpublished PhD dissertation; Berkeley: Graduate Theological Union and the University of California, 1991], p. 84, who also sees the book composed of two segments of seven sections each). Others more generally divide the book into seven sections, while making no attempt to enumerate any subdivisions in the 'unnumbered' sections. Among these Farrer's outline is most cogent: cf. chs. 1–3, 4–7, 8.1–11.14, 11.15–14.20, 15-18, 19-22). Nevertheless, Farrer's outline still encounters problems, among which is a lack of discernment of 'interlocking' transitions between sections, which makes it difficult to be

perspectives about the same general period of the future; it would be unexpected for a book like Revelation to model itself on Daniel's parallel structure and to have all the parallel sections also pertain to the very same general period of the future. Rather, it would seem more natural for the parallels to reflect an 'already-and-not-yet' temporal perspective, especially since John sees elsewhere that some of Daniel's significant future visions had begun to be fulfilled in Christ's first coming (see 1.7, 13; see further above on Chapter 3, sect. B). That the same phenomenon of recapitulation found in Daniel also occurs in other Jewish apocalyptic writings such as the *Sibylline Oracles* (the third sibyl),[158] the *Similitudes of Enoch*, and *4 Ezra* (3.1–9.22; 11.1–13.58)[159] likewise points to the similar phenomenon in Revelation.

2. *The Significance of 'Last' in Revelation 15.1 and of the Exodus Plague Background*

John sees in Revelation 15 'seven angels having seven last plagues', which is a further explanation of the immediately preceding 'great sign in heaven'. The wording πληγὰς ἑπτὰ τὰς ἐσχάτας could be translated 'seven plagues which are the last' (NASB, RSV, JB) or 'seven last plagues' (KJV).

A typical futurist, chronological sequence perspective of the seven bowls is that they come at the end of history after the events narrated in the seals and trumpets. In this respect, ἔσχατος ('last') would refer to the bowls as the last plagues which occur in history after the woes of seals and trumpets have taken place.[160] According to some, this seems to be the most natural reading of 'last'. Some qualify this slightly by seeing the bowls as the content of the seventh trumpet or third woe, just as they believe that the trumpets are the content of the seventh seal.[161]

precise about the exact beginning and ending of segments (as A.Y. Collins has pointed out). The outline preferred above represents an adjustment to Farrer's outline, for which there is not room here to discuss (see further Beale, *Book of Revelation*, 'Introduction').

158. So A.Y. Collins, *The Combat Myth in the Book of Revelation* (HDR, 9; Missoula, MT: Scholars Press, 1976), p. 43; J.J. Collins, *The Sibylline Oracles of Egyptian Judaism* (SBLDS, 13; Missoula, MT: Scholars Press, 1974), p. 37.

159. Cf. E. Breech, 'These Fragments I Have Shored against my Ruins: The Form and Function of 4 Ezra', *JBL* 92 (1973), pp. 267-74 (270).

160. Rissi, *Time and History*, p. 47.

161. So J.A. Seiss, *The Apocalypse: A Series of Special Lectures on the Revelation of Jesus Christ* (Grand Rapids: Eerdmans, 1966), p. 368; Beckwith, *Apoca-*

While such a futurist perspective is possible, ἔσχατος ('last') plausibly indicates the sequential order in which John saw the visions and not necessarily the chronological order of their occurrence in history. This would mean that the bowls are the "last" formal series of sevenfold visions John saw, after he had seen the visions of seals and trumpets (and perhaps the visions of chs. 12–14). Therefore, the bowls do not have to be understood as occurring as the last events of history but as the last of the formal sevenfold visions John saw, which are expanded by further visionary scenes in the following chapters.

This interpretation is supported by 15.5 which re-introduces the bowl visions with the phrase 'and after these things' (καὶ μετὰ ταῦτα). Throughout the Apocalypse the phrase 'after these things' indicates the sequential order in which John saw the visions but not necessarily the chronological order of their occurrence in history (so 4.1; 7.1, 9; 18.1; 19.1; see Rev. 4.1a). Therefore, v. 5 notes only that the bowls occurred last in the order of visions presented to John. Since v. 5 re-introduces the same vision which v. 1 began to introduce, it is reasonable to place 'and after these things I saw' (v. 5) in synonymous parallelism with 'and I saw another sign...seven last plagues' (v. 1)."Εσχατος ('last') plausibly is synonymous with μετὰ ταῦτα ('after these things').

Therefore, the introductory 'and I saw...seven last plagues' of v. 1 is expanded in the continued introduction of v. 5 to 'and after these things I saw', so that v. 1 also affirms that the bowls come last in the sequence of formal sevenfold visions seen by the seer. This means that the bowl judgments do not have to come chronologically after the series of judgments in chs. 6–14. The bowls go back in time and explain in greater detail the woes throughout the age and culminating in the final judgment. One of the indications of this is the observation that the final judgment has already been described as happening at the end of the seals (6.12-17; 8.1) and the trumpets (11.15-19), and most recently in 14.8-11 (the final punishment of Babylon and her followers) and 14.14-20.[162] Another hint of the temporal overlap between the bowls and earlier judgment series is that the word πληγή ('plague') refers to the sixth trumpet woe (9.20) and to the fourth bowl (16.9), as well as to the

---

lypse of John, pp. 669-71; Walvoord, *Revelation of Jesus Christ*, pp. 225-26; Ladd, *Revelation*, p. 203; Kraft, *Die Offenbarung des Johannes*, p. 201; Mounce, *Revelation*, p. 284; Johnson, *Revelation*, pp. 545-46.

162. An observation made by most commentators favoring 'synchronous parallelism' or 'recapitulation' (e.g. cf. Hendriksen, *More Than Conquerors*).

plagues which can come on the first century readers in their own lifetime, if they do not heed the book's warnings (22.18).

Alternatively 'last' may be a redemptive–historical reference to the last events of history. If so, the focus upon 'last' would not primarily be on the bowl plagues being only sequentially or chronologically last with respect to the previous two sevenfold judgments. Accordingly, the 'seven last plagues' could correspond to the ten plagues God brought against Egypt.[163] *Pesiqta de Rab Kahana*, *Piska* 7.11 affirms that the same ten plagues God sent against Egypt will be sent against Rome and Gog, and introduces the affirmation by saying 'with the very means by which He punished the former [Egypt] He will punish the *latter* [Rome]'; *b. Hul.* 92a affirms that Egypt drank 'the cup of staggering' at the time of the Exodus and will again 'with all the nations' at the end of history (for the equivalence of 'plagues' with 'cups' see Rev. 15.7-8). The Exodus judgments would be enacted against the world at the end of history when Israel would again be redeemed: so Mic. 7.10-17; *Targ. Jon. Zech.* 10.9-12; 1 QM11. 9-11; 14.1; *Apoc. Abr.* 29.15-16 and 30.1-8. According to Deut. 4.30, 8.16, 31.29 and 32.20, 'in the latter days' (ἐπ' ἐσχάτων τῶν ἡμερῶν) Israel was to be punished according to the pattern of the Egyptian plagues (Deut. 7.15 and 28.27, 59-60; note that Deut. 31.29 directly precedes a reference to the 'song' spoken by Moses in 31.30; likewise cf. Rev. 15.1 with 15.3).

These Old Testament–Jewish antecedents provide a typological and eschatological background against which the inherent idea of 'last' in Rev. 15.1 may well best be seen. This background makes plausible the suggestion that the plagues in Revelation are 'last' in the sense that they occur in the latter days (hence, 'seven eschatological plagues') in contrast to the former days when the Egyptian plagues occurred. John and the New Testament writers believed the latter days were inaugurated with Christ's first coming and will be culminated at his parousia (see on 4.1 at Chapter 3, sect. B.1.c!). Accordingly, the bowl plagues would extend throughout the course of the latter-day period, from Christ's first to his second coming. Chapter 16 bears out clearly that these are typological equivalents of the Egyptian plagues, as does the Exodus Red Sea imagery and context of 15.2-4 (on which see below). In Judaism and early Christian literature the Exodus plagues were also

---

163. So P. Mauro, *The Patmos Visions: A Study of the Apocalypse* (Boston: Hamilton, 1925), p. 457.

understood as typological of later plagues to come upon subsequent generations of humanity (for references see following excursus).

Rev. 15.1, 5-8 have introduced the seven bowl plagues. Chapter 16 explains the contents of each of these woes. Many commentators argue that the trumpets are different judgments than those of the bowls for the following reasons: (1) the first four trumpets appear only to affect nature, whereas the first four bowls affect wicked people; and (2) the first six trumpets are said to be partial in their effect, whereas the bowls seem to have universal effect. Another difference is that there is no parenthetical explanatory section after the sixth bowl as there is after the sixth seal and trumpet.

In response, the similarities of the trumpets and bowls overshadow the differences. The differences between the two seven-fold series are only highlighted because of the broader likenesses. It would be unusual for a writer to reproduce parallel visions with mechanical or photographic likeness. It is an overly literal and pedantic view to restrict the first four trumpets only to plagues against nature, since these plagues also certainly affect people, and may even best be seen to be symbolic for judgments against reprobate humanity. What the trumpets state in a highly figurative manner is stated more directly in the bowls.[164] However, this is not always true since the second and third trumpets are explicitly said to affect humanity, whereas the second bowl does not have such explicit comment (note the explicit mention of 'ships' and 'many men died' in 8.9-11). That the trumpets have partial affect ('a third') and the bowls universal affect may, but does not have to, indicate lack of identity. Rather, the difference in extent of effect may merely suggest that the trumpets are part of a larger process of judgment, which at the same time strikes the entire world. Therefore, the difference between the partial and total effect of the trumpets and bowls does not necessitate seeing the former as different judgments nor as chronologically preceding the latter.

Both trumpets and bowls present each of the plagues in the same order: plagues striking the (1) earth, (2) sea, (3) rivers, (4) sun, (5) realm of the wicked with darkness, (6) Euphrates (together with influencing the wicked by demons), and (7) world with the final judgment (with the same imagery of 'lightning and sounds and thunders and earthquake' and 'great hail').

---

164. See Sweet, *Revelation*, p. 242.

The overwhelming likeness of the trumpets and bowls is a result of both being modelled on the Exodus plagues. Each woe in both seven-fold series is an allusion to an Exodus plague (except for the sixth trumpet). Further, in each series seven angels execute the seven plagues. These observations point to the probability that the trumpet and bowl series are parallel literarily, thematically and temporally.[165] Because of the dominant likenesses, the burden of proof rests on those attempting to argue that the two sevenfold plague series are different.[166] The parallelism of the two series can be set out as follows:[167]

Comparative Outline of the Trumpet Series,
the Bowl Series and the Exodus Plagues

The Seven Trumpets	The Seven Bowls
1) Hail, fire and blood fall on the *earth*, one third of which is burned up.	A bowl is poured on the *earth*. Malignant sores come on men who had the mark of the beast and worshipped his image.
Seventh Exodus plague (Exod. 9.22ff.)	Sixth Exodus plague (Exod. 9.8ff.)
2) A blazing mountain falls into the *sea*. One third of the sea becomes *blood*, a third of *sea-creatures die*, and a third of ships are destroyed.	A bowl is poured on the *seas*. This becomes *blood*, and *every living thing in it dies*.
First Exodus plague (Exod. 7.17ff.)	First Exodus plague (Exod. 7.17ff.).
3) A blazing star (Wormwood) falls on a third of *rivers and fountains*, their waters are poisoned and many die.	A bowl is poured on *rivers and fountains*, and they become blood.
First Exodus plague (Exod. 7.17ff.)	First Exodus plague (Exod. 7.17ff.)
4) A third of *sun, moon and stars* is struck. Darkness results for a third of a night and day.	A bowl is poured on the *sun*, which scorches men with fire.
Ninth Exodus plague (Exod. 10.21ff.)	Seventh Exodus plague (Exod. 9.22ff.)

165. For further arguments see Beale, *Book of Revelation*, 'Introduction', *in loc.*; see Ladd, *Revelation*, p. 209, who disagrees with this conclusion.

166. See Beckwith, *Apocalypse of John*, pp. 672-73, 690, who acknowledges the similarities but does not want to conclude that the two series are essentially parallel.

167. As adapted from Beasley-Murray, *Revelation*, pp. 238-39, with changes.

5) The shaft of the pit is opened. Sun and air are *darkened* with smoke from which locusts emerge to *torment* men without the seal of God.	A bowl is poured on the throne of the beast. His kingdom is *darkened* and men are in *anguish*.
Eighth (Exod. 10.4ff.) and ninth Exodus plagues (Exod. 10.21ff.)	Ninth Exodus plague (Exod. 10.21ff.)
6) Four angels bound at *the Euphrates* are released, with their 200 million cavalry. A third of men is killed by them.	A bowl is poured on *the Euphrates*, which dries up for kings from the east. Demonic frogs deceive kings of the world to assemble for battle at Armageddon.
	Second Exodus plague (Exod. 8.2ff.)
7) *Loud voices in heaven* announce the coming of the kingdom of God and of Christ. *Lightning, thunder, earthquake* and *hail* occur.	A bowl is poured into the air, and a *loud voice from God's throne* announces, 'It is done.' *Lightning, thunder* and an unprecedented *earthquake* occur, and terrible *hail* falls.
Seventh Exodus plague (Exod. 9.22ff.) + Sinai theophanic description (Exod. 19.16-19)	Ninth Exodus plague (Exod. 9.22ff.) + Sinai theophanic description (Exod. 19.16-19)

The exact manner in which each parallel trumpet and bowl are related must await analysis elsewhere.[168] Generally, the first six trumpets and first five bowls cover the time between Christ's resurrection and his final parousia, while the last trumpet and bowl narrate the last judgment (the sixth bowl describes events directly preceding the last judgment). This does not mean there is a one-to-one correspondence between each parallel. However, they are similar enough to be considered as part of the same overall program of divine judgments occurring during the same general period. The phrase 'seven last plagues' in 15.1 was seen to refer, not to trials occurring after the seals and trumpets at the very end of history, but to the bowls coming last after the seals and trumpets in the sequence of formal sevenfold visions seen by the seer. They are 'last' in that they complete the thought revealed in the preceding woe visions (see further on 15.1). This means that the bowl judgments do not have to come chronologically after the series of judgments in chs. 6–14. The bowls go back in time and explain in greater detail the woes throughout the age, culminating in the final judgment.

168. See Beale, *Book of Revelation, in loc.*

The purpose of the recapitulation is to explain further the extent and application of God's latter-day Exodus judgments, an explanation that began with the portrayal of the trumpets. The trumpet visions may be compared to incomplete photographic snapshots and the bowls to fuller photographic pictures. Whereas only two trumpets explicitly identified those punished as unbelievers, six of the bowls clearly identify unbelievers as the ones afflicted. This implies too that even the unspecified trumpets are predominantly plagues directed against unbelieving humanity. Though even the first four trumpets affect some aspect of nature, and many commentators see them as mere warnings, the destruction wrought affects human beings in a harmful manner; this is the case, whether or not the first four trumpet plagues are taken literally or figuratively, though the latter is probable.

Some commentators argue that the bowls are judgments which come after the trumpets which are only warnings and not judgments: if people do not heed the warnings of the trumpets, they will be judged at a subsequent point by the bowl plagues. Of course, such a sequence could be one which is true in every generation, or it could refer to a sequence only in the last generation which experiences the Great Tribulation. Both the trumpets and the bowl plagues, however, are better viewed as judgments instead of mere warnings, which enhances further the parallelism between the two. This conclusion is based on the observation that the Exodus plagues are both a literary and *theological* model for the bowls.[169] The function of warning *is* expressed in 16.9, 11, where it says that none of the unbelievers 'repented', but the warning there functions within a larger framework of an already decided judgment. If the bowls were modelled only literarily on the Exodus plagues, then they could be viewed as mere warnings. But if the *theology* of the Exodus plagues has been formative behind the composition of the bowls and the *trumpets*, then they both should ultimately be understood as punishments which further harden people. They demonstrate God's uniqueness and incomparable omnipotence, as well as his righteous judgment (16.5-6). These plagues reveal hardness of heart and the fact that the ungodly are punished because of such hardness, which is expressed by their idolatry (16.2), persistent non- repentance (16.9, 11) and persecution of the saints (16.6).

---

169. For further development of this line of thought, see the excursus at the conclusion of this section, especially with respect to the theological background of the Exodus plague narratives.

Also, like the trumpets, the bowls are God's further answer to the saints' plea in 6.9-11 that their persecutors be judged. Such a link is apparent in 16.5-7 by reference to the 'altar' and to God as 'holy' and his judgments 'true'. This connection with 6.9-11 also explains why the bowls are not merely warnings but ultimately punishments and are called 'bowls of wrath' (16.1; cf. 15.1). Those undergoing the judgments of the bowl plagues are punished because they identify with the beast and not with the Lamb. John describes such people elsewhere as being predetermined to be influenced by the beast's deceptions (see 13.8b and 17.8), so that they worship him instead of the Lamb, they are intractably unrepentant, and they participate in the persecution of God's people.[170] Such an interpretative conclusion entails theological tensions revolving around divine sovereignty, human accountability and repentance.[171]

All of these temporal judgments climax in the great last judgment of the seventh bowl (16.17-21). The Exodus plagues are typologically broadened by the Old Testament to apply to later sinful generations of Israel in exile, as well as typologically applied by Judaism to unbelievers throughout the earth and to the ungodly living at the last stage of history.[172] Likewise, here the Exodus plagues are applied typologically

170. In this respect, see also the difficult 22.10-11; cf. A.Y. Collins, 'The History-of-Religions Approach to Apocalypticism and the "Angel of the Waters" (Rev. 16:4-7)', *CBQ* 39 (1977), pp. 367-81 (371-72).

171. For which there is not space to discuss.

172. The Exodus plagues are understood as a typological foreshadowing of later plagues, whose effect is to be escalated to the whole world (as recognized early by Irenaeus, *Adv. Haer.* 4.30.4, who sees the plagues happening again at the end; the Exodus plagues are also typologically broadened to apply to unbelievers throughout the earth in Josephus, *Ant.* 2.14.1; *T. Dan.* 5.8; *Exod. R.* 11.2; 12.4, 7; 14.3. In *Exod. R.* 11.2; 12.4; 13 the plague of fire and of insects is compared with the eternal judgment of hell which the wicked suffer. The Exodus plagues are also typologically broadened to apply to Israel in its land [cf. Amos 4.10] and in exile [Deut. 28.27-60]). Old Testament and Jewish tradition also believed that the Exodus judgments would be enacted against the world at the end of history when Israel would again be redeemed (Mic. 7.10-17; *Targ. Jon. Zech.* 10.9-12; 1QM 11.9-11; 14.1). *Apoc. Elij.* 2.44 typologically applies the plague of waters turning to blood (Exod. 7.19-20) to woes immediately preceding the appearance of the Antichrist. Similarly, the plague of darkness (Exod. 10.21-23) is applied to historical Rome (*Sib. Or.* 12.215-16). Josephus, *Ant.* 2.14.1 says that one of the purposes for recounting the narrative of the Exodus plagues is to warn 'mankind' in general that when they offend God like the Egyptians, they will be chastised in the same way (likewise

to the ungodly throughout the interadvent period in the first five bowls and to the wicked at the conclusion of history in the last two bowls. The result and goal of all seven trumpet judgments are not only to demonstrate God's incomparability and the just judgment of sinners, but also ultimately the glory of God (so 15.8; 16.9; cf. 11.13, 15-16; 15.4; 19.1-7). The number 'seven' is figurative and refers not to a mere seven specific woes but to the completeness and severity of these judgments upon the wicked (see further on 15.6).

Others see in the significance of 'last' in Rev. 15.1 that, whereas the trumpets primarily warned unbelievers, these plagues come last of all *throughout the age* and leave no more room for repentance, since rejection of the warnings has occurred.[173] While possible, this view is not preferable, since the trumpets not only warn but also are themselves woes which harden unbelievers and ripen them for judgment. Alternatively, 'last' could explain how the wrath revealed in the seals and trumpets *reaches its goal*.[174] This has some merit, since the bowl judgments in contrast to the other sevenfold series have more explicit statements about the purpose of divine judgments (i.e. to punish people for beast worship and persecution; cf. 16.2, 5-7, 19).

The bowls are 'last' in order of presentation of the visions 'because in them has been completed the wrath of God'. The bowls complement and round out the portrayal of divine wrath in the seals and trumpets. It is in this fuller presentation of punishment in the bowls that it can be said that God's wrath has been 'completely expressed'[175] or '*has reached its completion*' (ἐτελέσθη; JB, 'exhaust'; NEB, 'consummated'; RSV, 'ended'; NASB, 'finished'; KJV, 'filled up'). The full portrait of God's wrath will be finished when all the bowl visions have been painted on the heavenly canvas. The bowls are generally parallel thematically

---

Philo, *Somn.* 1.114, with respect to the plague of darkness in Exod. 10.21; cf. Philo, *Spec. Leg.* 2.188-92). In a similar manner *Apoc. Abr.* 29.15-16 and 30.1-8 universalize the Exodus plagues and apply them to the judgment of 'all earthly creation', which is associated with the sounding of a trumpet (31.1). Furthermore, the first four plagues mentioned there also emphasize famine conditions together with fire: cf. 30.4-5: 'sorrow from much need... fiery conflagrations for the cities ...destruction by pestilence...famine of the world'. Such sufferings would indicate one's separation from God and the beginning of judgment.

173. Hendriksen, *More than Conquerors*, p. 190; Morris, *Revelation*, p. 187.

174. Beasley-Murray, *Revelation*, p. 234.

175. R.G. Bratcher, *A Translator's Guide to the Revelation to John* (London: United Bible Societies, 1984), p. 124.

and temporally to the trumpets (and ultimately to the seals), which is borne out by their similarity.[176]

But the expression at the end of v. 1 may have no reference to any of the above noted nuances of τελέω which all revolve around the idea of 'completion'. The word could be rendered 'filled up' in a metaphorical manner, since it is parallel to 15.7 and 21.9:

> 15.1b: 'in them [the seven bowls] was *filled up* the wrath of God'.
> 15.7b: 'seven golden bowls *full* of the wrath of God'.
> 21.9:   'seven bowls *full* of the seven last plagues'.

In 15.7b and 21.9 the wording is metaphorical of bowls being filled up with the liquid (probably wine) of divine wrath, though this is a mixed metaphor, since 'wrath' is an abstract word (instead a pictorial word like 'wine' is expected). The parallelism suggests that the 'fulness' (τελέω) of 15.1 is the same as the 'fulness' (γέμω) of 15.7 and 21.9. This is a further development of God's 'cup of wrath' filled with 'the wine of wrath' in 14.10. The consequent meaning of the metaphor in 15.1 is that the seven bowls are referred to as 'last' because they portray the full-orbed wrath of God in a more intense manner than any of the previous woe visions. This conclusion does not significantly change the meaning of τελέω discussed directly above. Against this metaphorical view of τελέω is the fact that nowhere else among the seven other uses of the word in the book nor elsewhere in the New Testament does it have this metaphorical idea. Nevertheless, immediate context must always be decisive for meaning.

That both the majority of the trumpet and bowl judgments occur, not merely at the end of the age, but throughout the age extending from Christ's first advent to his final advent is apparent from a number of considerations, foremost of which is the significance of the use of Dan. 2.28-29, 45 in Rev. 1.1, 1.19, 4.1, and 22.6, which has been analyzed thoroughly above (in ch. 3, sect. B). There it was concluded that the Daniel 2 allusions in Revelation are intentional and draw with them the contextual idea of Daniel 2, and that the theme of Daniel 2 provides *a* framework of thought for the whole Apocalypse, that is, end-time judgment of cosmic evil and consequent establishment of the eternal kingdom. Whereas in Daniel 2, however, this judgment and kingdom were seen apparently to occur as two virtually simultaneous and brief

---

176. For argument in support of this point, see Beale, *Book of Revelation*, 'Introduction', *in loc.*

events at the very end of history, John understands the Daniel prophecy also as beginning its fulfillment at the end of history, but the end has been unexpectedly extended indefinitely.[177] This is an inaugurated latter-day perspective on Daniel which pervades the visions as well as the letters. Consequently, the visions should not be understood in an exclusively futuristic manner, but as also including significant sections pertaining to the eschatological past and present. The same judgment holds true for the sevenfold seals and the unnumbered visions of Revelation 12–14.

a. *Excursus on the Old Testament Background of the Trumpet Judgments.* The purpose of this excursus is to discuss the Old Testament background of the trumpet judgments which, like the bowls, are primarily designed to portray judgments and not primarily warnings.

(i). *The Background of the Exodus Plagues.* The trumpet judgments are sometimes understood as intended primarily to warn unbelievers that they will suffer the final judgment if they do not repent. The key to understanding the nature of these as 'warning judgments' is the Old Testament background which has been formative for the portrayal of the trumpets. The first five trumpets are patterned after five of the plagues inflicted upon the Egyptians immediately preceding Israel's Exodus: first trumpet (Exod. 9.22-25); second and third trumpet (Exod. 7.20-25); fourth trumpet (Exod. 10.21-23); and fifth trumpet (Exod. 10.12-15).[178] This broad influence can be discerned despite the different order and the fact that all the descriptions of the woes in Rev. 8.7–9.21 and 11.14-19 do not precisely correspond to those in Exodus.

God's overall intention in the plague narratives was to harden Pharaoh's heart so that he would not release Israel (Exod. 4.21) and so that God would have opportunity to perform his plague signs (Exod. 7.3; 10.1-2). Therefore, these signs were not intended to coerce Pharaoh into releasing Israel but functioned primarily to demonstrate Yahweh's incomparable omnipotence to the Egyptians (Exod. 7.5, 17; 10, 22; 8.6,

---

177. See Chapter 3, sect. D.3.b for the notion that the 'mystery' in Rev. 10.7 includes the idea that the eschatological period has been enigmatically lengthened, a concept also associated with 'mystery' in 1QpHab 7.7-8.

178. Cf. H.-P. Müller, 'Die Plagen der Apokalypse: Eine formgeschichtliche Untersuchung', *ZNW* 51 (1960), pp. 268-78.

18 [MT]; 9.16, 29; 10.1-2). God continued to harden Pharaoh's heart in order to continue to multiply his signs, otherwise Pharaoh would have let Israel go, and God would not have had occasion to demonstrate his omnipotence through the performance of the signs. The Exodus plagues also had the function of demonstrating the hardness of heart in Pharaoh and the majority of the Egyptians. In this light, they are also judgments executed against the Egyptians because of their callousness of heart. Indeed, Yahweh was judging the Egyptians because of their idolatry. This is discernible from observing that each plague is a judgment uniquely suited for a particular Egyptian god and is therefore meant as a polemic and judgment against that god.[179] Pharaoh and the Egyptians were also being punished because they were persecuting God's people.

The ultimate purpose of the plague signs was that Yahweh should be glorified. Even when God grants Pharaoh a change of heart so that he releases Israel, he hardens it again. The result of this last act of hardening results in the defeat of the Egyptians in the Red Sea, which results in God's glory (14.4, 8, 17). This is certainly the ultimate purpose of all of the plague signs and of the hardening of Pharaoh's heart (cf. 9.16). Therefore, the final defeat of the Egyptians at the Red Sea is but a culmination of the purpose inherent in all of the preceding plagues.

Consequently, while the Exodus plagues may be conceived as warnings, they are not warnings ultimately meant to cause Pharaoh and the majority of Egyptians to repent but to demonstrate that they are being judged because of their hardness of heart and to demonstrate Yahweh's incomparability and glory. At the heart of every plague sequence is Moses' command to let Israel go, followed by an indictment of Pharaoh and announcement of the coming judgment. This judgment will *definitely* come upon Pharaoh because he will refuse to release the people. The indictment assumes that Pharaoh will not release the people. This assumption is based on the knowledge that Pharaoh's heart is still in a hardened condition. Pharaoh's reaction to the signs is determined to be negative because his heart has been hardened by God. Although the plagues are warnings for which Pharaoh will be held accountable if he does not heed them, they are ultimately intended as judgments. For not only has God foreknown and predicted Pharaoh's obdurate response

---

179. E.g. J.J. Davis, *Moses and the Gods of Egypt* (Grand Rapids: Baker Book House, 1971).

(Exod. 3.19; 4.21; 7.3), he has also caused it (Exod. 4.21; 7.3).[180] Therefore, the plagues are better viewed not so much as warnings for the majority of Egyptians but as actual judgments, as borne out by further study of the plague narratives: cf. Exod. 7.14-25; 7.26–8.11 MT; 8.16-28; 9.1-7; 9.13-25; 10.12-20.[181]

On the other hand, note again Josephus's statement in *Ant.* 2.14.1 that one of the reasons for recounting the record of the Exodus plagues is to warn 'mankind' in general that when they offend God like the Egyptians they will be punished in the same way (cf. Amos 4.10). More pointedly, Philo, *Vit. Mos.* 1.95, says that one purpose of the plagues was to bring the Egyptians to their senses, and he subsequently notes that some 'were converted and brought to a wiser mind' (*Vit. Mos.* 1.147). These comments rightly recognize that the biblical text of Exodus implies that some Egyptians were converted by the plagues, so that the plagues *did* function for them as positive warnings (so Exod. 12.38). However, this does not contradict the preceding analysis, since the majority of the Egyptians did not repent. Consequently, it is still true to say that the purpose of the plagues for the *majority* was to harden them in their intractableness.

The Exodus plagues are both a literary and theological model for the trumpets. Therefore, the trumpet plagues are better viewed primarily as actual judgments on the majority of earth's inhabitants, though secondarily they are warnings for only a remnant. Their secondary function as warnings is indicated by the limitation of the judgments in Rev. 8.7–9.21, which implies that God is restraining his wrath to allow for repentance. Some who think that the main purpose of the trumpets is to warn appeal to 9.20-21, where it says that none of the unbelievers 'repented' from their sins.[182] Alternatively, this text could just as easily suggest that the overall purpose of the trumpets from God's perspective, after all, was to judge by hardening the hearts of unbelievers further. If the

180. So G.K. Beale, 'An Exegetical and Theological Consideration of the Hardening of Pharaoh's Heart in Exodus 4–14 and Romans 9', *Trinity Journal* 5 (1984), pp. 129-54, and J. Piper, *The Justification of God* (Grand Rapids: Baker Book House, 1983), pp. 139-51, who also discusses secondary sources in favor of and against this theologically charged conclusion.

181. So likewise C. Westermann, *Basic Forms of Prophetic Speech* (Philadelphia: Westminster Press, 1974), pp. 66, 217-18; cf. F. Hesse, *Das Verstockungsproblem im Alten Testament* (BZAW, 74; Berlin: A. Töpelmann, 1955), p. 51.

182. So Beasley-Murray, *Revelation*, p. 156.

trumpets are modelled only literarily on the Exodus plagues, then it is possible to view their ultimate aim as being admonitory. But if the theology of the Exodus plagues has been formative behind the composition of the trumpets, then they must ultimately be understood as punishments which further harden the hearts of the majority of people. The trumpets are woes not intended to coerce unbelieving idolaters into repentance but function primarily to demonstrate to them God's uniqueness and incomparable omnipotence. These plagues also function to demonstrate their hardness of heart and the fact that they are being punished because of such hardness, which is expressed by their persistence in idolatry (so 9.20-21!) and their persecution of the saints (cf. 6.9-11). Nevertheless, a remnant of unbelievers will repent in the face of these plagues, though that is not their primary function.

All of these temporal judgments climax in the great last judgment as described in the seventh trumpet (11.15-19). The Exodus plagues are probably understood by John as typological foreshadowings of punishments on the ungodly during the eschatological church age, which precede the final Exodus of God's people from this world to the new creation. The result and goal of all seven trumpet judgments are not only to demonstrate God's incomparability and the just judgment of sinners, but also above all they highlight the glory of God (so 11.13, 15-16; cf. 15.4; 19.1-7). These plagues are judicial indictments of coming punishments upon the persecutors of God's people because they have already refused to repent from their sin. The indictment assumes continued non-repentance because of a hardened attitude. Their reaction to the signs of woe is determined to be negative because they have not been given the 'seal' by God, which would enable them to respond in faith (cf. 7.1-8 and 9.4). Indeed, God intends that these plagues afflict only those both within and outside the visible community of faith who do not have God's protective seal. Israelites in Egypt who would not mark their doors with the lamb's blood would also suffer the fate of the unbelieving Egyptians.

This analysis is consistent with viewing the trumpets as God's answer to the saints' plea in 6.9-11 that their persecutors be punished. The connection with 6.9-11 also explains why the trumpets are not mainly warnings but punishments for the unrepentant persecutors and idolaters.

2. *The Old Testament Background of Trumpets.* The image of trumpets in the Old Testament and Judaism has a number of connotations, which are determined by the context in which the image appears. In the Old

Testament trumpets predominantly indicate: (1) a warning to repent; (2) judgment; (3) victory or salvation; (4) enthronement of Israel's king; (5) eschatological judgment or salvation; and (6) the gathering together of God's people.[183]

In the New Testament the trumpet is sounded to indicate the end-time coming of Christ and the gathering together of his people (Mt. 24.30-31; 1 Cor. 15.52; 1 Thess. 4.16). In the context of Revelation and against the background of the Exodus plagues, the emphasis with the trumpets is on judgment more than warnings to repent (trumpets in *Pseudo-Apoc. John* announce the last judgment). But since both the seals and the trumpets are trials which are unleashed because of the resurrection of Christ (cf. 5.5-6.1ff.), the trumpets must be seen as judgments ultimately executed as an expression of Christ's assumption of kingship and consequent sovereignty over history, as a result of the resurrection. We are reminded again in 8.1 with the revelation of the seventh seal that the exalted Lamb is still leading on the woeful events of history. The close relation of 8.1 to the trumpets in 8.6ff. points further to Christ being the one who ultimately unleashes the trumpet judgments as he did the seal woes. Rev. 8.2 clearly says that the seven angels received their power from God to execute the trumpet judgments (this is also supported by observing the use of the divine passive not only in 8.2 but likewise in 9.1, 3, 5).

In the Old Testament, trumpets also announced an alarm that holy battle was to be engaged against Israel's enemy or against Israel as God's enemy: e.g. Judg. 7.16-22; Jer. 4.5-21; 42.14; 51.27; Ezek. 7.14; Hos. 8.1; Joel 2.1; Zeph. 1.16. The background uppermost in mind for the trumpets is the story of the fall of Jericho, where the trumpets announced the impending victory of a holy war. This is evident from the parallelism of seven trumpets blown by seven priestly figures (equivalent to seven angels with seven trumpets in Rev. 8.2, 6ff.;[184] the priestly

---

183. Cf. Caird, *Revelation*, pp. 107-11; Beasley-Murray, *Revelation*, pp. 152-54; Num. 10.1-10; G. Friedrich, 'σάλπιγξ, κτλ.', *TDNT*, II, pp. 76-85; M.J. Harris, 'σάλπιγξ', *DNTT*, III, pp. 874-75; for survey of usage in Judaism cf. E.R. Goodenough, *Jewish Symbols in the Greco–Roman World* (Princeton, NJ: Princeton University Press, 1988), pp. 82-115.

184. So G.W. Buchanan, *The Book of Revelation: Its Introduction and Prophecy* (The Mellen Biblical Commentary, New Testament Series, 22; Lewiston, NY: Edwin Mellen Press, 1993), p. 204.

nature of the seven angels is supported from 15.5-6). The priests represent God's authority, which is symbolized by the ark with which they are formally associated (note the implied presence of the ark in Rev. 8.3-5 in the light of explicit reference in 11.19). In Joshua 6 God tells Joshua that He has decided that Jericho will fall at the hands of the Israelites. He commands Joshua to commission seven priests to take seven trumpets, position themselves in front of the ark and march around the city with the people following behind, once each day for six consecutive days. On the seventh day the priests and the people were to march seven times around the city. The seventh time around the priests were to blow their trumpets and the people were to shout. The result of this was that a severe earthquake would occur which would destroy the city. Joshua and the Israelites followed God's instructions and Jericho fell. Interestingly, there was 'silence' followed by a trumpet judgment, which is a pattern found in Rev. 8.1-5 ff.[185]

This background clarifies two important ideas necessary for understanding the trumpet woes in Revelation. First, the emphasis with the trumpets is on judgment more than warnings to repent. In fact, the Jericho account highlights the theological background of the Exodus plagues discussed above. That is, the trumpets blown by the priests, like the plagues on Egypt, are *not* warnings at all, but indicate ultimately only judgment, which God has already decided to bring upon his antagonists and those at enmity with his people. The background of the Egyptian plagues together with the fall of Jericho shows that the trumpets in Revelation primarily connote the idea of judgment.[186]

The second idea highlighted by the Joshua 6 model is that the first six trumpets in Revelation 8–9 are punishments preliminary to a climactic judgment. Strictly speaking, the first six trumpets in Joshua 6 were announcements of the judgment on the seventh day. However, they were also part of the process leading up to and necessary for the carrying out of the activities of the seventh day, which culminated in the decisive judgment of Jericho. Likewise, the initial six trumpets of the Apocalypse should be viewed as necessary preliminary woes leading up to and climaxing in a decisive judgment. The definitive judgment of the

---

185. Paulien, *Decoding Revelation's Trumpets*, p. 232.

186. This is contrary to the position of most commentators who see the primary thrust being warnings intended to induce genuine repentance (e.g. Sweet, *Revelation*, p. 161; Wilcock, *I Saw Heaven Opened*, p. 95; Ladd, *Revelation*, p. 124).

seventh trumpet is the last judgment at the end of history (see 11.15-19). At this time the 'Great City' (so 11.8), of which Jericho was an anticipatory type, will finally and decisively be destroyed, as described in 11.13: the phrase 'in that hour there was a great earthquake, and a tenth of the city fell' likely indicates the beginning of the final judgment and not some partial temporal trial, though the design of the present chapter does not allow space to develop that notion here). The trumpets metaphorically portray the trials which are destined to afflict the persecutors of God's people throughout the interadvent age, preceding and leading up to the last judgment.

In the light of 9.20-21 ('the rest...who were not killed by these plagues did not repent...'), the trumpets can be seen formally also as warnings to repent. As in the case of Jericho and the Egyptian plagues, however, they are warnings which are not primarily intended to induce repentance but are punishments for those who are intractably obdurate (as 9.20-21 shows) and for whom warnings will never be positively effective. That such a notion of punishments issued in the form of warnings which are not intended to be heeded ultimately by the majority is plausible in the light of the dual purpose of the original Exodus plagues (as discussed above in the first section of this excursus). Together with the idea of judgment, the trumpets at Jericho also indicated victory for God and his people. This confirms the same thrust with the trumpets in Revelation.

It is suitable that the trumpet judgments would be placed immediately after ch. 7, where the people of God have been portrayed as a fighting army (7.3-8), who conduct victorious holy war ironically by remaining faithful despite earthly suffering (e.g. 7.14).[187] The blowing of multiple trumpets, in contrast to only one trumpet, indicated a call to fight against the enemy in Num. 10.2-9. This suggests that the depiction of the war camp in Numbers 1–2ff., which was seen to lie behind the military organization at Qumran and behind Rev. 7.4-8, was also formative for Qumran's view of trumpets in the last battle (on which see directly below) and continues to be evoked in the trumpet woes of Revelation 8–9.

Earlier in this section (3.c) we observed that the saints' prayers from 6.9-11 for vindication against their persecutors is answered both in the final judgment of the seventh seal, as well as in the following trumpet

---

187. So, persuasively, Bauckham, *Climax of Prophecy*, pp. 210-37 (see the summary of his view in this respect above at Chapter 1).

woes. These prayers arise to God, and God responds to the prayers by causing inaugurated and final judgment on the earth. The trumpet afflictions coming on the heels of ch. 7 should be seen as another of the ways the saints carry on holy war: they pray that God's judicial decree will be carried out against their persecutors. The saints wage ironic warfare by means of sacrificial suffering, which makes their prayer of vindication acceptable to God (see 8.4). The integral relation of the believers' prayer for vindication is closely paralleled to the Qumran strategy for fighting the end-time battle. Part of the war plan was to write prayers for the destruction of the enemy on trumpets to be blown during the battle (on which see further below in this section). World disturbance and the apparently evil occurrences of history are not a sign that events are out of God's control, but are an expression of holy war, coming as a result of the church's prayers and God's sovereign response to those prayers.[188] Just as at Jericho, the saints do not directly fight in the battle, but wait on God to fight for them from heaven.

God typically fought Israel's holy wars from heaven through causing the elements of nature (inclement weather, etc.) to thwart the enemy. This is how he defeated the Egyptians, both through the ten plagues, and then at the Red Sea. Likewise, the sun, moon and hail were employed to defeat the Amorites (Josh. 10.10-15), and 'the stars fought from heaven' against the Canaanites, causing them to be defeated through a flood (Judg. 5.19-21). Some of the descriptions of victory in holy war are literal (Exod. 7–15), others figurative (Ps. 18.4-19), and sometimes the portrayals are a mixture of the two (as in Judg. 5), but most of the portrayals are figurative. Against this background, the portrayal of the trumpet plagues in chs. 8–9 with the same Old Testament imagery enhances further the notion that the trumpets depict God conducting holy war.

It is beyond coincidence that 'a very loud trumpet sound' summons Israel to Mount Sinai to acknowledge God's kingship and presence among them after the plagues of Egypt have been executed.[189] Indeed, Philo, *Spec. Leg.* 2.188-92, says the feast of 'Trumpets' was based on Exod. 19.16, where the trumpet was blown because it 'is the instrument used in war...for engaging battle and also for recalling the troops...to their respective camps'; the feast of 'Trumpets' expressed thanks 'to

---

188. T.F. Torrance, *The Apocalypse Today* (Grand Rapids: Eerdmans, 1959), pp. 60-61.

189. Exod. 19.6, 13-19; cf. Beasley-Murray, *Revelation*, p. 154.

God the peace-maker... who [first] destroys faction both in cities and in the various parts of the universe'. Philo adds that both the trumpet of Exod. 19.16 and these festive trumpets were directed 'partly to the nation [Israel] in particular, partly to all mankind in general'.

This Old Testament pattern of destructive plagues followed by the peace of kingship has been partially formative for John's introduction of the end-time kingship of God in Rev. 11.15-19 by the seventh trumpet following the plagues of the preceding trumpets. The presence of the Exodus background is clear from noticing that the theophanic description of Exod. 19.16, 18 ('sounds and lightning flashes... quaking') has been formative for the similar descriptions which both introduce (cf. Rev. 8.5) and conclude (cf. 11.19) the trumpet series.[190] It is appropriate that a trumpet sound would mark a transition between the defeat of Egypt and the imminent defeat of Jericho, all of which were conducted under God's military leadership.

The above theological conclusion about the trumpets as punitive judgments against hardened unbelievers, instead of mere warnings to induce repentance, is strikingly similar to the systematic use of trumpets in the last eschatological battle conducted by the saints of Qumran against the forces of Belial (so 1QM 3; 8.10–9.16; 10.6-8; 11.9-11; 16; 17.10-15; 18.3-5). This also is based partly on the episode of Joshua 6 and the narrative of Numbers 10 (note appeal to Num. 10.9 in 1QM 10, 6-8). Seven Aaronic priests are mentioned in the Qumran War Scroll, although only six have trumpets. These trumpets announce the judgment and defeat of the enemy, as is clear from the inscriptions which were to be written on them listed in 3.3-11 (e.g. 'to put to flight all who hate righteousness, and withdrawal of favours from those who hate God'; 'vengeance of his anger upon all the sons of darkness'; 'to destroy ungodliness'). This is emphasized by summarizing all the trumpets as 'trumpets of slaughter' (8.8-9; 9.1-2; 16.9). The very blowing of the trumpets themselves brings about part of the defeat. The defeat heralded by the trumpets also means that the saints 'shall be remembered before... God and shall be saved from [their]... enemies' (10.7-8). One of the Aaronic priests was to carry no trumpet but only to walk in front of all the troops 'to strengthen their hands in battle'. The other six were to sound their trumpets seven times for each assault which the troops of Qumran made against the enemy. The enemy would be routed

---

190. See further 4.5, 8.5 and 11.19, and Bauckham, *Climax of Prophecy*, pp. 202-204.

after the seventh assault, and the saints were to pursue them until they were finally destroyed (8.12–9.7).

In addition, seven Levitical priests were also appointed to go with the seven Aaronic priests, and they were assigned to carry seven 'horns'. These were to be blown during the battle in order to bring about victory by confounding the enemy (7.13-15; 8.9-10). This is related to the Talmudic reflection that a trumpet was to be blown on Tishri I, which in the rabbinic period came to be viewed as the day beginning the New Year. God was expected to judge all people on this day at the end of history. The purpose of blowing the trumpet on this last day was, not only to herald the last judgment, but also to confuse Satan (cf. *b. Roš. Haš.* 16a-b). Indeed, the trumpet symbol in post-biblical Judaism had a predominantly eschatological significance.[191] The trumpets and horns in the *War Scroll* do not produce a magical effect of victory nor do they signify that the saints on earth win the battle merely by their own efforts, but they indicate the ultimate fact that the defeat of the enemy is a result of God conducting battle from heaven through his angelic hosts (e.g. 1QM 9.10-16; 11.17–12.11). This judgment of the enemy is likened to that brought on Pharaoh and the Egyptians (11.9-11; 14.1). The main difference between the trumpet judgments in Qumran and Revelation is that the former immediately precedes the climax of history, whereas, on our reading, the latter encompass the whole of the church age. Only the last trumpet heralds the very end of history (although the seventh trumpet could have been imminent from John's perspective, as would then be the case with every Christian generation throughout the interadvent age).

Life of Adam and Eve (Apocalypse) 22.1-3 portrays 'the archangel …sounding his trumpet' to signal that God was about to pass 'sentence' and 'judgment' upon Adam and Eve, which occurs in direct connection with mention of them 'hiding' from God (23.1-2), a passage also alluded to in Rev. 6.17.

Possibly also in the background are the seven trumpets blown by the Levitical priests, which formed part of the music for the temple liturgy (1 Chron. 15.24; Neh. 12.41; note the association with the ark of God in the former text). These were blown each of the seven days of the week (cf. the context of 1 Chron. 15.24–16.7, 37; Neh. 12.41-47). Such trumpets were to 'be as a reminder of' Israel's needs 'before…God'

---

191. Goodenough, *Symbols*, pp. 11-113; cf. also Isa. 27.13; Joel 2.1, 15; Zeph. 1.16; Zech. 9.14; *Pss. Sol.* 11.1; *4 Ezra* 6.23.

and were to remind Israel to thank God for the way he had graciously remembered them in past times (e.g. 1 Chron. 16.4; Num. 10.10; Ps. 150).[192]

D. *The Use of* μυστήριον *in the Apocalypse and Elsewhere in the New Testament Against the Old Testament–Jewish Background*

The aim of this section is to analyze John's use of μυστήριον, to compare it with similar uses elsewhere in the New Testament, and to determine how these uses can be better understood in the light of the use of 'mystery' in the Old Testament and in early Judaism. Therefore, this is a selective, not exhaustive, survey of 'mystery' in the relevant literature.

1. *The Use of 'Mystery'* (רז *and* μυστήριον) *in the Old Testament and Early Judaism*

The first time that the word 'mystery' occurs in the Old Testament is in the book of Daniel, where it appears eight times in Daniel 2 (2.18-19, 27-30, 47) and once in Daniel 4 (4.6, MT). The 'mystery' in Daniel 2 refers apparently to both the content and the interpretation of Nebuchadnezzar's dream concerning the statue with four different metallic sections, all of which the king could not call to mind. The interpretation of the dream is that the four sections of the colossus represent four kingdoms, the first of which is the Babylonian. The focus of the dream and the interpretation, however, is on the fourth kingdom, since more discussion is dedicated to it than to any of the others and since it is the obvious climax of the vision and interpretation: God will destroy the fourth kingdom 'in the latter days'[193] and set up his kingdom forever

---

192. For broader background discussion of the trumpets cf. Caird, *Revelation*, pp. 107-11. See Paulien, *Decoding Revelation's Trumpets*, for a thorough analysis of the first four trumpets and their Old Testament–Jewish background, though important qualifications must be made about his approach (for evaluation see Beale, review of *Decoding Revelation's Trumpets: Literary Allusions and Interpretation of Revelation 8:7-12* [Andrews University Seminary Doctoral Dissertation Series, 21; Berrien Springs, MI: Andrews University Press, 1987], by J. Paulien, in *JBL* 111 [1992], pp. 358-61, and above at Chapter 1).

193. The phrase 'in the latter days' occurs in the Aramaic only once (2.28), though 'after this' in 2.29 and 2.45 appear to be eschatological synonyms, which is borne out by the LXX translation in 2.29 and 2.45 of ἐπ᾽ ἐσχάτων τῶν ἡμερῶν, though Theodotion renders the Aramaic 'after this' fairly literally by μετὰ ταῦτα

(Dan. 2.34-35, 40-45). The phrase 'latter days' is not merely a reference to the indefinite future, as it sometimes may be elsewhere in the
Old Testament, but is 'eschatological' because it refers primarily to the
end point of salvation history, which conforms to the way the equivalent Hebrew phrases are used in Dan. 8.17, 19, 10.14, and 11.40. Therefore, the revelation of the 'mystery' of Daniel 2 refers to the *hidden*
content and interpretation of the king's dream, and the primary focus of
the meaning of the dream was that in the end times God would destroy
the kingdom of evil and establish his own eternal kingdom.[194]

It is likely no coincidence that 'mystery' in Qumran sometimes refers
to an eschatological reality pertaining either to the defeat of the evil
kingdom or establishment of the divine kingdom, or that it is associated
with other Daniel allusions. The word רז appears in 1QS 3-4 three
times in connection with allusions to various aspects of the end-time
trial narrated in Daniel 12,[195] with overtones of Daniel 2. Just as the destruction of the evil world kingdoms in the end time formed the subject
of the 'mystery' in Daniel 2, so the subject of the 'mysteries' in 1QS is
likewise: 'But in His mysteries…God has set an end for the existence
of Perversity… He will destroy it forever' (1QS 4.18-19; likewise
3.23). And, as in Daniel, it is not merely God but his Spirit who reveals
the mysteries (cf. Dan. 4.6 [MT] and 1QS 4.6), though the same mysteries are hidden from the ungodly (1QS 9.18; 11.3, 5, 19). The fulfillment
of the Daniel 2 and 12 prophecy is to occur imminently in the midst of
the elect Essene community.[196] Similarly, 'mystery' in the *Hymns* Scroll
refers to the final end of the evil kingdom (1QH 4.26-28; 12.13, 20;
13.13), also in connection with the notion that there is a select group

---

(see on ch. 3.B.1 for textual comparisons of 2.28-29, 45 in the LXX and Theodotion). Though this is the focus of the narrative, it is apparent that even the first three
kingdoms are included implicitly in the eschatological time reference (see further
ch. 3.B.1).

194. 'Mystery' (רז) also occurs in Dan. 4.6 (MT) with reference only to the hidden interpretation of the king's prophetic dream which Daniel makes known to
him, though this dream does not concern explicit eschatological issues.

195. Cf. 'the man of insight' who is to 'instruct' in 3.13 (cf. Dan. 11.33; 12.10),
the 'time of the end' in 3.23 (Dan. 12.4, 6, 9), the 'periods of distress' in 3.23 (Dan.
12.1), and the 'prince of light' (Dan. 12.1). For further analysis of the Daniel parallels (including Aramaic and Hebrew comparisons) here and those mentioned elsewhere in the following discussion on Qumran, see Beale, *Use of Daniel*, pp. 23-42).
English translations of Qumran are from Dupont-Sommer, *Essene Writings*.

196. The use of רז in 1QS 9.18 has similar affinities with Daniel 12.

within the Qumran community who, as Dan. 11.33-35 and 12.3, 10 prophesied, would have insight and instruct others about the interpretation of eschatological happenings: for example, there will be 'destruction for all the peoples of the lands, to cut off at the time of judgment all who transgress... And through me you have illumined the face of many...for you have given me to know your marvellous mysteries' (1QH 4.26-28).

Comparable to 1QS 3-4, 1QM 17.9ff. also employs רז in close relationship to the tribulation and Michael's deliverance foreseen by Dan. 11.45–12.3, as well as to the idea of the defeat of evil and the reign of God's people in the eschaton from Daniel 2: the saints would suffer distress but be delivered from it, and would also participate in the establishment of God's kingdom (1QM 17.1-9). 1QM 14.9-10 appeals to the same Daniel background, and 'mystery' there refers to the 'dominion of Belial' and his 'hostility', from which true saints are protected so that they do not fall away from God's 'covenant'; they have even been protected from destructive 'spirits' (1QM 14.11). This covenantal protection finds consummate expression in God's resurrecting of the saints on the last day, and the judgment of the cosmic powers of evil, which 1QM 14.14-15 refers to as God's 'marvellous mysteries'.[197]

The word רז appears throughout the sect's writings to refer to Old Testament prophecies which are beginning fulfillment. In fact, 'mystery' could be paraphrased as 'prophecy' or, better, 'fulfilled prophecy' in most of its occurrences in Qumran. The reason for this is that it was inextricably linked originally with the revelation of Daniel's eschatological prophecy about the judgment of the opponents of God and the establishment of God's kingdom (i.e. it is virtually a metonymy of adjunct for fulfillment of prophecy). The most obvious examples of this are the repeated expressions 'the mystery to come' which may echo Dan. 2.28 and 2.29: 'mysteries...what is to be' (1QS 11.3-4; 1Q27 1.3 and 1.4; cf. the synonymous parallelism in the latter text of 'that which would befall them' and 'that shall come to pass' [1.5]).

---

197. The use of 'mystery' in 1QM 3.9 and 16.11 functions comparably in its respective contexts to that in columns 14 and 17, though the focus is on the victory of God. 1QS 27 also links 'mystery' to the defeat of evil in the latter days and the confirmation of the righteous, as well as affirming that the wicked will not be able to understand 'the mystery to come'; but the righteous are told how to discern the meaning of the 'mystery'.

Why did Qumran use 'mystery' instead of the more conventional 'prophecy' or 'fulfillment of prophecy' or 'what shall come to pass' or other equivalent phrases which are sometimes also used? Certainly, part of the reason is that 'mystery' in Daniel 2 also referred to the divinely inspired interpretation of the hidden meaning of a prophetic, symbolic revelation. Just as the prophet Daniel was given insight into the veiled mystery, so the Teacher of Righteousness was given insight, not only about the hidden meaning of Daniel's prophecies, but also about many other prophecies outside of Daniel. Qumran sometimes uses 'mystery' to connote fulfillment of prophecy because the Teacher of Righteousness and his followers believed that they had specially given insight into the meaning of the prophecies which the Old Testament prophets themselves did not have. The new insight which they had was the precise manner in which the prophecies were being fulfilled. First, the prophecies of Israel's salvation and deliverance from pagan oppression were being fulfilled, not in the nation in general, but in the Qumran covenanters in particular who represented the true remnant (e.g. cf. 'the remnant of your people' twice in 1QM 14.8-9). They were the true Israel out in the desert, and the religious leaders in Jerusalem were the covenant breakers who were compromising with the pagan oppressors (Rome) and were fulfilling the role of the covenantal 'hypocrites' (Dan. 11.30-35).[198] A good example of this is the *Habakkuk Pesher* which understands various verses from that Old Testament book to find specific concrete fulfillment in the Jewish compromisers, the Romans, and the elect of the Essene community.

An added dimension of why the particular word 'mystery' was used may also be because the prophecies were beginning fulfillment in an *unexpected* manner. One such use occurs with reference to Hab. 2.3, which says the fulfillment of the prophecy will assuredly come but there will be a period in which God's people must wait faithfully for it to happen. The Qumran commentator interprets this to mean that the eschatological climax of history is to occur within the generation of the covenanters; however, the 'mystery' is that 'the final time will last long ... for the mysteries of God are marvellous' (1QpHab 7.7; likewise, 7.9-14, where also 'mystery' appears). According to Old Testament–Jewish

---

198. See 4QpNah 1.2, where reference is made to the Greek king Demetrius 'who sought to enter Jerusalem on the counsel of those who *seek smooth things*',which is likely an allusion to Dan. 11.32 and which may refer either to compromising Hellenistic Jews or Pharisees (on this see further at sect. 2. below).

expectations, the final tribulation and defeat of ungodly forces in one final battle at the end of history apparently was to occur quickly (e.g. cf. Dan. 2.31-45; *4 Ezra* 11–13, and *2 Bar.* 36–42, which directly allude to Dan. 2 and 7). The Habakkuk commentator says that such a lengthening of an expected brief eschaton 'exceeds everything spoken of by the Prophets' (1QpHab 7.7-8), which is his way of saying that the revelation of the elongation is part of the unexpected aspect of fulfillment.

An especially striking feature reminiscent of Daniel 2 is the combination of פשרו with רז in 1QpHab 7.7-8 and 7.9-14: e.g. '*The interpretation of it* [פשרו] is that the final time will last long and will exceed everything spoken of by the Prophets; for the *mysteries* [רזי] of God are marvellous' (1QpHab 7.7-8).[199] Just as Daniel 2, so also 'the interpretation of mysteries' in 1QpHab 7 refers to special insight into prophetic visions pertaining to the latter days.

The use of 'mystery' (רז, μυστήριον, etc.) elsewhere in Jewish apocalyptic and Judaism is associated with eschatological issues in general and with the end-time coming of a messianic figure in particular.[200] For example, the use in *4 Ezra* 12.37-38 reflects the Daniel 'mystery' since the prophet Daniel is actually mentioned in 12.11, reference to 'mysteries' occurs in direct connection to clear allusions to Dan. 8.26, 11.33, and 12.3-4, 9, and all of this is set in an eschatological context.[201]

---

199. The root פשר occurs 33 times in Daniel, 31 of which are the noun form, and 14 of these have the 3 pers. sg. pronominal suffix (פשרה). In Dan. 2 רז appears 8 times and פשר 13. Though the two words do not occur in direct connection, they must be understood in the light of one another, since the 'mystery' includes both the content of the dream and its interpretation. The two words are most closely linked in Dan. 2.30 ('this *mystery* has not been revealed...but for the purpose of making the *interpretation* known') and 4.6 ('no *mystery* baffles you, tell the visions of my dream which I have seen, along with *its interpretation*', MT).

200. See R.E. Brown, *The Semitic Background of the Term 'Mystery' in the New Testament* (Biblical Series, 21; Philadelphia: Fortress Press, 1968), and M.N.A. Bockmuehl, *Revelation and Mystery in Ancient Judaism and Pauline Christianity* (WUNT, 2; Tübingen: J.C.B. Mohr [Paul Siebeck], 1990), who survey thoroughly these and other uses of 'mystery' in Qumran, Jewish Apocalyptic, the Apocrypha, Philo, Josephus, the Targums, and other early Jewish literature, as well as citing additional relevant bibliography. Also, for a discussion of 'mystery' in the Dead Sea Scrolls and the New Testament, see J. Coppens, ' "Mystery" in the Theology of Saint Paul and its Parallels at Qumran', in J. Murphy-O'Conner (ed.), *Paul and Qumran* (Chicago: The Priory Press, 1968), pp. 132-58.

201. See further Beale, *Use of Daniel*, pp. 122-29; see also Brown, *Semitic Background of the Term 'Mystery'*, p. 22.

Likewise, some of the references to 'mystery' in *1 Enoch* (chs. 46, 52, 71) have an eschatological background in Daniel, since they are used in conjunction with other Daniel allusions in the same context (such as 'son of man', 'ancient of days', etc.).[202] These uses pertain to something hidden which will be revealed in the eschaton.

2. The Use of μυστήριον *Elsewhere in the New Testament Outside of the Apocalypse*
Μυστήριον occurs 27 times in the New Testament. A feature noticeable in a number of the occurrences is that the word is directly linked with Old Testament quotations or allusions. In these cases, at least, 'mystery' appears in order to indicate two things: (1) that Old Testament prophecy is beginning fulfillment, and (2) that this fulfillment is unexpected from the former Old Testament vantage point. With respect to this last point, it is apparent that the various New Testament authors are exegeting Old Testament texts in the light of the Christ event and under the guidance of the Spirit, which result in new interpretative perspectives. While only a very few scholars have observed that μυστήριον occurs in direct connection to Old Testament references, I want to show that this occurs more than previously recognized.[203] Furthermore, prior studies of μυστήριον have not attempted a serious analysis of the Old Testament references which appear in close relationship to μυστήριον. The following analysis will attempt to do this in order to determine how this might shed further light on the use of μυστήριον in the New Testament.

a. The Use in Matthew 13 (and parallels in Mark 4.11 and Luke 8.10).
Μυστήριον is sandwiched in between the telling of the parable of the soils and the explanation of its interpretation in Mt. 13.11, which is part of a larger interlude of vv. 10-17. This interlude introduces, not only

202. See Beale, *Use of Daniel*, pp. 96-113; I suspect there are more uses of 'mystery' in *1 En.* 37–71 which reflect Daniel, but such a possibility must await more analysis; for skepticism of a Daniel influence behind 'mystery' in the *Similitudes*, cf. C. Caragounis, *The Ephesian* Mysterion (ConBNT, 8; Lund: C.W.K. Gleerup, 1977), pp. 128-29.
203. E.g. see Bockmuehl, *Revelation and Mystery*, who has observed this pattern more consistently and thoroughly than others in the Pauline uses; he also surveys all of Paul's references to μυστήριον; likewise, see Brown, *Semitic Background of the Term 'Mystery'*, who surveys all uses in the New Testament (see Bockmuehl and Brown for additional relevant bibliography).

the interpretation of the soils' parable, but also a number of other parables about the kingdom in vv. 24-52. The point of the interlude is to underscore the purpose of the parables.

Jesus' disciples ask him why he speaks in parables. His first response is: 'To you it has been given to know the mysteries of the kingdom of heaven, but to them it has not been given' (13.10). Verses 11-17 give reasons supporting this initial response, but we will focus only on the response because of the limited scope of the present discussion. The crucial word in the response is 'mysteries', which G.E. Ladd has briefly explained against the background of Daniel: he says that 'mystery' in Daniel refers to a divine revelation about eschatological matters which is hidden from human understanding, but then is revealed by God himself to the prophet, and he sees 'mystery' having the same general idea in Matthew and the rest of the New Testament.[204] The Old Testament, and especially Daniel, prophesied that the kingdom would come visibly, crush all opposition, judge all godless Gentiles, and establish Israel as a kingdom ruling over all the earth. The mystery is the revelation that 'in the person and mission of Jesus...the kingdom which is to come finally in apocalyptic power, as foreseen in Daniel, has in fact entered into the world in advance in a hidden form to work secretly within and among men'.[205]

In addition to the Daniel 2 background for 'mystery', the Isaiah 6 quotation in 13.14-15 further explains Jesus' initial response to the disciples,[206] as do the following parables in Matthew 13 which contain Old Testament allusions. Ladd explains how these parables in Mt. 13.18-52 explain the hidden or unexpected fulfillment of the beginning form of the prophesied Old Testament kingdom (note the explicit notion of 'hiddenness' in vv. 33, 44): instead of coming with external manifestations of power and forcibly imposing a kingdom on people, the kingdom rather concerns internal decisions of the heart to receive or not receive the message of the kingdom (the parable of the soils); consequently, the growth of the kingdom cannot be gauged by eyesight (parable of the leaven); final judgment has not yet come, so that the righteous and wicked are not yet separated from one another, but continue to co-exist until the very end of history (parable of the tares of the

204. Ladd, *Presence of the Future*, pp. 223-24; likewise A.E. Harvey, 'The Use of Mystery Language in the Bible', *JTS* NS 31 (1980), pp. 320-36 (333).

205. Ladd, *Presence of the Future*, p. 225.

206. The limits of the present study prevent analysis of the Isaiah 6 quotation.

field); the completed form of the kingdom is not established immediately, but begins very tiny, and then, after a process of growth, fills the
world (parable of the mustard seed); though the kingdom appears hidden, it is to be desired like a treasure or priceless pearl.[207]

Ladd's analysis of 'mystery' in Matthew 13 is astute and convincing.

b. *Romans 11.25-26*: '*For I do not wish you to be ignorant, brothers,
about this mystery, in order that you should not be wise among your-
selves, that a partial hardening has happened to Israel until the fulness
of the Gentiles should come in, and so all Israel will be saved.*' Romans
11.25-26 is one of the thorniest texts in the New Testament. Nevertheless, my study of Romans 11 must be abbreviated because of the limited scope of this chapter. Therefore, my point of departure is to begin
with Seyoon Kim's recent article on μυστήριον in Rom. 11.25, since he
summarizes the most relevant and recent studies on the subject, and my
own view can be understood better in the light of his conclusions.[208]

First, he reviews the conclusions from his earlier work, *The Origin of
Paul's Gospel*, where he plausibly argued that Paul interpreted his call
in view of Isaiah 49 (cf. Isa. 49.1, 5-6 in Gal. 1.15-16),[209] and, specifically, that his understanding of the 'mystery' in Rom. 11.25-26 originated, not only from meditation on Isaiah 49,[210] but also from reflection
on Isaiah 6 (see the parallels adduced from Isaiah 6 in Paul's letters).[211]
He then showed in his earlier book that the 'mystery' of Romans 11
and Paul's Gentile apostleship could be explained well against the background of Isaiah 6 and 49:[212] (1) God's hardening of Israel (Isa. 6.10);
(2) the 'until when' of Rom. 11.25 corresponds formally to the 'Lord,
how long?' and God's answer 'until when' (Isa. 6.11); (3) Paul's Gentile commission was linked logically with Israel's hardening: God has
hardened Israel in order to make a place for a Gentile mission in history

207. Ladd, *Presence of the Future*, pp. 229-42.

208. S. Kim, 'The "Mystery" of Rom 11.25-6 Once More', *NTS* 43 (1997), pp.
412-29.

209. He elaborates on the influence of Isa. 49.1-6 in Gal. 1–2: (1) Isa. 49.3 in
Gal. 1.24; (2) Isa. 49.4 in Gal. 2.2; cf. also Isa. 42.6-7 and 49.6 in 2 Cor. 4.4-6.

210. Kim says 'it is well known that Paul interpreted his apostolic call at the
Damascus christophany in the light of Isa 49.1-6' (Kim, '"Mystery"', p. 421).

211. Kim, '"Mystery"', p. 414. Especially see S. Kim, *The Origin of Paul's
Gospel* (Grand Rapids: Eerdmans, 1982), pp. 94-95.

212. See Kim's summary of this in Kim, '"Mystery"', pp. 414-15.

(Rom. 11.11-12, 15, 28-32), and, as long as Israel remains hardened, Paul must preach to them and be a light (2 Cor. 4.4-6) in order that God's salvation may reach to the ends of the earth (Isa. 49.6 = Acts 13.47; Isa. 42.6-7, 16 = Acts 26.18); (4) a hope for Israel's eventual salvation also can be understood against the background of both Isa. 6.13 and 49.5-6; (5) when the 'mystery' is seen in connection to Rom. 11.11, 13-14 and 15.15-16, 19, 23, it appears to reflect Paul's self-understanding that he was first accountable to go to the Gentiles but also responsible to play a key role in Israel's eventual salvation by means of his jealousy-provoking Gentile ministry (an implication illuminated by Isa. 49.5-6); and (6) Luke affirms that Paul appealed to Isa. 6.9-10 (Acts 28.25-28) in claiming that Israel's hardened response to the gospel led to Paul's mission among the Gentiles.

Developing his earlier conclusion about the 'mystery', Kim says the following about the result of the Damascus Road christophany:

> Once Paul realized God's call and sending to the gentiles and God's *Heilsplan* about the temporary hardening of Israel and about the order of salvation (the gentiles first and Israel at the end) by interpreting his experience in the light of the call narratives of Isaiah (Isa 6) and the *Ebed* (Isa 49), he could have been drawn to the passages like Isa 45.14-17, 20-5; 59.19-20; etc. as well as Deut 32.21, seeing them confirm that understanding of God's *Heilsplan*.[213]

Presumably, Kim believes that, as Paul reflected on Isa. 6.8-10, he saw the patterns of Isaiah's commission as being recapitulated in himself, so that he realized that, like Isaiah, Israel would also react in massive unbelief to his preaching, so that Paul would have to turn elsewhere for a reception of his message.[214] Likewise, consideration of Isa. 49.1-6 led Paul to believe that, like the prophesied Servant, his ministry to Israel would be rejected and that he would find success with Gentiles. Kim *implies* that the 'mystery' of Romans 11 involves, not only the zealous Pharisee's unexpected call and commission to the Gentiles on the Damascus Road, but also the unexpected way in which the Gentiles were being saved: Gentile first and then Jew, whereas the Old Testament prophetic pattern was Israel first and then Gentile.

---

213. Kim, '"Mystery"', p. 421. In addition to Isa. 45 and 59, Kim also has in mind Mic. 4.1-8.

214. Cf. Kim, *Origin of Paul's Gospel*, pp. 93-94.

Kim suggests the possibility that, after reflecting on Isaiah 6 and 49, Paul was led to other passages (Isaiah 45 and 59, as well as Deuteronomy 32 [cited above]) which confirmed him in his belief that God's plan all along had meant that Gentiles would be saved first, and then Israel's salvation would occur. The two Isaiah texts and Deuteronomy are appealed to as 'confirming' texts for Paul since some, apparently including even to some extent Kim,[215] see in them a *Heilsplan* order of salvation to Gentile first, followed subsequently by Israel's redemption. If this is an accurate tracing of the exegetical pathway followed by Paul, then it would seem that Paul should have been driven to the conclusion that there was no mystery about this order of salvation after all, because there were clear passages all along in the Old Testament which prophesied such a pattern.

Kim, however, does not draw this conclusion, perhaps because he sees that the order of Israel's salvation first and then that of Gentiles was so predominant in Jewish tradition that it had blinded early Judaism to the reversed order found in some of the above-mentioned Isaiah and Deuteronomy texts. If so, Paul's exegetical discoveries would, in effect, amount to the revelation of a 'mystery' since they would be reversing the dominant expectations of Jewish tradition and not necessarily that of the Old Testament itself.

Such an order of Gentile then Jew, however, is far from obvious in the passages adduced from Isaiah and Deuteronomy. Each of the passages cited in Isaiah 45 and 59 do mention Gentile salvation followed by a mention of Israelite salvation but there is no discernible intention to delineate a future historical order in these texts. These passages are more easily understood to indicate that the latter-day deliverance of God will include both Gentile and Israel. The clear pattern in the prophets, especially Isaiah, is that of Israelite salvation which then sparks off a movement of Gentiles streaming in to share in Israel's salvation; so Isa. 2.2-4;[216] 60.1-14; 61.1-6; Zech. 2.2-11; 8.11-23. Now, either there

---

215. Kim cites O. Hofius, 'Das Evangelium und Israel', O. Hufius (ed.), *Paulusstudien* (WUNT, 51; Tübingen: J.C.B. Mohr [Paul Siebeck], 1989), pp. 201-202. Though Kim acknowledges problems with Hofius's view, he does consider it a viable possibility (Kim, '"Mystery"', pp. 417 and, especially, 421 and 429).

216. God's blessing on Israel is before the blessing of Gentiles in the beginning of v. 2: 'The mountain of the house of the Lord will be established as the chief of the mountains... and all the nations will stream to it'; the Mic. 4.1-8 parallel to Isa. 2 is to be taken in the same way, despite the fact that Hofius adduces the same passage as a prooftext of Gentile–then–Israel salvation!

is an inherent contradiction between Isaiah 45 (and 59) and the other Isaiah (and Zechariah) texts just cited or one set of texts needs to be interpreted in the light of the other set. I contend that Isaiah 45 and 59 are best understood within the clearer framework of such texts as Isaiah 60 and 61, especially since any particular *Heilsplan* order is ambiguous at best in Isaiah 45 and 59.[217] If later-inserted chapter numbers are not considered, then one could more easily see Isa. 59.20-21 together with 60.1-3ff. forming a clear pattern of God's revelatory blessing first on Israel, which subsequently attracts Gentiles. This is significant because Isa. 59.20-21 is quoted in Rom. 11.26-27.

Kim also mentions the possibility that Paul's mind may have focused on Deut. 32.21 together with the Isaiah 45 and 59 texts, which would have further confirmed his new understanding of a 'Gentile first then Israel' salvation plan (cf. Rom. 10.19; 11.11, 14).[218] The Deuteronomy passage, however, says nothing about an order of salvation among Gentiles and Jews but merely that God would make Israel jealous with another nation and that he would 'provoke them to anger with a foolish nation'. In the context of Deuteronomy, this apparently referred to another nation which would invade Israel and take her into captivity; there is no hint in the Deuteronomy context about the conversion of or blessing upon Gentiles. Indeed, the reason given for the statement of Deut. 32.21 is: 'For a fire is kindled in My anger, and burns...and consumes... I will heap misfortunes on them' (Deut. 32.22-23; cf. 28.49-50). Nevertheless, that this is the way Paul understood the Deuteronomy text is clear from Rom. 10.19 and 11.11, 14. Consequently, the Deuteronomy passage is certainly part of the 'mystery' Paul has in mind in Romans 11, since the Old Testament reader would never have understood Deuteromony in this way, but Paul does because of the way he initially understood his call at the Damascus Road and, subsequently, because of the way Gentiles and Jews were, in fact, responding

217. Kim recognizes that Isa. 45.13 appears to indicate blessing on Israel first, then blessing of Gentiles in 45.14 ff. (Kim, '"Mystery"', p. 417), and even v. 14 itself refers to the nations coming to Israel because they have recognized first that 'God is with you [Israel]'; likewise, the 'him' of Isa. 45.24 is likely Israel and not God: 'Men will come to him, and all who were angry at him shall be put to shame'. Isa. 59.18-19 may refer merely to the 'fear' of nations who are in awe of God's mighty acts on behalf of Israel (cf. similarly Kim's query about Hofius's view of Isa. 59.19a [Kim, '"Mystery"', p. 417]).

218. Kim, '"Mystery"', pp. 418, 421, where Kim grants the plausibility of the suggestion by J. Jeremias.

to the gospel message. It is not clear that Kim sees the 'mystery' of Rom. 11.25 in this precise way with respect to Deuteronomy 32.

As far as I can determine, *the Old Testament evidence which Kim adduces does not* explain how Paul could have had a clear basis for explaining that the salvation plan all along was to be 'Gentiles first and Jews second'. Isaiah 6 and 49 together merely indicate that a remnant of Israel will believe and that Gentiles will also receive blessings, and, if an order were to be discerned in these two texts, it would be: (1) the remnant of Israel first, then (2) Gentiles (so Isa. 49.5-6), not the other way around. Neither do the texts from Isaiah 45, Isaiah 59, and Micah 4 indicate a Gentile-first-then-Israel order. And, one can see how Paul now understands Deuteronomy 32, but it certainly cannot be seen as a text which could give him a reasonable basis for discerning any order in the salvation of people groups.

Of course, one could contend, and some actually do, that Paul read into these Old Testament texts a new understanding which twisted their original meaning, and that Paul tries to justify such a procedure by calling his exegetically wild conclusions a 'mystery'. Kim, however, does not want to do this. As we mentioned, if Kim is right about these Old Testament texts and their meaning, then why would Paul select a word like 'mystery' in Rom. 11.25? Alternatively, some would contend that 'mystery' merely refers to a prophecy whose historical fulfillment had formerly been hidden in God's heavenly counsel and did not yet exist on earth, and that when it is fulfilled and becomes reality in history the 'mystery' has been revealed.[219] Kim appears, however, to want to fill the content of the 'mystery' with more than such a mere fulfillment meaning.

I have labored to summarize Kim's view and to raise a few questions about it, not because I think he is essentially wrong. I believe he is correct in seeing Isaiah 6 and 49 behind Paul's understanding of his Damascus experience and, therefore, behind the formulation of the 'mystery'. I do not think, however, that he has yet explained precisely enough the reason that Paul can see a 'Gentile-first-then-Israel' order of salvation, since the two Isaiah texts cannot bear the load of such a reversed understanding of the 'Israel-first-then-Gentiles' order of conversion found in the Old Testament prophets, at least in the way Kim has explained them. Is one left then only with the options that Paul, with

219. So, e.g., H. Ridderbos, *Paul* (Grand Rapids: Eerdmans, 1975), p. 46 (cf. also pp. 45-53).

respect to the 'mystery', either reads too much into the Old Testament in attempting to rationalize the order of salvation or that he is simply indicating fulfillment of prophecy without any reference to the unexpected manner of that fulfillment?[220]

I believe that the 'mystery' does involve an unexpected fulfillment and part of that unusual fulfillment concerns an apparent reversal in the order of salvation.[221] Some will conclude that Paul's exegetical attempt to justify such a fulfillment from the Old Testament was unsuccessful. There is reason to think, however, that Paul had good grounds from various Old Testament passages to formulate the mystery in the way he has. I lay out my own view of his reasoning in this respect in the following excursus.

220. In a private communication, Kim offers another alternative which was not explicit in his article: he affirms that the order in the Old Testament is (1) salvation of the remnant of Israel followed by (2) the salvation of the Gentiles, which is finally followed by (3) the salvation of the entire nation of Israel. Accordingly, the statements of 'Jew first, then Greek' in Rom. 1 and 15 (as well as Rom. 2 and 9) reflects parts (1) and (2) of the threefold pattern, while Gentile first, then Jew' reflects parts (2) and (3). I do not see the third part of the pattern in the Old Testament as Kim does; further exegesis of relevant Old Testament texts must be done to settle our different perspectives. I also do not see a (2)–(3) pattern in Rom. 11, but only a (1)–(2) pattern, so that the salvation of 'all Israel' in 11.26 refers, not to a salvation of the whole or majority of the nation at the end of the age, but to the total accumulation of the saved remnant of ethnic Israel throughout the interadvent period (a proposal which must await argumentation at a later point, though already argued for from various angles by, e.g., Hoekema, *Bible and the Future*, pp. 139-47, who also cites others contending for such a view; likewise, see O.P. Robertson, 'Is there a Distinctive Future for Ethnic Israel in Romans 11?', in K.S. Kantzer and S.N. Gundry (eds.), *Perspectives on Evangelical Theology* (Papers from the Thirtieth Annual Meeting of the Evangelical Theological Society; Grand Rapids: Baker Book House, 1979), pp. 209-27. If such an analysis of Rom. 11.25-26 is on the right track, then the precise nature of the 'mystery' is that the salvation of Gentiles throughout the interadvent period is the major device sparking off subsequent salvation of an accumulating Jewish remnant.

221. G. Bornkamm, 'μυστήριον', *TDNT*, IV, pp. 802-28 (822), comes close to implying this: 'Paul's interpretation is based on the fact that he sets the promise implied in the divine election of Israel in relation to what is on a human view the contradictory present'. In the above private correspondence, Kim also says that he holds to a notion of 'unexpectedness' in the 'mystery', though it is still unclear to me precisely how this is so.

Excursus on Paul's Understanding of the 'Mystery' in Romans 11.25.
My own view builds on Kim's outstanding insights about the Isaiah
background and explains how they, indeed, did provide Paul with an
understandable basis for positing an unexpected fulfillment of Old Testament prophecy concerning the order of salvation. My main thesis can
only be sketched here in brief form because of constraints of space, so
that thorough exegetical analysis and refinement must be done at some
later point. The basic thesis is that underlying Paul's view of the
'mystery' is the notion of Christ as the true Israel who first experienced
God's eschatological deliverance through resurrection and that Gentiles
were the subsequent predominant focus of benefitting from that deliverance. From this christological perspective the Old Testament order of
'Jew first, then Gentile' is fulfilled according to the expectation. Yet,
that Christ could sum up in himself the nation and be seen as fulfilling
the first part of the prophetic order about Israel's deliverance before
that of the Gentiles was likely included in part of Paul's understanding
of the 'mystery'. Who could have suspected that one person could
fulfill the prophecies about the nation?[222] Jesus as Israel's king could so
represent the nation because, not only was he her representative, as
were former Israelite kings, but his representative function was more
far reaching and exhaustive because all of the preceding kings were but
faint shadows pointing to him as divine messianic king (cf. Rom. 1.2-5;
9.5) who would bring Israel's and the Gentiles' history to an eschatological climax (Rom. 10.4). Interestingly, a similar narrowing of the
promised 'many' down to 'the one' occurs also in Gal. 3.16, 26-29 with
respect to the notion of the promises made to Abraham's 'seed'.[223]
Furthermore, the prophecy that the initial salvation of Israel would be a

---

222. It is possible that those first hearing and accepting the gospel at Pentecost
and shortly thereafter in Jerusalem (Acts 2–7) represent the beginning fulfillment of
the order of 'Jew first, then Gentile'. If so, however, it could still be an unexpected
fulfillment, since the Jewish believers were such a tiny group in comparison to the
nation Israel, and early Judaism (as well as many modern commentators) expected
that the Old Testament prophesied that the majority of Israel would be saved. On
the other hand, there are indications that the Old Testament does predict that only a
remnant in Israel will be saved, followed by Gentile salvation (cf. Isa. 65.1-17 and
66.7-23; Joel 2.28-3.2; Mic. 4.1-4 and 5.7-9; Zech. 8.6-23; 14.2-4, 16-21; cf. Isa.
10.20-22 with Isa. 11.1-5, 10-12, 16; cf. Isa. 4.3). The possible implications of such
a remnant expectation for the 'mystery' will have to be developed below.
223. On which see Wright, *Climax of the Covenant*, pp. 162-68.

remnant and not the majority of the people[224] is epitomized in Jesus, the remnant of one, who represents the true plural remnant of Israelite believers.

Alternatively, if looked at from an ethnic perspective, it did appear that Gentiles were the main ethnic group experiencing salvation, since only a remnant of ethnic Jews accepted Jesus as Messiah. Paul certainly hopes that this initial success of the gospel among ethnic Gentiles will 'provoke to jealousy' the ethnic Jews and so save some of them (Rom. 11.11-14). This apparent reversal in the prophesied order of salvation is also a part, indeed the dominant aspect, of the 'mystery'. This seeming reversal, however, cannot be seen separately from the christological vantage point as its foundation: as Gentiles are accepting the gospel message, they are corporately identified with their representative, Jesus the Messiah, the true Israel, and so Gentiles become true Israelites; the unbelieving ethnic Jews become as Gentiles, separated from the covenantal benefits (cf. Rom. 9.3-5; Eph. 2.12). Accordingly, the comparatively greater experience of ethnic Gentile salvation which Paul hopes will spur on subsequent ethnic Jewish blessing is, from the christological vantage point, another version of the prophesied order of 'Israel first, then Gentile' but this is now to be understood as 'true, spiritual Israel' first (equivalent to a large number of converted ethnic Gentiles and a much smaller number of ethnic Jews who come to belief), then true spiritual Gentiles (equivalent to ironically, the conversion of unbelieving ethnic Jews).

This also receives support from Rom. 9.24-26, where, again, the order of 'Jew then Gentile' (v. 24) is mentioned but Hos. 1.10 and 2.23 are cited to indicate that not only Jews but also Gentiles can fulfill the Hosea prophecy about the restoration of Israel (e.g. cf. v. 25a: 'I will call those who were not My people, "My people"'): when either Jews or Gentiles believe, they become a part of the fulfillment of the prophecy in Hosea 1-2 that *Israel* would be restored.[225] We have seen above

224. See the Old Testament passages cited directly above (to Isaiah, Joel, Micah and Zechariah).

225. Some understand Hos. being used merely as a comparison in application to Gentiles, so that there is no sense in which they fulfill the prophecy; in contrast, it is more likely that Hos. is seen as fulfilled in the remnant of Jewish believers and Gentiles because: (1) Hos. *is* a prophecy, and the burden of proof is on one to show that Paul's quotation of it does not involve prophetic fulfillment; (2) the following Old Testament quotations indicate prophetic fulfillment (cf. 9.27, 29, 33); (3) the use of ὡς in 9.25 in contrast to καθώς in 9.29 is not sufficient to differentiate the

how Paul could make such a hermeneutical move with respect to Gentiles being considered true Israel; the way is paved for the same kind of interpretative move in Rom. 2.28-29 ('he is not a Jew who is one outwardly... but he is a Jew who is one inwardly') and 9.6 ('for they are not all [true] Israel who are descended from Israel').

Consequently, the 'mystery' involves two vantage points, the christological and the ethnic, with the latter more in focus in Rom. 11.25. In Paul's theology in Romans and elsewhere, however, the christological perspective is dominant and the ethnic is subordinate and almost swallowed up within the christological (so Rom. 10.11-13). While this may seem hermeneutically strange and even complicated to think that *both* perspectives to some degree could be bound up in the mystery, it is supported by the following considerations:

(1) Paul begins and concludes Romans with a clear statement about 'Jew first, then Gentile' (Rom. 1.16; 2.9-10; 15.8-9; cf. Acts 3.26). On the other hand, he reverses the order in Rom. 11.11-31. Somehow, he believes that both are true. Does he contradict himself? This is a very difficult tension within Romans and I do not know of a satisfactory solution which has been yet proposed. I contend, however, that this ambivalence might best be explained by the twofold christological–ethnic perspective which he appears to maintain throughout Romans and many of his other epistles, though the former is the dominant lens. At the beginning and end of Romans Paul has an 'ethnic' perspective in line with the explicit expectation in the Old Testament, but in Romans 11 the christological lens may also be coming into play.

(2) The Isaiah background mentioned by Kim together with various passages in Romans point to a reasonable explanation of why he could use 'mystery' in this way. Kim contended that Isaiah 6 and 49 were combined in Paul's mind. Assuming the correctness of Kim's assertion, further analysis of the relation of these two texts appears to shed more light on the problem of the 'mystery'. First, Isaiah 6 concludes with the climactic picture of the nation's judgment being pictured as the burning of a tree in which only a 'stump' is subsequently left. Most commentators view this as a judgment in which only a remnant remains. If so, the reference in Isa. 11.1 and 11.10 may be a development of this remnant idea: 'Then a shoot will spring from the stem of Jesse, and a branch from his roots will bear fruit'; 'the nations will resort to the root of

former as a mere comparative use and the latter as a fulfillment use, since the two introductory words are probably synonymous.

Jesse'. The Isaiah 11 references themselves develop the explicit references to the 'returning remnant' in Isa. 10.21 ('a remnant will return')
and even earlier in 7.3 ('a remnant will return'), which itself is a likely
development of the image of Israel as the remains of a felled tree in
6.13 (and note that the image of 'felling trees' and a left-over part of a
tree trunk occurs both in 6.13 and 10.33–11.1!).[226] And the 'root' of
11.10 is closely associated with the Israelite 'remnant' in 11.11. In this
light, it is unlikely coincidental that the Servant of Isaiah 53 is called a
'root' and a 'shoot' (though the latter word in Hebrew is different from
that in 11.1). These links imply within Isaiah itself that the 'root' of Isaiah 11 (and, by implication, of Isaiah 53) is identified in some way as
the 'stump' of Isa. 6.13 or remnant of Isa. 7.3 and 10.2-22.

(3) In addition, Isa. 49.1-6 yields some interesting implications along
these lines. Isa. 49.3 refers to the Servant as 'My servant Israel'. Therefore, Isa. 49.3-6 portrays a faithful 'Servant Israel' restoring others, who
are also called 'the preserved ones of Israel', as well as the Gentiles. Of
course, the New Testament identifies Jesus as the Servant who fulfills
the mission to Israel and to the Gentiles (Lk. 2.32; Acts 26.23). If the
contextual idea of Isa. 49.3-6 is in mind in these passages, then Jesus is
'My servant Israel' who restores Israel and the nations. Furthermore,
the New Testament affirms that those who identify with Jesus the Servant and are corporately represented by him also can be viewed as
taking on the Servant's commission from Isa. 42.6 or 49.6, 8 (so Acts
13.47; 26.18 [cf. v. 23!], and 2 Cor. 6.1-2, all of which are applied to
Paul).

(4) In view of these connections already within Isaiah, and, again, assuming the correctness of Kim's proposal that the Isaiah texts *are* in
mind in Rom. 11.25, it seems plausible to think that Paul could have
observed the same thing in Rom. 11.25: that Jesus is the epitome of the
remnant, true Israel, who restores Israel and the nations. Is there any
actual evidence in Romans to encourage us that Paul, in fact, did think
along such lines? I believe there is.

(5) Rom. 15.8-9 refers to Christ who 'became a *servant* to the circumcision... to confirm the promises to the fathers, and for the Gentiles

---

226. I have found that J.F.A. Sawyer, '"My Secret is With Me" (Isaiah 24.16):
Some Semantic Links between Isaiah 24–27 and Daniel', in A.G. Auld (ed.),
Understanding Poets and Prophets: Essays in Honour of G.W. Anderson (JSOTSup,
152; Sheffield: JSOT Press, 1993), pp. 307-17 (309), also traces almost the identical relationship between Isa. 6, 10, and 11.

to glorify God...' Commentators have recognized that Jesus is being identified here as the 'Servant' of Isaiah 40–53, but I think we can pinpoint a more specific reference within that segment of Isaiah. Both Isa. 42.6 and 49.6 are unique within the book of Isaiah, since the explicit notions of (a) a 'servant' being commissioned as a 'light' to (b) restore 'Israel' first and (c) then the 'nations' are found only in these two texts. And this is just what we have in Rom. 15.8-9. One can only guess that this has not been recognized previously because the wording is not an exact verbal reproduction of either of the Isaiah texts. In this respect, Isa. 49.6 may be uppermost in mind because of the additional mention of Christ 'glorifying God' at the beginning of v. 7 which is also part of the Servant's purpose in Isa. 49.3-6 (cf. v. 3: 'You are My Servant Israel, in whom I will show My glory'; indeed, the idea of glorifying is found twice in Isa. 49.3-6, and at the end of Rom. 15.9 the Gentiles are said to glorify God, which is a second mention of 'glory' in Rom. 15.7-9).

Since Rom. 15.8-9 is one of the five places in Romans where Paul explicitly refers to an order of salvation (cf. Rom. 1.16; 2.9-10; 9.24; 11.11-31) and one of the other of these five passages is Romans 11, it is not far-fetched to believe that there is some link between the two passages, especially if Isaiah 49 is in the background of both texts.

(6) It is probably not coincidental that among the Old Testament texts adduced to explain the statement of the Isaianic 'Servant's' commission in 15.8-9 is Isa. 11.10 which Paul cites in Rom. 15.12: 'And again Isaiah says, There shall come the *root* of Jesse, and He who arises to rule over the Gentiles...' As we saw earlier, this Isaiah passage had close connections with the remnant theme of Isa. 6.13, 7.3, 10.20-22, and 53.2. The word 'root' was one of the images in which this connection consisted. The only other time 'root' (ῥίζα) appears with reference to a specific person in the New Testament is with respect to Jesus (Rev. 5.5; 22.16, both in allusion to Isa. 11.1, 10). Otherwise, it is a more general reference. The only other place the word occurs in Romans is in ch. 11 (11.16-18). Most have concluded that there 'root' refers to the 'fathers' to whom the promises of Israel's final salvation were made.[227] The reason for this identification is to be found in Rom. 11.28, where

---

227. E.g. J. Murray, *The Epistle to the Romans*, II (NICNT; Grand Rapids: Eerdmans, 1968), p. 85; J.D.G. Dunn, *Romans 9–16* (WBC, 38B; Dallas, TX: Word Books, 1988), p. 672; D.J. Moo, *The Epistle to the Romans* (NICNT; Grand Rapids: Eerdmans, 1996), pp. 699-701.

'for the sake of the fathers' is given as the reason for why God loves and has chosen Israel. Some commentators who favor a reference to the 'fathers', however, allow the notion that Christ is included in the reference to the 'root' in 11.16-18.[228]

Building on this last idea, I would go further and say that in 11.16-18 Christ is included as the apex or climax of the promises to the fathers, so that he is the focus of the 'root', as in Rom. 15.12. This is suggested by the following passages within Romans which view Christ as the climax of either the fathers' or Israel's hopes: Rom. 1.2 (Christ, 'promised beforehand through His prophets in the holy Scriptures'), Rom. 10.4 ('Christ is the end of the Law'), Rom. 15.8 ('Christ has become a servant to confirm the promises to the fathers'), and Rom. 9.5 (to the Israelites 'belongs the adoption as sons and the glory and the covenants and the giving of the Law and the [temple] service and the promises, whose are the fathers, and from whom is the Christ according to the flesh'). In fact, the reference to the promises to the fathers in 15.8 is another link between that segment and Rom. 11.16-18, 28, where, in both, the notion of promises to the fathers is directly linked to the image of a 'root'. Could Paul really use the present tense (βαστάζει) in 11.18 in referring to the 'root *supporting*' Gentiles and be thinking *only* of the promises to the fathers? Is it not plausible, indeed, probable, in view of the preceding considerations, that he also had in mind Christ as the fulfillment of those promises, and that it was ultimately fulfillment in him which made people 'holy' (so 11.16!), that only 'ingrafting' into the tree with him as the 'root' was genuine salvific connectedness (11.17-24; cf. Jn 15.1-8), and that it was he who was the ultimate salvific 'support' of believers (11.18). The notion of Christ as 'firstborn *among many brothers*' in Romans points further to Christ being the 'firstfruits' in 11.16a, which is in parallelism with 'root' in v. 16b (and the Spirit and Christ as 'firstfruits' respectively in Rom. 8.23 and 1 Cor. 15.20, 23 may enforce this).[229]

---

228. For the few commentators who see or allow reference to Christ see the citations in C.E.B. Cranfield, *Romans*, II (ICC; Edinburgh: T. & T. Clark, 1979), p. 565, and Moo, *Romans*, p. 699. E.g. also C. Maurer, 'ῥίζα', *TDNT*, VI, p. 989, who, while understanding the root primarily to refer to the fathers as originating possessors of the promises, states it in the following manner: the fathers are 'bearers of the promise *fulfilled in Christ*' (my italics).

229. Though some have identified 'firstfruits' in Rom. 11.16a with the first Jewish converts, since the word refers to 'first converts' elsewhere in Paul (Rom. 16.5; 1 Cor. 16.15; 2 Thess. 2.13). See further Moo, *Romans*, p. 700.

The use of 'root' in Rev. 22.16, in allusion to Isa. 11.1, 10, may have bearing on its use in Romans 15, and, therefore, possibly also in Romans 11: 'I am the root and the offspring of David, the bright morning star'. Interestingly, 'root' in Rev. 22.16 is not a metaphor of origin, as some view it[230] and as it possibly could be in Isa. 11.1, but it is a derivative image. The word 'root' is explained by the following 'offspring', so that it is a metaphorical synonym for descendent.[231] Ben Sirach 47.22 says God 'gave out of him [Jacob] a *root for David* [τῷ Δαυὶδ ἐξ αὐτοῦ ῥίζαν]'. In Sirach, 'root' is not that which gives rise to the rest of the organism, but that which branches out from a prior smaller growth. Further, the word in Sirach is in parallelism with σπέρμα ('seed') and ἔκγονος ('descendent'), both of which, especially the latter, are synonymous with γένος ('descendent') in Rev. 22.16. In addition, 'root' occurs again in Isa. 11.10 referring to the same figure of 11.1, and in 11.10 it is clearly a derivative metaphor. In 11.10 the 'root of Jesse' refers to a descendent from Jesse's line, not the originator of that line.[232] That genealogical derivation is the idea is even clearer from the LXX of Isa. 11.10. After 'root of [from] Jesse' (genitive of source), the LXX interprets the MT's 'will stand as a banner of the peoples' by 'the one *arising* to rule over the Gentiles' (cited by Rom. 15.12). Furthermore, 'root' also has the idea of 'sprout' or 'a growth from' in Isa. 5.24 and Isa. 53.2, in line with other similar metaphors. The main point of the title in Rev. 22.16 is to identify Jesus as the one who fulfills the prophecy that one of David's descendants would be the messiah.[233] Therefore, the genitival phrase in Rev. 22.16b should be rendered 'the root and the offspring *from* David'.

Allusion to Isa. 60.1-3 may be included together with Isa. 11.10 in Rev. 22.16: 'Arise, shine; for your light has come...nations will come to your light and kings to the *brightness* (λαμπρότητί) of your rising.' If both Isaiah texts are in John's mind, then they would function to

---

230. Beasley-Murray, *Revelation*, pp. 342-43, and Wilcock, *I Saw Heaven Opened*, pp. 217-18, contend.

231. Beckwith, The *Apocalypse of John*, pp. 777-78, compares Isa. 11.10 and Sir. 47.22, though without discussion.

232. So also Maurer, 'ῥίζα', p. 989.

233. So likewise T. Holtz, *Die Christologie der Apokalypse des Johannes* (TU, 85; Berlin: Akademie Verlag, 1971), pp. 151-52.

highlight Jesus as the one to whom the nations come for salvation, a theme just developed in 21.22-26.[234]

Now, this discussion of the derivative, not originative, nature of 'root', its identification with Jesus, and the connection with Gentile belief stemming from Jesus is just as applicable for Rom. 15.12. But is this notion relevant for Romans 11? The connections already drawn above between 11.16-18 and 15.7-12 point to a connection between the 'root' of Romans 11 and 15, especially the common idea of divine revelation resulting in Gentile belief. Intriguingly, in Rev. 22.16 Jesus is the fulfillment of Old Testament promises, and from this fulfillment is sparked Gentile blessing in allusion to Isa. 60.1-3; accordingly, Jesus is seen as the 'light' in Israel of Isa. 60.1-3, which enlightens the Gentiles. Is it coincidental that Rom. 11.26-27 quote the two verses directly preceding Isa. 60.1ff. (i.e. Isa. 59.20-21)?

If 'root' of Rom. 11 is derivative, especially in the sense of fulfillment of promises made to the fathers, and not originative, referring only to the fathers as those with whom the promises originated, as most commentators hold, then the plausibility of the 'root' being identified in some significant way with Christ is increased. What enhances this identification is that the usual Old Testament metaphor of 'root–branches–tree', which is seen underlying Paul's depiction in Rom. 11.14-24, is often understood prophetically in the Old Testament, so that the 'root' image is not backward looking but forward looking toward future fulfillment: so Isa. 27.6 ('In the days to come Jacob will take root, Israel will blossom and sprout; and they will fill the face of the world with fruit'.); Hos. 14.5-7 ('he [Israel] will take root...his shoots will sprout, and his beauty will be like the olive tree...they will blossom like the vine').[235] To these references should be added Isa. 37.31-32 which, in the midst of imagery about vineyards, says: 'And the surviving remnant of the house of Judah shall again take root downward and bear fruit upward. For out of Jerusalem shall go forth a remnant...' The reference

---

234. So Bauckham, *Climax of Prophecy*, pp. 322-26.

235. Cf. Jer. 11.16 which portrays the majority of Israel in Jeremiah's time as 'a green olive tree, beautiful in fruit' whose 'branches are worthless', and then depicts the prophet Jeremiah almost identically: 'the tree with its fruit' (Jer. 11.19). This shows that botanical imagery used of the nation can be applied to the faithful within the nation when the majority has become faithless; in this case, Jeremiah alone represents a remnant in the nation. Likewise, Ezek. 16.6-9 depicts Israel as a vine with sturdy roots spreading out with branches, but which will be judged by God. Cf. also Mal. 4.1.

to Isa. 27.6 is particularly relevant since Paul quotes from Isa. 27.9 in Rom. 11.27.[236]

What may further point to the 'root' as, at least partly, Christ is the application of the adjective 'rich' (πιότης)[237] to 'root' ('rich root'). Intriguingly, Christ is identified with 'richness' (using the πλοῦτος/πλου-τέω word group) in contexts like Romans 11 where the Jew–Gentile relationship in connection to 'mystery' is under discussion. In particular, Eph. 3.8 says that Paul was commissioned 'to preach to the Gentiles what is the unfathomable richness of Christ' which is in synonymous parallelism with the directly following statement in v. 9: 'to bring to light what is the administration of the *mystery* which for ages has been hidden in God...' (on which see analysis further below). Here the 'richness of Christ' is equated with the 'mystery' related to Jew and Gentile. Similarly, Col. 1.27 refers to 'what is the riches of the glory of this *mystery* among the Gentiles, which is Christ in you...', and 2.2 speaks of 'all the wealth coming from the full assurance of understanding, resulting from a knowledge of the *mystery* of God, [which is] Christ'. Rom. 10.12 says that 'there is no distinction between Jew and Greek; for the same Lord is Lord of all, abounding in riches for all who call upon Him'. Even closer, Rom. 11.12 refers to 'riches for the world' and 'riches for the Gentiles', which, in the light of 10.12, must certainly include an allusion not merely to salvation but salvation in Christ (cf. also 10.4-11). It is certainly not a giant step of faith to think that the reference in 11.17 to Gentiles becoming 'partakers... of the rich root of the olive tree' is a further development of the repeated expressions of 'riches for Gentiles' in v. 12 (whether or not πιότης is taken figuratively, though v. 12 suggests a metaphorical use).

The upshot of the discussion in this section is that Christ is a viable, if not probable, identification of 'root', or at least a significant part of the 'root', in Rom. 11.16-18. Possibly, commentators have been reticent to identify the 'root' as Christ because they see that 'root' in

236. In this respect, Moo, *Romans*, p. 729, sees Isa. 27.6 as contributing to part of the picture in 11.11-32.

237. J.P. Louw and E.A. Nida, *Greek–English Lexicon of the New Testament Based on Semantic Domains* (2 vols.; New York: United Bible Societies, 1988–89), I, p. 621, say that the word can mean 'rich, value, wealth', a metaphorical sense it had already acquired in secular literature, or it could be more literal, meaning 'fat, nutrionally rich, rich quality' (I, p. 36). If the former is in mind, then it would be generally synonymous with other words having the sense of exceptional value (I, pp. 620-22).

Romans 11 is part of Old Testament imagery different than that of Rom. 15.12, which is part of the specific imagery of Isa. 11.1, 10. We have labored, however, to show that this botanical imagery woven throughout Isaiah is linked conceptually, especially as an image of the remnant. Though neither Isa. 27.6 nor 37.31-32 has yet been discussed with respect to any potential relationship to Isaiah 6 or 11, the ch. 37 reference clearly alludes to a future Israelite remnant, and the parallelism of 27.6 with 37.31-32 suggests the same thing. Though Judaism could use 'root' with reference to the fathers,[238] the Old Testament never employs 'root' in this manner but uses the image with respect to Israel and especially the remnant of Israel, including the coming of the Davidic Messiah (Isa. 11.1, 10; 53.2). Throughout Romans 11 Paul has in focus Old Testament contexts, not unique streams of Jewish interpretation about the Old Testament.

(7) Finally, μυστήριον is found in Rom. 16.25-26: 'Now to Him who is able to establish you according to my gospel and *the preaching about Jesus Christ*, according to the revelation of the mystery which has been kept secret for long ages past, but now is manifested, and...has been made known to all the nations leading to the obedience of faith'. If Christ is the focus of this 'mystery' which concerns the Gentiles, which is clear, then it is plausible to think that he is, at least, included in the mystery of Rom. 11.25 which also has such clear reference to the Gentiles. Once we recall the Isaiah background of Rom. 11.25 and the links between Romans 11 and 15.7-9, 12, the plausibility is heightened. The 'mystery' of Romans 16, however, is stated only very generally, but probably has some idea of the reversal of salvific patterns discussed in ch. 11.

In summary, the 'mystery' of Rom. 11.25 involves two vantage points, the christological and the ethnic. The latter is the focus in Rom. 11.25, though the christological hovers in the background. The christological perspective is more explicit and the ethnic is almost swallowed up within the christological elsewhere in the book and in Pauline thought in general (so Rom. 10.11-13!). Though the preceding analysis has appeared involved, it is not beyond the kind of subterranean exegetical pathways which we might expect to find in Paul's mind, which is hinted at elsewhere in the New Testament (2 Pet. 3.15-16).

---

238. Moo, *Romans*, p. 699, cites such examples as *1 En.* 93.8; Philo, *Rer. Div. Her.*, 279, and *Jub.* 21.24 (though 'root' is not mentioned explicitly here).

c. *The Use in Romans 16.25-26*: '*Now to Him who is able to establish you according to my gospel and the preaching of Jesus Christ, according to the revelation of the mystery which has been kept secret for long ages past, but now is manifested, and by the Scriptures of the prophets, according to the commandment of the eternal God, has been made known to the nations unto obedience of faith.*' We have commented on this text briefly in the preceding section with respect to how it might relate to Rom. 11.25. It is important, however, to notice that μυστήριον is also employed here in direct connection to an Old Testament allusion, though this is usually not observed. Most acknowledge that the concluding phrase 'made known to the nations unto obedience of faith' is a paraphrastic repetition of Rom. 1.5, 'unto obedience of faith among the nations'. Some have observed that this expression in 1.5 is an allusion to Ps. 2.8 ('I will surely give the nations as your inheritance'), since Rom. 1.3-4 may well be an echo of Ps. 2.7 ('I will surely tell of the decree of the Lord: He said to Me, "You are my son, today I have begotten you"').[239] Such an allusion may be included in Rom. 1.5 *and* 16.16. There has also been suggestion that Gen. 49.10 lies behind the crucial phrase in Romans 1,[240] but this has not been explored in a trenchant manner nor has the proposal been made for Romans 16.

I want to set out the validity of the Genesis allusion for both Romans 1 and 16, and then discuss its interpretative significance in relation to the Psalm 2 allusion and, finally, to the meaning of the 'mystery' in Romans 16.

Genesis 49.10	Romans 1.4-5 (cf. almost identically 16.25)
'*Unto him* [the coming Israelite conqueror] will be *the obedience of the nations.*'	'*Jesus Christ*...through whom I received grace and apostleship *unto the obedience* of faith among all *the nations.*'

---

239. See D.B. Garlington, 'Obedience of Faith in the Letter to the Romans', *WTJ* 52 (1990), pp. 201-24 (203), and D.B. Garlington, *The Obedience of Faith* (WUNT, 38; Tübingen: J.C.B. Mohr [Paul Siebeck], 1991), pp. 237-43, and C. Anderson, 'Romans 1.1-5 and the Occasion of the Letter: The Solution to the Two-Congregation Problem at Rome', *Trinity Journal* 14 (1993), pp. 25-40 (33-38), and sources cited there.

240. See Garlington, 'Obedience of Faith in the Letter to the Romans', p. 203, who appears to see some degree of reference both to Gen. 49.10 and Ps. 2.8-9, but he only cites the references and does not develop his view; see also Anderson, 'Romans 1.1-5 and the Occasion of the Letter', p. 38, who elaborates more on a definite connection to Genesis 49.

Paul's rendering could be a paraphrastic translation from the Hebrew text (ולו יקהת עמים = εἰς ὑπακοὴν πίστεως ἐν πᾶσιν τοῖς ἔθνεσιν). Similarly, *Gen. R.* 93.8 and 97 also understood Gen. 49.10 of the MT to refer to 'the nations of the world',[241] and *Gen. R.* 99.8 paraphrases with 'all the nations'. Judaism also identified the conqueror of Gen. 49.9-10 with the Messiah.[242] The directly following context (vv. 11-12) of Gen. 49.10 is military imagery of an enemy's defeat and so indicates that the concluding phrase about the nations refers to the coming king's defeat of them in battle, and hence a forced obedience which is brought about among them.

The close resemblance of the two expressions in Romans 1 and 16 to the Hebrew text points to an allusion to Gen. 49.10, especially since Judaism and Rev. 5.5 identify the ruler of the Genesis passage respectively with the Messiah and Jesus. Such an allusion also fits nicely with Ps. 2.8, since both prophetically picture the forced submission of Gentiles by the Messiah. The Genesis background is also appropriate for the Romans 16 context for two reasons: (1) since virtually the identical phrase is found there; and (2) since Gen. 49.1 introduces the entire chapter as a prophecy which is to occur 'in the latter days' ('I will tell you what will befall you in the latter days'), and Rom. 16.25-26 speaks of 'the Scriptures of the prophets' which have been fulfilled 'now' at the turn of the ages.[243] In addition, *Targ. Neof.*, I, Gen. 49.1 twice calls the eschatological prophecy of Jacob a 'mystery', which is what Paul calls its fulfillment in Rom. 16.25.[244]

241. *Gen. R.* 97 (The Soncino Press edition) previously cited in this connection by Anderson, 'Romans 1.1-5 and the Occasion of the Letter', p. 38.

242. For this background, see Beale, *Book of Revelation, in loc.* at Rev. 5.5, B. Grossfeld, *The Targum Onkelos to Genesis* (The Aramaic Bible, VI; Wilmington, DE: Michael Glazier, 1988), p. 163, and Anderson, 'Romans 1.1-5 and the Occasion of the Letter', p. 38.

243. Anderson, 'Romans 1.1-5 and the Occasion of the Letter', p. 38, has made this observation previously with respect to Romans 1 but not Romans 16.

244. M. McNamara, *Targum Neofiti. I. Genesis* (The Aramaic Bible, 1A; Collegeville, MN: Liturgical Press, 1992), p. 215 (n. 1), sees the Targum at this point to be dependent on the use of 'mystery' in Dan. 2. Garlington, *Obedience of Faith*, p. 237, also contends that included in Paul's frame of reference in Rom. 1.5 is Num. 24.17-19 which prophesies that an Israelite conqueror will defeat Moab and Edom which represent oppressive Gentile powers. There is no doubt that the Numbers text is explicitly alluding to Gen. 49.9-10 for the following reasons: (1) the virtually verbatim wording of Gen. 49.9 and Num. 24.9, 'He couches, he lies down as a lion, and as a lion who dares rouse him?'; (2) the use of 'scepter' in Gen. 49.10

Again, we see 'mystery' attached closely to an Old Testament reference, perhaps even two references if Psalm 2 is also in mind. And, also again, the reason for the link of 'mystery' to the Old Testament, is not merely to indicate that prophecy has been fulfilled but to say something about the manner of the fulfillment. How so? Genesis 49 and Psalm 2 (as well as, perhaps, Num. 24) agree that when the eschatological king of Israel comes, he will bring about a forced submission of the Gentile enemies. Paul, no doubt, still holds this to be true: it will happen at the very end of history, when Jesus returns to establish consummately the eternal kingdom already inaugurated. On the other hand, he sees that the two prophecies (or, at least, Gen. 49) have already begun fulfillment at Christ's first coming but in an unanticipated manner: antagonistic Gentiles have begun to yield themselves voluntarily to the Messiah's reign by the 'obedience of faith', that is, 'by the obedience which consists in faith and the obedience which is the product of faith'.[245] It was a 'mystery' from the Old Testament perspective that Genesis 49 (Ps. 2 and Num. 24) could be speaking about voluntary obedience of Gentile enemies, but now Paul sees that this mysterious prophecy has begun fulfillment unexpectedly by Gentiles being taken into 'captive obedience' through trusting in the preaching about the Christ.[246]

If this is a correct analysis, then it is understandable to think that Paul was interpreting Genesis 49 in the light of his acquaintance with Isaiah's prophecies about Gentiles voluntarily responding positively to God's revelation in Israel (e.g. Isa. 11; 49.6-7; 60–61; 66.18-21),[247] especially

and Num. 24.17; (3) both the Gen. and Numbers texts identify their respective prophecies to be about 'the latter days' (cf. Num. 24.14); (4) Num. 24.8, like Gen. 49, also explicitly refers to the 'nations' as Israel's enemies who are to be defeated. In addition to these links between Gen. 49 and Num. 24, Paul's inclusion of a possible reference to the Num. text in Rom. 1.5, as well as in 16.25, could be enhanced by noticing that *Targ. Neof.*, I, Num. 24, like *Targ. Neof.* I, Gen. 49, also refers to the prophecy there as one which will occur in 'the last days' (24.14) and which is a part of the 'mysteries of prophecy' (24.4, 16; likewise *Targ. Ps.-Jon.* Num. 24).

245. For this understanding of the genitival phrase, see Garlington, 'Obedience of Faith in the Letter to the Romans', pp. 223-24.

246. Cf. Garlington, 'Obedience of Faith in the Letter to the Romans', p. 203, though he does not relate this to the 'mystery'.

247. *Gen. R.* 97 (on which see the note to Anderson above) understands the phrase 'until Shiloh come' of Gen. 49.10 to indicate 'that all the nations of the world will bring a gift to Messiah the son of David', and then appeals to the Gentile hope of Isa. 18.7 in support; *Gen. R.* 99.8 interprets the clause 'unto him will be the obedience of the peoples' of Gen. 49.10 to refer to 'him to whom the nations of the

since echoes of the imagery of a military defeat of Gentiles from Gen. 49.11-12 appears to be found in the midst of some of these prophecies (cf. Isa. 60–61 and 66.18-21 with 63.1-6, though this latter text is about the Gentiles' defeat).[248] Paul's positive view of Gen. 49.10 also may have been inspired by the LXX rendering of 'expectation' (προσδοκία) in place of the Hebrew's 'obedience',[249] since this may have conjured up a more positive notion of the prophetic 'looking for' or hope by Gentiles or 'expectation of a faithful response by Gentiles'.[250] That Paul has something from the Old Testament in mind is apparent from his statement that the mystery 'now has *been manifested by means of the Scriptures of the prophets*' (which is in syntactical parallelism with 'by means of having been made known according to the commandment of the eternal God unto obedience of faith unto all the gentiles'). The phrase increases the parallelism with Romans 1: cf. 1.1-2, 'the gospel of God which he announced beforehand through his prophets in the holy Scriptures'. Whether or not there was a positive pre-Christian understanding of Gen. 49.10 cannot be known for certain; if so, Paul's view of Genesis 49 might not have been quite as novel. As noted earlier,

world will flock', and supports it by the prooftext of Isa. 11.10 ('The root of Jesse, that stands for an ensign of the peoples, unto him shall the nations seek'). A similar link was made in Epiphanius (2.136; on which see below).

248. Probably because of a link already between Gen. 49 and Isa. 63, the *Pal. Targ*. Gen. 49.11 alludes to Isa. 63.2 in describing the Messiah's defeat of the enemy: 'his *garments, dipped [or 'rolled', m'g 'gyn] in blood*, are like the outpressed juice of grapes' [Etheridge edition]; so also *Targ. Neof.*, I, uses the same verb 'dipped'). The *Pal. Targ*. Gen. 49.11 also alludes to Isa. 63.3, paraphrasing 'sprinkled' with 'dipped'.

249. In line with the MT, *Targ. Onq*. Gen. reads 'and him shall nations obey' (Grossfeld, *Targum Onkelos to Genesis*, p. 158), *Targ. Neof.*, I, *Gen*. has 'to him shall all the kingdoms be subject' (McNamara, *Targum Neofiti. I. Genesis*, p. 220) and *Targ. Ps.-Jon. Genesis* renders 'because of whom the people will pine away (or 'melt away') (M. Maher, *Targum Pseudo-Jonathon: Genesis* [The Aramiac Bible, 1B; Collegeville, MN: Liturgical Press, 1992], p. 159).

250. Though this word typically connotes 'looking for, expectation, whether in hope or fear, but more commonly fear' (so H.G. Liddell and R.Scott, *A Greek–English Lexicon* (Oxford: Clarendon Press, 1973), p. 1507. Nevertheless, Epiphanius (2.136) renders positively the last clause of Gen. 49.10 as επ αυτου εθνη ελπιουσιν ('in him the nations will hope') in the light of Isa. 11.10 (ἐπ' αὐτῷ ἔθνη ἐλπιοῦσιν), which is also quoted in Rom. 15.12.

the 'mystery' of Rom. 16.25 may also include the notion of 11.25 concerning the reversal in the order of salvation.[251]

d. *The Use in Ephesians 1.9 and 3.3, 9.* μυστήριον first appears in Ephesians in 1.9, where merely the notion of God 'making known the mystery of His will' is found. The essential idea is that God has revealed something in redemptive history which was not formerly known. Whether or not this refers to mere fulfillment of prophecy or also the manner in which prophecy has been fulfilled cannot be decided from the immediate context. Eph. 3.3, 9, however, help answer this. Paul says 'according to a revelation the mystery was made known to me …[that is that] the Gentiles are fellow-inheritors and fellow-members of the body and fellow-partakers of the promises *in Christ Jesus* through the gospel' (3.3, 6).

The mention of the 'mystery' in ch. 3 continues the preceding discussion of Eph. 2.14-15, where it says that Christ made Jew and Gentile one 'by having loosed the dividing wall of the barrier' and 'by having nullified in his flesh the Law of commandments in decrees'. This likely focuses not so much on the redemptive significance of Christ's death (as the parallel in Col. 2.13-14, in fact, does) but on one of the crucial sociological results of that death. Christ's death has effected a change in how people now define themselves, especially with respect to the nationalistic tags which formerly defined Israel as a peculiar ethnic nation. Paul says that Christ's death in some way rendered the Law ineffective.

This refers not to Christ's nullification of the whole Law, but only part of the Law, as I believe the remainder of Ephesians bears out, since Paul repeatedly quotes and alludes to Old Testament moral Law. Christ has abolished that part of the Law which divided Jew from Gentile so that they could become one. Gentiles no longer need to adopt the signs and customs of national Israel to become true Israelites in the latter days, as the Old Testament and Judaism expected, but they need only have Christ as their identification mark: they do not need to move to geographical Israel to become Israelites, but they need only move to

251. Aquila reads σύστημα instead of προσδοκία in Gen. 49.10 which carries the nuance of a 'composite' or 'complete whole', with the resulting sense of 'and to him will be the *complete body* of the nations'. Such an exegetical tradition could have been associated easily with the similar expression in Rom. 11.25, 'until the fulness of the nations has come in'.

Jesus, the true Israel; they do not need to be circumcised in flesh but in the heart by Christ's death, which was their true circumcision, since it cut them off from the old world and set them apart to the new (cf. Col. 2.10-14; Gal. 6.14-15); Gentiles do not need to make pilgrimage to Israel's temple to get near to God, but they merely need to make pilgrimage to Jesus, the true temple, of which the Ephesian Christians were a part (see Eph. 2.20-22).

The parallel passage to Eph. 2.13-18 in Colossians 2 defines the 'decrees' (δόγμα) of Eph. 2.15 which Christ abolished as the external nationalistic expressions of the Law: food, drink festivals, new moons, or Sabbaths (see Col. 2.15-17, 20-21). Col. 2.20-21 even refers to these 'decrees' with the verbal form of δόγμα: '[why] do *you submit yourself to decrees* [δογμαίζω]—do not handle, do not taste, do not touch, which things are all destined for perishing with the consuming, according to the commandments and doctrines of men'.

What is then the precise significance of defining the 'mystery' in Eph. 3.6 as Gentiles being 'fellow-heirs and fellow-members of the body and fellow-partakers of the promise in Christ Jesus'? It is that Gentiles no longer need to adopt the customs and outward signs of national Israel to become true Israelites. But how can they be true Israel without adopting the old Israelite tags? The most plausible answer is that Jesus the Messiah is true Israel, and since there is only one Messiah, there can only be one people of God. Christ is now the only 'tag' with which one needs to be identified. This is why Eph. 2.15-18 speak of the result of Christ's death being that Jew and Gentile have become 'one new man', 'one body', and exist in the sphere of 'one Spirit'. This 'one new man' and 'one body' is none other than the body of Christ: Jew and Gentile are one because they are now incorporated and identified with Christ (which is also clear from comparing 1.20-21 with 2.5-6). Gentiles can be 'fellow-inheritors and fellow-members of the body and fellow-partakers of the promises in Christ Jesus' along with Jewish Christians because the promises and inheritance of Israel have been inaugurated in Christ, the Israelite king who represents all true Israelites.

What is the essence of the 'mystery' in Ephesians 3? It was not as clear in the Old Testament that when the Messiah would come the theocracy of Israel would be so completely reconstituted that it would continue only as the new organism of the Messiah (Jesus), the true Israel. In him Jews and Gentiles would be fused together on a footing of complete equality through corporate identification.[252] Some commentators have seen the mystery consisting of complete spiritual equality among humanity, but, as far as I can determine, none have recognized that the basis for such equality lies in the one person 'Christ Jesus' as the true Israel, since there can be no distinguishing marks in him but only unity.

C.C. Caragounis has shown through ten significant parallels that behind the use of 'mystery' in Ephesians 3 stands the background of 'mystery' in Daniel 2.[253] For example, the expression κατὰ ἀποκάλυψιν ἐγνωρίσθη μοι τό μυστήριον in Eph. 3.3 appears to reflect the similar phrase in Dan. 2.28 (Theodotion): ἀποκαλύπτων μυστήρια καὶ ἐγνώρισε τῷ βασιλεῖ. What added significance could the Daniel background contribute to what we have concluded so far about the 'mystery'? As in Daniel, the mystery concerns the Messiah's establishment of Israel's kingdom following his defeat of evil rulers (Eph. 1.9, 20-22) in the end time (Eph. 1.10; 3.5. 10 ['now']; cf. Gal. 4.4). In this light, the 'mystery' in Ephesians 3 is explaining the new entrance requirements for becoming a part of the Israelite kingdom prophesied in Daniel 2: submission only to Jesus the Israelite king, not to the ethnic identification marks of the Mosaic Law.[254] That the subject of the kingdom of

252. So similarly W. Hendriksen, *New Testament Commentary: Exposition of Ephesians* (Grand Rapids: Baker Book House, 1967), pp. 153-55, whose comments have helped to clarify my own conclusion, though he is not clear about whether Christ is the 'new organism' or the church. Cf. F.F. Bruce, *The Epistles to the Colossians, to Philemon, and to the Ephesians* (NICNT; Grand Rapids: Eerdmans, 1984), p. 314, who says the mystery is that the complete lack of discrimination between Jew and Gentile was not foreseen. R.L. Saucy, 'The Church as the Mystery of God', in C.A. Blaising and D.L. Bock (eds.), *Dispensationalism, Israel and the Church* (Grand Rapids: Zondervan, 1992), pp. 127-55 (149-51), says that a secondary nuance of the Eph. 3 mystery indicates unanticipated fulfillment in the sense that Gentiles are being saved though Israel's salvation is being set aside for the most part, and in the sense that the Old Testament expected only one age of fulfillment but Ephesians pictures two such ages. I find neither of these notions present in Eph. 3.

253. Caragounis, *Ephesian 'Mysterion'*, pp. 123-26.

254. In this respect, J.W. Bowker, 'Mystery and Parable', *JTS* NS 25 (1974), pp. 304-308, shows that early Judaism (Philo and Josephus) and rabbinic writings use 'mystery' (μυστήριον and *mysteyrin*) to refer to the 'distinctive marks of Israel' and 'rites of initiation' which only Israel possessed and understood, and from which the nations were excluded and did not understand. He has not related this to Eph. 3, but it poses an intriguing possibility in the light of my preceding analysis

Israel is at issue is pointed to not only by the background of Daniel and the reference to 'in Messiah [Israel's anointed king] Jesus' in v. 6, but also by noticing that the reference to 'fellow-*inheritors*...in Christ Jesus' in 3.6 is expanded in 5.5 by reference to 'having an *inheritance in the kingdom* of Christ'. That the subject of Gentiles being now related to Israel is in mind in 3.6 is also apparent from 2.12, where Gentiles who do not believe are viewed as separated from the following three realities which are put in synonymous parallelism: (1) 'without Christ', (2) 'alienated from the commonwealth of Israel', and (3) strangers of the covenants of promise'. To be without Christ is to be separated from Israel and from participation in her promises, and 3.6 presents Gentiles as sharers both in Messiah and in the 'promises', which must be the same as the promises of 2.12. That Gentiles can be considered true Israel is apparent from recognizing that the Isa. 57.19 prophecy of Israel's restoration can be applied to Gentiles (Eph. 2.17) and that they can be seen as a part of Israel's inaugurated end-time temple (Eph. 2.20-22).[255] The presence of the Old Testament background in close association with 'mystery', as elsewhere in the New Testament, indicates that the ὡς in 3.5 ('[the mystery of Christ...] *as* now revealed') is comparative, indicating partial but not full revelation of the mystery in the Old Testament.[256] Therefore, the notion of Christ as true Israel makes good sense of the meaning of the 'mystery' in Ephesians 3.

In Eph. 6.19 Paul requests that the readers pray that he would be empowered 'to make known with boldness the *mystery* of the gospel'. This may be such a general use that not much can be concluded about the

and in view of Harvey, 'Use of Mystery Language in the Bible', pp. 330-36, who contends (with respect to Mk 4.11) that μυστήριον has a Semitic background, yet retains 'some of the force which it would normally have had in the mind of a Greek-speaking reader'. Such lines of thought, however, cannot be explored here.

255. The cumulative force of the argument in this section points in the opposite direction of Saucy, 'Church as the Mystery of God', pp. 127-55, who contends, among other things, that the 'mystery' has nothing to do with Gentiles becoming a part of true Israel.

256. In contrast to C.C. Ryrie, 'The Mystery in Ephesians 3', *BSac* 123 (1966), pp. 24-31 (29), who contends that ὡς has a 'declarative force' of only adding additional information or that it has the notion of 'but', both senses of which would be very rare meanings of the word and, therefore, demand the burden of proof. The usual use of the word and the Old Testament background in Eph. 2–3 together are difficult hurdles for such a view to overcome.

precise nature of the mystery. On further examination, however, there appear to be the following verbal links with the ch. 3 'mystery':

Ephesians 3.2-3, 8-9, 12	Ephesians 6.19
τῆς χάριτος τοῦ θεοῦ τῆς <u>δοθείσης</u> <u>μοι</u>... <u>ἐγνωρίσθη μοι τὸ μυστήριον</u>; <u>τοῖς ἔθνεσιν εὐαγγελίσασθαι</u>... τίς ἡ οἰκονομία <u>τοῦ μυστηρίου</u>; ἐν ᾧ ἔχομεν τὴν <u>παρρησίαν</u>.	ἵνα <u>μοι δοθῇ</u>... ἐν <u>παρρησίᾳ γνωρίσαι</u> <u>τὸ μυστήριον</u> τοῦ <u>εὐαγγελίου</u>

At the end of his epistle, Paul wants to return to the grand theme of the revelation of the 'mystery of the gospel' to Gentiles, which he elaborated on in ch. 3, so that the 'mystery' has the same notion in ch. 6 and ch. 3.

e. *The Use in Ephesians 5.32*. Paul quotes Gen. 2.24 about man and woman becoming 'one flesh', and says that 'this mystery is great, but I am speaking with reference to Christ and the Church'. Again, we see μυστήριον directly connected with a reference to an Old Testament passage, so that we should not be surprised if we find that it is an inspired exegesis of that text in the light of the redemptive–historical happenings of the Christ event. This time neither Daniel 2 nor any other Old Testament prophecy is in mind, rather a summarizing description from the conclusion of Genesis 2 about men and women leaving their families and forming new families.

What is the 'mystery' about the Genesis 2 statement? Paul is saying that what appeared to be a pattern describing only the human institution of marriage, now, in view of Christ's coming and the formation of his church, this description was not merely applicable only to the marriage of a man and a woman. The continual pattern of a man leaving his family and becoming one with a wife contains within it a reflection of a grander marriage: Christ leaving his heavenly home and Father and becoming one with the church. Until the end of history, Christians are to view their own marriages in this manner: husbands should sacrifice for their wives in order to reflect what Christ has done, and wives should 'fear' their husbands in order to reflect what the church has done with respect to Christ (and should do). Such an understanding would not have been obvious to the Old Testament writer or reader of Gen. 2.24, but now, retrospectively, on the other side of Christ's cross and resurrection and by the revelation of the Spirit (cf. Eph. 3.5), it can be seen how such a meaning could organically grow out the Genesis text.

Christ is the ultimate, eschatological 'man' (ideal Adam) and the church is the ultimate, eschatological bride (e.g. 2 Cor. 11.2-3; Rev. 19.7-9; 21.2, 9-27!).

If μυστήριον is associated with prophetic fulfillment, as in Matthew 13, Romans 11, and Ephesians 3, then Gen. 2.24 would be seen as a typological prophecy, much like Hos. 11.1 in Mt. 2.15, whereby a historical pattern (in this case marriage) from Old Testament history foreshadows or adumbrates some redemptive event in the New Testament age.[257]

How could the use of μυστήριον in Eph. 5.32 be related to that in ch. 3? Both concern unity of diverse groups: Jews and Gentiles on the one hand, and married men and women on the other. Paul is concerned to say, not only that Christ has inaugurated the unity of fragmented humanity in general (Jew and Gentile), but he also has begun to put back together the broken relationships within the family in particular.[258] In both cases, Paul sees that the way Christ has fulfilled Old Testament expectations and historical patterns is unexpected and mysterious from a Jewish perspective. How fitting for Paul to appeal to a pre-fall creation text about unity in marriage as a prototype for the unity of Christ and the church in the new creation: husbands and wives now are motivated to maintain unity, not only because this is the original purpose of marriage according to Gen. 2.24, but also because they have the model of Christ and the church to follow as the paradigm for marriage relationships for those living in the new creation, to which Gen. 2.24 ultimately pointed.[259]

f. *The Use in Colossians.* Μυστήριον appears in Col. 1.26, 27, 2.2, and 4.3. The well-known verbal parallels between Col. 1.26 and Eph. 3.3-11. would suggest that the 'mystery' of Colossians has the similar con-

---

257. Cf. Bockmuehl, *Revelation and Mystery*, p. 204, who views Eph. 5.32 as inspired exegesis of Gen. 2.24, drawing out a deeper meaning which is prophetically typological in nature (and cites others generally following this view). Cf. A.J. Kosternberger, 'The Mystery of Christ and the Church: Head and Body, "One Flesh"', *Trinity Journal* 12 NS (1991), pp. 79-94, e.g., p. 94, and T. Moritz, *A Profound Mystery: The Use of the Old Testament in Ephesians* (NovTSup, 85; Leiden: E.J. Brill, 1996), p. 142-46, who are skeptical about a typological sense.

258. An insight I have subsequently also found in Kostenberger, 'Mystery of Christ and the Church', p. 94.

259. Moritz, *Profound Mystery*, p. 146 n. 124, comes close to saying this, which is not consistent with his reticence about a typological view of Gen. 2.24.

tent as that in Ephesians 3. The explicit identification of the 'mystery' in Col. 1.27 as '*Christ* in you [the Gentiles]', and the similar identification in 2.2, points to the same kind of mystery as in Ephesians 3: Jews and Gentiles are fused together on a footing of complete religious equality by means of corporate identification in Jesus the Messiah, the true Israel. This is a 'mystery' because it was not clear in the Old Testament that Israel's theocracy would be so thoroughly transformed that it would find its continuation only in the sphere of the Messiah himself.

In this regard, recall that Col. 2.16-22 was parallel with Eph. 2.14-18, the latter of which underscores that Christ's coming did away with the former ethnic markers of God's people and replaced them with Christ, which is key to understanding the mystery of Ephesians 3. Col. 2.16-22 emphasizes the same thing, where the Mosaic Laws pertaining to 'food or drink or Jewish festivals or new moons or Sabbath days' are no longer binding because they must now be seen as only 'shadows' pointing toward Christ, who is the eschatological 'substance' of these things. Believers have 'died with Messiah' to these things which were so important to Israel's old world but no longer are crucial for membership in God's true end-time people (vv. 20-22). It was a mystery that Gentiles could become a part of latter-day Israel by not submitting to the identification marks of the old theocracy but only submitting to and having the Messiah as their sole identification.

g. *The Use in 2 Thessalonians 2.7.* In 2 Thess. 2.1-12 Paul warns the Thessalonians not to be deceived about when the 'day of the Lord' (the final coming of Christ and the end of history) will come. Apparently, there were false teachers who were claiming that the last coming of Christ had already arrived. Perhaps, similar to the Corinthian heresy of over-realized eschatology, the false teachers claimed that the spiritual resurrection had occurred and that, therefore, Christ had already come to raise his people to glory.

Paul tells the readers that there is a telltale sign by which they can know whether or not the end has come: has the 'man of lawlessness' yet come? Paul says he has not yet come but will in the future. Therefore, neither has the end yet come. When this 'antichrist' figure finally appears, he will attempt to pass himself off as divine. He will be a deceiver but will not succeed ultimately because Christ will come and judge him. Commentators are generally agreed that part of the description of this enemy of God is drawn from Daniel 11, along with other apocalyptic traditions:[260]

Daniel 11.31, 36	2 Thessalonians 2.3-4
'forces from him will arise, desecrate the sanctuary fortress, and do away with the regular sacrifice...they will set up the abomination of desolation' (v. 31); 'he will exalt and magnify himself above every god; he will speak extraordinary things against the God of gods...' (v. 36).	'the man of lawlessness...who opposes and exalts himself above every so-called God or object of worship, so that he sits in the temple of God, proclaiming himself to be God'.

In addition, the expression 'man of lawlessness (ἀνομίας)' echoes Dan. 12.10-11 (Theodotion) which is strikingly similar to Dan. 11.29-34 (Theodotion) and refers to the end-time trial as a time when 'the *lawless ones* will do *lawlessness*, and the *lawless ones*[261] will not understand', and this doing of lawlessness is directly linked, if not partly explained, by 'the time of the removal of the perpetual sacrifice, when the abomination of desolation shall be set up'.[262]

According to the eschatological scenario of Dan. 11.30-45, a final opponent of God will attack the covenant community. The attack is to take two forms: (1) a subtle attack of deception by influencing with 'smooth words' some within the community 'who forsake the holy covenant' (v. 30) and 'who act wickedly toward the covenant' to become 'godless' themselves (v. 32), to compromise, and to foster deception

---

260. E.g. C.A. Wanamaker, *Commentary on 1 & 2 Thessalonians* (NIGTC; Grand Rapids: Eerdmans; Exeter: Paternoster Press, 1990), pp. 245-46; cf. D. Wenham, *Paul* (Grand Rapids: Eerdmans, 1995), pp. 316-19, for the influence of the synoptic eschatological discourse; L. Hartman, *Prophecy Interpreted*, pp. 198-205, sees influence from Daniel, other Old Testament texts, and the synoptic eschatological discourse.

261. Three times forms of ἄνομος and its verb form occur in Dan. 12.10 and once in Dan. 11.32 in the version of Theodotion.

262. Among those who discern some degree of Daniel influence, see O. Betz, 'Der Katechon', *NTS* 9 (1963), pp. 282-84; F.F. Bruce, *1 & 2 Thessalonians* (WBC 45; Dallas: Word Books, 1982), p. 168; Marshall, *1 and 2 Thessalonians*, pp. 190-91; Wanamaker, *1 & 2 Thessalonians*, pp. 246-47; Hartman, *Prophecy Interpreted*, pp. 198-205.

and further compromise among others;[263] Daniel says that 'many will join with them [the faithful] in *hypocrisy*', claiming to be faithful but who are not (v. 34); and (2) the end-time opponent will persecute those who remain faithful to God's covenant (vv. 33-35, 44). This eschatological antagonist will appear openly before the community by 'exalting and magnifying himself above every god', and then will meet his final end under God's judicial hand (v. 45).

Though Paul says the Danielic 'man of lawlessness' has not yet come, he nevertheless claims there is a sense in which he has come: 'For the mystery (μυστήριον) of lawlessness is *already* at work'.[264] As with the other New Testament uses of μυστήριον, again we find it used in close connection with Old Testament references, this time allusions to Daniel. We should not be surprised to find μυστήριον in association with Daniel 11 here when it is recalled that μυστήριον in the Old Testament has an eschatological meaning only in Daniel 2, that it is used eschatologically in Qumran sometimes in association with other Daniel allusions, and that Matthew 13 (and par.) and Ephesians 3 actually use μυστήριον against its Daniel 2 backdrop. In fact, Qumran even uses 'mystery' in connection with Daniel 11–12 and with respect to the theme of the latter-day trial and the forces antagonistic to God's people, especially their judgment.[265] A close parallel is 1QM 14.9-10 which alludes to Dan. 11.45–12.3, and applies 'mystery' to the 'dominion of Belial' and his 'hostility' from which true believers are protected so that they do not fall away from God's 'covenant'. They have even been protected from destructive 'spirits' (1QM 14.11), from whom Paul is also trying to protect them: 'that you may not be quickly shaken...by a spirit' (1 Thess. 2.2).

---

263. In Dan. 11.32 the LXX and Theodotion have the Jewish apostates instead of the evil king as the subject of the seductive activity within the covenant community. F.M. Cross, *The Ancient Library of Qumran* (Garden City, NY: Doubleday, 1961), pp. 122-23, thinks that the reference in 4QpNah 1.2 to the Greek king Demetrius 'who sought to enter Jerusalem on the counsel of those who *seek smooth things*' is an allusion to Dan. 11.32, and he conjectures that it refers either to Hellenistic Jews or Pharisees. Note that the latter-day opponent in Dan. 8.23-25 also will be 'ambiguous of speech', 'will corrupt...the holy people', and 'through his shrewdness he will cause deceit to succeed by his influence', and then he will be judged.

264. The limited scope of the present study prohibits discussion of the identification of the 'restrainer' in the conclusion of vv. 6-7.

265. See the earlier analysis in Qumran (above at Chapter 3, sect. D.1).

Why does Paul, however, refer to 'mystery' in 1 Thess. 2.7? The reason is that he understands the Daniel 11 prophecy to be commencing fulfillment in the church community of the Thessalonians in an enigmatic manner, not clearly foreseen by Daniel. Whereas the final foe of Daniel 11 was to appear in full force and openly to all eyes ('to exalt and magnify himself') when he would attempt to deceive and persecute, now Paul sees that, though this fiend has not yet come visibly for the final denouement, he is nevertheless 'already at work' in the covenant community through his deceivers; from Daniel we expect that when the fiend's deceivers are on the scene, so would he be very manifestly. The revealed 'mystery' is that the prophecy of Daniel 11 is beginning unexpectedly because the devilish foe has not yet come in bodily form but he is already inspiring his 'lawless' works of deception through false teachers. Therefore, the Thessalonian Christians must not think that the Antichrist's deception will come only when he comes in the flesh at the very end of the age, but they must be on their guard *now* in order that they will not be deceived by his unusual, invisible coming through his deceptive emissaries.

Hence, Paul, again, is interpreting Old Testament prophecy in the light of how he sees it beginning to be fulfilled in a startlingly unusual manner.

h. *Other Uses of μυστήριον in the New Testament Outside of the Apocalypse.* A number of additional New Testament uses of μυστήριον are still unaccounted for: five occurrences in 1 Corinthians (2.7; 4.1; 13.2; 14.2; 15.51) and two in 1 Timothy (3.9, 16).[266] Interestingly, two of these uses are found in direct connection with Old Testament references. In 1 Cor. 2.6-8 Paul says he speaks 'wisdom in a mystery', a wisdom which the 'rulers of this age' do not understand and which God 'predestined before the ages'. The preceding context reveals that the cross is the focus of the mystery (cf. 1.18-25; 2.2): that 'Messiah crucified' is 'the power of God and the wisdom of God' (1.24). That divine power and wisdom would be revealed through offering salvation to humanity by a crucifixion of the true Messiah was considered foolishness according to the ungodly world's standard of thinking (whether Jewish or Greek). It is true that Jewish readers of such passages as Isaiah 53, Dan. 9.26, and Zech. 12.10 should not have been caught totally

---

266. I do not view the uses in 1 Timothy as associated with the specific notion of fulfillment of prophecy, as found elsewhere in the present analysis.

off guard about this, since they could have discerned a promise in these passages of the Messiah's death resulting in salvation. On the other hand, even the Old Testament would not have prepared the Jew for what happened with Christ, since nowhere is there the notion that the Messiah would rule *powerfully in the midst of his death, as Jesus did.* The demonstration of divine power in the midst of weakness is clearly in view together with God's wisdom, though the latter is underscored (note δύναμις four times in 1.18, 24; 2.4, 5 [and synonyms in 1.25, 26, 27]; σοφία appears 15 times in 1.18–2.16 and σοφός five times).

This view of the 'mystery' fits with the preceding studies of its use elsewhere in the New Testament, since, again, there is an unexpected idea of fulfillment. The fact that Paul explains the 'mystery' further by adducing an Old Testament quotation reflects additional resemblance with the other uses analyzed. Though the precise source of the quotation is unclear, the gist of it is that people of the old covenant, especially those who rejected Christ, could not perceive who he really was, but those who truly loved God were able to understand. Also, the mention of a 'mystery' which is 'hidden' from worldly rulers and divinely decreed in combination with 'wisdom' and God 'revealing' through the 'Spirit' (cf. 1 Cor. 2.10-16) in the eschatological age (cf. 1 Cor. 2.6-7) certainly has echoes of the use of 'mystery' in Daniel 2 and 4.[267] If Daniel 2 is in the background, then the idea of the prophesied eschatological kingdom coming in power would be in mind, especially the unusual manner in which that power has been manifested in Christ's death at the inauguration of the ages.

'Mystery' in 1 Cor. 15.51 refers to the future transformation of believers' bodies at the very end of the age which will enable them to 'inherit the kingdom of God' in its final form (v. 50). There should be no surprise that, as before, 'mystery' is linked with the Old Testament. It could be connected in some way with the quotations of Isa. 25.8 and Hos. 13.14 in vv. 54-55. On the other hand, G.D. Fee argues that the 'content of the "mystery" is the concept of believers being transformed

267. See Caragounis, *Ephesian* Mysterion, pp. 124-25, where most of the ten parallels for Dan. 2 and Eph. 3 are also relevant for 1 Cor. 2. In addition, Brown, *Semitic Background of the Term 'Mystery'*, cites Dan. 2.27-28 as a parallel for 1 Cor. 2.7-8: 'Wise men...cannot show to the king the mystery which the king has asked, but there is a God in heaven who reveals mysteries'; cf. 1 Cor. 2.7-8: 'we speak God's wisdom in a mystery...[the wisdom] which none of the rulers of this age has understood'.

"so as to bear the likeness of the man [Christ = Last Adam] of heaven"', which has been the topic of vv. 45-49.[268] If Fee is correct, which is likely, then the 'mystery' of v. 51 is linked to the quotation of Gen. 2.7 in 15.45: 'So also it is written, "the first Man, Adam, became a living soul"'.

Paul, as elsewhere, may be exegeting the Old Testament as a result of his new knowledge of Christ's resurrection and its implications for Christ as the last Adam, especially as this was revealed to him on the Damascus Road.[269] Richard Gaffin even suggests that the wording directly following the Gen. 2.7 quotation ('The last Adam [became] a life-giving Spirit') is actually part of Paul's paraphrase of Genesis, expanded in the light of Christ's resurrection.[270] Whether or not this is the case, Paul sees that God's breathing of earthly life into the first Adam contains an antithetical pattern of the glorious and heavenly resurrection life imparted to the last Adam. This is certainly not a clear idea which could have been seen, nor can be seen, in Gen. 2.7, apart from the Christian presupposition that Jesus the Messiah was a last Adam figure, not only in his earthly life, but in his resurrection state, which was the beginning of a new creation. Just as the first Adam was given one kind of life at the beginning of the first creation, so the last Adam is given another kind of life at the beginning of the new creation. Underlying such thinking is, not only Paul's new understanding of Christ's resurrection and Christ as the last Adam and possessor of the end-time image of God, but also the notion of *'Endzeit als Urzeit'*.[271] Eschatology is protology, which means that the goal of all redemptive history is to return to the primal condition of creation from which mankind fell[272]

268. G.D. Fee, *The First Epistle to the Corinthians* (NICNT; Grand Rapids: Eerdmans, 1987), p. 801.

269. Kim, *Origin of Paul's Gospel*, pp. 186-268.

270. R.B. Gaffin, *The Centrality of the Resurrection* (Grand Rapids: Baker Book House, 1978), pp. 9-82; likewise E.E. Ellis, *Paul's Use of the Old Testament* (Grand Rapids: Baker Book House, 1981 [1957]), p. 143.

271. As far as I am aware, this was first established in scholarship as a significant idea by the work of H. Gunkel, *Schöpfung und Chaos in Urzeit und Endzeit* (Göttingen: Vandenhoeck & Ruprecht, 1895), e.g., pp. 367-70. Gunkel himself was reflecting the same idea found already in the *Barn.* 6.13, 'behold, I make the last things as the first things'. For the specific application of a schema of *Urzeit* = *Endzeit* to Paul's first Adam—last Adam correspondences and antitheses, see Kim, *Origin of Paul's Gospel*, pp. 186-87, 260.

272. So Allison, *End of the Ages*, p. 91.

and then go beyond it to a more heightened state, which the first creation did not reach.[273] In this respect, in the light of Adam's 'fall', Paul
probably reasoned that a 'first' implied a 'last', who would remedy the
ruin ushered in by the first.

Paul even says that the process of death launched by the first Adam
contains a logical necessity that the last Adam would bring about resurrection from the dead: *'because* (ἐπειδὴ) through a man [came] death,
also [consequently, καὶ) through a man [came] the resurrection of the
dead' (v. 21; v. 22 further reiterates the idea). It is understandable how
Paul can go from such reasoning to then interpreting Gen. 2.7 as providing a basis for deducing the conclusion about Christ, albeit understood retrospectively in view of the new age. Since Paul calls this a
'mystery', a highly charged prophetic fulfillment word in Qumran and
the New Testament, it is even plausible that he sees in the first Adam
(and in Gen. 2.7) a pattern which adumbrated what had happened in
Christ. Paul elsewhere refers to the first Adam as a 'type' of the last
Adam (Rom. 5.14), which, at least, refers to the analogy between the
representative effects of the first Adam's sinful acts and of the last
Adam's righteous acts,[274] but also plausibly includes the notion that
Paul believed that the first Adam foreshadowed the last Adam. We
have seen a similar interpretative approach to the same chapter of Genesis in Ephesians 5, where Paul's view of Gen. 2.24 is called a revealed
'mystery'.

In 1 Cor. 13.2 and 14.2 Paul says respectively that prophets 'know all
mysteries' and 'speak mysteries'.[275] There is some debate about the
precise identification of these 'prophets',[276] but it is likely that they are

---

273. See Kim, *Origin of Paul's Gospel*, pp. 187-92, for this hope in Judaism,
though here it was viewed more as a hope for restoration of the pre-fall state, not so
much an ultimate excelling of such a state. Vos believes that Paul wanted to
demonstrate that God, from the beginning, had made provision for Adam to have a
'higher kind of body' which he did not receive, and so from the time of the Fall the
provision awaited another who had to come and receive it (Vos, *Pauline Eschatology*, pp. 169-70, followed by Gaffin, *Centrality of the Resurrection*, p. 82).

274. So Ridderbos, *Paul*, pp. 57, 61.

275. 1 Cor. 14.2 likely refers to tongues as uninterpreted prophecy (cf. vv. 3-
5ff.; so, e.g., R.B. Gaffin, *Perspectives on Pentecost* [Phillipsburg, NJ: Presbyterian
and Reformed Publishing, 1979], pp. 56-58).

276. Gaffin, *Perspectives on Pentecost*, pp. 55-116, contends that the prophets
in Corinth, as well as elsewhere in the New Testament, were on an authoritative par
with Old Testament prophets and New Testament apostles, whereas W.A. Grudem,

New Testament prophets who not only foretell but also forthtell by receiving revelations from God and proclaiming them to the church. Since μυστήριον is used often elsewhere in the New Testament to indicate the meaning of Old Testament prophecy in the light of the Christ event, there is no reason why it should not have the same sense in these two passages. I do not believe it takes a great leap of faith to accept such an understanding in 13.2 and 14.2. Likewise, 1 Cor. 4.1 refers to Paul and the apostles as 'stewards of the mysteries of God', which is virtually identical to Eph. 3.9, where Paul refers to his ministry as making known the 'stewardship of the mystery'. 1 Cor. 4.1 is probably a general reference to Paul's prophetic office of interpreting and proclaiming the gospel, especially in the light of the Old Testament promissory background. The identical expression in Eph. 3.9 supports such a meaning.[277]

3. *The Use of* μυστήριον *in the Apocalypse*
a. *Revelation 1.19-20*: *'Write, therefore, what you have seen and what they are and what is about to come to pass after these things. The mystery of the seven stars...'* We have established in Chapter 3 (sect. B) that Dan. 2.28-29, 45 is the clear background for the last phrase of Rev. 1.19 ('what is about to come to pass after these things'). That μυστήριον in v. 20 comes directly after the allusion to Dan. 2.28-29 in v. 19 can hardly be accidental, since the same phrases appear in direct connection in Dan. 2.28 and 2.29. Since 'mystery' occurs with an eschatological sense only in Daniel, its appearance in Rev. 1.20 in such a context confirms its link to that Old Testament book. Perhaps the syntactical awkwardness of beginning v. 20 with 'the mystery' without any transitional wording was designed to make it more easily recognizable as a clear part of the larger Daniel 2 allusion which concludes v. 19.[278]

The Gift of Prophecy in 1 Corinthians (Washington, DC: Universtiy Press of America, 1982), argues that the prophets in 1 Corinthians 14 had a lesser degree of authority, so that truth had to be 'sifted out' from error in the various utterances which each prophet gave.

277. Cf. also Fee, *First Epistle to the Corinthians*, p. 160, whose assessment is generally in line with the preceding analysis: Paul is 'one who has the Spirit, [and] has been given to understand God's plan of salvation, long hidden to human minds but now revealed in Christ'.

278. We will find that the solecisms of Revelation have a similar function of making readers pause to recognize more easily Old Testament allusions. Τò μυστήριον ('the mystery') occurs in the Greek Old Testament only in Daniel and

Furthermore, there are definite links between the use of μυστήριον in Rev. 1.20 and that in Matthew 13, where also we saw allusion to Daniel 2 behind Matthew's use of μυστήριον. That Matthew 13 is in the immediate background in the use of 'mystery' in Rev. 1.20 is observable from the following parallels, as we noticed in the Chapter 3 discussion: (1) that μυστήριον in both Matthew 13 and Revelation 1–3 occurs after an initial parabolic portrayal and before the formal interpretation of that portrayal to indicate that the hidden meaning of the preceding parable will be unveiled (cf. Mt. 13.11 and Rev. 1.13-19, 1.19-20 [and chs. 2–3]); (2) both uses of μυστήριον are linked to an interpretation of the Old Testament (respectively, of Isaiah 6 in Matthew and of several Old Testament allusions, including some from Isaiah 44–49, in Rev. 1.12-18); (3) the hearing formula at the conclusion of each of the letters in Revelation 2–3 is dependent, at least in part, on the same formula in Matthew;[279] (4) indeed, μυστήριον itself in Mt. 13.11 and Rev. 1.19-20 is a conscious allusion to Dan. 2.28-29, 45, where the word occurs also in reference to the prophetic vision conveyed through symbols and concerning the establishment of the end-time kingdom of God, a topic also of primary concern to these New Testament texts (Mt. 13.11, 19ff.; Rev. 1.6, 9);[280] (5) strikingly, both Matthew and Revelation employ μυστήριον, not only to refer formally to the hidden meaning of pictorial language but also to connote what kind of meaning the pictorial language conveys: that the prophesied messianic kingdom has begun fulfillment in an unexpected, even ironic manner,[281] whereas in Daniel 2 'mystery' has to do formally only with the hidden meaning of a symbol whose interpretation has eschatological significance.

---

12 times in the apocrypha: cf. μυστήρια ('mysteries') and τὸ μυστήριον following ἃ δεῖ γενέσθαι ('what must come to pass') in Dan. 2.28-30, while μυστήρια ('mysteries') precedes the same phrase in 2.28a. Brown, *Semitic Background of the Term 'Mystery'*, p. 36, sees a 'connection' between v. 20a and Dan. 2 because of the similarity of usage, and Swete, *Apocalypse*, cxxxvii, has seen explicit allusion to the 'mystery' of Dan. 2.29 in v. 20a, but neither see allusion to Dan. 2.28-29, 45 in v. 19c. The margin of Kilpatrick's edition of the Greek New Testament is the only source indicating allusion to Dan. 2.29 in *both* v. 19c and v. 20a.

279. E.g. cf. Rev. 2.7 ('the one having an ear, let him hear') with Mt. 13.9, 43 ('the one having ears, let him hear').

280. For argument concerning the allusion to Dan. 2 in Mt. 13, cf. Ladd, *Presence of the Future*, p. 225, and in Rev. 1 see Chapter 3, sect. B above.

281. Cf. Mt. 13.19-23, and the analysis of Ladd, *Presence of the Future*, pp. 218-42, as well as Rev. 1.9 and the analysis of Beale, *Use of Daniel*, pp. 176-77.

Particularly striking in comparison to Revelation 1 is this last observation about the 'mysteries of the kingdom' in Mt. 13.11 (par.), referring *both* to the hidden meaning of Jesus' parables and to their interpretation concerning the unexpected form of the kingdom, which was beginning fulfillment. The parables especially highlight the unanticipated nature of the initial phase of the kingdom: it was beginning small rather than large, growing not visibly but invisibly, allowing the godly and the wicked to continue to co-exist for a longer than expected time before rewards and punishments are meted out, etc.

The notion of unexpected fulfillment is seen vividly in the preceding context of Rev. 1.20. According to 1.7, Christ fulfills Dan. 7.13 in an unforeseen progressive manner and the Zechariah 12 prophecy of Israel's salvation is fulfilled in the Gentile-dominated church instead of ethnic Israel (on which see Chapter 2, sect. D.4.a.(1)). John understands that the Old Testament prediction of the rule of the saints has reached its initial fulfillment (so Rev. 1.6, 9). The ideas of 'tribulation' and 'kingdom', discussed separately in the Old Testament (especially in Dan. 7), have been merged into a unified, ironic concept, as expressed best by 1.9: 'I John, your brother and fellow-partaker in the tribulation and kingdom and perseverance in Jesus.' Those reigning in the kingdom were, at the same time, experiencing tribulation; in fact, ruling in the kingdom occurred partly by persevering through tribulation. Rev. 1.13-16, 20 show the 'son of man' in a *present* position of sovereignty among the weak and suffering churches (lampstands) of his kingdom, bringing into sharper focus the unexpected form in which the expected Danielic kingdom has reached its initial fulfillment.[282]

μυστήριον ('the mystery') has been taken over from Daniel precisely at 1.20 to emphasize the ironic nature of the fulfillment and its reversal of expectations, as was the case also in Matthew 13. 'Mystery' in Rev. 1.20 refers most explicitly to the hidden symbolic meaning of the stars and lampstands, which are about to be interpreted respectively as 'angels and churches'. 'Mystery' also suggests, however, that the connotation of unexpected, end-time fulfillment is included in the meaning of the stars and lampstands, to which the overall context of ch. 1 points. Indeed, as we have seen, μυστήριον occurs elsewhere in the New Testament, even in addition to Matthew 13, to indicate fulfillment of prophecy in an unexpected manner (e.g. Rom. 11.25; 1 Cor. 2.7;

---

282. See Beale, *Use of Daniel*, pp. 154-77, for the dominant influence of Dan. throughout Rev. 1.

Eph. 3.3-11; 2 Thess. 2.7). And we will see the same thing again elsewhere in Revelation.

μυστήριον indicates that in some way the earthly church (lampstands) and her heavenly correspondence (stars)[283] in 1.20 are part of
the unexpected, initial realization of, not only the kingdom anticipated
by Daniel 2 and 7, but also the temple prophecy of Zechariah 4. This
unusual 'mysterious' form of the emerging eschatological temple in
Revelation 1 needs elaboration. The first image John sees in Rev. 1.12
is that of 'seven golden lampstands' (v. 12b), which has its general
background in Exodus 25, 37 and Numbers 8, but the image is more
specifically drawn from Zech. 4.2, 10. Thorough analysis of the lampstand and star imagery has been conducted earlier in the present
work,[284] so only a summary is needed here.

In Zech. 4.2-6 the lampstand with its seven lamps is figurative: the
lampstand as part of the temple furniture stands for the whole temple,
which by extension also represents faithful Israel (cf. Zech. 4.6-9) who
is required to live '"not by [earthly] might nor by power, but by My
Spirit" says the Lord' (Zech. 4.6). Jewish exegetical tradition also
understood the lampstand of Zechariah to represent all the righteous
living throughout Israel's history. The lampstand in the Tabernacle and
temple was in God's presence, and the light which shone from it represented the divine presence. Similarly, the lamps on the lampstand in
Zech. 4.2-5 are interpreted in 4.6 as representing God's presence or
Spirit, which was to empower Israel (the lampstand) to finish re-building the temple, despite opposition (cf. Zech. 4.6-9). So eschatological
Israel, the church, is to derive its strength from the Spirit, the divine
presence, before God's throne in its drive to stand against the world's
opposition and establish itself as God's temple.[285] Just as in Zechariah
the beginning establishment of the physical temple faced opposition, so
the spiritual beginning of the new temple faces opposition. The idea
of the lamps on the lampstand representing God's presence with the
church is also underscored by 11.4, where the 'lampstands...stand before the Lord of the earth'.

283. See Chapter 2, sect. D.4.a.(ii) for the 'seven stars' as the heavenly reality
corresponding to the earthly 'lampstands'.
284. See Chapter 2, sect. D.4.a.(ii).
285. In 1.4 and 4.5 the seven lamps are identified as the Spirit, as in Zech. 4 (see
1.4).

Consequently, against the Zechariah 4 background, the picture of the churches as lampstands identifies her with the beginning form of the end-time temple,[286] though she is such because she is identified with Christ, whose resurrection was the establishment of the new temple (Jn 2.19-22; cf. Rev. 21.22). The 'lampstand' (the church) is given power by 'the seven lamps' on it, a power primarily to witness as a light uncompromisingly to the world so that the powers of evil would not prevail against the building of God's temple, the true Israel. The new, spiritual temple of the church appears as small, insignificant, weak and vulnerable to the world's opposition.

This beginning fulfillment of prophecies about the Old Testament temple was unexpected because the temple of the new age was apparently to be *completely built* as a *physical* structure in glory immediately when the Messiah would come and the new creation would arrive (as in Ezek. 40–48; Hag. 2.9).[287] Therefore, it is this hidden form of the temple, along with the unusual form of the kingdom mentioned earlier, that μυστήριον refers to in Rev. 1.20. Kingdom and temple are not two separate realities in this case, but the mystery form of the temple is itself an ironic expression of the kingdom.

b. *Revelation 10.6b-7*: '*time will be no longer but in the days of the voice of the seventh angel when he should be about to sound, then will be completed the mystery of God, as He announced to His servants the prophets.*' Verses 6-7 are an oath which an angel makes before God which is modelled on a similar oath made by an angel in Dan. 12.7,

286. Elsewhere early Christianity identifies the church as the temple of God: 1 Cor. 3.16-17; 6.19; 2 Cor. 6.16; Eph. 2.21-22; 1 Pet. 2.5; Ignatius, *Eph.* 9; Ignatius, *Eph.* 15.

287. Judaism expected the physical temple of Zech. 4 to be finished when the Messiah would come; see Chapter 2, sect. D.4.a.(ii) for references in Judaism which understood that Zech. 4 and 6, as well as Isa. 53.5, prophesied the Messiah's rebuilding of the temple. The same lampstand imagery of Rev. 1 appears also in Rev. 11.3-4 in connection to temple imagery derived from Ezek. 40 (on which see further Beale, *Book of Revelation, in loc.*). It is quite possible, if not likely, that the use of Zech. 4 in Rev. 1 is not merely analogical, but that the prophecy that Zerubbabel would begin and finish the building of the second temple was understood by John as a typological foreshadowing of the new temple envisioned in Rev. 1 and elsewhere in the book, which finds consummation in Rev. 21.1–22.5. If this is so, then 'mystery' in Rev. 1.20 may include reference to the unexpected fulfillment of the Zech. 4 prophecy in the church, as I have argued in this section.

though the idea has been altered somewhat. The content of the oath follows a description of God as creator. In Dan. 12.6 the prophet asks the angel 'how long will it be until the end of these wonders?', which refer to future events of tribulation, judgment of evildoers, the resurrection, and establishment of God's kingdom. The oath of Dan. 12.7 is the angel's answer to this question: '*that it would be for a time, times and half a time*, and as soon as they finish shattering the power of the holy people, all these events will be completed'. In contrast to Daniel, the angelic oath of Rev. 10.6 reads '*that time shall be no longer*'. This is not to be understood in a philosophical sense that there will be an abolition of time at the end of history, which is replaced by timelessness, as some understand it. Such a doctrine may be deducible on the basis of other biblical and apocalyptic texts concerning the non-temporal aspect of the eternal state (e.g. *2 En.* 33.2; 65.7). Instead, the phrase expresses primarily the idea that there is a predetermined time in the future when God's purposes for history will be completed.[288] The expression could be translated 'there will be *delay* no longer'.[289] The point is that *when God has decided to terminate history, there will be no delay in doing so*.

A parallel between 10.7 and 6.11 shows that the content of the mystery in ch. 10 concerns God's decree that the saints suffer, which leads directly to the judgment of their persecutors: compare 6.11, 'yet a little time until [their sufferings] should be fulfilled' with 10.6b-7 'that time shall be no longer...when...the mystery of God is fulfilled'. In 6.10 the saints ask 'how long' it will be before God judges their oppressors. The divine response is that the judgment and the saints' vindication will be for 'yet a little time until' the decreed sufferings (or full number) of 'their servants, even their brothers who are about to be killed even as themselves, should be fulfilled'. Rev. 10.6-7 affirms that, in response to the prayers of the saints (6.10), the final judgment will begin without delay only when all believers whom God has decreed to suffer finally fulfill their destiny.[290]

---

288. See J. Barr, *Biblical Words for Time* (SBT, 33; London: SCM Press, 1962), p. 76.

289. χρονίζω has the meaning of delay in Hab. 2.3, where the fulfillment of the prophetic vision 'will not delay' when the appointed time should arrive for its execution; so likewise Mt. 25.5; 24.48; Heb. 10.37.

290. Likewise Kiddle and Ross, *Revelation*, pp. 172-73; cf. J.P. Heil, 'The Fifth

Apparently, from the saints' perspective who cry out 'how long', the intervening time before final judgment has been a long time, but from God's perspective it is short (perhaps according to the principle of 2 Pet. 3.4-9 and Ps. 90.4, 13). The elongation of the interadvent period may well be included as a part of the 'mystery' which is being completed. According to Old Testament prophecy, the events of the end-time apparently would take place quickly and climactically, followed by the destruction of the cosmos and its recreation. One would never have assumed that an unusually extended period would transpire between the coming of the Messiah and the final judgment of the wicked. The new temporal perspective is unexpected and, therefore, a 'mystery' from the Old Testament viewpoint, which now has been revealed. Such an understanding of the 'mystery' has also been observed in 1QpHab 7 (see above at Chapter 3, sect. D.1) and in Matthew 13, where the force of the parable of the tares of the field was that, though the kingdom has begun, the final judgment has been put off for an unknown but unusually prolonged time. The parable of the mustard seed, sandwiched between the telling and the explanation of the tares of the field in Matthew 13, also enforces the notion that an unexpected period must transpire before the growth of the kingdom is completed.

The more precise meaning of the phrase 'that time shall be no longer' in Rev. 10.6 is given in v. 7, which unpacks further how the meaning of the oath from Daniel is being understood. The prophecy of Dan. 11.29–12.13 concerned the end-time suffering and persecution of God's people, God's destruction of the enemy, and the setting up of the kingdom. Dan. 12.7 says that the judgment of Israel's persecutor (cf. 11.32-45) will occur after the enemy finishes 'shattering' them. The prophetic events were to lead up to and result in the consummation of history. Dan. 12.7 says these prophetic events would occur during 'a time, times, and half a time', after which God's prophetic plan would 'be completed'. The occurrence of ἐτελέσθη ('completed') in Rev. 10.7 betrays the continuing thought of Dan. 12.7: cf. συντελεσθήσεται ('will be completed') of Dan. 12.7 (LXX).

Daniel 'could not understand' this prophecy fully (cf. Dan. 12.7-8). He asks the angel *how long* it would be until the prophecy would be fulfilled (Dan. 12.6) and *how* (the 'outcome of') it would be fulfilled

(Dan. 12.8). The angel tells Daniel that he will not be able to understand these things because the full meaning of the prophecy was to be
'concealed and sealed up until the end time', when finally it would be
fulfilled and all would be revealed to the 'wise' (*maskilim*) living at the
end of time (Dan. 12.9).

In contrast to the oath of Daniel 12, the angel's oath in Revelation 10
begins an emphasis upon *when* and *how* the prophecy will be completed, which is amplified in ch. 11. The prophecy of Dan. 11.29–12.13
will be fulfilled, and history will come to an end when the seventh
angel sounds his trumpet (i.e. historical 'time shall be no longer').[291]

The point of asserting that there will be no delay in Rev. 10.6 is to
affirm that the consummation of God's covenantal plan for history,
which was prophesied to Daniel, will finally reach fulfillment. The
phrase 'then the mystery of God is completed' in 10.7 further elaborates on the words 'time shall be no longer' in v. 6 (the καὶ is not a
mere conjunctive but a temporal consecutive, 'then'): not everyone is
able to penetrate the meaning of the historical 'time' leading up to the
end, since it is enveloped in a 'mystery'. God has hidden the meaning,
so that it is mysterious. Only those to whom God reveals the mystery
can understand the meaning of this history. Whereas Daniel could not
understand, now the angel is commencing to reveal its meaning to John
and the churches to whom he is writing, but the ungodly within and
outside the church will not understand.

---

291. The introductory words '*in the days of* the voice of the seventh angel' may
mean that the sounding of the seventh trumpet embodies a span of time and is not
one distinctive act. On this basis Charles, Ladd (*Revelation*, p. 145), and others
identify its content too broadly with the seven bowls or with a final, brief period of
tribulation; G.H. Lang, *The Revelation of Jesus Christ* (London: Oliphants, 1945),
pp. 180-81, agrees, adducing the verbal similarities of Mt. 13.4 and Lk. 21.7 as
support, but he draws too much out of the grammatical parallels. Charles (Charles,
Revelation, I, pp. 263-66) sees that vv. 6-7 focus on the idea that when a point in
history is reached when the Antichrist is ordained to come on the scene, he will
appear without delay, and the final tribulation will begin. The view represented by
Charles is plausible on the basis that the phrase '*in the days* of the voice of the seventh angel *when he is about* to sound' refers precisely to a brief period of trial
immediately before the consummation of history, which is signaled by the last
trumpet. But this may be overly precise and even may be an inaccurate translation.
Therefore, it is not merely the last stage of tribulation which is to come without
delay but the very end of all history (so also Beckwith, *Apocalypse*, pp. 582-83).

John views the 'times, time and half a time' of Dan. 12.7 as the inter-advent age beginning from the time of Christ's resurrection and leading up to the final judgment.[292] This identification of the threefold time formula from Daniel is deducible especially from 12.4-6, where the period begins from the time of Christ's ascension and refers to the church's time of suffering (so also 12.14). The same meaning is apparent for the equivalent phrase 'forty-two months' in 13.5, which describes the time of the beast's blasphemous and persecuting activities. This is indicated by the combined references to (1) the dragon 'making war with the rest of her [the woman's] seed' (12.18) (2) followed by reference to the beast's 'fatal wound' (13.3) which reflect the *proto-evangelium* in Gen. 3.15 and which began to be fulfilled through Jesus' death and resurrection.[293] That Christ is the one in view who inflicted the beast with such a fatal blow at the cross is apparent from the mention in 13.14 that a 'sword' was the instrument of the beast's 'fatal wound'; [294] elsewhere in Revelation 'sword' often signifies Jesus' judgment of his enemies.[295] In this light, Jesus is also the one who wields the sword which struck the beast in 13.14. One of the heads of the beast is depicted as 'slain' because of Christ's death and resurrection, as 2.5, 10-12 together with 1.5 and 5.9 bear out (cf. also the resurrection in 12.5 with the mention of the Devil being cast out of heaven and being overcome in 12.10-12). This is consistent with other New Testament testimony affirming that Christ's death and resurrection defeated the Devil.[296] This means that the defeat in mind here is more likely the

292. See further on the use of the phrase and its equivalents in 11.3, 12.6, 14, and 13.5; in this respect, see elaboration by Beale, *Book of Revelation, in loc.*

293. See Sweet, *Revelation*, p. 210. Cf. also Rom. 16.20: 'And the God of peace will soon crush Satan under your feet', which is presumably based on Jesus' prior defeat of the Devil.

294. Literally the Greek reads 'plague [πληγή] of death; everywhere else in Revelation πληγή (usually rendered 'plague') is a punishment inflicted by God (so 11 times and the verb in 8.12).

295. These judgments by Jesus are either in the present (1.16; 2.12, 16) or future (19.15, 21), though these passages employ the synonym ῥομφαία and not μάχαιρα, as in 13.14; cf. Minear, *I Saw a New Earth*, pp. 25-254. The future judgment by Jesus in Rev. 19 is at the very end of history as a part of the last judgment. Therefore, more likely in mind in 13.3 is Jesus' judgment of the beast, who is the earthly representative of the dragon, at the cross.

296. For other references affirming that Christ's coming was designed to nullify the purposes of Satan, see Mt. 12.28-29; Jn 12.31; 16.11; Acts 10.38; 2 Cor. 4.4-6;

victory over the Devil at the cross than some punishment of an evil historical figure (like Nero or someone else; though constraints of space do not allow argument for this).

Therefore, Rev. 10.6-7 is speaking of the end of the period of the entire interadvent age of the church, which is the end of history.[297]

The reason the revelation of the mystery can now finally be made is that the death, resurrection and exaltation of Christ have inaugurated the latter days and the fulfillment of the prophecies from Daniel which were to occur at the end. Christ's removing of the seals from the scroll in ch. 5 connoted precisely the same idea of new revelation due to the inauguration of the latter-day prophecies from Daniel 12; the very notion of 'sealing' Daniel's prophecy 'until the end time' in Dan. 12.4, 9 involves an eventual unsealing, which is what Revelation 5 has in mind.[298] Consequently, the seals of Daniel 12 which are removed in Revelation 5 would appear to be equivalent to the Daniel 2 'mystery' which is revealed in 10.7, which is pointed to by the clear allusion to Dan. 12.7 in 10.6-7.

Therefore, the fulfillment of the prophetic mystery of the interadvent age will be completed when 'time will be no longer'. 'The mystery of God' extends from the time of Christ's exaltation (or ministry) until the consummation of history, which will occur at the sounding of the seventh trumpet. This means God's prophetic mystery began to be revealed at Christ's first coming. The striking parallel of 10.6-7, 11 with Rom. 16.25-26 points to this conclusion: 'Now to him who is able to establish you according to the *revelation of the mystery* which has been kept secret for long ages past, but now is manifested, and by the Scriptures of *the prophets*, according to the *commandment* of the *eternal*

Eph. 6.10-18; 1 Jn 3.8; 4.4; 5.19; cf. also the end-time expectation of God's destruction of the Devil and his designs in Isa. 27.1 (which, in fact, may be echoed in Rev. 13.1); 1QH 3.29-36; *T. Jud.* 25.3; *T. Levi* 18.12; *Asc. Isa.* 7.9-12.

297. The end of the period according to the LXX is the conclusion of Israel's exile, which is an early interpretation of Dan. 12.7 supporting the notion that John has in mind the end of true Israel's (the church's) exile on earth, not merely the end of a brief final time of tribulation. In place of the concluding phrase of Dan. 12.7 (MT), 'as soon as they finish shattering the power of the holy people, all these events will be completed', the LXX has '[then will be] the completion of the severe diaspora [cf. Theodotion] of the holy people, and then all these things will be completed'.

298. See Beale, *Book of Revelation, in loc.* at Rev. 5.1-5, 9.

God, has been *made known to the nations...*' (the reference to μυστή-ριον in Eph. 3.3-6 functions similarly in this respect).

Μυστήριον is an allusion to Dan. 2.28-30 which is borne out by re-calling that only in Daniel 2 does 'mystery' have reference to a proph-ecy with eschatological meaning. Furthermore, μυστήριον clearly forms part of an allusion to Dan. 2.28-30 in Rev. 1.20, and in 17.5, 7 it is part of an allusion to Dan. 4.6. In addition, we have seen that it was not unusual in Qumran to combine the Daniel 2 'mystery' with allu-sions to Daniel 12, as well as with the notion of 'delay'.[299]

Not only does the revelation of the mystery involve answering Daniel's question of *when* his prophecies would be fulfilled (that is, they have commenced fulfillment at Christ's death and resurrection), but also the precise manner of their fulfillment is now part of the mys-tery which is made known. Verse 7 is interpreting Dan. 12.7b, which foretells that the kingdom of evil will not be defeated until it finishes defeating 'the power of the holy people'. *The angel is explaining that this prophecy is coming to pass in a mysterious manner.* How so? The broad context of Revelation 10, to be analyzed further below, suggests that the prophecy of God's defeat of the evil kingdom is being ironi-cally fulfilled by this evil kingdom's apparent physical victory over the saints. God's people are already beginning to win spiritually in the midst of their physical defeat. Their enemies are already beginning to lose spiritually in the midst of their apparent physical victory. Unbe-lievers begin to undergo unseen loss, since their persecuting activities begin to lay the basis for their ultimate punishment. Such antagonistic actions also betray their allegiance to and identification with Satan, who has already begun to be judged at the cross and resurrection. They also already stand under this inaugurated judgment. 'The persecution of the church is thus the secret weapon by which God intends to win his vic-tory over the church's persecutors'.[300] At the second coming this judg-ment is consummated.

---

299. The difference, however, between 1QpHab 7.6-14 and Rev. 10.7 is that the former underscores the idea of delay and the latter that of the end of delay; never-theless, 6.11 also underscores the notion of delay, which 10.7 then sees as coming to an end.

300. So Caird, *Revelation*, p. 128, who also proposes a similar link with Daniel 12, as discussed above.

The mysterious nature of the saints' victory is to be understood through the ironic way in which Christ obtained victory through his apparent defeat by the same evil kingdom. But where in ch. 10 is there any hint of such an ironic victory either of Christ or of the saints? The legitimacy of this comparison is based on the observation that ch. 10 is parallel to ch. 5 and is to be interpreted in its light, especially with respect to the 'books' in each chapter. However, the similarities are so striking that a close connection between the two scrolls is probable.[301] The link is confirmed by noticing the following parallels: (1) not only are both 'books opened', but also (2) they are held by Christ (in 10.1ff.), (3) who is compared to a lion; (4) both are allusions to the scroll of Ezekiel 2, (5) are associated with a 'strong angel', who 'cries out', and (6) with God, who 'lives forever and ever', and (7) both books are directly related to the end-time prophecy of Daniel 12; (8) in both visions someone approaches a heavenly being and takes a book out of the being's hand; (9) part of the prophetic commission of John in both visions is stated in near identical language ('I heard a voice from heaven speaking': cf. 10.4 and especially 10.8 with 4.1); (10) finally, both scrolls concern the destiny of 'peoples and nations and tongues and tribes [kings]'.[302]

These parallels indicate that the essential themes associated with the book of Revelation 5 are relevant for Revelation 10. In ch. 5 Christ's death was already a beginning victory because he was a 'faithful witness' resisting the spiritual defeat of compromise (1.5) and because he was accomplishing the redemption of his people by paying the penalty of their sin (so 5.9-10; 1.5-6). Jesus' death was also a victory because it was an initial step leading to the resurrection (1.5; 5.5-8). Likewise, ch. 10 is saying that those believing in Christ will follow in his footsteps. Their defeat is also an initial victory because they are faithful witnesses withstanding the spiritual defeat of compromise and their death is a spiritual resurrection, when they receive a crown of victory (2.10-11).

There is one difference between the scrolls of ch. 5 and here, yet even this suggests the ironic interpretation just given. The 'scroll' in ch. 5 is called a βιβλίον, whereas in 10.2, 9-10 it is called a βιβλαρίδιον, 'a little scroll'. The similarities between the scrolls together with this

---

301. So also P. Prigent, *L'Apocalypse de Saint Jean* (Paris: Delachaux & Niestlé, 1981), p. 151.

302. 'Kings' in Rev. 10.11 replaces 'tribe' in the formula of Rev. 5.9, but even in the directly following 5.10 'kingdom' and the saints' reign is mentioned.

small difference connote that, just as Christ, so Christians have their 'book', which is also symbolic of their purpose: they are to reign ironically as Christ did by being imitators on a small scale of the great cosmic model of the cross. And this may be why Christ, or perhaps his representative angel, is portrayed as a large, cosmic figure overshadowing the earth.

Therefore, the little book is a new version of those same purposes symbolized by the ch. 5 book in so far as they are to be accomplished by the people of God.[303] The reason that the scroll of ch. 10 is also referred to once somewhat inconsistently as a βιβλίον (v. 8) shows the two books are generally the same. The interchangeable use of the two Greek words serves to highlight the connection of the βιβλαρίδιον of ch. 10 with the βιβλίον of ch. 5. Therefore, this is a clue enabling the reader not to think that the ch. 10 scroll is a totally different kind of book from that of ch. 5, but only one on a smaller scale.[304] John wants to underscore the fact that this is a 'little book' in comparison to the big book of ch. 5, and that it is modelled on that big book.[305]

This understanding of the 'mysterious' way in which the Daniel 12 prophecy is being fulfilled is pointed to not only by the parallels with ch. 5 but by the following context of 11.1-13. There also, the persecution and defeat of the witnessing church is the means leading to its resurrection and its enemies' defeat.[306]

303. So Caird, *Revelation*, p. 126; similarly C. Brütsch, *Die Offenbarung Jesu Christi*, I (Zürcher Bibelkommentare; Zürich: Zwingli-Verlag, 1970), pp. 401, 407-408; Prigent, *L'Apocalypse*, p. 152.

304. Cf. also Sweet, *Revelation*, p. 177.

305. Mazaferri, *Genre of the Book of Revelation*, pp. 267-69, and Bauckham, *Climax of Prophecy*, pp. 244-60, contend that βιβλαρίδιον, though diminuitive in form, has lost any diminuitive notion, and, therefore, does not mean 'little book' but merely 'book'. Partly on this basis, they conclude that βιβλίον and βιβλαρίδιον are synonynmous and without any distinction, so that the two books of Rev. 5 and 10 are completely identical. Such a conclusion could but does not necessitate a difference in the conclusion drawn in the present discussion (for elaboration of the different views of the 'books' of Rev. 5 and 10 and the possible interpretative consequences, see Beale, *Book of Revelation, in loc.*

306. The parallel between 10.7 and 6.11 (above) shows, at the least, that the content of the mystery in ch. 10 concerns God's overt decree that the saints suffer, which leads directly to the final judgment of their persecutors. In this respect, the phrase 'the mystery of God is fulfilled' of 10.7 is paralleled and interpreted by '[the sufferings of God's people through which they persevere and which is their ironic victory] should be fulfilled' of 6.11.

Therefore, revelation of the mystery in 10.7 involves not only the idea that fulfillment of prophecy has begun (as some commentators affirm) but also concerns the formerly hidden, even unexpected and ironic manner in which prophecy would be fulfilled.

c. Revelation 17.5, 7: 'And upon her forehead a name written, a mystery, Babylon the Great, the mother of harlots and of the abominations of the earth... And the angel said to me, "why have you marvelled? I will tell you the mystery of the woman and of the beast who is carrying her".' Revelation 17.1-2 portrays an angel telling John that he will show the seer 'the judgment of the great whore... with whom the kings of the earth fornicated' and from whom the nations became drunk 'from the wine of her fornication'. Verse 4 pictures her riding on a scarlet beast, which shows her alliance and close relationship with the beast. Verse 5 presents her attired in majestic dress, holding a cup which is 'full of abominations and the unclean things of her fornication'. The kings' and the nations' acquiescence to the 'fornication' refers not to literal immorality but figuratively to acceptance of the religious and idolatrous demands of the ungodly earthly order. The economic interpretation of the nations' intoxicating passion and the kings' immoral desire for Babylon is clear from 18.3, 9-19, where the same phrases for immorality and intoxication of 17.2 are equated with terms for economic prosperity, and the nations' loyalty to Babylon lay in her ability to provide economic prosperity for them.

In the conclusion of 17.5 the woman, 'Babylon the Great', is given an additional description: 'the mother of the harlots and of the abominations of the earth'. As in v. 4, the combination of these two words 'abomination' and 'harlot' (equivalent to one committing fornication) probably refers to idol worship, as they so often did in the Old Testament.[307] That she is 'mother' of idolaters connotes her authoritative influence over and inspiration of the system of idolatry which was an integral part of economic involvement. She expresses herself throughout the ages in ungodly economic-religious institutions and facets of culture.

---

307. πορνεία and πορνεύω elsewhere in the book are figurative expressions for idolatry (so 2.14, 20-21; cf. 9:21; see on 14.8; 17.2). βδελυγμάτων in 17.4 establishes beyond doubt the connection with an idolatrous influence, since this is one of the common words for idol or idolatrous sacrifice in the LXX (so βδέλυγμα occurs at least 47 times out of an approx. 122 times total uses).

Some commentators have observed that the Babylonian whore has been set in explicit contrast to the woman–mother (12.1-6, 14-17) and the Lamb's bride (19.7-8; 21.2, 10),[308] which indicates the following: (1) her transtemporal nature, since the woman of chs. 12, 19, and 21 spans the church age;[309] (2) that she spawns faithless children in contrast to the woman who bears faithful seed; and (3) that she is ultimately motivated by Satan in contrast to the woman motivated by Christ, so that the whore has a religious side in addition to its economic focus.

The nature of the woman is revealed in greater detail in v. 5 by the name written on her forehead. Names written on 'foreheads' in the book reveal the true character of people and their ultimate relationship, whether to God (7.3; 14.1; 22.4) or Satan (13.16; 14.9; 20.4). Likewise, the 'name having been written on the forehead' of the whore reveals her seductive and idolatrous character, which further identifies her to be on the side of the beast. The depiction may reflect the practice of Roman whores who purportedly had their names written on bands across their forehead, though the validity of the references attesting this are doubtful (except perhaps for Seneca the Elder, *Controversiae* 1.2.7). Those who corporately compose the bride of the Lamb and have 'his name on their foreheads' (22.4) are especially set in contrast to the whore.

The first part of the name is 'Babylon the Great', which is an allusion to Dan. 4.27 (4.30, LXX, Eng.), which occurs also in 14.8. The name in Daniel 4 is part of the king's self-praise for which he is soon judged. Likewise, the end-time Babylon is on the verge of judgment for its pride and evil. The prefixing of 'mystery' (μυστήριον) to the title confirms the Daniel background, since 'mystery' also occurs in Dan. 4.9 (Theodotion) as an introduction to the narration of Nebuchadnezzar's pride and subsequent judgment. Furthermore, 'mystery' (μυστήριον) in the LXX occurs with an eschatological sense only in Dan. 2.28-29, 45 (and appears rarely elsewhere in the Old Testament; see on 1.20; 10.7). In Rev. 17.5 'mystery' also has end-time associations, since the primary subject of the whole vision is the destruction of Babylon immediately preceding Christ's coming (cf. 17.10-18). Indeed, 'mystery' has been used previously with end-time connotations in 1.20 and 10.7. Both 10.7 and 17.5 overtly refer to the mystery as something

308. That an intentional contrast is intended is evident from the strikingly identical introductory vision formulas of 17.1 and 21.9-10.

309. Cf. Johnson, *Revelation*, p. 556.

prophetic which will be (or is being) fulfilled according to God's word (cf. 17.17).

In 17.7 'mystery' is used again to refer to the hidden meaning of the symbolism of, not only the woman, but also the beast, which the angel explains in vv. 8-18. This is not merely referring to the fulfillment of end-time events on the stage of history which have been prophesied and whose realization has hitherto been hidden in the decretive counsels of God, but the revealing of the unanticipated or ironic manner in which such events will unravel. In 1.20 and 10.7 the 'mystery' involved the unexpected way in which Daniel's prophecy about the establishment of Israel's latter-day kingdom and temple, and the defeat of evil empires, was beginning fulfillment. As we have seen, the notion of μυστήριον in both Revelation texts is that the kingdom begins ironically through the suffering of Christ and his people (e.g. cf. 1.5-6, 13-14 with 1.20; see on 1.20 and conclusion to Rev. 1).

Rev. 17.8-18 is also termed a 'mystery' because it reveals the unexpected way in which the kingdom of evil will begin to be defeated: it will turn against itself and start to self-destruct even before Christ returns. The political side of the evil system (the beast and his allies) will turn against the religious–economic side and destroy it: 'they will hate the harlot, and they will make her desolated and naked and they will eat her flesh and burn her with fire' (17.16). Old Testament prophecy did not foresee in such detail the events leading up to the close of the age but only generally expected that God, or his Messiah, would decisively defeat the entire forces of evil at a climactic battle at the very end. Who could have expected that the way God would commence the defeat of the kingdom of evil at the end of history would be by making that kingdom divide within itself and fight against itself?[310]

4. *Conclusion*

Most scholars have viewed many of the uses of μυστήριον in the New Testament to refer primarily to Old Testament prophecies whose historical fulfillment had formerly been hidden in the inaccessible heavenly counsels of God. And the 'revelation' of such mysteries refers, not merely to the uncovering of information related to certain facts or events, 'but the appearance itself, the becoming historical reality of that

---

310. For generalized antecedents of eschatological civil war in the OT without the kind of specificity in Rev. 17.16-17 see Beale, *Book of Revelation*, in *loc.* at Rev. 17.17.

which until now did not exist as such, but was kept by God, hidden, held back'.[311] In this connection, Bockmuehl says that Paul believed that formerly the meaning of the Old Testament was concealed until the time of its prophetic fulfillment, which was in Christ. He goes further and says that Paul viewed Christ as the hermeneutical key to rereading the Old Testament (e.g. 2 Cor. 1.20), so that 'the true meaning of the Old Testament has only now been uncovered in Christ',[312] yet the Old also casts light on the New.[313] Bockmuehl apparently believes that Paul's new revelation allowed him to perceive reference to Christ in certain Old Testament passages which otherwise one would never suspect are speaking about Christ. Such new meaning is the result of revelation of an Old Testament mystery. Bockmuehl's analysis, however, does not go much beyond these conclusions to explain in more detail these 'newer' meanings.

Seyoon Kim showed promising signs of penetrating Paul's thinking on the 'mystery' of Romans 11 by implicitly discussing the general idea of unexpected fulfillment of Old Testament prophecy. Nevertheless, his precise understanding of this, in my view, still needs sharpening, though his thought-provoking position on the 'mystery' of Romans 11 is the foundation upon which my own view of Romans 11 has been built. George Ladd in his study of Matthew 13 is the only one I have discovered so far who has explicitly identified the 'mystery', not merely with prophecy formerly hidden in heaven but now fulfilled in earthly history, but more specifically *with an unexpected fulfillment of prophecy*. True, Bockmuehl's view could be understood to include the notion that Christ is the unexpected fulfillment of the Old Testament, but he never terms it this way and he never analyzes the contexts of the Old Testament citations or allusions to define precisely their prophetic meaning in order then to determine how Paul understands the fulfillment to be unexpected. He merely says generally (in his introduction

311. Ridderbos, *Paul*, p. 46 (cf. pp. 45-53), who represents the general position among scholars; this is also the overall thrust of the conclusions of Brown, *Semitic Background of the Term 'Mystery'*. For a listing of others holding this position, see Kim's earlier work, *Origin of Paul's Gospel*, p. 74, whose own position there does not appear to advance much beyond this definition. Saucy, 'Church as the Mystery of God', pp. 144-55, adopts Ridderbos's definition as the primary meaning for 'mystery' in Eph. 3.3, 4, 9.

312. Bockmuehl, *Revelation and Mystery*, p. 156.

313. Bockmuehl, *Revelation and Mystery*, pp. 153-56.

to his study of Paul) that Christ is the new meaning of the Old Testament or is the key to rereading it.

My own investigation has not discovered anything new in early Jewish uses.[314] The study has confirmed the conclusion reached earlier by others that the notion of 'mystery' in the New Testament has its roots not in the Hellenistic mystery religions but in the Old Testament, in line generally with early Judaism's eschatological usage of the term and concept.[315] In contrast to the conclusions of preceding studies, I have tried to point out that the consistent trend in New Testament uses of μυστήριον not only refer to fulfillment in general but also focus on the kind of fulfillment which is often unexpected in comparison to what one would have expected in the pre-Christian era as a mere reader of the Old Testament prophecies which are referred to by Paul in direct connection with μυστήριον. The New Testament's christological and eschatological presuppositions (on which see at ch. 2), based on the revelation of Christ's acts in history and the historical response to those acts, are the justification of such readings; indeed, Christ and the New Testament writers would see such apparently unexpected fulfillments as not a twisting of the Old Testament Scripture but organic outgrowths of it, as the bud is related to the opened flower. John's uses in Revelation are no exceptions to usage elsewhere in the New Testament, but fall in line with the other uses.

314. However, the brief analysis of the use of 'mystery' in Qumran showed that sometimes 'mystery' occurs in close association with other allusions to Daniel, especially Dan. 11–12, which commentators have not observed; this analysis is a summary of an earlier study in my *Use of Daniel*, pp. 12-42; A.Y. Collins objected to my earlier conclusion that there was really a Daniel background to the use of 'mystery' in Qumran because she was unconvinced of the validity of the other Daniel allusions which I argued lay in close proximity to the use of רז. She, however, merely states her disagreement by asserting that similar vocabulary and ideas do not indicate literary dependence. In response, what other criteria can one use? Certainly these are correct criteria; she merely is not convinced of the evidence I adduce (Collins, review of, *Use of Daniel*, pp. 734-35). I remain convinced of my earlier analysis, which is broadly pointed to also by general acknowledgement that the Qumran community was saturated with an eschatological atmosphere and had its inception with the hasidim who were obsessed with Daniel: so, e.g., F.F. Bruce, *New Testament History* (Garden City, NY: Doubleday, 1971), pp. 100-103; Cross, *Ancient Library of Qumran*, pp. 113, 131-32, 198-200).

315. So cf., e.g., the studies of Bornkamm, Brown, Coppens, Caragounis, and Bockmuehl, who have shown especially that the Pauline uses do not have the background of the Greek mystery religions but a Semitic background.

E. *The Old Testament Background of Revelation 3.14:*
The Already and Not Yet New Creation of Revelation

1. *Introduction*[316]

Christ describes Himself in Rev. 3.14 as 'the Amen, the faithful and
true witness, the beginning of the creation of God'. Commentators have
suggested a variety of backgrounds for the threefold title. The purpose
of this study is to review these proposals and argue in support of one of
them.

2. *The Proposal that an Old Testament or Jewish Exegetical Tradition*
Based on Proverbs 8, Proverbs 14 and Genesis 1 Stands Behind the
Title of Revelation 3.14

About 30 years ago L.H. Silberman[317] argued that the phrase 'the
Amen' of Rev. 3.14 is a mistransliteration of the Hebrew אמון ('master
workman'), which is employed to describe Wisdom in Prov. 8.30
('Then I [wisdom] was beside Him [at creation], as a master workman'), and which refers to Torah in the midrash on Gen 1.1 in *Gen. R.*
1.1. He also argued that the following titles in Rev 3.14, 'the faithful
and true witness' and 'the beginning of the creation of God', respectively, are drawn from the Hebrew of Prov. 14.25 (עד אמת, 'faithful
witness') and 8.22 (ראשית דרכו, 'beginning of his ways'). To buttress
his view he noted that the midrash on Genesis 1 equates the 'beginning
of his ways' (from Prov. 8.22) and 'master builder' (from Prov. 8.30),
since both are applied to the Torah.[318] Silberman concluded by proposing that Rev. 3.14 must have read in a Hebrew antecedent, 'Thus says

---

316. An earlier version of this chapter was read at the Summer, 1993, annual
meeting of the Tyndale Fellowship for Biblical Research (New Testament section)
in Cambridge and at the Fall, 1993, annual meeting of the Society of Biblical Literature in Washington, DC. I am grateful to participants at these meetings for their
comments.

317. L.H. Silberman, 'Farewell to O AMHN', *JBL* 82 (1963), pp. 213-15,
building on an earlier article by C.F. Burney (C.F. Burney, 'Christ as the *APXH* of
Creation', *JTS* 27 [1926], pp. 160-77).

318. P. Trudinger, 'O AMHN (Rev. 3: 14) and the Case for a Semitic Original
of the Apocalypse', *NovT* 14 [1972], pp. 277-79, agrees with Silberman's analysis.
Silberman could also have cited Midr. Tanhuma, Genesis, Parashah 1.5 on Gen.
1.1ff., Pt. 5, which is virtually identical to *Gen. R.* 1.1 in its use of Prov. 8.22 and
8.30.

the Master Workman, the faithful and true witness, the foremost of his creation'.

J.A. Montgomery had proposed years before Silberman a similar but more simple background: that Rev. 3.14 is directly dependent on Prov. 8.22, 30.[319] In particular, he argued that John in rabbinic fashion changed the vocalization of אָמוֹן ('master builder') in Prov. 8.30 to אָמֵן. This would mean that John understood wisdom in that passage as the 'Amen', and immediately applied it as a title to Christ in Rev. 3.14. In more straightforward fashion than either Silberman or Montgomery, other commentators have proposed that Col. 1.18 and Rev. 3.14 are parallel, that both depend directly on Prov. 8.22 and are employed polemically against Jewish–Gnostic ideas about Jesus as a mediating power, but not as a supreme one.[320] Still others have denied any dependence on Col 1.15, 18 and have seen only a reference to Prov. 8.22, with the emphasis of ἀρχή being on Christ's temporal priority to the original creation.[321]

Indeed, apparently unnoticed so far, the Targum to Prov. 8.22 translates the Hebrew 'The Lord possessed me [Wisdom] at the beginning of his way' by 'God created me [Wisdom] at *the beginning of his creation*', which is closer to the wording of Rev. 3.14 ('beginning of the creation of God') than any other recently proposed Jewish-Old Testament parallels. However, also unobserved by later-twentieth century commentators, and even nearer still to the language of Rev. 3.14, are two passages interpreting Gen. 1.2-3 from the *Pesiqta Rabbati* (Friedmann edition) cited by Adolph Schlatter: 'from the beginning of the creation of the world the King Messiah was born' (*Pes. R.*, *Piska* 33.6 = מחחלת בריתו של עולם נולד מלך המשיח‎ ἀπ' ἀρχῆς κτίσεως κόσμου ἐγεννήθη ὁ βασιλεὺς ὁ Χριστός; almost identical wording is repeated later in the same section of *Pesiqta Rabbati*, *Piska* 33.6).[322]

---

319. J.A. Montgomery, 'The Education of the Seer of the Apocalypse', *JBL* 45 (1926), pp. 70-81 (73).

320. E.g. C. Hemer, *The Letters to the Seven Churches of Asia in their Local Setting* (JSNTSup, 11; Sheffield: JSOT, 1986), pp. 186-87.

321. T. Holtz, *Die Christologie der Apokalypse des Johannes*, pp. 144-47.

322. Schlatter, *Das Alte Testament in der johanneischen Apokalypse*, pp. 43-44. Likewise J. Gill, *An Exposition of the New Testament. III. The Revelation of St. John the Divine* (Philadelphia: W.W. Woodward, 1811), p. 723, cites the Zohar, fol. 77.1 on Gen. 24.2: 'this is Metatron (or the Mediator), the servant of God...for he is the beginning of the creation of God, who rules over all that he has'.

3. *The Proposal of an Isaiah Background for the Title of Revelation 3.14*

a. *Problems With a Proverbs—Original Creation Background for Revelation 3.14.* The proposal of Silberman, and others like it cited above, is possible. However, in addition to the overly complex nature of his view and the problems of dating the Jewish tradition, there are other factors which raise questions about the proposal. First, 'wisdom' of Prov. 8.22, 30 is never explicitly identified with the Messiah in Judaism, though there may be a broader thematic wisdom tradition which has messianic connotations. Second, nowhere else in Revelation is Christ equated with Torah, as would be the case in Rev. 3.14, if the Genesis 1–Proverbs 8 background were explicitly present. Third, regardless of the relationship of Rev. 1.5 and 3.14 to Col. 1.15-18, both Revelation texts first and primarily are to be interpreted by their immediate contexts in Revelation. In this respect, 3.14 is designed to be a literary development of Christ's title in 1.5.[323] Now it is clear there that Jesus as 'faithful witness' and 'first-born of the dead' in 1.5 is related *not to the original creation* but to his ministry, death and resurrection. Therefore, the self-description 'the Amen, the Faithful and True Witness' in 3.14a is an expansion of 'faithful witness' in 1.5. That 3.14 is developing 1.5 in some way is apparent, since all of the introductory self-ascriptions in the seven letters quote or allude to descriptions or quotations of Christ from ch. 1.

In addition, the second part of 3.14, 'the beginning of the creation of God', is also evidently a development of the phrase 'first-born of the dead' in 1.5, which in 1.5 also immediately follows the expression 'the faithful witness'. The variant εκκλησιας ('church') for κτίσεως ('creation') is secondary because of weak MS support (read only by א) and because it may have been an unintentional misreading of κτίσεως (the resulting reading of א is 'the beginning of the church'). However, the variant may not have been accidental, since the scribe may well have been trying to conform it to the parallel of Col. 1.15 and 18, where respectively Christ as 'first-born of all creation' is interpreted by Christ as 'the head of the body, which is the church'. At the least, the variant reading would have come to represent an early interpretation of the

323. So also N. Brox, *Zeuge und Märtyrer* (SANT, 5; Munich: Kösel-Verlag, 1961), p. 98.

verse as Christ being the beginning, not of the original creation, but of the newly created church or the new age of the church.

Therefore, in contrast to what many commentators think, this is not a reference linking Jesus to the original creation in Genesis 1 or in Proverbs 8, but is an interpretation of Jesus' resurrection from 1.5.[324] Jesus' resurrection is viewed as being the beginning of the *new* creation, which is parallel with Col. 1.18b: compare 'first-born of all creation' (πρωτότοκος πάσης κτίσεως) in Col. 1.15b, which likely refers to the original creation of Genesis, and 'the beginning, the first-born from the dead' (ἀρχή, πρωτότοκος ἐκ τῶν νεκρῶν) in Col. 1.18b, which refers to the resurrection as a new cosmic beginning, as evident not only by the link with Col. 1.15-17 but also 1.19-20, 23.[325]

The conclusion that the title 'beginning of the creation of God' in 3.14 is an interpretative development of 'first-born of the dead' from 1.5 is confirmed by the observation that ἀρχή ('beginning') and πρωτότοκος ('first-born') are generally related in meaning and especially used together almost synonymously in Col. 1.18b (ἀρχὴ, πρωτότοκος ἐκ τῶν νεκρῶν) to refer to Christ's sovereign position in the new age, as a result of the resurrection. In addition, the titles of Christ in Rev. 22.13 ('the *first* and the last, the *beginning* and the end') use ἀρχὴ ('beginning') synonymously with πρῶτος ('first'). It is not inconceivable that in 3.14 ὁ ἀρχὴ ('the beginning') could be an interpretative development not only of ὁ πρωτότοκος ('the first-born') in 1.5b but also the immediately following phrase ὁ ἄρχων ('the ruler') at the end of 1.5. If so, it might be an interpretative pun (ראשׁית ['beginning'] and ראשׁ ['ruler'] are based on the same root, and both ἀρχή [approx. 75 times] and ἄρχων [approx. 90 times] typically translate ראשׁ in the

324. So likewise only Burney, 'Christ as 'APXH', p. 177, and S.M. Gilmour, 'The Revelation to John', in C.M. Laymon (ed.), *The Interpreter's One-Volume Commentary on the Bible* (Nashville: Abingdon Press, 1971), pp. 945-68 (952); M. Rist, 'The Revelation of St. John the Divine', *IB*, XII, pp. 347-613 (396), sees both ideas of original and new creation included, as does most recently Krodel, *Revelation*, p. 142, and M.R. Mulholland, *Revelation* (Grand Rapids: Zondervan, 1990), p. 133, all of whom appear to have been anticipated by Gill, *Revelation of St John*, p. 722.

325. Note 2 Cor. 5.15, 17 where Jesus' resurrection is understood as bringing about a 'new creation' (cf. the linking ὥστε); so Eph. 1.20-23; 2.5-6, 10.

LXX).[326] That is, Christ as 'first-born from the dead and ruler of the kings of the earth' in Rev. 1.5 is interpreted in Rev. 3.14 as the sovereign inaugurator of the new creation.[327]

If there is such a double sense behind ἀρχή, then τῆς κτίσεως may be both a partitive genitive ('beginning among the creation'), as well as an objective genitive ('ruler over the creation'). Consequently, the title 'beginning of the creation of God' refers not to Jesus' sovereignty over the original creation but to his resurrection as demonstrating that he is the *inauguration* of and *sovereign* over the new creation.[328]

b. *The Proposal of an Isaiah Background for Revelation 3.14*

(i). *Allusion to the New Creation Prophecy of Isaiah 65.16-18.* Many commentators have concluded that behind the title ὁ Ἀμήν stands Isa. 65.16 ('the God of *amēn* [אָמֵן]'),[329] although little exegetical argumentation is adduced in support of the contention, and the Isaianic connection is never related to the idea of the creation in the second clause of Rev. 3.14. A few commentators have suggested, also without further discussion, that the full clause 'The Amen, the faithful and true witness' is an expanded translation of the Isaianic 'Amen'.[330] Consequently, the

---

326. Cf. Burney, 'APXH', pp. 176-77, and Holtz, *Christologie*, p. 147, for further evidence that ἀρχή can include both ideas of 'beginning' and 'sovereign head' in Col. 1.18, Rev. 3.14 and elsewhere.

327. It is also possible that Christ is presented in this way as a polemic against the idea that the emperor's birthday marked the beginning of a new creation of the Roman empire. The Roman governor of the province of Asia during the reign of Augustus declared that 'the birthday of the most divine Caesar' was 'equivalent to *the beginning of all things, and he has restored...every form that had become imperfect and fallen...Therefore people would be right to consider this to have been *the beginning of the breath of life* for them'. The assembly of the province of Asia also honored Augustus because 'the birthday of the god marked for the world *the beginning* of good tidings' (for the translations and fuller contexts of these quotations see S.R.F. Price, *Rituals and Power* [Cambridge: Cambridge University Press, 1984], p. 55).

328. Likewise Lohmeyer, *Die Offenbarung des Johannes*, p. 38, and Mulholland, *Revelation*, p. 133, who understand Rev. 3.14 as referring to new creation.

329. E.g. Hemer, *Letters to the Seven Churches*, p. 185, says 'Christ is equated with the "God of Amen" of Isa 65:16'; likewise Kiddle and Ross, *Revelation*, p. 57.

330. The following see the threefold title of Rev. 3.14 as an expanded translation of 'Amen' in Isa. 65.16: M. Rissi, *The Future of the World: An Exegetical*

suggestion of an Isaiah allusion has seemed superficial and the purported Isaiah background perhaps viewed as an echo.[331]

However, there is evidence that the Isaiah text is the *primary* source for the titles in Rev. 3.14. The present analysis will offer the following seven lines of argument in support of an allusion to Isa. 65.16, most of which have been hitherto unobserved: (a) the evidence of Septuagint usage in general; (b) the evidence of the Septuagintal versions of Isa. 65.16 specifically; (c) the use of 'Amen' as a name or attribute of God only in Isa. 65.16 and Rev. 3.14; (d) the phrase 'the beginning of the creation of God' in Rev. 3.14b best suits an Isa. 65.16ff. background, (e) as does the immediate context of 3.14 and (f) unique parallels elsewhere in the wider context of the book; (g) the word 'witness' is rooted in another Isaiah context parallel with that of Isa. 65.16ff.

(a) *Evidence of Septuagint Usage in General.* The three descriptions 'the Amen, the faithful and true' are not distinct, but generally overlap in meaning to underscore the idea of Jesus' *faithfulness* in testifying to his Father during his earthly ministry and that he continues as such a witness. In fact, ὁ Ἀμήν ('the Amen') is a semitic equivalent to the Greek 'faithful' (πιστός), as well as 'true' (ἀληθινός), which is evident from the Septuagint's typical translation of verbal and nominal forms of the root אמן ('to be faithful') mainly by πιστός,[332] but also sometimes by ἀληθινός.[333] Therefore, the threefold name could be an independent, expanded translation of Isaiah's 'Amen'.

Study of Rev. 19:11–22:15 (SBT, Second Series 23; London: SCM Press, 1972), p. 21; H. Schlier, 'ἀμήν', *TDNT*, I, p. 337; H. Bietenhard, 'ἀμήν', *NIDNTT*, I, p. 99.

331. The only exception to this, which came to my notice after completing an initial draft of the present study, is Fekkes, *Isaiah and Prophetic Traditions*, pp. 137-38, who offers two brief arguments in support of an Isaiah allusion behind 'Amen' (see nn. 344 and 347 below), though he does not see 'faithful and true' as based on Isaiah.

332. See the numerous examples in E. Hatch and H.A. Redpath, *A Concordance to the Septuagint* (Graz–Austria: Akademische Druck, 1954), II, pp. 1138-39; likewise see on 'πίστις', II, p. 1138.

333. See examples in Hatch and Redpath, *Concordance to the Septuagint*, I, p. 54, and in particular note the LXX rendering of אמן in Isa 65.16 twice by ἀληθινός; similarly see p. 54, on ἀληθῶς (especially in Jer. 35[28].6, where it renders אמן), and p. 53, on ἀλήθεια. See also below on the translations of Isa. 65.16 by Aquila and Symmachus.

(b) *Evidence of Septuagintal Versions in Isa. 65.16 in Particular.* To-gether with Rev. 1.5 (and the allusion there to Ps. 88.38 [= 89.38, MT]), the Old Testament Greek versions of Isa. 65.16 likely have significant relevance for understanding the formulation of the title in Rev. 3.14. First, the Hebrew text refers twice to God as 'the God of *truth* [or "Amen", אָמֵן]', which is translated in the following ways by different versions of the Septuagint: τὸν θεὸν τὸν ἀληθινόν (LXX); ἐν τῷ θεῷ πεπιστωμένως (Aquila);[334] ἐν τῷ θεῷ 'ἀμήν (Symmachus; Theodotion also reads 'ἀμήν).[335]

Most commentators omit notice that all three words in Rev. 3.14a are essentially attested in extant versions of Isa. 65.16 (though πιστός is not identical to Aquila or MS 86 [see n. 334]). Some earlier commenta-tors observe the versional readings of Isa. 65.16, but do not conclude that they have relevance for understanding the composition of the threefold title in Rev. 3.14.[336] Though not observed even by those few suggesting that the threefold name is an expanded translation of Isa. 65.16,[337] the versional evidence demonstrates the plausibility that Rev. 3.14 could well have expanded Isa. 65.16 in the same threefold manner. In this light, the title ὁ μάρτυς ὁ πιστὸς καὶ ἀληθινός ('the faithful and true witness') in Rev. 3.14 is best taken as an interpretative translation

334. The full translation of Aquila is, 'by which the one blessing himself in the earth will be blessed *faithfully* by God', so that πεπιστωμένως functions adver-bially, but still refers to the faithfulness of God. Jerome reflects Aquila's rendering by reading the adverb *fideliter*, and MS 86 similarly reads πεπιστωμένος for the first 'Amen' of Isa. 65.16.

335. Symmachus could be rendered in one of two ways, since 'ἀμήν is indeclin-able: (1) 'by which the one blessing himself upon the earth will be blessed by the God of Amen', or (2) 'by which the one blessing himself will be blessed by God, amen' (Field's edition of Origin's Hexapla punctuates in the latter way). In the former it is an adjective for God, while in the latter it is a response by God to his prior assertion, which would still refer to his faithfulness in fulfilling his promises. The Vulgate likewise reads *amen* twice, and Theodotion and MS 86 read 'ἀμήν for the second 'Amen' of the Isaiah text (for full data see the Göttingen LXX apparatus edited by J. Ziegler).

336. So Swete, *Apocalypse* (London: Macmillan, 1906), p. 58, as well as Sil-berman, 'Farewell to O AMHN', p. 213 and Prigent, *L'Apocalypse De Saint Jean*, pp. 75-76, though they note only the readings of Symmachus and the LXX. Charles, *Revelation*, p. 94, cites the LXX, Aquila and Symmachus, but merely concludes that only 'ἀμήν in Rev. 3.14 is derived from Isa. 65.16, and does not comment on 'faithful and true'.

337. See references at n. 330.

of אָמֵן ('Amen' = ἀμήν) from Isa. 65.16. Perhaps 'Amen' is placed first followed by 'faithful and true' to show that the latter clause is an interpretative expansion of the Isaianic 'Amen'.

The formulation could be an independent, amplified rendering of the Isaiah text.[338] Or, similarly, 'faithful' from Rev. 1.5 has been taken and now understood in the light of Isaiah's 'Amen'; 'True' has been taken from Rev. 3.7, where it occurred already as a rendering of 'faithful' from 1.5, and was added as part of the expansion in 3.14. Yet another possibility is that the three different readings of the LXX, Aquila, Symmachus and Theodotion were already extant in the first century in earlier versional forms or represented prior exegetical traditions on Isa. 65.16, and that the Rev. 3.14 rendering was 'sparked off' by and composed under the influence of such prior versions or traditions.[339]

---

338. Even different English versions render אָמֵן in almost identical ways as Rev. 3.14 and the Septuagint versions: Douay and NEB = 'Amen'; NRSV and Moffat = 'faithfulness' or 'faithful'; KJV, RSV, NIV, NASB, JB = 'true'. BDB, p. 53, cites the same three possibilities of translation for Isa. 65.16.

339. There is consensus that the Septuagint of Isaiah was translated before the first Christian century (e.g. see H.B. Swete, *Introduction to the OT in Greek* [Cambridge: Cambridge University Press, 1902], pp. 24-25; S. Jellicoe, *The Septuagint and Modern Study* [Oxford: Clarendon Press, 1968], p. 67). Therefore, at least one of the Old Testament Greek readings of Isa. 65.16 was extant before the first century AD (probably ἀληθινός of the LXX). The precise dates of Aquila's, Theodotion's and Symmachus' translations are after the usually accepted 95 AD date of Revelation.

Aquila's work is typically placed around 130 AD, Theodotion's toward the end of that century and that of Symmachus about 200 AD. Such close chronological proximity to Revelation, especially on Aquila's and Theodotion's part (see below), makes plausible that their readings may have existed earlier in some versional or traditional form. There is also geographical proximity, since 'Ur–Theodotion' had been current for a long time in Asia Minor prior to the end of the second century AD (Jellicoe, *Septuagint*, p. 89), and possibly Aquila's translation had influence there, since he was from Pontus (Sinope) in Asia Minor (Swete, *Introduction to the OT in Greek*, p. 31). The three were not independent translators, but were revisors of prior Old Testament Greek translations. Aquila was revising in order to produce a more literal translation of the Hebrew. Interestingly, his work has been seen to reflect 'the exegetical tradition of the school of Jamnia' (Swete, *Introduction to the OT in Greek*, p. 458; cf. pp. 32, 41). Symmachus is generally known as a 'dynamic equivalent' translator. Some of his readings pre-date the first century AD (Jellicoe, *Septuagint*, p. 96). Symmachus' translation also shows a knowledge of previous Greek versions (B.J. Roberts, *The OT Text and Versions* [Cardiff: University of

It is difficult to decide whether or not the enlarged rendering was done independently or dependently. The latter is an attractive possibility, since it seems more than coincidental that the four Greek versions of Isa. 65.16 together have virtually the same amplified renderings as that of Rev. 3.14, which many, on superficial grounds, have concluded is linked in some way to אָמֵן in the same Isaiah passage. Whichever is the case, the articulation of the heavenly Christ's name through an exegesis of Old Testament texts has affinities with the practice in Judaism of formulating personal names for angels on the basis of exegeting Old Testament texts.[340]

What enhances the notion that the three readings existed in some form prior to the second century AD is that the Hebrew אָמֵן could be pointed in three possible ways, which correspond at least to two and possibly three of the Greek Old Testament versional readings and to Rev. 3.14.[341]

(c) *The Use of 'Amen' as a Name or Attribute of God Only in Isaiah 65.16 and Revelation 3.14*. In both the Hebrew and Greek Old Testament 'Amen' is an utterance acknowledging the sovereign word of God or is a concluding response of the believing community to a prayer.[342] In all of its Old Testament uses outside of Isaiah 65 (23 times in Hebrew and 8 times in Greek [15 times including Aq., Theodotion,

---

Wales, 1951], p. 126), a thoroughgoing use of Hebrew and Greek sources 'as quarries from which he...carefully selects the stones', and his work reveals 'extensive knowledge of current Jewish exegesis' (Jellicoe, *Septuagint*, pp. 98-99; likewise Roberts, *The OT Text*, p. 126). Though Theodotion's version is dated toward the end of the second century, it is acknowledged that his work was a recension of a translation made in the early second century BC, usually now referred to as Ur-Theodotion. The primary basis for positing the early existence of Ur-Theodotion is the appearance of Theodotonic readings in the New Testament (especially Dan. allusions in Rev. and the earliest Fathers; see Jellicoe, *Septuagint*, pp. 83-94).

340. For the practice in Judaism see S. Olyan, *A Thousand Thousands Served Him* (TSAJ, 36; Tübingen: J.C.B. Mohr [Paul Siebeck], 1993), who notes that these angelic name formulations were sometimes based on an exegetical expansion of divine attributes from the Hebrew Old Testament, which would seem to have relevance especially for the expansions of the divine name 'Amen' in Isa. 65.16.

341. In addition to אָמֵן, cf. also אֹמֶן ('faithfulness') and אֱמוּן ('firmness, faithfulness'); see A. Jepsen, "amen', *TDOT*, I, pp. 320-22 (322) and the apparatus of *BHS* on Isa. 65.16.

342. Jepsen, "amen', pp. 320-22.

Symm.]) it confirms an assertion by someone. ἀμήν is used likewise about 125 times in the New Testament outside of Rev. 3.14 either to confirm the truth of Jesus' sayings (in the Gospels) or as a concluding response to an assertion or a prayer (predominately in the Epistles).[343] The only exceptions to this use in the Old Testament and the New Testament are Isa. 65.16 (twice) and Rev. 3.14, where in both passages 'Amen' is a name or attribute respectively of God and Christ. That such a predicative use occurs only in Isa. 65.16 and Rev. 3.14 points further to a close, integral link between the two texts.[344]

(d) *The Phrase 'The Beginning of the Creation of God' in Revelation 3.14 best suits an Allusion to Isaiah 65.16-17.* The 'blessing' of the 'God of Amen', which is only generally referred to in Isa. 65.16, is precisely understood in the following verse of Isaiah 65 to be that of the new creation which he will bring about: 'For behold, I create a new heavens and a new earth' (Isa. 65.17). Also to be noted is the identity of Isa. 65.16 with 65.17, which lies in the repeated phrase in the second line of each verse, 'the former troubles (or 'things') are forgotten' (or 'shall not be remembered'; *Exod. R.* 23.11 applies the language of Isa. 65.16 to 'the Messianic Age'). Similarly, the mention of 'the creation of God' directly after calling Christ 'the Amen...' follows the same sequence of concepts seen above in Isa. 65.16 and 65.17.

(e) *Evidence in the Immediate Context Pointing to an Isaiah Allusion in Revelation 3.14.* That Isaiah 65 is in mind is confirmed also by recognizing that just two verses earlier in Rev. 3.12 allusion has been made to Isa. 65.15 (cf. LXX), where Christ refers to his 'new name', by which his eschatological people likewise will be identified ('I will write upon him...My new name'),[345] and in 3.14 this name is revealed as 'the Amen, the Faithful and True'. Indeed, this conforms to the pattern of

---

343. Cf. Bietenhard, 'ἀμήν', pp. 97-99.

344. After finishing the rough draft of this article, I read J.A. Alexander, *Commentary on the Prophecies of Isaiah* (Grand Rapids: Zondervan, 1953 [orig. 1846–47]), p. 451, who comes close to making the same point; even more recently my attention has been drawn to the work of Fekkes, *Isaiah and Prophetic Traditions*, pp. 137-38, who independently confirms the same point.

345. The allusion to Isa. 65 in Rev. 3.12 is acknowledged by many commentators and probably includes Isa. 62.2, where the end-time status of God's people also will be indicated by conferring on them a 'new name'. Note the same allusion to Isa. 62.2 and 65.15 in Rev. 2.17.

Isa. 65.15-16 (LXX), where in v. 15 God prophesies that his 'servants will be called by a new name', and v. 16 says they will be associated with his name of 'True [Amen and Faithful]' because they will be blessed by Him (or will bless Him).[346]

The intense focus on this section of Isaiah is likewise evident from noticing allusion to other related texts of Isaiah in Rev. 3.7, 9 (e.g. Isa. 60.14; 49.23; 43.4). Furthermore, the threefold name for God in Rev. 1.4 and 1.8, and for Christ in 1.17-18 derives from Isa. 41.4, 43.10, 44.6 and 48.12.

(f) *Evidence in the Wider Context of the Book Pointing to an Isaiah Allusion in Revelation 3.14.* Indeed, the divine name 'the Beginning and the End' in Rev. 21.6, which is based on Isa. 41.4, 44.6 and 48.12 (all have variant forms of God saying 'I am the first and the last'), is directly appended to allusions from Isa. 43.18 (in Rev. 21.4), Isa. 43.19 and 65.16 (in Rev. 21.5). Corroboration also comes from Rev. 21.5a, where the one 'on the throne' says Ἰδοὺ καινὰ ποιῶ πάντα ('Behold, I make all things new'), a reference, not only to Isa. 43.19, but also 65.17, and then he refers to this declaration in 21.5b as οἱ λόγοι πιστοὶ καὶ ἀληθινοί εἰσιν ('these words are faithful and true'). The declaration of 'making all things new' is a development of the earlier allusion to Isa. 65.17 in Rev. 21.1: 'And I saw a new heaven and a new earth'. In this light, it is not accidental that in 21.6 God or Jesus is called 'the beginning' (ἡ ἀρχὴ). In view of the above discussion of 3.14, such language in 21.6 may imply that the hoped for new creation of 21.1, 4-5 has already been inaugurated by Jesus' resurrection.

---

346. The context of Isa. 65.15 primarily contrasts God's faithful servants in Israel with Israelites who compromise by dedicating meals and cup offerings to idols and false gods (vv. 3-4, 7, 11). *Targ. Isa.* 65.4 is applied to those who pay homage to a memorial erected in honor of the emperor Tiberias (so Chilton, *Isaiah Targum*, p. 123). In the eschaton the faithful will be comforted from their former troubles (Isa. 65.13-19) by 'eating' and 'drinking', whereas the compromisers will be punished because they will 'prepare a table for the Devil and fill up the drink-offering for Fortune' (v. 11). Perhaps the context of idolatrous feasts in Isaiah 65 made it even more attractive to appeal to, since emperor worship pervaded all aspects of society and idolatrous trade guild banquets were one of the problematic situations facing the seven churches, including Laodicea (e.g. Rev. 2.14, 20; see Hemer, *Letters to the Seven Churches*, pp. 107-23). In this respect, Christ's promise in 3.20 that he will 'dine' with the faithful takes on more significance.

The Isaianic-new creation link between 3.14 and 21.1, 4-5 is further apparent from observing that of the three times the phrase πιστὸς καὶ ἀληθινός ('faithful and true') occurs elsewhere in the book outside of 3.14, one serves as an introductory affirmation of the truth that God will 'make *all* things new' (21.5), and a second (22.6) functions likewise as an emphatic conclusion to the same discussion of the new creation in 21.5–22.5 (although in 21.5 and 22.6 the words are in the plural). The other occurrence of the phrase in 19.11 is not explicitly linked with a new creation idea, though it is also a title for Christ. The title in 19.11 underscores his function in executing end-time judgment, which is directly linked in the following context with the destruction of the cosmos and its re-creation (cf. 20.11–22.5).[347] All three of these occurrences underscore assurance that Old Testament prophecy about new creation and judgment will be fulfilled.

(g) Conclusion
A seventh line of evidence confirming an Isaiah allusion in Rev. 3.14 is the recognition that the mention of 'witness' also derives from a parallel new creation passage elsewhere in Isaiah (for full analysis see directly below, sect. 2).

Therefore, according to Rev 1.5 and 3.14, Jesus' resurrection has launched the fulfillment of Isaiah's prophecy of the new creation.[348] 2 Cor. 5.14-17 also understands that the resurrection of Christ inaugurated the new creation prophesied by Isa. 43.19 and 65.17.[349] In this connection, the Targumic rendering of 'God of truth' from Isa. 65.16 (MT) by 'living [קים] God' is striking, since the name in Rev. 3.14 is applied to Christ as the resurrected and 'living' Lord (Christ is referred

---

347. A. Farrer, *A Rebirth of Images: The Making of St. John's Apocalypse* (Boston: Beacon Press, 1963), pp. 280-81, sees Isa. 65.13-18 as the background for 'Amen', and 'Faithful and True' in Rev. 19.4, 11, which he sees being applied to Christ in future fulfillment of Isaiah's prophecy that God would be called these names in the new world. However, Farrer does not relate this to Rev. 3.14.

Recently Fekkes, *Isaiah and Prophetic Traditions*, p. 138, in arguing for dependence of 'Amen' in 3.14 on Isa. 65.16 also independently has pointed out a few of the allusions observed above to confirm the point (Isa. 65.15, 65.17 and 65.16c respectively in Rev. 3.12, 21.1 and 21.4).

348. In an obscure commentary on Revelation, Mauro, *Patmos Visions*, pp. 129-30, comes close to suggesting this conclusion as a possibility, although his discussion is brief.

349. On this see Beale, 'Old Testament Background of Reconciliation'.

to as 'living' [ζῶν] two times in the preceding context [Rev. 1.18a, 1.18b] and once as he who 'came to life' [ἔζησεν in 2.8]). Likewise, the parallel new creation prophecy of Isa. 66.22 well could refer to the resurrection of Israel: 'for as the new heaven and new earth, which I make, remain before Me, so will your seed *stand*' (στήσεται, which also could be translated 'come up', 'remain'). Later Judaism also understood Isa. 65.17 and 66.22 to pertain to the final resurrection (see *T. d. Eliyy.*, p. 86;[350] *T. d. Eliyy.*, *PRE*, S, p. 31; cf. *Midr. Ps.* 46.2). Rev. 3.14 appears to be in line with both early and late Judaism's interpretation of these Old Testament texts as resurrection prophecies. That resurrection and new creation go hand-in-hand is logical, since the resurrection of the saints is *the* means by which people become part of the new creation.

Therefore, Jesus as the principle, origin or source of the original creation is not in mind, but Jesus as the inaugurator of the new creation is the focus. The genitive construction τῆς κτίσεως ('of the creation') is best taken as a partitive genitive like the phrase 'Christ... *the first fruits of those sleeping*' in 1 Cor. 15.20. Christ's resurrection is the beginning of a much larger new creation to come. Implicit in the idea of ἡ ἀρχὴ may be, not only that of inauguration, but also supremacy over, as well as temporal priority, as evident from the parallel of Col. 1.18 and especially from Rev. 1.5, where 'first-born from the dead' is directly explained by 'ruler of the kings of the earth'.[351] Some commentators who assume that τῆς κτίσεως τοῦ θεοῦ ('of the creation of God') refers to the original creation do not like the translation of 'beginning' for ἀρχή because they think this would necessitate viewing Jesus as a created being along with the rest of creation.[352] However, seeing the phrase as a reference to the new creation results in the different understanding for which we have argued. The message about the new creation (21.5), and of the book in general (22.6), is referred to as 'faithful and true' because it is from Jesus who is 'faithful and true' (19.9, 11; 3.14; cf. 1.5).

350. References to *Tanna debe Eliyyahu* are from the Braude and Kapstein translation (Philadelphia: Jewish Publication Society of America, 1981).

351. For the idea of temporal priority in Jewish and Greek literature cf. Holtz, *Christologie*, pp. 145-46.

352. E.g. Ladd, *Revelation*, p. 65.

(ii). *Allusion to the Role of 'Witness' to the New Creation in Isaiah 43.10-13.* The only part of the title in Rev. 3.14 which has not been accounted for from an Old Testament background in our analysis is the word 'witness'. The simplest way to account for the word in 3.14 is that it is merely repeated from Rev. 1.5 without any further Old Testament background inspiring its re-appearance. No doubt, commentators are right in seeing Ps. 88(89).27 (28), 37 as the basis for the statement in Rev. 1.5 that Christ is a 'faithful witness', 'firstborn' and 'ruler of the kings of the earth', since all three of these phrases from Rev. 1.5 also occur in the Psalm. The immediate context of the Psalm speaks of David as an 'anointed' king, who will reign over all his enemies and whose seed will be established on his throne forever (Ps. 88[89].19-32, LXX; Judaism understood Ps. 89.28 messianically [*Exod. R.* 19.7; perhaps *Pes. R.* 34.2]). John views Jesus as the ideal Davidic king on an escalated eschatological level, whose death and resurrection have resulted in his eternal kingship and in the kingship of his 'beloved' people (cf. Rev. 1.5b), which is developed in v. 6. Ὁ πρωτότοκος refers to a high, privileged position as a result of the resurrection from the dead (i.e. a position with respect to the Old Testament idea of primogeniture, especially in the context of royal succession [Ps. 89.27-37 is developing this idea from 2 Sam. 7.13-16 and Ps. 2.7-8]).

The Psalm uses both 'firstborn' and the phrase 'higher than the kings of the earth' to refer to the coming Davidic king. However, the wording 'faithful witness' in the Psalm (89.37) is used in the expression 'as the moon is established forever, even as the witness is faithful in heaven'. Just as the moon will endure as long as creation lasts as a testimony to God's faithfulness, so will David's royal seed sit on a throne forever. Though Rev. 1.5 likely derived the phrase 'faithful witness' from the Psalm, the actual reference in the Psalm is not to the coming Davidic king but a metaphor of the certainty of the coming king's enduring reign.

This Psalm background is likely carried over from Rev. 1.5 into Rev. 3.14. However, there is an additional Old Testament background for the idea of 'faithful witness', especially in the context of the expression in Rev. 3.14, which is highlighted there more than Ps. 89.37. The LXX of Isa. 43.10 says, 'you [Israel] be My witnesses, and I am a witness, says the Lord God, and My servant whom I have chosen'. Likewise 43.12-13 (LXX) is parallel with 43.10 and has, 'you [Israel] are My witnesses, *and I am a witness, says the Lord God, even from the beginning*' (κἀγὼ μάρτυς, λέγει κύριος ὁ θεός, ἔτι ἀπ' ἀρχῆς). Though some LXX MSS in 43.12 omit μάρτυς, λέγει,[353] μάρτυς still could be implied or assumed.

What is striking is that Israel, God and the Servant are all called 'witnesses'. Indeed, the Targum interprets 'My servant' as 'My servant *the Messiah*'. To what are Israel, God and the Servant or Messiah to witness? In context, it is evident that they are primarily witnesses to God's past act of redemption at the Exodus (43.12-13, 16-19) and, above all, to God's coming act of restoration from exile, which is to be modelled on the former redemption from Egypt.[354] Isa. 43.18-19 refers to the coming restoration as none other than a new creation: 'Do not remember the first things, nor consider the beginning things. Behold, I create new things'. Therefore, Israel, God and the Messiah are to be witnesses of the future restoration and new creation. Isa. 44.6-8 also says Israel is a 'witness' both to God's past act of creation and his coming deliverance of the nation from exile. Both Isa. 43.10-13 and 44.6-8 also underscore the notion that the witness is against the idols who cannot compare with the true God and his sovereign acts (on which see further below at end of sect. 3).

Especially noteworthy is the observation that the 'witness' by Israel, God and the Servant (Messiah) in Isa. 43.10-13 is to events 'from the beginning' (ἀπ' ἀρχῆς; likewise Isa. 44.8), which are linked with the yet-future new creation, to which they are likewise to bear witness. This phrase 'from the beginning', and like formulations of ἀρχή in various contexts of Isaiah (LXX), refer to the 'beginning' at the first creation (40.21; 42.9; 44.8; 45.21; 48.16) or the 'beginning' when God created Israel as a nation at the Exodus (41.4; 43.9, 13; 48.8, 16; 51.9; 63.16, 19). But the point of saying that God is a 'witness... still [yet, even]

___

353. The preferred reading of the Göttingen LXX textual apparatus retains μάρτυς, λέγει, but cites the following MSS supporting omission of the phrase: S *O'''* *L'''*- 86ᶜ C 198 393 410 449′ 544 965 (vid.) Sypᵃ ᵇ Syl Eus. Tht. Hi. = 𝔐; MSS in Holmes and Parsons supporting the μάρτυς reading are XII, 26, 49, 86, 106, 239, 306, Alex., 233. Even if μάρτυς were omitted, the text could also be translated 'you are My witnesses, and I am the Lord God [or, and I the Lord God am a witness] even from the beginning', but either way there is an implied verb in the second clause.

354. *b. Ber.* 13a sees both an Exodus and Babylonian exile background for Isa. 43.18-19, whereas the majority of Jewish commentators see only the latter setting for Isa. 65.16-17 and 66.22 [*Exod R.* 23.11; *Deut. R.* 10.4; *Lam. R.* 1.2, § 23; *Pes. R.*, *Piska* 29/30B.4; *PRE* 51]).

from the beginning' in the LXX of 43.12-13 (κἀγὼ μάρτυς… ἔτι ἀπ᾽ ἀρχῆς) is to emphasize the witness to God's past acts of redemption as new creations as the basis for his future act of redemption as an escalated new creation. God has been a witness to his past acts of creating the cosmos and of creating Israel as a nation at the Exodus, and he will be a witness *yet* again to another creation.

The emphasis on the continuing divine witness is brought out by the implied verb 'to be' followed by ἔτι in Isa. 43.12-13: 'and I am a witness… even [still, yet] from the beginning' (or ἔτι ἀπ᾽ ἀρχῆς could be rendered '*ever since* the beginning').[355] In this respect, note elsewhere in Isaiah the use of the present tense of εἰμι + ἔτι denoting a situation from the past (the reality of the one God) as continuing on into the present and future in contrast to other gods which have not existed in the past, do not exist and will never exist.[356]

Therefore, the emphasis lies on Israel, God and the Servant being 'witnesses' to the coming new creation as another 'beginning' in the nation's history and in cosmic history. It is in this sense that the nation was not to focus any longer on witnessing primarily to past redemptive events but to the future one, since all earlier ones paled in comparison with that which was to come (so Isa. 43.18-19; 65.16-17). All earlier covenantal and redemptive events eventually issued into sin and exile, and it is this condition which is to be forever abolished in the new covenantal age (1QH 13.11-13 interprets Isa. 43.19 in this manner).

The 'witness' of Isa 43.10, 12 is to be understood as a *true witness* because of the directly preceding contrast with Isa 43.9, where the 'witnesses' (μάρτυρας) of the nations (= false idols or prophets) are commanded by Isaiah *to hear the truth* (ἀκουσάτωσαν ἀληθῆ) and *to speak the truth* (εἰπάτωσαν ἀληθῆ [אמת = 'truth']). The repetiton of ἀληθής highlights the exhortation that the witnesses be *true*.[357] It is not by happenstance that Judaism viewed the witness of Isa. 43.12 as a *true witness*, since it is explicitly contrasted in the midrashim with those who bear 'false witness' (*Lev. R.* 6.1 and 21.5).

---

355. Cf. LSJ, p. 703.

356. Cf. Isa. 45.5, 45.6a, 45.6b and 45.18, though these uses could denote comparative degree ('besides'; see LSJ, p. 703; cf. BAGD, p. 315).

357. The first ἀληθής of Isa. 43.9 (LXX) is read only by MSS 26, 41, 106, 198, 233, Alexandrinus (so the Holmes and Parsons apparatus) and Sinaiticus[2] (so Hatch and Redpath, *Concordance to Septuagint, in loc*).

In the light of the above discussion of Isa. 43.10-12, it is not coincidental that the Palestinian and Jerusalem Targum to Deut. 32.1-2 interpret the MT as portraying Moses as a 'witness' who calls forth the present creation as a 'witness' to the forthcoming new creation, which is formulated explicitly on the basis of Isa. 65.17: 'I have prepared *to create a new heavens and a new earth*' (in the next line of the Targum 'Isaiah the prophet' is even identified as speaking this prophecy). The cosmic witness is said not to 'taste death in this world', but will 'be renewed in the world to come' (Palestinian Targ.; likewise Jerusalem Targ.) The Jerusalem Targum in its paraphrase of Deut. 32.4 ('God of *faithfulness*') goes on and calls God 'a *faithful* God and *true*', perhaps further influence from Isa. 65.16.

It is this Isaiah background of Israel, God and the Servant being a witness primarily to the coming new creation which likely lies behind the statement in Rev. 3.14 that Christ is 'the Amen, the faithful and true witness...the beginning of the creation of God'.[358] Rev. 3.14 stands in the same line of thought as the Targumic tradition on Deut. 32.1-4, which combines the same three Isaianic ideas of witness, new creation and God as faithful and true, and has added the notion that the cosmic 'witness' will not 'taste death in this world', but will 'be renewed in the world to come'. Christ was a cosmic witness who did taste death, though not permanently because he was raised from the dead as 'the beginning of a new creation' to which he was, in an ultimate sense, an undying witness (Rev. 1.18; 2.8).

---

358. Jewish exegetes interpreted Isa. 43.10, 12 to refer to Israel's duty to 'witness' to God as Creator of the cosmos (*Mek., Tract. Baḥodesh* 8.87-93, and *Tract. Shabbata* 1.45-50) or to witness to the Exodus–Sinai revelation, which the first generation failed to do (*Exod. R.* 29.5; *Lev. R.* 6.1 and 6.5; *Pes. K.*, Piska 12.6). *Targ. Isa.* 43.10-13 includes both ideas in the witness. The witness of Isa. 43.12 is understood in Judaism as a *faithful witness*, since it is explicitly contrasted with those who bear 'false witness' (*Lev. R.* 6.1 and 21.5). Some even saw Isa. 43.10 as having its ultimate reference point in the future resurrection at the end of the age (*Gen. R.* 95.1; *Tanḥ.*, Genesis, Parashah 11.9 on Gen. 46.28 ff., Pt. 1). The above references of faithful witnessing to the first creation or to the final resurrection is strikingly parallel to Rev. 3.14, where Christ is the faithful witness, not only to God during his earthly ministry, but also of his own resurrection as the beginning of the new creation. It is important to recall at this point that Isa. 65.17 and 66.22 are viewed as referring to the final resurrection, which shows further affinities between Judaism's view of these Isaiah passages and that of the use in Rev. 3.14 (see *T. d. Eliyy.*, p. 86; *T. d. Eliyy., PRE*, S, p. 31; *Midr. Ps.* 46.2).

His witness to the new creation set in motion the fulfillment of Isaiah 43.10-19.[359] As the representative messianic servant, he sums up in himself true Israel in his role as witness, in addition to being identified as the Lord of Isa. 65.16-17, who himself is the Creator. Therefore, Jesus was a witness, not only to God during his earthly ministry, but also to the inauguration of the new creation as true Israel, the messianic servant and as the Lord. And, as we have seen, the beginning phase of the new creation to which he witnesses is his own resurrection.[360] He himself *is* the beginning of the new creation and he is also witness to it.

Discernment of the new creation background of Isa. 43.10-19 is confirmed by recalling that 43.18-19 is the closest parallel in the entire book of Isaiah to the other new creation prophecies in 65.16-17[361] and 66.22, which have been alluded to in Rev. 3.14a.[362] The presence of an

359. It is surprising that Isa. 43 apparently has not been recognized heretofore as the background for the 'witness' in Rev. 3.14. Brox, *Zeuge und Märtyer*, pp. 144-50, discusses the idea of witness in Isa. 43–44, but does not link it as background for Rev. 3.14. My former students B. Lee and S.T. Um brought to my attention that 'witness' in Isa. 43.10-13 might be related to Rev. 3.14, but they had not noticed its close link with new creation in Isa. 43.18-19 nor the other relevant Jewish material nor Isa. 65 allusions in Rev. 3.14, which confirms their suggestion.

360. Likewise Rissi, *Future of the World*, p. 21. That the 'witness' is primarily to fulfillment of Old Testament prophecy in Jesus' resurrection is apparent from the use of 'faithful and true' in Rev. 19.11, 21.5 and 22.6, which respectively refer to an assurance that Christ will fulfill Old Testament prophecy about final judgment and that God will fulfill Old Testament prophecy about the new creation (see above Chapter 3 sect. E.3.b.[1][f]). That a witness to the resurrection is, at the least, allowed is apparent from: (1) the consistent use of the μάρτυς word group throughout the book to refer to testimony about Christ in general, which certainly includes his resurrection; (2) since the *risen* Christ's affirmation of himself as a 'witness' in 3.14 is so generally stated, it is probable that the reference includes his role as a witness to God's revelatory work at the resurrection and its subsequent effects.

361. The only passages in Isaiah where 'My servant' (עבדי) is equated with 'My chosen' (בחירי) are Isa. 43.10, 20 and 65.14-15, which may have been catch-words further facilitating an association of the two contexts (though עבד is sg. in the former and plural in the latter).

362. Like Rev. 3.14, Jewish exegetical tradition sometimes understood Isa. 65.17-18, and its parallel in 66.22, as having inaugurated application to the present: *Gen. R.* 1.13; *Lev. R.* 29.12 ('The Holy One said, "I will consider it as though you have this day [the annual festival day of the New Year] been made before Me, as though this day I had created you as a new being"'); *Pes. K.*, *Piska* 23 is virtually identical to the preceding *Lev. R.* reference; *Tanḥ.*, Genesis, Parashah 1.9 on Gen. 1.1ff., Pt. 9; *T. d. Eliyy.*, p. 83 and cf. p. 92.

Isaiah 43 allusion is confirmed further by recalling that Isa. 43.18-19 is also combined with Isa. 65.16-17 in Rev. 21.1, 4-5, which is also placed together with 'faithful and true' in 21.5 (see above on sect. 3.b[1][f]). Paul likewise combines the same Isaiah 43 and 65 allusions in his new creation reference in 2 Cor. 5.17 (on which see n. 368 above).

Perhaps the added adjective 'true' (ἀληθινός) designates Jesus as the genuine or authentic witness in contrast to fleshly Israel as false witnesses (cf. Jesus as 'true', without the addition of 'faithful', in Rev. 3.7 in contrast to those in 3.9 'who call themselves Jews, and they are not, but they lie'!). The phrase 'true' likely includes more than mere moral and cognitive truth, but also the idea of authentic in the redemptive–historical sense of Jesus being *true* Israel by fulfilling the Isa. 43.10-19 prophecy about God and Israel's witness to the new creation. In contrast to unfaithful Israel, he fulfilled the prophecy by perfectly testifying to the new creation both before and after his resurrection. In this manner, he demonstrated himself to be the true Israel prophesied by Isaiah.[363] This attribute of authenticity may also be viewed against the Isaiah background of God saying that Israel should be a faithful witness in contrast to the nations as false witnesses to their idols or their idols themselves being false witnesses, which the nations mistakenly believe to be the 'truth' (ἀληθῆ; Isa. 43.9). Therefore, Christ is the 'true witness' after which all other faithful witnesses are modelled (for this reason Jesus may call Antipas, who was martyred for his faith, only 'My

Isa. 43.19, 65.17 and 66.22 are viewed as a prophecy of the future numerous times in early Judaism (see additional references at n.367 below). The Isaiah texts also are used often to refer to the prophetic future in the later midrashic literature: *Exod. R.* 23.11; *Num. R.* 23.4; *Deut. R.* 10.4; *Lam. R.* 1.2, § 23; *Mek.* 18.111-14; *Sifre Deut., Piska* 47; 306; *Pes. R., Piska* 29/30B.4 and 44.7; *PRE* 51; *T. d. Eliyy.*, p. 4; *T. d. Eliyy., Zuṭa, EZ*, p. 178; *T. d. Eliyy., PRE, S*, p. 31; *Tanḥ.* Genesis, Parashah 1.20 on Gen. 2.4ff., Pt. 9.

363. In addition to Rev. 3.7, 9, Rev. 15.3, 16.7, 19.2, 19.11, 21.5 and 22.6 also generally refer to Jesus or God as 'true' because they will fulfill Old Testament prophecy in the future; note ἀληθινον in Jn 1.9; 6.32; 15.1 for 'true' in John's Gospel as the contrastive antitype to Israel, also used like Rev. 3.7, 9, and 3.14. Cf. also ἀλήθεια in Jn 1.17; 4.23-24. P.E. Hughes, *The Book of Revelation* (Grand Rapids: Eerdmans, 1990), pp. 63-64, notes that 'Amen' in 3.14 may well have the same above idea of fulfilling prophetic promises in Christ and hence confirming them, as also in 2 Cor. 1.20, especially in the light of the uses of 'Amen' elsewhere in the book at the conclusion of segments concerning either inaugurated or future fulfillment of Old Testament prophecy (Rev. 1.6-7; 5.14; 7.12; 19.4; 22.20). Likewise Boring, *Revelation*, p. 88.

faithful witness' [Rev. 2.13], but not *'true* witness', since only Jesus fulfilled the prophecy, though the two words could be generally synonymous).[364]

It is likely not coincidental that the problem with the Laodicean Christians lay in their willingness to identify in some way with the trade guilds and their patron deities. Perhaps this identification merely consisted in identifying with the guilds and not testifying to their faith in Christ as a polemic against the guilds' loyalty to their patron deities who purportedly were responsible for the economic prosperity of each trade. Loyalty to these deities usually included professions of loyalty to the imperial cult. This background of idolatry may have been an additional reason attracting attention to Isa. 43.10-13, since it portrays Israel as 'witnessing' to the true God and against false deities (so likewise Isa. 44.6-11). Indeed, the double reference to 'the God of truth' in Isa 65.16 is set in contrast to false deities only four verses earlier (65.11; cf. also Targ. Isa., which refers to 'idols' and 'gods' associated with Rome). Similarly, the Targumic combination of an undying 'witness' to a new creation together with God as 'faithful and true' is set in a context intended as a polemic against idolatry in Israel (so the Palestinian and Jerusalem Targum to Deut. 32.1-2; cf. MT of Deut. 32.12-18).

4. *Conclusion*

There have been various proposals concerning the Old Testament and Jewish background of the christological title in Rev. 3.14. Proposals of a background in wisdom literature of the Old Testament and Judaism have been examined and found not completely satisfactory.

A number of commentators have noted that the phrase 'God of Amen' in Isa. 65.16 lies behind the title 'the Amen', and some have seen the following clause 'the faithful and true witness' as an expansion of Isaiah's 'Amen'. However, little exegetical data have hitherto been adduced in favor of the plausibility of these suggestions, so that for the most part they have lacked persuasiveness. Nor are those appealing to the Isaiah background able to account for the word 'witness' and the concluding phrase 'the beginning of the creation of God'.

However, the suggestion is confirmed that 'faithful and true' is, not only a legitimate interpretative expansion of 'Amen' in Isa. 65.16, but, also the full threefold wording is likely based on that Old Testament

---

364. Could ὁ μάρτυς μου in Rev. 2.13 also be an allusion to Isa. 43.10, 12 ([ἐ]μοι μάρτυρες [twice])?

passage. This confirmation comes from further scrutiny of the LXX in general and of the Greek Old Testament versions of Isa. 65.16 in particular, as well as observing the unique predicative use of 'Amen' together with analysis of the immediate and broad contexts of Rev. 3.14. In addition, the Isa. 65.16-17 background well accounts for the conclusion of Rev. 3.14, 'the beginning of the creation of God'. In view of the conclusion that Isa. 65.16 lies behind the first clause of Rev. 3.14, it is probable that the prophecy about the new creation in Isa. 65.17 lies behind the final clause in Rev. 3.14, 'the beginning of the creation of God'. And, lastly, the Isaiah background also accounts for the idea of 'witness', since the other parallel new creation prophecy in Isaiah 43 affirms that 'the Servant Messiah' would be a witness to the new creation, which is even associated with being a witness of 'the beginning' (cf. Isa. 43.10-17 with 43.18-19).[365]

It is possible that the Old Testament Genesis 1-wisdom background concerning *the original creation*, especially in Prov. 8.22 (e.g. the targumic tradition), could still lie behind Rev. 3.14 as supplemental to the Isaiah background and as transformed to apply to the new creation. The plausibility of such a transformation is increased by recognizing that later Jewish tradition saw in Gen. 1.1-4 a prophetic hint of the Messiah's *name (Gen. R.* 1.4)[366] and of his coming work of redemption (*Pes.*

---

365. Contra the recent evaluation of Fekkes, *Isaiah and Prophetic Traditions*, pp. 110-12, this conclusion makes more attractive the suggestion of some that standing behind 'faithful witness' in Rev. 1.5 is either the use of 'witness' in Isa. 43.9-10 (+ Isa. 44.8-9) or in Isa. 55.4 ('I have made him [David] a testimony [μαρτύριον]...a prince [ἄρχοντα] and a commander to the Gentiles'); in support of the former see Kraft, *Die Offenbarung des Johannes*, p. 26, W.H. Brownlee, 'Messianic Motifs of Qumran and the New Testament', *NTS* 3 (1956–57), pp. 195-210 (208), and A.A. Trites, *The New Testament Concept of Witness* (SNTSMS, 31; Cambridge: Cambridge University Press, 1976), p. 159, the last suggesting only the possibility of the Servant's role of witness in Isa. 40–55 as part of the background both in Rev. 1.5, 3.14 and throughout the book; in support of the Isa. 54 influence see J. Massingberd Ford, *Revelation* (Garden City, NY: Doubleday, 1975), p. 380, Swete, *Apocalypse*, p. 7 (who includes Prov. 14.5), and above all Schüssler Fiorenza, *Priester für Gott*, pp. 199-200 (who includes Ps. 89). This is striking when it is recalled that Rev. 3.14 develops 1.5, as argued above and acknowledged by many commentators.

366. Though not explicitly citing Gen. 1, the following Jewish texts also understand that 'the name of the Messiah' existed directly before the creation of the world: *Midr. Ps.* 72.6; 90.12; *T. d. Eliyy.*, p. 160; *PRE* 3; b. *Ned.* 39b; b. *Pes.* 54a; cf. also *Midr. Ps.* 93.3.

R., Piska 33.6, and *Piska* 36.1-2; cf. *Gen. R.* 3.6). This tradition even affirmed that 'from the beginning of the creation of the world the King Messiah was born' (*Pes. R., Piska* 33.6; see also *Pes. R., Piska* 36.1-2). Most intriguingly, the midrashic tradition on Gen. 1.1 adduces the new creation prophecies of Isa. 65.17 and 66.22, and asserts that the new creation had already been created in some sense (probably potentially as a thought in God's mind) when God brought the first creation into being (*Gen. R.* 1.13; *Tanh.*, Genesis, Parashah 1.9 on Gen. 1.1ff., Pt. 9).[367]

Therefore, the use of Isaiah 43 and 65 in Rev. 3.14 indicates that Christ is the true Israel and the divine 'Amen, the faithful and true witness' to his own resurrection as 'the beginning of the new creation of God', in inaugurated fulfillment of the Isaianic new creation prophecies.[368]

367. Jewish literature generally identified 'wisdom' of Prov. 8.22, 30 as Torah (*Gen. R.* 85.9; *Mek.*, Tract. Shirata 9.122-24; *Sifre. Deut., Piska* 309 and 317; Minor Tracts. Tal., *Kalla* 54a; *T. d. Eliyy.*, p. 71; *T. d. Eliyy.*, Pirke Derek 'Eres, S, p. 20; *T. d. Eliyy. Zuta*, EZ, p. 171). In particular, Jewish tradition held that Torah-Wisdom of Prov. 8.22 was created before the rest of creation, and, hence, was the beginning of the creation (*Gen. R.* 1.1; 1.8; 8.2; *Exod. R.* 30.9; *Lev. R.* 19.1; *Cant. R.* 5.11§1; *b. Ned.* 39b; *b. Pes.* 54a; Minor Tracts. Tal., *ARN* 29a; *Tanh.*, Genesis, Parashah 1.5 on Gen. 1.1ff., Pt. 5; *Sifre. Deut Piska* 37; *T. d. Eliyy.*, p. 112 and p. 160).

However, in Judaism neither Prov. 8.22 nor Prov. 8.30 are ever identified with the Messiah or the new creation.

368. In contrast to Rev. 3.14, but like Rev. 21.1, 4-5 (which also alludes to Isa. 43.18-19 and 65.16-18), some sectors of Judaism, in reflection on Isa. 65 (or Isa. 43), conceived of the new creation as yet future: *Jub.* 1.29; 4.26; *1 En.* 45.4-5; 72.1; 91.16; *2 Bar.* 32.1-6; 44.12; 57.2; *4 Ezra* 7.75; Targ. Pal. and Jerus. Deut. 32.1; *Targ. Hab.* 3.2; Irennaeus, *Contra Haer.* 5.36.1; for reference to a like renewal in the future but not necessarily in allusion to Isaiah cf. *Targ. Onq. Deut.* 32.12; *Targ. Jer.* 23.23; *Targ. Mic.* 7.14; *b. Sanh.* 92b, 97b. Cf. 2 Pet. 3.5-13; Mt. 19.28. John likely viewed Rev. 21.1, 4-5 as the consummation of a process mentioned as beginning in 3.14.

Chapter 4

THE INFLUENCE OF THE OLD TESTAMENT UPON
THE SYMBOLISM OF REVELATION

A. *Symbolism as the Predominant Mode of Communication in
Revelation: The Old Testament Background of Revelation 1.1*

Revelation 1.1 introduces the book, not only by using the word 'apocalypse', but also by saying that God 'made known' to John the contents
of the book through an angel. The translation 'made known' is a rendering of the Greek word σημαίνω (so RSV, NRSV, NEB, JB, NIV). The
standard New Testament Greek lexicon[1] defines the word in Rev. 1.1 as
'make known', 'report', or 'communicate', while acknowledging that
the word can connote 'foretell', 'mean', or 'signify' elsewhere outside
the New Testament. Almost all of these definitions generally connote
the idea of communication, though the precise nature of the communication is left undefined.

However, in order to understand fully the word, its role in the immediate context must be recalled. The word is part of a clear allusion to
Dan. 2.28-30, 45, since the clauses 'revelation... God showed... what
must come to pass... and He *made known* [σημαίνω]' occur together
uniquely only in Daniel 2 and Rev. 1.1.[2]

Σημαίνω in Daniel 2 is a translation of the Aramaic ידע ('to make
known'), which is translated by γνωρίζω ('to make known') in the Old
Testament Greek version of Theodotion. However, in both the Aramaic
and Theodotion the kind of communication is not left undefined but is

---

1. BAGD, p. 747.
2. For in-depth textual demonstration that these combined clauses in 1.1 are
referring to Daniel 2 see on Chapter 3 (sect. B), where it was argued that Dan. 2.28-
29, 45 is the clear background for the last phrase of v. 19 ('what is about to come to
pass after these things'); similarly, see the further analysis above at Chapter 2, sect.
D.5.b. σημαίνω also occurs not only in Dan. 2.45 (LXX) but also at Dan. 2. 23, 30
(LXX) as a part of the introduction to the narration by Daniel of the king's dream.

explained by the context of the vision to be a symbolic communication by means of a dream vision. In Dan. 2.23, 30, and 45 the word is employed to describe the symbolic dream vision which King Nebuchadnezzar saw. For example, Dan. 2.45 says, 'The great God has *made known* to the king what must come to pass in the latter days', and God made it known by means of a symbolic vision and interpretation of that vision. The revelation was not abstract but was pictorial. The king saw a huge statue composed of four sections of different metals: gold, silver, bronze and iron. The image was smashed by a rock which grew until it became a mountain filling the earth. Daniel recounts the symbolic vision seen by the king and then interprets it: each section of the colossus represented a major world kingdom, the last of which would be defeated and replaced by God's eternal kingdom.

In this light, the likely reason that the LXX translator did not choose γνωρίζω but σημαίνω to render the Aramaic verb 'make known' was to underscore the precise kind of communication under discussion in Daniel 2, which was symbolic communication. σημαίνω can overlap with the more general and abstract idea of 'make known' in the sense of 'indicate', 'declare', 'be manifest'.[3] However, its concrete and, at least, equally used sense is that of 'show by a sign', 'give [or make] signs [or signals]', or 'signify' (the latter of which is chosen by the Douay, KJV and NASB [marg.] translations for Rev. 1.1). It is this idea of symbolic communication which σημαίνω typically has when it is not used with the general sense of 'make known'. Both the abstract and concrete senses are found in the Greek Old Testament (LXX). Of the five other times the verb is used in the New Testament, twice it has the sense of 'make known' (Acts 25.27), though one of these may have the nuance of symbolic information (if Acts 11.28 is parallel with the prophetic mode of symbolic revelation by the same prophet in Acts 21.10-11); three other uses are by John's Gospel in summarizing Jesus' *pictorial* description of crucifixion (Jn 12.33; 18.32; 21.19). The gospel writers use the noun form σημεῖον repeatedly to refer to Jesus' miracles which were outward 'signs' or 'symbols' of his attributes and mission.[4]

---

3.   See BAGD above and LSJ, p. 1592. The verb does have the more general sense in Dan. 2.15 (LXX).

4.   E.g. Jesus' healing of the dying boy in Jn 4.46-54 is an action symbolizing his ability to give spiritual life, as well as literal resurrection life, to all, in the light of the context of Jn 5.19-29; the 'sign' of feeding the five thousand symbolized his

The symbolic use of σημαίνω in Daniel 2 defines the use in Rev. 1.1 as referring to symbolic communication and not mere general conveyance of information. Therefore, John's choice of σημαίνω over γνωρίζω ('make known') is not haphazard but intentional. This conclusion is based on the supposition that John uses Old Testament references with significant degrees of awareness of Old Testament context, for which the present work argues trenchantly.[5]

That σημαίνω means 'communicate by symbols' in Rev. 1.1 is confirmed also by noticing its parallelism with δείκνυμι ('to show') in the first clause of v. 1: 'The revelation of Jesus Christ which God gave to Him *to show* to His servants'. This word 'show' is not a synonym with other words meaning 'make known', though it could be used in that manner in other contexts. Rather, here it refers to a revelation through the medium of symbolic, heavenly visions communicated through an angel. This meaning of δείκνυμι as 'show' is clarified from its remaining seven uses in the book, where it clearly has this idea (4.1; 17.1; 21.9-10; 22.1, 6, 8; e.g. 17.1: 'I will *show* you the judgment of the great harlot who sits on many waters'). In each of the remaining cases a symbolic vision is distinctly the object 'shown'. John's repeated response in these contexts is that he 'saw' these pictorial revelations (e.g. 17.3, 6; 21.22; 22.8); the section of visions is punctuated throughout by the refrain 'and I saw' (καὶ εἶδον). It is fitting that σημαίνω is parallel with δείκνυμι in 1.1, since virtually the same parallelism is observable between δηλόω ('to show', or 'to reveal') and σημαίνω in Dan. 2.28-30 (LXX).

The significance of this brief study of Rev. 1.1 bears upon one's overall hermeneutical approach to interpreting the Apocalypse. Some commentators contend that since Revelation sometimes explicitly explains the meaning of an image in a vision, there is a 'presumption that, where

---

ability to give spiritual, salvific nourishment; cf. K.H. Rengstorf, 'σημεῖον', *TDNT*, VII, pp. 229-59. For examples of σημαίνω with the general sense of 'make known' in the contemporary literature see the LXX of Exod. 18.20; 1 Esd. 2.2; 8.48; Est. 2.22; for examples of the concrete, figurative use see the LXX references to 'signalling' by a trumpet blow (e.g. Num. 10.9; Jos. 6.8; Judg. 7.21; Job 39.24-25; Jer. 4.5; Ezek. 33.3, 6) or making signals with one's foot (Prov. 6.13).

5.   On which see further Chapter 2 ('The Various Ways John Uses the Old Testament') above and the numerous exegetical test cases throughout Beale, *Book of Revelation*.

expressions are not explained, they can normally be interpreted according to their natural [i.e., "literal"] meaning, unless the context clearly indicates otherwise'.[6] Therefore, a number of commentators in both popular and scholarly circles contend that one should interpret literally at most places in the book unless forced to interpret symbolically by clear indications of context.[7]

The results of the above analysis of Rev. 1.1, however, indicate that this rule should be turned on its head: we are told in the book's introduction that the majority of the material in it is revelatory symbolism (1.12-20 and 4.1–22.5 at the least). Hence, the predominant manner by which to approach the material will be according to a non-literal interpretative method. Of course, there are parts which are not symbolic, but the essence of the book is figurative. Where there is lack of clarity about whether or not something is symbolic, the scales of judgment should be tilted in the direction of a non-literal analysis. The purported presumption that a minority of formally explicit explanations of images indicates that the unexplained images are to be taken 'literally' is contradicted by even literal interpreters who acknowledge throughout the book the symbolic meaning of images which have no explicit explanation attached: e.g. the Lamb and lion (Rev. 5), the 'book' (Rev. 5), the 'woman' (Rev. 12), God's throne, one 'hour' of testing (Rev. 3.10), a sword proceeding out of Christ's mouth (Rev. 1.16; 2.16; 19.15), the 'one hour' of Babylon's desolation (Rev. 18), etc. Furthermore, symbolic genre elsewhere in biblical literature can be detected where images are clearly figurative but there are no formal explanatory formulas.

B. *The Hearing Formula in the Letters of Revelation and its Implications for the Purpose of Symbolism in the Visionary Portion of the Book*[8]

The role of the seven letters of Revelation 2–3 in relation to the entire book has been debated. Some have thought that the primary purpose of the letters is to convey the condition of the first-century churches, and,

6.   J. Walvoord, *Revelation of Jesus Christ*, p. 30.

7.   The most recent commentator who takes this approach is Thomas, *Revelation 1–7*, e.g., pp. 35-38.

8.   An earlier version of this article appeared in a *Festshrift* for John Sweet, on behalf of whose honour I was happy to be able to contribute an article. He has given wise and invaluable guidance to me, not only in my doctoral work, but also in my research on John's Apocalypse during the past decade.

by implication, the pre-eschatological condition of the church throughout the ages until the beginning of the final tribulation, directly preceding Christ's final coming. Others have thought that the primary purpose
of the letters is to express the major themes of the following visionary
portion of the book (Rev. 4–21), both of which exhibit an 'already-and-
not-yet' end-time perspective.[9] This essay sets out to argue the plausibility of the latter view, and to propose in particular that the letters,
especially their repeated conclusions, anticipate the symbolic visions
and even explain the theological purpose of the visions.

1. Introduction to the Letters

a. *The Relation of the Letters to the Rest of the Book.*[10] Phrases and
concepts from the letters are related to the introductory vision of ch. 1,
to the visions of chs. 4–20 and to the concluding scene of the new creation in 21.9–22.5.[11] The express development of the son of man vision
(1.9-20) throughout the letters makes more viable the proposal that the
letters function in the same manner in relation to the remainder of the
book. Such a proposal best explains the presence of phrases and concepts from the letters in the following visionary portion. The son of
man vision is primarily developed in the introductions of the letters
(although it is developed also in the body of some of the letters and in
subsequent parts of the book). The concluding promises of the letters
overtly anticipate the end of the book and the final paradisial vision (cf.
chs. 19–22).[12] Even the deceptive threats to the churches are echoed
again in the concluding description of the character of those who posed
the threat and will consequently experience the 'second death' (see

9.   For a fuller discussion of both views and their respective supporters see the
Introduction (especially the 'The Structure and Plan of John's Apocalypse') to
Beale, *Book of Revelation*, and *passim*.

10.   For discussions of the historical background of the letters in their Asia
Minor context, see Sir William Mitchell Ramsay, *The Letters to the Seven
Churches of Asia and their Place in the Plan of the Apocalypse* (London: Hodder &
Stoughton, 1904); Hemer, *Letters to the Seven Churches* (cf. sources cited therein;
Hemer's is the most thorough of all sources); Beale, review of Hemer's *Letters to
the Seven Churches*, and the more recent positive assessment of Hemer by C.H.H.
Scobie, 'Local References in the Letters to the Seven Churches', *NTS* 39 (1993),
pp. 606-24 and, Price, *Rituals and Power*.

11.   See Beale, *Book of Revelation* (Introduction).

12.   Sweet, *Revelation*, p. 77; Minear, *I Saw a New Earth*, p. 61.

21.8). This observation points still further to the plausibility that the body of the letters is integrally related to the body of the book. This accords with the fact that John places the visions within the framework of the traditional Christian letter form with an extended introduction (chs. 1–3), concluding admonitions (22.7, 11, 14, 17-19) and benediction (22.20-21).[13]

One of the main features of the typically Pauline epistolary pattern is that the themes of the introductions are developed throughout the body of the letter.[14] This feature is also true of the Apocalypse to some degree. It is clear that the introductions of the seven letters and the introductory son of man vision pertain to the same general time period and mutually interpret one another, as primarily do also the conclusions of the seven messages and the book's final vision of bliss. This points to the likelihood that the same relationships cohere between the body of the letters and the visionary body of the book. It is in this sense that we can call the letters the literary microcosm of the entire book's macrocosmic structure.

An important issue for brief consideration is whether or not the symbols which appear in the letters should be interpreted primarily by the context of the ch. 1 vision or mainly by the historical context of the letters themselves. In particular, should the various descriptions of Christ in chs. 1–3 be interpreted by the historical situation in which these images have their origin or from the Old Testament literary context from which they also come? There is likely a reciprocal interpretative relationship between the ch. 1 vision and the letters. Therefore, the historical background of the churches and the Old Testament literary background mutually interpret one another.[15]

b. *The Literary Structure of the Letters and the Function of the Hearing Formula Therein.* Although 1.9-20 is best considered a call narrative and, therefore, a separate introductory unit, it should also be viewed as part of the larger literary segment of 1.9–3.22. This is clear from the fact that the command to write in 1.11 and 1.19 is repeated at the beginning of each of the letters, as is also a description from some facet of

---

13. So E. Schüssler Fiorenza, 'Apocalyptic and Gnosis in the Book of Revelation', *JBL* 92 (1973), pp. 565-81 (575).

14. Cf. P.T. O'Brien, *Introductory Thanksgivings in the Letters of Paul* (NovTSup, 49; Leiden: E.J. Brill, 1977).

15. Cf. further Beale, review of *Letters to the Seven Churches*, by Hemer.

the son of man vision, which is usually developed later in the body of each letter.[16]

There have been different proposals for the structure which is common to all seven letters.[17] Generally speaking, each letter typically can be divided into seven divisions, although there is sometimes slight alteration: (1) command to write to an angel of a church; (2) a self-description by Christ from ch. 1 introduced by the introductory formula 'these things says [the one]' (τάδε λέγει); (3) a commendation of a church's good works (lacking in the letter to Laodicea); (4) an accusation because of some sin; (5) an exhortation to repent with a warning of judgment or an encouragement (element 4 and the second part of 5 are lacking in the letters of Smyrna and Philadelphia, since they are seen as faithful; elements 3–5 could be viewed as one section introduced by οἶδα ['I know'] followed by commendations or accusations with corresponding encouragements or exhortations to repent to avoid judgment) (6) exhortation to discern the truth of the preceding message ('he who has an ear...'); and (7) a promise to the conquerors.

Each message can also be divided into four broad sections: (1) commission formula with christological descriptions; (2) an 'I know' section (typically containing elements of praise, exhortation and accusation, perhaps including calls for repentance, threats of judgment, and promises); (3) exhortation to discern; and (4) exhortation to conquer.[18]

The logical flow of thought in each letter generally conforms to the following pattern: (1) Christ presents himself with certain attributes (particularly suitable to the situation of each church, faith in which provides the basis for overcoming the specific problem faced); (2) the situation and the particular problem are reviewed (introduced by 'I know'); (3) on the basis of the situation and problem, Christ issues either an encouragement to persevere in the face of conflict (for faithful churches)

---

16. For the relation of the christological introductions to the body of the letters cf. B. Gerhardsson, 'Die christologischen Aussagen in den Sendschreiben', in A. Fuchs (ed.), *Theologie aus dem Norden* (SNTU, Serie A, Band 2; Linz, Austria: Plöchl, Freistadt. 1977), pp. 142-66.

17. See D.E. Aune, *Prophecy in Early Christianity and in the Ancient Mediterranean World* (Grand Rapids: Eerdmans, 1983), pp. 275-78; *idem*, 'The Form and Function of the Proclamations to the Seven Churches (Revelation 2–3)', *NTS* 36 (1990), pp. 182-204.

18. So Aune, *Prophecy in Early Christianity*, pp. 275-78, and appendix at the end of his book.

or to repent in order to avoid judgment (for unfaithful churches); (4) then, both the prior situation and problem, together especially with the corresponding encouragements to persevere or exhortations to repent, form the ground for Christ issuing a call for the churches to respond by heeding ('hearing') either the preceding encouragement or exhortation; and (5) on the basis of a positive response (equivalent to 'hearing' followed by 'overcoming'), Christ promises the inheritance of eternal life with him, which uniquely corresponds to Christ's attributes or to the churches' situation (the hearing formula still functions as a ground clause, together with overcoming, even when placed after the promise in the last four letters).

In view of the similar logical development and theme of all of the letters, the general main point of chs. 2–3 can be formulated in the following manner: *Christ encourages the churches to witness, warns them about compromise, and exhorts them to 'hear' and to overcome compromise in order to inherit the promise of eternal life with him.*

Therefore, the logical flow of each letter climaxes with the promise of inheriting eternal life with Christ, which is the main point of each letter. The body of each letter provides the basis upon which the Spirit calls the churches to respond by 'hearing', which should inextricably result in overcoming, the consequence of which is inheriting the respective promises.

The concluding 'hearing' exhortations are not merely addressed to each particular church but 'to [all] the churches'. Although each letter is addressed to the particular situation of a church, it is relevant for the needs of all 'seven' of the churches, and probably, by implication, for the universal church or church 'at large'.[19]

Three general divisions can be discerned among the seven churches. The first and last are in danger of losing their very identity as a Christian church. Therefore, they are exhorted to repent in order to prevent their judgment and to inherit the promises which genuine faith deserves. The churches addressed in the three central letters have to varying degrees some who have remained faithful and others who are compromising with pagan culture. Among these, Pergamum is in the best condition and Sardis is in the worst. These churches are exhorted to purge the elements of compromise from their midst in order to avert

19. See 1.4 for this figurative significance of 'seven', and commentators who understand it this way: e.g. Caird, *Revelation*.

judgment on the compromisers (and probably also themselves) and to inherit the promises due those who overcome compromise. The second and sixth letters are written to churches which have proved themselves faithful and loyal to Christ's 'name' even in the face of persecution from both Jews and pagans. Even though they are 'poor' and 'have little power', they are encouraged to continue persevering as the 'true Israel', since more trials will confront them. They are to endure with the hope that they will inherit the promises of eternal salvation (both will receive a 'crown').[20]

In this light, the condition of the churches is presented in the literary form of a chiasm: a b c c c b a. The significance of this is that the Christian church *as a whole* is perceived as being in poor condition, since not only are the healthy churches in a minority but also the literary pattern points to this emphasis because the churches in the worst condition form the literary boundaries of the letters and the churches with serious problems form the very core of the presentation. This is highlighted by recognizing that at the center of the middle letter stands a general statement that 'all the churches will know' that Christ is the omniscient judge of his unfaithful followers (2.23). The reference in 2.23 is conspicuous because the only other collective reference to the churches occurs repeatedly at the conclusion of each letter.[21]

All of the letters deal generally with the issue of witnessing for Christ in the midst of a pagan culture.[22] The churches with problems are all exhorted to strengthen their witness in various ways and the two churches without problems are encouraged to continue to persevere in the faithful witness which they had been maintaining. Consequently, the hearing formula functions to exhort Christians to witness despite the temptations to compromise.

c. *The Literary Genre of Revelation 2–3 and the Function of the Hearing Formula.* The seven letters do not technically correspond to the typical epistolary form and, therefore, are better referred to as 'proph-

---

20. For further discussion of these three divisions see Kiddle and Ross, *Revelation*, pp. 19-65.

21. Cf. Mulholland, *Revelation*, p. 112.

22. So Beale, *Book of Revelation*, *in loc.* on Rev. 2–3 for argumentation of this point.

etic messages'.[23] There has also been a recent attempt at a rhetorical analysis of chs. 2–3.[24]

W.H. Shea has proposed that five essential segments are observable, which thematically reflect the fivefold ancient Near Eastern-Old Testament covenant form imposed upon Israel by Yahweh in Exodus 21ff. and throughout Deuteronomy: (1) preamble (the words of Christ ['these things says'] and his descriptive titles from ch. 1); (2) prologue ('I know your works...', which include the two sections labelled above as commendation and accusation); (3) stipulations (expressions built around variants of 'therefore...repent', along with other hortatory words); (4) witness to the covenant ('hear what the Spirit says to the churches'); and (5) concluding blessings and curses ('to him who overcomes I will give...').[25]

Shea's proposal is overstated, since a verse-by-verse study exposes a number of exceptions to the overall pattern.[26] Nevertheless, a qualified version of Shea's view is plausible. Although he does not attempt to fit into his scheme the initial command to write, the addition of such a command is natural since it occurs in contexts where Yahweh is addressing his covenant to Israel through his covenant messengers (whether Moses or the later prophets; see the Old Testament background of 1.11).[27] Furthermore, the blessings and cursings are separated in the letters, the latter typically occurring as a conclusion of the 'stipulations' section. Because each of these sections begins with a set

---

23. See F. Hahn, 'Die Sendschreiben der Johannesapokalypse: Ein Beitrag zur Bestimmung prophetischer Redeformen', in G. Jeremias, H.-Kuhn and H. Stegemann (eds.), *Tradition und Glaube* (Göttingen: Vandenhoeck & Ruprecht, 1971), pp. 357-94; L. Hartman, 'Form and Message: A Preliminary Discussion of "Partial Texts" in Rev 1–3 and 22.6ff.', in J. Lambrecht (ed.), *L'Apocalypse johannique et l'Apocalyptique dans le Nouveau Testament* (BETL, 53; Gembloux: Duculot; Leuven: Leuven University Press, 1980), pp. 129-49; U.B. Müller, *Prophetie und Predigt im Neuen Testament* (SNT, 10; Gütersloh: Gerd Mohn, 1975), pp. 47-100; Aune, *Prophecy in Early Christianity*, pp. 274-79, who also provides a summary and evaluation of Hahn's and Müller's discussions; R.L. Muse, 'Revelation 2–3: A Critical Analysis of Seven Prophetic Messages', *JETS* 29 (1986), pp. 147-61.

24. See J.T. Kirby, 'The Rhetorical Situations of Revelation', *NTS* 34 (1988), pp. 197-207.

25. Shea, 'Covenantal Form of the Letters to the Seven Churches'.

26. So Aune, 'Form and Function of the Proclamations to the Seven Churches', p. 182.

27. Beale, *Use of Daniel*, p. 172 n. 46.

formula, they are best seen as the five literary divisions of each letter, although certainly the initial formulaic command to write must be included as a sixth element in the pattern.

That the proposed covenantal scheme forms at least part of the general background is supported by several factors. *First*, the fivefold covenant pattern has also been observed to be influential for the book as a whole;[28] in this respect, of particular note is the conclusion of the book in 22.7b, 18-19, part of which alludes to Deut. 4.2, and 22.16-20, where an angel, the Spirit, the church, and Jesus are formally termed 'witnesses'. *Second*, the high degree to which allusion is made elsewhere in the book to Old Testament phrases and themes permits the plausibility of the employment of such a major theme as this. *Third*, the covenant theme is a particularly appropriate one, since Jesus is now viewed with attributes of Yahweh who is addressing the churches, which are now also seen as the continuation of true Israel. For example, Jesus introduces himself (τάδε λέγει) with a stock formula from the prophets of the Old Testament which was used to introduce the prophetic sayings of the Lord to Israel: τάδε λέγει κύριος ('these things says the Lord'; the Old Testament formula occurs 95 times in Ezekiel and Jeremiah, and 29 times in the Minor Prophets). The recapitulation of the covenant formula is suitable because a new covenant community has now been inaugurated to be the continuation of the true people of God. If the church is faithful, it will inherit the covenantal blessings of the new creation originally promised to Israel (e.g. see Isa. 40–60).[29] But unfaithfulness will bring the curse of being excluded from the blessings.

D.E. Aune has thoroughly discussed the multiple genre of the seven letters.[30] In particular, he has argued that the literary genre of chs. 2–3 is 'that of the *royal* or *imperial edict*, while the *mode* is that of the prophetic form of speech called the *parenetic salvation–judgment oracle*'.[31] If

---

28. See Strand, 'Further Note on the Covenantal Form in the Book of Revelation', pp. 251-64.

29. Cf. W.J. Dumbrell, *The End of the Beginning* (Homebush West, Australia: Lancer, 1985), pp. 183-96.

30. Aune, 'Form and Function of the Proclamations to the Seven Churches', who also proposes a sevenfold or eightfold literary structure different from that discussed above.

31. Aune, 'Form and Function of the Proclamations to the Seven Churches', p. 183, and *passim*.

the background of the pagan royal edict genre is in mind, then Christ would be presenting himself as a king addressing his subjects. Furthermore, he would be portraying himself as the true sovereign in contrast to the pseudo-kingship of the Roman emperor.[32] This perspective need not exclude the covenantal form discussed above, since the covenantal background would enhance the Old Testament prophetic speech form, which itself was a development of the covenantal cursings and blessings of Exodus and Deuteronomy.

In the light of the above analysis, the hearing formula functions as the Spirit's witness to Christ's (the King's) new covenant ('hear what the Spirit says to the churches') to exhort true Israel to faithfulness to her acknowledged Lord.

2. The Exegetical and Theological Significance of the Formula 'the One Having Ears Let Him Hear' in the Letters and its Relation to the Apocalypse as a Whole

a. *The Background of the Hearing Formula.* This formula has its background in the synoptics and the Old Testament, where in both cases it occurs in connection with symbolic or parabolic revelation. In the Old Testament it refers to the effect which the symbolic revelation of the prophets had on the Israelites. The primary function of the prophets Isaiah, Jeremiah, and Ezekiel was to warn Israel of its impending doom and divine judgment. They delivered their warnings initially in a rational and sermonic way, exhorting the audience about their sin and reminding them about their past history in which God had judged their fathers because of the same kind of selfish disobedience. But these prophetic messengers had little success because of Israel's idolatrous allegiances, spiritual lethargy and stiff-necked attitude against changing the ways to which they had grown accustomed. They had become spiritually hardened to rational, historical and homiletical warning methods.

As a consequence, the prophets began to take up different forms of warning. They started to employ symbolic action and parable in order to get attention.[33] But such a change in warning form is effective only with those who already have spiritual insight. Symbolic parables cause

32. Aune, 'Form and Function of the Proclamations to the Seven Churches', pp. 199, 204.

33. David L. Jeffrey, 'Literature in an Apocalyptic Age', *Dalhousie Review* 61 (1981), pp. 426-46, first attracted my attention to this transition in the prophets.

those who 'have ears to hear and hear not' to misunderstand further. The literary form of symbolic parable (e.g. *mašal*) 'appears whenever ordinary warnings are no longer heeded' (cf. Mt. 13.10)[34] and no warning will ever be heeded by hardened people who are intent on continuing in disobedience. This is the point of Isa. 6.9-10, where the prophet is commissioned to tell Israel to '*keep on listening* but do not perceive...render the hearts of this people insensitive, *their ears dull*... lest they... *hear with their ears*...and repent and be healed'.

Isaiah's preaching is intended as a judgment to blind and deafen the majority in Israel and to have a positive effect only on the remnant (cf. chs. 7-8).[35] His message in chs. 1–5 is predominantly a non-parabolic warning of judgment and promise of blessing conditional on repentance. Then the parabolic message comes in 7.3 and 8.1-4, which has already been anticipated by the vineyard parable in 5.1-7. The parabolic aspect of the prophet's message is then closely linked to the hardening commission of Isa. 6.9-10 and, therefore, may be considered one of the means by which the people are to be blinded and deafened (which is viewed as beginning fulfillment, e.g., in Isa. 42.20 ['your ears are open but none hears'] and 43.8).

Yet the parables are also intended to have a jolting effect on the remnant who have become complacent among the compromising majority. Israel did not want to hear the truth, and, when it was presented straightforwardly to convict them of sin, they would not accept the fact of their sin. The parables, however, functioned to awake those among the true, righteous remnant from their sinful anesthesia. The same pattern found in Isaiah is apparent in Ezekiel, where the Isaianic hearing language occurs in Ezek. 3.27 (ὁ ἀκούων ἀκουέτω: 'he who hears, let him hear'), followed directly by the prophet's first parable, and in 12.2 (ὦτα ἔχουσιν τοῦ ἀκούειν, καὶ οὐκ ἀκούουσιν: 'they have ears to hear, but they do not hear'), followed immediately in vv. 3-16 by a parabolic act before onlooking Israel (for similar wording to Ezekiel's hearing forumlae cf. Jer. 5.21; 17.22-23). Ezekiel's usage is a development of that already found in Isaiah.

The shock effect of the parables on the believing yet sinfully complacent remnant is a phenomenon observable also in the case of Nathan's parable addressed to David, after he had sinned by committing adultery

---

34. So Jeffrey, 'Literature in an Appocalyptic Age'.
35. For sources discussing aspects of the exegetical and theological problems in Isa. 6.9-10, see Beale, 'Isaiah VI 9-13', pp. 257-78.

with Bathsheba and killing her husband, Uriah. David was not ready to hear an outright, direct accusation. He had become spiritually anesthetized to his spiritual and moral decline. Therefore, Nathan the prophet uses the approach of symbolic language (cf. 2 Sam. 12.1-9, 13-15). The symbolic story catches David off-guard. It causes him to focus objectively on the meaning of the story because he does not think it is related to him personally. Only after he had fully understood the pictorial story and felt its emotive impact, does Nathan then apply it to David. And then David is pierced to the heart and is able to accept the accusation of his sin and repent.

Against this background, Jesus' use of the hearing formula is not novel but in line with the Old Testament prophetic pattern. In the majority of New Testament uses the phrase 'the one having ears, let him hear' (cf. Mt. 13.9-17, 43, and the almost identical form in Mk 4.9, 23; Lk. 8.8) is a direct development of Isa. 6.9-10 and has the dual function of signifying that parabolic revelation is intended to enlighten the genuine remnant but blind those who, though they confess outwardly to be part of the covenant community, are really unbelievers (Mt. 7.15-23): compare Mt. 13.9-16 and the use in conjunction with a parable in Lk. 14.35 (see also Mt. 11.15 in connection with Isaianic prophecy).[36]

Isa. 6.9-10 is likely reflected in the repeated call to 'hear' in John's letters. However, discernment of the Matthew 13 background as lying primarily behind the hearing formula in the letters of Revelation is apparent from recognizing that the same wording is found in both the Matthean and the Johannine formulae. An additional connection is observable from the following parallels: (1) that μυστήριον ('mystery') in both Matthew 13 and Revelation 1–3 occurs after an initial parabolic portrayal and before the formal interpretation of that portrayal to indicate that the hidden meaning of the preceding parable will be unveiled (cf. Mt. 13.11 and Rev. 1.13-19, 1.19-20 [and chs. 2–3]); (2) both uses of μυστήριον are linked to an interpretation of the Old Testament (respectively, of Isa. 6 in Mt. and of several Old Testament allusions, including some from Isa. 44–49, in Rev. 1.12-18); (3) indeed, μυστήριον itself in Mt. 13.11 and Rev. 1.20 is a conscious allusion to Dan. 2.28-29, 45, where the word occurs in reference to the prophetic vision concerning the establishment of the end-time kingdom of God, a topic also of primary concern to these two New Testament texts (Mt. 13.11,

---

36. For uses in the Apocrypha in connection with parables, see Aune, 'Form and Function of the Proclamations to the Seven Churches', p. 194.

19ff.; Rev. 1.6, 9);[37] strikingly, both Matthew and Revelation employ μυστήριον, not only to refer to the hidden meaning of pictorial language but also to connote that the prophesied messianic kingdom has begun fulfillment in an unexpected, even ironic, manner.[38]

There is consensus that the repeated hearing formula in Revelation 2–3 is an allusion to the synoptic formula, though commentators appear to assume the validity of this rather than providing the analysis of parallels cited above. Some interpreters contend that the contextual use of the phrase in the synoptics has been lost sight of and that the use of the formula has lost the idea of hardening or blinding which it had in the synoptics.[39] In addition, however, to the above-noted affinities to Matthew 13, the numerous repetitions of the hearing formula at the same concluding point in each of the letters suggest further that the phrase is not a mere early Christian stock-in-trade reflection of the gospel expression, but is utilized quite consciously, so that awareness of its synoptic context is, at least, plausible.[40] Therefore, as in Isaiah 6 and the synoptics, the formula refers to the fact that Christ's message will enlighten some but blind others.

Ezek. 3.27 is also likely in the background, since its wording is not only most similar to the saying in both Matthew and Revelation, but in Ezek. 3.22-27 this formula is also said to be the very words of the Spirit and of Yahweh, as well as of the human prophet, as in the Revelation formulae (where John writes, and yet what he writes is also presented as the words of Christ *and* the Spirit). The emphasis of the formula in the Ezekiel context is upon Israel's refusal to listen and consequent judgment, though the notion of a righteous remnant responding to the hearing exhortation is included in the context (cf. 3.17-21; 9.4-8; 14.12-23).

Now, however, the formula of Revelation is addressed to the church, which is the continuation of the true covenant community from the Old Testament. But like Israel, the church has also become compromising,

---

37. For argument concerning the allusion to Dan. 2 in Mt. 13, cf. Ladd, *Presence of the Future*, p. 225, and in Rev. 1 see Chapter 3, sect. B above.

38. Cf. Mt. 13.19-23, and the analysis of Ladd, *Presence of the Future*, pp. 218-42, as well as Rev. 1.9 and the analysis of Beale, *Use of Daniel*, pp. 176-77. See also Chapter 3, sect. D above.

39. E.g. see A.-M. Enroth, 'The Hearing Formula in the Book of Revelation', *NTS* 36 (1990), pp. 598-608.

40. So Vos, *Synoptic Traditions in the Apocalypse*, pp. 73-75.

spiritually lethargic, and has entertained idolatrous allegiances, so that the parabolic method of revelation is instituted. The parables throughout the book not only have a judicial effect on the unbelieving but are meant also to shock believers caught up in the church's compromising complacency by revealing to them the horrific, beastly nature of the idolatrous institutions with which they are beginning to associate. As in Isaiah, Ezekiel, and Jeremiah, John is addressing a covenant community, the majority of which is unfaithful and compromising in one way or another.

It is true that the hearing formula is stated more positively ('he who *has* an ear let him hear') in Revelation than in Isaiah 6 ('make heavy their ears...lest...they hear with their ears'). Nevertheless, the positive formulation occurs also in Ezekiel 3 and Matthew 13 with awareness still, as in Isaiah, that the majority would not respond positively, but only the authentic remnant would be able to 'hear'.[41] Whether or not John's warning was met with the same negative response by the majority is not known. Nevertheless, since he stands squarely in the prophetic tradition of Isaiah, Ezekiel, and Jesus in his use of the parables, we should not be overly optimistic about thinking that there was an overwhelmingly positive response (likewise, 2 Tim. 1.15 pessimistically narrates that 'You are aware of the fact that all who are in Asia turned away from me [Paul]'). Just as the parables signalled imminent judgment for the majority of Israel in the past, so likewise the heavenly parables of John probably functioned for the majority of the church and the world. In this respect, it is likely that John held a 'remnant' concept as did the Old Testament prophets and Jesus. The hearing formula was one of the means by which he called out the remnant from among the compromising churches.

---

41. Ezek. 3.27b was changed from an expression of non-repentance ('and he who refuses, let him refuse') into a positive statement of repentance by the Targumist, who apparently could not resist altering such a negative exhortation: 'let him who will refrain, let him refrain *from sinning*'. This conforms also to a general tendency in the early versions of Isa. 6.9-10, as well as to post-biblical Judaism's interpretation of the same Isaiah text, to soften the original Hebrew text by shifting the ultimate cause for the condition of hardening away from God to Israel (so C.A. Evans, *To See and Not Perceive: Isaiah 6.9-10 in Early Jewish and Christian Interpretation* [JSOTSup, 64; Sheffield: JSOT Press, 1989], p. 164, and *passim*); some rabbis even understood Isa. 6.9-10 to imply forgiveness (Evans, *To See and Not Perceive*, p. 145).

b. *An Example of the 'Shock-Effect' Function of the Apocalyptic Parables.* An example of the jarring role of the heavenly parables for the readership occurs in Revelation 2 and 17. In Revelation 2, Christ addresses a sinful situation in which the Christians have become spiritually anesthetized. The Christians in Thyatira may have thought it was wrong for 'Jezebel' to teach a more lax morality and that it was religiously allowable to worship idols together with Jesus (Rev. 2.19-20). The idols she was teaching about were economic idols, like Baal was for the Israelites. Israel did not deny Yahweh but they worshipped Baal for prosperity of the economy. 'Jezebel' was teaching something similar.

The Thyatiran Christians, however, 'tolerated' her teaching. Though they may have disagreed with her views, the church officials did not think it was destructive enough to disallow her from teaching any more within the church.

John wants to shock the sluggish Christians so that they will discern the gravity of the situation. Therefore, in Revelation 17 John paints Jezebel in her 'true colors'. For example, the phrase 'they will eat her flesh' (τὰς σάρκας αὐτῆς φάγονται) in Rev. 17.16 is reminiscent of Jezebel's destiny in 2(4) Kgs 9.36: 'they...will eat the flesh of Jezebel' (καταφάγονται... τὰς σάρκας Ἰεζάβελ).' Jezebel's destruction likewise happened according to the 'word of the Lord' (4 Kgs 9.36), as is true of Babylon in Rev. 17.17.[42]

Though past commentators have tended to identify Babylon either only with ungodly Roman culture or only with the apostate church or only with apostate Israel, it is better to see these identifications as not mutually exclusive (most interpreters have preferred an identification with the sinful Roman society). Nevertheless, the wicked religious–economic culture of the evil Roman world system is the focus in Revelation 17, and the apostate church and unbelieving Israel are included with it, in as much as they have become a part of the sinful world system. In this light, the link between Babylon and Jezebel in Revelation 2 suggests that Jezebel more precisely represents the apostate sector of

42. Mauro, *Patmos Visions*, p. 490; Chilton, *Days of Vengeance*, p. 439 and Ruiz, *Ezekiel in the Apocalypse*, p. 367, see a connection between the 4 Kgs text and Rev. 17.16. See Beale, *Book of Revelation*, in discussion of Rev. 17, where 11 additional parallels are drawn between the Harlot Babylon and Jezebel in 1 and 2 Kgs.

the church through which the religious–economic system of the ungodly Greco–Roman (Babylonian) society makes its incursions into the
church and establishes a fifth columnist movement.

Therefore, the point in Rev. 2.19-24 is this: as long as the church of
Thyatira allows 'Jezebel' to teach such things within the confines of the
church, the church itself is beginning to have spiritual intercourse with
the Devil's whore and with the devilish beast himself, upon whose back
she rides in ch. 17. She is the opposite of the pure woman of Rev. 12.1-
2 who symbolizes the pure, true people of God. John is saying to the
Christians in Thyatira: 'Oh, you want to tolerate this teaching which
you do not think is too bad—well, if you do, you are dealing with the
Devil himself, and you will be destroyed.' What they thought was insignificant compromise and sin was really a crack in their spiritual
dikes which could have let through a flood of spiritual evil, overwhelming them (cf. Rev. 12.15).

The hearing formulae of the letters are linked partially to Christ and
his address in the letters, and, therefore, also to the symbolic son of
man vision (1.9-20), which forms a literary unity with chs. 2–3. This
formula also anticipates the visionary parables of chs. 4–21, including
those of ch. 17, which are likewise intended to have the dual revelatory
function mentioned above. This is suggested further by the use of the
same formula in 13.9, εἴ τις ἔχει οὖς ἀκουσάτω ('if anyone has ears,
let him hear'), which, together with the exhortations of 13.10, are parenthetical addresses to the present readership.[43] The likely reason that
the formula appears in ch. 13 is to awaken Christians to the lethal spiritual threat of economic compromise with the ungodly world system.
The exhortation is intended to strengthen the resolve of saints not to be
taken in by the wiles and seductions of the 'beast', who is the same
figure upon whose back the Babylonian whore, Jezebel, rides in ch. 17.
Together they are a formidable political and cultural duo in exerting
pressure to compromise economically, and, hence, theologically.

The response of 'wisdom' (σοφία) and 'understanding' (νοῦς) needed
to comprehend the 'number of the beast' in Rev. 13.18 is understood

---

43. Similar developments from the letters in the visionary segment are 14.12,
14.13, 16.15a, and 16.15b (cf. respectively 2.13, 19; 2.10-11; 2.5, 16; 3.17-18).
Rev. 13.18 and 17.9 are also present tense exhortations to discern, essentially synonymous with the formulae in the letters and in 13.9, 10c. Note below the close
relation of the formula in 13.10c with 13.9 and 13.18, 17.9 (cf. Sweet, *Revelation*,
p. 82; Beale, 'Danielic Background').

best as being an intended sobering effect of the shocking parabolic portrayals of the beast both in 13.1-8 and 13.11-17.[44] If the saints are sufficiently jolted by the apocalyptic parables, they will have such perception, and will not be deceived as others (cf. Rev. 13.3-8).

The same response in 17.9 (with the introductory ὧδε ['here', as also in 13.18!] plus σοφία ['wisdom'] and νοῦς ['mind']) has the identical meaning as in 13.18, which further binds the themes of the two passages together. It serves to exhort Christians not to be taken in by the beast's deceptions like the rest of 'the earth-dwellers' (17.8). It also functions to exhort them to perceive the symbolic meaning of the beast's 'seven heads', which continues the idea from 17.7-8 about the state's deception (see on 17.9-10). Outside of 13.18 and 17.9, σοφία ('wisdom') occurs only in 5.12 and 7.12, where 'wisdom' is attributed to the Lamb's ability to plan and execute redemptive history from his throne. The parabolic depictions of chs. 13 and 17 serve to shake believers out of worldly-mindedness and to view matters from the perspective of the divine throne (e.g. see Rev. 4–5). Possessing such a divine perspective is tantamount to having the 'wisdom' and 'understanding' (13.18 and in 17.9) which enables them to know the Lamb's wise plan and be prepared to discern divine imposters and their propagandists.[45]

It is unlikely coincidental that μυστήριον ('mystery') also occurs in Revelation 17 in a similar manner as it does in Revelation 1–3 (cf. 1.20 with 17.5, 7): both occur after an initial parabolic vision as a transition to the interpretation; in both passages 'mystery' describes a hidden meaning of a symbolic portrayal based on the Old Testament and which needs further revelatory interpretation.

Furthermore, Rev. 17.6-7 explicitly underscores the shock effect of the apocalyptic parables by narrating John's own reaction of alarm at the vision: 'And I was astonished with great astonishment while beholding it [the vision].' And the angel said to me, "Why have you become astonished?"

The angel's question, 'Why have you become astonished?', is not merely a question about why the seer was amazed at the unusual vision. Rather, several ideas are evoked by the question. The same language of

44. For fuller discussion of the combined use of σοφία and νοῦς, see Beale, 'Danielic Background'.

45. Cf. Ruiz, *Ezekiel in the Apocalypse*, p. 207, upon which this observation about the use of σοφία is based.

'amazement' in Dan. 4.17a, 19a (LXX) also expressed a fearful and troubled spirit.[46] The Aramaic expresses the idea of being 'appalled' (cf. שמם in Dan. 4.16, MT).[47] In response to the horrific vision of Daniel 4, 'Daniel...was appalled...and his thoughts troubled him'. In Daniel the idea of 'appalled' should be understood in the sense of 'shock and fear'. Likewise, John expresses fear about the nightmarish vision he has just seen concerning the horrible nature of the beast and woman, and their persecution. Perhaps, part of what contributed to his troubled spirit was shock and fear over the blasphemous claims of the beast and the severe persecution envisioned.

Also, contributory to the seer's shock may have been the parabolic portrayal of Babylon in the guise of a religiously faithful figure. She was attired in 17.4 almost identically to the bride-city of Christ in Revelation 21, who was 'adorned in precious stone' (21.19), pearls and gold (21.18-21), as well as having been 'clothed in linen' (cf. 18.16 and 19.8!). The fact that the linen is defined as the 'righteous deeds of the saints' in 19.8 may have momentarily led John to think that Babylon was not all bad but had some attractive spiritual features. Enhancing such an impression may have been the fact that the high priest in the Old Testament is described also as adorned with 'gold, purple, scarlet, linen, and [precious] stones', which are likewise applied to the bridal city in 21.18-21.

In contrast, the beast is 'full of blasphemous names' (17.3), the cup in the woman's hand is 'full of abominations and the unclean things of her immorality' (17.4), she is called 'the mother of harlots and of the abominations of the earth' (17.5), and the woman he saw was 'drunk from the blood of the saints and from the blood of the witnesses of Jesus' (17.6).

Consequently, John may have been temporarily captivated by what appeared, in part, to be a spiritually attractive figure and was blinded to the full, true, ungodly nature of the harlot. In fact, as noted already, part of the depiction of the Babylonian woman is taken from the Old Testament portrayal of Jezebel (see 17.16!). Since Jezebel also stands as the model for a party of false teachers in Rev. 2.20, the point in Rev. 17.6-7 would be that even John is shocked to discover that the Jezebel

---

46. Cf. Theodotion of Dan. 4.16; cf. ἐθαύμασα...θαῦμα μέγα ('I marvelled greatly') of Rev. 17.6 with Dan. 4.17a (LXX), σφόδρα ἐθαύμασα ('I marvelled exceedingly'), and 4.19a (LXX), μεγάλως δὲ ἐθαύμασεν ('he marvelled greatly').

47. Cf. Thompson, *Apocalypse and Semitic Syntax*, p. 12

party, which is passing itself off as a group of Christian teachers, is none other than pseudo-Christian; indeed, Jezebel is none other than Babylon herself in the midst of the church, who eventually will be judged along with persecutors from outside the church. Therefore, at least part of the prophet's shock was the result of theological dissonance produced by the combination in one parabolic figure of sinful and apparently righteous features.[48]

Chapters 13 and 17 are only two examples illustrating the function of John's parables. The symbols have a twofold effect: they either enforce the anesthetized condition of people so that they continue in blissful ignorance of their sin (cf. Rom. 1.21-32) or they shock people out of their spiritual anesthesia. That metaphorical communication could have the greater potential to shake true believers out of lethargy is understandable because, unlike abstract communication, symbols operate at not only a cognitive level but also an emotive. Consequently, what is understood is also felt. It is the emotive level which has more potential to jar people so that they can re-focus on the cognitive and perceive better the reality of their dangerous situation. In addition to knowing that there was significant suffering in Nazi concentration camps, if Christians in Germany could have seen pictures of what was really occurring they might have been moved to react against this reality more than they did. It is one thing to hear abstract explanations about the devastation of the atomic bombs dropped on Japan in World War II, but quite another to see actual pictures of this devastation. Pictorial representation makes a greater impact than mere abstract communication, and this is one of the reasons that it is used in the Apocalypse.

3. Conclusion: The Hearing Formula and the Significance of its Old Testament and Gospel Background
The preceding analysis suggests that the symbolic visions of chs. 4–21 are parabolic portrayals of the more abstract, propositionally expressed exhortations, warnings and promises of the letters, so that the latter

---

48. If the notions of 'fearful' and 'perplexed' are preferable over 'admired', then the verb θαυμάζω probably conveys a different notion in 17.6-7 than in 17.8: John's fearful and puzzled reaction in contrast to the ungodly world's admiration for the beast in 17.8. The reason for the difference, despite close contextual ties between the uses, could lie in the former being an allusion to Dan. 4 and the latter not part of such an allusion; for further discussion of the thorny lexical issue see Beale, *Book of Revelation, in loc.* on Rev. 17.

interpret the former and *vice versa*. This thesis finds corroboration in the visions of trumpets and bowls being modelled, not coincidentally, on the Exodus plague signs, which functioned originally to harden the hearts of Pharaoh and the Egyptians but to convey revelation and salvation to Israel. This model is now applied to the church and the world, which dovetails with our suggested use of Christ's parabolic 'hearing' formula. Therefore, there is a theological reason for the presence of so much symbolic communication in Revelation.

Recalling that the hearing formula is rooted ultimately in Isa. 6.9-10 helps explain why it is used in a context of compromise with idols. Just as idols have eyes but cannot see and ears but cannot hear, so Isa. 6.9-10 describes apostate Israelites likewise to indicate figuratively that the idols which they had revered, they had come to resemble spiritually (so also Ps. 115.4-8; 135.15-18). They had become as spiritually lifeless as their idols. In fact, the overwhelming Old Testament use of the basic phraseology 'having ears but not hearing' refers to unrepentant members of the covenant community who had become as spiritually lifeless as the idols which they had insisted on continuing to worship.[49] Though the seven churches have not yet finally capitulated to the idols of the culture, some are in the process of doing so, while others are facing the temptation.

Therefore, the hearing formula is suitably addressed to the churches in the midst of this idolatrous atmosphere in order to warn them not to become identified with the idols and the mores of the surrounding idolatrous culture. In this light, 'hearing' refers figuratively to perceiving truth and desiring to respond in obedience to it (cf. Rev. 1.3; 22.17; Ezek. 44.5 and *Sifre Deut.*, *Piska* 335).

In conclusion, the repeated hearing formulae underscores the Spirit's exhortation that the churches be loyal to their sovereign Lord despite temptations to compromise by participating in idolatry and threats of persecution. They are to express their loyalty by means of being faithful witnesses to Christ, which necessitates no compromise with idolatry. John's strategy to move the readers to this ethical–theological goal is to address them through the medium of prophetic parabolic communication. Such a medium had already been used by the Old Testament prophets and by Jesus to move the remnant in Israel away from its idolatry and self-serving economic sin, which may suggest that John

49. For the full exegetical argument for this in Isa. 6 and elsewhere in the Old Testament, see Beale, 'Isaiah VI 9-13: A Retributive Taunt Against Idolatry'.

also held a remnant theology. And, just as parables signalled imminent judgment for the majority of Israel in the past, so likewise the apocalyptic parables of Revelation function for the majority of the church and the world. Nevertheless, the hearing formula is an exhortation conveying both notions of salvation and judgment. Consequently, the formula anticipates the symbolic communication of chs. 4–21.

Chapter 5

THE INFLUENCE OF THE OLD TESTAMENT ON THE GRAMMAR
OF REVELATION: SOLECISMS IN REVELATION AS SIGNALS
FOR THE PRESENCE OF OLD TESTAMENT ALLUSIONS
(A SELECTIVE ANALYSIS OF REVELATION 1–22)

Introduction[1]

Much research has been invested in analyzing John's grammar, especially his unusual grammatical and syntactical constructions, often referred to as solecisms.[2] The purpose of this chapter is to offer a new perspective by which a programmatic solution to the majority of the significant solecisms can be achieved and which provides a perspective through which better to view John's peculiar Greek usage.

A. A Brief Survey of Past Relevant Study of the Grammar
in the Apocalypse

As early as the first half of the third century Dionysius of Alexandria (d. 264/265 AD) observed that John's 'use of the Greek language is not accurate, but that he employs barbarous idioms, in some places committing downright solecisms' (cited by Eusebius, *Hist. Eccles.* 7.25. 26-27). Other modern scholars have accused John of writing poor Greek. The most thorough and important studies of John's grammar

---

1. Earlier drafts of this chapter were read in the Fall Term of 1994 at the New Testament Colloquium of the Boston Theological Institute and also at the 'Biblical Greek Language and Linguistics Section' of the 1995 SBL Annual Meeting. I am grateful for comments made by members of these seminars, as well as the editorial comments by Greg Goss.

2. For a brief overview of twentieth-century discussion representing a variety of approaches to the problem of the solecisms see Murphy, 'Book of Revelation', pp. 190-91.

are those by Moses Stuart (mid-nineteenth century)[3] and R.H. Charles (early twentieth century),[4] as well as G. Mussies' massive study (latter part of the twentieth century).[5]

B. *The Solecisms of the Apocalypse as Signals for the Presence of Old Testament Allusions*

Various explanations have been proposed for the grammatical irregularities in the Apocalypse. Some have concluded that the solecisms are errors, resulting from John's imperfect knowledge of Greek.[6] Others have attributed the unusual constructions to John's writing in Greek but thinking according to the standards of Hebrew grammar and being influenced to significant degrees by Semitic style.[7] There has rightly been a reaction against understanding John's language as 'Jewish Greek', especially conceived of as a distinct dialect and reflecting a

3. Stuart, *Commentary on the Apocalypse*, II, pp. 232-57: 'Peculiar Characteristics of the Language and Style of the Apocalypse'.

4. Charles, *Revelation*, I, pp. cxvii-clix: 'A Short Grammar of the Apocalypse'.

5. G. Mussies, *The Morphology of Koine Greek as Used in the Apocalypse of St. John: A Study in Bilingualism* (NovTSup, 27; Leiden: E.J. Brill, 1971); cf. also W. Bousset's introductory section entitled 'Die Sprache der Apokalypse' in his commentary: W. Bousset, *Die Offenbarung Johannis* (Göttingen: Vandenhoeck & Ruprecht, 6th edn, 1906), pp. 159-79.

6. E.g. E.C. Selwyn, *The Christian Prophets and the Prophetic Apocalypse* (London: Macmillan, 1900), p. 258.

7. So Charles, *Revelation*, I, pp. cxlii-cxliv, followed similarly by Nigel Turner, in J.H. Moulton, W.F. Howard and Nigel Turner, *A Grammar of New Testament Greek. IV. Style* (Edinburgh: T. & T. Clark, 1976), pp. 146-58, and Thompson, *Semitic Syntax*, e.g., p. 108 (who both include Aramaic together with Hebrew influence as a factor); generally also Swete, *Apocalypse*, pp. cxiii-cxxv; Ozanne, 'Language of the Apocalypse'; C.C. Torrey, *The Apocalypse of John* (New Haven: Yale University Press, 1958), contended that Revelation had been translated into Greek from Aramaic; similarly, R.B.Y. Scott, *The Original Language of the Apocalypse* (Toronto: Toronto University Press, 1928), argued that the book had been translated into Greek from Hebrew (for brief but pointed critique of both Torrey and Scott, see Ozanne, 'Language of the Apocalypse', pp. 3-4); see S.E. Porter, 'Language of the Apocalypse in Recent Study', pp. 583-84, for a listing of other works supporting the general notion that John's style was significantly affected by Semitic influence; cf. also G. Mussies, 'The Greek of the Book of Revelation', in J. Lambrecht (ed.), *L'Apocalypse johannique et l'Apocalyptique dans le Noveau Testament* (BETL, 53; Gembloux: Duculot; Leuven: Leuven University Press, 1980), pp. 167-77; Sweet, *Revelation*, p. 16.

unique Hebrew grammatical structure. Instead, the irregularities have been viewed by a number of scholars neither as mistaken slips of the pen, nor as Semitisms, but reflecting categories of unusual, though acceptable, Greek syntax, attested also in contemporary Hellenistic Greek.[8] Some have understood the difficult expressions partly as due to *constructio ad sensum*,[9] which is quite plausible: e.g. 1.20a; 2.27; 4.4; 5.6; 6.1; 13.3a; 17.3; 21.12-14. A recent proposal has suggested that the solecisms are the result of John's own attempt to write in the dominant language of the ruling Greco-Roman powers, but to do so in idiosyncratic grammar in order to 'decolonialize' the language and to express an incipient insurgent protest statement against these imperialist powers.[10]

Apparently unrecognized for the most part previously, a significant number of these irregularities occur in the midst of Old Testament allusions. Accordingly, a number of the expressions appear irregular because John is carrying over the exact grammatical form of the Old Testament wording (often from the Greek Old Testament and its various versions, or sometimes from the Hebrew).[11] He does not change

8. E.g. so Porter, 'Language of the Apocalypse in Recent Study'; Nigel Turner, in J.H. Moulton, W.F. Howard and Nigel Turner, *A Grammar of New Testament Greek. III. Syntax* (Edinburgh: T. & T. Clark, 1963), p. 315 (Moulton and Howard's view, but apparently not Turner's); Porter, *Verbal Aspect in the Greek of the New Testament*, pp. 111-61, which is a sweeping evaluative survey of past studies on various degrees of Semitic influence on verbal aspect throughout the New Testament; G.H.R. Horsley and S.R. Llewelyn, *New Documents Illustrating Early Christianity* (7 vols.; North Ryde, NSW, Australia: The Ancient History Documentary Research Centre, 1981–[1989]), V, pp. 5-48, which is also a general evaluative survey of the debate about Semitic influence upon Greek throughout the New Testament, especially the notion that there was a 'Jewish Greek' dialect or language.

9. So A.T. Robertson, *A Grammar of the Greek New Testament in the Light of Historical Research* (New York: Hodder & Stoughton, 1914), p. 135; likewise Stuart, *Apocalypse*, I, pp. 236-38. For explanations of some of these 'constructions from sense', see the commentary by Beale, *Book of Revelation*, in loc, on 5.6; 13.3a; 17.3; 21.12-14.

10. A.D. Callahan, 'The Language of the Apocalypse', *HTR* 88 (1995), pp. 453-70.

11. After finishing a rough draft of this section, I read Bauckham, *Climax of Prophecy*, p. 286, and M. Wilcox, 'The Aramaic Background of the New Testa-

the grammatical form of the Old Testament wording to fit the immediate syntactical context of Revelation, so that the Old Testament expression 'sticks out like a sore thumb'. This creates 'syntactical dissonance', whereby, for example, there is lack of concord in case or
gender. Just as often, the precise grammar from the Old Testament
passage is not retained, but stylistic Semitisms or Septuagintalisms are
incorporated in order to create the dissonance. This 'dissonance' is one
of the ways that John gets the readers' attention, causing them to focus
on the phrase and to recognize more readily the presence of an Old
Testament allusion. The exegetical analysis in the concluding part of
this chapter indicates that a significant number of Revelation's solecisms function in the above manner to signal Old Testament allusions:
see below, especially on 1.4; 1.5; 2.13; 4.1; 11.15; 12.5; 12.7; 14.7;
14.20; 20.2.[12]

The majority of the solecisms examined consist of a violation of concord, whether in case, number, gender or person. Other unusual grammatical features, sometimes included in discussions of the solecisms,
are better categorized as peculiar variations in style but do not approach
outright transgressions of more ordinary grammatical rules, examples
of which are the following: (1) resumptive pronouns (e.g. 3.8; 7.9);
(2) the use of participles as verbs or the resolution of a participle into a
finite verb in a following clause (e.g. with respect to the latter cf. 1.5-6;
2.20); (3) the mixing of different verb tenses and moods without any
explicit reason for the alteration (e.g. 21.24-27); (4) stylistic expressions which seem to express Hebraisms or Aramaisms (e.g. Rev. 4.9-

---

ment', in D.R.G. Beattie and M.J. McNamara (eds.), *The Aramaic Bible* (JSOTSup,
166; Sheffield: JSOT Press, 1994), pp. 362-78 (370), who come close to this conclusion. The former says, 'Unusual and difficult phrases in Revelation frequently
turn out to be Old Testament allusions', though he appears not to be discussing
solecisms, since he adduces only two examples, and these are not grammatical solecisms. Wilcox similarly says with respect to the New Testament in general, 'Infe-
licities in the Greek may also at times mask allusions to Scripture, or in some cases,
to midrashic material linked to Scripture, but not immediately identifiable as
Scripture', though he adduces only one example, which also does not involve a
grammatical irregularity.

12. Because of space, only ten of the clearest solecisms in this respect are analyzed below; eight others are surveyed in a following excursus. The solecisms discussed in this chapter are representative of others (see further Beale, *Book of Revelation, in loc.* on excursuses at Rev. 1.10-12; 2.20; 10.2, 8; 19.6; 19.20; though less
certain, see also 11.4).

10).[13] Some of the clear solecisms are difficult to account for according to any theory.[14]

Ruiz argues that the idiosyncratic solecisms are intended to stop the reader and confound a natural understanding of particular portions of the Revelation text.[15] The present discussion indicates that no such hermeneutical intention is present, though a significant number of the solecisms do cause the reader to pause and to reflect on the wording in order to point the reader back to a particular Old Testament reference in order better to understand the meaning of the phrase in Revelation. In the nineteenth century, Stuart argued that the syntactical peculiarities were intended to cause readers to take closer notice of the clause at hand (especially when they were appositional or explanatory clauses), and so were due to rhetorical purposes.[16] The present conclusions refine this assessment. Some, but not most, of the solecisms which can be traced to Old Testament influence could also be explained as due to *constructio ad sensum*. Furthermore, even when both an explanation of *constructio ad sensum* and Old Testament influence are possible, it may be preferable to opt for the latter as the reason for the solecism, since the very presence of an Old Testament allusion could provide more objective evidence for recognition whereas recognizing a *constructio ad sensum* involves more subjective evaluation. On the other hand, it is not unthinkable that there could be an Old Testament allusion together with a *constructio ad sensum*, the latter of which might be responsible for the unusual syntax.

Some deny that the solecisms of Revelation reflect any Hebrew or Semitic style, while others contend that such style is the complete explanation for the peculiarities, while still others conclude that the expressions reflect both an irregular but attested Hellenistic (or Koine, vernacular) idiom *and* a Semitic style.[17] Robertson comes closest to the

---

13. For further examples of each of these preceding four categories see P.M. Bretscher, 'Syntactical Peculiarities in Revelation', *CTM* 16 (1945), pp. 95-105.

14. E.g. 14.12 and 11.18. However, 14.12 may be due to a rhetorical use by which a discordant nominative (especially the nominative form of the participle) introduces an explanatory clause in order to highlight the explanation before the readers' eyes (cf. Stuart, *Apocalypse*, I, p. 235). The irregularity in 11.18 merely may be due to stylistic variation.

15. Ruiz, *Ezekiel in the Apocalypse*, p. 220.

16. Stuart, *Apocalypse*, I, p. 235.

17. Robertson, *Grammar of the Greek New Testament*, pp. 135-37; cf. also

solution when he says that 'it is not so much particular Hebraisms that meet us in the Apocalypse as the flavour of the LXX whose words are interwoven in the text at every turn'.[18]

In the light of the following analysis, and in confirmation of Robertson's general proposal, we will see that stylistic Septuagintalisms sometimes have been incorporated into the text of Revelation. They have been incorporated not simply to reflect an Old Testament Greek style, but to indicate the presence of an actual Old Testament allusion. It is true that one could say that such Septuagintalisms 'fall within the range of possible registers' of first-century Greek usage.[19] The question, however, is not about a mere few grammatical irregularities but the great number of the difficulties, and the frequency of the phenomena in comparison with other works.[20] Furthermore, why does John use such peculiar language on occasion and yet keep the rules of standard Hellenistic Greek most of the time? The explanation is that these peculiarities at just these points are not mere reflections of unusual though possible registers of Greek usage, but are stylistic Septuagintalisms; such semi-irregular Hellenistic expressions may occur more frequently in Revelation because they would have felt natural for the author as a result of his Hebrew and especially Old Testament Greek background.[21] Other cases of John's solecisms are even to be more specifically explained as grammatically awkward because they are parts of actual Old Testament verbal allusions carried over in their original syntactical form as they stood in the Old Testament passage. The overall purpose

B. Fanning, *Verbal Aspect in New Testament Greek* (Oxford: Clarendon Press, 1990), pp. 271-74.

    18. Robertson, *Grammar of the Greek New Testament*, p. 136.

    19. As Porter, 'Language of the Apocalypse in Recent Study', p. 603, says in response to attempts to explain John's Greek as influenced by a grammatical system of Hebrew.

    20. So Roberston, *A Grammar of the Greek New Testament*, pp. 414, 136.

    21. Cf. Fanning, *Verbal Aspect in New Testament Greek*, p. 273; Wilcox, 'Aramaic Background of the New Testament', pp. 367-68, cites the Babatha Archive papyri, dated at the end of the first century AD, where Aramaic is rendered into Greek. He observes that the evidence there demonstrates that when Aramaic is put into Greek, it resembles closely New Testament Semitisms often attributed to Septuagintal influence. In this light, he cautions against assuming pervasive LXX influence over Hebrew or Aramaic. His caution is, perhaps, well taken, though his warning is not relevant in those places of Revelation where a solecism occurs in the midst of or in direct connection with an Old Testament allusion based on the LXX.

of these Septuagintalisms, stylistic Semitisms, and awkward Old Testament allusions was probably to create a 'biblical' effect in the hearer and, hence, to show the solidarity of his writing with that of the Old Testament.[22]

The following section in the remainder of this study inductively attempts to demonstrate the above deductive analysis: that a significant number of the Apocalypse's grammatical solecisms indicates the presence of Old Testament allusions. The following solecisms which are analyzed appear to be representative of others which also could have been discussed below (with respect to which see above on n. 12).

C. *Exegetical Analysis of Some of the Well-Known Solecisms in the Apocalypse which Points to their Use as Signals for the Presence of Old Testament Allusions* [23]

1. *Solecisms Involving an Irregular Use of Nouns in the Nominative Case.*

a. *Revelation 1.4*: ἀπὸ ὁ ὢν καὶ ὁ ἦν καὶ ὁ ἐρχόμενος. The clause ἀπὸ ὁ ὢν ('from the one who is') is the first and most famous solecism of the Apocalypse, since a genitive construction should follow ἀπό. It is also one of the clearest Old Testament allusions in the book. Does the Old Testament allusion have any significant bearing upon the grammatical irregularity? Before answering this, the Old Testament allusion must be clarified.

The complete threefold clause in Rev. 1.4, 'the one who is and who was and who is coming', is a reflection of Exod. 3.14 together with Isaiah's twofold and threefold temporal descriptions of God (cf. Isa. 41.4; 43.10; 44.6 48.12), which themselves may be developed reflections on the divine name in Exod. 3.14. The name of Exod. 3.14 was also expanded in a twofold and threefold manner, not only by Isaiah, but also by later Jewish tradition, which is understandable since the verb form 'I am' (אהיה in Hebrew, or 'I will be') is repeated three times

---

22. See above at Chapter 2, sect. D.8, following Sweet, *Revelation*, p. 16.

23. For discussion of the immediate and broad contexts of each of the following passages in which solecisms occur, as well as further analysis of some of the Old Testament allusions involved, see Beale, *Book of Revelation*; also, see the introductory section therein on 'The Grammar of the Apocalypse' for a text-critical analysis of the most significant solecisms (25 examples are surveyed).

in Exod. 3.14: (1) 'I am He who is and who will be' (*Targ. Ps.-J. Exod. 3.14*); (2) 'I am now what I always was and always will be' *Exod. R. 3.6; The Alphabet of Rabbi Akiba*; likewise *Midr. Ps.* 72.1); (3) 'I am he who is and who was and I am he who will be' (*Targ. Ps.-J. Deut.* 32.39; see likewise the gloss to *Targ. Neof., I, Exod.* 3.14). In *Mek., Tract. Shirata* 4.25-32, as well as *Tract. Baḥodesh* 5.25-31, the similar threefold formula describes the God of the Exodus in direct linkage with Deut. 32.39.[24]

Among the preceding references, Rev. 1.4 most resembles the targumic expression in Deut. 32.39. It is unlikely, however, that John is dependent only on the Deut. 32.39 reference,[25] since the first and last elements of that formula are not the same. Consequently, he is more likely familiar with the general tradition represented by the above texts (especially Old Testament texts) which expands Exod. 3.14.[26] A similar threefold formula is found also in pagan Greek literature as a title of the gods,[27] which may have sparked John's appeal to the Jewish formulae as an apologetic.

Since a genitive construction should follow ἀπό in the phrase ἀπὸ ὁ ὤν, scribes tried to correct the apparent mistake by adding θεου ('of God', 𝔐 [a] t; Vic Prim) after the preposition. But it would be a blunder of modern thinking to judge this as a mistake of one who did not know his Greek very well. In this particular instance, as often elsewhere, commentators generally acknowledge that the 'incorrect' grammar is intentional, since John keeps the grammatical rules most of the time. The phrase ὁ ὤν is probably taken from Exod. 3.14 and John keeps it in the nominative in order to highlight it as an allusion to Exodus.[28] John's

---

24. The Shirata reference is also linked to a similar threefold formula based on Isa. 41.4; note the threefold formula based on Isa. 44.6 in *Gen. R.* 80 1.2, *Deut. R.* 1.10, and *Cant. R.* 1.9 § 1; for a similar threefold formula for God without reference to a precise Old Testament text see Josephus, *Apion* 2.190; *Ant.* 8.280; *Aristob.* 4.5; *Sib. Or.* 3.16; cf. Rom. 2.36.

25. Contra Trudinger, 'Old Testament in the Book of Revelation', p. 87.

26. So similarly Delling, 'Zum Gottesdienstlichen Stil der Johannes-Apokalypse', pp. 124-26; cf. discussion of the targumic references by McNamara, *New Testament and the Palestinian Targum*, pp. 105-12.

27. Stuart, *Apocalypse*, II, p. 16; cf. also J. Moffatt, *Revelation*, p 21; Lohmeyer, *Die Offenbarung des Johannes*, pp. 168, 179, 181, and McNamara, *New Testament and the Palestinian Targum*, p. 102; for early patristic references see Charles, *Revelation*, II, pp. 220-21.

28. So also J.H. Moulton, W.F. Howard and Nigel Turner, *A Grammar of New*

emphasis stems from the fact that ὁ ὤν occurs twice in Exod. 3.14 as an explanation of the divine name Yahweh.

Furthermore, it is possible that the full threefold phrase became a general title for God in Judaism (cf. above),[29] and this would have been reason enough for the author to maintain the nominatives. Some grammarians,[30] however, note that 'names are usually cited in the case required by the construction; only rarely are they introduced independently in the nominative'.[31] Beckwith,[32] Robertson,[33] and others argue unnecessarily that John considered the LXX paraphrase of the divine name as an indeclinable noun, since the unchangeable form would have suited better the majesty, sovereignty, and unchangeableness of God. If such is the case, the same kind of grammatical irregularity has the same significance for the Devil's name in 20.2![34]

Possible also is the suggestion that John employs such kinds of constructions here and elsewhere as Hebraisms (in Hebrew the noun in the indirect cases is not inflected).[35] John's purpose in doing so, as suggested above, would be to create a 'biblical' effect upon the reader and thereby to show the solidarity of his work with that of God's revelation in the Old Testament. Unconvincing is Mussies,[36] who speculates without any manuscript evidence that after ἀπό was written the name of God to which ὁ ὤν was put in apposition, and that the name was 'effaced by

---

Testament Greek. II. *Accidence and Word-Formation* (Edinburgh: T. & T. Clark, 1929), p. 154; Laughlin, *Solecisms of the Apocalypse*, p. 12; Stuart, *Apocalypse*, II, p. 15, suggests that the indeclinability of the name YHWH in the same Old Testament passage may have enforced this.

29. Cf. H.E. Dana and J.R. Mantey, *A Manual Grammar of the Greek New Testament* (Toronto: Macmillan, 1927), p. 70.

30. F. Blass and A. Debrunner, *A Greek Grammar of the New Testament and Other Early Christian Literature* (ed. R.W. Funk; Chicago: University of Chicago Press, 1961), § 143.

31. Blass and Debrunner (*Greek Grammar*, § 143) cite Rev. 1.4, but it is unclear whether they consider the threefold clause in Rev. 1.4 as an exception to the rule or as maintaining the nominative because it is based on a rabbinical exegesis of Exod. 3.14, or both.

32. Beckwith, *Apocalypse of John*, p. 424.

33. Robertson, *Grammar of the Greek New Testament*, pp. 270, 414, 459, 574-75.

34. Cf. Sweet, *Revelation*, p. 65, and the analysis of 20.2 below.

35. So Charles, *Revelation*, I, p. 13.

36. Mussies, *Morphology*, p. 94.

thumbing or by decay of the scroll', and that scribes misconstrued ὁ ὤν as originally having been written directly following the preposition.

The most probable explanation, however, for the nominative is that it is intended to reflect an allusion to Exod. 3.14.

Excursus on Revelation 1.4: a Comparison with John 8.58. There is a striking similarity between Rev. 1.4 and Jn 8.58. Both refer to the divine name from the Old Testament, especially from Isaiah (see above), which itself is most likely based on Exod. 3.14.[37] Rev. 1.4 cites the ὁ ὤν part of the Exodus formula (though not found explicitly in Isaiah) and draws attention to it by expressing it in an awkward, apparently syntactically incorrect manner. Jn 8.58 alludes in some degree to the ἐγὼ εἰμί part of the name in Exodus (ἐγὼ εἰμί ὁ ὤν), though the primary source drawn from is Isa. 43.10, 13 which has paraphrastically developed Exod. 3.14.[38] Similarly, the syntax of the wording in Jn 8.58 is also extremely clumsy, if not bordering on being incorrect: πρὶν Ἀβραὰμ γενέσθαι ἐγὼ εἰμί, which is best rendered 'before Abraham was born, I am'. There are much better, even more correct, ways of saying the same thing, among which, for example are: 'before Abraham was born, *I already existed*' (= ἤδη ἤμην), or 'before Abraham was born, *I existed from the beginning*' (= ἤμην ἀπ᾽ ἀρχῆς), or 'before Abraham was born, *I existed from the generations of old*' (= ἤμην ἀπὸ γενεῶν ἀρχῆς), or '*I am he; before me* Abraham *did not exist*' (= ἐγὼ εἰμι· ἔμπροσθέν μου οὐκ ἐγένετο). What compounds the awkwardness of the expression is that, among the 13 'I am' statements by Jesus in the Gospel of John,[39] only Jn 8.58 clearly can have no predicate. All the others either have an implied predicate ('I am *he*' or 'it is *I*') or an explicit predicate (e.g. 'I am *the true vine*').[40] There is no possibility,

---

37. See P.B. Harner, *The 'I Am' of the Fourth Gospel* (Facet Books, Biblical Series, 26; Philadelphia: Fortress Press, 1970), pp. 6-16, who observes that Isaiah 41–52 is in the background of John's 'I am' statements (including Jn 8.58), as well as more generally possibly Exod. 3.14, and that Exod. 3.14 also influenced the LXX translators of Isa. 41–52.

38. D.M. Ball, *'I Am' in John's Gospel* (JSNTSup, 124; Sheffield: Sheffield Academic Press, 1996), pp. 188-98, argues persuasively that Isa. 43.10, 13 is, at least, the primary focus of Jn 8.58.

39. See R.E. Brown, *The Gospel According to John I–XII* (AB, 29; Garden City, NY: Doubleday, 1966), pp. 53-538, who also notes additional 'borderline' uses.

40. Brown, *Gospel According to John*, p. 533, contends that 8.24 and 8.28, as

however, of even reading in an implied predicate in Jn 8.58 to smooth out the awkwardness, as is the case in the other implied predicate nominative uses (i.e. it cannot be translated 'before Abraham was born, I am *he*' [or 'it is *I*']).

Such unusual use of ἐγώ εἰμί in Jn 8.58 probably highlights it as an allusion to Isa. 43.10, 13 specifically,[41] and generally to the numerous repetitions of ἐγώ εἰμί with reference to God in Isaiah 41–52; indeed, ἐγώ εἰμί occurs with reference to God 21 times in Isaiah 41–52.[42] Especially awkward uses occur in Isa. 43.25, 45.19, and 51.12, where ἐγώ εἰμι ἐγώ εἰμι appears, and it is translated emphatically by English translations of the LXX ('I, even I, am...');[43] likewise, some English versions of the Hebrew equivalent (אנכי אנכי) in the same passages (i.e. Isa. 43.11, 25; 51.12) give an emphatic rendering: 'I, even I' (e.g. NIV, NASB). Other English versions, however, render more literally: 'I, I am' (e.g. RSV; Douay).[44] These three ἐγώ εἰμι ἐγώ εἰμι clauses are significant since they occur only here in Isaiah and nowhere else in the entire Old Testament (the same is true of אנכי אנכי, which occurs only in Isa. 43.11, 25, and 51.12). The first ἐγώ εἰμί in each of these three texts may be intended to be understood absolutely and not merely as part of an emphatic expression, so that the wording may best be rendered 'I am, I am...' Isa. 46.4 and, especially, Exod. 3.14 may also be in mind, since these also appear to be very awkward uses of 'I am', apparently being the only 'I am' expressions which are used absolutely (with no implied predicate nominative) in addition to the three just

---

well as 13.19, also have no predicate, but this is not necessarily true, since a predicate is plausible in each case (i.e., 'I am he'); cf. the allusions to Isa. 41–52 generally and the wording there, above all Isa. 43.10, 13, where a predicate is very possibly implied or there could be intentional ambiguity, with the divine name implied; in the cases of Jn 8.24, 28 a predicate may be implied or, again, there may be intentional ambiguity.

41. See above on n. 38, and Ball, *'I Am' in John's Gospel*, pp. 188-98, who argues that Isa. 43.10 is the primary allusion in Jn 8.24 and 8.28, though he allows that other parallel passages from the broader Isaiah and Old Testament contexts could also be in the field of reference.

42. Outside of these 21 uses, the phrase does not occur elsewhere at all in Isa. 41–52.

43. *The Septuagint Version of the Old Testament and Apocrypha with an English Translation* (Grand Rapids: Zondervan, 1972).

44. Douay actually has 'I am, I am' in the first two texts, and 'I, I myself' in the third.

noted above.[45] Consequently, the absolute use of ἐγὼ εἰμί in Jn 8.58 may be intended to reflect Isa. 43.10, 13 together with the absolute use in the LXX of Isa. 43.25 (and, perhaps, 45.19; 51.12) and the awkward uses of 'I am' in the Hebrew of Exod. 3.14. Could the three occurrences of ἐγώ εἰμι ἐγώ εἰμι in Isaiah echo the awkwardly twice repeated אהיה ('*I am* who *I am*') of Exod. 3.14a, *and* the absolute use of אהיה in Exod. 3.14b ('say this to the sons of Israel, *I am* has sent me to you')?

Therefore, both Rev. 1.4 and Jn 8.58 make use of different parts of the same divine name from the same Old Testament books, and do so in an intentionally awkward syntactical manner, which causes the reader/hearer to be jarred and to focus more on the expression, with hopes that its Old Testament background could be more readily recognized. Jn 8.58 is an intriguing and unique construction which is similar to Rev. 1.4 and which points further to the solecism in Rev. 1.4 as functioning to signal an Old Testament allusion (could it also be a subtle pointer, together with additional observations by other commentators, to common authorship?).[46]

b. *Revelation 1.5*: ἀπὸ Ἰησοῦ Χριστοῦ, ὁ μάρτυς ὁ πιστός, ὁ πρωτότοκος τῶν νεκρῶν. The phrase ὁ μάρτυς ὁ πιστός ὁ πρωτότοκος ('the faithful witness, the first-born') is nominative but should be genitive (following ἀπὸ Ἰησοῦ Χριστοῦ). The phrase is an allusion to 'the faithful witness' of Ps. 88.38 (= 89.38, MT) (LXX), which refers specifically to the unending witness of the moon, and which is compared to the unending reign of David's seed on his throne (likewise Ps. 88.30 [= 89.20, MT]). Just as *Exod. R.* 19.7 applies the 'first-born' from Ps. 89.28 (MT) to the 'King Messiah', and *Gen. R.* 97 sees Ps. 89.37 (MT) as a messianic prophecy, so John applies the phrase directly to the Messiah's own faithful witness which led to establishment of his eternal kingship.

---

45. The future tense of εἰμί would be natural in Isa. 46.4 instead of the unexpected present: 'until you have grown old, I am [*he*]', though the use may not have to be viewed in an absolute sense.

46. See, e.g., S.S. Smalley, 'John's Revelation and John's Community', *BJRL* 69 (1987), pp. 549-71; V.S. Poythress, 'Johannine Authorship and the Use of Intersentence Conjunctions in the Book of Revelation', *WTJ* 47 (1985), pp. 329-36; P. Whale, 'The Lamb of John: Some Myths about the Vocabulary of the Johannine Literature', *JBL* 106 (1987), pp. 289-95.

Like the solecism in 1.4 following ἀπό, the phrase here is probably kept in the nominative because it is part of the very wording of the Old Testament allusion, which was also in the nominative in its Old Testament context: the LXX of Ps. 88.38 (= 89.38, MT) has ὁ μάρτυς... πιστός, while v. 27 (28 [Eng.]) of the Psalm has πρωτότοκον. The author likely wants to keep the nominative to direct attention to the Old Testament allusion, as well as perhaps because, like the phrase in v. 4, it *may* have been a name for the Messiah, as noted above;[47] there is not, however, enough evidence that it was a name at this time.[48] Consequently, 'first-born' has been changed from its Old Testament accusative form either because it had become a name, or, more probably, to conform to the nominative of 'the faithful witness' (ὁ μάρτυς ὁ πιστός) in the Greek Old Testament text.

c. *Revelation 2.13*: ἐν ταῖς ἡμέραις Ἀντιπᾶς ὁ μάρτυς μου ὁ πιστός μου. The phrase Ἀντιπᾶς ὁ μάρτυς μου ὁ πιστός μου ('Antipas My witness, My faithful one') directly following ἐν ταῖς ἡμέραις ('in the days') could be classified as a Semitism which 'contravenes Greek syntax', since the nominative Ἀντιπᾶς is a declinable name and should be in the genitive (Ἀντιπᾶ),[49] as should the following ὁ μάρτυς... ὁ πιστός.[50] Even if the name were indeclinable, it would still stand in a genitival relationship with 'in the days', as should the appositional ὁ μάρτυς ...ὁ πιστός.[51] It is unlikely that the proper name should be considered a nominative of appellation, since indeclinable proper nouns are typically assigned the case demanded by their use in the clause.[52] Consequently,

47. Whether in Judaism, or formulated newly by John; likewise Turner, in Moulton, Howard and Turner, *Grammar*, III, p. 314; Laughlin, *Solecisms of the Apocalypse*, p. 15, is the only one I have subsequently found to come closest to my conclusion: 'The phrase...is directly quoted from the LXX of Ps. 89:37.'

48. Cf. further Blass and Debrunner, *Greek Grammar of the New Testament*, § 143, discussed above at 1.4, with respect to the general rule that names are cited in the case required by the syntactical context.

49. J.H. Moulton, W.F. Howard and Nigel Turner, *A Grammar of New Testament Greek*. I. *Prolegomena* (Edinburgh: T. & T. Clark, 1907), p. 12.

50. See also Blass and Debrunner, *Greek Grammar of the New Testament*, § 53-55.

51. Cf. B.M. Metzger, *A Textual Commentary on the Greek New Testament* (London: United Bible Societies, 1971), p. 734.

52. J.A. Brooks and C.L. Winbery, *Syntax of New Testament Greek* (Washington: University Press of America, 1979), p. 5.

the modifying phrase 'my faithful witness' cannot be construed as being nominative because it purportedly modifies a nominative of appellation.

Rather, like the solecisms in 1.4 and 1.5, which also should have been in the genitive, this phrase occurs in the nominative because it is part of the same Old Testament allusion as 1.5, where ὁ μάρτυς ὁ πιστός ('faithful witness') also occurs in allusion to the nominative ὁ μάρτυς...πιστός of Ps. 88.37 (LXX = 89.38, Eng.) (see on 1.5 at Chapter 5, sect. C.1.b. above). Again, the awkward nominative is a device directing attention to the Old Testament allusion, as well as to the first occurrence of the phrase in 1.5, in order to make clear the identification of Antipas' faithful witness with that of Jesus.[53] Therefore, it is unlikely that Ἀντιπᾶς is a careless slip for Ἀντιπᾶ[54] nor that it is a mere feature of the uneducated *koine* style.[55]

It is theoretically possible that the name is a generally indeclinable Semitic name, since some Hellenized Semitic names were sometimes declined and sometimes not,[56] but apparently no examples of 'Antipas' have yet been found which are indeclinable. Furthermore, the common practice with Hellenized Semitic personal names ending with nominative -ας was to decline them according to the first declension (-ας, -α, etc.).[57] However, even if the name were indeclinable, the reason that the following clause ('My witness, My faithful one') has been attracted to the indeclinable nominative name needs more explanation than that it was accidental, since the almost identical clause in 1.5 modifies Ἰησοῦ Χριστοῦ, but its case *is* different.[58]

---

53. Indeed, the other Old Testament text lying behind the idea of 'faithful witness' is Isa. 43.10-12, which repeats twice that the Israelites were to be 'My witnesses' (ἐμοὶ μάρτυρες, the latter also in the nominative) together with God and his servant in the new age of redemption (see further above on Chapter 3, sect. E.3.b.(ii), 'The Old Testament Background of Rev. 3.14: The Already and Not Yet New Creation of Revelation').

54. As Robertson, *Grammar of the Greek New Testament*, p. 255, and Moulton, Howard and Turner, *Grammar*, IV, pp. 146-47, conjecture.

55. Moulton, Howard and Turner, *Grammar*, IV, pp. 146-47.

56. Mussies, *Morphology*, p. 94, and G. Mussies, 'Antipas (Rev. 2:13b)', *NovT* 7 (1964), pp. 242-44; cf. Robertson, *Grammar of the Greek New Testament*, p. 255.

57. So Blass and Debrunner, *Greek Grammar of the New Testament*, § 53-55; Charles, *Revelation*, I, p. 52, following Lachmann and others, is so convinced of the declinability of the name that he proposes the conjectural emendation of Ἀντιπᾶ.

58. Scribes tried to smooth out the reading by adding 'in which' (αις or εν αις)

d. *Revelation 12.7*: ὁ Μιχαὴλ καὶ οἱ ἄγγελοι αὐτοῦ τοῦ πολεμῆσαι. There is a grammatical difficulty in the phrase ὁ Μιχαὴλ καὶ οἱ ἄγγελοι αὐτοῦ τοῦ πολεμῆσαι, since the nominative (ὁ Μιχαὴλ καὶ οἱ ἄγγελοι) serves as the subject of the infinitive, instead of the normal accusative. The articular genitival infinitive (τοῦ πολεμῆσαι), as is often the case, merely may denote the *result* of the initial clause, 'And there came about war in heaven, *so that* Michael and his angels *waged war* in heaven'. More generally, Robertson,[59] on analogy with classical usage, takes the construction as a 'loose infinitive of design' in 'explanatory apposition to πόλεμος', while Moffatt is content to refer to the construction as 'syntactical laxity'.[60] In line with Robertson, Porter refers to the construction as a 'strictly independent' infinitive, which he classifies as part of a larger category of independent infinitives 'long… recognized in both earlier and later ancient Greek'.[61] The majority of examples of independent infinitives adduced in Goodwin,[62] however, form part of idiomatic parenthetical expressions used in speaking or writing to qualify something which has been spoken or written;[63] for example Herodotus uses the infinitive absolute in a very specific manner, often in idiomatic expressions and primarily in the following three kinds of statements about his historical research: (1) when making methodological statements of '*general purport* about his own method', or (2) about problems confronting him in evaluating his sources of information, or (3) when he makes a 'bare *statement of fact* about the

before Antipas, but the attempt was unsuccessful, since the genitive of the name and of its appositional clause is still required (see Metzger, *Textual Commentary*, p. 734). Stuart, *Apocalypse*, II, pp. 71-72, tries hesitatingly to solve the syntactical problem by reading in the imperfect ἦν, 'even in the days in which Antipas [was] my faithful martyr', though he acknowledges the problems with this (likewise, but more confidently, F. Düsterdieck, *Critical and Exegetical Handbook to the Revelation of John* [H.A.W. Meyer's Commentary on the New Testament, XI; trans. H.E. Jacobs; Winona Lake, IN: Alpha Publications, 1980 1st English edn; Edinburgh: T. & T. Clark, 1883], p. 143, and Gill, *Exposition of the New Testament*, III, p. 709).

59. Robertson, *Grammar of the Greek New Testament*, p. 1066.

60. Moffatt, *Revelation*, p. 426.

61. Porter, *Verbal Aspect in the Greek of the New Testament*, p. 377.

62. William W. Goodwin, *Syntax of the Moods and Tenses of the Greek Verb* (Boston: Ginn, 1890), pp. 310-13, cited in Porter, *Verbal Aspect in the Greek of the New Testament*, p. 377.

63. Likewise H.W. Smyth, *Greek Grammar* (Cambridge, MA: Harvard University Press, 1984), p. 447.

problems involved in *obtaining...specific* information.[64] A number of examples cited by Porter are idioms of greeting. No doubt, there are examples of independent infinitives which are not idiomatic, but the question is whether these are typical in any period of Greek. More data must be adduced and evaluated than hitherto before this could be demonstrated conclusively. The infinitive of Rev. 12.7 does not occur as part of such specialized or idiomatic expressions as noted above.

Therefore, while it is possible that the construction of 12.7 reflects exceptional broader Greek style, or that it is a lax expression, these explanations do not account sufficiently for the unusual construction of the nominative (ὁ Μιχαὴλ καὶ οἱ ἄγγελοι) serving as the subject of the infinitive, instead of the normal accusative. Moule's explanation is that this is a reflection of John's 'barbarous Greek'.[65] But this may be an exceptional formulation, which proves the general rule. In this respect, the strange syntax may be the result of an attempt to transcribe literally an unusually vivid vision.[66] Some MSS (𝔓⁴⁷ ℵ 𝔐) omit the genitive article τοῦ before the infinitive πολεμῆσαι, though this is likely to be an attempt to smooth out the difficulty by simplifying the grammar.

The nominative also can be accounted for grammatically, however, by seeing the construction as a complementary or epexegetical infinitive with γίνομαι repeated from the first part of the verse in the more personalized third person plural form of a verb like ἔρχομαι, ἐξέρχομαι or ἀνίστημι (e.g. ἐγένετο πόλεμος ἐν τῷ οὐρανῷ, ὁ Μιχαὴλ καὶ οἱ ἄγγελοι αὐτοῦ [ἦλθον] τοῦ πολεμῆσαι).[67] Or, as Swete proposes, ἐγένετο may be repeated from the first part of the verse directly before ὁ Μιχαὴλ: 'there arose war in heaven; there arose Michael and his angels to make war'.[68] Implied but elided verbs are typical both in Revelation and in Paul, as well as in the New Testament in general.[69] In either of the two proposals of supplied verbs, the nominative is not

64. P. Stork, *The Aspectual Usage of the Dynamic Infinitive in Herodotus* (Groningen: Bouma's Boekhuis, 1982), p. 107; cf. pp. 89-108 (cited also by Porter, *Verbal Aspect in the Greek of the New Testament*, p. 377).

65. C.F.D. Moule, *An Idiom Book of New Testament Greek* (Cambridge: Cambridge University Press, 1953), p. 129.

66. So Farrer, *Revelation*, p. 146.

67. In Rev. 14.15 a number of MSS have the articular genitival infinitive also functioning epexegetically or complementarily to ἔρχομαι.

68. Swete, *Apocalypse*, p. 153.

69. Cf. Blass and Debrunner, *Greek Grammar of the New Testament*, § 479-83 on ellipses.

awkward, since it serves as the subject of the implied ἦλθον or ἐγένετο followed by its completing infinitive.[70]

In addition to the above explanations, plausible also is the solution which views the construction as reflective of a Hebrew idiom where the subject preceding the *lamed*-prefix (*le*) plus infinitive occurs. Indeed, in these instances the LXX reproduces the wording literally with a nominative subject preceding an articular genitival infinitive, just as in Rev. 12.7 (e.g. Hos. 9.13; Ps. 24.14; I Chron. 9.25; Eccles. 3.15). And just as the idiom in the LXX reproductions conveys the idea of necessity, some suggest the same nuance is included here: 'Michael and his angels *had to make war*'.[71] In addition to these examples from the LXX, τοῦ plus the infinitive elsewhere renders *lamed*-plus infinitive, though the same Aramaic construction occurs numerously and the same construction is found in Classical and Hellenistic Greek.[72]

The attempt by Charles and others to explain the articular genitival infinitive as reflecting an idiomatic Hebrew–LXX Semitism appears to be on the right track. However, the Semitism is not likely due to a general Semitic influence upon John, but is to be accounted for more precisely on the basis of the specific allusion to Dan. 10.20 (from either the Hebrew or Greek Old Testament text), which is present in Rev. 12.7. There also Theodotion renders *lamed*-plus infinitive by genitive plus infinitive, which serves as epexegetical or complementary to the preceding verb 'return' in the phrase ἐπιστρέψω τοῦ πολεμῆσαι ('I will return to make war'). The first person singular 'I', which is assumed in the verb 'return' in Dan. 10.20, is closely associated with none other than Michael (cf. Dan. 10.21), and this best accounts for 'Michael' being used in the nominative in Rev. 12.7 in allusion to the same Daniel text.

Likewise, οὐκ plus the aorist ἴσχυσεν ('they were not strong enough') in Rev. 12.8 may be regarded as reflecting Semitic style,[73] but

70. Contra Charles, *Revelation*, I, p. 322; Thompson, *Semitic Syntax*, p. 62, notes that a nominative is the subject of an articular genitival infinitive in listings of Hoskier's variant readings of 4.11, 5.3, 9.6 and 12.2 (see Hoskier, *Concerning the Text of the Apocalypse*, II, *in loc.*).

71. So Charles, *Revelation*, I, p. 322; Mussies, *Morphology*, p. 96; Thompson, *Semitic Syntax*, pp. 60-63; Blass and Debrunner, *Greek Grammar of the New Testament*, § 400, 7-8; cf. Moule, *Idiom Book*, p. 129.

72. Cf. Thompson, *Semitic Syntax*, p. 61, and Robertson, *Grammar of the Greek New Testament*, p. 1066.

73. As contends Thompson, *Semitic Syntax*, pp. 40-41, and similarly Charles, *Revelation*, I, pp. 324-25.

it is more precisely the result of an explicit allusion to Dan. 7.21 (beginning in v. 7b; cf. MT, and Theodotion [ἴσχυσεν]),[74] which underscores the presence of the Dan. 10.20 allusion. In both instances of Rev. 12.7-8 the same wording of the Old Testament text is preserved, despite reflecting somewhat awkward (in the case of 12.8) or unusual Greek syntax (in the case of 12.7), in order to highlight for the reader the Daniel background.

e. *Revelation 20.2*: ἐκράτησεν τὸν δράκοντα, ὁ ὄφις ὁ ἀρχαῖος'. The nominative phrase ὁ ὄφις ὁ ἀρχαῖος in 20.2 is a solecism (so A 1678 1778 2080), since following the accusative τὸν δράκοντα it should also be accusative. The irregularity could be understood as the nominative of appellation, but probably is not, since there is no early extant evidence of the existence of such a name for the Devil (*Sib. Or.* 5.29 identifies Nero as 'a direful serpent'; *b. Soṭ.* 9.b and *b. Sanh.* 29.a call the Devil respectively 'the primeval serpent' and 'the ancient serpent'). Furthermore, both ὄφις and ἀρχαῖος are declined according to the various cases elsewhere in the New Testament, even when referring to the Devil (e.g. note Rev. 12.9, 15 where the nominative ὄφις is used and then in 12.14 the genitive form is used, all with reference to the Devil). The reason for writing an original nominative is to conform the name to the same nominative phrase in 12.9 (ὁ δράκων...<u>ὄφις ὁ ἀρχαῖος</u>), thus identifying the passage even further with 12.7-11.[75]

This signposting function of the solecism fits with our observations of other solecisms throughout the book which have the same function, usually with respect to Old Testament allusions. Such a grammatical irregularity in this passage is also designed to attract the reader to the earlier occurrence of Satan's title in 12.9; the device apparently had its desired effect on later scribes, as testified to by MSS 051. 2030. 2377 𝔐K syh, which add the phrase ο πλανων την οικουμενην ολην after ὁ Σατανᾶς in order to conform the passage yet more with the wording of the ch. 12 text, which has the identical phrase. Together with reference to Rev. 12.9, the phrase in Rev. 20.2 may include allusion to Genesis 3, where the precise nominative form ὁ ὄφις occurs four times (and τῷ ὄφει twice), to which Rev. 12.9 alludes. The striking change to the nominative in 20.2 may highlight the Genesis 3 background more,

74. Cf. also Charles, *Revelation*, I, pp. 324-25.
75. Cf. the somewhat different reasoning of Metzger, *Textual Commentary*, p. 764, which would still lead to the same conclusion.

which may be made explicit by the directly following addition of 'ancient' (ἀρχαῖος also in the nominative).

2. *Solecisms Involving an Irregular Use of the Nominative Case or of Gender in an Introductory Participial Form of λέγω*

a. *Revelation 4.1*: ἡ φωνὴ ἡ πρώτη ἣν ἤκουσα ὡς σάλπιγγος λαλούσης μετ᾽ ἐμοῦ λέγων. The participle λαλούσης ('speaking') should be accusative in concord with ἣν, which itself is a relative pronoun referring back to ἡ φωνή, 'the voice'. Later scribes changed λαλούσης to an accusative in line with ἣν (e.g. ℵ gig Prim Ambr); others changed it to a nominative, apparently intending to conform it to the nominative φωνὴ preceding the accusative relative (e.g. 2329 *pc*[76]). Despite these notable attempts to correct the text, the irregularity of 4.1 is intentional. For the rationale, especially with respect to the unusual genitive participle as an indicator of an allusion to Exod. 19.16-19, see 1.10b-11, where the feminine participle λεγούσης ('saying') has been assimilated to the genitive case of the feminine σάλπιγγος ('trumpet'), though its antecedent appears to be the feminine, accusative φωνήν ('voice'). Therefore, in 1.10-11 λεγούσης is out of concord with φωνήν, since the former is genitive and the latter is accusative. The irregular assimilation of λεγούσης to σάλπιγγος may be intended to highlight the trumpet sound of the voice in order to underscore even more the Exodus 19 background (e.g. LXX), where Moses and Israel did not precisely hear Yahweh's voice as great but 'the voice of the trumpet sounded great' (Exod. 19.16) and 'the voices of the trumpet were going on very much louder' (Exod. 19.19).[77] Therefore, the same syntactical phenomenon of 1.10-11 has been repeated in 4.1.

In addition, the following participle, λέγων in Rev. 4.1, should be feminine nominative in line with φωνή, but is masculine (scribes tried to conform it accordingly to the feminine λέγουσα: ℵ¹𝔐ᴬ). Many grammarians see the use of the nominative λέγων probably as a Semitism, representing the indeclinable לֵאמֹר, as it does in the LXX; see likewise 5.11-12; 11.1, 15; 14.6-7 (see on 14.7 below).[78] Porter acknowledges

---

76. See further Hoskier, *Concerning the Text of the Apocalypse*, II, p. 120, for additional MSS supporting both changes.

77. For further analysis of the solecism in 1.10-11, especially with respect to the legitimacy of categorizing the phraseology as a 'solecism', see Beale, *Book of Revelation, in loc.*, excursus on 1.10-11.

78. E.g. Moulton, Howard and Turner, *Grammar*, III, p. 315.

'at most' only 'LXX enhancement', pointing out that all periods of Greek use λέγων this way;[79] however, his evidence is fragmentary. The use is probably better referred to as an intentional stylistic Septuagintalism[80] (here and throughout the book), since of the 870 times the infinitive construct לֵאמֹר occurs in the MT, 770 are rendered in the LXX by λέγων,[81] and because the word is always used in Revelation in conjunction with an Old Testament allusion. Here, the Septuagintal idiom further attracts attention to the Exodus 19 allusion, especially since it introduces the phrase 'come up [ἀνάβα]', which likely alludes to God's command to Moses in Exod. 19.24, 'come up' (ἀνάβηθι); an allusion to Dan. 2.28-29, 45 also directly follows in Rev. 4.1.[82]

M. Wilcox has observed that, as in the LXX, the expression 'saying' (λέγων, λέγουσα) introduces direct speech in the Babatha Archive, which is a document dating at the end of the first century AD where Aramaic is rendered into Greek.[83] In the LXX the Greek λέγων is a translation of לֵאמֹר and in the Babatha Archive it is a rendering of Aramaic לְמֵימַר, and it is likely not a Septuagintalism in the Archive. In this light, Wilcox cautions against assuming that λέγων in the New

79. Porter, *Verbal Aspect in the Greek of the New Testament*, pp. 138-39.

80. There is debate about the distinction between a Semitism and a Septuagintalism. A viable definition of 'Semitism' is an 'un-Greek' construction produced by an overly literal rendering of either a Hebrew or Aramaic source, whether oral or written. A 'Septuagintalism' is discerned by recognizing both a deviation from idiomatic Greek and from Semitic constructions. A 'Septuagintalism is a construction in the LXX of prominence disproportionate to other Hellenistic Greek usage' (Porter, *Verbal Aspect in the Greek of the New Testament*, p. 118, where also possible examples of Septuagintalisms or Septuagintal enhancements are discussed: e.g. pp. 120-26, 133, 138-39). In particular, the clearest Septuagintalisms are those syntactical peculiarities that are not dependent on or imitative of Semitic syntax but reflect language, 'used to render Semitic constructions into Greek in one of the translation styles in the Septuagint' (D.D. Schmidt, 'Semitisms and Septuagintalisms in the Book of Revelation', *NTS* 37 [1991], pp. 592-603 (594), upon which discussion in this note is also broadly based.). On the distinction between a Semitism and a stylistic Septuagintalism, see further Beale, *Book of Revelation*, Introduction ('The Grammar of the Apocalypse').

81. Porter, *Verbal Aspect in the Greek of the New Testament*, p. 138.

82. Cf. Swete, *Apocalypse*, p. 66, and Beckwith, *Apocalypse of John*, p. 495, who see λέγων as masculine because of the author's attempt to align gender with the male person behind the voice (φωνή).

83. Wilcox, 'Aramaic Background of the New Testament', pp. 367-68.

Testament as an introduction to direct discourse is always a Septuagintalism, but could be from Hebrew or Aramaic influence.[84]

A Septuagintal influence in the present case of Rev. 4.1, however, is further confirmed from the consideration of the same kind of solecism below in Rev. 11.15 and 14.7 (on which see below).

b. *Revelation 11.15*: ἐγένοντο φωναὶ μεγάλαι ἐν τῷ οὐρανῷ λέγοντες. Some MSS read the masculine participle λέγοντες (A 2053. 2351 𝔐ᴬ), while others have the feminine λέγουσαι (𝔓⁴⁷ ℵ C 051. 1006. 1611. 1841. 2329. 2344 𝔐ᴷ). It is hard to decide the original reading on external grounds since good witnesses are divided in attestation. However, the masculine reading is certainly the most difficult and best explains how the feminine developed. There would have been more of a scribal tendency to change the masculine to the feminine in order to bring the participle into agreement with the preceding feminine φωναὶ μεγάλαι, which is the subject of the participle. This lack of concord is a characteristic feature of the Apocalypse (see below), and it is always accompanied with scribal tendencies to smooth out the awkwardness. An original masculine may have resulted from John's understanding of the voices as emanating from masculine beings.[85]

Alternatively, this could be an instance of the indeclinable form being equivalent to the Semitic לאמר. As such, it could be a stylistic Septuagintalism, serving to introduce the Old Testament allusion, attracting attention to it through its irregular Greek grammatical form. In this respect, interestingly, λέγοντες also introduces the Song of Moses (Exod. 15.1: 'they spoke, *saying*'), which is significant, since part of that Song is alluded to in Rev. 11.15 (on which see below): cf. Exod. 15.18, κύριος βασιλεύων τὸν αἰῶνα καὶ ἐπ' αἰῶνα. The same participial form is also found earlier in Daniel 2 as part of an introductory question that the entire revelatory dream of Daniel 2 be made known (Dan. 2.7 [LXX]: 'they answered a second time, *saying*'). This is relevant since the prophecy of Dan. 2.44 (Theodotion), ἀναστήσει ὁ θεὸς τοῦ οὐρανοῦ βασιλείαν ἥτις εἰς τοὺς αἰῶνας, may also be evoked by the phrase ἐγένετο ἡ βασιλεία...τοῦ κυρίου...βασιλεύσει εἰς τοὺς

---

84. In response to Wilcox, see Beale, *Book of Revelation*, Introduction ('The Grammar of the Apocalypse').

85. Cf. Robertson, *General Epistles and the Revelation of John*, p. 384; Stuart, *Apocalypse*, II, p. 240; note mention of the elders in v. 16 and the introduction of their praise in v. 17a with λέγοντες.

αἰῶνας τῶν αἰώνων at the conclusion of Rev. 11.15 (cf. also Dan. 7.14, 27). The redundant לֵאמֹר (directly following a verb of speaking) is translated hundreds of times in the LXX by λέγων, λέγοντες, and λέγουσα (often indeclinable), and the same phenomenon occurs in Rev. 5.9; 6.10; 7.2-3, 10, 13; 14.18; 15.3; 17.1; 18.2, 15-16, 18; 19.17; 21.9.[86] Especially striking is the observation of Rev. 15.3, where the redundant expression ᾄδουσιν τὴν ᾠδὴν Μωυσέως... λέγοντες (also virtually identical to Rev. 5.9) directly alludes to the Song of Moses in Exod. 15.1, demonstrating that this precise Old Testament passage is clearly in John's mind elsewhere in the book.

c. *Revelation 14.(6-)7*: (εἶδον ἄλλον ἄγγελον . . . ἔχοντα εὐαγγέλιον) λέγων ἐν φωνῇ μεγάλῃ. The original introductory λέγων in Rev. 14.7 has been changed to λέγοντα by some scribes in order to harmonize with the preceding accusative ἔχοντα, which also describes the angel in v. 6 (so 𝔓[47] 051. 1611. 2053). λέγων could well be in the nominative because it may represent the indeclinable לֵאמֹר,[87] or, more likely, the Septuagintal rendering of the Hebrew typically by a Greek nominative, as in 4.1; 5.11-12; 11.1, 15; (see discussion on 4.1 above at Chapter 5, sect. C.2.a.). This may be a stylistic enhancement from the Septuagint in order to signal to the hearer/reader that the background for v. 7 is to be sought in the Greek Old Testament of Daniel 4, which is alluded to in Rev. 14.6-7. It is appropriate that λέγων introduces an allusion to Daniel 4, since λέγων conspicuously introduces an almost identical angelic command to Nebuchadnezzar to 'give glory to the Most High' in Dan. 4.34 (LXX):

---

86. So Thompson, *Semitic Syntax*, p. 70; for statistics of LXX occurrence see Porter, *Verbal Aspect in the Greek of the New Testament*, pp. 138-39, who also contends that parallels of the pleonasm occur in 'all periods of Greek', though he has not shown it was a much used idiom in all periods, as in the LXX; nevertheless, his conclusion that the pleonasm could be a 'well-accepted Greek idiom enhanced by the LXX' is an acceptable qualification of Thompson (see also on the discussion of 4.1 above).

87. Moulton, Howard and Turner, *Grammar*, II, p. 454; Moulton, Howard and Turner, *Grammar*, III, p. 315; Moulton, Howard and Turner, *Grammar*, IV, p. 155; cf. M. Zerwick, *Biblical Greek* (Scripta Pontificii Instituti Biblici, 114; Rome: Pontifical Biblical Institute, 1963), § 14.

Daniel 4.34 (LXX)	Revelation 14.6-7
ἰδοὺ ἄγγελος εἷς ἐκάλεσέ με ἐκ τοῦ οὐρανοῦ λέγων, Ναβουχοδονοσορ, δούλευσον τῷ θεῷ... δὸς δόξαν τῷ ὑψίστῳ ('behold, an angel called me from heaven, saying, "Nebuchadnezzar, serve God... give glory to the Most High"'). LXX of Dan. 4.37a expands on v. 34 partly by the following wording: ἀπὸ τοῦ φόβου αὐτοῦ τρόμος εἴληφέ με ('from *fear of him* trembling gripped me'). Theodotion of Dan. 4.14 also has ἐφώνησεν ἐν ἰσχύι ('he [an angel] cried loudly')!	εἶδον ἄλλον ἄγγελον... ἐν μεσουρανήματι... λέγων ἐν φωνῇ μεγάλῃ, Φοβήθητε τὸν θεὸν καὶ δότε αὐτῷ δόξαν ('I saw another angel... in mid-heaven... saying in a great voice, "fear God and give to him glory"').

The close parallels point to the likelihood that λέγων is not a general Semitism nor merely a general Septuagintal stylistic enhancement but is actually part of the allusion to Dan. 4.34 (LXX). Therefore, the more precise reason that λέγων is in the nominative instead of accusative is to maintain part of the Old Testament's exact grammatical form in order to create 'syntactical dissonance', so that the hearer/reader would be alerted to recognize more easily the allusion to Daniel 4.

That 14.6-7 alludes to Dan. 4.34 (LXX, not Theodotion) receives striking confirmation from the recognition that 14.6-8 is also based on a series of expressions from Daniel 4 about Nebuchadnezzar:[88]

(1)   an angel commands him to 'give glory to the Most High' (δὸς δόξαν τῷ ὑψίστῳ, Dan. 4.34, LXX; and for the notion of 'fearing' God, see v. 37a);

(2)   the king gives 'praise to the one having made the four-part cosmos' (αἰνῶ τῷ κτίσαντι τὸν οὐρανὸν καὶ τὴν γῆν καὶ τὰς θαλάσσας καὶ τοὺς ποταμούς, Dan. 4.37, LXX);

(3)   the angelic declaration to humanity through the fourfold formula of universality ('every nation and tribe and tongue and people') is based on the same repeated formula in Daniel, two

88. See Beale, 'Text of Daniel in the Apocalypse', pp. 541-42; cf. W. Altink, '1 Chronicles 16:8-36 as Literary Source for Revelation 14:6-7', *AUSS* 22 (1984), pp. 187-96, who attempts to propose 1 Chron. 16.8-36 as background.

of which occur in the LXX of Dan. 4.1, 37b (see, e.g., also Rev. 5.9);

(4)   the use of 'hour' (ὥρα) as the time of the latter-day judgment is based on the repeated eschatological use of the same word in Daniel, which is unique to the remainder of Old Testament usage; the approaching time of the Babylonian king's judgment is described as an 'hour' (Dan. 4.17a, LXX).[89] The closest verbal parallel from Daniel for the phrase 'the hour of his judgment came' (ἦλθεν ἡ ὥρα τῆς κρίσεως αὐτοῦ) in Rev. 14.7 is Dan. 11.45, LXX: 'the hour of his end will come', ἥξει ὥρα τῆς συντελείας αὐτοῦ), which refers to the final judgment of God's end-time opponent (cf. also Ezek. 7.7; 22.3);

(5)   both passages mention 'Babylon the Great' (see Dan. 4.27 of the MT = 4.30 of the LXX and Theodotion; so Rev. 1.8).

3. Solecisms Involving an Irregular Use of Gender in Adjectival Forms

a. *Revelation 12.5*: ἔτεκεν υἱὸν ἄρσεν. The masculine υἱὸν followed by the neuter pronominal adjective ἄρσεν ('male son') appears to be irregular, since adjectives should be in the same gender as nouns which they modify. Could John's penchant for alluding to the Old Testament be helpful in explaining this problem?

The language of the woman 'bearing the male child' is reminiscent of Isa. 7.14, 66.7 and Mic. 5.3-4 (cf. 12.2).[90] Allusion specifically to Isa. 66.7 is evident from the following observations:

(1)   the verbal similarity between 12.2, 5 (ὠδίνουσα...τεκεῖν... καὶ ἔτεκεν υἱὸν ἄρσεν) and Isa. 66.7 (ὠδίνουσαν τεκεῖν... καὶ ἔτεκεν ἄρσεν; this clause is repeated in 66.8, with ἄρσεν being replaced by τὰ παιδία);

(2)   the combination of 'son' and 'male' in Rev. 12.5 is based, at least in part, on the close parallelism of Isa. 66.7 with 66.8 in the MT:

Isaiah 6.7	Isaiah 66.8
'she travailed, she brought forth . . . she gave birth to a male [זכר].'	'Zion *travailed, she also brought forth her sons* [pl. of בן].'

---

89. For fuller discussion of the Old Testament background of ὥρα and its use in Revelation see Beale, 'Text of Daniel in the Apocalypse', pp. 541-42.

90. BAGD, p. 110, prefer Isa. 66.7.

In addition to the verbal parallelism, the singular 'male' of
66.7 is replaced in 66.8 with the plural 'sons', both apparently
referring to Israel.

(3)   The phrase in Isaiah is part of a prophecy figuratively describing that Jerusalem will be like a reborn child when God restores Israel from captivity (see Isa. 66:8-14) and brings about
a new creation (cf. Isa. 66.22; 65.17-23). Allusion to an Isaiah
restoration and new creation prophecy here anticipates the
even clearer allusion to an Isaiah restoration promise later in
ch. 12 (see 12.14) and to the new creation allusion to Isa.
65.17 in Rev. 21.1. Isaiah's national promise is applied here to
Christ as an individual, presumably because he is the ideal
Israel and represents the nation as their king, as the Psalm 2
enthronement citation, which also occurs in 12.5, indicates.[91]
Indeed, the Psalm 2 reference is applied both to Christ and the
believer in 2.26-27 (cf. the identification of the reign of both
in 1.5-6, 9; 5.5-12)!

(4)   The depiction of the woman as having 'fled' (ἐξέφυγε) and
consequently successfully bearing offspring (Isa. 66.7) best
explains the image in Rev. 12.6 of 'the woman [who] fled
[ἔφυγεν]', ensuring the welfare of her offspring (so 12.13-17).

John may intentionally have the neuter pronominal adjective ἄρσεν
(instead of the masculine) irregularly modify the masculine υἱόν. As
observed above in the textual comparisons of Revelation 12 and Isaiah
66, the unusual grammar reflects the actual wording of the Isaiah text,
where *both* the mention of 'male' and the corporate plural of 'son' (or
'child') occur in synonymous phrases expressing Jerusalem bearing in
travail. That John has not made a careless grammatical blunder is clear
from 12.13, where the masculine τὸν ἄρσενα *is correctly* used.[92]

On the other hand, some do not see a grammatical incongruity in
the use of ἄρσεν, but view it as a noun in apposition to 'son', further

---

91. See *Midr. Ps.* 2.9, which interprets the Son of Ps. 2.7 and the son of man in
Dan. 7.13 as Israel, and equates the figures of the two texts with the nation as God's
'first-born' in Exod. 4.22.

92. Cf. also Torrey, *Apocalypse of John*, p. 51, and Blass and Debrunner, *Greek
Grammar of the New Testament*, § 136, who have concluded independently that the
difficult neuter ἄρσεν is to be accounted for as an allusion to Isa. 66.7 of the LXX.

describing it.[93] J. Fekkes thinks this finds possible justification in 12.13 where ἄρσενα is used substantivally. But this still leaves unanswered the question why the neuter occurs in 12.5 and masculine in 12.13; in addition, the substantival use normally would be articular, as in 12.13. Furthermore, in other combinations of υἱός plus ἄρσην, which are rare, the latter is masculine and adjectival, and υἱός has the general sense of child, that is, 'male child': Tob. 6.12 (Siniaticus; see Göttingen *Septuaginta* apparatus); CPR 28.12;[94] PSI 9.1039.36.[95]

b. *Revelation 14.19*: ἔβαλεν εἰς τὴν ληνὸν τοῦ θυμοῦ τοῦ θεοῦ τὸν μέγαν. Rev. 14.19 refers to the 'great winepress' as part of imagery expressing divine judgment. The word ληνός ('winepress') is feminine but followed by an irregular masculine modifier: τὴν ληνὸν... τὸν μέγαν ('*the great* winepress').

Mussies suggests that John's unusual shift to the masculine τὸν μέγαν is due to conforming it to the 'more important component of the word group'[96] (if so, it would be conformed to τοῦ θυμοῦ or τοῦ θεοῦ). Lenski suggests that the adjective 'the great' is in the masculine (τὸν μέγαν) instead of the feminine to emphasize the appositional phrase,[97] while Beckwith conjectures that the author put τὸν μέγαν in the accusative as a result of having been so caught up in focusing on the meaning of the symbol as expressed in the apposition.[98] A weakening in the distinction of gender also reflects Hebrew style.[99] Some MSS (𝔓[47]

93. So J. Fekkes, *Isaiah and Prophetic Traditions*, pp. 183-84, who lists others in agreement.

94. Cf. J.H. Moulton and G. Milligan, *The Vocabulary of the Greek New Testament* (Grand Rapids: Eerdmans, 1972), p. 79.

95. LSJ, p. 1847. The references to Tobit, CPR, and PSI are cited in Fekkes, *Isaiah and Prophetic Traditions*, p. 184. There are apparently only three other extant references in Greek (so TLG): Hippolytus, *De antichristo* 60.8 and 61.10, both of which quote Rev. 12.5 and have υἱὸν ἄρσενα, perhaps following the secondary textual tradition which changes the neuter to masculine, seeing ἄρσενα as adjectival. Also, Theodoret, *Interp. Jer.* 81.616.34, who cites Jer. 20.15 (MT = 'male–son'; LXX = ἄρσεν) as υἱὸς ἄρσην ('male–child'), again with ἄρσην functioning as an adjective.

96. Mussies, *Morphology*, p. 139.

97. R.C.H. Lenski, *The Interpretation of St. John's Revelation* (Minneapolis: Augsburg, 1963), p. 450.

98. Beckwith, *Apocalypse of John*, p. 664.

99. *Gesenius' Hebrew Grammar* (eds. E. Kautzsch and A.E. Cowley; Oxford: Clarendon Press, 1910), § 110 *k*, 135 *o*, 144 *a*, 145 *p, t, u*.

1611 *pc*) change τὸν μέγαν to του μεγαλου in order to make it conform with the immediately preceding τοῦ θυμοῦ τοῦ θεου reading either 'the great wrath of God' or 'the wrath of the great God'. Some MSS (e.g. 181. 424. 468) omit μέγας altogether, presumably because of the lack of concord with anything which precedes or because of the separation from ληνός, or both.

Revelation 14.19 has several close Old Testament parallels. Cf. Joel 4.13b, πατεῖτε, διότι πλήρης ἡ ληνός, with Rev. 14.20a, ἐπατήθη ἡ ληνὸς...καὶ ἐξῆλθεν αἷμα ἐκ τῆς ληνοῦ. In connection with the treading of the wine press, cf. also LXX Lam. 1.15 (ληνὸν ἐπάτησεν Κύριος) and LXX Isa. 63.2-3: 'Why are your garments red...as though fresh from a *wine press* [πατητοῦ ληνοῦ]? [*I am*] *full of that which is trodden* (πλήρης καταπεπατημένης)...*I trampled* [κατεπάτησα] them in my fury... and brought down their *blood* [αἷμα] to the earth'.

Could this Old Testament background shed light on the problem of the feminine ληνός in Rev. 14.19 being followed by the discordant masculine modifier: τὴν ληνὸν...τὸν μέγαν (though ℵ for 1006. 1841. 1854. 2053. al. gig syᵖʰ correct with the feminine form την μεγαλην)? The feminine is the typical construction in biblical literature, though the masculine of ληνός occurs rarely, as in Isa. 63.2,[100] which may have influenced the use of the same gender of τὸν μέγαν in 14.19 (Gen. 30.38, 41, also contain a masc. form of ληνός). In fact, Stuart suggests that to τὸν μέγαν at the end of v. 19 should be added an elliptical masculine ληνόν, so that the final clause becomes epexegetical of the earlier τὴν ληνὸν, which could be even closer to the thought of the LXX of Isaiah (see further below).[101] Laughlin notes that the feminine τὴν ληνὸν followed by the masculine τὸν μέγαν [ληνόν] is a construction suggested by the similar pattern of the Hebrew feminine פורה ('wine-press') followed by the masculine pronominal suffix (appended to a verb) in Isa. 63.2-3: 'I have trodden the *winepress* [פורה] ... And *I will tread them* [ואראמסם] in My anger...'[102] John's addition of 'great' to Isaiah's 'winepress' imagery of the Hebrew text could be following early exegetical tradition which also added similar intensifying adjectives: note 'full' (πλήρης) in the LXX of Isa. 63.3a above; the same wording of the LXX Isaiah text could read v. 3a as part of the question begun in v. 2: 'Why...is your raiment as from a trodden winepress, [which is]

100. See above, and Robertson, *Grammar of the Greek New Testament*, p. 253.
101. Stuart, *Apocalypse*, II, p. 303.
102. Laughlin, *The Solecisms of the Apocalypse*, p. 13.

full of that which is trodden?' The Targumic version reads: 'why will...plains *gush forth* like wine in the press? Behold, as grapes trodden in the press, so shall slaughter *increase...*'

Conclusion

Various explanations have been proposed for the syntactical solecisms of the Apocalypse, prominent among which are: (1) that they are the result of carelessness or ignorance; (2) that they are due to various degrees of Semitic or Septuagintal influence generally; (3) that they are mere reflections of somewhat unusual but attested Hellenistic Greek; and (4) that many are explainable as being the result of the phenomenon sometimes referred to as *constructio ad sensum*.

This chapter has attempted to offer a new approach, though it is to be considered as a sub-category of the second alternative above, which has attempted to solve the solecism problem by turning to a Semitic or Septuagintal background *in general*. Evidently unrecognized for the most part previously, a significant number of the syntactical irregularities, occur in the midst of specific Old Testament allusions. A significant number of the solecisms have been analyzed in the preceding segment of this essay which, it has been contended, are representative of others for which there was not space to study. In this respect, a number of the expressions appear irregular because John is carrying over the exact grammatical form of the Old Testament wording in order to create 'syntactical dissonance', which causes the reader/hearer to pause and increases their chances of recognizing the unusual wording to be an Old Testament allusion. Sometimes the precise grammar from the Old Testament passage is not retained, but stylistic Semitisms or, more usually, Septuagintalisms are incorporated in order to create the dissonance, so that the fuller clause of which the solecism is a part can more quickly be recognized as an Old Testament allusion.

Excursus to Solecisms in the Apocalypse as Signals for the Presence of Old Testament Allusions

The following are plausible examples of further instances of solecisms which point to the existence of Old Testament allusions, but which are not as clear-cut as the above examples. In contrast to many of the above examples, all of the syntactical irregularities below do not correspond to a particular grammatical form of the allusion in its Old Testament context, but, nevertheless, the awkwardness may still be generally intended as a way to cause the reader to pause and to draw attention to the Old Testament reference.

Revelation 1.13, 15

The accusative υἱὸν ('son') following ὅμοιον ('like') is a solecism since the dative usually follows.[103] Accordingly, scribes changed υἱὸν to the dative υιω (A C 1006. 1854. 2053. 2062. 2351. 𝔐ᴬ), whereas the original, harder accusative reading has been retained by ℵ 1841. 2050. 2329 𝔐ᴷ. The identical phenomenon occurs in 14.14 with the same Dan. 7.13 'son of man' allusion.[104] Mussies explains that the accusative υἱὸν has been attracted to its complement ὅμοιον as a stylistic imitation of the Semitic כ ('like'), which formed one word with a following substantive.[105] Just as possibly, the irregularity may be designed to get the reader's attention and direct it back to the Old Testament (in this case Daniel), as in Rev. 1.4-5.

Could it be also that the genitive πεπυρωμένης ('fired') following the dative καμίνῳ ('furnace') is an irregular construction designed similarly to attract attention to the Old Testament allusion repeated three times in Theodotion of Dan. 3.21, 23 and 26 (93), where the word for 'fire' and 'burning' following 'furnace' is also in the genitive: τῆς καμίνου τοῦ πυρὸς τῆς καιομένης (though in Daniel the noun form πῦρ occurs instead of the participial form, and this is intensified by a genitive participial form of καίω)? Scribes tried to correct the solecism by changing to πεπυρωμενω (ℵ 2050. 2053. 2062 pc) in line with καμίνῳ or to πεπυρωμενοι (𝔐) in line with the subject of the clause. It is also possible that the genitival participle is a genitive absolute ('his feet were like bronze as when it is fired in a furnace').[106]

Revelation 3.12

The appositional clause ἡ καταβαίνουσα ('which descends') is nominative but should be genitive, since it modifies τῆς καινῆς Ἰερουσαλὴμ

---

103. Turner, *Style*, p. 150.

104. An observation which J. Schmid sees as favoring the originality of the solecism, though the very difficulty of the reading itself enhances this judgment (J. Schmid, *Studien zur Geschichte des griechischen Apokalypse-Textes* [3 vols.; Münchener Theologische Studien; Munich: K. Zink, 1955]), II, p. 249.

105. Mussies, *Morphology*, p. 139.

106. So Thomas, *Revelation 1-7*, p. 102.

('of the New Jerusalem').[107] The irregularity, however, this time is neither a Septuaginalism nor correspondent with anything specifically in the Old Testament text (though, could Isa. 64.1 have influenced a nominative construction: 'Oh that you would tear the heavens [and] *come down*'?); nevertheless, the irregular syntax may still be used intentionally to draw attention to the Old Testament allusion, as observed above already several times in chs. 1–2 and elsewhere throughout the book (John maintains concord in the almost identical phrase in 21.2). In this case, the indeclinable name Jerusalem (standing in a genitival position) is part of an allusion to Isa. 62.2 and 65.15 (on the validity of the allusion see discussion of 2.17 and 3.12 at Chapter 2, sect. D.5.a above). In Isa. 62.1-6 redeemed Israel of the future is referred to figuratively as 'Jerusalem' which God 'will call...by a new name' (cf. similarly 65.15-19, where Jerusalem also is equated figuratively with God's servants, who 'will be called a new name').

Grammatically zealous copyists smoothed out the syntactical incongruity either by altering the nominative phrase to the genitive της καταβαινουσης (א²) or by changing it to a relative pronoun plus finite verb (η καταβαινει, 'which descends').

Revelation 5.6a
The masculine participle ἔχων ('having') is to be preferred over the neuter participle (εχον) on the basis of external MS evidence (only 𝔐 supports the neuter reading); furthermore, the masculine is preferable to the neuter because it would be more likely that it would have been changed to a neuter (rather than the other way around) to conform with the neuter construction ἀρνίον ἑστηκὸς ὡς ἐσφαγμένον ('a lamb standing as slain'). The reason for the abrupt change may be because the lamb represents a masculine person (Jesus), but, if this were the case, why the directly preceding two participles have not also been changed from neuter to masculine is more difficult to explain.[108]

The awkward syntax may not be due to a mere *constructio ad sensum* but may also serve to indicate an Old Testament allusion to Dan. 7.7, especially in the light of the following analysis of the nature of the allusion (though the grammatical form of Rev. 5.6 is not identical to that of Dan. 7.7). The lamb's 'seven horns' may be linked to the beast's horns

---

107. E.g. see Blass and Debrunner, *Greek Grammar of the New Testament*, § 136 (1).
108. See also Thomas, *Revelation 1–7*, p. 392.

of Daniel 7. In particular, the lamb may mimic the beast with horns in Dan. 7.7-8, 20, 24, since the lamb appears to be a substitute image for the son of man in Dan. 7.13 (one could even possibly discern seven remaining horns on the beast in Dan. 7.8 after three had been uprooted from the prior ten).[109] The unusual ἔχων may be a way of attracting attention to εἶχε of Dan. 7.7 (LXX): the beast '*had* ten horns'. In Rev. 5.6 ἔχων may even be a verbal use of the participle (the same point could likewise be made about the neuter εχον): 'he had seven horns', which is reflected in some Armenian versions and an Arabic version (which have the equivalent of the aorist ἔσχε ['he had']).[110]

The same kind of mimicking phenomena employing the metaphor of horns occurs in *1 En.* 90.9-13, 16, *T. Jos.* 19.6-8, and in *Gen. R.* 99.2, in the last of which the descendant of Judah as a lion (Gen. 49) is said to defeat the Babylonian lion of Dan. 7.4, and in the following lines the descendant of Joseph with horns (Deut. 33.17) is said to oppose Rome, which is portrayed with the horns of the fourth beast in Dan. 7.20. In Rev. 5.6 ironic parody is expressed by portraying the Messiah in his defeat of the enemy by means of the same imagery of Daniel 7 which is applied to the beast in describing his defeat of the saints. The same way in which the enemy would try to subdue God's people would be used by God to subdue his enemy, even to the extent of resembling the enemy's likeness. This mimicking figuratively emphasizes divine justice, which often mocks those who attempt to thwart God's purposes (e.g. Ps. 2.1-5). The Lamb's coming and receiving of authority enhances this idea, since it is also an ironic parody of the Danielic beasts' coming and reception of authority in Dan. 7.3-7 and in Revelation 13, as confirmed from observing that the reception of authority in the case of each beast and the Lamb results in universal sovereignty (cf. 13.7b, 14-16 with 5.9b).

The plausibility of this parody is increased with the mention of the beast who had a *slain* head, which had been healed (13.3), and the beast with 'horns like a lamb' (13.11), which show that the beast also mimics Christ for his devious purposes. The Lamb may be portrayed as standing on the sea or beside it, since both are directly before the divine throne (cf. 4.6; 5.6-7), and the saints 'who had come off victorious from the beast...[are] standing on the sea of glass' (15.2). Therefore,

109. This possibility was made known to me through an oral communication by R.T. France in 1978, though he gave no evaluation of it.

110. So Hoskier, *Concerning the Text of the Apocalypse*, II, p. 149.

the Lamb is on or by the sea to indicate that he had defeated the satanic beast in his own watery abode.

This suggestion about the Old Testament background of Rev. 5.6 as an explanation of the awkward ἔχων is made more attractive by the following observations: (1) the notion that the 'sea' in 4.6 is partially allusive to the sea in Dan. 7.3 and (2) that the overall structure of Revelation 4–5 is modelled upon the outline of Dan. 7.9-27.[111] Therefore, despite the fact that the grammatical form of Rev. 5.6 is not identical to that of Dan. 7.7, its grammatical incongruity still may serve to jolt the reader and draw attention to Daniel in a way that using a regular grammatical form would not have done.

Revelation 5.12
The participle λέγοντες ('saying') is masculine but should be feminine in concord with the gender of φωνὴν in v. 11 ('voice') or, more probably the feminine gender of 'myriads...and thousands'. Perhaps the form occurs because: either (1) John may view the multitudes of v. 11 as masculine persons, and now they become the focus of the action and by *constructio ad sensum* the participle is put in the masculine;[112] or (2) it is in agreement with ὁ ἀριθμὸς ('the number') as a noun of multitude;[113] or (3) possibly the form is an indeclinable Septuagintalism equivalent to the Hebrew לאמר; as can be observed elsewhere in the book, the apparently irregular gender may be an attention-getting device, drawing further attention to the Old Testament (Dan. 7.10) allusion. In addition, in Dan. 7.10 the angelic service to God is contrasted directly with that of the beast in 7.11, who spoke defiantly in a 'voice of great words' (φωνῆς τῶν λόγων τῶν μεγάλων). Could the heavenly host's 'speaking in a great voice' (λέγοντες φωνῇ μεγάλη) in Rev. 5.12 be a polemical counterpart? If so, such a use would be consistent with the same phenomenon of parody based on Dan. 7.8 which may be present in 5.6 (on which see the preceding analysis of Rev. 5.6 above).

---

111. See further Beale, 'The Problem of the Man from the Sea in IV Ezra 13', where the same Daniel parody is argued for in 4 *Ezra* 13.1ff., and Beale, *Use of Daniel*, pp. 181-228.

112. Cf. similarly Stuart, *Apocalypse*, II, p. 134.

113. Stuart, *Apocalypse*, II, p. 134.

Revelation 7.4-8

The participle ἐσφραγισμένοι ('sealed') is nominative, but should be genitive, modifying the directly preceding τῶν ἐσφραγισμένων ('of the ones sealed'). Some solve the problem by saying that the nominative participle functions as a finite passive verb, under the influence of the Aramaic use of participles as verbs.[114] A more probable reason for the grammatical awkwardness is to introduce and draw attention to the inclusio formed by δώδεκα χιλιάδες ἐσφραγισμένοι ('12,000 sealed') in v. 5a and v. 8c, which plausibly reflects a similar inclusio of the numbering of the tribes of Israel in Num. 1.19 ('he [Moses] numbered them') and 1.44 ('Moses and Aaron numbered [them]'; likewise LXX). The change to the nominative participle may even echo the passive of the verb used in 1.19 (LXX, 'were numbered') and the passive participle in 1.44 (MT, 'were numbered') at the end of the inclusio of the Numbers text.

That this analysis of the purpose of the grammatical irregularity is viable is pointed to further by R. Bauckham.[115] The 144,000 is a figurative number for the totality of the redeemed, who have been formed as an army to conduct spiritual or ironic holy war by winning the victory of faith in the midst of physical suffering (cf. 7.13-14).

According to Bauckham, the evidence for the view is primarily four-fold.[116]

(1)   The purpose of numbering for a census in the Old Testament was always for counting up the military force of the nation: e.g. Num. 1.3, 18, 20, etc.; 26.2, 4; 1 Chron. 27.23; 2 Sam. 24.1-9 (the use of a 'thousand' in Revelation 7 may also have a military connotation, as in Num. 1; 31.14, 48; etc.).[117] For example, the purpose in the wilderness was to organize a military force to conquer the promised land; likewise, when David

114. Thompson, *Semitic Syntax*, pp. 66-69.

115. Bauckham, *Climax of Prophecy*, pp. 217-29, who has argued convincingly that the numbering of Rev. 7.4-8 suggests that those numbered are an army; so also, in less-developed form, by Valentine, 'Theological Aspects of the Temple Motif', pp. 219-23.

116. The following four points by Bauckham have been summarized already at Chapter 2.A.4 above, but are restated here to underscore the presence of the Old Testament background which is relevant for the overall point being made in this segment.

117. So Boring, *Revelation*, p. 131.

took his census in 2 Samuel 24, it was for the purpose of reckoning the military strength of Israel. The repeated phrases ἐκ φυλῆς ('from the tribe of') in Rev. 7.4-8 may echo the almost identical repeated phrase ἐκ τῆς φυλῆς ('from the tribe of') from Num. 1.21, 23, etc. (in addition to Bauckham's observations, note also the phrase 'of the sons of Israel' in Num. 2.32 and the same phrase in Rev. 7.4).

(2) This is suggested further by the fact that those counted in the Old Testament were males of military age, and the 144,000 in Rev. 14.1-4 are 'male virgins'.

(3) The military census of Numbers 1 has influenced the account in 1QM of the Qumran community's understanding of the future, imminent messianic war, when they would re-conquer the land of promise. For instance, 1QM organizes the army of the Qumran sect into the traditional grouping of 12 tribes (2.2-3, 7; 3.13-14; 5.1-2; 6.10; 14.16).

(4) There is evidence that the end-time expectation of the return of the ten tribes also included a hope that they would take part in a final war to defeat decisively God's enemies (though this point is less convincing, except for the appeal to Isa. 11.14, which is preceded by reference to 'the root of Jesse', probably alluded to in Rev. 5.5). Together with Isa. 11.14, Bauckham's last point finds more support from Isa. 14.2 and Mic. 5.6-9, the latter of which refers to a 'ruler in Israel' from 'Judah', whose 'exoduses are from *the beginning*' (5.2), who will 'shepherd His flock' (5.4), which is called 'the tribes of Israel' (4.14, LXX), 'the sons of Israel' (5.3), a 'remnant … *as lambs*' and a 'remnant…*as a lion*'(5.6-7, LXX). These Old Testament prophetic descriptions behind Rev. 7.3-8 not only provide more rationale for why Judah is placed first in the tribal list but also hint at an identification of a remnant from 'every tribe of the sons of Israel' in Rev. 7.3-8 both with 5.5 and the group in 7.9ff., who are also alluded to as sheep who will be shepherded (7.17).[118]

---

118. For further interpretative implications for this approach to Rev. 7.4-8 ff., see Bauckham, *Climax of Prophecy*, pp. 217-29.

Revelation 7.9

There are three grammatical incongruities in 7.9. First, there is the re-dundant pronoun: '*which* no one was able to number *it*' (a similar re-dundancy occurring also in 7.2). This is likely a stylistic Semitism (see, e.g., Rev. 3.8 and 13.8b, and elsewhere in the book). Secondly, the sin-gular παντὸς plus singular ἔθνους (= 'every nation') is followed by discordant plural terms for groups of people (καὶ φυλῶν καὶ λαῶν καὶ γλωσσῶν), which forces the translator to understand παντὸς as a plural (= 'and all tribes and peoples and tongues'; note also the following dis-cordant plural participles). Thirdly, following the nominative participle ἑστῶτες ('standing') is the accusative περιβεβλημένους ('clothed'), which also should be nominative in line with the case of the preceding participle. Some solve the difficulty by saying that the author carries over εἶδον ('I saw') from the beginning of v. 9, so that the second par-ticiple is accusative because it is seen as the object of the initial verb. However, this does not explain why the first participle is nominative and not also accusative. Some suggest that the second participle is an accusative absolute, reflecting a Semitic verbal style, which would enhance the Old Testament color of v. 9.[119]

Bauckham asserts that Rev. 7.9 alludes precisely to the form of the patriarchal promise occurring in Gen. 17.4-6, 35.11 and 48.19, where the patriarchs are referred to as being progenitors of a multitude 'of nations'.[120] He highlights Gen. 17.4, where he sees 'a multitude of na-tions' (πλῆθος ἐθνῶν) reflected in John's 'a great multitude... from all nations' (ὄχλος πολύς... ἐκ παντὸς ἔθνους). Bauckham views the Gen-esis 17 allusion being signposted in Rev. 7.9 by the placing of 'nations' (ἔθνους) first, which is unique among the same fourfold formulae repeated elsewhere in the book (see below), and by the grammatical awkwardness setting 'nations' apart from the rest of the members of the formula. He concludes that the significance of this is that '7.9 as a reinterpretation of 7.4-8 indicates not so much the replacement of the national people of God as the abolition of its national limits', which is consistent with 21.12, 24-26, where the gates of the new Jerusalem have 'the names of the twelve tribes' and remain open for the nations to enter. Furthermore, the formula of 7.9 is set apart from the rest, since it has a mixture of singular and plural, which is unique among all the oth-ers, which either use only plurals (11.9; 17.15) or only singulars (5.9;

119. So Thompson, *Semitic Syntax*, pp. 78-79.
120. Bauckham, *Climax of Prophecy*, pp. 224-25.

13.7; 14.6). The irregularity of the redundant pronoun and the participial lack of concord may be stylistic signposts further hinting that an Old Testament allusion was to be recognized.

Closer to Rev. 7.9 than Gen. 17.4 or any other of the above Genesis promises is a textual tradition in Gen. 22.17-18: 'your seed...*which cannot be numbered because of the multitude* [ητις ουκ (εξ)αριθμηθησεται απο του πληθους][121]...and in your seed will be blessed *all the nations* [πάντα τὰ ἔθνη]. If John were alluding to this textual tradition, then he would be seeing that the blessing upon the nations which results from the multiplied Israelite seed is that the nations themselves become identified as a part of Israel.

Revelation 8.9
The solecism τὰ ἔχοντα ψυχάς ('the ones having life') occurs here, which, instead of being nominative, should be in the genitive in agreement with its antecedent τῶν κτισμάτων ('of the creatures'). The lack of agreement may be due to Semitic influence, since Hebrew had fewer declined forms than Greek. In particular, the phrase may reflect Gen. 1.20,[122] where the phrase חיה נפֶשׁ (lit., 'soul of life' = 'having a soul of life') is undeclined according to Hebrew conventions, but according to syntactical position is in apposition to the cognate accusative שֶׁרֶץ ('swarming things').

Revelation 9.14
The mention that four angels had been held back at the 'great river Euphrates' evokes the Old Testament prophecy of a northern enemy beyond the Euphrates, whom God would bring to judge sinful Israel,[123] as well as other ungodly nations around Israel.[124] In both cases, the invaders were characterized as a terrifying army on horses arising from the north.[125]

---

121. Cf. this textual variant in the LXX textual apparatus *in loc.* in J.W. Wevers (ed.), *Genesis* (Septuaginta. Vetus Testamentum Graecum Auctoritate Academiae Scientiarum Gottingensis, 1; Göttingen: Vandenhoeck & Ruprecht, 1974), Tht I 196 661.

122. So Paulien, *Decoding Revelation's Trumpets*, pp. 252-53.

123. Cf. Isa. 7.20; 8.7-8; 14.29-31; Jer. 1.14-15; 4.6-13; 6.1, 22; 10.22; 13.20; Ezek. 38.6, 15; 39.2; Joel 2.1-11, 20-25.

124. Isa. 14.31; Jer. 25.9, 26; 46–47; 50.41-42; Ezek. 26.7-11; from Israel's vantage point the Euphrates ran both north, as well as east.

125. Isa. 5.26-29; Jer. 4.6-13; 6.1, 22; 46–47; 50.41-42; Ezek. 26.7-11; 38.6, 15;

The strongest Old Testament echo comes from Jeremiah 46, which portrays the coming judgment on Egypt: the army of horsemen from the north are like serpents, innumerable locusts, having breastplates (cf. 46.4, 22-23) and being 'by the River Euphrates' (ἐπὶ τῷ ποταμῷ Εὐφράτῃ; 46[26].2; likewise 46.6, 10). In John's time the Parthian threat from beyond the Euphrates was identified with this Old Testament tradition; this invasion was also to be instigated by angels (*1 En.* 56.5-8).[126] Mention of the 'Euphrates' anticipates the battle of the sixth bowl, where the Euphrates is also mentioned.[127] Indeed, the sixth trumpet and sixth bowl describe 'the same event from different points of view'.[128]

As in the Old Testament parallels of the northern invader, so here it is God who ultimately unleashes the corrupt angelic invaders. These angels could be identified as the angelic counterparts to the wicked nations who dwelt at or north of this boundary (e.g. Dan. 10.13, 20-21). The fact that the four angels of Rev. 9.14 are at the particular locality of the Euphrates reflects the end-time expectations concerning the direction from which the final onslaught of the satanic enemy against the whole world would come.

Two characteristic solecisms occur here. The accusative masculine λέγοντα ('saying') has its antecedent in the accusative feminine φωνὴν ('voice'). The participle may be masculine in order to agree with the masculine gender of the angel (ὁ ἄγγελος) behind the voice (v. 13). Or, the irregularity may function generally to get the reader's attention and prepare them to recognize an Old Testament allusion in v. 14 (i.e., to Jeremiah 46 [= 26 in LXX]; for fuller discussion of the function of irregular participial uses of λέγω, see the discussion above in this chapter of 1.11; 4.1; 11.15; 14.7; though here the participle is accusative and not nominative, as in the above cases). The nominative ὁ ἔχων ('the one having') has its antecedent in the dative ἀγγέλῳ ('angel'). The

39.2; Hab. 1.8-9; cf. *Ass. Mos.* 3.1; LXX of Amos 7.1 pictures an army like locusts 'coming from the east'.

126. In *2 Bar.* 6 four angels, representing the Babylonians, are standing at the four corners of Jerusalem prepared to destroy the city at the appointed time.

127. A.Y. Collins, 'Apocalypse (Revelation)', in R.E. Brown, J.A. Fitzmeyer and R.E. Murphy (eds.), *The New Jerome Biblical Commentary* (Englewood Cliffs, NJ: Prentice–Hall, 1990), pp. 994-1016 (1007).

128. Collins, 'Apocalypse (Revelation)', p. 1007. On the link with the sixth bowl see further Beale, *Book of Revelation, in loc.* at 9.19.

nominative may be used because this may have been conceived of as an angelic title in John's eyes. The phrase 'the one having the trumpet' is best considered syntactically parenthetical,[129] referring back to the nominative 'the sixth trumpet angel' in v. 13a.

---

129. So Prigent, *L'Apocalypse de Saint Jean*, p. 144.

Chapter 6

THE BEARING OF THE OLD TESTAMENT ON THE INTERPRETATION OF THE MILLENNIUM IN REVELATION 20.1-7

Introduction

There are three predominant views of the millennium, though within each perspective there are wide variations of interpretation which cannot be cataloged here. Some believe that the millennium will occur after the second coming of Christ. This view is traditionally known as premillennialism.[1] Postmillennialism has held that the millennium occurs toward the end of the church age, and that Christ's climactic coming will occur at the close of the millennium. Others believe that the millennium started at Christ's resurrection and will be concluded at his final coming. This view has been called amillennialism. It is better to refer to this third view more simply as 'inaugurated millennialism',

---

1.   Most recently, J.W. Mealy has offered his own novel view of premillennialism (Mealy, *After the Thousand Years*, whose most striking points are: (1) during the thousand years all of the saints reign over a fully recreated earth (Rev. 20.4, 5b-6); (2) at the conclusion of the thousand years Satan is released from his confinement along with the dead nations of 19.15-21 who are resurrected in fulfillment of 20.5a, and, again, he deceives them so that they rebel against Christ a second time (20.5a, 7-8); (3) then both Satan and the nations are judged a second time (20.9-10); everything after 20.10 recapitulates so that (4) 20.11-12 repeats the first judgment of 19.11–20.4; (5) 20.13-15 is another version of the second judgment at the end of the millennium already described in 20.7-10; and (6) the picture of the new Jerusalem in Rev. 21 recapitulates the parousia when the reign of the saints together with God and Christ is established (cf. 19.7-9; 20.4, 5b-6). For a further summary and evaluation of Mealy's thesis see G.K. Beale 'Review Article: J.W. Mealy, *After the Thousand Years*', *EQ* 66 (1994), pp. 229-49, and note some of the following discussions below which apply to his view where it overlaps with traditional premillennialism.

since 'amillennial' is vaguer ('amillennial' literally means 'no millennium'). Postmillennialism and amillennialism have approached the passage more consistently according to a symbolic interpretation.[2]

It is important to remember the genre of Revelation in approaching Rev. 20.1-6, especially the programmatic nature of 1.1, which states the general symbolic nature of the communication from the mediating angel to John. Further, the repeated introductory 'I saw' phrases (or similar expressions) throughout the book introduce symbolic visions (e.g. see on 4.1ff.; 12.1-3; 13.1-3; 14.1; 17.1-3; etc.).[3] Since 'I saw' (εἶδον) introduces both vv. 1-3 and vv. 4-6, we can assume that there are *at least* three levels of communication in vv. 1-6: (1) a visionary level, which consists of the actual visionary experience which John had in seeing resurrected people and the other objects of his vision; (2) a referential level, which consists of the particular historical identification of the resurrected people and the other objects seen in the vision; and (3) a symbolic level, which consists of what the symbols in the vision connote about their historical referents.[4] Literal interpreters of the majority of the book, and of Rev. 20.1-6, especially among more popular commentators, formally acknowledge these distinctions in generally approaching the book's interpretation. At significant points throughout, however, including Rev. 20.1-6, they typically neglect the visionary and symbolic levels of communication by collapsing them into the referential, historical level.[5]

2. For overview of the above three millennial positions, variants within each, and a listing of commentators see Brütsch, *Die Offenbarung Jesu Christi*, II, pp. 344-58, and Walvoord, *Revelation of Jesus Christ*, pp. 282-90. For a wider survey of bibliography and millennial positions pertaining to Rev. 20 not referred to herein see Beale, *Book of Revelation, in loc.* Some premillennarians view 21.9–22.5, 14-15 as a further description of the millennium in 20.4-6, with 21.1-5 a description of the postmillennial new creation (Beasley-Murray, *Revelation*, pp. 314-18). But there is no evidence that the portrayal of the new Jerusalem in 21.9-22.5, 14-15 is a recapitulation of 20.4-6 nor that it is different from the eternal new Jerusalem just described in 21.1-5 (so also Johnson, *Revelation*, p. 580).

3. See discussion of 1.1 in Chapter 4, sect. A above.

4. These distinctions generally follow the analysis of V.S. Poythress, 'Genre and Hermeneutics in Rev 20:1-6', *JETS* 36 (1993), pp. 41-54, on which see for further discussion.

5. See further Poythress, 'Genre and Hermeneutics', pp. 49ff., particularly for examples of such an approach.

Assuming the validity of these distinctions in Rev. 20.1-6, John, for example, employs the words '1000 years', 'resurrection', and 'life' because he saw, at the *visionary level*, people who were resurrected and were given life for a 1000 years. Because the objects he sees and what he hears are seen and heard within the context of a vision, these objects are not *first* to be understood literally but viewed as symbolically portrayed and communicated, which is the *symbolic level* of the vision. That this vision is shot through with symbols is apparent merely by recalling the obvious symbolic nature of such words as 'chain', 'abyss', 'dragon', 'serpent', 'locked', 'sealed' and 'beast'. Therefore, the words 'resurrection' and 'life', for example, do not by themselves give a clue about whether the visionary, symbolic portrayal has a one-to-one (literal) correspondence to its historical referent together with a figurative meaning or has only an indirect figurative relation. Careful exegesis must decide in each case.

Before analyzing specific issues and verses in the passage, it will be helpful briefly to recall the contextual setting of Revelation 20. Rev. 20.1-10 is a part of the larger literary segment extending from 17.1 to 21.8. The first sections of the literary unit have been the announcement of the fall of Babylon at the end of time (ch. 17), elaboration of Babylon's fall, especially the responses drawn forth both from unredeemed and redeemed multitudes (18.1–19.10), and Christ's judgment of the ungodly world forces at the end of history (19.11-21).

The precise thematic and temporal relationship of ch. 20 to ch. 19 is hotly debated. However, the following exegesis of Revelation 20 will attempt to adduce exegetical argument in favor of the conclusion that 20.1-6 refers to the course of the interadvent age and temporally precedes the narration of final judgement in chs. 17–19, while, on the other hand, 20.7-15 recapitulates the description of final judgment in 19.11-21. The following exegetical idea for Rev. 20.1-15 can be formulated: *the millennium is inaugurated during the interadvent age by God's limitation of Satan's deceptive powers (vv. 1-3) and by deceased Christians being vindicated through reigning in heaven (vv. 4-6), and it is concluded by a resurgence of Satan's deceptive assault against the Church (vv. 7-8) and the final judgment (vv. 9-15).*[6] The focus of the following study will be on the issue of the millennium in vv. 1-7, so

---

6.   See Beale, *Book of Revelation, in loc.*, for indepth argument in favor of this idea, which is aligned most with historic 'amillennialism', but the view elaborated in the following analysis is better termed inaugurated millennialism.

that only parts of the preceding idea will be elaborated upon, especially those parts upon which John's use of the Old Testament has special bearing.

The only hope of obtaining any clarity about this explosively debated segment is to interpret it primarily in the light of its closest parallels elsewhere in the book and, secondarily, other parallels in the New Testament and Old Testament.

A. *The Bearing of the Old Testament on Revelation 20.1-3:*
The Millennium is Inaugurated During the Interadvent Age
by God's Curtailment of Satan's Ability to Deceive the Nations
and to Annihilate the Church

Introduction
Many think that this section and the following verses record historical events which come after the episode of judgment in 19.11-21.[7] The primary evidence adduced for this view is the series of conjunctions punctuating 19.11–20.15. These conjunctions are understood to indicate historical sequence in 19.11-21, and the continued use of the identical conjunctions in 20.1-15 is said to function most probably in the same historical manner, so that ch. 20 must record events in history which will occur after those of ch. 19.[8]

On closer analysis the argument is not as forceful as might initially appear. First, 'and' (καί) throughout the book can indicate either historical sequence or visionary sequence. More often than not the conjunction indicates visionary sequence as a transitional device either between major literary segments or between smaller units of material within the larger segments. Where historical sequence is indicated, it is typically found within the larger segments as a transition between verses or even phrases. Each overall context must determine which use is in mind. That the conjunctions signify historical sequence in 19.11-21 does not

---

7. E.g. Merril C. Tenney, 'The Importance and Exegesis of Rev. 20, 1-8', *BSac* 111 (1954), pp. 140-42.

8. Note the καί ('and') throughout; e.g. Schnackenburg, *God's Rule and Kingdom of Jesus Christ*, pp. 340-41; Walvoord, *Revelation*, p. 289; J.F. Walvoord, 'The Theological Significance of Revelation 20:1-6', in S.D. Toussaint and C.H. Dyer (eds.), *Essays in Honor of J. Dwight Pentecost* (Chicago: Moody Press, 1986), pp. 228-29; Mounce, *Revelation*, p. 352; J.S. Deere, 'Premillennialism in Revelation 20:4-6', *BSac* 135 (1978), pp. 60-63.

bear up under more precise scrutiny of καί in 19.11-21. Only 3 out of the 35 conjunctions in 19.11-21 clearly indicate sequence in historical time (cf. the initial καί in vv. 20a, 21a, 21b; perhaps also v. 14a). The remaining conjunctions serve only as visionary linking devices. On the other hand, the majority of the 'ands' in ch. 20 do indicate historical sequence, though there are exceptions which mark visionary or mere thematic sequence (vv. 2b, 4b, 6, 8b, 13-14).

In which of the two categories does the initial 'and' of 20.1 belong? Does it indicate continued historical sequence following on the heels of 19.21 or does it merely serve as a more general transition between visions? If the latter is the case, then more trenchant exegetical work must be done in order to clarify where the vision fits in the historical scheme of the Apocalypse. A close examination of the conjunctions in 19.11–20.15 cannot solve the problem one way or another. Other contextual evidence must be considered.

Elsewhere in the book, however, when 'and' (καί) is directly followed by an angelic descent ('and I saw an angel descending from heaven') or ascent, without exception it introduces a vision either suspending the temporal historical progress of a preceding section and introducing a section synchronous with the preceding (see 10.1) or reverting to a time anterior to a preceding section (see 7.2 and 18.1, where, as in 10.1 and 20.1, in each case the angel is described as 'having' something). Indeed, the majority of commentators, regardless of their interpretive approach to the book, acknowledge this function of the phrase in 7.2, 10.1, and 18.1, but no one until recently has applied the parallels to 20.1.[9] Early scribal tradition identified 20.1 with these earlier three parallels in the book.[10] Therefore, it is quite plausible that the introductory phrase in 20.1 functions like those in chs. 7, 10 and 18. Whether it introduces visions synchronously parallel to 19.11-21 or temporally prior to that section must be decided by the following context, though it will be argued here that vv. 1-6 are likely prior and vv. 7-15 temporally parallel.

---

9.   So R.F. White, 'Reexamining the Evidence for Recapitulation in Rev 20:1-10', *WTJ* 51 (1989), pp. 337-43. Likewise, see Beale, *Book of Revelation*, respectively on 10.1, 7.2 and 18.1 *in loc.*

10.   א[2] 2050 together with other minuscules and Vulgate, Syriac and Sahidic witnesses add ἄλλον before ἄγγελον to conform it to the three parallels which all have ἄλλον.

1. *Additional Introductory Observations Supporting a Non-Sequential Temporal Relationship of Revelation 20.1-10 to 19.11-21*

a. *The Allusion to Ezekiel 38–39 in Both Revelation 19.17-21 and 20.8-10.* First, the repeated allusion from Ezekiel 38-39 in Rev. 20.8-10 to the battle of Gog and Magog against the saints points to the likelihood that 20.8-10 is a recapitulation of the same battle narrated in 19.17-21, where also allusions are made to the same battle of Ezekiel 38–39 together with the virtually identical expression 'gather them together unto the war'.[11] Indeed, both 19.17-21 and 20.8-10 recount the same battle of 16.12-16, which is highlighted by the same phrase 'gather them together unto *the* battle' (συναγαγεῖν αὐτοὺς εἰς τὸν πόλεμον, though 19.19 varies insignificantly).[12] And, if 20.1-6 precedes the time of 20.7-10, and if 19.17-21 is temporally parallel to the battle of 20.7-10, then 20.1-6 is temporally prior to the battle of 19.17-21.

Nevertheless, some commentators unsuccessfully see two future, separate battles fulfilling the one battle prophesied in Ezekiel 38–39,[13] or that Ezekiel 38–39 has mythical significance with many possible historical applications,[14] or that the battle of 19.17-21 is a fulfillment of the Ezekiel prophecy but that of 20.8-10 is either not related to the Ezekiel passage at all,[15] or is described with the Ezekiel imagery but not considered a formal fulfillment, since John purportedly often engages in 'a free-and-easy use of [Old Testament] sources' which bear no close connection to their original Old Testament contexts.[16]

With respect to the last notion, Webb contends, in particular, that John employs Gog and Magog, not with a specific idea of fulfillment of the Ezekiel prophecy, but only with the broad, paradigmatic meaning of

---

11. See 20.8-10; for corroboration see White, 'Recapitulation', pp. 326-28.

12. So also Lenski, *Interpretation of St. John's Revelation*, p. 600; see 16.14 and 19.19.

13. Kiddle and Ross, *Revelation*, p. 398; R.H. Alexander, 'A Fresh Look at Ezekiel 38 and 39', *JETS* 17 (1974), pp. 157-69 (168-69); Mealy, *After the Thousand Years*, pp. 130-33; 187-88.

14. Caird, *Revelation*, p. 256.

15. Cf. Walvoord, *Revelation of Jesus Christ*, p. 303; C.L. Feinberg, *Millennialism: The Two Major Views* (Chicago: Moody Press, 1980), p. 327.

16. So W.J. Webb, 'Revelation 20: Exegetical Considerations', *The Baptist Review of Theology / La Review Baptiste de Théologie* 4 (1994), pp. 7-39 (11), whose contention about John's use of the Old Testament is argued against by the overall thrust of the present work (especially see on Chapter 2 above).

forces who are 'the enemies of God's people', similar to the way he refers to Sodom and Egypt in Rev. 11.8 or to Babylon in Rev. 16.19.[17] This is possible but improbable for three reasons:

(1)   in contrast to Sodom, Egypt and Babylon, Gog and Magog are part of a specific prophecy about the latter days, which has remained unfulfilled; unless there is clear indication otherwise, John should be understood as using the Ezekiel wording with its prophetic sense in mind;

(2)   most commentators of all millennial perspectives agree that already in Rev. 19.17-21 John views the Ezekiel 39 prophecy as being specifically fulfilled at a precise time in the future; unless there is clear indication otherwise, it is unlikely John would change his understanding of Ezekiel 39 within the short space of only seven verses. Put another way, it is best to interpret later uses of Old Testament allusions in Revelation by earlier, clear uses of allusions in Revelation from the same Old Testament context.

(3)   Finally, that John has in mind a specific prophecy–fulfillment connection with Ezekiel 38–39 is borne out by the broader context of Revelation 20–21, where a fourfold ending of the book reflects the ending of Ezekiel 37–48: resurrection of God's people (Rev. 20.4b; Ezek. 37.1-14), messianic kingdom (Rev. 20.4b-6; Ezek. 37.15-28), final battle against Gog and Magog (Rev. 20.7-10; Ezek. 38–39), and final vision of the new temple and new Jerusalem, described as a restored Eden and sitting on an exceedingly high mountain (Rev. 21.1–22.5; Ezek. 40–48).[18]

Others have tried to distinguish the battle in Ezekiel 38–39 from that in Revelation 20 by noting that in Ezek. 39.4 the enemy invaders are destroyed as they 'fall upon the mountains of Israel' (likewise 39.17) and in Rev. 20.9 they are destroyed by 'fire'.[19] This observation serves,

17. Webb, 'Revelation 20', pp. 11-13.

18. See J. Lust, 'Order of the Final Events in Revelation and in Ezekiel', p. 179, for references to those observing the pattern; similarly R.F. White, 'Making Sense of Rev 20:1-10? Harold Hoehner Versus Recapitulation', *JETS* 37 (1994), pp. 543-44.

19. So H.W. Hoehner, 'Evidence from Revelation 20', in D.K. Campbell and J.L. Townsend (eds.), *A Case for Premillennialism: A New Consensus* (Chicago: Moody Press, 1992), p. 258.

however, not to distinguish the two portrayals, but to identify them as the same, since Ezek. 38.21 (cf. 39.17-21) states that God slays the enemy with a sword 'on all my mountains' (likewise 39.17, 'sacrifice on the mountains of Israel'), and Ezek. 38.22 and 39.6 says that God defeats the same enemy by fire.[20] The two depictions in Ezekiel are different metaphorical ways of underscoring *the same defeat* of the enemy by God. In fact, these two metaphorical versions of the same battle in Ezekiel are reflected in the two battles of Rev. 19.17-21 and 20.7-9; in the former the enemy is destroyed by a sword, and in the latter the foe is defeated by fire.[21]

Neither is there sufficient basis for distinguishing the Ezekiel prophecy from Revelation 20 because Gog and Magog come from the north in Ezekiel 38–39, and apparently and implicitly also in Revelation 19, but in Revelation 20 Gog and Magog are identified with all nations of the earth.[22] Rev. 19.15-21 refers to 'the nations' in general as the antagonists of Christ, not nations from the north, so that they are not necessarily different from the nations in 20.8.[23] Indeed, Rev. 19.15 refers to 'the nations' as part of an allusion to Isa. 11.4 and Ps. 2.9, which have a universal perspective of the nations; in the former Isaiah refers to 'earth' in place of John's 'nations' and in the latter the 'nations' are explained further as 'the ends of the earth'. Therefore, if Revelation 19 is alluding to the Ezekiel battle, there is no reason to distinguish Revelation 19 from Revelation 20 on the basis of a different geographical perspective of Ezekiel's enemy. Both Revelation accounts are probably universalizing the enemy of Ezekiel, but this should not lead to the conclusion that John is developing Ezekiel contrary to its original contextual intention.[24]

Webb tries to undergird the idea that the two battles are multiple fulfillments by ingeniously observing that John sees a multiple dimension of fulfillment of other Old Testament prophecies elsewhere in the book:[25] for example the inaugurated fulfillment of Dan. 7.13 in

---

20. So White, 'Hoehner Versus Recapitulation', p. 543.
21. White, 'Hoehner Versus Recapitulation', p. 543.
22. Against Hoehner, 'Evidence from Rev. 20', p. 258.
23. So White, 'Hoehner Versus Recapitulation', p. 543; see Rev. 20.8.
24. On which see further Beale, *Book of Revelation, in loc.*, on 20.8 for the rationale.
25. Webb, 'Revelation 20', pp. 12-13.

Rev. 1.13 (applying to Jesus' present reign) and its exclusively future fulfillment in 14.14 (applying to his final coming in judgment).[26] Among a number of other examples would be Isa. 49.2, which John conceives as beginning fulfillment in Jesus (Rev. 1.16), as potentially continuing fulfillment whenever churches become unfaithful and deserve judgment (2.12, 16), and as finding complete fulfillment at Christ's final coming in judgment (19.15, 21). Could the allusions to Ezekiel 38–39 in Revelation 19 and 20 be further examples respectively of inaugurated fulfillment followed by final fulfillment?

A negative answer to the question is likely, since the defeat of the ungodly forces in 19.17-21 appears to be complete and definitive, whereas other cases of inaugurated Old Testament prophecies in the book do not evoke such specific finality. Furthermore, these other examples are not multiple fulfillments but inaugurated fulfillments, whose inauguration continues over an extended period of time, and then is concluded by a consummate fulfillment. On the other hand, if the Ezekiel 38–39 battle episodes in Revelation 19 and 20 do display such a relationship of inauguration followed by consummation, one would expect to find the portrayal in Rev. 20.7-9 to appear as a continuation of the battle in 19.17-21, or some explicit indication of continuation would be needed. Not only does it not appear that Rev. 20.7-8 picks up where Rev. 19.21 left off, but the battle of 20.7-10 has a beginning, just like that of 19.17-21. In particular, the very same language describing the commencement of the battle in 19.19 is repeated again in 20.8. Furthermore, this language is based on the same allusion from Ezek. 38.2-8 and 39.2, together with passages from Zechariah 12–14 (12.3-4; 14.2, 13-14 and Zeph. 3.8), which also stand behind the parallel phrases in Rev. 16.14 and 19.19 (see further the Old Testament background of 16.14, 19.19, 20.8,[27] and directly below, point # [c]). Indeed, the same depiction of the battle in 16.14 would mean, according to Webb's analysis, that what appears to be three final, climactic versions of the same battle must be construed as three chronologically subsequent phases of one battle or three different battles. Such a creative analysis is possible but does not appear probable, especially in the light of the following considerations (points c–f directly below, as well as the remainder of the chapter).

26. In this respect, see discussion on 1.7 in Chapter 2 above.
27. Though there is not space to argue this further here, see Beale, *Book of Revelation*, on 16.14, 19.19, and 20.8.

Consistent with some of the directly preceding options attempting to distinguish the battles of Revelation 19 and 20 is the proposal that one of the battles is against demonic forces and the other against human forces.[28] For example some view 'Gog and Magog' in 20.8 as ghostly and demonic forces similar to those in 9.1-11 and 9.13-19.[29] Interestingly, the parallel narrative of 16.13-14 depicts demonic involvement, but there the demons do not do battle but gather the kings of the earth for battle and are not to be equated with them. Therefore, the suggestion that ch. 19 is about a battle against human armies and that ch. 20 is about battle against demonic armies fares no better than the above similar proposals for the same reasons.

b. *The Connection Between Recapitulation in Ezekiel 38–39 Itself and Revelation 19.17–20.10.* Ezekiel 39 recapitulates the same battle narrated in Ezekiel 38. This would suggest that if John is following any model in Rev. 19.17-21 and 20.7-10, he would be following the generally acknowledged pattern of recapitulation in Ezekiel 38–39 (see further below on 20.5-6 for the broader similarity between 20.4–22.5 and Ezek. 37–48 [sect. B.1.b]). Indeed, recapitulation is typical elsewhere in Ezekiel, as well as in the other prophetic books of the Old Testament.

A minority of commentators argue that Ezekiel 38 prophesies a different battle from that of ch. 39.[30] Little evidence is adduced in favor of this. According to J.W. Mealy, Rev. 19.17-21 refers to the Ezekiel 39 attack which occurs at Christ's parousia and launches the millennium and 20.8-10 alludes to the Ezekiel 38 attack which occurs after the millennium. Mealy supports this view by saying merely that Ezekiel 38 and 39 are to be distinguished from one another because Ezekiel 39.23-29 concludes with a reflection on God's restoration of Israel, so that the attack in ch. 39 must occur around the time of that restoration, whereas the attack in ch. 38 occurs *after* Israel has been restored to the land and has enjoyed a long period of peace there.[31]

---

28. E.g. G.A. Krodel, *Revelation* (Augsburg Commentary on the New Testament; Minneapolis: Augsburg Publishing House, 1989), p. 337.

29. Rissi, *Future of the World*, pp. 35-36, 99, and literature cited therein.

30. So older source critics (cited in G.A. Cooke, *The Book of Ezekiel* [ICC; Edinburgh: T. & T. Clark, 1936], pp. 407-408), as well as, more recently, Alexander, 'Ezekiel 38 and 39', pp. 168-69, and Mealy, *After the Thousand Years*, pp. 130-33, 187-88.

31. Mealy, *After the Thousand Years*.

Mealy's view is not an unimaginable scenario for Ezekiel 38–39, but more exegetical argument is needed to make it plausible than the bare two or three sentences stated.[32] Mealy cites no more evidence nor does he cite any Old Testament commentaries or periodical literature in support of his view.

In contrast to Mealy's assessment, there is nothing in ch. 38 to indicate clearly that there is a *long period* of peace after Israel's restoration. Ezek. 38.8 does say that 'After many days you will be summoned; in the latter years you will come into the land that is restored'; however, the introductory time reference probably does not refer to 'days' and 'years' from the time after Israel's restoration, but merely that Gog will attack Israel during the general period of 'the last days' (found verbatim in 38.16), which is generally also the time of the restoration. The phrases 'latter days', 'after these things', etc. typically in prophetic literature serve as introductory temporal phrases to indicate the same general eschatological period of restoration of Israel and judgment of the nations.[33] Such phrases often do not refer to a sequential, chronological distinction to the immediately preceding narrative but to the thematic idea of the latter times in general, which can overlap temporally with the preceding or following context.[34] Therefore, Gog's attack comes at some period around the same time as the restoration (though the New Testament context of Revelation clarifies that the attack occurs at the end of the latter-day inter-advent age of true Israel's [i.e. the Church's] time of restoration, which was inaugurated through Christ's redemptive work).

Indeed, the consensus opinion by more recent major Old Testament commentators is that Ezek. 39.1-20 recapitulates ch. 38 and that the

---

32. Kiddle and Ross, *Revelation of St. John* [London: Hodder & Stoughton, 1940], p. 398, is cited by Mealy as agreeing that John had this view of Ezek. 38–39, though Kiddle and Ross add 'such exegesis of a prophetic oracle seems utterly pointless and misleading to our generation; it arises out' of a 'rabbinical method of reasoning'.

33. So, e.g, for the former cf. Dan. 2.28; 10.14; the two kinds of phrases are used synonymously in the same contexts, both referring to restoration; Jer. 30.24 and 31.33; Jer. 48.47 and 49.6; Isa. 2.2 and 1.26; Hos. 3.5b and 3.5a; and Ezek. 38.16 and 38.8 appear to fall into precisely the same pattern.

34. E.g. for elaboration of such uses of the phrase 'after this' in the prophets see further W.A. VanGemeren, 'The Spirit of Restoration', *WTJ* 50 (1988) pp. 81-102 (84-90).

two chapters prophesy two versions of the same attack.[35] The concluding mention of restoration at the end of Ezekiel 39 is a flashback to
other hopes recorded earlier in Ezekiel 34–37. Such kinds of flashbacks
are characteristic of Ezekiel and prophetic literature. Most see the concluding comments about restoration from exile in 39.25-29 as a summary or retrospective reflection on the same theme in chs. 34–37,
serving as a transition between 34.1–39.24 and chs. 40–48.[36] Ezek.
39.1-8ff. is most naturally taken as a continuation of the narrative in ch.
38. There is no break between the two chapters to hint at the kind of
temporal dislocation which Mealy wants to see.[37] He does admit telli-
ngly that his explanation of Ezekiel results in a 'rather cryptic double
presentation' by the prophet.[38] The burden of proof rests on someone
wanting to see different attacks, since on the surface they appear to be
the same.

Another possible, though less clear, line of analysis is to see Ezekiel
39 recapitulating ch. 38, as above, but being fulfilled in the Selucid
forces of Antiochus IV Epiphanes in the second century BC, who are
typological of the forces at the end of history which will attempt to annihilate the church.[39]

35. Cooke, *Ezekiel*, pp. 406-408, 417-18; J.W. Wevers, *Ezekiel*, pp. 286, 294;
W. Zimmerli, *Ezekiel* (2 vols.; Hermeneia; Philadelphia: Fortress Press, 1969), II,
p. 298; D. Stuart, *Ezekiel* (The Communicator's Commentary, 18; Dallas, TX,
Word Books, 1989), pp. 351-63; L.C. Allen, *Ezekiel 20–48* (WBC, 29; Dallas, TX:
Word Books, 1990), pp. 207-209; cf. W. Eichrodt, *Ezekiel* (Philadelphia: Westminster Press, 1970), pp. 521, 527, whose conclusions line up generally with the
preceding.
36. E.g. Cooke, *Ezekiel*, p. 422; Eichrodt, *Ezekiel*, p. 529; Allen, *Ezekiel*,
pp 208-209.
37. For the view that Ezek. 38–39 is one coherent thematic presentation of eight
cartoon-like snapshots of only *one* event, see recently D. Block, 'Gog and Magog
in Ezekiel's Eschatological Vision', Tyndale Old Testament Lecture delivered at
the Tyndale Fellowship Triennial Conference on Eschatology (Swanwick, Great
Britain, July, 1997), published subsequently as 'Gog and Magog in Ezekiel's Eschatological Vision' in K.E. Brower and M.W. Elliott (eds.), *The Reader Must
Understand* (Leicester: Apollos [Inter-Varsity], 1997), pp. 85-116. This lecture and
article anticipate his forthcoming commentary on Ezekiel in the NICOT commentary series (vol. 2; Grand Rapids: Eerdmans, 1998).
38. Mealy, *After the Thousand Years*, p. 187.
39. J.G. Aalders, *Gog en Magog en Ezechiël* [Kampen: Kok, 1951], and
T. Boersma, *Is the Bible a Jigsaw Puzzle? ...An Evaluation of Hal Lindsey's Writings* (St. Catherine's, Ontario: Paideia, 1978), pp. 120-25.

c. *The Relationship of Revelation 16.12-16, 19.19 and 20.8.* Thirdly, not only do Rev. 16.12-16, 19.19-20 and 20.8 have in common the same language describing the gathering together of forces for the war (noted above), but they also share the notion that the forces gathered have been *deceived* into participating. This enforces the impression that Satan's *deception* of the nations in 20.8 'to gather them together for the war' is the same event as the *deception* of the nations in 16.12-16 and 19.19, where respectively demons 'gather them together for the war' of Armageddon and 'the kings of the earth and their armies 'are gathered together to make war' (the latter in connection with mention of the false prophet's deceptive activities, though not as directly stated in 19.19-20). And, just as the war of Armageddon in ch. 16 is followed with a description of the destruction of the cosmos (16.17-21), so likewise does a vision of the dissolution of the world follow the final battle of 20.7-10, which suggests further the synchronous parallelism of the two segments.[40] Some identify the defeated forces of 19.17-21 as demonic and the forces of 20.7-10 as their human counterparts, defeated after the intervening millennium.[41] But there is not enough evidence to make such a distinction. Not only do the two texts allude to Ezekiel 38–39 but they also refer to the oppressive multitudes as 'the nations' (τὰ ἔθνη; Rev. 19.15; 20.8). More likely, the nations in both passages refer to identical groups, as argued further below.

d. *The Relationship of the 'Nations' in Revelation 19.13-20 to the 'Nations' in 20.3.* Another observation points to a non-sequential chronological relationship of Revelation 19–20. If 20.1-3 chronologically follows 19.17-21, then there is an incongruity, since 'it makes no sense to speak of protecting the nations from deception by Satan in 20.1-3 after they have just been both deceived by Satan (16.13-16, cf. 19.19-20) and destroyed by Christ at his return in 19.11-21 (cf. 16.15a, 19)'.[42]

In conjunction with the preceding arguments in favor of chronological sequence between 19.17-21 and 20.1-3, some contend that 20.3 and 20.8 show there are survivors left among the nations who will be gathered again to fight one more battle. But it should be asked how there could be any survivors left among the rebellious nations of 19.11-21

40. Cf. White, 'Hoehner Versus Recapitulation', pp. 331-36.
41. Cf. Johnson, *Revelation*, p. 587.
42. White, 'Hoehner Versus Recapitulation', p. 321.

after Christ's absolute victory over them (19.21 says 'the *rest* were killed')? The likely answer is that the description of 19.15-21 leaves no room for any survivors.[43]

Nevertheless, one possible answer is that the 'nations' mentioned in 20.3 are a remnant of the rebellious forces who never entered the final battle but now are able to believe as a result of the removal of the deceptive powers;[44] or, similarly, a conceivable response is that only the wicked among the nations were destroyed in 19.19-21, so that the nations in 20.3 are the saints who are from among the nations.[45] At the close of the millennium, the descendants of these Christians will be deceived into fighting against Christ again. But, in the light of the absolute defeat recorded in 19.21 and the inclusive reference to 'nations' in 19.15 (especially in view of the universal connotation of 'nations' in the Ps. 2.8 background there), and in view of the overall analysis so far, the burden of proof rests on those attempting to argue this. In merely 4 of 23 occurrences outside of 20.3 (15.4 [?]; 21.24, 26; 22.2) do 'the nations' (plural of ἔθνος or its singular form) explicitly refer to saints, as revealed by each respective context; in all other uses outside of 20.3 and the above 4 verses, 'the nations' are distinguished from those who have been redeemed.[46] Consequently, it is unlikely that 'the nations' in 20.3 refer to redeemed people, especially since the phrase 'the nations' in the immediate context refers to unbelievers (19.15; 20.8).[47]

The notion that the antagonists in 19.17-21 are human, whereas in 20.7-10 they are only demonic, also does not fit with the climactic nature of the defeat in ch. 19. Furthermore, in both the battles of chs. 19 and 20 the enemies are not distinguished but both are called 'the nations' and refer to the same human enemy prophesied about in Ezekiel 38–39. For the same reason, the attackers could not be demons accompanying the spirits of deceased unbelievers, which is also implausible since there is no Old Testament, Jewish or Christian parallel for such a notion anywhere.[48]

43. So also Mealy, *After the Thousand Years*, pp. 90-91, citing as well Schüssler Fiorenza.
44. So Ladd, *Revelation*, p. 263; Mounce, *Revelation*, p. 353.
45. Hoehner, 'Evidence from Revelation 20', p. 252.
46. White, 'Hoehner Versus Recapitulation', p. 540.
47. White, 'Hoehner Versus Recapitulation', p. 541.
48. Mealy, *After the Thousand Years*, pp. 122-23.

e. *The Relation of Revelation 15.1 and 16.17-21 to 19.19-21 and 20.8-9.* Since Rev. 19.19-21 brings to conclusion the 'plot line' commenced but dropped after 16.16, then the Messiah's wrath in 19.19-21 coincides with the seventh plague of divine wrath in 16.17-21. On this basis, Christ's wrath in 19.19-21 ought to occur within the time scope of the seven bowl plagues, which 15.1 says 'brings to conclusion the wrath of God'; Rev. 19.19-21 overlaps at least with the sixth and seventh bowl woe. If so, then the event of fiery destruction in 20.9 likely should also be included within the temporal framework of 'the seven last plagues' in 15.1, especially in the light of the argument so far in this chapter. *There is no evidence anywhere in Revelation (excluding the present debated text of 20.1-10) that divine wrath could be directed against the nations after the seventh plague, which coincides with Christ's second coming in judgment.* Therefore, 20.8-9 probably cannot be another instance of divine wrath exercised against the nations *after* the events of the sixth and seventh bowl plagues and the synchronous events of 19.19-21, since the seven bowl plagues are said to '*bring to conclusion the wrath of God' against the ungodly nations.*[49]

f. *The Relation of the Structure of Daniel 7 to that of Revelation 19.11–20.6.* Some contend that 19.11–20.6 is sequential because it follows the sequential chronological pattern of Daniel 7 (esp. Dan. 7.11-27):[50] (1) destruction of the beast and (2) reign of the saints.[51] However, Daniel 7 itself exhibits a clear structure of recapitulation, repeating narratives about the persecution and kingdom of the saints (7.8, 13-14, 19-22, 23-25, 27), as well as the judgment of the beast (7.9-11, 26). Furthermore, that there is no concern to develop a precise, linear chronological understanding of Daniel 7 in the Apocalypse is evident from such texts as Rev. 1.13ff., which pictures the Son of Man already reigning in the midst of the first-century churches in beginning fulfillment of Dan. 7.13; likewise, Rev. 5.9-10 shows the church is already beginning to fulfill the Dan. 7.18, 22, 27 prophecy that the saints would reign. In addition, the 'opening of the books' of Dan. 7.10, which precedes the beast's judgment in Daniel, follows his judgment in Rev. 20.12, where

49. So White, 'Hoehner Versus Recapitulation', pp. 547-48.

50. So Deere, 'Premillenialism', pp. 60-61; J.L. Townsend, 'Is the Present Age the Millennium?' *Bibliotheca Sacra* 140 (1983), p. 213.

51. Deere, 'Premillennialism', p. 60.

it is applied to unbelievers. Rev. 22.5 applies the terminology of ruling from Daniel and Rev. 20.4-6 to the eternal state.

B. *The Bearing of the Old Testament on the Interpretation of Revelation 20.4-6: The Millennium is Inaugurated for Deceased Saints during the Interadvent Age by the Resurrection of their Souls, Placing Them in the Heavenly Status of Having Authority with Christ as Priests and Kings Over Spiritual Death (Revelation 20.4-6)*

1. *Interpretation of Revelation 20.4-6*

a. *Interpretation of Revelation 20.4.* The focus on what has taken place in the abyss in Rev. 20.1-3 is shifted to what has happened in heaven as a result of the binding of Satan. Verse 4 portrays the effects for the community of saints which have occurred because of Satan's fall in vv. 1-3. The main point of v. 4 is to explain that Satan's fall is a judgment upon him which vindicates the saints; their vindication is positively demonstrated by the facts of their resurrection and their reigning on thrones with Christ.

The events of both vv. 1-3 and vv. 4-6 occur during the same period, which is referred to as '1000 years'. That this is not a literal chronological number is apparent from: (1) the figurative use of numbers consistently elsewhere in the book; (2) the figurative nature of much of the immediate context ('chain', 'abyss', 'dragon', 'serpent', 'locked', 'sealed', 'beast'); (3) the predominantly figurative tone of the entire book (so 1.1); (4) the figurative use of the number '1000' in the Old Testament; and (5) the use in Judaism and early Christianity of '1000' years as a figure for the eternal blessing of the redeemed.[52]

The first effect of the Devil's fall into the abyss is that Christians are enabled to sit on thrones, which is explained at the conclusion of v. 4 as their ability to reign with Christ because they 'came to life' from the dead. Subsequent comment must clarify whether or not this resurrection and reign is physically literal or figurative and whether or not it occurs on earth or in heaven. There can be little doubt that beings sitting on 'thrones' do not refer to beings sitting on literal pieces of furniture, but a figurative way of referring to beings who reign over a kingdom.

---

52. See sect. C below ['The Bearing of Old Testament and Jewish Background on the Question of the Literal or Figurative Meaning of the "One Thousand Years" in Revelation 20.1-7 and in Early Christian Literature'] for the last two points.

Another effect of Satan's fall is that 'judgment was given for the saints' (κρίμα ἐδόθη αὐτοῖς). There are at least four possible identifications of these figures who sit on the 'thrones'.

(1)   They may refer only to martyrs[53] or to all of God's people who will assist him in the final judgment (cf. Lk. 22.30; 1 Cor. 6.2; Rev. 2.26-27; 19.14); Mounce identifies the saints with those of Dan. 7.27, who, in turn, he identifies with the 'court' in Dan. 7.26 which judges.[54]

(2)   The 'thrones' and those who 'sat on them' are the angelic court of Daniel 7 who declare the final judgment against the satanic fiend in vindication of the saints whom he oppressed; this would be in correspondence to Dan. 7.9-11: 'thrones were set up...the court sat...the beast was slain' (cf. Dan. 7.26; *Midr. Ps.* 4.4 identifies the court as angelic).

(3)   The court is composed only of angels but the angels represent saints.

(4)   The court in Rev. 20.4 probably includes exalted believers *along with* angels, since the same scene of figures ('elders') sitting on heavenly thrones in Rev. 4.4 included angels, who corporately represent exalted saints.[55] This receives support by observing that the only places outside of 20.4 in the book where the plural of 'throne' occurs are in 4.4 and 11.16, where it is elders who sit on the thrones (*b. Sanh.* 38b views the court of Dan. 7.9-10 as consisting of God, angels, and the Davidic messiah, while *b. Ḥag.* 14a sees only God and the messiah sitting on the plural thrones).

This last identification is preferable, though the focus is primarily on saints themselves. The focus on saints is evident from the third phrase of v. 4: 'judgment was passed for *them* (αὐτοῖς), where 'them' refers to saints (see below the allusion to Dan. 7.22). The antecedent of 'them' must be in 'they sat', which clearly places the saints on the 'thrones'. That the word 'them' appears abruptly without any antecedent is improbable. Argument could even be made in favor of three distinct

53. Rist, 'Revelation of St. John the Divine', p. 520; Bratcher, *Translator's Guide*, p. 167.
54. Mounce, *Revelation*, p. 355; so similarly Johnson, *Revelation*, p. 582.
55. See Beale, *Book of Revelation*, on 4.4 and 11.16, for full argumentation.

groups in v. 4: judges, martyrs, and non-compromisers, the last two on whose behalf judgment has been passed.[56]

The inaugurated judgment against Satan (vv. 1-3) has been executed on behalf of God's people. The judgment presumably has already been passed by the divine court in heaven. This is suggested by Dan. 7.9-27, where the heavenly court is distinct from the saints on whose behalf the court declares the judgment. But the first three expressions of Rev. 20.4 underscore the fact that the saints have become part of the heavenly court so that their co-reign with Christ in vv. 4 and 6 is partly judicial in nature. When saints are translated to heaven at death they join Christ on his judicial throne to rule over the enemy in inaugurated fulfillment of the promise given to 'overcomers' in 3.21 and 2.26-27, though these promises will also reach complete fulfillment at the final resurrection of the saints: compare 3.21, 'to the one overcoming I will give to him to sit with me on my throne, as I overcame and sat with my Father on his throne' (so likewise Mt. 19.28; Lk. 22.30). That those who reign with Christ (Rev. 20.4c, 6) are the same ones who sit on thrones and judge in v 4a is also pointed to by Lk. 22.30 (= Mt. 19.28), where the future reign of Jesus' followers is to be carried out by exercising judgment: 'you will sit on thrones judging the twelve tribes of Israel'.[57] The way they actually carry out their reign with him is likely through agreement with and praise of his judicial decisions (cf. Rev. 19.1-6), which is consummated by their witness being a basis for Christ's judgment of the ungodly at the end of the age (e.g. cf. 11.3-13; 17.14; 19.14-15).[58] This is consonant with biblical literature elsewhere in which there is an interrelationship between judging and ruling, especially with respect to God.[59] Consequently, the saints are pictured as beginning to reign and to execute the judicial function which they will carry out consummately at the end of the age in fulfillment of Dan. 7.22 (so also Lk. 22.30; 1 Cor. 6.2; *1 En.* 38.5; 48.9; 95.3; 98.12).

The corporate identification of saints with the angelic judges is also part of the reason why they can be pictured as sitting on the seats of the heavenly court. A better translation of κρίμα ἐδόθη αὐτοῖς would be

---

56. Cf. A.H. Lewis, *The Dark Side of the Millennium* (Grand Rapids: Baker Book House, 1980), p. 57.

57. So Beckwith, *Apocalypse of John*, p. 739.

58. Cf. Hoekema, *Bible and the Future*, pp. 230-31.

59. See F. Büchsel, 'κρίνω', *TDNT*, III, pp. 923, 933-41; V. Herntrich, 'The OT Term מִשְׁפָּט', *TDNT*, III, pp. 923-33.

'judgment was passed [against the Devil] on their [the saints] behalf' (or 'for them', αὐτοῖς as a dative of advantage). This rendering is confirmed by Dan. 7.22 [Theodotion], to which partial allusion is also made here: 'judgment was passed in favor of the saints' (τὸ κρίμα ἔδωκεν ἁγίοις; the phrase εἶδον θρόνους of Rev. 20.4a widens the allusion to include Dan. 7.9).[60] The majority of versions and commentators understand that in Dan. 7.22 the judgement is executed *on behalf of the saints* for their vindication.[61] The vindication in Daniel 7 was a necessary condition enabling the saints to assume kingship together with the son of man (cf. 7.13-14, 18, 27). The judgment of the evil kingdoms paves the way for the son of man and his saints to reign (Dan. 7.11-14, 18, 27). As in Rev. 20.4, so in Dan. 7.22 the 'judgment' is followed by the mention of the 'saints possessing the kingdom'. Though the word κρίμα can simply mean 'judgment' (so Rev. 17.1), the use in Dan. 7.22 (Greek OT) and in Rev. 18.20 indicates the meaning here of 'judicial vindication' (see 18.20; the only other use of κρίμα in the book is at 17.1).

The clear connection between the martyr portrayals of Rev. 6.9 and 20.4 (see below) confirms this meaning, since 6.10 is the first formal call for the saints' vindication ('how long...will you not judge and avenge our blood?'). Rev. 20.4 is not a first answer to that initial petition but an expansion of the answer already implicit in 6.11, where the white robes and the 'rest' are the beginning of the answer (as also is 'rest' in 14.13). Therefore, Rev. 20.4-6 is not a consummate answer to the plea of Rev. 6.10,[62] since our contextual analysis argues against that; if the incipient form of the divine answer in 6.11 is acknowledged, there should be no problem in seeing 20.4-6 as part of that non-consummate response. This expanded answer to 6.11 is not really new since saints have already been called priests and a kingdom in 1.6 and 5.10. However, some see these earlier texts as affirming that, while the saints exercise priesthood, they only have a claim to Christ's rule but do not actually exercise that rule until the consummated age.[63]

60. Also Kraft, *Die Offenbarung des Johannes*, p. 256.

61. Though a minority of commentators favor 'judgment was given to the saints'; e.g. J.A. Montgomery, *A Critical and Exegetical Commentary on the Book of Daniel* (ICC; Edinburgh: T. & T. Clark, 1979), pp. 309-10.

62. Against the argument of Schüssler Fiorenza, *Priester*, p. 324.

63. E.g. Schüssler Fiorenza, *Priester*, pp. 330, 338 and against Schüssler Fiorenza see discussion of 1.6 and 5.10 above at Chapter 3, sect. A.9 c.ii.

The same pattern of Daniel 7 is evident in Rev. 20.1-4, where the casting down of Satan is the inaugurated judgment enabling the saints to commence their reign in incipient fulfillment of Dan. 7.22. Hence, their thrones indicate primarily their kingship, which is in line with the other uses of throne elsewhere in the book as a symbol of God's, Christ's or the elders' kingship.[64]

The ones identified as sitting on the thrones are those who had not compromised with the idolatrous system of the beast because the Devil's deceptive tactics against them had been restrained (vv. 1-3).[65] First, they are referred to as 'the souls of the ones who had been beheaded on account of the witness of Jesus and on account of the word of God'. The closest parallel to this is 6.9, where John sees 'the souls of the ones slain on account of the word of God and on account of the witness'. These were believers who had died while holding to their faith despite persecution and whose souls had been translated to heaven in order to receive rest from the Lord (see on 6.9-11). The same kind of scene is probably in view in 20.4-6.

Though 'soul' (ψυχή) can be a substitute for 'living body' (8.9; 12.11; 16.3; cf. 18.13), here its combination with 'beheaded' is best suited to indicate a distinction between soul and body, as the almost identical combination 'souls of the ones having been slain' in 6.9 clearly indicates.[66] If such a distinction of soul and body is not held, an awkward picture emerges: 'bodies of beheaded people'. Rev. 18.13 could also make a distinction between the 'bodies and the souls of men' (cf. the questionable parallel language of Rom. 2.9). The non-corporeal sense of 'soul' is suggested further by its close connection to thrones which are in heaven, not on earth (see below). Assuming that Rev. 6.9 is in mind, the change from 'those having been slain' (τῶν ἐσφαγμένων) to 'those having been beheaded' (τῶν πεπελεκισμένων) could specify that only actual martyrs are meant but more likely the expression is figurative for varying kinds of persecution. The phrase in 6.9 was figurative for all degrees of persecution up to death,[67] which 1.9

---

64. So Schüssler Fiorenza, *Priester*, p. 304.

65. The Syriac, Arabic and Ethiopic versions identify the 'them' of v. 4a as different from the directly following 'souls' (see John Gill, *An Exposition of the New Testament. III. The Revelation of St. John the Divine* [Philadelphia: William W. Woodward, 1811]), p. 859.

66. So Hendriksen, *More Than Conquerors*, p. 230.

67. E.g. on 6.9, 11 see Beale, *Book of Revelation, in loc.*

and 12.11 substantiate, where also the phrases 'on account of the word of God and the witness of Jesus' and 'on account of their witness' respectively occur (see also 2.10 for degrees of persecution up to death). At the very least, decapitation is not merely in mind, since Christians were killed in other ways as well (e.g. crucifixion).

Therefore, the parallel with 6.9 suggests strongly that the scene here is also picturing deceased saints reigning in heaven and not on earth (so likewise 7.14-17). They remained faithful to death, whether or not that death came through martyrdom or other forms of suffering. The heavenly location of the thrones in 20.4 is apparent from the observation that 42 of the 46 times 'throne[s]' (θρόνος) occurs elsewhere in the book, it is clearly located in heaven.[68] The remaining three uses refer either to Satan's or the beast's throne, which is likewise not earthly but located in a spiritual dimension.[69] The 'thrones' in Dan. 7.9 also appear to be in heaven (cf. Dan. 7.10-13).

There is debate about the additional phrases describing those occupying the thrones in the last half of Rev. 20.4, but this cannot be addressed here.

b. *The Interpretation of Revelation 20.5-6.* Verse 4 has affirmed that the saints' exercise of judgment, coming to life and reigning with Christ are effects of the binding of Satan in vv. 1-3. Now, these effects are interpreted further to be the 'first resurrection' and its attendant blessing of being 'priests', protected from the 'second death' and of reigning as kings. The reference to 'holy' could refer to the believers' holy priesthood,[70] though more likely it is synonymous with the preceding 'blessing' and pertains to their favored position, which here refers to their being immune to the second death, as well as being priests and kings. Their resurrection existence is the basis upon which the second death 'has no authority' over them. They have overcome any threat of the second death, which is to say that they have authority over it.

This authority over the second death, or the result of this authority, is expressed in the phrase 'they will be priests of...Christ and they will

---

68. So Hendriksen, *More Than Conquerors*, p. 230; Morris, *Revelation*, p. 236; though the throne in 22.1 and 22.3 is located in the new heavens and earth.

69. See M. Gourges, 'The Thousand-Year Reign (Rev. 20:1-6): Terrestrial or Celestial?', *CBQ* 47 (1985), pp. 676-81, for summary of arguments for and against a heavenly setting for 20.4-6, though he favors the former.

70. Cf. Prigent, *L'Apocalypse de Saint Jean*, p. 312.

reign with him'. Their priestly status means they serve in the presence of God, whereas those suffering the second death will be separated from God forever (see 20.10, 14-15; 21.3, 7-8, 27; 22.14-15). Their position as kings demonstrates that they 'will reign with Christ' and win victory forever over the second death (cf. 2.10-11; 3.21). The statement in 22.5 that the saints 'will reign forever and ever' in eternity is a continuation of the reign begun during the millennial period and is not to be superimposed on 20.4-6 as if the two reigns were identical in time.[71] Just as the Devil's captivity is limited to a thousand years, the saints *intermediate* reign is likewise limited, but is followed by a *consummate* stage of reigning in eternity.[72]

The background for the dual office of priesthood and kingship is based, not only on Exod. 19.6 (see Rev. 1.6; 5.10), but also on Isa. 61.6, which refers to the end-time restoration of God's people when the entire nation 'will be called the priests of the Lord'.[73] The Targumic version of Isa. 61.3-6 adds that the whole nation will not only be priests, but also be 'true princes' wearing 'a diadem'. Interestingly, Zech. 6.13 refers to a messianic-like figure who will 'rule on his throne' and 'he will be a priest on his throne', which may stand behind Christ's dual role at points throughout Revelation, with which the saints are corporately identified; of particular relevance may be *Targ. Isa.* 22.21-25, which also explicitly attributes to Eliakim ruling and priestly roles, and these roles of Eliakim in the Isaiah 22 passage are seen by Rev. 3.7 as an anticipatory analogue to Christ's roles.

In 1.6 and and 5.10 saints have been said only to be 'priests *to God*', but now it is said that they will be 'priests of God and *of Christ*'. The additional mention that believers will also be priests serving Christ suggests that Christ is on a par with God, which is underscored elsewhere in the book: e.g. 5.13-14; 7.9-17.[74]

As noted in 20.1, the 'thousand years' of Satan's imprisonment and the saints' reign with Christ is often understood to commence with Christ's final coming, so that the dead raised to life in v. 4 begin to reign at the time of this coming and the 'rest of the dead' of v. 5 will 'come to life' at the completion of the millennial period. Accordingly,

71. As does, e.g., Schüssler Fiorenza, *Priester*, pp. 293, 322-23.
72. Against Schüssler Fiorenza, *Revelation*, p. 107.
73. Cf. Schüssler Fiorenza, *Priester*, pp. 336-38.
74. So A. Vanhoye, *Old Testament Priests and the New Testament* (Petersham, MA: St Bede's, 1986), pp. 302-303; cf. Rev. 22.3-4.

the period is sometimes understood as a literal thousand years, though many view it as a figurative period during which people will reign on the earth and not in heaven. Furthermore, this premillennial view interprets both the 'coming to life' of the righteous in v. 4 and that of the ungodly in v. 5 as literal physical resurrections, whereas historic amillennialism has understood the first resurrection as spiritual and the second as physical.

One of the most substantial arguments in favor of the premillennial interpretation is based on the observation that the coming to life of 'the rest of the dead' mentioned in v. 5a is clearly a physical resurrection (about which there is apparent unanimous agreement by all commentators). If the physical resurrection of the wicked is described with 'they came to life' (ἔζησαν) and the identical word describes the resurrection of the saints in v. 4, then the resurrection of v. 4 must also be a physical resurrection. The often-quoted dictum of H. Alford is appealed to in support of this: 'If, in a passage where *two resurrections* are mentioned... [if] the first resurrection may be understood to mean *spiritual* rising with Christ, while the second means *literal* rising from the grave; —then there is an end of all significance in language, and Scripture is wiped out as a definite testimony to anything.'[75] Mounce notes likewise that if 'they came to life' in v. 4 'means a spiritual resurrection... then we are faced with the problem of discovering within the context some persuasive reason to interpret the same verb differently within one concise unit. No such reason can be found'.[76]

A word study of ἀνάστασις ('resurrection') is adduced in further support of the literal interpretation of the initial resurrection in v. 4, which is formally called 'the first resurrection' (ἡ ἀνάστασις ἡ πρώτη) in vv. 5-6. ἀνάστασις appears 41 times in the New Testament and means a physical resurrection with but 2 exceptions (Lk. 2.34; Jn 11.25). In this light, it would appear probable that the term has a literal meaning in Rev. 20.5-6.[77] According to this perspective, the word ζάω ('to live'), found in both vv. 4 and 5, should also be understood literally in the same way. Indeed, it also can be found with the literal meaning both inside and outside of the book.

75. Alford, *Greek Testament*, p. 732; appealed to recently, e.g., by Hoehner, 'Evidence from Revelation 20', p. 254.
76. Mounce, *Revelation*, p. 356.
77. So Deere, 'Premillenialism', p. 71.

In contrast to the literal approach, it is important to recognize that ἀνάστασις ('resurrection') is found in Revelation only in 20.5-6. In addition, the ordinal 'first' (πρῶτος) with 'resurrection' occurs nowhere else in the Old Testament or New Testament. This is a hint that lexical studies of words expressing the idea of 'first' and 'second' need to be conducted in order to understand the full meaning of 'resurrection' in the present context (so see below). In addition, ζάω ('to live') has a more fluid range of meaning both outside and within the Apocalypse (for the sense of physical resurrection outside the book, cf. Mt. 9.18; Rom. 14.9; 2 Cor. 13.4). Within the book it sometimes refers to physical resurrection (1.18; 2.8) or generally to some form of physical existence (16.3; 19.20), but more often has a figurative connotation of spiritual existence, especially with respect to God's attribute of timeless existence (so 6 times). In 3.1 the word refers to spiritual life (and the uses in 7.17 and 13.14 are likely also figurative).

Most striking, however, is the observation elsewhere in the New Testament that ἀνάστασις ('resurrection') and ζάω ('live', or ζωή ['life']) together with other synonyms are used interchangeably to refer both to spiritual and physical resurrection *within the same immediate context*. Rom. 6.4-13 reads:

> just as Christ was *raised* from the dead...so also we should walk in newness *of life*. For if we have become united with the likeness of his death, certainly also we will be in the likeness of his *resurrection*... For if we have died with Christ, we believe that also *we will live* with him...but the life *he* [Christ] *lives, he lives* to God. So also you reckon yourselves to be dead to sin but *living* to God in Christ Jesus...present yourselves to God as *those alive* from the dead.

(Compare similarly Rom. 8.10-11). Likewise, Jn 5.24-29 has the following:

> the one believing him who sent me has eternal *life* and does not come into judgment, but has passed from death into *life*...an hour is coming and now is when the dead will hear the voice of the Son of God and the ones hearing *will live*. For just as the Father has *life* in himself, so also he has given the Son to have *life* in himself...an hour is coming in which all those in the tombs will hear his voice, and they will come forth, those having done good deeds unto a *resurrection of life*, those having practised evil deeds unto a *resurrection* of judgment.

These observations do not demonstrate that the same words in Rev. 20.4-6 mean both spiritual and physical resurrection, but only that they can have that dual meaning elsewhere in the *same* context, which dilutes the principial hermeneutical objection noted by Alford above. Some commentators have observed, however, that there are indications within 20.4-6 that the words, in fact, do have the same interchangeable meaning; this view has been worked out most thoroughly by M.G. Kline, though he was anticipated by some earlier interpreters.[78] The following analysis is a summary of Kline's perspective.

It is clear that 'the second death' in v. 6 refers to a spiritual death of the unrighteous involving conscious, eternal suffering (see 20.10, 14-15, though this cannot be argued in depth here). On the other hand, the death of the righteous mentioned in v. 4 (e.g. 'the souls of those *be-headed*') refers to a literal, physical death. Therefore, there is a *first death* of believers which is physical and different in nature from the *second death* of unbelievers, which is spiritual. Now, if there are two different kinds of deaths, it is plausible that the resurrections would reflect the dual nature of the deaths. The resurrection of believers is spiritual, whereas the resurrection of unbelievers is physical. The passage would then reflect the following chiasm:

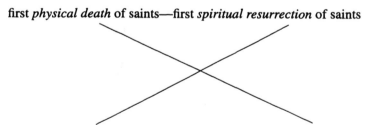

first *physical death* of saints—first *spiritual resurrection* of saints

second *physical resurrection* of wicked—second *spiritual death* of wicked

Ironically, the first physical death of saints translates them into the first spiritual resurrection in heaven, whereas the second physical resurrection translates the ungodly into the second spiritual death. This interpretation suits the thought of 20.6, since a first, eternal, spiritual resurrection is the minimal condition needed to prevent one from suffering a second, eternal, spiritual death. As the bodily resurrection of the

---

78. M.G. Kline, 'The First Resurrection', *WTJ* 37 (1975), pp. 366-75. Kline's view was anticipated by Hengstenberg, *Revelation of St. John*, II, p. 359; Swete, *Apocalypse*, p. 263 (followed by Prigent, *L'Apocalypse*, p. 312) and, to some extent, R. Summers, *The Life Beyond* (Nashville, TX: Broadman, 1959), pp. 86-90; R. Summers, 'Revelation 20: An Interpretation', *RevExp* 57.2 (1960), pp. 181-82.

wicked shows, bodily resurrection by itself does not provide protection against the second death.

The qualitative distinction between the two resurrections is also suggested by the qualitative antithesis between the 'first' (old) creation and second (new) creation in 21.1, where the former was pre-consummate or incomplete, while the latter consummate or complete. Strikingly, in 21.4-8 there is a formal antithesis between 'the [first physical] death' and 'the second [spiritual] death'. In 21.4 physical 'death' is the focus of the phrase 'the *first things* have passed away' which is contrasted with 'the second [spiritual] death' (21.8), which is associated in some way with the consummate condition of 'the new things' of the eternal new creation (21.5), though lying outside the boundaries of that new world. Rev. 21.1, 4 are a clear allusion to Isa. 65.16-17, where the same qualitative contrasts occur between the 'first affliction' or 'former' earth and 'a new heaven and a new earth'. Isa. 66.22 affirms that one of the qualitative differences is that 'the new heaven and new earth' will 'remain' forever in contrast to the former which passed away.[79] P.S. Minear is generally supportive by concluding that the distinction between 'first' and 'second' or between 'old' and 'new' throughout Revelation does not express temporal succession but qualitative antithesis, the difference between that which is transient and that which is eternally enduring.[80]

At least four possible objections can be lodged against this position (the first three as set forth by J.R. Michaels).[81]

(1) First, the fact that there is no formal reference to a '*first* (physical) death' or to a '*second* (physical) resurrection' suggests that these concepts may not really be in mind. If so, then the above-proposed ironic antitheses would not be evident. As noted already, however, the concepts are clearly stated in the text and the following context of ch. 21 actually uses the language of 'first' with physical death in antithesis to 'second (spiritual) death'.

(2) Second, the idea that the 'second death' is not literal but spiritual restricts the nature of that death too much. Does it not also include the physical existence of the reprobates who have been resurrected?

79. Kline, 'First Resurrection', pp. 366-67.

80. Minear, 'Cosmology of the Apocalypse', pp. 23-37, 261-62.

81. J.R. Michaels, 'The First Resurrection: A Response', *WTJ* 39 (1976), pp. 100-109.

Further, if the 'second death' means spiritual death, does not this mistakenly presuppose that those suffering it once possessed spiritual life? Those especially who understand the 'second death' to be annihilation and not eternal, conscious torment, would underscore the physical as well as the spiritual nature of the death. This would mean that there is less of an antithesis between the death in 20.4a and 20.6b.

On the other hand, I believe that a careful exegesis of 14.10-11 and 20.10 demonstrates the probability that the 'second death' is primarily a conscious suffering for eternity, which does not include physical destruction, though physical suffering could be included.[82] That the 'second death' must logically presuppose a first spiritual life is not a necessary logical deduction, especially if John's intention is to express paradoxical or ironic relationships between the two lives and deaths. Furthermore, elsewhere spiritual death does not presuppose a prior spiritual life (e.g. Eph. 2.1, 5; Col. 2.13).

(3) A third objection to the supposition of a 'first' spiritual resurrection followed by a second physical resurrection is that it is inconsistent to maintain that the first resurrection in vv. 4, 5b-6 fits the transitory pre-consummation pattern of the 'old–new'/'first–second' redemptive-historical antithesis, since this resurrection purportedly is the beginning of a resurrection which endures for eternity. But the inconsistency is resolved by understanding that the intermediate state of the soul's resurrection is, indeed, an incomplete state, since these souls await the final, consummated physical resurrection in the new heavens and earth. True, the soul's condition of 'life' will continue forever, but it will not continue in a non-corporeal form.[83] Further, even those souls translated into the immediate presence of God must wait for the redemptive-historical fulfillment of judgment before they can rest fully.

(4) A final objection to this version of the inaugurated millennial view is that the intermediate state is never called a 'resurrection' elsewhere in the Old Testament or New Testament. But this is not strictly true (on which see further below).

82. See further Beale, *Book of Revelation, in loc.*
83. See Michaels, 'First Resurrection: A Response', for other objections to Kline, and cf. M.G. Kline, 'The First Resurrection: A Reaffirmation', *WTJ* 37 (1976), pp. 110-19, for amplification of the above responses to Michaels.

c. *Additional Observations Supporting the Above Analysis of Revelation 20.4-6*

(i). *The Significance of 'First–Second' and 'Old–New' Antitheses Elsewhere in Old Testament, New Testament and Jewish Literature.* The preceding analysis is in line with similar 'first–second' and 'old–new' contrasts elsewhere, such as with the 'first Adam' and 'last Adam' in 1 Cor. 15.22, 42-49 and with the 'old (first) covenant' and 'new (second) covenant' in Heb. 8.6–10.9. The first Adam had a perishable, inglorious body and he brought death, whereas the last Adam had an imperishable and glorious body and he brought eternal life. The first covenant was temporary and led to death (e.g. Heb. 8.13), while the second was eternal and led to life. Neither in Revelation nor 1 Corinthians nor Hebrews does 'first' (πρῶτος) function as an ordinal in a process of counting things which are *identical in kind*.[84]

Likewise Hag. 2.6-9 (LXX) says that after God 'will shake the heaven and the earth', he will make the glory of 'the last' temple 'more than the first' temple. In the same vein *T. Benj.* 9.2 asserts that 'the latter temple will exceed the former in glory'. In Isa. 43.18-19 and 65.16-17 πρῶτος and πρότερος stand in contrast to καινός to refer to the 'former' old creation which will be replaced by a new, everlasting creation (cf. Isa. 65.19-22 and 66.22 for the eternal aspect).[85]

84. This paragraph follows Kline, 'First Resurrection', pp. 367-69.

85. Similarly, 1QH 13.11-13, by partial allusion to Isa. 43.19, affirms, 'they shall recount Thy glory in all Thy dominion... For Thou hast caused them to see what they had not known [by bringing to an end the] former [things] and by creating things that are new, by setting aside the former covenants and by [set]ting up that which shall remain for ever. For Thou art a God of eternity... and shalt be for ages without end'. In addition, note the following references employing the 'former–latter'/'first–last' language with the same significance as the above references, especially with respect to the enduring temple of the new creation in contrast to the temporary temple of the old creation: (1) CD (Ms. A) 3.19, 'He built for them a sure house in Israel such as did not exist from former times till now' (in contrast with 'end of days' in 4.4); (2) *Jub.* 1.27-29, 'from the first creation until my sanctuary is built in their midst forever' at the time of 'the new creation' (translation from Charlesworth, *OTP*, II, p. 54); (3) *1 En.* 14.15-16, 'there was a second house, greater than the former... in every respect it so excelled in splendour and magnificence and extent'; (4) *1 En.* 90.28-29, 'they folded up that old house... the Lord... brought a new house greater and loftier than the first, and set it up in the place of the first which had been folded up: all its pillars were new, and its

(ii). *The Bearing of the Broader Fourfold Ending of Revelation which is Based on the Ending of Ezekiel.* The broader fourfold ending of Revelation reflects the ending of Ezekiel 37–48: resurrection of God's people (Rev. 20.4a; Ezek. 37.1-14), messianic kingdom (Rev. 20.4b-6; Ezek. 37.15-28), final battle against Gog and Magog (Rev. 20.7-10; Ezek. 38–39) and final vision of the new temple and new Jerusalem (21.1–22.5; Ezek. 40–48).[86] In the light of the structural parallelism, the word ἔζησαν ('they came to life') in Rev. 20.4 is to be seen as an echo of Ezek. 37.10 (LXX), where the very same verb (ἔζησαν) is used (so also Ezek. 37.6, 14 [LXX], though using a future tense form). If the parallelism is intentional, then it would support a spiritual resurrection in Rev. 20.4-6 because the resurrection of Ezekiel 36–37 is also spiritual, or, at least, metaphorical in picturing Israel's coming restoration from Babylonian captivity as a resurrection.[87] Indeed, as is clearly the case in Ezekiel 37, it is possible that the vision of Rev. 20.4-6 is a picture of deceased saints being bodily resurrected, but this picture is to be interpreted symbolically as a spiritual resurrection.[88] This approach would be a partial answer to the literalist objection that a bodily resurrection *must* be envisioned. The Ezekiel prophecy is universalized and applied to the church. This is pointed to by the fact that the language of 'priests, kingdom, and reigning' in 20.4-6 is alluding to Exod. 19.6 and Dan. 7.27 which originally referred to ethnic Israel and which have already been applied to the church's present existence in Rev. 1.6, 9 and 5.9-10! The overall analysis given so far in this chapter on 20.1-6 also favors an application to the church and not to ethnic Israel.

ornaments were new and larger than those of the first, the old one which he had taken away'; Tob. 14.4-5, 'they shall build a temple, but not like to the first', which was 'burned' (cf. Tob. 13.13-18).

86. See Lust, ' The Order of the Final Events in Revelation and in Ezekiel', p. 179, for references to those observing the pattern.

87. For the similar point see A. Feuillet, *The Apocalypse* (Staten Island, NY: Alba House, 1965), p. 121, Brütsch, *Die Offenbarung Jesu Christi*, p. 340, and R.F. White, 'The Millennial Kingdom-City: Epic Themes, Ezek 36–39, and the Interpretation of Rev 20:4-10' (A paper delivered at the Annual Meeting of the Evangelical Theological Society, November, 1991).

88. So similarly A. Pieters, *The Lamb, the Woman and the Dragon: An Exposition of the Revelation of St. John* (Grand Rapids: Zondervan, 1937), pp. 293-94, 320, though without reference to Ezek. 37; cf. similarly L. Gry, *Le millénarisme dans ses origines et son développement* (Paris: Picard & Fils: 1904), p. 60.

Ezekiel 37.10 has already been applied in Rev. 11.11 to connote figuratively the church's continued existence, vindication, and release from the world's captivity into the immediate presence of God.[89] Similar to Ezekiel 37, Hos. 6.2 (LXX) figuratively uses resurrection terminology to refer to Israel's restoration from captivity: ἀναστησόμεθα καὶ ζησόμεθα ('we will arise and live'). Here, as in Rev. 20.4-6, the same root words are used in synonymous parallelism. The figurative uses in Ezekiel 37 and Hosea 6 are significant because in Rev. 6.9-10 and 7.14-17 saints are seen entering the blessed state of heaven after having come out of the afflictions of the world, which in both passages are described with Old Testament portrayals of Israel's affliction in captivity. Hence, plausibly also in Revelation 20 the exalted saints are viewed as latter-day Israel being restored, or figuratively resurrected, into the immediate presence of God out from the captivity of the world. Schüssler Fiorenza says, on the other hand, that, even if John alludes to Ezekiel 37, he conceives of the resurrection as literal, according to the pattern of the same wording in Rev. 2.8 and the Christian tradition behind it.[90]

(iii). *The Bearing of the Idea That Biblical Literature Elsewhere Affirms Only One Physical Resurrection at the Very End of the Age.* The above understanding of Rev. 20.4-6 is consistent with the view reflected elsewhere in the Old Testament and New Testament that there will be only *one* physical resurrection which will occur at the conclusion of history: see Isa. 26.19-21; Dan. 12.2; Jn 5.28-29; Acts 24.15; 2 Thess. 1.7-10; cf. Jn 6.39-40, 44, 54 (so also *1 En.* 51; *4 Ezra* 7.32; 14.35; *2 Bar.* 42.8; *Sib. Or.* 4.179-82; *Ps.-Philo* 3.10). This final resurrection is mentioned again in 20.12-15, which includes the physical resurrection of the saints along with the unrighteous. Rev. 20.5a mentions only the physical resurrection of the wicked to stress that they do not share in the first spiritual resurrection. In the light of 20.12-15, and the consensus of relevant

89. See on 11.11 in Beale, *Book of Revelation, in loc.*
90. Schüssler Fiorenza, *Priester*, p. 318. Judaism also believed that Ezek. 37.10 and Hos. 6.2 could be prophesying a literal resurrection of dead bodies at the end of history (for Ezek. 37.10 see *Tanḥ* Genesis, parashah 7.1; *Sib. Or.* 2. 221-24; 4.181-82; *PRE* 33; as well as Irenaeus, *Adv. haer.* 5.15.1; so likewise various parts of the Ezek. 37.1-14 vision in *Pes. R.* 1.6; *Gen. R.* 14.5; *Lev. R.* 14.9; *Deut. R.* 7.6; for Hos. 6.2 see *Targ. Hos.* 6.2; *Gen. R.* 56.1; Midr. Rab. *Deut. R.* 7.6; *Esth. R.* 9.2; *y. Ber.* 5.2[(I.B)]; *y. Ta'an.* 1.1[(II.B)]; *Sifre Deut. Piska*, 329; *T. d. Eliyy.*, p. 29; for the same view of Ezek. 37.5 see *y. Šeq.* 3.3[(VI.I)]; *y. Šab.* 1.3[(VIII.L)].

biblical evidence elsewhere, the physical resurrection of unbelievers in 20.5a should be seen as part of the general physical resurrection of all humanity at the end of the age, which, therefore, implicitly includes the physical resurrection of saints.

Therefore, the premillennial affirmation of two physical resurrections, respectively at the beginning and end of the millennium, is inconsistent with the biblical view elsewhere.

C. *The Bearing of Old Testament and Jewish Background on the Question of the Literal or Figurative Meaning of the 'One Thousand Years' in Revelation 20.1-7 and in Early Christian Literature*

Some understand all of vv. 4-6 as forecasting a literal fulfillment of Old Testament prophecies about a literal, earthly messianic reign (e.g. Ps. 2; Isa. 2.1-4; 4.1-6; 11.1-16; Jer. 23.5-8; Ezek. 37.24-28; 40–48; Dan. 2 and 7; Zech. 14). Consequently, a 'literal' hermeneutical approach also demands taking the millennial period literally.[91] However, such a hermeneutical perspective is debated, since many contend that New Testament authors sometimes understand fulfillment of the Old Testament in the New Testament non-literally.[92] Furthermore, many Old Testament prophecies could be viewed as having literal fulfillment in a newly created cosmos instead of in a millennium in the old cosmos.[93]

Walvoord argues that the 1000 years is literal since John mentions it both in the vision (vv. 4-5) and in the interpretation of the vision (v. 6; actually vv. 5-6 compose the interpretative comment).[94] But this assumes that figures of speech cannot be used in interpretative comments. Indeed, in the interpretative comment on v. 3 in v. 7 the figurative word 'prison' is found (so also cf. 'first-fruits' in 14.4; etc). G.W. Buchanan also takes the number literally.[95]

Some contend that the number '1000' is used only literally, whether in quantitative or temporal designations.[96] Walvoord says since all the other numbers in Revelation are literal, so also must be the thousand

---

91. E.g. J.F. Walvoord, 'The Millennial Kingdom and the Eternal State', *BibSac* 123 (1966), pp. 291-300; Hoehner, 'Evidence from Revelation 20', pp. 248-50.

92. E.g. LaRondelle, *Israel of God*; Beale, 'Did Jesus and his Followers Preach the Right Doctrine from the Wrong Texts?'

93. E.g. Hoekema, *Bible and the Future*, pp. 274-87.

94. Walvoord, *Revelation of Jesus Christ*, p. 293.

95. Buchanan, *Book of Revelation*, pp. 518ff.

96. E.g. Deere, 'Premillennialism', p. 70, who provides no demonstration.

years.[97] However, the programmatic use of σημαίνω ('signify') in 1.1 with reference to the whole book encourages the reader to expect a predominance of symbolic over literal language, including numbers.[98] Contrary to assertions otherwise, the number 1000 can be used figuratively. Indeed, multiples of 1000 have already been so used (see on 5.11; 7.4-9; 9.16; 14.1), as they are also in 21.16 (see also 11.3; 12.6 and 14.20, where χιλιάς with other numbers is likely figurative).[99]

Webb contends that the 1000 years is figurative and refers to saints physically reigning on the earth for a *long time*, since the 1000 years stands in contrast to a 'short time' in 20.3.[100] Assuming the correctness of this conclusion, Webb argues that an amillennial perspective would have to view Rev. 20.3-6 as expressing a delayed or postponed coming of Christ, which would be in virtual irreconcilable tension with the imminent expectation of the parousia elsewhere in the book (e.g. 6.10-11). It is certainly possible that the figurative significance of the number is that of a 'long time', and, if so, it would stand in tension with other imminence passages in the book. However, this would not be fatal to an amillennial view, since there are other New Testament passages which could be considered to express a delay before Christ's coming, which also stand in tension with imminence texts in their respective books (cf. Mt. 25.5 vs. 24.36-44; cf. also Lk. 12.41-48; 19.11-13).[101]

On the other hand, that the 1000 years represents mainly the notion of a *long time* is not necessarily the case, since the 'short time' appears to refer to an extremely brief transitional period directly following the millennium and immediately preceding the consummation. Indeed, 3.10 and 17.12 refer to the transitional period as 'the hour' or 'one hour'. Therefore, potentially and theoretically, the 1000 years could represent a year in contrast to a few days or months of the 'short time'. What

---

97. J.F. Walvoord, 'The Theological Significance of Revelation 20:1-6', in S.D. Toussaint and C.H. Dyer (eds.), *Essays in Honor of J. Dwight Pentecost* (Chicago: Moody Press, 1986), pp. 231; so also Hoehner, 'Evidence from Revelation 20', p. 249.

98. See on 1.1 at Chapter 4, sect. A above.

99. See Beale, *Book of Revelation*, for analysis supporting figurative uses in these passages.

100. Webb, 'Revelation 20', pp. 26-29.

101. See further Hoekema, *Bible and the Future*, pp. 109-28.

time period is being contrasted with the 'short time' is relative depending on the actual duration of the 'short time'. Therefore, on an amillennial (i.e. inaugurated millennial) reading, Rev. 20.3-6 does not necessarily express a clear concept of a delay of the parousia. The primary
point of the 1000 years is probably not to connote figuratively a long
time but the thematic idea of the ultimate victory of Christians who
have suffered. This is consistent with the use of other large numbers in
the book, where the largeness of the number figuratively connotes
themes. For example, the length, width, and height of the walls of the
New Jerusalem respectively is 'fifteen hundred miles [= 12,000 stadia]';
the idea is not literally that of very long, very wide and very high, but
the *completeness of God's people*, who are the city (see 21.12-16, 18-
20). The city's wall of 144 cubits does not indicate literally a very high
wall but the *absolute security* of God's people in the new creation (see
21.17-20). On the other hand, large numbers elsewhere in Revelation
can have the figurative idea of a very large group (e.g. 5.11; 9.16).
Context must decide in each case.

The number '1000' is often used both as a literal temporal and non-
temporal indicator in the Old Testament and New Testament.[102] Especially noteworthy is 1 Chron. 16.15-17 (= Ps. 105.8-10), where God's
'covenant forever' and his 'everlasting covenant' are equated with 'the
word which He commanded to a thousand generations'. Whether or not
'a thousand years' in Ps. 90.4 and 2 Pet. 3.8 are literal or figurative is
debated, though the latter is probable, as attested by early Jewish interpretation of Ps. 90.4: Wis. 18.9-11 substitutes 'a few years' for the
'thousand years' of Psalm 90, while *2 Bar.* 48.12-13 and *Ps.-Philo*
19.13a respectively substitute 'hours...and days' and 'this age [reading
seculum instead of *celum* (heaven)]'. Likewise figurative is CD (Ms. A)
7.5-6: 'the covenant of God is assurance that they *will live for a thousand generations* [= eternal life]'; 4QpPs. 37 2.1 also asserts the following: 'the converts of the desert who *will live for a thousand generations*...[and to them will belong all the glory]...for ever'.

In Judaism there are numerous traditions about the nature and length
of the future messianic reign. Some speculated that there would be no
messianic reign at all, while others proposed periods of an intermediate

---

102. See non-temporal figurative uses in Deut. 1.10-11; 32.30; Josh. 23.10; Job
9.3; 33.23; Ps. 68.17; Ps. 50.10; Song 4.4; Isa. 7.23; Isa. 30.17; 60.22 (LXX); Dan.
7.10; Amos 5.3. For temporal figurative uses see Deut. 7.9; Ps. 84.10; Eccles. 6.6;
7.28; *Jub.* 30.20.

reign from 40 to 365,000 years. Only two rabbis calculate the period to be '1000' years.[103] R. Eliezer b. Hyrcanus (c. 90 AD) represents the earliest attested view of a 1000 year reign, a conception which he likely learned from earlier rabbinic tradition[104] (cf. *b. Suk.* 28a). Samaritan tradition also held to a 1000 year messianic reign.[105] Other estimates in years are: (1) 60, (2) 70, (3) 100, (4) 365, (5) 400, (6) 600, (7) 2000, (8) 4000, and (9) 7000 (see the surveys of rabbinic views in *b. Sanh.* 97a-b; *b. Sanh.* 99a; *Midr. Ps.* 90.17; *Pes. R., Piska* 1, though some see the last as estimating the time leading up to the coming of Messiah). All of these may have been conceived of as reckonings of literal years, but all are also multiples of ten and potential candidates as figurative numbers of completeness. The 365 and 365,000 years presumably are intensifications of the 365-day cycle of the year, and, likewise are potentially figurative for annual completeness. Charles contends that all Jewish views of an intermediate messianic reign were understood to take place on a literal earth, and that John has the same view.[106]

The only other use of the millennial period is clearly figurative for the complete perfection of the eternal time of blessing for God's people: *Jub.* 23.27-30 says, 'And the days shall begin to grow many and increase amongst those children of men till their days draw nigh to *one thousand years*, and to a greater number of years than [before] was the number of the days. And there shall be no old man...And all their days they shall complete and *live* in peace and joy...and rejoice with joy for ever and ever'. The number of a 'thousand' in this passage is derived from *Jub.* 4.29-30, which alludes to Isa. 65.22 (LXX: 'For as the days of the tree of life shall be the days of my people, they shall long enjoy the fruits of their labors'):

> Adam died...he lacked seventy years of one thousand years; for one thousand years are as one day [= Ps. 90.4] in the testimony of the heavens, and therefore was it written concerning the tree of knowledge: "On

103. R. Eliezer b. Hyrcanus cited in *Midr. Pss.* 90.17; R. Eliezer [= b. Jose the Galilean], cited in *Pes. R. Piska* 1; cf. *b. Sanh.* 97a, where a 1000 year reign is implied from the teaching of Rab. Kaṭṭina.

104. So Str-Bill, III, pp. 826-27.

105. See J.W. Bailey, 'The Temporary Messianic Reign in the Literature of Early Judaism', *JBL* 53 (1934), pp. 179-80.

106. Charles, *Revelation*, II, pp. 184-85 (likewise Webb, 'Revelation 20', pp. 32-33, who argues that, since Rev. 20.1-3 and 20.7-9 take place on earth, 20.4-6 probably also takes place on earth).

the day you eat thereof you shall die". For this reason he did not complete the years of this day; for he died during it.

Jubilees understands that the ideal life of the probationary period
('day') in Eden should have been 1000 years (so also *Gen. R.* 19.8;
Num. R. 5.4; *Midr. Ps.* 25.8 on the basis of Ps. 90). Therefore, the
Jubilees text concludes that the future messianic reign must achieve
what Adam did not. *Jubilees* bases this on three pieces of evidence: (1)
Adam's age at death, which did not quite reach 1000 years; (2) Isa.
65.22, which prophesies that the messianic age will last as long as the
ideal meant for the first paradise (cf. likewise *T. Levi* 18.8-13); and (3)
Ps. 90.4 (the *Jubilees* tradition of the ideal millennial span of the first
paradise is reflected in Irenaeus [*Adv. haer.* 5.23.2]). At least in part,
Jub. 23.27-30 was influenced to conceive of this millennium figuratively because of the Psalm 90 formula, whereas early fathers like Justin
Martyr (*Dial.* 81) used the same reasoning to formulate a literal premillennial perspective.[107]

In another context similar to *Jubilees* 23 the evil spirits and reprobates will 'be bound...to the end of all generations...and then all the
righteous escape, and they shall live till they beget thousands of children and all their days of their youth and their old age shall they complete in peace' (1 En. 10.14-17). Both Jubilees and *1 Enoch* picture the
saints 'completing' their days of blessedness for eternity (cf. further
1 En. 10.22). *1 Enoch* has this happening at the same time as the evil
spirits are 'bound'.

On the basis that 'a thousand years is like one day' (Ps. 90.4), *2
Enoch* 25–33 appeals to the seven days of creation in Genesis 1 and
affirms that history will follow the same sevenfold pattern, the consequent reckoning of the historical age being 7000 years and a following
'eighth day', referring apparently to eternity.[108] In connection with the

107. Cf. likewise Hippolytus (*Fragments on Daniel* 2.4-6), and possibly
Methodius (*Banquets of the Ten Virgins* 9.1; *Extracts from the Work on Things
Created* 9), though they may reflect a similar line of interpretation as in *Barn.* 15 or
perhaps Irenaeus; see further Daniélou, *Theology of Jewish Christianity*, pp. 390-
96, on which this paragraph is based.

108. See Wikenhauser, 'Weltwoche und tausendjähriges Reich', for a survey of
how Psalm 90 and the days of creation influenced the church Fathers of the third
and fourth centuries with respect to the duration of world history and the question
of chiliasm.

same tradition, *Barnabas* 15 reckons history to last 6000 years at the conclusion of which

> the Lord will bring all things to an end; for the day with Him signifies a thousand years...in six thousand years all things will be brought to an end...but what I have made [the sabbath of the last thousand years], when I have set all things at rest, I will make the beginning of the eighth day which is the beginning of another world.

The sabbath of the last thousand years merges into the eternity of the eighth day, 'in which also Jesus rose from the dead'. The last thousand years is figurative for the saints' eternal rest and the eighth day of Christ's resurrection becomes figurative, not merely for eternity, but for the age of the saints' resurrection which commences eternal rejoicing.[109] Irenaeus, *Adv. haer.* 5.28.3 and 5.33-36 may follow the same line of thought in *Barnabas* 15, though his view seems inconsistent and the consensus is that he was a premillennialist.

Testament of Isaac 6–8 speaks of a 'millennial banquet' (6.13, 22; 8.6), which possibly is to be enjoyed by departed souls beginning at the point of their death. This is suggested by noting that at death these souls inherit 'the kingdom of heaven' (6.22; 7.2; 8.5), which appears to be synonymous with 'the millennial banquet' in 8.6. In fact, at the time that Isaac's soul went to heaven, he experienced 'the fulfillment of his covenant forever' (7.2). Alternatively, and perhaps more plausibly, the millennium could refer to final, eternal bliss, which starts at some future eschatological time when the souls will 'celebrate...in the everlasting light in the kingdom'. The *Testament of Isaac* text fits better into a view that the millennium refers to the soul's bliss after death or into a conception akin to that of *Barnabas* 15 rather than conforming to a typical premillennial belief. *Apoc. Elij.* 5.36-39 may represent premillennial thought, though it could reflect a similar theological tendency as in Barnabas 15, as suggested by word order and the possible equation of eternity with the millennium: 'On that day... He [Christ] will burn the earth. He will spend a thousand years upon it...he will create a new

---

109. See Daniélou, *Theology of Jewish Christianity*, pp. 396-401, and Kromminga, *Millennium in the Church*, pp. 29-40, for a similar view of *Barn.* 15; for discussion of other viewpoints on *Barnabas* see Mealy, *After the Thousand Years*, p. 48, who himself sees the last thousand years in *Barnabas* as the *beginning* of the eternal age but not co-extensive with it, which is plausible; see Kromminga, *Millennium in the Church, passim*, for a thorough survey of the doctrine from the Apostolic Fathers up to the twentieth century.

earth... He will rule with his saints...while they are *always* with the angels and they are with Christ for a thousand years.' The mention of 'day' followed by 'thousand years' could echo the Psalm 90 formula.[110] But Justin Martyr, *Dial.* 70-71, clearly testifies to a classic form of early premillennialism, while acknowledging that 'many who belong to the pure and pious faith, and are true Christians' disagreed with his view.

The millennium of Revelation 20 could be associated broadly with early rabbinic tradition of a 1000 year reign,[111] and especially the tradition reflected in *Jubilees, 2 Enoch*, and *Barnabas*. If so, it would not be a period of a literal '1000 years' but would represent a long epoch which would be the last of world history;[112] Schüssler Fiorenza sees the tradition in *Jubilees, 2 Enoch*, and *Barnabas* as influential and argues for a thematic rather than temporal meaning of the 1000 years, viewing it as emphasizing end-time rule by Christ and his saints.[113] Another reason for her view is that she sees Rev. 22.5 as referring also to the millennial reign but there also it is said to be an eternal reign.[114] On the other hand, the 1000 years of Revelation 20 do not appear to be equivalent with eternity as in *Jubilees* 23 or *Barnabas*.[115]

The three elements of (1) the binding of evil heavenly beings, (2) the messianic reign, and (3) a thousand year epoch are found together nowhere in Judaism outside of Rev. 20.1-6. These elements have been combined in Revelation 20 to indicate that Christ's death and resurrection have inaugurated both the binding of Satan and the era of the

---

110. Note the above wording in *Apoc. Elij.*, as possibly implied by O.S. Wintermute, 'Apocalypse of Elijah', *OTP*, I, pp. 721-53 (753).

111. Bailey, 'Temporary Messianic Reign', p. 187.

112. So Bailey, 'Temporary Messianic Reign'; Prigent, *L'Apocalypse de Saint Jean*, p. 304; cf. Mounce, *Revelation*, pp. 357-59; most recently, B.W. Snyder, 'How Millennial is the Millennium? A Study in the Millennial Background of the 1000 Years in Revelation 20', *Evangelical Journal* 9 (1991), pp. 51-74 (70-71).

113. Schüssler Fiorenza, *Priester*, pp. 293, 321-24.

114. Schüssler Fiorenza, *Priester*, pp. 293, 322-23.

115. For a thorough yet concise survey of possible Jewish parallels to the millennium of Rev. 20 see broadly Str-B, IV, pp. 799-1015, and, more specifically Str-B, III, pp. 823-27 (the latter briefly summarized in English by Beasley-Murray, *Revelation*, pp. 288), as well as R.H. Charles, *Eschatology: The Doctrine of a Future Life in Israel, Judaism and Christianity* (New York: Schocken Books, 1963 [1913]), pp. 219-20, 239-40, 270-73, 301-302, 324-37; Bailey, 'Temporary Messianic Reign'; Snyder, 'How Millennial is the Millennium?'

saints' reign with Christ.[116] If the reign in 20.4-6 has been influenced by the general Jewish idea of an intermediate reign on earth, then the intermediate period is plausibly now the so-called church age and the reign takes place in heaven, though 1.6 and 5.10 show that it also takes place on earth among those who are regenerate.

116. So Snyder, 'How Millennial is the Millennium?', pp. 70-71.

BIBLIOGRAPHY

Aalders, J.G., *Gog en Magog in Ezechiël* (Kampen: Kok, 1951).

Alexander, J.A., *Commentary on the Prophecies of Isaiah* (Grand Rapids: Zondervan, 1953 [orig. 1846–47]).

Alexander, R.H., 'A Fresh Look at Ezekiel 38 and 39', *JETS* 17 (1974), pp. 157-69.

Alford, H., *The Greek Testament*. IV. *Epistles of St. John and Jude: And the Revelation* (Cambridge: Deighton, Bell, 1866).

Allen, L.C., *Ezekiel 20–48* (WBC, 29; Dallas, TX: Word Books, 1990).

Allison, D.C., *The End of the Ages Has Come* (Philadelphia: Fortress Press, 1985).

—'Eschatology', in Green, McKnight and Marshall (eds.), *Dictionary of Jesus and the Gospels*, pp. 206-209.

Altink, W., '1 Chronicles 16:8-36 as Literary Source for Revelation 14:6-7', *AUSS* 22 (1984), pp. 187-96.

Anderson, C., 'Romans 1.1-5 and the Occasion of the Letter: The Solution to the Two-Congregation Problem at Rome', *Trinity Journal* 14 (1993), pp. 25-40.

Auld, A.G., *Understanding Poets and Prophets: Essays in Honour of G.W. Anderson* (JSOTSup, 152; Sheffield: JSOT Press, 1993).

Aune, D.E., 'Apocalypticism', in Hawthorne, Martin and Reid (eds.), *Dictionary of Paul and his Letters*, pp. 25-35.

—'The Form and Function of the Proclamations to the Seven Churches (Revelation 2–3)', *NTS* 36 (1990), pp. 182-204.

—*Prophecy in Early Christianity and in the Ancient Mediterranean World* (Grand Rapids: Eerdmans, 1983).

Bailey, J.W., 'The Temporary Messianic Reign in the Literature of Early Judaism', *JBL* 53 (1934), pp. 170-87.

Balch, D.L., E. Ferguson and W.A. Meeks (eds.), *Greeks Romans, and Christians: Essays in Honor of A.J. Malherbe* (Minneapolis: Fortress Press, 1990).

Baldwin, J.G., *Daniel* (Leicester: Inter-Varsity Press, 1978).

—*Haggai, Zechariah, Malachi* (London: Tyndale Press, 1972).

Ball, D.M., *'I Am' in John's Gospel* (JSNTSup, 124; Sheffield: Sheffield Academic Press, 1996).

Bandstra, A.J., 'History and Eschatology in the Apocalypse', *Calvin Theological Journal* 5 (1970), pp. 180-83.

—' "A Kingship and Priest": Inaugurated Eschatology in the Apocalypse', *Calvin Theological Journal* 27 (1992), pp. 10-25.

Barr, J., *Biblical Words for Time* (SBT, 33; London: SCM Press, 1962).

Barrett, C.K., 'The Eschatology of the Epistle to the Hebrews', in Davies and Daube (eds.), *The Background of the New Testament and its Eschatology*, pp. 363-93.

Bauckham, R.J., *The Climax of Prophecy: Studies in the Book of Revelation* (Edinburgh: T. & T. Clark, 1993).

—'The Eschatological Earthquake in the Apocalypse of John', *NovT* 19 (1977), pp. 224-33.

—'The Great Tribulation in the Shepherd of Hermas', *JTS* 25 (1974), pp. 27-40.

—*Jude, 2 Peter* (WBC, 50; Waco, TX: Word Books, 1983).

—'Synoptic Parousia Parables and the Apocalypse', *NTS* 23 (1977), pp. 162-76.

—*The Theology of the Book of Revelation* (Cambridge: Cambridge University Press, 1993).

Bayer, H.F., 'Christ-Centered Eschatology in Acts 3:17-26', in Green and Turner (eds.), *Jesus of Nazareth: Lord and Christ*, pp. 236-50.

Beale, G.K., *The Book of Revelation* (NIGTC; Grand Rapids: Eerdmans; Carlisle: Paternoster, 1998).

—'The Danielic Background for Revelation 13:18 and 17:9', *TynBul* 31 (1980), pp. 163-70.

—'Did Jesus and his Followers Preach the Right Doctrine from the Wrong Texts? An Examination of the Presuppositions of Jesus' and the Apostles' Exegetical Method', *Themelios* 14 (1989), pp. 89-96.

—'An Exegetical and Theological Consideration of the Hardening of Pharaoh's Heart in Exodus 4–14 and Romans 9', *Trinity Journal* 5 (1984), pp. 129-54.

—'The Influence of Daniel upon the Structure and Theology of John's Apocalypse', *JETS* 27 (1984), pp. 413-23.

—'The Interpretative Problem of Rev. 1:19', *NovT* 34 (1992), pp. 360-87.

—'Isaiah VI 9-13: A Retributive Taunt against Idolatry', *VT* 41 (1991), pp. 257-78.

—' "Kings of Kings and Lord of Lords" in Rev. 17:14', *NTS* 31 (1985), pp. 618-20.

—'The Old Testament Background of Reconciliation in 2 Corinthians 5–7 and its Bearing on the Literary Problem of 2 Corinthians 6:14-18', *NTS* 35 (1989), pp. 550-81.

—'The Old Testament Background of Rev. 3:14', *NTS* 42 (1996), pp. 133-52.

—'The Problem of the Man from the Sea in IV Ezra 13 and its Relation to the Messianic Concept in John's Apocalypse', *NovT* 25 (1983), pp. 182-88.

—'A Reconsideration of the Text of Daniel in the Apocalypse', *Bib* 67 (1986), pp. 539-43.

—*The Use of Daniel in Jewish Apocalyptic Literature and in the Revelation of St. John* (Lanham, MD: University Press of America, 1984).

—'The Use of Daniel in the Synoptic Eschatological Discourse and in the Book of Revelation', in Wenham (ed.), *Gospel Perspectives. V. The Jesus Tradition outside the Gospels*, pp. 129-53.

—'[The Use of the Old Testament in] Revelation', in Carson and Williamson (eds.), *It Is Written: Scripture Citing Scripture*, pp. 318-36.

—'Review Article: J.W. Mealy *After the Thousand Years*', *EvQ* 66 (1994), pp. 229-49.

—Review of *Decoding Revelation's Trumpets: Literary Allusions and Interpretation of Revelation 8:7-12* (Andrews University Seminary Doctoral Dissertation Series, 21; Berrien Springs, MI: Andrews University Press, 1987), by J. Paulien, in *JBL* 111 (1992), pp. 358-61.

—Review of *The Letters to the Seven Churches of Asia in their Local Setting* (JSNTSup, 11; Sheffield: JSOT Press, 1986), by C.J. Hemer, in *Trinity Journal* 7 (1986), pp. 107-11.

Beale, G.K., (ed.), *Right Doctrine from Wrong Texts? Essays on the Use of the Old Testament in the New* (Grand Rapids: Baker Book House, 1994).

Beasley-Murray, G.R., *The Book of Revelation* (London: Marshall, Morgan & Scott, 1974).

Beattie, D.R.G., and M.J. McNamara (eds.), *The Aramaic Bible* (JSOTSup, 166; Sheffield: JSOT Press, 1994).

Beckwith, Isbon T., *The Apocalypse of John* (New York: Macmillan, 1919).

Betz, O., 'Der Katechon', *NTS* 9 (1963), pp. 282-84.

Bietenhard, H., 'ἀμήν', in *NIDNTT* I, pp. 97-99.

Blaising, C.A., and D.L. Bock (eds.), *Dispensationalism, Israel and the Church* (Grand Rapids: Zondervan, 1992).

Blass, F., and A. Debrunner, *A Greek Grammar of the New Testament and Other Early Christian Literature* (ed. R.W. Funk; Chicago: University of Chicago Press, 1961).

Block, D., 'Gog and Magog in Ezekiel's Eschatological Vision', Tyndale Old Testament Lecture delivered at the Tyndale Fellowship Triennial Conference on Eschatology (Swanwick, Great Britain, July, 1997).

—'Gog and Magog in Ezekiel's Eschatological Vision', in K.E. Brower and M.W. Elliott (eds.), *The Reader Must Understand* (Leicester: Apollos [Inter-Varsity], 1997), pp. 85-116.

Bockmuehl, M.N.A., *Revelation and Mystery in Ancient Judaism and Pauline Christianity* (WUNT, 2; Tübingen: J.C.B. Mohr [Paul Siebeck], 1990).

Bøe, A.S., 'Bruken av det Gamle Testamente i Johannes' Åpenbaring', *Tidsskrift for Teologi og Kirke* 63 (1992), pp. 253-69.

Boersma, T., *Is the Bible a Jigsaw Puzzle... An Evaluation of Hal Lindsey's Writings* (St Catherines, Ontario: Paideia, 1978).

Boismard, M., ' "L'Apocalypse" ou "Les Apocalypses" de St Jean', *RB* 56 (1949), pp. 530-32.

Boring, M.E., *Revelation* (The Interpretation Series; Louisville: John Knox Press, 1989).

Bornkamm, G., 'μυστήριον', in *TDNT*, IV, pp. 802-28.

Bousset, W., *Die Offenbarung Johannis* (Göttingen: Vandenhoeck & Ruprecht, 6th edn, 1906).

Bowker, J.W., 'Mystery and Parable', *JTS* NS 25(1974), pp. 300-17.

Bowman, J.W., 'The Revelation to John: Its Dramatic Structure and Message', *Int* 9 (1955), pp. 436-53.

Bratcher, R.G., *A Translator's Guide to the Revelation to John* (London: United Bible Societies, 1984).

Breech, E., 'These Fragments I Have Shored Against My Ruins: The Form and Function of 4 Ezra', *JBL* 92 (1973), pp. 267-74.

Bretscher, P.M., 'Syntactical Peculiarities in Revelation', *CTM* 16 (1945), pp. 95-105.

Brown, C., 'The Parousia and Eschatology in the NT', *NIDNTT*, II, pp. 901-35.

Brooks, J.A., and C.L. Winbery, *Syntax of New Testament Greek* (Washington: University Press of America, 1979).

Brown, R.E., *The Epistles of John* (AB, 30; Garden City, NY: Doubleday, 1982).

—*The Gospel According to John I-XII* (AB, 29; Garden City, NY: Doubleday, 1966).

Brown, R.E., J.A. Fitzmeyer, and R.E. Murphy (eds.), *The New Jerome Biblical Commentary* (Englewood Cliffs, NJ: Prentice–Hall, 1990).

—*The Semitic Background of the Term 'Mystery' in the New Testament* (Biblical Series, 21; Philadelphia: Fortress Press, 1968).

Brownlee, W.H., 'Messianic Motifs of Qumran and the New Testament', *NTS* 3 (1956–57), pp. 195-210.

Brox, N., *Zeuge und Märtyer* (SANT, 5; Munich: Kösel, 1961).

Bruce, F.F., *The Epistles to the Colossians, to Philemon, and to the Ephesians* (NICNT; Grand Rapids: Eerdmans, 1984).
—'Eschatology in Acts', in Gloer (ed.), *Eschatology and the New Testament: Essays in Honor of G.R. Beasley-Murray*, pp. 51-63.
—1 & 2 Thessalonians (WBC, 45; Dallas, TX: Word Books, 1982).
—*New Testament Development of Old Testament Themes* (Grand Rapids: Eerdmans, 1970).
—*New Testament History* (Garden City, NY: Doubleday, 1971).
Brütsch, C., *Clarte de l'Apocalypse* (Geneva: Labor et Fides, 1955).
—*Die Offenbarung Jesu Christi*, I–II (Zürcher Bibelkommentare; Zürich: Zwingli-Verlag, 1970).
Buchanan, G.W., *The Book of Revelation: Its Introduction and Prohecy* (The Mellen Biblical Commentary, New Testament Series, 22; Lewiston: Mellen Biblical Press, 1993).
Büchsel, F., 'κρίνω', in *TDNT*, III, pp. 923, 933-41.
Burney, C.F., 'Christ as the *APXH* of Creation', *JTS* 27 (1926), pp. 160-77.
Buzzard, A., 'Acts 1:6 and the Eclipse of the Biblical Kingdom', *EvQ* 66 (1994), pp. 197-215.
Cadbury, H.J., 'Acts and Eschatology', in Davies and Daube (eds.), *The Background of the New Testament and its Eschatology*, pp. 300-21.
Caird, G.B., *A Commentary on the Revelation of St. John the Divine* (London: A. & C. Black; New York: Harper & Row, 1966).
—*The Language and Imagery of the Bible* (Philadelphia: Westminster Press, 1980).
Callahan, A.D., 'The Language of the Apocalypse', *HTR* 88 (1995), pp. 453-70.
Cambier, J., 'Les images de l'Ancien Testament dans l'Apocalypse de Saint Jean', *NRT* 77 (1955), pp. 113-22.
Campbell, D.K., and J.L. Townsend (eds.), *A Case for Premillennialism: A New Consensus* (Chicago: Moody Press, 1992).
Caragounis, C., *The Ephesian* Mysterion (ConBNT, 8; Lund: C.W.K. Gleerup, 1977).
Carlston, C.E., 'Eschatology and Repentance in the Epistle to the Hebrews', *JBL* 78 (1959), pp. 296-302.
Carmignac, J., 'La notion d'eschatologie dans la Bible et à Qumran', *RevQ* 7 (1969), pp. 17-31.
Carnegie, D.R., 'The Hymns in Revelation: Their Origin and Function' (Unpublished PhD dissertation for the British Council for National Academic Awards [supervision under the London Bible College], 1978).
—'Worthy is the Lamb: The Hymns in Revelation', in Rowden (ed.), *Christ the Lord*, pp. 243-56.
Carroll, J.T., *Response to the End of History: Eschatology and Situation in Luke–Acts* (Atlanta: Scholars Press, 1988).
Carson, D.A. (ed.), *From Sabbath to Lord's Day* (Grand Rapids: Zondervan, 1982).
—*The Gagging of God* (Grand Rapids: Zondervan, 1996).
Carson, D.A. and H.G.M. Williamson (eds.), *It Is Written: Scripture Citing Scripture. Essays in Honour of Barnabas Lindars* (Cambridge: Cambridge University Press, 1988).
Casey, J.S., 'Exodus Typology in the Book of Revelation' (PhD dissertation, Southern Baptist Theological Seminary, Louisville, Kentucky, 1981).

Charles, R.H., *A Critical and Exegetical Commentary on the Revelation of St. John* (2 vols.; Edinburgh: T. & T. Clark, 1920).

—*Eschatology: The Doctrine of a Future Life in Israel, Judaism and Christianity* (New York: Schocken Books, 1963 [1913]).

Charlesworth, J.H. (ed.), *The Messiah* (Minneapolis: Fortress Press, 1992).

Chilton, B.D., *The Isaiah Targum* (The Aramaic Bible, II; Wilmington, DE: Michael Glazier, 1987).

Chilton, D.C., *The Days of Vengeance* (Fort Worth, TX: Dominion Press, 1987).

Collins, A.Y., *The Apocalypse* (New Testament Message, 22; Wilmington, DE: Michael Glazier, 1979).

—'Apocalypse (Revelation)', in Brown, Fitzmeyer, and Murphy (eds.), *The New Jerome Biblical Commentary*, pp. 996-1016.

—*The Combat Myth in the Book of Revelation* (HDR, 9; Missoula, MT: Scholars Press, 1976).

—*Crisis and Catharsis* (Philadelphia: Westminster Press, 1984).

—'The History-of-Religions Approach to Apocalypticism and the "Angel of the Waters" (Rev. 16:4-7)', *CBQ* 39 (1977), pp. 367-81.

Review of *Use of Daniel in Jewish Apocalyptic Literature and the Revelation of St. John* (Lanham: University Press of America, 1984), by G.K. Beale, in *JBL* 105 (1986), pp. 734-35.

—'The "Son of Man" Tradition and the Book of Revelation', in Charlesworth (ed.), *The Messiah*, pp. 536-68.

Collins, J.J., *The Apocalyptic Vision of the Book of Daniel* (HSM, 16; Missoula, MT: Scholars Press, 1977).

—*The Sybylline Oracles of Egyptian Judaism* (SBLDS, 13; Missoula, MT: Scholars Press, 1974).

Comblin, J., *Le Christ dans l'Apocalypse* (Bibliotheque de Théologie, Théologie Biblique 6.3; Paris: Desclée de Brouwer, 1965).

Cooke, G.A., *The Book of Ezekiel* (ICC; Edinburgh: T. & T. Clark, 1936).

Coppens, J., ' "Mystery" in the Theology of Saint Paul and its Parallels at Qumran', in J. Murphy-O'Conner (ed.), *Paul and Qumran* (Chicago: The Priory Press, 1968), pp. 132-58.

Cranfield, C.E.B., *Romans*, II (ICC; Edinburgh: T. & T. Clark, 1979).

Cross, F.M., *The Ancient Library of Qumran* (Garden City, NY: Doubleday, 1961).

Cullmann, O., *Christ and Time* (Philadelphia: Westminster Press, 1964).

Dana, H.E., and J.R. Mantey, *A Manual Grammar of the Greek New Testament* (Toronto: Macmillan, 1927).

Daniélou, J., *The Theology of Jewish Christianity: the Development of Christian Doctrine before the Council of Nicaea*, I (Chicago: H. Regnery, 1964).

Davids, P. and R.P. Martin (eds.), *Dictionary of the Later New Testament and its Developments* (Downers Grove, IL: InterVarsity Press, 1997).

Davies, W.D., and D. Daube (eds.), *The Background of the New Testament and its Eschatology: Studies in Honour of C.H. Dodd* (Cambridge: Cambridge University Press, 1956).

Davis, J.J., *Moses and the Gods of Egypt* (Grand Rapids: Baker Book House, 1971).

Deere, J.S., 'Premillennialism in Revelation 20:4-6', *BSac* 135 (1978), pp. 58-73.

Delling, G., 'Zum Gottesdienstlichen Stil der Johannes-Apokalypse', *NovT* 3 (1959), pp. 107-37.

Dennison, C.G., and R.C. Gamble (eds.), *Pressing toward the Mark* (Philadelphia: Committee for the Historian of the Orthodox Presbyterian Church, 1986).

Dittmar, W.D., *Vetus Testamentum in Novo* (Göttingen: Vandenhoeck & Ruprecht, 1903).

Dodd, C.H., *According to the Scriptures* (New York: Charles Scribner's Sons, 1953).

Donaldson, T.L., 'Parallels: Use, Misuse and Limitations', *EvQ* 55 (1983), pp. 193-210.

Draper, J.A., 'The Heavenly Feast of Tabernacles: Revelation 7.1-17', *JSNT* 19 (1983), pp. 133-47.

—'The Twelve Apostles and the Foundation Stones of the Heavenly Jerusalem and the Foundation of the Qumran Community', *Neot* 22 (1988), pp. 41-63.

Dumbrell, W.J., *The End of the Beginning* (Homebush West, Australia: Lancer, 1985).

—'The Purpose of the Book of Isaiah', *TynBul* 36 (1985), pp. 111-28.

Dunn, J.D.G., *Romans 9–16* (WBC, 38B; Dallas, TX: Word Books, 1988).

Dupont-Sommer, A., *The Essene Writings from Qumran* (trans. G. Vermes; Oxford: Basil Blackwell, 1961).

Düsterdieck, F., *Critical and Exegetical Handbook to the Revelation of John* (H.A.W. Meyer's Commentary on the New Testament, XI; trans. H.E. Jacobs; Winona Lake, IN: Alpha Publications, 1980; ET T. & T. Clark, 1883).

Eichrodt, W., *Ezekiel* (Philadelphia: Westminster Press, 1970).

Eliade, M., *The Myth of the Eternal Return* (London: Routledge & Kegan Paul, 1955).

Ellingworth, P., *The Epistle to the Hebrews* (NIGTC; Grand Rapids: Eerdmans; Carlisle: Paternoster Press, 1993).

Ellis, E.E., *Paul's Use of the Old Testament* (Grand Rapids: Baker Book House, 1981 [1957]).

—'Present and Future Eschatology in Luke', *NTS* 12 (1965), pp. 27-41.

Enroth, A.-M., 'The Hearing Formula in the Book of Revelation', *NTS* 36 (1990), pp. 598-608.

Epp, E.J., and G.W. MacRae (eds.), *The New Testament and its Modern Interpreters* (Atlanta, GA: Scholars Press, 1989).

Evans, C.A., *To See and Not Perceive: Isaiah 6.9-10 in Early Jewish and Christian Interpretation* (JSOTSup, 64; Sheffield: JSOT Press, 1989).

Fanning, B., *Verbal Aspect in New Testament Greek* (Oxford: Clarendon Press, 1990).

Farrer, A., *A Rebirth of Images: The Making of St. John's Apocalypse* (Boston: Beacon Press, 1963).

—*The Revelation of St. John the Divine* (Oxford: Clarendon Press, 1964).

Fee, G.D., *The First Epistle to the Corinthians* (NICNT; Grand Rapids: Eerdmans, 1987).

Feinberg, C.L., *Millennialism: The Two Major Views* (Chicago: Moody Press, 1980).

Fekkes, J., *III Isaiah and Prophetic Traditions in the Book of Revelation: Visionary Antecedents and their Development* (JSNTSup, 93; Sheffield: JSOT Press, 1994).

Ferguson, E., 'Was Barnabas a Chiliast? An Example of Hellenistic Number Symbolism in Barnabas and Clement of Alexandria', in Balch, Ferguson, and Meeks (eds.), *Greeks, Romans, and Christians*, pp. 157-67.

Feuillet, A., *The Apocalypse* (Staten Island, NY: Alba House, 1965).

Ford, D., *The Abomination of Desolation in Biblical Eschatology* (Washington, DC: University Press of America, 1979).

—*Daniel* (Nashville: Southern Publishing Association, 1978).

Ford, J. Massingberd, *Revelation* (AB, 38; Garden City, NY: Doubleday, 1975).

France, R.T., *Jesus and the Old Testament* (London: Tyndale Press, 1971).

Francis, F.O., 'Eschatology and History in Luke–Acts', *JAAR* 37 (1969), pp. 49-63.

Franklin, E., 'The Ascension and the Eschatology of Luke–Acts', *SJT* 23 (1970), pp. 191-200.

Fransen, I., 'Cahier de Bible: Jésus, le Témoin Fidèle (Apocalypse)', *BVC* 16 (1956–57), pp. 66-79.

Friedrich, G., 'σάλπιγξ, κτλ.', in *TDNT*, VII, pp. 71-88.

Fuchs, A. (ed.), *Theologie aus dem Norden* (SNTU, Serie A, Band 2; Linz, Austria: Plöchl, Freistadt, 1977).

Gaffin, R.B., *The Centrality of the Resurrection* (Grand Rapids: Baker Book House, 1978).

Gaffin, R.B. (ed.), *Perspectives on Pentecost* (Phillipsburg, NJ: Presbyterian and Reformed Publishing, 1979).

—*Redemptive History and Biblical Interpretation: The Shorter Writings of Geerhardus Vos* (Phillipsburg, NJ: Presbyterian and Reformed Publishing, 1980).

—'A Sabbath Rest Still Awaits the People of God', in Dennison and Gamble (eds.), *Pressing toward the Mark*, pp. 33-51.

Gangemi, A., 'L'utilizzazoine del Deutero-Isaia nell'Apocalisse di Giovanni', *Euntes Docete* 27 (1974), pp. 109-44, 311-39.

Garlington, D.B., *The Obedience of Faith* (WUNT, 38; Tübingen: J.C.B. Mohr [Paul Siebeck], 1991).

—'Obedience of Faith in the Letter to the Romans', *WTJ* 52 (1990), pp. 201-24.

Gärtner, B., *The Temple and the Community in Qumran and the New Testament* (SNTSMS, 1; Cambridge: Cambridge University Press, 1965).

Gaventa, B.R., 'The Eschatology of Luke–Acts Revisited', *Encounter* 43 (1982), pp. 27-42.

Gerhardsson, B., 'Die christologischen Aussagen in den Sendschreiben', in Fuchs (ed.), *Theologie aus dem Norden*, pp. 142-66.

Gesenius, William, *Gesenius' Hebrew Grammar* (eds. E. Kautzsch and A.E. Cowley; Oxford: Clarendon Press, 1910).

Giblin, C.H., *The Book of Revelation* (Good News Studies, 34; Collegeville, MN: Liturgical Press, 1991).

Giles, K., 'Present–Future Eschatology in the Book of Acts (I)', *RTR* 40 (1981), pp. 65-71.

—'Present–Future Eschatology in the Book of Acts (II)', *RTR* 41 (1982), pp. 11-18.

Gill, John, *An Exposition of the New Testament. III. The Revelation of St. John the Divine* (Philadelphia: William W. Woodward, 1811), pp. 691-886.

Gilmour, S.M., 'The Revelation to John', in C.M. Laymon (ed.), *The Interpreter's One-Volume Commentary on the Bible*, pp. 945-68.

Gloer, W.H. (ed.), *Eschatology and the New Testament: Essays in Honor of G.R. Beasley-Murray* (Peabody, MA: Hendrickson, 1988).

Goodenough, E.R., *Jewish Symbols in the Greco–Roman World* (Princeton, NJ: Princeton University Press, 1988).

Goodwin, William W., *Syntax of the Moods and Tenses of the Greek Verb* (Boston: Ginn, 1890).

Goppelt, L., 'τύπος', in *TDNT*, VIII, pp. 246-59.

—*Typos* (Grand Rapids: Eerdmans, 1982).

Gottwald, N.K., *The Hebrew Bible—A Socio-Literary Introduction* (Philadelphia: Fortress Press, 1985).

Goulder, M.D., 'The Apocalypse as an Annual Cycle of Prophecies', *NTS* 27 (1981), pp. 342-67.

Gourges, M., 'The Thousand-Year Reign (Rev. 20:1-6): Terrestrial or Celestial?', *CBQ* 47 (1985), pp. 676-81.

Gowan, D.E., *Eschatology in the Old Testament* (Philadelphia: Fortress Press, 1986).

Gray, D.A., 'The Day of the Lord and its Culmination in the Book of Revelation (Related to the Theology of Hope)' (PhD dissertation; Manchester: University of Manchester, 1974).

Green, J.B., S. McKnight and I.H. Marshall (eds.), *Dictionary of Jesus and the Gospels* (Downers Grove, IL: InterVarsity Press, 1992).

Green, J.B. and M. Turner (eds.), *Jesus of Nazareth: Lord and Christ* (Grand Rapids: Eerdmans, 1994).

Grossfeld, B., *The Targum Onkelos to Genesis* (The Aramaic Bible, 6; Wilmington, DE: Michael Glazier, 1988).

Grudem, W.A., *The Gift of Prophecy in 1 Corinthians* (Washington, DC: University Press of America, 1982).

Gruenler, Royce G., *Meaning and Understanding* (Grand Rapids: Zondervan, 1991).

Gry, L., *Le millénarisme dans ses origines et son développement* (Paris: Picard & Fils, 1904).

Gundry, R.H., *The Church and the Tribulation* (Grand Rapids: Zondervan, 1973).

Gunkel, H., *Schöpfung und Chaos in Urzeit und Endzeit* (Göttingen: Vandenhoeck & Ruprecht, 1895).

Günther, H.W., *Der Nah—und Enderwartungshorizont in der Apokalypse des heiligen Johannes* (FzB, 41; Würzburg: Echter Verlag, 1980).

Hahn, F., 'Die Sendschreiben der Johannesapokalypse: Ein Beitrag zur Bestimmung prophetischer Redeformen', in Jeremias, Kuhn, and Stegemann (eds.), *Tradition und Glaube*, pp. 357-94.

—*The Titles of Jesus in Christology* (London: Lutterworth, 1969).

Hailey, H., *Revelation* (Grand Rapids: Baker Book House, 1979).

Harner, P.B., *The 'I Am' of the Fourth Gospel* (Facet Books, Biblical Series, 26; Philadelphia: Fortress Press, 1970).

Harris, M.J., 'σάλπιγξ', in *NIDNTT*, III, pp. 873-74.

Hartman, L., 'Form and Message: A Preliminary Discussion of "Partial Texts" in Rev 1–3 and 22.6ff', in Lambrecht (ed.), *L'Apocalypse johannique et l'Apocalyptique dans le Nouveau Testament*, pp. 129-49.

—*Prophecy Interpreted* (ConBNT, 1; Lund: C.W.K. Gleerup, 1966).

Harvey, A.E., 'The Use of Mystery Language in the Bible', *JTS* NS 31 (1980), pp. 320-36.

Hatch, E., and H.A. Redpath, *A Concordance to the Septuagint and the Other Greek Versions of the Old Testament*, I–II (Graz–Austria: Akademische Druck–U. Verlagsanstalt, 1954).

Hawthorne, G.F. (ed.), *Current Issues in Biblical and Patristic Interpretation* (Grand Rapids: Eerdmans, 1975).

Hawthorne, G.F., R.P. Martin and D.G. Reid (eds.), *Dictionary of Paul and his Letters* (Downers Grove, IL: InterVarsity Press, 1993).

Hays, R.B., *Echoes of Scripture in the Letters of Paul* (New Haven: Yale University Press, 1989).

Heil, J.P., 'The Fifth Seal (Rev 6,9-11) as a Key to Revelation', *Bib* 74 (1993), pp. 220-43.

Hemer, C.J., *The Letters to the Seven Churches of Asia in their Local Setting* (JSNTSup, 11; Sheffield: JSOT Press, 1986).

Hendriksen, W., *More than Conquerors: An Interpretation of the Book of Revelation* (Grand Rapids: Baker Book House, 1962).

—*New Testament Commentary: Exposition of Ephesians* (Grand Rapids: Baker Book House 1967).

Hengstenberg, E.W., *The Revelation of St. John*, I–II (New York: R. Carter and Brothers, 1853).

Hennecke, E., *New Testament Apocrypha* (2 vols.; ed. and rev. W. Schneemelcher; trans. R.McL. Wilson; Philadelphia: Westminster Press, 1963).

Herntrich, V., 'The OT Term מִשְׁפָּט', in *TDNT*, III, pp. 923-33.

Hesse, F., *Das Verstockungsproblem im Alten Testament* (BZAW, 74; Berlin: Alfred Töpelmann, 1955).

Hill, D., 'The Spirit and the Church's Witness: Observations on Acts 1:6-8', *IBS* 6 (1984), pp. 16-26.

Hirsch, E.D., *The Aims of Interpretation* (Chicago: University of Chicago Press, 1976).

—*Validity in Interpretation* (New Haven: Yale University Press, 1967).

Hoehner, H.W., 'Evidence from Revelation 20', in D.K. Campbell and J.L. Townsend (eds.), *A Case for Premillennialism: A New Consensus*, pp. 235-62.

Hoekema, A.A., *The Bible and the Future* (Grand Rapids: Eerdmans, 1979).

Hofius, O., 'Das Evangelium und Israel', in O. Hofius (ed.), *Paulusstudien*, pp. 175-202.

Hofius, O. (ed.), *Paulusstudien* (WUNT, 51; Tübingen: Mohr [Paul Siebeck], 1989).

Holman, C.L., *The Origin of Christian Eschatology* (Peabody, MA: Hendrickson, 1996).

Holtz, T., *Die Christologie der Apokalypse des Johannes* (TU, 85; Berlin: Akademie Verlag, 1971).

Horbury, W., and B. McNeil (eds.), *Suffering and Martyrdom in the New Testament* (Cambridge: Cambridge University Press, 1981).

Horsley, G.H.R., and S.R. Llewelyn, *New Documents Illustrating Early Christianity* (7 vols.; North Ryde, NSW, Australia: The Ancient History Documentary Research Centre, 1981–).

Hoskier, H.C., *Concerning the Text of the Apocalypse* (2 vols.; London: Bernard Quaritch, 1929).

Howard, G., 'Eschatology in the Period between the Testaments', in Lewis (ed.), *The Last Things*, pp. 60-73

Hughes, P.E., *The Book of the Revelation* (Grand Rapids: Eerdmans, 1990).

Hühn, E., *Die alttestamentlichen Citate und Reminiscenzen im Neuen Testament* (Tübingen: J.C.B. Mohr [Paul Siebeck], 1900).

Hultberg, A., 'The Significance of Zech. 12:10 for the Theology of the Apocalypse' (A paper presented at the 47th Annual Meeting of the Evangelical Theological Society, Philadelphia, PA, 16 November 1995).

Hurst, L.D., 'Eschatology and "Platonism" in the Epistle to the Hebrews', in Kent Harold Richards (ed.), *SBLSP 23* (Chico, CA: Scholars Press, 1984), pp. 41-74.

Jeffrey, David L., 'Literature in an Apocalyptic Age', *Dalhousie Review* 61 (1981), pp. 426-46.

Jellicoe, S., *The Septuagint and Modern Study* (Oxford: Clarendon Press, 1968).

Jenkins, F., *The Old Testament in the Book of Revelation* (Marion, IN: Cogdill Foundation Publications, 1972).

Jepsen, A., ' 'amen', in *TDOT*, I, pp. 320-22.

Jeremias, G., H.-Kuhn and H. Stegemann (eds.), *Tradition und Glaube* (Göttingen: Vandenhoeck & Ruprecht, 1971).

Johnson, Alan, *Revelation* (The Expositor's Bible Commentary, 12; Grand Rapids: Zondervan, 1981).

Kantzer, K.S., and S.N. Gundry, (eds.), *Perspectives on Evangelical Theology* (Papers from the Thirtieth Annual Meeting of the Evangelical Theological Society; Grand Rapids: Baker Book House, 1979)

Keel, O., *The Symbolism of the Biblical World* (New York: Crossroad, 1985).

Keil, C.F., *Biblical Commentary on the Book of Daniel* (Biblical Commentary on the Old Testament; Grand Rapids: Eerdmans, 1971).

Kiddle, Martin, and M.K. Ross, *The Revelation of St. John* (MNTC; London: Hodder & Stoughton, 1940).

Kim, S., 'The "Mystery" of Rom 11.25-26 Once More', *NTS* 43 (1997), pp. 412-29.

—*The Origin of Paul's Gospel* (Grand Rapids: Eerdmans, 1982).

Kirby, J.T., 'The Rhetorical Situations of Revelation', *NTS* 34 (1988), pp. 197-207.

Klassen, W., and G.F. Snyder (eds.), *Current Issues in New Testament Interpretation: Festschrift for O.A. Piper* (New York: Harper & Row, 1962).

Klein, W.W., C.L. Blomberg and R.L. Hubbard, *Introduction to Biblical Interpretation* (Dallas, TX: Word Books, 1993).

Kline, M.G, 'The First Resurrection', *WTJ* 37 (1975), pp. 366-75.

—'The First Resurrection: A Reaffirmation', *WTJ* 37 (1976), pp. 110-19.

—*Images of the Spirit* (Grand Rapids: Baker Book House, 1980).

—*The Structure of Biblical Authority* (Grand Rapids: Eerdmans, 1972).

—'The Structure of the Book of Zechariah', *JETS* 34 (1991), pp. 179-93.

König, A., *The Eclipse of Christ in Eschatology* (Grand Rapids: Eerdmans; London: Marshall, Morgan & Scott, 1980).

Kostenberger, A.J., 'The Mystery of Christ and the Church: Head and Body, "One Flesh"', *Trinity Journal* 12 NS (1991), pp. 79-94.

Kraft, H., *Die Offenbarung des Johannes* (HNT, 16a; Tübingen: Mohr [Paul Siebeck], 1974).

Kreitzer, L.J., 'Eschatology', in Hawthorne, Martin, and Reid (eds.), *Dictionary of Paul and his Letters*, pp. 253-69.

—'Parousia', in Davids and Martin (eds.), *Dictionary of the Later New Testament and its Developments* (1997).

Krodel, G.A., *Revelation* (Augsburg Commentary on the New Testament; Minneapolis: Augsburg, 1989).

Kromminga, D.H., *The Millennium in the Church* (Grand Rapids: Eerdmans, 1945).

Kuhn, K.G., 'Gog-Magog', in *TDNT*, I, pp. 789-91.

Kurz, W.S., 'Acts 3:19-26 as a Test of the Role of Eschatology in Lukan Christology', in Paul J. Achtemeier (ed.), *SBLSP 11* (Missoula, MT: Scholars Press, 1977), pp. 309-23.

Ladd, G.E., *A Commentary on the Revelation of John* (Grand Rapids: Eerdmans, 1972).

—'Eschatology and the Unity of the New Testament Theology', *ExpTim* 68 (1957), pp. 268-78.

—*Presence of the Future* (Grand Rapids: Eerdmans, 1974).

Lambrecht, J. (ed.), *L'Apocalypse johannique et l'Apocalyptique dans le Nouveau Testament* (BETL, 53; Gembloux: Duculot; Leuven: Leuven University Press, 1980).

Lancellotti, A., 'L'antico testamento nell'apocallise', *RivB* 14 (1966), pp. 369-84.

Lang, G.H., *The Revelation of Jesus Christ* (Letchworth, Hertfordshire: Garden City Press; London: Oliphants, 1945).

LaRondelle, H.K., *The Israel of God in Prophecy* (Berrien Springs, MI: Andrews University Press, 1983).

Läuchli, S., 'Eine Gottesdienststruktur in der Johannesoffenbarung', *TZ* 16 (1960), pp. 359-78.

Laughlin, T.C., *The Solecisms of the Apocalypse* (Princeton, NJ: Princeton University Press, 1902).

Laymon, C.M. (ed.), *The Interpreter's One-Volume Commentary on the Bible* (Nashville: Abingdon Press, 1971).

Lenglet, A., 'La structure litteraire de Daniel 2–7', *Biblica* 53 (1972), pp. 169-90.

Lenski, R.C.H., *The Interpretation of St. John's Revelation* (Minneapolis: Augsburg, 1963).

Lewis, A.H., *The Dark Side of the Millennium* (Grand Rapids: Baker Book House, 1980).

Lewis, J.P. (ed.), *The Last Things: Essays Presented to W.B. West, Jr.* (Austin, TX: Sweet Publishing, 1972).

Lincoln, A.T., *Paradise Now and Not Yet* (SNTSMS, 43; Cambridge: Cambridge University Press, 1981).

—'Sabbath, Rest, and Eschatology in the New Testament', in Carson (ed.), *From Sabbath to Lord's Day*, pp. 197-220.

Lindars, B., *New Testament Apologetic* (Philadelphia: Westminster Press, 1961).

—'The Place of the Old Testament in the Formation of New Testament Theology', *NTS* 23 (1977), pp. 59-66.

Lindsey, H., *There's a New World Coming* (New York: Bantam Books, 1975).

Lohmeyer, E., *Die Offenbarung des Johannes* (HNT, 16; Tübingen: J.C.B. Mohr [Paul Siebeck], 1970).

Lohse, E., 'Die alttestamentliche Sprache des Sehers Johanne: Textkritische Bemerkungen zur Apokalypse', *ZNW* 52 (1961), pp. 122-26.

—*Die Offenbarung des Johannes* (Göttingen: Vandenhoek & Ruprecht, 1960).

Longenecker, R., 'Can We Reproduce the Exegesis of the New Testament?', *TynBul* 21 (1970), pp. 3-38.

Longman, T., 'The Divine Warrior: The New Testament Use of an Old Testament Motif', *WTJ* 44 (1982), pp. 290-307.

Louw, J.P., and E.A. Nida, *Greek–English Lexicon of the New Testament Based on Semantic Domains*, I–II (2 vols.; New York: United Bible Societies, 1988).

Lövestamm, E., 'Apokalypsen 3:8b', *SEÅ* 30 (1965), pp. 91-101.

Luomanen, P.(ed.), *Luke–Acts* (Helsinki: The Finnish Exegetical Society, 1991).

Lust, J., 'The Order of the Final Events in Revelation and in Ezekiel', in Lambrecht (ed.), *L'Apocalypse johannique et l'Apocalyptique dans le Nouveau Testament*, pp. 179-83.

MacRae, G.W., 'Heavenly Temple and Eschatology in the Letter to the Hebrews', *Semeia* 12 (1978), pp. 179-99.

Maher, M., *Targum Pseudo–Jonathan: Genesis* (The Aramaic Bible, IB; Collegeville, MN: Liturgical Press, 1992).

Marconcini, B., 'L'utilizzazione del T.M. nelle citazioni isaiane dell'Apocalisse', *RevB* 24 (1976), pp. 113-36.

Marshall, I.H., *1 and 2 Thessalonians* (NCB; Grand Rapids: Eerdmans; London: Marshall, Morgan & Scott, 1983).

—*The Epistles of John* (NICNT; Grand Rapids: Eerdmans, 1978).

—'Slippery Words', *ExpTim* 89 (1978), pp. 264-69.

Mattill, A.J., *Luke and the Last Things* (Dillsboro, NC: Western North Carolina Press, 1979).

Maurer, C., 'ῥίζα', in *TDNT*, VI, pp. 985-90.

Mauro, P., *The Patmos Visions: A Study of the Apocalypse* (Boston: Hamilton, 1925).

Mazzaferri, F.D., *The Genre of the Book of Revelation from a Source-Critical Perspective* (BZNW, 54; Berlin: W. de Gruyter, 1989).

McCartney, D., and C. Clayton, *Let the Reader Understand* (Wheaton, IL: Bridgepoint: Victor Books, 1994).

McComiskey, T.E., 'Alteration of OT Imagery in the Book of Revelation: Its Hermeneutical and Theological Significance', *JETS* 36 (1993), pp. 307-16.

McDowell, E.A., *The Meaning and Message of the Book of Revelation* (Nashville, TX: Broadman, 1951).

McKelvey, R.J., *The New Temple* (Oxford: Oxford University Press, 1969).

McNamara, M., *The New Testament and the Palestinian Targum to the Pentateuch* (AnBib, 27; Rome: Pontifical Biblical Institute, 1966).

—*Targum Neofiti*. I. *Genesis* (The Aramaic Bible, IA; Collegeville, MN: Liturgical Press, 1992).

McRay, J., 'Charismata in Second-Century Eschatology', in Lewis (ed.), *The Last Things*, pp. 151-68.

Mealy, J.W., *After the Thousand Years* (JSNTSup, 70; Sheffield: JSOT Press, 1992).

Metzger, B.M., *A Textual Commentary on the Greek New Testament* (London: United Bible Societies, 1971).

Michaels, J.R., 'The Centurion's Confession and the Spear Thrust', *CBQ* 29 (1967), pp. 102-109.

—'Eschatology in 1 Peter III.17', *NTS* 13 (1967), pp. 394-401.

—'The First Resurrection: A Response', *WTJ* 39 (1976), pp. 100-109.

—'Revelation 1:19 and the Narrative Voices of the Apocalypse', *NTS* 37 (1991), pp. 604-20.

Michel, O., 'ναός', in *TDNT*, IV, pp. 880-90.

Minear, P.S., 'The Cosmology of the Apocalypse', in Klassen and Snyder (eds.), *Current Issues in New Testament Interpretation*, pp. 23-37.

—*I Saw a New Earth: An Introduction to the Visions of the Apocalypse* (Washington: Corpus Books, 1969).

Moffatt, J., *The Revelation of St. John the Divine* (The Expositor's Greek Testament, 5; Grand Rapids: Eerdmans, 1970).

Montgomery, J.A., *A Critical and Exegetical Commentary on the Book of Daniel* (ICC; Edinburgh: T. & T. Clark, 1979).

—'The Education of the Seer of the Apocalypse', *JBL* 45 (1926), pp. 70-81.

Moo, D.J., *The Epistle to the Romans* (NICNT; Grand Rapids: Eerdmans, 1996).

Moritz, T., *A Profound Mystery: The Use of the Old Testament in Ephesians* (NovTSup, 85; Leiden: E.J. Brill, 1996).

Morris, L., *The Revelation of St. John* (Grand Rapids: Eerdmans, 1980).

Moule, C.F.D., *An Idiom Book of New Testament Greek* (Cambridge: Cambridge University Press, 1953).

—'Influence of Circumstances on the Use of Eschatological Terms', *JTS* 15 (1964), pp. 1-15.

J.H. Moulton, and G. Milligan, *The Vocabulary of the Greek New Testament* (Grand Rapids: Eerdmans, 1972).

J.H. Moulton, W.F. Howard and Nigel Turner, *A Grammar of New Testament Greek*. I. *Prolegomena* (Edinburgh: T. & T. Clark, 1906).

—*A Grammar of New Testament Greek*. II. *Accidence and Word-Formation* (Edinburgh: T. & T. Clark, 1929).

—*A Grammar of New Testament Greek*. III. *Syntax* (Edinburgh: T. & T. Clark, 1963).

—*A Grammar of New Testament Greek*. IV. *Style* (Edinburgh: T. & T. Clark, 1976).

Mounce, R.H., *The Book of Revelation* (NICNT; Grand Rapids: Eerdmans, 1977).

Moyise, S., *The Old Testament in the Book of Revelation* (JSNTSup, 115; Sheffield: Sheffield Academic Press, 1995).

Mulholland, M.R., *Revelation* (Grand Rapids: Francis Asbury Press of Zondervan Publishing House, 1990).

Müller, H.-P., 'Die Plagen der Apokalypse; Eine formgeschichtliche Untersuchung', *ZNW* 51 (1960), pp. 268-78.

Müller, U.B., *Prophetie und Predigt im Neuen Testament* (SNT, 10; Gütersloh: Gerd Mohn, 1975).

Murphy, F.J., 'The Book of Revelation', *CR:BS* 2 (1994), pp. 181-225.

Murphy-O'Conner, J. (ed.), *Paul and Qumran* (Chicago: The Priory Press, 1968).

Murray, J., *The Epistle to the Romans* (NICNT; Grand Rapids: Eerdmans, 1968).

Muse, R.L., 'Revelation 2–3: A Critical Analysis of Seven Prophetic Messages', *JETS* 29 (1986), pp. 147-61.

Mussies, G., 'Antipas (Rev. 2:13b)', *NovT* 7 (1964), pp. 242-44.

—'The Greek of the Book of Revelation', in Lambrecht (ed.), *L'Apocalypse johannique et l'Apocalyptique dans le Noveau Testament*, pp. 167-77.

—*The Morphology of Koine Greek as Used in the Apocalypse of St. John: A Study in Bilingualism* (NovTSup, 27; Leiden: E.J. Brill, 1971).

Nielsen, A.E., 'The Purpose of the Lucan Writings with Particular Reference to Eschatology', in Luomanen (ed.), *Luke–Acts*, pp. 76-93.

O'Brien, P.T., *Introductory Thanksgivings in the Letters of Paul* (NovTSup, 49; Leiden: E.J. Brill, 1977).

Olyan, S., *A Thousand Thousands Served Him* (TSAJ, 36; Tübingen: J.C.B. Mohr [Paul Siebeck], 1993).

Ozanne, C.G., 'The Language of the Apocalypse', *TynBul* 16 (1965), pp. 3-9.

Parker, H.M., 'The Scripture of the Author of the Revelation of John', *Iliff Review* 37 (1980), pp. 35-51.

Pate, C.M., *The End of the Ages Has Come: The Theology of Paul* (Grand Rapids: Zondervan, 1995).

Paulien, J., *Decoding Revelation's Trumpets: Literary Allusions and Interpretation of Revelation 8:7-12* (Andrews University Seminary Doctoral Dissertation Series, 21; Berrien Springs, MI: Andrews University Press, 1987).

—'Elusive Allusions: The Problematic Use of the Old Testament in Revelation', *BibRes* 33 (1988), pp. 37-53.

Penner, T.C., *The Epistle of James and Eschatology* (JSNTSup, 121; Sheffield: Sheffield Academic Press, 1996).

Pieters, A., *The Lamb, the Woman and the Dragon: An Exposition of the Revelation of St. John* (Grand Rapids: Zondervan, 1937).

Piper, J., *The Justification of God* (Grand Rapids: Baker Book House, 1983).

Porter, S.E., 'The Language of the Apocalypse in Recent Study', *NTS* 35 (1989), pp. 582-603.

—*Verbal Aspect in the Greek of the New Testament, with Reference to Tense and Mood* (Studies in Biblical Greek, I; New York: Peter Lang, 1989).

Poythress, V.S., 'Genre and Hermeneutics in Rev 20:1-6', *JETS* 36 (1993), pp. 41-54.

—'Johannine Authorship and the Use of Intersentence Conjunctions in the Book of Revelation', *WTJ* 47 (1985), pp. 329-36.

Price, S.R.F., *Rituals and Power* (Cambridge: Cambridge University Press, 1984).

Prigent, P., *L'Apocalypse de Saint Jean* (Paris: Delachaux & Niestlé, 1981).

—*Apocalypse et Liturgie* (Cahiers Théologiques, 52; Paris: Delachaux & Niestlé, 1964).

Pryor, N., 'Eschatological Expectations in the Old Testament Prophets', in Lewis (ed.), *The Last Things*, pp. 32-59.

Rad, G. von, *Old Testament Theology* (2 vols.; New York: Harper & Row Publishers, 1962, 1965).

Ramsay, Sir William Mitchell, *The Letters to the Seven Churches of Asia and their Place in the Plan of the Apocalypse* (London: Hodder & Stoughton, 1904).

Rengstorf, K.H., 'σημεῖον', in *TDNT*, VII, pp. 229-59.

Ridderbos, H., *Paul* (Grand Rapids: Eerdmans, 1975).

Rissi, M., *The Future of the World: An Exegetical Study of Rev. 19:11–22:15* (SBT Second Series, 23; London: SCM Press, 1972) (Expanded and Revised Version of an Original German Edition).

—*Time and History: A Study on the Revelation* (Richmond, VA: John Knox Press, 1966).

Rist, M., 'The Revelation of St. John the Divine' (IB, 12; Nashville: Abingdon Press, 1957), pp. 347-613.

Roberts, B.J., *The OT Text and Versions* (Cardiff: University of Wales, 1951).

Robertson, A.T., *The General Epistles and the Revelation of John* (Word Pictures in the New Testament, 6; Nashville: Broadman Press, 1933).

—*A Grammar of the Greek New Testament in the Light of Historical Research* (New York: Hodder & Stoughton, 1914).

Robertson, O.P., 'Is there a Distinctive Future for Ethnic Israel in Romans 11?', in Kantzer and Gundry (eds.), *Perspectives on Evangelical Theology*, pp. 209-27.

Robinson, W.C., 'Eschatology of the Epistle to the Hebrews: A Study in the Christian Doctrine of Hope', *Encounter* 22 (1961), pp. 37-51.

Roloff, J., *Revelation* (Minneapolis: Fortress Press, 1993).

Rowden, H.H. (ed.), *Christ the Lord: Studies Presented to D. Guthrie* (Downers Grove, IL: InterVarsity Press, 1982).

Ruiz, J.-P., *Ezekiel in the Apocalypse: The Transformation of Prophetic Language in Revelation 16,17–19,10* (European University Studies, 23.376; Frankfurt am Main: Peter Lang, 1989).

Russell, R., 'Eschatology and Ethics in 1 Peter', *EvQ* 47 (1975), pp. 78-84.

Ryrie, C.C., 'The Mystery in Ephesians 3', *BSac* 123 (1966), pp. 24-31.

Sabourin, L., 'The Eschatology of Luke', *BTB* 12 (1982), pp. 73-76.

Sandmel, S., 'Parallelomania', *JBL* 81 (1962), pp. 1-13.

Satake, A., *Die Gemeindeordnung in der Johannesapokalypse* (WMANT, 21; Neukirchen–Vluyn : Neukirchener Verlag, 1966).

Saucy, R.L., 'The Church as the Mystery of God', in Blaising and Bock (eds.), *Dispensationalism, Israel and the Church*, pp. 127-55.

Sawyer, J.F.A., ' "My Secret is with Me" (Isaiah 24.16): Some Semantic Links between Isaiah 24–27 and Daniel', in Auld (ed.), *Understanding Poets and Prophets: Essays in Honour of G.W. Anderson*, pp. 307-17.

Schlatter, A., *Das Alte Testament in der johanneischen Apokalypse* (BFCT, 16.6; Gütersloh: Bertelsmann, 1912).

Schlier, H., 'ἀμήν', in *TDNT*, I, p. 337.

Schmid, Josef, *Studien zur Geschichte des griechischen Apokalypse-Textes* (Münchener Theologische Studien, 1.1, 1.2, 2; Munich: K. Zink, 1955).

Schmidt, D.D., 'Semitisms and Septuagintalisms in the Book of Revelation', *NTS* 37 (1991), pp. 592-603.

Schnackenburg, R., *God's Rule and Kingdom* (New York: Herder & Herder, 1963).

Scholer, D.M., 'Sins within and Sins without: An Interpretation of 1 John 5:16-17', in Hawthorne (ed.), *Current Issues in Biblical and Patristic Interpretation*, pp. 230-46.

Schüssler Fiorenza, E., 'Apocalyptic and Gnosis in the Book of Revelation', *JBL* 92 (1973), pp. 565-81.

—'Apokalypsis and Propheteia: Revelation in the Context of Early Christian Prophecy', in Lambrecht (ed.), *L'Apocalypse johannique et l'Apocalyptique dans le Nouveau Testament*, pp. 105-28.

—*The Book of Revelation: Justice and Judgment* (Philadelphia: Fortress Press, 1985).

—*Preister für Gott: Studien zum Herrschafts und Priestermotiv in der Apokalypse* (Münster: Aschendorff, 1972).

—*Revelation: Vision of a Just World* (Proclamation Commentaries; Minneapolis: Fortress Press, 1991).

—'Revelation', in Epp and MacRae (eds.), *The New Testament and its Modern Interpreters* (Atlanta: Scholars Press, 1989), pp. 407-27.

Scobie, C.H.H., 'Local Reference in the Letters to the Seven Churches', *NTS* 39 (1993), pp. 606-24.

Scott, E.F., *The Book of Revelation* (London: SCM Press, 1939).

Scott, R.B.Y., *The Original Language of the Apocalypse* (Toronto: Toronto University Press, 1928).

Seiss, J.A., *The Apocalypse: A Series of Special Lectures on the Revelation of Jesus Christ* (Grand Rapids: Eerdmans, 1966).

Selwyn, E.C., *The Christian Prophets and the Prophetic Apocalypse* (London: Macmillan, 1900).

—'Dialogues on the Christian Prophets', *Expositor*, Sixth Series 5 (1902), pp. 321-43.

—'Eschatology in 1 Peter', in Davies and Daube (eds.), *The Background of the New Testament and its Eschatology*, pp. 394-401.

The Septuagint Version of the Old Testament and Apocrypha with an English Translation (Grand Rapids: Zondervan, 1972).

Shea, W.H., 'The Covenantal Form of the Letters to the Seven Churches', *AUSS* 21 (1983), pp. 71-84.

Shütz, R., *Die Offenbarung des Johannes und Kaiser Domitian* (FRLANT, 32; Göttingen: Vandenhoeck & Ruprecht, 1933).

Silberman, L.H., 'Farewell to O AMHN', *JBL* 82 (1963), pp. 213-15

Silva, M., *Biblical Words and their Meaning* (Grand Rapids: Zondervan, 1983).

—'Perfection and Eschatology in Hebrews', *WTJ* 39 (1976), pp. 60-71.

Sims, J.H., *A Comparative Literary Study of Daniel and Revelation* (Lewiston: Mellen Biblical Press, 1994).

Smalley, S.S., *1, 2, 3 John* (WBC, 51; Waco, TX: Word Books, 1984).

—'John's Revelation and John's Community', *BJRL* 69 (1987), pp. 549-71.

Smith, C.R., 'Revelation 1:19: An Eschatologically Escalated Prophetic Convention', *JETS* 33 (1990), pp. 461-66.

Smith, R.H., 'The Eschatology of Acts and Contemporary Exegesis', *CTM* 29 (1958), pp. 641-63.

—'History and Eschatology in Luke–Acts', *CTM* 29 (1958), pp. 881-901.

Smyth, H.W., *Greek Grammar* (Cambridge, MA: Harvard University Press, 1984).

Snyder, B.W., 'Combat Myth in the Apocalypse: The Liturgy of the Day of the Lord and the Dedication of the Heavenly Temple' (Unpublished PhD dissertation; Berkeley: Graduate Theological Union and the University of California, 1991).

—'How Millennial is the Millennium? A Study in the Millennial Background of the 1000 Years in Revelation 20', *Evangelical Journal* 9 (1991), pp. 51-74.

Stork, P., *The Aspectual Usage of the Dynamic Infinitive in* Herodotus (Groningen: Bouma's Boekhuis, 1982).

Strand, K.A., 'A Further Note on the Covenantal Form in the Book of Revelation', *AUSS* 21 (1983), pp. 251-64.

Stuart, D., *Ezekiel* (The Communicator's Commentary, 18; Dallas, TX: Word Books, 1989).

Stuart, M., *Commentary on the Apocalypse*, I-II (Andover: Allen, Morrell & Wardwell; New York: M.H. Newman, 1845).

Summers, Ray, 'Revelation 20: An Interpretation', *RevExp* 57 (1960), pp. 176-83.

—*The Life Beyond* (Nashville, TX: Broadman, 1959).

Sweet, J.P.M., 'Maintaining the Testimony of Jesus: The Suffering of Christians in the Revelation of John', in Horbury and McNeil (eds.), *Suffering and Martyrdom in the New Testament*, pp. 101-17.

—*Revelation* (SCM Pelican Commentaries; London: SCM Press, 1979).

Swete, H.B., *The Apocalypse of St. John* (London: Macmillan, 1906).

—*Introduction to the OT in Greek* (Cambridge: Cambridge University Press, 1902).

Taylor, J.B, *Ezekiel* (Leicester: Inter-Varsity Press, 1969).

Tenney, Merril C., 'The Importance and Exegesis of Rev. 20, 1-8', *BSac* 111 (1954), pp. 137-48.

—*Interpreting Revelation* (Grand Rapids: Eerdmans, 1957).

Thomas, R.L., 'The Chronological Interpretation of Revelation 2–3', *BSac* 124 (1967), pp. 321-31.

—'The Kingdom of Christ in the Apocalypse', *The Masters Seminary Journal* 3.2 (1992), pp. 117-40.

—*Revelation 1–7: An Exegetical Commentary* (Chicago: Moody Press, 1992).

Thompson, S., *The Apocalypse and Semitic Syntax* (SNTSMS, 52; Cambridge: Cambridge University Press, 1985).

Torrance, T.F., *The Apocalypse Today* (Grand Rapids: Eerdmans, 1959).

Torrey, C.C., *The Apocalypse of John* (New Haven: Yale University Press, 1958).

Toussaint, S.D., 'The Eschatology of the Warning Passages in the Book of Hebrews', *GTJ* 3 (1982), pp. 67-80.

Townsend, J.L., 'Is the Present Age the Millennium?' *Bibliotheca Sacra* 140 (1983), pp. 206-204.

Townsend, J.T., 'Education: Greco-Roman Period', in *ABD*, II, pp. 12-17.

Toussaint, S.D., and C.H. Dyer (eds.), *Essays in Honor of J. Dwight Pentecost* (Chicago: Moody Press, 1986).

Trites, A.A., *The New Testament Concept of Witness* (SNTSMS, 31; Cambridge: Cambridge University Press, 1976).

Trudinger, P., 'O AMHN (Rev. 3:14) and the Case for a Semitic Original of the Apocalypse', *NovT* 14 (1972), pp. 277-79.

—'Some Observations Concerning the Text of the Old Testament in the Book of Revelation', *JTS* 17 (1966), pp. 82-88.

Unnik, W.C. van, 'A Formula Describing Prophecy', *NTS* 9 (1962–63), pp. 86-94.

—*Het Godspredikaat 'Het Begin en het Einde' bij Flavius Josephus en in de Openbaring van Johannes* (Mededelingen der Koninklijke Nederlandse Akademie van Wetenshappen, afd. Letterkunde, Nieuwe Reeks-deel, 39.1; Amsterdam: Noord-hollandsche Uitgevers-Maatschappij, 1976).

—*Sparsa Collecta 2* (NovTSup, 30; Leiden: E.J. Brill, 1980).

Valentine, J., 'Theological Aspects of the Temple Motif in the Old Testament and Revelation' (Unpublished PhD dissertation; Boston, MA: Boston University Graduate School, 1985).

VanGemeren, W.A., 'The Spirit of Restoration', *WTJ* 50 (1988), pp. 81-102.

Vanhoye, A., *Old Testament Priests and the New Testament* (Petersham, MA: St Bede's, 1986).

—'L'utilisation du livre d'Ezéchiel dans l'Apocalypse', *Bib* 43 (1962), pp. 436-76.

Vogelgesang, J.M. 'The Interpretation of Ezekiel in the Book of Revelation' (Unpublished PhD dissertation; Cambridge, MA: Harvard University, 1985).

Vos, G., 'The Eschatological Aspect of the Pauline Conception of the Spirit', in Gaffin (ed.), *Redemptive History and Biblical Interpretation: The Shorter Writings of Geerhardus Vos*, pp. 91-125.

—'Eschatology and the Unity of New Testament Theology', *ExpT* 68 (1957), pp. 268-78.

—*The Pauline Eschatology* (Grand Rapids: Baker Book House, 1979).

Vos, L.A., *The Synoptic Traditions in the Apocalypse* (Kampen: Kok, 1965).

Waal, C. van der, *Openbaring van Jezus Christu: Inleiding en Vertaling* (Groningen: De Vuurbaak, 1971).

Wainwright, G., *Eucharist and Eschatology* (New York: Oxford University Press, 1981).

Walvoord, J.F., 'The Millennial Kingdom and the Eternal State', *BSac* 123 (1966), pp. 291-300.

—*The Revelation of Jesus Christ* (London: Marshal, Morgan & Scott, 1966).

—'The Theological Significance of Revelation 20:1-6', in Toussaint and Dyer (eds.), *Essays in Honor of J. Dwight Pentecost*, pp. 227-38.

Wanamaker, C.A., *Commentary on 1 & 2 Thessalonians* (NIGTC; Grand Rapids: Eerdmans; Exeter: Paternoster Press, 1990).

Webb, W.J., 'Revelation 20: Exegetical Considerations', *The Baptist Review of Theology/La Review Baptiste de Théologie* 4 (1994), pp. 7-39.

Wenham, D., 'Being "Found" on the Last Day: New Light on 2 Peter 3:10 and 2 Corinthians 5:3', *NTS* 33 (1987), pp. 477-79.

—*Paul* (Grand Rapids: Eerdmans, 1995).

Wenham, D. (ed.), *Gospel Perspectives. V. The Jesus Tradition Outside the Gospels* (Sheffield: JSOT Press, 1985).

Westermann, C., *Basic Forms of Prophetic Speech* (Philadelphia: Westminster Press, 1974).

Wevers, J.W., *Ezekiel* (NCB; London: Thomas Nelson, 1969).

Wevers, J.W. (ed.), *Genesis* (Septuaginta. Vetus Testamentum Graecum Auctoritate Academiae Scientiarum Gottingensis, 1; Göttingen: Vandenhoeck & Ruprecht, 1974).

Whale, P., 'The Lamb of John: Some Myths about the Vocabulary of the Johannine Literature', *JBL* 106 (1987), pp. 289-95.

White, R.F., 'Making Sense of Rev 20:1-10? Harold Hoehner Versus Recapitulation', *JETS* 37 (1994), pp. 539-51.

—'The Millennial Kingdom-City: Epic Themes, Ezek 36–39, and the Interpretation of Rev 20:4-10' (A paper delivered at the Annual Meeting of the Evangelical Theological Society, November 1991).

—'Reexamining the Evidence for Recapitulation in Rev 20:1-10', *WTJ* 51 (1989), pp. 319-44.

Wikenhauser, A., 'Das Problem des tausendjährigen Reiches in der Johannes-Apokalyse', *Römische Quartalschrift* 40 (1932), pp. 13-25.

—'Weltwoche und tausendjähriges Reich', *Tübinger Theologische Quartalschrift* 127 (1947), pp. 399-417.

Wilcock, M., *I Saw Heaven Opened* (London: Inter-Varsity Press, 1975).

Wilcox, M., 'The Aramaic Background of the New Testament', in Beattie and McNamara (eds.), *The Aramaic Bible*, pp. 362-78.

Wintermute, O.S., 'Apocalypse of Elijah', in *OTP*, I, pp. 721-53.

Woods, C., 'Eschatological Motifs in the Epistle to the Hebrews', in Lewis (ed.), *The Last Things*, pp. 140-51.

Wright, N.T., *The Climax of the Covenant* (Minneapolis: Fortress Press, 1992).

—*The New Testament and the People of God* (Minneapolis: Fortress Press, 1992).

Zerwick, M., *Biblical Greek* (Scripta Pontificii Instituti Biblici, 114; Rome: Pontifical Biblical Institute, 1963).

Zimmerli, W., *Ezekiel*, II (2 vols.; Hermeneia; Philadelphia: Fortress Press, 1969).

RABBINIC WRITINGS

OTHER ANCIENT SOURCES

INDEX OF AUTHORS

JOURNAL FOR THE STUDY OF THE NEW TESTAMENT
SUPPLEMENT SERIES

CPSIA information can be obtained at www.ICGtesting.com
Printed in the USA
LVOW07s0852090815

449425LV00006B/47/P